Middle School 3-2

학교시험 완벽대비

2학기 전과정

적중 100 plus

영어 기출문제집

중 3

시사 | 송미정

Best Collection

구성과 특징

교과서의 주요 학습 내용을 중심으로 학습 영역별 특성에 맞춰 단계별로 다양한 학습 기회를 제공하여
단원별 학습능력 평가는 물론 중간 및 기말고사 시험 등에 완벽하게 대비할 수 있도록 내용을 구성

Words & Expressions

Step1   Key Words 단원별 핵심 단어 설명 및 풀이
         Key Expression 단원별 핵심 숙어 및 관용어 설명
         Word Power 반대 또는 비슷한 뜻 단어 배우기
         English Dictionary 영어로 배우는 영어 단어

Step2   실력평가 단원별 수시평가 대비 주관식, 객관식 문제풀이

Step3   서술형 대비 학업성취도 및 수행능력평가 대비 서술형 문제풀이

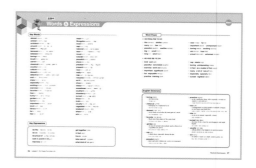

Conversation

Step1   핵심 의사소통 소통에 필요한 주요 표현 방법 요약
         핵심 Check 기본적인 표현 방법 및 활용능력 확인

Step2   대화문 익히기 교과서 대화문 심층 분석 및 확인

Step3   교과서 확인학습 빈칸 채우기를 통한 문장 완성 능력 확인

Step4   기본평가 시험대비 기초 학습 능력 평가

Step5   실력평가 단원별 수시평가 대비 주관식, 객관식 문제풀이

Step6   서술형 대비 학업성취도 및 수행능력평가 대비 서술형 문제풀이

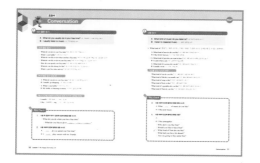

Grammar

Step1   주요 문법 단원별 주요 문법 사항과 예문을 알기 쉽게 설명
         핵심 Check 기본 문법사항에 대한 이해 여부 확인

Step2   기본평가 시험대비 기초 학습 능력 평가

Step3   실력평가 단원별 수시평가 대비 주관식, 객관식 문제풀이

Step4   서술형 대비 학업성취도 및 수행능력평가 대비 서술형 문제풀이

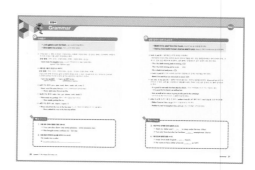

Reading

Step1   구문 분석 단원별로 제시된 문장에 대한 구문별 분석과 내용 설명
         확인문제 문장에 대한 기본적인 이해와 인지능력 확인

Step2   확인학습A 빈칸 채우기를 통한 문장 완성 능력 확인

Step3   확인학습B 제시된 우리말을 영어로 완성하여 작문 능력 키우기

Step4   실력평가 단원별 수시평가 대비 주관식, 객관식 문제풀이

Step5   서술형 대비 학업성취도 및 수행능력평가 대비 서술형 문제풀이
         교과서 구석구석 교과서에 나오는 기타 문장까지 완벽 학습

Composition

|영역별 핵심문제|

단어 및 어휘, 대화문, 문법, 독해 등 각 영역별 기출문제의 출제 유형을 분석하여 실전에 대비하고 연습할 수 있도록 문제를 배열

|단원별 예상문제|

기출문제를 분석한 후 새로운 시험 출제 경향을 더하여 새롭게 출제될 수 있는 문제를 포함하여 시험에 완벽하게 대비할 수 있도록 준비

|서술형 실전 및 창의사고력 문제|

학교 시험에서 점차 늘어나는 서술형 시험에 집중 대비하고 고득점을 취득하는데 만전을 기하기 위한 학습 코너

|단원별 모의고사|

영역별, 단계별 학습을 모두 마친 후 실전 연습을 위한 모의고사

INSIGHT on the textbook

교과서 파헤치기

- **단어Test1~3** 영어 단어 우리말 쓰기, 우리말을 영어 단어로 쓰기, 영영풀이에 해당하는 단어와 우리말 쓰기
- **대화문Test1~2** 대화문 빈칸 완성 및 전체 대화문 쓰기
- **본문Test1~5** 빈칸 완성, 우리말 쓰기, 문장 배열연습, 영어 작문하기 복습 등 단계별 반복 학습을 통해 교과서 지문에 대한 완벽한 습득
- **구석구석지문Test1~2** 지문 빈칸 완성 및 전문 영어로 쓰기

Lesson **5**

Look Inside You

의사소통 기능

- 설명 요청하기
  A: What does "pull myself together" mean?
  B: It means "to calm down."

- 대안 묻기
  A: Are there any other sauces?
  B: Sorry. Those are the only two we have.

언어 형식

- 관계대명사 what
  What you draw and how you draw it are related to your personality.

- 현재완료진행형
  Doctors **have been using** various drawing tests to better understand people.

Words & Expressions

Key Words

- **above**[əbʌ́v] 전 ~ 위에
- **active**[ǽktiv] 형 활동적인
- **against**[əgénst] 전 ~에 반대하여
- **annoyed**[ənɔ́id] 형 짜증이 난
- **app**[æp] 명 앱, 응용 프로그램
- **article**[ɑ́ːrtikl] 명 기사
- **attention**[əténʃən] 명 주의, 집중
- **below**[bilóu] 전 ~ 아래에
- **bright**[brait] 형 밝은, 긍정적인
- **calm**[kɑːm] 형 차분한
- **careful**[kɛ́ərfəl] 형 주의 깊은
- **cheerful**[tʃíərfəl] 형 발랄한, 쾌활한
- **closely**[klóusli] 부 면밀히, 밀접하게
- **comfortable**[kʌ́mfərtəbl] 형 편한, 편안한
- **creative**[kriéitiv] 형 창의적인
- **crowd**[kraud] 명 사람들, 군중
- **culture**[kʌ́ltʃər] 명 문화
- **curious**[kjúəriəs] 형 호기심이 있는
- **delay**[diléi] 동 미루다, 연기하다
- **dependent**[dipéndənt] 형 의존적인
- **detail**[ditéil] 명 세부 사항
- **difference**[dífərəns] 명 다름, 차이점
- **draw**[drɔː] 동 (그림을) 그리다, (관심 등을) 끌다
- **drop**[drɑp] 명 방울
- **emotion**[imóuʃən] 명 감정
- **express**[iksprés] 동 표현하다
- **focus**[fóukəs] 동 집중하다
- **future**[fjúːtʃər] 명 미래
- **friendly**[fréndli] 형 친절한
- **frightened**[fráitnd] 형 겁먹은, 두려워하는
- **heavy**[hévi] 형 심한, 거센
- **hold**[hould] 동 들다
- **hopeful**[hóupfəl] 형 희망찬
- **imagination**[imædʒənéiʃən] 명 상상, 상상력
- **independent**[ìndipéndənt] 형 독립적인, 자립심이 강한
- **language**[lǽŋgwidʒ] 명 언어
- **light**[lait] 형 가벼운
- **loudly**[láudli] 부 큰 소리로
- **magazine**[mǽgəzìn] 명 잡지
- **means**[miːnz] 명 수단, 방법
- **meaning**[míːniŋ] 명 의미
- **nervous**[nə́ːrvəs] 형 불안해[초조해/두려워] 하는
- **opinion**[əpínjən] 명 의견
- **personality**[pə̀ːrsənǽləti] 명 성격
- **peaceful**[píːsfəl] 형 평화로운
- **popular**[pɑ́pjulər] 형 인기 있는
- **possible**[pɑ́səbl] 형 가능한
- **protection**[prətékʃən] 명 보호
- **raise**[reiz] 동 기르다
- **realistic**[rìːəlístik] 형 현실적인
- **reasonable**[ríːzənəbl] 형 합리적인
- **recipe**[résəpi] 명 조리[요리]법
- **reduce**[ridjúːs] 동 줄이다
- **relate**[riléit] 동 ~을 관련[연결]시키다
- **relax**[rilǽks] 동 (긴장을) 늦추다, 휴식을 취하다
- **scary**[skɛ́əri] 형 무서운, 겁나는
- **seat**[siːt] 명 자리, 좌석
- **shy**[ʃai] 형 수줍어하는
- **situation**[sìtʃuéiʃən] 명 상황, 환경
- **spicy**[spáisi] 형 매운
- **stressful**[strésfəl] 형 스트레스가 많은
- **study**[stʌ́di] 동 연구하다, 살피다
- **sweat**[swet] 명 땀, 식은땀
- **try**[trai] 동 (시험 삼아) 해 보다
- **type**[taip] 명 유형
- **useful**[júːsfəl] 형 유용한, 도움이 되는
- **various**[vɛ́əriəs] 형 여러 가지의, 다양한
- **zone**[zoun] 명 구역

Key Expressions

- **according to** ~에 따르면, ~에 따라
- **at the same time** 동시에, 함께
- **be ready to** ~할 준비가 되다
- **be related to** ~와 연관되다
- **deal with** ~을 다루다, ~을 처리하다
- **draw attention to oneself** 자신에게 관심을 끌다
- **for example** 예를 들어
- **get along** (사람들과) 잘 어울리다
- **have to do with** ~와 관련되다
- **in other words** 다시 말하면
- **on the other hand** 반면에, 한편으로는
- **participate in** ~에 참가하다
- **see A as B** A를 B로 보다
- **sold out** 매진된, 다 팔린

Word Power

※ 서로 비슷한 뜻을 가진 어휘

- □ **various** (여러 가지의) – **diverse** (여러 가지의)
- □ **scary** (무서운) – **horrifying** (무서운)
- □ **popular** (인기 있는) – **well-liked** (인기 있는)
- □ **personality** (성격) – **character** (성격)

- □ **useful** (도움이 되는) – **helpful** (도움이 되는)
- □ **reduce** (줄이다) – **lessen** (줄이다)
- □ **nervous** (걱정하는) – **anxious** (걱정하는)
- □ **reasonable** (합리적인) – **logical** (타당한)

※ 서로 반대의 뜻을 가진 어휘

- □ **above** (~ 위에) ↔ **below** (~ 아래에)
- □ **comfortable** (편안한) ↔ **uncomfortable** (불편한)
- □ **difference** (다름, 차이) ↔ **similarity** (유사, 비슷함)
- □ **dependent** (의존적인) ↔ **independent** (독립적인)

- □ **future** (미래) ↔ **past** (과거)
- □ **heavy** (무거운) ↔ **light** (가벼운)
- □ **hopeful** (희망찬) ↔ **hopeless** (절망적인)

※ 동사 → 명사

- □ **imagine** (상상하다) → **imagination** (상상)
- □ **create** (창조하다) → **creation** (창조)
- □ **attend** (주의를 기울이다) → **attention** (주의)

- □ **express** (표현하다) → **expression** (표현)
- □ **protect** (보호하다) → **protection** (보호)
- □ **relate** (관련시키다) → **relation** (관련)

English Dictionary

- □ **attitude** 태도
  → the way you think and feel about someone or something
  당신이 어떤 사람이나 사물에 대해 생각하거나 느끼는 방식

- □ **calm** 차분한
  → not excited, nervous, or upset
  흥분하거나 긴장하거나 화내지 않는

- □ **difference** 다름, 차이점
  → something that makes one thing or person not the same as another thing or person
  한 사물이나 사람을 다른 사물이나 사람과 같지 않게 만드는 것

- □ **express** 표현하다
  → to show or make known a feeling, an opinion, etc. by words, looks or actions
  말, 표정 또는 행동으로 감정, 의견 등을 표시하거나 알려주다

- □ **frightened** 겁먹은, 두려워하는
  → feeling or showing fear
  두려움을 느끼거나 드러내는

- □ **hopeful** 희망찬
  → believing that something you want will happen
  당신이 원하는 일이 일어날 것이라고 믿는

- □ **independent** 독립적인, 자립심이 강한
  → not requiring or relying on other people for help or support
  다른 사람에게 도움이나 지원을 구하거나 의지하지 않는

- □ **personality** 성격
  → the set of emotional qualities, ways of behaving, etc., that makes a person different from other people
  어떤 사람을 다른 사람과 구별시켜 주는 일련의 감정적인 특성, 행동 방식 따위

- □ **reasonable** 합리적인
  → fair and sensible
  타당하고 분별 있는

- □ **reduce** 줄이다
  → to make something smaller in size, amount, number, etc.
  어떤 것의 크기, 양, 수 등이 작아지게 하다

서답형

01 다음 짝지어진 단어의 관계가 같도록 빈칸에 알맞은 말을 쓰시오.

> future : past = dependent : _____

02 다음 영영풀이가 가리키는 것을 고르시오.

> the set of emotional qualities, ways of behaving, etc., that makes a person different from other people

① detail
② expression
③ attitude
④ opinion
⑤ personality

 03 다음 중 밑줄 친 부분의 뜻풀이가 바르지 <u>않은</u> 것은?

① The price was quite <u>reasonable</u>. (합리적인)
② Let me write a <u>recipe</u> for you. (조리법)
③ Please <u>hold</u> this box for a while. (들다)
④ Television is an effective <u>means</u> of communication. (의미)
⑤ You should <u>focus</u> more on your studies. (집중하다)

서답형

04 다음 우리말에 맞게 빈칸에 알맞은 말을 쓰시오. (2 단어)

> 표가 매진되어서 나는 그 콘서트에 갈 수 없었다.
> ➡ I couldn't go to the concert because the tickets were _____ _____.

서답형

05 다음 영영풀이에 해당하는 단어를 쓰시오. (주어진 철자로 시작할 것)

> the way you think and feel about someone or something

➡ a_____

 06 다음 주어진 문장의 밑줄 친 express와 <u>다른</u> 의미로 쓰인 것은?

> In class, we learned how to <u>express</u> our opinions clearly.

① I <u>expressed</u> concern about the changes.
② Teenagers often have difficulty <u>expressing</u> themselves.
③ My twins <u>express</u> their feelings in the paintings.
④ I'm going to travel by <u>express</u>.
⑤ Words cannot <u>express</u> how happy I am now.

서답형

07 다음 우리말에 맞게 빈칸에 알맞은 단어를 쓰시오.

(1) 우리는 삼림 보호를 위한 법률을 만들어야 한다.
➡ We should make a law for the _____ of forests.

(2) 이 상황에서는 그것이 좋은 생각인 것 같다.
➡ In this _____, I think that would be a good idea.

(3) 이 두 단어 사이에는 의미상 차이가 없다.
➡ There's no _____ in meaning between these two words.

01 다음 짝지어진 두 단어의 관계가 같도록 빈칸에 알맞은 말을 쓰시오. (주어진 철자로 시작할 것)

> heavy : light = difference : s_____

02 다음 빈칸에 알맞은 단어를 〈보기〉에서 골라 쓰시오.

> ┤ 보기 ├
> focus   opinion   raise   details

(1) His boss checked the _____ before the meeting.

(2) My personal _____ doesn't matter in this situation.

(3) You should take responsibility when you _____ a dog.

(4) You should _____ more on your studies.

03 다음 우리말에 맞게 빈칸에 알맞은 말을 쓰시오.

(1) 이 두 개의 버튼을 동시에 눌러 주세요.
  ➡ Please press these two buttons _____ _____ _____ _____ .

(2) 후기들에 따르면, 이 영화는 흥미로울 것이 틀림없다.
  ➡ _____ _____ the reviews, this movie must be interesting.

(3) 이번 행사에 참여할 뜻이 있으면 언제든지 전화 주세요.
  ➡ Please call me anytime if you want to _____ _____ this event.

04 다음 제시된 의미에 맞는 단어를 주어진 철자로 시작하여 빈칸에 쓰고, 알맞은 것을 골라 문장을 완성하시오.

> • r_____ : fair and sensible
> • f_____ : feeling or showing fear
> • r_____ : to make something smaller in size, amount, number, etc.

(1) Ellen was _____ to speak in public.

(2) He is a very _____ man.

(3) We'll need to _____ the weight by half.

05 두 문장이 같은 의미가 되도록 빈칸을 채우시오.

> There are now several different types of cars which are eco-friendly.
> = There are now _____ cars which are eco-friendly.

06 다음 우리말과 일치하도록 주어진 단어를 모두 배열하여 영작하시오.

(1) Jake는 혼자 살 준비가 되지 않았다. (not / is / Jake / live / on / to / ready / own / his)
  ➡ _____

(2) Jane은 화가 난 개들을 다루는 방법을 안다. (knows / with / how / Jane / deal / to / dogs / angry)
  ➡ _____

(3) 그건 문화와 관련이 있을지도 모른다. (with / it / have / may / to / culture / do)
  ➡ _____

Conversation

1 설명 요청하기

> A: What does "pull myself together" mean? 'pull myself together'가 무엇을 의미하니?
> B: It means "to calm down." 그것은 '진정하는 것'을 의미해.

■ What does ~ mean?은 '~가 무엇을 의미하니?'라는 뜻으로 상대방에게 설명을 요청할 때 쓸 수 있는 표현이다. What is the meaning of ~?, What do you mean by ~?, 또는 Could[Can] you explain what ~ mean(s)?, Could[Can] you tell me the meaning of ~? 등으로 바꿔 쓸 수 있다.

■ 상대방의 질문에 설명할 때는 It means ~.(그것은 ~을 의미한다.)로 답한다. 상대방이 질문한 것에 모른다고 답할 때는 I'm sorry, but I don't know what it means., Sorry, but I'm not sure what it means. 등으로 답할 수 있다.

■ 상대방의 말을 듣고 더 설명해 달라고 할 때는 Could[Can] you tell me more about ~?이라고 한다. 좀더 공손하게 표현하여 Can 대신 Could나 Would를 사용할 수도 있다. tell 대신 explain을 써서 Could[Can] you explain that more, please?라고 할 수 있다.

설명 요청하기

- What does ~ mean? ~가 무엇을 의미하니?
- What is the meaning of ~? ~의 의미가 무엇이니?
- What do you mean by ~? ~의 의미가 무엇이니?
- Could[Can] you explain what ~ mean(s)? ~가 무슨 의미인지 설명해 줄 수 있니?
- Could[Can] you tell me the meaning of ~? ~의 의미를 설명해 줄 수 있니?

핵심 Check

1. 다음 대화의 순서를 바르게 배열하시오.

A: Hi, Jack! How are you doing?

(A) It means I'm really happy and excited.

(B) I'm on cloud nine! I got a concert ticket for my favorite band.

(C) What does 'on cloud nine' mean?

➡ _____

② 대안 묻기

A: Are there any other sauces? 어떤 다른 소스들도 있나요?

B: Sorry. Those are the only two we have. 죄송합니다. 저것들이 저희가 가진 오직 두 가지입니다.

- Are there any other ~?는 '다른 ~가 있나요?'라는 뜻으로 대안을 묻는 표현이다. Do you have any other ~?로 바꿔 쓸 수 있다.

  - A: Are there any other games? 어떤 다른 게임들은 없니?
    B: We can play a card game. 카드 게임을 할 수 있어.

  - A: Do you have any other drinks? 어떤 다른 음료가 있나요?
    B: We have apple juice, too. 사과 주스도 있습니다.

대안 묻기 유사 표현

- What else? 그 밖에 무엇이 있을까?

- Is there anything else that I can do? 내가 할 수 있는 그 밖의 것이 있니?

- Instead of it, what can I do? 그것 대신에 나는 무엇을 할 수 있을까?

핵심 Check

2. 다음 대화의 빈칸에 들어갈 알맞은 것은?

   A: Are there _____ other buses to our school?

   B: No, Bus Number 5 is the only one.

   ① many   ② some   ③ each

   ④ any   ⑤ these

3. 다음 대화의 밑줄 친 우리말에 맞도록 단어들을 순서대로 배열하시오.

   A: Let's go to the museum by bus.

   B: Well, 그곳에 도착하는 다른 방법이 있니?(other / get / there / are / ways / to / any / there)

   A: We can take a taxi.

   ➡ _____

Real-Life Zone

> **Hajun:** Look! ❶I found this test on an app that tells what kind of person you are. ❷Do you want to try it?
>
> **Emma:** Sure. Sounds like fun.
>
> **Hajun:** Okay, listen. What are you afraid of? ❸Choose one of these: crowds, spiders, or dark places.
>
> **Emma:** I hate dark places. I cannot sleep without a night light on. ❹ What does that mean?
>
> **Hajun:** It says you are full of imagination. ❺That's why you fill dark places with all kinds of scary things.
>
> **Emma:** That's very interesting. What about you? ❻Is there anything you are afraid of?
>
> **Hajun:** I chose dark places too. But I don't think I have a big imagination.
>
> **Emma:** This is fun. I want to do some more. ❼Are there any other tests we can take?
>
> **Hajun:** Sure. This app has a lot of them.

하준: 봐! 네가 어떤 종류의 사람인지 말해주는 앱에서 이 검사를 발견했어. 한 번 해볼래?
Emma: 물론이지. 재미있겠다.
하준: 응, 들어봐. 당신이 두려워하는 것은 무엇입니까? 이들 중 하나를 고르세요. 군중, 거미, 또는 어두운 곳.
Emma: 나는 어두운 곳을 싫어해. 나는 야간등을 켜놓지 않고는 잘 수 없어. 그것은 무엇을 의미하니?
하준: 그것은 네가 상상력이 풍부하다는 것을 말해줘. 그것이 네가 어두운 곳을 온갖 종류의 무서운 것들로 채우는 이유야.
Emma: 매우 흥미롭구나. 너는 어때? 너는 두려워하는 것이 있니?
하준: 나도 어두운 곳을 골랐어. 그렇지만 나는 내가 상상력이 풍부하다고 생각하지 않아.
Emma: 이거 재미있다. 더 하고 싶어. 우리가 할 수 있는 다른 검사들이 있니?
하준: 물론이지. 이 앱에는 많은 검사가 있어.

❶ what kind of person you are는 간접의문문으로 동사 tell의 목적어이다.
❷ it은 this test를 가리킨다.
❸ one of+복수명사: ~ 중의 하나
❹ 상대방에게 설명을 요청할 때 쓰는 표현이다.
❺ That's why ~.: 그것이 ~한 이유이다., fill A with B: A를 B로 채우다
❻ be afraid of: ~을 두려워하다
❼ Are there any other ~?(다른 어떤 ~가 있니?): 대안을 물을 때 사용한다.

Check(√) True or False

(1) Emma doesn't want to take a personality test on an app.   T ☐ F ☐

(2) Hajun doesn't think he has a big imagination.   T ☐ F ☐

Listen & Speak 2 A-2

> **B:** Jane, what are you reading?
>
> **G:** I'm reading an interesting magazine. ❶It says colors can change people's feelings.
>
> **B:** That's surprising.
>
> **G:** Yes. ❷For example, the color red can help us focus better.
>
> **B:** Are there any other useful colors?
>
> **G:** Yes. ❸The color blue helps people relax.

B: 제인, 무엇을 읽고 있니?
G: 나는 흥미로운 잡지를 읽고 있어. 이것이 말하길 색깔은 사람들의 기분을 바꿀 수 있대.
B: 그거 놀랍네.
G: 응. 예를 들어, 빨간색은 우리가 집중을 더 잘하도록 도와준대.
B: 다른 유용한 색깔들은 있니?
G: 응. 파란색은 사람들이 편안하도록 도와줘.

❶ It says ~.: ~라고 쓰여 있다, ~라고 한다.
❷ for example: 예를 들어(=for instance), help+목적어+목적격보어(동사원형): ~가 …하는 것을 돕다
❸ relax: 편안하게 하다

Check(√) True or False

(3) Colors can change people's feelings.   T ☐ F ☐

(4) The color red can help people relax.   T ☐ F ☐

Listen & Speak 1 Listen

1. G: ❶What does "be in a cold sweat" mean?
   B: ❷It means "to be nervous or frightened before doing something."
2. B: What does "feel blue" mean?
   G: ❸It means "to feel sad."
3. G: What does "have a long face" mean?
   B: ❸It means "to look sad."
4. B: What does "throw up one's hands" mean?
   G: ❹It means "to give up."

❶ What does ~ mean?: ~가 무엇을 의미하니?
❷ It means ~.: 그것은 ~을 의미한다. / frightened: 겁먹은, 무서워하는
❸ feel/look+형용사: ~하게 느끼다/보이다
❹ give up: 포기하다

Listen & Speak 1 A

1. G: Hi, Jack! How are you doing?
   B: I'm on cloud nine! I got a concert ticket for my favorite band.
   G: What does "on cloud nine" mean?
   B: It means I'm really happy and excited.
2. G: ❶I took a personality test today. I had to draw a house.
   B: A house?
   G: Yeah. ❷According to the test, you can tell a lot about a person by their drawing. Here's mine.
   B: Interesting. So what do these big windows mean?
   G: ❸They mean I'm open to other people.

❶ take a test: 시험을 보다, 시험을 치르다
❷ according to: ~에 따르면 / tell: 알다, 판단하다
❸ They는 these big windows를 가리킨다.

Listen & Speak 2 Listen

1. M: Sorry. The tickets for the blue zone are all sold out.
   G: ❶Are there any other seats?
   M: Yes, we have some tickets for the red zone.

2. W: What would you like on your hot dog? We have spicy sauce and sweet sauce.
   B: Are there any other sauces?
   W: Sorry. ❷Those are the only two we have.
3. M: What would you like to drink? A soft drink maybe?
   G: Are there any other drinks? Soft drinks have too much sugar in them.
   M: We have apple juice too.
4. W: ❸This is the most popular cap in our store.
   B: Are there any other colors?
   W: Sure, we have lots more. They're over here. I'll show you.

❶ Are there any other seats?=Do you have any other seats?
❷ Those: spicy sauce and sweet sauce
❸ the most popular: 가장 인기 있는

Listen & Speak 2 A-2

M: EDPI Test Center. Do you want to learn more about yourself? We have many kinds of personality tests. ❶If there are any other tests you want to learn more about, we are here to help you.
B: Hi, ❷I'm calling to take a personality test. ❸ Can I do one this afternoon?
M: Sure, you can come any time before 5 o'clock.

❶ we are here to ~: 우리는 ~하기 위해 여기에 있다
❷ I'm calling to ~.: 나는 ~하기 위해 전화를 걸고 있다.
❸ one=a personality test

Wrap Up 1~2

B: ❶What's your blood type?
G: Type A. Why?
B: I'm reading an article. ❷It says that blood type tells something about your personality.
G: Wow. Then what does type A mean?
B: ❸People with blood type A are calm. They are good listeners, too.

❶ blood type: 혈액형
❷ It says ~.: ~라고 한다. / personality: 성격
❸ 주어가 People with blood type A이므로 복수동사 are가 쓰였다. / with: ~을 가진 / calm: 차분한

● 다음 우리말과 일치하도록 빈칸에 알맞은 말을 쓰시오.

Listen & Speak 1 Listen

1. **G:** What does "be in a cold sweat" _____?
   B: It means "to be _____ or _____ before _____ something."
2. **B:** What _____ "feel blue" _____?
   G: It means "to _____ _____."
3. **G:** What _____ "have a long face" _____?
   B: It _____ "to _____ _____."
4. **B:** What _____ "throw up one's hands" _____?
   G: It _____ "to _____ _____."

Listen & Speak 1 A

1. **G:** Hi, Jack! _____ are you _____?
   B: I'm on cloud nine! I got a concert ticket _____ my favorite band.
   G: What _____ "on cloud nine" _____?
   B: It _____ I'm really _____ and _____.
2. **G:** I took a _____ _____ today. I _____ _____ draw a house.
   B: A house?
   G: Yeah. _____ _____ the test, you can tell _____ _____ about a person _____ their drawing. Here's _____.
   B: Interesting. So what _____ these big windows _____?
   G: They _____ I'm open to _____ people.

Listen & Speak 2 Listen

1. **M:** Sorry. The tickets for the blue zone are all _____ _____.
   G: Are there any _____ _____?
   M: Yes, we have _____ _____ for the red zone.
2. **W:** What would you like on your hot dog? We have _____ sauce and _____ sauce.
   B: Are there any _____ _____?
   W: Sorry. Those are the _____ two we have.
3. **M:** What _____ you _____ drink? A soft drink _____?
   G: Are there any other drinks? Soft drinks have _____ _____ in them.
   M: We have apple juice _____.
4. **W:** This is _____ _____ _____ cap in our store.
   B: Are there any _____ _____?
   W: Sure, we have _____ more. They're _____. I'll show you.

해석

1. **G:** 'be in a cold sweat'가 무엇을 의미하니?
   B: 그것은 '무언가 하기 전에 긴장하거나 겁을 먹는 것'을 의미해.
2. **B:** 'feel blue'가 무엇을 의미하니?
   G: 그것은 '슬프게 느끼는 것'을 의미해.
3. **G:** 'have a long face'가 무엇을 의미하니?
   B: 그것은 '슬퍼 보이는 것'을 의미해.
4. **B:** 'throw up one's hands'가 무엇을 의미하니?
   G: 그것은 '포기하는 것'을 의미해.

1. **G:** 안녕, 잭! 어떻게 지내니?
   B: 나는 날아갈 것 같아! 내가 가장 좋아하는 밴드의 콘서트 티켓을 얻었어.
   G: 'on cloud nine'이 무엇을 의미하니?
   B: 그것은 내가 아주 기쁘고 들떠 있다는 뜻이야.
2. **G:** 나 오늘 성격검사를 했어. 나는 집을 그려야 했어.
   B: 집?
   G: 응, 그 시험에 따르면 그림을 통해서 사람의 많은 것을 알 수 있대. 여기 내 것이 있어.
   B: 흥미롭구나. 그러면 이 큰 창문들은 무엇을 의미하니?
   G: 그들은 내가 타인에게 열려 있다는 것을 의미해.

1. **M:** 죄송합니다. 파란 구역의 표는 매진입니다.
   G: 다른 자리가 있나요?
   M: 네, 빨간 구역의 표가 좀 있습니다.
2. **W:** 핫도그에 무엇을 올릴까요? 저희에겐 매운 소스와 달콤한 소스가 있습니다.
   B: 다른 소스들도 있나요?
   W: 죄송합니다. 이것들이 저희가 가진 오직 두 가지입니다.
3. **M:** 무엇을 마시겠습니까? 혹시 탄산음료를 마시겠어요?
   G: 다른 음료가 있나요? 탄산음료에는 지나치게 많은 설탕이 들어 있어요.
   M: 사과 주스도 있습니다.
4. **W:** 이것은 우리 가게에서 가장 인기 있는 모자예요.
   B: 다른 색도 있나요?
   W: 물론이죠. 우리는 더 많이 가지고 있어요. 그것들은 이쪽에 있어요. 제가 보여드릴게요.

Listen & Speak 2 A

1. B: Jane, what are you _____?

   G: I'm reading an interesting magazine. It _____ colors can change _____ _____.

   B: That's _____.

   G: Yes. _____ _____, the color red can _____ _____ _____ better.

   B: Are there any other _____ _____?

   G: Yes. The color blue _____ people _____.

2. M: EDPI Test Center. Do you want to learn _____ about _____? We have many _____ _____ personality tests. If there are any _____ _____ you want to learn more about, we are here to help you.

   B: Hi, I'm calling to _____ a personality _____. Can I do one this afternoon?

   M: Sure, you can come any time _____ 5 o'clock.

Real-Life Zone

Hajun: Look! I found this test on an app that tells _____ _____ _____ person you are. Do you want _____ _____ it?

Emma: Sure. Sounds _____ fun.

Hajun: Okay, listen. What are you _____ _____? Choose _____ _____ these: crowds, spiders, or dark places.

Emma: I hate _____ _____. I cannot sleep _____ a night light _____. What does that _____?

Hajun: It _____ you are _____ _____ imagination. _____ _____ you _____ dark places _____ all kinds of _____ _____.

Emma: That's very interesting. What _____ you? Is there _____ you are _____ _____?

Hajun: I chose dark places too. But I don't think I have a _____ _____.

Emma: This is fun. I want to do some more. Are there _____ _____ _____ we can take?

Hajun: Sure. This app has _____ _____ _____ them.

Wrap Up 1~2

B: What's your _____ _____?

G: Type A. Why?

B: I'm reading _____ _____. It _____ that blood type tells something about _____ _____.

G: Wow. Then what does _____ _____ mean?

B: People _____ blood type A are _____. They are good listeners, _____.

해석

1. B: 제인, 무엇을 읽고 있니?
   G: 나는 흥미로운 잡지를 읽고 있어. 이것이 말하길 색깔은 사람들의 기분을 바꿀 수 있대.
   B: 그거 놀랍네.
   G: 응. 예를 들어, 빨간색은 우리가 집중을 더 잘하도록 도와준대.
   B: 다른 유용한 색깔들도 있니?
   G: 응. 파란색은 사람들이 편안하도록 도와줘.
2. M: EDPI 검사 센터입니다. 자신에 대해 더 알고 싶으신가요? 우리는 여러 종류의 성격검사를 가지고 있습니다. 당신이 더 알아보고 싶은 검사가 있다면 우리는 이곳에서 당신을 도와드리겠습니다.
   B: 안녕하세요. 성격검사를 받기 위해 전화드렸습니다. 오늘 오후에 하나 해 볼 수 있을까요?
   M: 물론입니다. 5시 전에 아무 때나 오시면 됩니다.

하준: 봐! 네가 어떤 종류의 사람인지 말해주는 앱에서 이 검사를 발견했어. 한 번 해볼래?
Emma: 물론이지. 재미있겠다.
하준: 응, 들어봐. 당신이 두려워하는 것은 무엇입니까? 이들 중 하나를 고르세요. 군중, 거미, 또는 어두운 곳.
Emma: 나는 어두운 곳을 싫어해. 나는 야간등을 켜놓지 않고는 잘 수 없어. 그것은 무엇을 의미하니?
하준: 그것은 네가 상상력이 풍부하다는 것을 말해줘. 그것이 네가 어두운 곳을 온갖 종류의 무서운 것들로 채우는 이유야.
Emma: 매우 흥미롭구나. 너는 어때? 너는 두려워하는 것이 있니?
하준: 나도 어두운 곳을 골랐어. 그렇지만 나는 내가 상상력이 풍부하다고 생각하지 않아.
Emma: 이거 재미있다. 더 하고 싶어. 우리가 할 수 있는 다른 검사들이 있니?
하준: 물론이지. 이 앱에는 많은 검사가 있어.

B: 너의 혈액형은 무엇이니?
G: A형이야. 왜?
B: 내가 기사 하나를 읽고 있어. 거기에서 말하길 혈액형이 너의 성격에 대해 무언가 말해준다.
G: 와. 그러면 A형은 무엇을 의미하니?
B: 혈액형이 A형인 사람들은 차분해. 그들은 또한 남의 말을 잘 들어주는 사람이기도 해.

[01~02] 다음 대화를 읽고, 물음에 답하시오.

W: What would you like on your hot dog? We have spicy sauce and sweet sauce.
B: (A)Are there any other sauces?
W: Sorry. (B)Those are the only two we have.

01 위 대화의 밑줄 친 (A)의 의도로 알맞은 것은?

① 이유 묻기   ② 대안 묻기
③ 조언 구하기   ④ 허락 요청하기
⑤ 추천 부탁하기

02 위 대화의 밑줄 친 (B)Those가 가리키는 말을 쓰시오.

➡ _____

03 다음 대화의 빈칸에 알맞은 것은?

A: What does "have a long face" mean?
B: _____

① That's what I mean.   ② I feel so bad.
③ It means "to look sad."   ④ I said, "have a long face."
⑤ You can say that again.

04 다음 대화의 순서를 바르게 배열하시오.

(A) They mean I'm open to other people.
(B) A house?
(C) Interesting. So what do these big windows mean?
(D) I took a personality test today. I had to draw a house.
(E) Yeah. According to the test, you can tell a lot about a person by their drawing. Here's mine.

➡ _____

01 다음 중 짝지어진 대화가 <u>어색한</u> 것은?

① A: What does "have a long face" mean?
　　B: It means "to look sad."
② A: Are there any other sauces?
　　B: Sorry. Those are the only two we have.
③ A: What do you mean by that?
　　B: It means "to give up."
④ A: What does that mean?
　　B: He seems to understand you.
⑤ A: Let's watch this movie.
　　B: Are there any other movies?

[02~06] 다음 대화를 읽고 물음에 답하시오.

G: I took a personality test today. I had to draw a house.
B: A house?
G: Yeah. According to the test, you can tell a lot about a person ＿＿(A)＿＿ their drawing. Here's mine.
B: Interesting. So (B)<u>what do these big windows mean?</u>
G: (C)<u>They</u> mean I'm open to other people

02 위 대화의 빈칸 (A)에 알맞은 것은?

① on　　　　　② by
③ into　　　　④ with
⑤ from

서답형
03 위 대화의 밑줄 친 (B)를 다음과 같이 바꿔 쓸 때 빈칸에 알맞은 말을 쓰시오.

what is the ＿＿＿＿＿ of these big windows?

서답형
04 위 대화의 밑줄 친 (C)They가 가리키는 말을 쓰시오.

➡ ＿＿＿＿＿＿＿＿＿＿＿＿＿

서답형
05 위 대화에서 다음 영영풀이에 해당하는 단어를 찾아 쓰시오.

expressing thoughts and feelings in a direct and honest way

➡ ＿＿＿＿＿＿＿＿＿＿＿＿＿

06 위 대화의 내용과 일치하지 <u>않는</u> 것은?

① 소녀는 오늘 성격검사를 했다.
② 소녀는 성격검사에서 집을 그렸다.
③ 그림을 통해서 사람에 대해 많은 것을 알 수 있다.
④ 소녀는 큰 창문들을 그렸다.
⑤ 큰 창문들은 타인에 의해 괴롭힘을 당한다는 의미이다.

서답형
07 다음 대화가 자연스럽게 이어지도록 순서대로 배열하시오.

(A) Hi, Jack! How are you doing?
(B) It means I'm really happy and excited.
(C) What does "on cloud nine" mean?
(D) I'm on cloud nine! I got a concert ticket for my favorite band.

➡ ＿＿＿＿＿＿＿＿＿＿＿＿＿

[08~10] 다음 대화를 읽고 물음에 답하시오.

> B: Jane, what are you reading?
> G: I'm reading an interesting magazine. (①)
> B: That's surprising. (②)
> G: Yes. (③) For example, the color red can help us focus better. (④)
> B: <u>다른 어떤 유용한 색깔들이 있니?</u> (useful / any / there)
> G: Yes. The color blue helps people relax. (⑤)

08 위 대화의 ①~⑤ 중 다음 문장이 들어갈 위치로 알맞은 곳은?

> It says colors can change people's feelings.

①   ②   ③   ④   ⑤

서답형

09 위 대화의 밑줄 친 우리말을 주어진 단어를 이용해 영작하시오.

➡ _____

10 위 대화의 내용과 일치하지 <u>않는</u> 것은?

① Jane은 흥미로운 잡지책을 읽고 있다.
② 잡지는 색깔과 사람들의 기분에 관한 것이다.
③ Jane은 이미 색깔이 어떻게 사람의 감정에 영향을 미치는지 알고 있었다.
④ 빨간색은 사람들이 보다 더 집중하도록 도와준다.
⑤ 사람들은 파란색으로 편안함을 느낄 수 있다.

[11~13] 다음 대화를 읽고 물음에 답하시오.

> M: EDPI Test Center. Do you want to learn more about yourself? We have many kinds of personality tests. If there are ___(A)___ tests you want to learn more about, we are here to help you.
> B: Hi, I'm calling to take a personality test. Can I do (B)<u>one</u> this afternoon?
> M: Sure, you can come ___(C)___ before 5 o'clock.

11 위 대화의 빈칸 (A)와 (C)에 알맞은 말이 바르게 짝지어진 것은?

① another – any time
② any other – a little time
③ any more – some time
④ any other – any time
⑤ some more – any time

서답형

12 위 대화의 밑줄 친 (B)one이 가리키는 말을 찾아 쓰시오.

➡ _____

13 위 대화의 내용과 일치하지 <u>않는</u> 것은?

① M은 EDPI 적성검사 센터의 직원이다.
② 검사 센터에는 많은 종류의 검사가 있다.
③ B는 적성검사를 신청하기 위해 검사 센터를 방문했다.
④ B는 오늘 오후에 적성검사를 받고 싶어 한다.
⑤ B는 5시 이전에 아무 때나 센터에 방문하면 된다.

[01~04] 다음 대화를 읽고 물음에 답하시오.

Hajun: Look! I found this test on an app that tells what kind of person you are. Do you want to try (a)it?

Emma: Sure. Sounds like fun.

Hajun: Okay, listen. What are you afraid of? Choose one of (A)[this / these]: crowds, spiders, or dark places.

Emma: I hate dark places. I cannot sleep without a night light (B)[on /off]. What does that mean?

Hajun: It says you are full of imagination. That's why you fill dark places (C)[of / with] all kinds of scary things.

Emma: That's very interesting. What about you? Is there anything you are afraid of?

Hajun: I chose dark places too. But I don't think I have a big imagination.

Emma: This is fun. I want to do some more. (b)우리가 할 수 있는 다른 검사들이 있니? (take / there / any)

Hajun: Sure. This app has a lot of them.

01 위 대화의 밑줄 친 (a)it이 가리키는 말을 영어로 쓰시오.

➡ _____

02 위 대화의 (A)~(C)에서 어법상이나 문맥상 알맞은 단어를 골라 쓰시오.

(A) _____ (B) _____ (C) _____

03 위 대화의 밑줄 친 (b)의 우리말을 주어진 단어를 이용하여 영작하시오.

➡ _____

04 What does it mean to you if you hate dark places? Answer in English.

➡ _____

[05~08] 다음 대화를 읽고 물음에 답하시오.

B: What's your blood type?

G: Type A. Why?

B: I'm reading an article. It says that blood type tells something about your personality.

G: Wow. 그러면 A형은 무엇을 의미하니?

B: People with blood type A are calm. They are good listeners, too.

05 What are the boy and the girl talking about?

➡ _____

06 What's the girl's blood type?

➡ _____

07 Write down the personality of people with blood type A. Answer in Korean.

➡ _____

08 위 대화의 밑줄 친 우리말을 영어로 쓰시오.

➡ _____

① 관계대명사 what

> • **What** you draw and how you draw it are related to your personality.
> 당신이 무엇을 그리는지 그리고 그것을 어떻게 그리는지는 당신의 성격과 관련이 있습니다.

■ 관계대명사 what은 '～인 것', '～하는 것'으로 해석한다.
- I know **what** you did yesterday. 나는 네가 어제 한 것을 알고 있다.

■ 선행사를 포함하는 관계대명사로 풀어서 표현하면 the thing(s) that[which]로 쓸 수 있다.
- I can't hear the thing. + You said the thing. 나는 그것을 들을 수 없다. + 너는 그것을 말했다.
  = I can't hear the thing that you said.
  = I can't hear **what** you said.

  cf. The rain shows the stress the person **who** drew the picture is under. 비는 그림을 그린 사람이 받고 있는 스트레스를 보여 줍니다. (관계대명사 who의 선행사는 the person이고 who는 형용사절을 이끔.)

  Tell me the story **which** you have heard. 당신이 들은 이야기를 나에게 말해 주세요.
  (관계대명사 which의 선행사는 the story이고 which는 형용사절을 이끔.)

■ 관계대명사 what은 명사절로 주어, 목적어, 보어 역할을 한다.
- You can pick the thing. + You want the thing.
  = You can pick the thing which you want.
    (관계대명사 which의 선행사는 the thing이다.)
  = You can pick **what** you want. 너는 네가 원하는 것을 고를 수 있다.
    (관계대명사 what은 what 앞에 위치한 주절의 동사 pick의 목적어(명사)와 관계사절의 동사 want의 목적어 역할을 한다.)
- He wanted to have **what** they had found. 그는 그들이 발견한 것을 가지기를 원했다.

핵심 Check

1. 다음 괄호 안에서 알맞은 것을 고르시오.
   (1) This is (that / what) made him happy.
   (2) (That / What) she says is not important.

② 현재완료진행형

> • Doctors **have been using** various drawing tests to better understand people.
> 의사들은 사람들을 더 잘 이해하기 위해 다양한 그림 그리기 검사를 사용해 오고 있습니다.

■ 현재완료진행형은 현재완료(have/has+p.p.) + 현재진행형(be+~ing)으로 'have[has]+been+~ing'로 쓰고, '(과거부터 지금까지) ~해 오고 있다'로 해석한다.
- • Lisa **has been learning** English since she was ten. Lisa는 10살 때부터 영어를 배워오고 있다.

■ 과거에 시작되어 현재도 지속되는 일을 표현할 때 쓰고, 기간을 나타내기 위해 'for, how long, since' 등을 함께 쓸 수 있다.
- • He **has been playing** the guitar for two straight hours. 그는 2시간 연속으로 기타를 치고 있다.
- • My sister **has been playing** the piano since this morning. 언니는 오늘 아침부터 피아노를 치고 있다.

■ 현재완료진행형의 축약형은 "'ve['s]+been+~ing"로 쓴다.
- • We've **been waiting** for Paul for 50 minutes. 우리는 50분 동안 Paul을 기다리고 있다.
- • My dad's **been looking** for his cellphone since yesterday evening.
  아버지는 어제 저녁부터 그의 휴대폰을 찾고 있다.

■ 부정문은 'have/has not been ~ing'로 쓴다.
- • She **hasn't been working** for two weeks. 그녀는 2주 동안 일을 하지 않고 있다.

■ 의문문은 'have/has+주어+been ~ing ~?'로 쓴다.
- • How long **have** you **been learning** Spanish? 당신은 얼마나 오랫동안 스페인어를 배우고 있나요?

■ 인식, 소유, 감정 등을 나타내는 동사는 현재완료진행형으로 쓰지 않는다.
- • I **have wanted** to meet you since I was young. 나는 어렸을 때부터 너를 만나고 싶었다.
  → I have been wanting to meet you since I was young. (✗)

핵심 Check

2. 다음 괄호 안에서 알맞은 말을 고르시오.
   (1) I (have been living / am living) in America for three years.
   (2) He (has drawing / has been drawing) a plan for the new city hall.

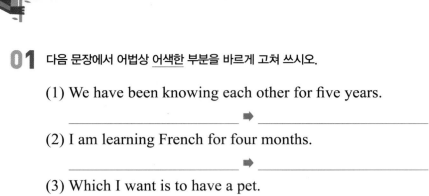

01 다음 문장에서 어법상 <u>어색한</u> 부분을 바르게 고쳐 쓰시오.

(1) We have been knowing each other for five years.

_____ ➡ _____

(2) I am learning French for four months.

_____ ➡ _____

(3) Which I want is to have a pet.

_____ ➡ _____

(4) I remember which I saw at the beach.

_____ ➡ _____

02 두 문장을 한 문장으로 쓰시오. (관계대명사 what을 사용할 것)

> • You need the thing.
> • You can tell me the thing.

➡ _____

03 다음 우리말에 맞게 괄호 안에 주어진 어구를 바르게 배열하시오.

(1) 점심때부터 내내 비가 내리고 있다. (be, since)

➡ _____

(2) 그들은 1시간 동안 달리고 있다. (be, run)

➡ _____

(3) Paul이 요리한 것은 피자였다. (what, cook)

➡ _____

(4) 나는 아들이 진짜로 필요한 것을 사줬다. (what, need)

➡ _____

(5) Suji는 1년 동안 영어를 공부하고 있다.

➡ _____

01 다음 문장에서 어법상 틀린 부분을 찾아 바르게 고쳐 쓰시오.

> My mom has cooking beef stew in the kitchen for two hours.

_____ ➡ _____

[02~03] 다음 글을 읽고 물음에 답하시오.

> I was not really good at English. (A)[That / What] I have done to improve it is to read a lot of books in English, and I could get better grades. Still, I _____(study) English at least one hour a day.

서답형
02 괄호 (A)에서 알맞은 것을 고르시오.

➡ _____

서답형
03 '공부해 오고 있는 중이다'라는 의미가 되도록 주어진 단어를 이용하여 빈칸을 채우시오.

➡ _____

04 다음 중 어색한 문장을 고르시오.

① He is the only person that I can trust.
② Sam and Son bought a swimming suit that could minimize resistance against water.
③ I don't care what people say.
④ I told you everything what I know.
⑤ The artists are drawing what they see.

*minimize: 최소화하다 *resistance: 저항

05 다음 문장과 같은 뜻을 지닌 문장을 고르시오.

> The thing which he said is true.

① Which he said is true.
② What he said is true.
③ Who he said is true.
④ Whom he said is true.
⑤ That he said is true.

06 다음 빈칸에 들어갈 말로 알맞은 것을 고르시오.

> Jay is the most brilliant student _____ I've taught.

① that   ② what
③ which   ④ the thing
⑤ the thing which

서답형
07 다음 〈보기〉의 두 문장을 관계대명사를 사용하여 한 문장으로 영작하시오.

┤ 보기 ├
• She bought a luxurious house.
• It has a huge pool.

➡ _____

_____

[08~09] 다음 글을 읽고 물음에 답하시오.

_____(A)_____ I do when I'm stressed out is to watch comedy movies. I _____(B)_____ (do) that since last month. It is a very helpful way to release my stress.

08 빈칸 (A)에 들어갈 적절한 단어는?

① Which   ② What   ③ When
④ How   ⑤ That

서답형
09 괄호 안의 단어를 활용하여 빈칸 (B)에 현재완료진행형을 쓰시오.

➡ _____

서답형
10 다음 우리말과 같은 뜻이 되도록 괄호 안의 단어를 활용하여 현재완료진행 형태로 문장을 완성하시오.

3일 동안 비가 오고 있다. (rain)

➡ _____

중요
11 다음 우리말에 맞게 영작할 경우 어법상 어색한 것을 고르시오.

① 영어를 얼마나 오래 공부해 왔니?
  → How long have you been studying English?
② 나는 너를 찾고 있었어.
  → I have been looking for you.
③ 그녀는 3시간 동안 페인트칠을 하고 있다.
  → She painted for 3 hours.
④ 나는 2시간 동안 운동하고 있습니다.
  → I have been working out for 2 hours.
⑤ 그녀는 오늘 아침부터 기타를 치고 있습니다.
  → She has been playing the guitar since this morning.

12 우리말에 맞게 영작하고자 할 때 빈칸에 들어갈 말로 알맞은 것은?

나는 지난주부터 이 책을 읽고 있다.
➡ I _____ this book since last week.

① read   ② was reading
③ reading   ④ am reading
⑤ have been reading

13 다음 우리말을 바르게 영작한 것을 모두 고르시오.

내가 필요한 것은 바로 너의 도움이다.

① What I need is your help.
② Which I need is your help.
③ The thing which I need is your help.
④ That I need is your help.
⑤ Who I need is your help

중요
14 다음 빈칸에 들어갈 말로 바르게 짝지어진 것을 고르시오.

• _____ makes me happy is to play soccer. • The book _____ he wrote was a big hit.

① That – that   ② That – what
③ What – that   ④ What – what
⑤ Which – that

서답형
15 우리말에 맞게 괄호 안의 어휘들을 배열하여 영작할 때, 8번째 단어를 쓰시오.

John과 Paul이 먹고 싶은 것은 프라이드 치킨이다. (John, Paul, want, is, to, what, and, eat, fried chicken)

➡ _____

16 다음 우리말과 같은 뜻이 되도록 괄호 안의 단어를 활용하여 조건에 맞게 빈칸을 채우시오.

(1) 우리는 학교에서 많은 다양한 종류의 활동들을 하고 있다. (현재완료진행형)

➡ We _____(do) a lot of different kinds of activities at school.

(2) 내 친구들이 나에 대해 말하는 것은 꽤 달랐다.

➡ _____(what) about me was quite different.

(3) 나는 5년 동안 고양이를 키우고 있다. (현재완료진행형)

➡ I _____(raise) a cat for five years.

(4) 3일 동안 눈이 오고 있다. (현재완료진행형)

➡ It _____(snow) for three days.

(5) 내가 원하는 저녁식사는 중국 음식이다.

➡ _____(what) for dinner is Chinese food.

(6) Jane과 Jay가 볼 것은 판타지 영화이다.

➡ _____(what, see) is a fantasy movie.

17 다음 중 어법상 어색한 것을 고르시오.

① I have been planting trees with my friends since then.
② I've been living in Australia for 20 years.
③ Jason hasn't been feeling well since this morning.
④ She was working very hard recently.
⑤ I've been looking for this.

18 다음 중 어법상 올바른 것을 모두 고르시오.

① We have planting flowers regularly there.
② Harry has been waiting for the bus for 30 minutes.
③ Nathan worked on the project since 2019.
④ He has been watched TV since this morning.
⑤ She has been driving since she was 20.

19 다음 중 어색한 것을 고르시오.

① Don't forget that I said.
② She did what she had to do.
③ I will cook my daughter what she wants to eat.
④ What they needed was just a bottle of water.
⑤ The girl is watching a movie that makes her excited.

20 우리말에 맞게 괄호 안의 단어를 활용하여 빈칸을 채우시오. (현재완료진행형으로 쓸 것)

Tom은 2시간 동안 컴퓨터 게임을 하고 있다. (play)

➡ Tom _____ computer games for two hours.

01 우리말에 맞게 괄호 안의 단어를 활용하여 빈칸을 채우시오.

> 그림은 종종 당신의 마음속에 당신이 느끼고 있는 것과 밀접하게 관련되어 있다.
> ➡ A picture is often closely related to
> _____ (what, feel) in your
> mind.

02 밑줄 친 (A) 대신 들어갈 수 있는 것을 쓰시오.

> (A)The thing which I want to have is a computer.

➡ _____

03 관계대명사 what과 괄호 안의 단어를 활용하여 영작하시오.

(1) 나는 네가 원하는 것을 알아. (want, 5 단어)
   ➡ _____

(2) 이것이 바로 내가 의미하는 것이야. (mean, 5 단어)
   ➡ _____

(3) 내가 하는 것을 해 봐. (do, 4 단어)
   ➡ _____

(4) Suji가 영화관에 타고 갈 것은 버스이다. (take, 10 단어)
   ➡ _____

04 그림을 참고하여 우리말과 같도록 괄호 안의 단어를 활용하여 영작하시오.

> 그들은 30분 동안 치킨을 먹고 있다.
> (eat, for, 8 단어)

➡ _____

05 괄호 안의 단어를 활용하여 우리말에 맞게 영작하시오.

> 난 네가 지난여름에 한 일을 알고 있다. (know, do)

➡ _____

06 다음 우리말을 괄호 안의 어휘를 활용하여 영작하시오.

> 나는 사람들이 말하는 것에 신경 쓰지 않는다.
> (care, say)

(1) (관계대명사 what을 사용할 것)
   ➡ _____

(2) (which를 사용할 것)
   ➡ _____

07 그림에 맞게 괄호 안의 단어를 활용하여 영작하시오.

(1) John은 2시간 동안 노래를 부르고 있다. (7 단어)

➡ _____

  (sing)

(2) 그들은 1시간 동안 다트 게임을 하고 있다.

  (8 단어)   *darts: 다트 게임

➡ _____

  (play, darts)

(3) 그들이 원하는 것은 이야기하고 노는 것이다.

  (8 단어)

➡ _____

  (want, talk and play)

08 다음 우리말을 괄호 안에 주어진 어휘와 주어진 조건에 맞춰 영작하시오.

> 난 네가 요즘 무엇을 하고 있는지 알아.
> (know, do)

(1) (the thing which 사용)

  ➡ _____

(2) (관계대명사 what 사용)

  ➡ _____

09 괄호 안의 단어를 어법에 맞게 배열하시오.

> _____(I, to, what, finish, have) by three o'clock is an essay for homework. However, I do not have enough time to finish it. _____(have, writing, I, been) it for an hour, but I just wrote two sentences. I need more time!

10 괄호 안의 단어를 활용하여 우리말에 맞게 영작하시오.

> John이 Sally와 하고 싶은 것은 영화를 보는 것이다. (what, do, see)

➡ _____

11 다음 우리말에 맞게 괄호의 단어를 활용하여 빈칸을 채우시오.

(1) 나는 오늘 아침부터 숙제를 해오고 있는 중이다.

  ➡ I _____(do) my homework since this morning.

(2) 나는 가까운 장래에 회사가 어떻게 될지 알고 있다.

  ➡ I know _____ (what, become) in the near future.

Reading

Drawing the Mind

Everything you do says something about you. The language you use,
앞에 관계대명사 that 생략
the clothes you wear, and even the pets you raise somehow show what
의문형용사 what으로 시작하는 간접의문문
kind of person you are.

The things you draw are not much different. What you draw and how
별로 주어
you draw it are related to your personality. Doctors have been using
it=what you draw 동사 현재완료진행형
various drawing tests to better understand people.
목적을 나타내는 부사적 용법

One of those tests is the Draw-a-Person-in-the-Rain (DAPR) test.
Study the pictures below.
아래에, 밑에

The person in Drawing A is holding an umbrella in a light rain. On
the other hand, the person in Drawing B is in a heavy rain and has no
umbrella. Also, there are dark clouds above the person in Drawing B.
~ 위에
What can these differences mean?

First, the rain shows the stress the person who drew the picture is
앞에 관계대명사 that이나 which 생략
under. The bigger the drops are or the more heavily the rain is falling,
the+비교급 ~, the+비교급 ...: ~하면 할수록 더 ...하다
the bigger the stress is. The clouds mean problems waiting to happen,
현재분사: problems를 수식
so a big cloud shows the drawer is not very hopeful about the future.
그래서

---

even 심지어
raise 기르다
somehow 어떻게든, 왠지
be related to ~과 관련이 있다
personality 인격, 성격
various 다양한
light 가벼운
on the other hand 한편에
be under stress 스트레스를 받다

확인문제

● 다음 문장이 본문의 내용과 일치하면 T, 일치하지 <u>않으면</u> F를 쓰시오.

1 We can understand you by everything you do. ☐

2 The things you draw aren't related to your personality. ☐

3 A big cloud means the drawer's hope about the future. ☐

Second, the umbrella means the protection <u>the person has</u> in a
앞에 관계대명사 that이나 which 생략
stressful situation. A big umbrella shows that the drawer has a lot of
plans or protection. If there's no umbrella in the drawing, the drawer
does not have any means to <u>deal</u> with difficult situations.
means를 수식하는 형용사적 용법

Third, the details in the drawing of the person <u>have to do with</u> the
~와 관계가 있다
drawer's attitude under stress. For example, someone who draws a
person <u>without a face</u> does not want to draw people's attention to
a person을 수식하는 형용사구
<u>himself or herself</u>. Someone who draws the person on the right side of
재귀대명사로 전치사 to의 목적어
the paper is ready to meet the future. <u>On the other hand,</u> someone who
반면에
draws the person on the left side <u>may</u> be worried about things that <u>have</u>
추측을 나타내는 조동사　　　　　　　　　완료를 나타내는 현재완료
<u>happened</u> in the past.

These are some of the possible meanings of each part of the
drawings. Now, go back and look at the two drawings. <u>Try reading</u>
try+-ing: ~해 보다
them <u>yourself</u>. Can you understand what kind of person drew each
강조 용법으로 쓰이는 재귀대명사
<u>one</u>? What's your opinion?
= drawing

protection 보호

stressful 스트레스를 주는

means 수단

detail 상세

attitude 태도

deal with ~을 처리하다, 헤쳐 나가다

draw one's attention 사람의 주의를 끌다

happen 일어나다

possible 가능한

be ready to ~할 준비가 되다

확인문제

- 다음 문장이 본문의 내용과 일치하면 T, 일치하지 <u>않으면</u> F를 쓰시오.

1 A small umbrella shows that the drawer has many plans. ☐

2 A big umbrella means more protection than a small umbrella. ☐

3 Someone who draws a person without a face wants to be well known. ☐

4 There are some of the possible meanings of each part of the drawings. ☐

● 우리말을 참고하여 빈칸에 알맞은 말을 쓰시오.

Drawing the Mind

마음 그리기

1 Everything you do _____ _____ about you.

1 당신이 하는 모든 행동은 당신에 대해 말해 줍니다.

2 The language you _____, the clothes you _____, and _____ the pets you _____ somehow show _____ _____ _____ person you are.

2 당신이 사용하는 언어, 당신이 입는 옷, 그리고 당신이 기르는 애완동물까지도 당신이 어떤 종류의 사람인지 보여 줍니다.

3 The things you _____ are not _____ different.

3 당신이 그리는 그림도 마찬가지입니다.

4 _____ you draw and _____ you draw it _____ _____ _____ your personality.

4 당신이 무엇을 그리는지 그리고 그것을 어떻게 그리는지는 당신의 성격과 관련이 있습니다.

5 Doctors have been using various drawing tests _____ _____ _____ people.

5 의사들은 사람들을 더 잘 이해하기 위해 다양한 그림 그리기 검사를 사용해 오고 있습니다.

6 _____ of _____ _____ is the Draw-a-Person-in-the-Rain (DAPR) test.

6 이런 검사들 중 하나는 빗속의 사람 그리기 검사입니다.

7 Study the pictures _____.

7 아래의 그림들을 연구해 봅시다.

8 The person in Drawing A is _____ an umbrella in a _____ rain.

8 A 그림 속의 사람은 가벼운 빗속에서 우산을 들고 있습니다.

9 On the _____ _____, the person in Drawing B is in a _____ rain and has _____ umbrella.

9 반면에, B 그림 속의 사람은 거센 빗속에서 우산을 가지고 있지 않습니다.

10 Also, there are dark clouds _____ the person in Drawing B.

10 또한, 검은 구름들이 B 그림의 사람 머리 위에 있습니다.

11 What can these _____ _____?

11 이런 차이는 무엇을 의미하는 걸까요?

12 First, the rain shows the stress the person _____ drew the picture is _____.

12 첫 번째, 비는 그림을 그린 사람이 받고 있는 스트레스를 보여 줍니다.

13 _____ _____ the drops are or _____ _____ _____ the rain is falling, _____ _____ the stress is.

13 빗방울의 크기가 크면 클수록, 혹은 비가 더 세게 내리면 내릴수록 스트레스는 더 큽니다.

14 The clouds mean problems _____ to _____, so a big cloud shows the drawer is not very _____ about the _____.

14 구름은 앞으로 벌어질 문제를 의미하기 때문에, 큰 구름은 그림을 그린 사람이 미래에 대해 그다지 희망적이지 않다는 것을 나타냅니다.

15 _____, the umbrella means the _____ the person has in a _____ situation.

16 A _____ umbrella _____ that the drawer has a lot of _____ or _____.

17 If there's no umbrella in the _____, the drawer does not have any _____ to _____ _____ difficult situations.

18 _____, the _____ in the drawing of the person _____ _____ _____ with the drawer's _____ under stress.

19 For _____, someone _____ draws a person _____ a face does not want to draw people's _____ to _____ or _____.

20 Someone _____ draws the person on the _____ side of the paper _____ _____ _____ meet the future.

21 On the other _____, someone who draws the person on the left side _____ be _____ about things that have _____ in the past.

22 These are some of the _____ _____ of each _____ of the drawings.

23 Now, go _____ and look _____ the two drawings.

24 Try _____ them _____.

25 Can you understand _____ _____ of person drew _____ _____?

26 What's your _____?

15	두 번째, 우산은 스트레스를 받는 상황에서 그 사람이 가지고 있는 보호 기제를 의미합니다.
16	큰 우산은 그림을 그린 사람이 많은 계획이나 보호 기제를 가지고 있음을 보여 줍니다.
17	만약 그림에 우산이 없다면, 그 그림을 그린 사람은 어려운 상황을 헤쳐 나갈 어떤 방법도 가지고 있지 않습니다.
18	세 번째, 그림 속 사람의 세부적인 것들은 그 그림을 그린 사람이 스트레스를 받을 때의 태도와 관련이 있습니다.
19	예를 들어, 얼굴이 없는 사람을 그린 사람은 사람들의 관심을 끌기를 원하지 않습니다.
20	사람을 종이의 오른쪽에 그린 사람은 미래를 맞이할 준비가 되어 있습니다.
21	반면에, 사람을 왼쪽에 그린 사람은 과거에 일어났던 일에 대해 걱정하고 있을 수도 있습니다.
22	이것들은 그림 각 부분의 가능한 의미 풀이 중 일부입니다.
23	이제, 돌아가서 두 그림을 보세요.
24	그 그림들을 스스로 읽으려고 시도해 보세요.
25	당신은 각 그림을 그린 사람이 어떤 사람인지 알 수 있나요?
26	당신의 의견은 어떤가요?

우리말을 참고하여 본문을 영작하시오.

Drawing the Mind

1 당신이 하는 모든 행동은 당신에 대해 말해 줍니다.

➡ _____

2 당신이 사용하는 언어, 당신이 입는 옷, 그리고 당신이 기르는 애완동물까지도 당신이 어떤 종류의 사람인지 보여 줍니다.

➡ _____

3 당신이 그리는 그림도 마찬가지입니다.

➡ _____

4 당신이 무엇을 그리는지 그리고 그것을 어떻게 그리는지는 당신의 성격과 관련이 있습니다.

➡ _____

5 의사들은 사람들을 더 잘 이해하기 위해 다양한 그림 그리기 검사를 사용해 오고 있습니다.

➡ _____

6 이런 검사들 중 하나는 빗속의 사람 그리기 검사입니다.

➡ _____

7 아래의 그림들을 연구해 봅시다.

➡ _____

8 A 그림 속의 사람은 가벼운 빗속에서 우산을 들고 있습니다.

➡ _____

9 반면에, B 그림 속의 사람은 거센 빗속에서 우산을 가지고 있지 않습니다.

➡ _____

10 또한, 검은 구름들이 B 그림의 사람 머리 위에 있습니다.

➡ _____

11 이런 차이는 무엇을 의미하는 걸까요?

➡ _____

12 첫 번째, 비는 그림을 그린 사람이 받고 있는 스트레스를 보여줍니다.

➡ _____

13 빗방울의 크기가 크면 클수록, 혹은 비가 더 세게 내리면 내릴수록 스트레스는 더 큽니다.

➡ _____

14 구름은 앞으로 벌어질 문제를 의미하기 때문에, 큰 구름은 그림을 그린 사람이 미래에 대해 그다지 희망적이지 않다는 것을 나타냅니다.

➡ _____

15 두 번째, 우산은 스트레스를 받는 상황에서 그 사람이 가지고 있는 보호 기제를 의미합니다.

➡ _____

16 큰 우산은 그림을 그린 사람이 많은 계획이나 보호 기제를 가지고 있음을 보여 줍니다.

➡ _____

17 만약 그림에 우산이 없다면, 그 그림을 그린 사람은 어려운 상황을 헤쳐 나갈 어떤 방법도 가지고 있지 않습니다.

➡ _____

18 세 번째, 그림 속 사람의 세부적인 것들은 그 그림을 그린 사람이 스트레스를 받을 때의 태도와 관련이 있습니다.

➡ _____

19 예를 들어, 얼굴이 없는 사람을 그린 사람은 사람들의 관심을 끌기를 원하지 않습니다.

➡ _____
_____

20 사람을 종이의 오른쪽에 그린 사람은 미래를 맞이할 준비가 되어 있습니다.

➡ _____

21 반면에, 사람을 왼쪽에 그린 사람은 과거에 일어났던 일에 대해 걱정하고 있을 수도 있습니다.

➡ _____
_____

22 이것들은 그림 각 부분의 가능한 의미 풀이 중 일부입니다.

➡ _____

23 이제, 돌아가서 두 그림을 보세요.

➡ _____

24 그 그림들을 스스로 읽으려고 시도해 보세요.

➡ _____

25 당신은 각 그림을 그린 사람이 어떤 사람인지 알 수 있나요?

➡ _____

26 당신의 의견은 어떤가요?

➡ _____

[01~03] 다음 글을 읽고 물음에 답하시오.

(①) Everything you do says something about you. (②) The language you use, the clothes you wear, and even the pets you raise somehow show what kind of person you are. (③) ⓐ you draw and ⓑ you draw it are related to your personality. (④) Doctors have been using various drawing tests to better understand people. (⑤)

01 위 글의 ①~⑤ 중 다음 주어진 문장이 들어갈 알맞은 곳은?

The things you draw are not much different.

①   ②   ③   ④   ⑤

서답형
02 위 글의 빈칸 ⓐ와 ⓑ에 알맞은 말을 쓰시오.

ⓐ _____ ⓑ _____

중요
03 위 글의 뒤에 이어질 내용으로 가장 알맞은 것은?

① 행동과 성격의 관계
② 집에서 기르는 애완동물의 종류
③ 취미로 그림 그리기
④ 나쁜 성격 고치기
⑤ 그림으로 사람의 성격을 이해하기

[04~07] 다음 글을 읽고 물음에 답하시오.

One of those tests is the Draw-a-Person-in-the-Rain (DAPR) test. Study the pictures below.

The person in Drawing A is holding an umbrella in a light rain. ⓐ , the person in Drawing B is in a heavy rain and has no umbrella. Also, there are dark clouds above the person in Drawing B. What can these differences mean?

First, the rain shows the stress the person who drew the picture is ⓑ . The bigger the drops are or the more heavily the rain is falling, the bigger the stress is. The clouds mean problems (A)wait to happen, so a big cloud shows the drawer is not very hopeful about the future.

04 위 글의 빈칸 ⓐ에 들어갈 말로 적절한 것은?

① At last   ② That is
③ On the whole   ④ For example
⑤ On the other hand

05 위 글의 빈칸 ⓑ에 들어갈 말로 적절한 것은?

① on   ② over
③ under   ④ across
⑤ among

서답형

06 위 글의 밑줄 친 (A)를 알맞은 형으로 고치시오.

➡ _____

중요

07 위 글의 내용과 일치하지 <u>않는</u> 것은?

① 그림 A에서는 비가 적게 오고 있다.
② 그림 B에서는 비가 많이 오고 있다.
③ 그림 B에 있는 사람의 머리 위에는 어두운 구름이 보인다.
④ 비가 많이 내릴수록 그림 속의 사람은 많은 스트레스를 받는다.
⑤ 그림 속의 큰 구름은 미래에 대한 도전을 나타낸다.

[08~10] 다음 글을 읽고 물음에 답하시오.

Second, the umbrella means the protection the person has in a ⓐstress situation. A big umbrella shows that the drawer has a lot of plans or protection. If there's no umbrella in the drawing, the drawer does not have any means ⓑto deal with difficult situations.

서답형

08 위 글의 밑줄 친 ⓐstress를 알맞은 형으로 고치시오.

➡ _____

09 위 글의 밑줄 친 ⓑ와 용법이 같은 것은?

① My hope is to work as a doctor in Africa.
② It's time to go to bed now.
③ My job is to report the news.
④ The boys hoped to find the hidden treasure.
⑤ Kate went to a shopping mall to buy clothes.

서답형

10 What does a big umbrella show? Answer in Korean.

➡ _____

_____

[11~14] 다음 글을 읽고 물음에 답하시오.

Third, the details in the drawing of the person have to do ①<u>with</u> the drawer's attitude ②<u>under</u> stress. (A)(For example / On the other hand), someone who draws a person without a face does not want to draw people's attention ③<u>at</u> himself or herself. Someone who draws the person on the right side of the paper is ready to meet the ___ⓐ___. (B)(For example / On the other hand), someone who draws the person on the left side ⓑ<u>may</u> be worried ④<u>about</u> things that have happened ⑤<u>in</u> the past.

11 위 글의 밑줄 친 전치사 ①~⑤ 중 어법상 어색한 것은?

①   ②   ③   ④   ⑤

서답형

12 위 글의 괄호 (A)와 (B)에서 각각 알맞은 것을 고르시오.

(A) _____

(B) _____

서답형

13 위 글의 빈칸 ⓐ에 본문에 나오는 단어의 반의어를 쓰시오.

➡ _____

중요

14 위 글의 밑줄 친 ⓑmay와 용법이 같은 것은?

① You may come in if you wish.

② May she rest in peace!

③ The rumor may be false.

④ May I take a picture here?

⑤ You may stay at this hotel for a week.

[15~16] 다음 글을 읽고 물음에 답하시오.

These are ①some of the possible meanings of each ②part of the drawings. Now, go back and look ③at the two drawings. Try ④to read them yourself. Can you understand ⑤what kind of person drew each ⓐone? What's your opinion?

15 위 글의 밑줄 친 ①~⑤ 중 어색한 것을 올바르게 바꾼 것은?

① any   ② parts

③ for   ④ reading

⑤ which

서답형

16 위 글의 밑줄 친 ⓐone이 가리키는 것을 영어로 쓰시오.

➡ _____

[17~20] 다음 글을 읽고 물음에 답하시오.

__(A)__ you do says __(B)__ about you. The language you use, the clothes you wear, and even the pets you raise somehow show ⓐ당신이 어떤 종류의 사람인지. The things you draw are not much different. ____ⓑ____ you draw and how you draw it are related to your ⓒpersonal. Doctors have been using various drawing tests to better understand people.

중요

17 위 글의 빈칸 (A)와 (B)에 알맞은 것으로 짝지어진 것은?

① Everything – anything

② Everything – something

③ Nothing – something

④ Something – anything

⑤ Nothing – everything

서답형

18 위 글의 밑줄 친 ⓐ를 영어로 옮기시오. (6 words)

➡ _____

19 위 글의 빈칸 ⓑ에 알맞은 것은?

① What   ② That

③ Whom   ④ Why

⑤ Which

서답형

20 위 글의 밑줄 친 ⓒ를 알맞은 형으로 고치시오.

➡ _____

[21~26] 다음 글을 읽고 물음에 답하시오.

First, the rain shows the stress the person ___(A)___ drew the picture is under. ⓐThe bigger the drops are or the more heavily the rain is falling, the bigger the stress is. The clouds mean problems waiting to happen, ___(B)___ a big cloud shows the drawer is not very hopeful about the future.

Second, the umbrella means the protection the person has in a stressful situation. A big umbrella shows that the drawer has ⓑa lot of plans or protection. If there's no umbrella in the drawing, the drawer does not have any means to deal ___(C)___ difficult situations.

21 위 글의 빈칸 (A)에 알맞은 것은?

① what
② who
③ whom
④ how
⑤ which

서답형

22 밑줄 친 ⓐ와 같은 뜻이 되도록 다음 문장의 빈칸에 알맞은 말을 쓰시오.

_____ the drops are _____
_____.

23 위 글의 빈칸 (B)에 알맞은 것은?

① so
② or
③ but
④ for
⑤ because

서답형

24 위 글의 밑줄 친 ⓑ를 한 단어로 바꿔 쓰시오.

➡ _____

25 위 글의 빈칸 (C)에 알맞은 것은?

① at
② to
③ from
④ for
⑤ with

중요

26 위 글의 내용과 일치하지 않는 것은?

① 비는 그림을 그린 사람이 받고 있는 스트레스를 보여 준다.
② 빗방울이 크면 스트레스도 더 크다.
③ 구름은 앞으로 벌어질 문제를 의미한다.
④ 우산은 스트레스를 받는 상황에서 그 사람이 가지고 있는 보호 기제를 의미한다.
⑤ 큰 우산은 그림을 그린 사람이 더 많은 문제를 가지게 될 것을 의미한다.

[27~28] 다음 글을 읽고 물음에 답하시오.

These are some of the possible meanings of each part of the drawings. Now, go back and look at the two drawings. Try reading ⓐthem yourself. ⓑCan you understand what kind of person drew each one? What's your opinion?

서답형

27 위 글의 밑줄 친 ⓐ가 가리키는 것을 영어로 쓰시오.

➡ _____

서답형

28 위 글의 밑줄 친 ⓑ를 우리말로 옮기시오.

➡ _____
_____

[01~04] 다음 글을 읽고 물음에 답하시오.

One of those tests is the Draw-a-Person-in-the-Rain (DAPR) test. Study the pictures below.

The person in Drawing A is holding an umbrella in a light rain. On the other ⓐ , the person in Drawing B is in a ⓑ rain and has no umbrella. Also, there are dark clouds above the person in Drawing B. What can these ⓒ mean?

01 위 글의 빈칸 ⓐ에 알맞은 말을 쓰시오.

➡ _____

02 위 글의 빈칸 ⓑ에 본문에 나오는 단어의 반의어를 쓰시오.

➡ _____

03 위 글의 빈칸 ⓒ에 different를 알맞은 어형으로 바꿔 쓰시오.

➡ _____

04 주어진 단어를 활용하여 다음 물음에 영어로 답하시오.

> Q: What are above the person in Drawing B? (there, 4 words)

➡ _____

[05~08] 다음 글을 읽고 물음에 답하시오.

Third, the details in the drawing of the person have to do ⓐ the drawer's attitude under stress. For example, someone who draws a person without a face does not want to draw people's attention to ⓑhim or her. Someone who draws the person on the right side of the paper is ready to meet the future. On the other hand, someone who draws the person on the left side may be worried about things that ⓒ(are happened / have happened) in the past.

05 위 글의 빈칸 ⓐ에 알맞은 전치사를 쓰시오.

➡ _____

06 위 글의 밑줄 친 ⓑ를 알맞게 고치시오.

➡ _____

07 위 글의 괄호 ⓒ에서 알맞은 것을 고르시오.

➡ _____

08 사람을 종이의 오른쪽에 그린 사람은 무엇을 맞이할 준비가 되었는지 우리말로 간단히 쓰시오.

➡ _____

[09~12] 다음 글을 읽고 물음에 답하시오.

(A)당신이 하는 모든 것은 당신에 대해 무엇인가를 말해 줍니다. The language you use, the clothes you wear, and even the pets you raise somehow show what kind of person you are. (B)The things you draw are not much different. What you draw and how you draw ⓐit are related to your personality. Doctors have been using various drawing tests to better understand people.

09 주어진 단어를 활용하여 밑줄 친 우리말 (A)를 영어로 쓰시오.

(everything, something, 7 words)

➡ _____

10 위 글의 밑줄 친 (B)가 구체적으로 의미하는 것을 우리말로 쓰시오.

➡ _____
_____

11 위 글의 밑줄 친 ⓐit이 가리키는 것을 우리말로 쓰시오.

➡ _____

12 Why have doctors been using various drawing tests? Answer in English with a full sentence.

➡ _____
_____

[13~15] 다음 글을 읽고 물음에 답하시오.

First, the rain shows the stress the person who drew the picture is under. (A)The bigger the drops are or the more heavily the rain is falling, bigger the stress is. The clouds mean problems (B)(waiting, waited) to happen, so a big cloud shows the drawer is not very hopeful about the future.

Second, the umbrella means the protection the person has in a (C)(stressed / stressful) situation. A big umbrella shows that the drawer has a lot of plans or protection. If there's no umbrella in the drawing, the drawer does not have any means to deal with difficult situations.

13 위 글의 밑줄 친 (A)에서 어법상 어색한 것을 고쳐 다시 쓰시오.

➡ _____
_____

14 위 글의 괄호 (B)에서 알맞은 것을 고르시오.

➡ _____

15 위 글의 괄호 (C)에서 알맞은 것을 고르시오.

➡ _____

해석

Before You Read

A picture is often closely related to what you're feeling in your mind. When
관계대명사   시간 부사절
you draw a picture, it shows your feelings. In other words, your various

feelings can be expressed through pictures. Therefore, you can find out other
          조동사+be+p.p. 수동태

people's feelings if you pay careful attention to their drawings.

구문해설 • in other words: 다시 말해서 • pay attention to: ~에 관심을 기울이다

그림은 종종 네 마음속에 느끼고 있는 것과 밀접한 관계가 있다. 네가 그림을 그릴 때, 그것은 너의 감정들을 나타낸다. 다시 말해서, 너의 다양한 감정들은 그림을 통해 표현될 수 있다. 그러므로 너는 다른 사람들의 그림에 주의 깊게 관심을 기울인다면 그들의 감정을 이해할 수 있다.

Writing Workshop

This year, we have been doing a lot of different kinds of activities at school.
               현재완료진행형   = many
Today, we had to talk about our own personalities and then talk about a
                                                      had to에 연결되는 동사원형
friend's personality. I saw myself as shy and friendly. What my friend said
              재귀목적어   선행사를 포함하는 관계대명사
about me was quite different. She said I am active and curious because I get

along well with others and am in lots of clubs.
              = other people

구문해설 • activity: 활동 • personality: 성격, 개성 • shy: 수줍은 • active: 활동적인
        • curious: 호기심이 많은

올해, 우리는 학교에서 많은 다양한 종류의 활동들을 해 오고 있다. 오늘 우리는 우리 자신의 성격과 친구의 성격에 대해 말해야 했다. 나는 내 자신이 수줍음이 많고 친절하다고 생각했다. 나에 대해 내 친구가 말한 것은 매우 달랐다. 그녀는 내가 활동적이고 호기심이 많다고 말했는데, 그 이유는 내가 다른 사람들과 잘 지내고 많은 동아리에 속해 있기 때문이라고 했다.

Wrap Up 3~4

G: I need to go to Daegu today, but there are no train tickets left. Are there any
   ~해야 한다   Are there any other ~?: 다른 ~가 있니?
   other ways to get there?

B: You can take a bus. It's fast and comfortable.

G: That's a great idea. I'll do that.

구문해설 • take a bus: 버스를 타다 • comfortable: 편리한

G: 나는 오늘 대구에 가야 하지만 남아 있는 기차표가 없어. 거기로 가는 다른 방법이 있을까?
B: 버스를 탈 수 있어. 그것은 빠르고 편해.
G: 좋은 생각이야. 그렇게 할게.

Words & Expressions

01 다음 짝지어진 단어의 관계가 같도록 빈칸에 알맞은 말을 쓰시오.

future : past = above : _____

02 다음 영영풀이에 해당하는 단어로 적절한 것은?

not requiring or relying on other people for help or support

① dependent   ② realistic
③ reasonable   ④ hopeful
⑤ independent

03 다음 빈칸에 공통으로 들어갈 말로 적절한 것은?

• A turtle is covered _____ a hard shell.
• Counselors deal _____ many kinds of problems.

① on   ② in   ③ at
④ by   ⑤ with

04 다음 중 밑줄 친 부분의 뜻풀이가 바르지 <u>않은</u> 것은?

① The bakery had so many different <u>types</u> of cookies. (유형)
② Emma's hands were soaked in <u>sweat</u> during the test. (땀)
③ Many Koreans enjoy eating <u>spicy</u> food like *tteokbokki*. (매운)
④ The price of this chair is very <u>reasonable</u>. (합리적인)
⑤ Kevin's parents were <u>against</u> his plan to travel alone. (~에 찬성하는)

05 다음 빈칸에 들어갈 말로 적절한 것은?

My friend is handsome and has a good _____.

① rest   ② personality
③ difference   ④ protection
⑤ situation

06 다음 문장에 공통으로 들어갈 말을 고르시오.

• I _____ a hamster as my pet.
• Please _____ your hand if you know the answer.

① hang   ② raise   ③ have
④ hold   ⑤ keep

07 다음 우리말과 같도록 빈칸에 알맞은 말을 〈보기〉에서 골라 쓰시오. (필요시 형태를 바꿀 것)

┌─ 보기 ─┐
have to do with / in other words / get along with

(1) Kate는 너무 친절하고 인기가 있어서 모든 사람과 잘 어울린다.
➡ Kate is so kind and popular that she _____ everyone.
(2) 다시 말하면, 각각의 색은 우리의 정신에 영향을 끼친다.
➡ _____, each color affects our mind.
(3) 그 음악은 오늘 축제와 관련이 있다.
➡ The music _____ the festival toady.

Conversation

[08~09] 다음 대화를 읽고 물음에 답하시오.

G: I took a personality test today. (①)

B: A house? (②)

G: Yeah. (③) According to the test, you can tell a lot about a person by their drawing. Here's mine. (④)

B: Interesting. So (A)what do these big windows mean? (⑤)

G: They mean I'm open to other people.

08 위 대화의 ①~⑤ 중 다음 문장이 들어갈 알맞은 곳은?

> I had to draw a house.

①   ②   ③   ④   ⑤

09 위 대화의 밑줄 친 (A)와 같은 의미가 되도록 괄호 안에 주어진 단어를 이용하여 문장을 완성하시오.

➡ _____ these big windows?
(meaning / is)

➡ _____ these big windows?
(by / mean)

[10~11] 다음 대화를 읽고 물음에 답하시오.

G: I need to go to Daegu today, but there are no train tickets left. 거기로 가는 다른 방법이 있을까? (get / ways / there / other / are / any / to / there)

B: You can take a bus. It's fast and comfortable.

G: That's a great idea. I'll do that.

10 위 대화의 밑줄 친 우리말과 같은 뜻이 되도록 괄호 안의 단어를 알맞게 배열하시오.

➡ _____

11 How will the girl go to Daegu? Answer in English. (5 words)

➡ _____

[12~13] 다음 대화를 읽고 물음에 답하시오.

B: What's your blood type?

(A) Wow. Then what does type A mean?

(B) Type A. Why?

(C) (a)People with blood type A is calm. They are good listeners, too.

(D) I'm reading an article. It says that blood type tells something about your personality.

12 위 대화의 (A)~(D)의 순서를 바르게 배열한 것은?

① (B) – (A) – (C) – (D)
② (B) – (D) – (A) – (C)
③ (C) – (B) – (D) – (A)
④ (D) – (B) – (A) – (C)
⑤ (D) – (B) – (C) – (A)

13 위 대화의 밑줄 친 (a)에서 어법상 틀린 부분을 찾아 바르게 고쳐 쓰시오.

_____ ➡ _____

[14~16] 다음 대화를 읽고 물음에 답하시오.

M: EDPI Test Center. Do you want to learn more about yourself? We have many kinds of personality tests. If there are any other tests you want to learn more about, we are here (A)help you.

B: Hi, I'm calling (B)take a personality test. Can I do one this afternoon?

M: Sure, you can come any time before 5 o'clock.

14 When does the boy want to take a personality test? Answer in English.

➡ _____

15 위 대화의 밑줄 친 (A)와 (B)를 알맞은 형태로 쓰시오.

(A) _____ (B) _____

16 Write the purpose of the boy's telephone call. Answer in Korean.

➡ _____

Grammar

17 다음 우리말에 맞게 괄호 안의 단어를 활용하여 빈칸을 채우시오.

(1) 의사들은 사람들을 더 잘 이해하기 위해 다양한 그리기 검사를 사용하고 있다. (3 단어)

➡ Doctors _____ (use) various drawing tests to better understand people.

(2) 좋은 친구를 사귀는 것이 나를 행복하게 하는 것이다.

➡ Having good friends is _____ _____ (what).

(3) Fred는 2010년 이후로 서울에서 살고 있다. (3 단어)

➡ Fred _____ (live) in Seoul since 2010.

(4) 이것이 내가 생활비를 벌기 위해서 할 수 있는 일이다.

➡ This is _____ (what) to make a living. *make a living: 생활비를 벌다

18 다음 중 어법상 올바른 문장을 고르시오.

① What people want to see is the letter that Gogh wrote.

② They need a specialist what can handle the challenging situation. *specialist: 전문가

③ I used to wear the red shoes the thing which my cousin liked.

④ You can order that you want to eat.

⑤ I want to know that they did.

19 우리말과 같은 뜻이 되도록 괄호 안의 어휘를 배열하여 영작하시오.

> 그들이 원하는 것은 약간의 음식이다. (food, they, is, what, some, want)

➡ _____

20 다음 우리말에 맞게 괄호 안의 단어를 활용하여 빈칸을 6단어로 채우시오.

> 이것이 내가 말하려고 하던 것이다.

➡ This is _____. (what)

21 다음 우리말과 같은 뜻이 되도록 괄호 안의 단어를 활용하여 문장을 완성하시오.

(1) 그것은 그들이 원했던 것이 아니다. (what을 이용하여 쓸 것.)

➡ That isn't _____ _____ _____.

(2) 우리는 5년 동안 서로를 알아 왔다. (완료형을 이용하여 쓸 것.)

➡ We _____ _____ (know) each other for five years.

(3) 나는 작년부터 그 프로젝트를 작업해 오고 있다. (진행형을 이용하여 쓸 것.)

➡ I ＿＿＿＿＿ ＿＿＿＿＿ ＿＿＿＿＿ (work) on the project since last year.

(4) 내가 하는 말을 믿으세요. (what을 이용하여 쓸 것.)

➡ Believe ＿＿＿＿＿ ＿＿＿＿＿ ＿＿＿＿＿.

22 그림의 상황에 맞게 괄호 안의 단어를 활용하여 빈칸을 채우시오.

I ＿＿＿＿＿＿＿＿＿＿ (know) what I can do first.

23 괄호 안의 단어를 활용하여 우리말에 맞게 빈칸을 채우시오.

(1) 나는 그가 하는 말을 믿을 수가 없다. (what)

➡ I can't believe ＿＿＿＿＿ ＿＿＿＿＿ ＿＿＿＿＿.

(2) 나는 네가 발견했던 것을 알고 있었다. (know)

➡ ＿＿＿＿＿ ＿＿＿＿＿ ＿＿＿＿＿ you had found.

24 다음 두 문장을 관계대명사 what을 사용하여 한 문장으로 만드시오.

- Henry couldn't understand the thing.
- The teacher said it.

➡ ＿＿＿＿＿＿＿＿＿＿＿＿＿＿＿

[25~28] 다음 글을 읽고 물음에 답하시오.

　One of those tests is the Draw-a-Person-in-the-Rain (DAPR) test. Study the pictures below.
　(①) The person in Drawing A is holding an umbrella in a ＿ⓐ＿ rain. (②) On the other hand, the person in Drawing B is in a heavy rain and has no umbrella. (③) What can these differences mean? (④)
　First, the rain shows the stress the person who drew the picture is under. (⑤) The bigger the drops are or the more heavily the rain is falling, the bigger the stress is. The clouds mean problems waiting to happen, so a big cloud shows the drawer is not very ⓑhope about the future.

25 위 글의 ①~⑤ 중 다음 주어진 문장이 들어갈 알맞은 곳은?

Also, there are dark clouds above the person in Drawing B.

① 　　② 　　③ 　　④ 　　⑤

26 위 글의 빈칸 ⓐ에 본문에 나오는 단어의 반의어를 쓰시오.

➡ ＿＿＿＿＿＿＿＿＿＿＿

27 위 글의 밑줄 친 ⓑhope를 알맞은 형으로 바꿔 쓰시오.

➡ ＿＿＿＿＿＿＿＿＿＿＿

28 다음 중 위 글의 내용을 바르게 이해하지 <u>못한</u> 사람은?

① Amelia: 그림 A의 사람은 가벼운 빗속에서 우산을 들고 있어.

② Brian: 그림 B의 사람은 거센 빗속에서 우산을 가지고 있지 않아.

③ Chris: 검은 구름들이 그림 B의 사람 머리 위에 있어.

④ David: 비는 그림을 그린 사람이 받는 스트레스를 보여 줘.

⑤ Eden: 큰 구름은 그림을 그린 사람의 미래에 대한 도전 의식을 나타내.

[29~32] 다음 글을 읽고 물음에 답하시오.

Third, the details in the drawing of the person have to do with the drawer's attitude ___ⓐ___ stress. ___(A)___ example, someone who draws a person without a face does not want to draw people's attention to himself or herself. Someone who draws the person on the right side of the paper is ready to meet the future. ___(B)___ the other hand, someone who draws the person on the left side may be worried about things that have happened in the ___ⓑ___ .

29 위 글의 빈칸 ⓐ에 적절한 것은?

① on   ② to
③ over   ④ among
⑤ under

30 위 글의 빈칸 (A)와 (B)에 적절한 것으로 짝지어진 것은?

① To – On   ② For – To
③ For – At   ④ For – On
⑤ With – To

31 위 글의 빈칸 ⓑ에 본문에 나오는 단어의 반의어를 쓰시오.

➡ _____

32 What is someone who draws the person on the right side of the paper ready to meet? Answer in English.

➡ _____

[33~35] 다음 글을 읽고 물음에 답하시오.

(①) This year, we have been doing a lot of different kinds of activities at school. (②) Today, we had to talk about our own personalities and then talk about a friend's personality. (③) ___ⓐ___ my friend said about me was quite different. (④) She said I am active and ___ⓑ___ because I get along well with others and am in lots of clubs. (⑤)

33 위 글의 ①~⑤ 중 다음 주어진 문장이 들어갈 알맞은 곳은?

I saw myself as shy and friendly.

①   ②   ③   ④   ⑤

34 위 글의 빈칸 ⓐ에 적절한 것은?

① That   ② How
③ Who   ④ What
⑤ Which

35 위 글의 빈칸 ⓑ에 다음 영영풀이에 해당하는 단어를 철자 c로 시작하여 쓰시오.

interested in something and wanting to know more about it

➡ _____

01 출제율 90%

다음 중 짝지어진 단어의 관계가 <u>다른</u> 하나는?

① heavy – light
② future – past
③ various – diverse
④ calm – excited
⑤ carefully – carelessly

02 출제율 95%

다음 빈칸에 알맞은 말이 바르게 짝지어진 것은?

- I saw myself _____ shy and friendly.
- I want to deal _____ two other issues.

① as – to   ② with – of
③ as – about   ④ with – as
⑤ as – with

03 출제율 90%

다음 문장의 빈칸에 〈영어 설명〉에 해당하는 알맞은 단어를 쓰시오. (주어진 철자로 시작할 것)

The sky darkened and a few d_____ of rain fell.

〈영어 설명〉 a very small amount of liquid that falls in a rounded shape

04 출제율 95%

다음 밑줄 친 부분과 바꿔 쓸 수 있는 것은?

They all burst out laughing <u>at the same time</u>.

① completely   ② carefully
③ significantly   ④ consequently
⑤ simultaneously

[05~06] 다음 대화를 읽고 물음에 답하시오.

B: Jane, what are you reading?
G: I'm reading an interesting magazine. (①)
B: That's surprising. (②)
G: Yes. For example, the color red can help us focus better. (③)
B: Are there any other useful colors? (④)
G: Yes. The color blue helps people relax. (⑤)

05 출제율 100%

위 대화의 ①~⑤ 중 다음 문장이 들어갈 위치로 알맞은 곳은?

It says colors can change people's feelings.

①   ②   ③   ④   ⑤

06 출제율 90%

위 대화에서 다음 영영풀이에 해당하는 단어를 찾아 쓰시오.

to become or make someone become calmer and less worried

➡ _____

07 출제율 90%

다음 대화의 빈칸에 주어진 말을 이용해서 쓰시오.

G: What does "have a long face" mean?
B: It means ' _____ . (sad, 3 words)

➡ _____

[08~10] 다음 대화를 읽고 물음에 답하시오.

G: I __(A)__ a personality test today. I had to draw a house.

B: A house?

G: Yeah. __(B)__ the test, you can tell a lot about a person by their drawing. Here's mine.

B: Interesting. So what do these big windows __(C)__ ?

G: They mean I'm open to other people.

출제율 100%

08 위 대화의 빈칸 (A)와 (C)에 알맞은 말이 바르게 짝지어진 것은?

① made – have
② threw – mean
③ had – take
④ took – mean
⑤ had – have

출제율 90%

09 위 대화의 빈칸 (B)에 '~에 따르면'이라는 어구를 두 단어로 쓰시오. (철자 A로 시작할 것)

➡ _____

출제율 95%

10 What do the big windows that the girl drew mean? Answer in Korean.

➡ _____

출제율 95%

11 〈보기〉 중 알맞은 단어를 골라 빈칸을 채우시오.

┌─── 보기 ───┐
│   what   that   │
└──────────┘

(1) Everybody _____ I know is honest and kind.

(2) He gave me _____ I wanted.

출제율 95%

12 괄호 안의 단어를 사용하여 우리말에 맞게 현재완료진행형 문장을 쓰시오.

┌─────────────────────┐
│ 비가 3시간 동안 심하게 내리고 있다. │
│ (rain, heavily)   │
└─────────────────────┘

➡ _____

출제율 100%

13 다음 중 어법상 어색한 문장을 고르시오.

① I have been knowing him since my childhood.
② She has been crying since last night.
③ I have been studying Spanish for 5 years.
④ I've been reading the book you lent me.
⑤ He has been collecting stamps since he was eight.

출제율 95%

14 괄호 안의 단어를 활용하여 우리말에 맞게 빈칸을 채우시오.

(1) 그것은 그들이 원했던 집이 아니다. (that)
➡ That isn't the house _____.

(2) 그 여인은 자기가 필요한 것을 말했다. (what)
➡ The woman said _____.

(3) 나는 지난해부터 여기에서 일하고 있는 중이다. (work)
➡ I _____ here since last year.

✏️ 출제율 95%

15 다음 그림을 보고 괄호 안의 단어를 활용하여 빈칸을 채우시오. (현재완료진행형으로 쓸 것.)

We _____ (discuss) the problems for one hour.

[16~17] 다음 글을 읽고 물음에 답하시오.

(A)이것들은 그림들 각 부분의 가능한 의미 풀이 중 일부입니다. Now, go back and look ①at the two drawings. Try ②reading them ③yourself. Can you understand ④what kind of person drew ⑤both one? What's your opinion?

✏️ 출제율 90%

16 위 글의 밑줄 친 (A)를 주어진 단어를 이용하여 영어로 옮기시오.

some, possible, meanings, each, drawings

➡️ _____

_____

✏️ 출제율 95%

17 위 글의 밑줄 친 ①~⑤ 중 어법상 어색한 것은?

①   ②   ③   ④   ⑤

[18~21] 다음 글을 읽고 물음에 답하시오.

This year, we have been doing ⓐa lot of different kinds of activities at school. Today, we had to talk about our own personalities and then talk about a friend's personality. I saw myself as shy and friendly. What my friend said about me was quite ___ⓑ___. She said I am active and curious because I get along well with others and am in lots of clubs.

I=Minsu

✏️ 출제율 95%

18 위 글의 밑줄 친 ⓐ 대신 쓸 수 있는 것은?

① few   ② little
③ enough   ④ many
⑤ much

✏️ 출제율 95%

19 위 글의 빈칸 ⓑ에 알맞은 것은?

① strange   ② same
③ different   ④ essential
⑤ important

✏️ 출제율 100%

20 위 글의 내용과 일치하지 <u>않는</u> 것은?

① 민수의 학교에서는 많은 종류의 활동을 해 오고 있다.
② 그들은 자신의 성격과 친구의 성격을 말하는 활동을 가졌다.
③ 민수는 자신이 수줍음을 탄다고 생각했다.
④ 민수의 친구는 민수가 소극적인 성격이라고 말했다.
⑤ 민수는 많은 동아리에 가입하고 있다.

21 출제율 90%

Why did Minsu's friend say he is active and curious?
Answer in English.

➡ _____

_____

[22~27] 다음 글을 읽고 물음에 답하시오.

First, the rain shows the stress the person who drew the picture is under. (A)As the drops are bigger or the rain is falling more heavily, the stress is bigger. The clouds mean problems waiting to happen, so a big cloud shows the drawer is not very ___(B)___ about the future.

Second, the umbrella means the protection the person has in a stressful situation. A big umbrella shows (C)that the drawer has a lot of plans or protection. ___(D)___ there's no umbrella in the drawing, the drawer does not have any means to deal with difficult situations.

22 출제율 90%

위 글의 밑줄 친 (A)를 'the+비교급 ~, the+비교급 …' 구문을 써서 바꿔 쓰시오.

➡ _____

_____

23 출제율 95%

위 글의 빈칸 (B)에 알맞은 것은?

① careful   ② promising
③ hopeful   ④ essential
⑤ exciting

24 출제율 95%

위 글의 밑줄 친 (C)와 용법이 같은 것은?

① It is strange that she doesn't come.
② I know that you don't like cats.
③ Look at the trees that stand on the hill.
④ It was here that she first met Mike.
⑤ This is the doll that my mother made for me.

25 출제율 95%

위 글의 빈칸 (D)에 알맞은 것은?

① If   ② As
③ Since   ④ While
⑤ Although

26 출제율 100%

위 글의 내용과 일치하지 <u>않는</u> 것은?

① 빗방울이 클수록 스트레스도 크다.
② 구름은 어떤 문제들이 발생할 것을 의미한다.
③ 큰 구름은 미래에 나쁜 일이 발생할 것을 나타낸다.
④ 우산은 스트레스를 주는 상황에서 사람을 보호해 준다는 것을 의미한다.
⑤ 우산을 가지고 있지 않은 사람은 어려운 상황을 극복할 용기가 있음을 나타낸다.

27 출제율 90%

What does a big umbrella show? Answer in Korean.

➡ _____

_____

01 다음 대화의 빈칸에 괄호 안의 단어를 이용하여 〈조건〉에 맞게 알맞은 말을 쓰시오.

(1)

> A: What does "feel blue" mean?
> B: It means '_____'. (sad, 3 words)

(2)

> A: What does "throw up one's hands" mean?
> B: It means '_____'. (give, 3 words)

[02~03] 다음 대화를 읽고 물음에 답하시오.

> B: Jane, what are you reading?
> G: I'm reading an interesting magazine. It says colors can change people's feelings.
> B: (A)That's surprising.
> G: Yes. For example, the color red can help us focus better.
> B: Are there any other useful colors?
> G: Yes. The color blue helps people relax.

02 What is the magazine about?

➡ _____

03 위 대화의 밑줄 친 (A)That이 가리키는 것을 우리말로 쓰시오.

➡ _____

04 괄호 안의 단어를 활용하여 문장을 완성하시오. (관계대명사 that이나 what을 사용할 것.)

(1) 그가 음악을 사랑하는 바로 그 사람이다. (the very)

➡ _____

(2) 당신이 원하는 것을 고르세요. (pick)
➡ Please _____.

(3) 그것은 그가 사랑하는 바로 그 음악이다. (the very)

➡ _____

(4) 네가 가지고 온 것을 보여 줘. (bring)
➡ Show me _____.

05 우리말에 맞게 〈보기〉의 단어를 활용하여 배열하시오.

> ┤ 보기 ├
> months, the, do, I, course, have, for, been, six

> 나는 6개월 동안 그 과정을 밟아 왔다.

➡ _____

06 다음 우리말에 맞게 괄호 안의 단어를 활용하여 영작하시오. (9 단어)

> 그는 2시간 동안 버스를 타고 있다. (take, for)

➡ _____

Everything you do says ①something about you. The language you use, the   (A)   you wear, and even the pets you raise somehow show what kind of person you are. (B)The things you draw are not much different. What you draw and ②how you draw it are related to your personality. Doctors ③have been using various drawing tests to better understand people.

One of those tests ④are the Draw-a-Person-in-the-Rain (DAPR) test. Study the pictures below.

The person in Drawing A is holding an umbrella in a light rain. On the other hand, the person in Drawing B is in a heavy rain and has no umbrella. Also, there are dark clouds ⑤above the person in Drawing B. What can (C)these differences mean?

07 위 글의 밑줄 친 ①~⑤ 중 어법상 어색한 것을 바르게 고쳐 쓰시오.

➡ _____ ➡ _____

08 위 글의 빈칸 (A)에 다음 영영풀이에 해당하는 단어를 쓰시오.

> the things that people wear, such as shirts, coats, trousers, and dresses

➡ _____

09 위 글의 밑줄 친 (B)가 의미하는 것을 우리말로 쓰시오.

➡ _____

_____

10 위 글의 밑줄 친 (C)these differences가 구체적으로 가리키는 것을 우리말로 쓰시오.

➡ _____

_____

_____

[11~12] 다음 글을 읽고 물음에 답하시오.

Third, (A)the details in the drawing of the person have to do with the drawer's attitude under stress. For example, someone who draws a person without a face does not want to draw people's attention to himself or herself. Someone who draws the person on the right side of the paper is ready to meet the future. On the other hand, someone who draws the person on the left side may be (B)worry about things that have happened in the past.

11 위 글의 밑줄 친 (A)로 알 수 있는 것을 우리말로 쓰시오.

➡ _____

_____

12 위 글의 밑줄 친 (B)를 알맞은 형으로 고치시오.

➡ _____

01 다음은 아래 그림에 대한 해석이다. (1)~(3)을 적절한 순서로 배열하시오.

(1) In addition, the drawer does not want to draw attention to himself or herself.

(2) Since the person in the picture is standing on the left side and has no umbrella in the heavy rain, it shows that the person who drew the picture is under a lot of stress.

(3) The drawer does not seem to have a lot of plans and any means to protect himself or herself against stressful situations.

02 다음 〈보기 A〉와 〈보기 B〉에서 알맞은 말을 하나씩 골라 (1)번과 같이 관계대명사를 이용한 문장을 완성하시오.

보기 A	보기 B
have for lunch	the doll
like to do	bread and milk
have to do	do one's homework
have in my pocket	watch movies

(1) What I had for lunch was bread and milk.

(2) _____

(3) _____

(4) _____

03 다음 〈보기〉와 같이 SNS 자기 소개글을 써 보시오.

보기

I like sweet chocolate and cute cats. I've been raising a cat for five years. I call her Wendy. I'm open to making new friends. Follow me, and I'll follow you back.

I like (A)_____. I've been (B)_____.
What I (C)_____. I'm open to making new friends. Follow me, and I'll follow you back.

단원별 모의고사

01 밑줄 친 부분과 바꿔 쓸 수 있는 말을 고르시오.

> I've always been <u>frightened</u> of dogs.

① bored   ② excited   ③ angry
④ worried   ⑤ scared

02 다음 빈칸에 들어갈 말을 고르시오.

> She tries to _____ attention to herself by wearing bright clothes.

① have   ② draw
③ find   ④ take
⑤ make

03 다음 빈칸에 들어갈 말을 〈보기〉에서 찾아 쓰시오.

> ┌── 보기 ──┐
>
> at   in   off   to   out

(1) All of the tickets were sold _____.
(2) She didn't participate _____ the meeting.
(3) Everything went according _____ the plan.

04 다음 영영풀이에 해당하는 단어를 고르시오.

> needing someone or something else for support, help, etc.

① useful   ② trustful
③ serious   ④ dependent
⑤ disappointed

05 다음 우리말에 맞도록 빈칸에 알맞은 말을 쓰시오.

(1) 내가 하찮은 세부 사항까지 일일이 기억하지는 못해.
  ➡ I can't remember every little _____.
(2) 기자들은 그 정치인이 하는 말에 집중했다.
  ➡ The reporters paid _____ to what the politician said.
(3) 삶에 대해 긍정적인 태도를 가지는 것이 좋을 것이다.
  ➡ It would be good to have a positive _____ toward life.

[06~07] 다음 대화를 읽고 물음에 답하시오.

> G: Hi, Jack! (A)<u>How are you doing</u>?
> B: I'm on cloud nine! I got a concert ticket for my favorite band.
> G: What does "on cloud nine" mean?
> B: It means (B)_____.

06 위 대화의 밑줄 친 (A)와 바꿔 쓸 수 있는 말을 <u>모두</u> 고르시오.

① How's it going?
② What's going on?
③ How have you been?
④ How is it done?
⑤ Is anything the matter?

07 위 대화의 빈칸 (B)에 알맞은 것은?

① I feel depressed.
② I'm really angry.
③ I'm nervous and scared.
④ I'm really happy and excited.
⑤ I'm so bored and lonely.

[08~11] 다음 대화를 읽고 물음에 답하시오.

Hajun: Look! I found this test on an app that tells what kind of person you are. Do you want to try it?

Emma: Sure. Sounds like fun.

Hajun: Okay, listen. What are you afraid of? Choose one of these: crowds, spiders, or dark places.

Emma: I hate dark places. I cannot sleep without a night light on. What does that mean?

Hajun: It says you are full of imagination. That's (A)[why / because] you fill dark places with all kinds of scary things.

Emma: That's very interesting. What about you? (a)너는 두려워하는 것이 있니?

Hajun: I chose dark places (B)[too / either]. But I don't think I have a big imagination.

Emma: This is fun. I want to do some more. Are there any (C)[other / another] tests we can take?

Hajun: Sure. This app has a lot of them.

08 위 대화의 밑줄 친 (a)의 우리말과 같은 뜻이 되도록 주어진 단어를 바르게 배열하시오.

there / are / you / anything / of / is / afraid

➡ _____

09 위 대화의 괄호 (A)~(C)에서 알맞은 것을 골라 쓰시오.

➡ (A) _____ (B) _____ (C) _____

10 위 대화에서 다음 영영풀이에 해당하는 단어를 찾아 쓰시오.

the ability to form a picture in your mind of something that you have not seen or experienced

➡ _____

11 위 대화의 내용과 일치하지 <u>않는</u> 것은?

① Emma는 성격 테스트를 받고 싶어 한다.
② Emma는 어두운 장소를 싫어한다.
③ Emma는 불을 켜 놓고 잠을 잘 수 없다.
④ 하준이는 자기가 상상력이 풍부하다고 생각하지 않는다.
⑤ 앱에는 다른 성격검사들이 많이 있다.

12 다음 우리말에 맞게 괄호 안의 어휘와 관계대명사 what과 the thing which를 활용하여 빈칸에 알맞은 말을 쓰시오.

(1) 이것은 내가 좋아하는 것이다. (like)

➡ _____

(2) 그녀가 말했던 것은 사실이야. (be, true)

➡ _____

(3) 나는 다채로운 것이 좋아. (like, colorful)

➡ _____

13 우리말과 일치하도록 할 때 빈칸에 알맞은 것은?

그녀는 2012년 이후로 영어를 가르치고 있다.
➡ She has _____ English since 2012.

① teach
② been teaching
③ teaching
④ been taught
⑤ be taught

14 다음 중 어법상 <u>어색한</u> 것은?

① This is what I can do to help you.

② I want to do well what I have to do.

③ I'll tell you what he likes.

④ I can't catch that you are saying.

⑤ That she loved him made me surprised.

15 다음 중 빈칸에 들어갈 말로 적절한 것을 고르시오.

> They have been waiting for Minsu _____ thirty minutes.

① since   ② in

③ on   ④ for

⑤ during

16 빈칸에 들어갈 알맞은 것을 고르시오.

> 나는 그를 5년 동안 알고 지냈다.
> ➡ I have _____ him for 5 years.

① known   ② been knowing

③ know   ④ knowing

⑤ be known

17 우리말에 맞게 괄호 안의 단어를 배열하시오.

> 요리사가 휴가를 떠나서 음식점 문이 닫혀 있다.
> (so, the, has, cook, a, been, vacation, the, taking, is, restaurant, closed)

➡ _____

_____

18 다음 우리말에 맞게 괄호 안의 단어를 활용하여 두 가지로 영작하시오.

> 내가 관심 있는 것은 기타 연주하는 법을 배우는 것이다. (be interested in)

➡ _____

➡ _____

_____

19 다음 그림을 보고 빈칸을 채우시오.

> _____ I ordered is a glass of apple juice.

20 다음 우리말에 맞게 괄호 안의 단어를 활용하여 빈칸을 채우시오.

> 아이들이 두 시간째 피구를 하고 있습니다. (play)
> *dodgeball 피구
> ➡ The children _____ _____ _____ dodgeball _____ two hours.

21 다음 그림을 보고 괄호 안의 단어를 활용하여 우리말에 맞게 빈칸을 채우시오.

> Jake는 오늘 아침부터 몸이 안 좋았습니다. (feel, sick)
> ➡ Jake _____ _____ _____ _____ _____ _____ _____.

[22~25] 다음 글을 읽고 물음에 답하시오.

This year, we ①have been doing a lot of different kinds of activities ②at school. Today, we had to talk about our own personalities and then talk about a friend's personality. I saw ③myself as shy and ⓐfriend. ④What my friend said about me was quite different. She said I am active and curious because I get ⓑ_____ well with ⑤other and am in lots of clubs.

22 위 글의 밑줄 친 ①~⑤ 중 어법상 어색한 것은?

①   ②   ③   ④   ⑤

23 위 글의 밑줄 친 ⓐfriend를 알맞은 형으로 고치시오.

➡ _____

24 위 글의 빈칸 ⓑ에 알맞은 것은?

① on   ② about
③ up   ④ along
⑤ over

25 위 글의 필자의 성격에 관한 질문에 우리말로 답하시오.

필자의 생각: ➡ (1) _____
                 (2) _____
친구의 생각: ➡ (1) _____
                 (2) _____

[26~29] 다음 글을 읽고 물음에 답하시오.

Everything you do says something about you. The language you use, the clothes you wear, and ⓐeven the pets you raise somehow show what kind of person you are. The things you draw are not much different. What you draw and how you draw it are related ⓑ_____ your personality. Doctors have been using various drawing tests ⓒto better understand people.

26 위 글의 밑줄 친 ⓐeven과 같은 뜻으로 쓰인 것은?

① He never even opened the letter.
② You know even less about it than I do.
③ 4, 6, 8, 10 are all even numbers.
④ Our scores are now even.
⑤ You need an even surface to work on.

27 위 글의 빈칸 ⓑ에 알맞은 것은?

① on   ② to   ③ up
④ at   ⑤ from

28 위 글의 밑줄 친 ⓒ와 용법이 같은 것은?

① We wished to reach the North Pole.
② He made a promise to come again.
③ To live without air is impossible.
④ He worked hard to support his family.
⑤ We decided to go fishing in the river.

29 위 글에서 어떤 사람인지 알 수 있는 정보로 언급되지 <u>않은</u> 것은?

① the language you use
② the pets you raise
③ the food you eat
④ the clothes you wear
⑤ the drawings you draw

Lesson 6

Buy and Sell Wisely

 의사소통 기능

- 허가 여부 묻기

  A: Do you mind if I lean my seat back?

  B: No, not at all.

- 제안, 권유, 요청에 답하기

  A: Can I look around the stage?

  B: I'm sorry. I'm afraid you can't. It's open only for the actors.

 언어 형식

- as+형용사/부사의 원급 + as

  My old bike is almost **as good as** a new one.

- 과거완료

  He realized what he **had done** wrong.

Words & Expressions

Key Words

- **accept** [æksépt] 동 받아들이다
- **account** [əkáunt] 명 은행 계좌
- **act** [ækt] 동 행동하다
- **add** [æd] 동 더하다
- **advertisement** [ædvərtáizmənt] 명 광고
- **ahead** [əhéd] 부 앞으로
- **angle** [æŋgl] 명 각도
- **attractive** [ətræktiv] 형 매력적인
- **buyer** [báiər] 명 구매자
- **category** [kǽtəgɔ̀:ri] 명 범주, 부류
- **comment** [kámənt] 명 언급
- **contact** [kántækt] 명 연락, 접촉
- **customer** [kʌ́stəmər] 명 고객
- **deliver** [dilívər] 동 배달하다
- **description** [diskrípʃən] 명 묘사
- **dig** [dig] 동 (땅을) 파다, (땅에서) 캐다
- **excellent** [éksələnt] 형 훌륭한, 탁월한
- **excuse** [ikskjú:z] 동 (무례나 실수 등을) 용서하다
- **expectation** [èkspektéiʃən] 명 기대
- **experience** [ikspíəriəns] 명 경험 동 경험하다
- **finally** [fáinəli] 부 결국에
- **greedy** [grí:di] 형 욕심 많은
- **grocery** [gróusəri] 명 식료품, 식료품점
- **hasty** [héisti] 형 성급한
- **however** [hauévər] 부 그러나, 하지만
- **indoors** [indɔ́:rz] 형 실내의
- **lend** [lend] 동 빌려주다
- **maybe** [méibi:] 부 아마도
- **mix** [miks] 동 섞다
- **normally** [nɔ́:rməli] 부 보통, 보통 때는
- **pass** [pæs] 동 (시간이) 흐르다, 지나가다
- **possible** [pásəbl] 형 발생 가능한, 있을 수 있는
- **post** [poust] 동 (안내문 등을) 게시하다
- **posting** [póustiŋ] 명 게시 글
- **realize** [rí:əlàiz] 동 깨닫다
- **receive** [risí:v] 동 받다
- **recommend** [rèkəménd] 동 추천하다
- **reply** [riplái] 명 답장, 대답
- **ride** [raid] 동 (자전거 등을) 타다
- **sadly** [sǽdli] 부 슬프게
- **sale** [seil] 명 할인 판매
- **savings** [séiviŋz] 명 예금
- **scratch** [skrætʃ] 명 긁힌 자국
- **search** [sə:rtʃ] 동 찾다, 검색하다
- **seem** [si:m] 동 ~처럼 보이다, ~인 것 같다
- **sell** [sel] 동 팔다
- **several** [sévərəl] 형 몇몇의
- **shiny** [ʃáini] 형 빛나는
- **shut** [ʃʌt] 동 닫다
- **sink** [siŋk] 동 가라앉다
- **steal** [sti:l] 동 훔치다
- **suddenly** [sʌ́dnli] 부 갑자기
- **through** [θru:] 전 ~을 통해
- **tip** [tip] 명 조언, 정보
- **ugly** [ʌ́gli] 형 못생긴
- **used** [ju:st] 형 중고의

Key Expressions

- **a whole day** 하루 종일
- **act fast** 빠르게 움직이다[행동하다]
- **as good as** ~ ~만큼 좋은
- **ask for** ~을 요청하다
- **at first** 처음에는
- **compared to** ~ ~에 비교해서
- **from different angles** 다른 각도에서
- **get a reply** 답장을 받다, 댓글이 달리다
- **go up** 올라가다
- **good for** ~ ~에 좋은
- **grow up** 성장하다
- **hand over** ~을 건네 주다
- **have an idea** 생각이 있다
- **online market** 인터넷 시장
- **plan to** ~ ~할 계획이다
- **push down** 밀어 내리다
- **take a photo of** ~ ~의 사진을 찍다
- **the number of** ~ ~의 수/숫자
- **think about** ~에 대해 생각하다
- **this time** 이번에
- **this year** 올해

Word Power

※ 서로 비슷한 뜻을 가진 어휘

- ☐ **attractive** 매력적인 – **charming** 매력 있는
- ☐ **excellent** 훌륭한, 탁월한 – **outstanding** 눈에 띄는, 저명한
- ☐ **greedy** 욕심 많은 – **avaricious** 탐욕적인
- ☐ **maybe** 아마도 – **probably** 아마도

- ☐ **description** 묘사 – **explanation** 설명
- ☐ **finally** 결국에 – **eventually** 결국, 마침내
- ☐ **hasty** 성급한 – **hurried** 서둘러 하는
- ☐ **used** 중고의 – **second-hand** 중고의

※ 서로 반대의 뜻을 가진 어휘

- ☐ **ahead** 앞으로 ↔ **behind** 뒤에, 뒤떨어져
- ☐ **buyer** 구매자 ↔ **seller** 판매자
- ☐ **greedy** 욕심 많은 ↔ **generous** 후한, 관대한
- ☐ **indoors** 실내의 ↔ **outdoors** 외부의, 야외에서

- ☐ **attractive** 매력적인 ↔ **unattractive** 매력적이지 않은
- ☐ **excellent** 훌륭한, 탁월한 ↔ **terrible** 형편없는
- ☐ **hasty** 성급한 ↔ **slow** 느린
- ☐ **shut** 닫다 ↔ **open** 열다

※ 비교급 ❶ 형용사 +-er

- ☐ **big** + **-er** → **bigger** 더 큰
- ☐ **fast** + **-er** → **faster** 더 빠른, 더 빠르게
- ☐ **happy** + **-er** → **happier** 더 행복한
- ☐ **simple** + **-er** → **simpler** 더 단순한

- ☐ **cheap** + **-er** → **cheaper** 더 저렴한
- ☐ **funny** + **-er** → **funnier** 더 재밌는
- ☐ **heavy** + **-er** → **heavier** 더 무거운
- ☐ **ugly** + **-er** → **uglier** 더 못생긴

※ 비교급 ❷ more + 형용사

- ☐ **more** + **attractive** → **more attractive** 더 매력적인
- ☐ **more** + **dangerous** → **more dangerous** 더 위험한
- ☐ **more** + **popular** → **more popular** 더 인기있는
- ☐ **more** + **intelligent** → **more intelligent** 더 똑똑한

- ☐ **more** + **charming** → **more charming** 더 매력적인
- ☐ **more** + **expensive** → **more expensive** 더 비싼
- ☐ **more** + **important** → **more important** 더 중요한
- ☐ **more** + **interesting** → **more interesting** 더 흥미로운

English Dictionary

- ☐ **accept** 받아들이다
  → to agree to take something; to say yes to an offer or invitation
  어떤 것을 취하기로 동의하다; 제안이나 초대에 응하다

- ☐ **account** 은행 계좌
  → an arrangement with a bank to keep your money there and to allow you to take it out when you need to
  돈을 유지하고 필요할 때 꺼내 쓰기 위한 은행과의 계약

- ☐ **act** 행동하다
  → to behave in the stated way; to do something for a particular purpose or to solve a problem
  언급된 방식으로 행동하다; 문제를 해결하기 위해 또는 특정 목적을 위해 어떤 일을 하다

- ☐ **comment** 언급
  → something that you say or write to express your opinion
  의견을 표현하기 위해 하는 어떤 말이나 글

- ☐ **contact** 연락, 접촉
  → communication with someone, especially by speaking or writing to them regularly
  정기적으로 말하거나 씀으로써 어떤 사람과 의사소통하는 것

- ☐ **excuse** 용서하다
  → to forgive someone 어떤 사람을 용서하다

- ☐ **expectation** 기대
  → the feeling that good things are going to happen in the future
  좋은 일이 미래에 일어날 것이라는 느낌

- ☐ **experience** 경험
  → the process of getting knowledge or skill from doing, seeing, or feeling things
  사물들을 보거나 하거나 느낌으로써 오는 지식이나 기술을 얻는 과정

- ☐ **normally** 보통, 보통 때는
  → in the usual or expected way 보통의 혹은 예상되는 방식으로

- ☐ **search** 찾다, 검색하다
  → to look somewhere carefully in order to find something
  무언가를 찾기 위해 주의 깊게 어느 곳을 보다

- ☐ **ugly** 못생긴
  → unpleasant to look at; not attractive
  보기에 즐겁지 않은; 매력적이지 않은

- ☐ **used** 중고의
  → not new 새것이 아닌

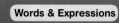
서답형

01 다음 짝지어진 단어의 관계가 같도록 빈칸에 알맞은 말을 쓰시오.

> greedy : generous = indoors : _____

02 다음 영영풀이가 가리키는 것을 고르시오.

> to agree to take something; to say yes to an offer or invitation

① accept   ② contact

③ excuse   ④ experience

⑤ receive

03 다음 중 밑줄 친 부분의 뜻풀이가 바르지 <u>않은</u> 것은?

① His <u>account</u> was deliberately ambiguous. (은행 계좌)

② The photo was taken from an unusual <u>angle</u>. (각도)

③ The company promises to <u>deliver</u> my order within 48 hours. (배달하다)

④ The bank refused to <u>lend</u> the money to us. (빌려주다)

⑤ How many hits has this <u>posting</u> had? (게시 글)

서답형

04 다음 우리말을 주어진 어휘를 이용하여 영작하시오.

(1) 우리는 여러분을 새로운 고객으로 맞이하고 싶습니다. (customer, welcome)

➡ _____

(2) Peter는 수년 동안 그 식료품점에서 물건을 샀다. (grocery, shop, years)

➡ _____

서답형

05 다음 문장의 빈칸에 들어갈 말을 〈보기〉에서 골라 쓰시오. (필요하면 어형 변화를 할 것.)

> ─┤ 보기 ├─
> act / several / used / sale / realize / post

(1) We all should _____ the seriousness of this crime.

(2) Many _____ stores have books that are hard to find at regular stores.

(3) The scandal was in the headlines for _____ days.

(4) The test results will be _____ on the Internet.

06 다음 문장의 빈칸 (A)~(B)에 각각 공통으로 들어갈 말이 바르게 짝지어진 것은?

> • Many French people say that red wine is good ___(A)___ you.
> • Ask ___(A)___ a refund if the order is faulty.
> • As we go ___(B)___, the air grows colder.
> • Children grow ___(B)___ so fast these days.

① for – down   ② for – to

③ for – up   ④ to – down

⑤ to – up

01 다음 짝지어진 단어의 관계가 같도록 빈칸에 알맞은 말을 쓰시오.

> heavy : heavier =
> charming : _____

02 다음 주어진 우리말에 맞게 빈칸에 알맞은 말을 쓰시오.

(1) 이것은 심각한 문제이다. 우리는 그것에 대해 생각할 시간이 더 필요하다.

➡ This is a serious issue; we need more time to _____ _____ it.

(2) 우리는 월요일에 그들을 만날 때 서류를 건네주어야 한다.

➡ We have to _____ _____ the documents when we meet them on Monday.

(3) 그녀는 이번에는 반드시 시험에 통과할 작정이다.

➡ She is determined to pass the test _____ _____.

03 다음 영영풀이에 맞는 단어를 쓰시오.

> something that you say or write to express your opinion

➡ _____

04 우리말과 일치하도록 주어진 단어를 모두 배열하여 영작하시오.

(1) 나는 갑자기 나도 모르게 길을 뛰어 내려가고 있었다.

(found, down, I, the, myself, street, suddenly, running)

➡ _____

(2) 그녀는 처음에는 그 일이 피곤하다는 것을 알았지만, 곧 익숙해졌다.

(she, found, got, she, the, job, soon, used, it, at, to, first, but, tiring)

➡ _____
_____

(3) 그 건물의 지반이 내려앉기 시작한다.

(the, the, building, of, is, to, foundations, sink, starting)

➡ _____

05 다음 문장의 빈칸에 들어갈 말을 〈보기〉에서 골라 쓰시오.

> ┤ 보기 ├
> have an idea / act fast / compared to / take a photo of / as good as

(1) The photographer is allowed to _____ any type of car and sell them.

(2) It's too bad every day can't be _____ today.

(3) I _____ that my ex-boyfriend is still living somewhere near here.

 06 다음 우리말에 맞게 주어진 어구를 사용하여 영작하시오.

(1) 그녀는 아카데미 시상식에서 상을 받기 위해 앞으로 나갔다. (step up, receive)

➡ _____

(2) Julia는 영화 부문에서 대상을 받았다. (category, the grand prize)

➡ _____

(3) 눈 때문에 사람들이 그녀가 매력있다고 느끼는 거야. (attractive, the reason)

➡ _____

Conversation

1 허가 여부 묻기

> **A** Do you mind if I lean my seat back? 제가 좌석을 뒤로 젖혀도 될까요?
> **B** No, not at all. 네. 그럼요.

■ 상대방에게 허락 여부를 묻는 표현으로는 "Can I ~?", "Do you mind if I ~?", "Would you mind if I ~?"와 같은 표현을 사용할 수 있다. 이때 "Can I ~?"보다 정중한 표현으로 "Do/Would you mind if I ~?"를 사용한다.

■ 이외에도 상대방에게 허가를 묻는 표현으로는 다음과 같은 표현이 있다.
  • Can I open the window?
    = Do you mind my opening the window?
    = Do you mind if I open the window?
    = Would you mind if I open the window?

■ "Do you mind if I ~?"에서 'mind'는 '~하기를 꺼려하다, 언짢아하다'라는 뜻이다. 따라서 "Yes, I do."라고 답하면 꺼려한다는 의미이므로 상대방의 요청에 거절하는 의미이다. 반면에 "No, I don't.", "Not at all."이라고 답하면 상대방의 요청을 허락한다는 의미이다.

Do you mind if I ~? 물음에 답하기

  • 승낙할 때
    No, not at all. / Certainly not. / Of course not. / No, I don't. / No problem. / Sure. / Go ahead.
  • 거절할 때
    Yes, I do. / Sorry, but ~. / I'm afraid I ~.

핵심 Check

1. 다음 대화의 빈칸 (A)에 들어갈 말로 적절한 것은? (2개)
   A: _____(A)_____ I shut the blinds?
   B: No, go ahead.
   ① Can   ② Could
   ③ Do you mind   ④ Do you mind if
   ⑤ Would you mind if

2 제안, 권유, 요청에 답하기

> **A** Can I look around the stage? 제가 무대를 둘러봐도 될까요?
>
> **B** I'm sorry. I'm afraid you can't. It's open only for the actors.
> 죄송하지만, 그러실 수 없습니다. 배우들만 출입할 수 있어요.

■ '제가 ~을 해도 될까요?'라고 허락을 구하는 표현은 'Can I ~?'를 사용하여 말할 수 있으며 'May I ~?'로 바꿔 쓸 수 있다.

- **A:** Can I take pictures during the play?
- **B:** I'm sorry. I'm afraid you can't. It can disturb other people.

Can I ~?로 물음에 답하기

- 승낙할 때

Yes, you can. / Of course. / Why not? / Sure. / Be my guest. / Do as you wish.

- 거절할 때

No, you can't. / I'm sorry. You can't. / I'm sorry, but I'm afraid you can't.

제안, 권유, 요청하는 질문에 답하기

- 승낙할 때

Sure. / Of course. / Certainly. / Why not? / No problem.

- 거절할 때

I'm sorry, but you can't[may not]. / I'm afraid you can't. / I'm afraid not. / No way! / You can't do that. / Not right now.

핵심 Check

2. 다음 밑줄 친 우리말을 주어진 단어를 이용하여 영작하시오.(4 words)

   A: Can I sit anywhere I want?

   B: I'm sorry. <u>미안하지만, 그럴 수 없습니다.</u>(afraid) Your seat number is on your ticket.

   ➡ _____

Real-Life Zone

Ben: Wow! This comic book is really hard to find. ❶Do you mind if I take a look at it?

Dana: ❷Not at all. It's one of ❸my favorites. I've read it maybe a hundred times.

Ben: ❹I've been looking all over for it. Can you lend it to me?

Dana: ❺I'm afraid I can't. Actually, it's not mine. It's my sister's. Sorry.

Ben: Oh, that's okay. I understand.

Dana: You know, if you really want it, you should check used bookstores online.

Ben: ❻Used bookstores online? I've never thought of that. That's a good idea.

Dana: ❼Let's look together. Oh, here's one! It says it's "like new." What do you think?

Ben: Great! And it's cheap! ❽I'll get it. Thanks!

Ben: 와, 이 만화책 정말 찾기 힘든 건데. 내가 좀 봐도 되니?

Dana: 그럼. 이것은 내가 제일 좋아하는 것들 중 하나야. 아마 백 번 정도 읽었을 걸.

Ben: 난 이걸 찾아 샅샅이 살펴봤어. 나에게 빌려줄 수 있니?

Dana: 미안하지만 안 돼. 사실, 이게 내것이 아니야. 언니 거야. 미안.

Ben: 어, 괜찮아. 이해해.

Dana: 있잖아, 네가 진짜 갖고 싶으면 인터넷 중고 서점을 확인해 봐.

Ben: 인터넷 중고 서점? 그건 생각해보지 못했네. 좋은 생각이다.

Dana: 같이 찾아보자. 아, 여기 하나 있다! "거의 새 제품"이라고 하네. 어떻게 생각해?

Ben: 좋아! 그리고 저렴하네! 이거 살게. 고마워!

❶ Do you mind if ~?는 상대방에게 무언가 허가 받을 때 사용하는 표현이다. ❷ 상대방이 Do you mind if ~?로 물어봤을 경우, 승낙하면 대답은 No, I don't. 혹은 Not at all.이라고 표현한다. ❸ favorite: 좋아하는 것, 좋아하는 사람 ❹ 현재완료진행 구문으로, 과거에서부터 현재까지 계속되고 있음을 나타낸다. ❺ I'm afraid I can't.는 허락을 구하는 상대방의 말에 정중하게 거절하는 표현이다. ❻ used : 중고의 (=second-hand 중고의) ❼ Let us ~가 줄여진 문장으로, let은 목적보어로 동사원형을 취한다. ❽ I'll get it.은 '내가 살게.' 혹은 '내가 받을게.'라는 표현이다.

Check(√) True or False

(1) Both Dana and Ben like to read the same comic book.   T ☐ F ☐

(2) Dana will lend the comic book to Ben.   T ☐ F ☐

Wrap Up 1-2

B: The toy on your desk is so cute. ❶Do you mind if I take a look at it?

G: ❷Not at all. It's called a *maneki-neko*, or a good luck cat. My friend bought it for me when she went to Japan.

B: Why is it putting its hand up?

G: ❸That means it is bringing you money.

B: Really? That's interesting. Could you ask your friend ❹where she got it? I'm going to Japan next week and I'd like to get one.

G: ❺I'm sorry. I'm afraid I can't. I ❻lost contact with her.

B: 네 책상에 있는 장난감 너무 귀엽다. 내가 좀 봐도 되겠니?

G: 그럼. 마네키네코, 즉 행운의 고양이라고 불려. 내 친구가 일본에 갔을 때 사줬어.

B: 저건 왜 손을 올리고 있는 거니?

G: 그건 너에게 돈을 가져다준다는 의미야.

B: 정말? 흥미롭다. 네 친구한테 어디서 샀는지 물어봐 줄 수 있니? 나 다음 주에 일본 가는데 하나 사고 싶어서.

G: 미안하지만 안 되겠어. 연락이 끊어졌거든.

❶ Do you mind if I ~? 표현은 Would you mind if I ~?라는 더 정중한 표현으로 대체할 수 있다. ❷ 이때 대답은 부정으로 해야지 상대방의 허락을 승낙하는 것이 된다. ❸ That은 행운의 고양이가 손을 들고 있는 것을 가리키는 대명사이다. ❹ 의문사 where를 이용한 간접의문문으로, 본인에게 직접적으로 물어 보는 경우 Where did you get it?으로 표현할 수 있다. ❺ 상대방의 요청을 정중하게 거절하는 표현이다. ❻ lose contact with ~와 연락이 끊기다

Check(√) True or False

(3) The toy is called a *maneki-neko*, which means a good luck cat.   T ☐ F ☐

(4) The girl knows where her friend is living now.   T ☐ F ☐

Listen & Speak 1 Listen

1. **M:** Do you mind if I ❶lean my seat back?
   G: ❷No, not at all.
2. **B:** Mom, do you mind if I use your smartphone?
   W: ❸No, I don't mind.
3. **G:** Do you mind if I change seats with you?
   B: ❹I'm sorry. I'm with my friend.
4. **B:** Do you mind if I shut the blinds?
   G: No, ❺go ahead.

❶ lean one's seat back 좌석을 뒤로 젖히다
❷ 상대방이 Do you mind if I ~?로 허락을 구하는 경우, 상대방에게 승낙할 때 사용할 수 있는 표현이다.
❸ Do you mind if ~?라고 상대방이 묻는 경우 mind는 '꺼리다, 언짢아하다'라는 뜻을 갖기 때문에, 부정의 표현으로 대답해야 상대방의 말을 승낙하는 것이 된다.
❹ 상대방의 말을 거절할 때는 정중한 표현으로 "I'm sorry."를 쓸 수 있다.
❺ go ahead : 진행하세요, 계속 하세요

Listen & Speak 1 A-1

B: Excuse me. I want to ❶return these sneakers.
W: Okay. Can I ask ❷why you want to return them?
B: There's dirt on them and ❸I haven't even worn them yet.
W: ❹Do you mind if I have a look?
B: Not at all. Here.

❶ return 반납하다, 반품하다
❷ 의문사 why가 쓰인 간접의문문으로, 직접의문문으로 바꿀 경우 Why do you want to return them?이라고 표현할 수 있다.
❸ 현재완료 용법으로, 이 문장에서는 과거에서부터 지금까지 신발을 신어 본 적이 없다는 의미로 사용되었다.
❹ Do you mind if I ~?는 더 정중한 표현인 Would you mind if I ~?로 대체할 수 있다.

Listen & Speak 1 A-2

M: ❶What can I help you with?
G: ❷I'd like to open a bank account. What should I do?
M: First, you need to ❸fill out this form.
G: Sure. Do you mind if I use your pen?
M: Not at all.

❶ 상대방에게 도움을 제안하는 표현으로 'What can I do for you?'라는 표현으로 대체할 수 있다.
❷ 'I would like to open ~'의 줄임말이다.
❸ fill out ~을 채우다, 기입하다

Listen & Speak 1 B-1

A: Do you mind if I lean my seat back?
B: ❶No, not at all.

❶ 'No, I don't mind at all.'의 줄임말이다.

Listen & Speak 1 B-2

A: ❶Do you mind if I change seats with you?
B: No, not at all.

❶ Do you mind changing seats with me?라고 바꿔 쓸 수 있다.

Listen & Speak 1 B-3

A: Do you mind if I eat this snack here?
B: ❶No, go ahead.

❶ go ahead: 진행하세요, 계속 하세요

Listen & Speak 2 Listen

1. **G:** Can I ❶look around the stage?
   M: ❷I'm sorry. I'm afraid you can't. It's open only for the actors.
2. **B:** Can I take pictures during the play?
   W: I'm sorry. I'm afraid you can't. It can ❸disturb other people.
3. **B:** Can I sit ❹anywhere I want?
   M: I'm sorry. I'm afraid you can't. Your seat number is on your ticket.

❶ look around 둘러보다
❷ 영어 표현에서 상대방의 말을 거절할 때에는 'I'm sorry.'를 덧붙여 정중하게 표현한다.
❸ disturb 방해하다
❹ anywhere 어디든, 아무데나

Listen & Speak 2 A-1

G: Look! This jacket is really cute. Let's ❶ check out this store.

B: Wait, ❷I'm afraid we can't take our drinks inside.

G: But I haven't finished ❸mine yet.

B: Let's finish our drinks first. Then we can go inside.

❶ check out 살펴보다
❷ '음료를 내부로 가지고 들어갈 수 없어서 유감이다'라는 표현이다.
❸ my drink를 가리킨다.

 Listen & Speak 2 A-2

G: Minho, can you come with us to the game expo this Sunday?

B: ❶I'd love to, but I'm afraid I can't. I have an important test next week.

G: ❷That's too bad. They're having a special show of various games.

B: Yeah, I've heard it's really great. ❸What about going with me next Saturday then?

G: Sure. Let's go together next Saturday.

❶ 상대방의 말을 거절할 때, 'I'd love to, but I'm afraid I can't.'라는 표현을 쓴다.
❷ '그것 참 안됐다.'라는 의미이다.
❸ 상대방에게 무언가를 제안할 때 What about ~ing?를 쓸 수 있다. 이때 Why don't we ~?로 대체 가능하다.

 Listen & Speak 2 B-1

A: ❶Can I look around the stage?

B: I'm sorry. I'm afraid you can't. It's open only for the actors.

❶ Do you mind if I look around the stage?로 바꿔 쓸 수 있다.

 Listen & Speak 2 B-2

A: Can I use this coupon?

B: ❶I'm sorry. I'm afraid you can't. The coupon is only for online orders.

❶ 영어 표현에서는 상대방의 말을 거절할 때는 정중하게 'I'm sorry.'를 덧붙인다.

 Listen & Speak 2 B-3

A: ❶Can I seat anywhere I want?

B: I'm sorry. I'm afraid you can't. Your seat number is on your ticket.

❶ Do you mind if I seat anywhere I want?라고 바꿔 쓸 수 있다.

 Wrap Up 3

B: I want to buy some traditional Korean gifts for my friends. Where's a good place to buy ❶ them?

G: ❷Have you been to Insa-dong? They have lots of traditional Korean things there.

B: ❸No, I've never been there.

G: ❸How about I take you there this Friday afternoon?

B: Oh, I'm afraid I can't. I have other plans. ❹ What about Saturday?

G: That's fine with me.

❶ 앞에서 언급된 some traditional Korean gifts를 가리킨다.
❷ 현재완료의 경험 용법으로, '~에 다녀온 적 있니?'라고 해석된다.
❸ How about ~?은 보통 뒤에 목적어로 동명사(~ing)나 명사를 취하지만, 여기서는 접속사 that이 생략되어 있는 문장이 사용되었다.
❹ What about ~?: ~은 어때?

다음 우리말과 일치하도록 빈칸에 알맞은 말을 쓰시오.

Listen & Speak 1 Listen

1. **M:** Do you mind if I _____ my seat back?
   G: No, not _____ _____.
2. **B:** Mom, do you _____ if I use your smartphone?
   W: No, I _____ mind.
3. **G:** Do you mind if I _____ _____ with you?
   B: I'm sorry. I'm with my friend.
4. **B:** Do you mind if I _____ the blinds?
   G: No, go _____.

Listen & Speak 1 A-1

B: _____ me. I want to _____ these sneakers.
W: Okay. Can I ask _____ you want to return them?
B: There's dirt on them and I _____ even _____ them yet.
W: Do you _____ if I have _____ _____?
B: Not at _____. _____.

Listen & Speak 1 A-2

M: _____ can I help you with?
G: I'd like to _____ a bank account. What _____ I do?
M: First, you need to _____ out this _____.
G: Sure. Do you mind if I _____ your pen?
M: Not at all.

Listen & Speak 1 B-1

A: Do you mind if I lean my seat back?
B: No, not _____ _____.

Listen & Speak 1 B-2

A: _____ you _____ if I change seats with you?
B: No, not at all.

Listen & Speak 1 B-3

A: _____ you mind if I _____ this snack here?
B: No, go _____.

해석

1. **M:** 제가 좌석을 뒤로 젖혀도 될까요?
   G: 네, 그럼요.
2. **B:** 엄마, 제가 이 스마트폰을 사용해도 될까요?
   W: 그래, 그러렴.
3. **G:** 저랑 좌석을 바꾸실 수 있을까요?
   B: 죄송하지만, 친구랑 같이 있어서요.
4. **B:** 제가 블라인드를 쳐도 될까요?
   G: 그럼요, 하세요.

B: 실례합니다. 이 운동화 반품하고 싶은데요.
W: 알겠습니다. 왜 반품하고 싶으신지 물어봐도 될까요?
B: 먼지가 묻어 있고요, 저는 아직 안 신어 봤어요.
W: 제가 좀 봐도 될까요?
B: 그럼요. 여기 있습니다.

M: 무엇을 도와 드릴까요?
G: 은행 계좌를 열고 싶은데요. 뭘 하면 될까요?
M: 우선, 이 양식을 작성해 주세요.
G: 그럼요. 제가 펜을 써도 될까요?
M: 그럼요.

A: 제가 좌석을 뒤로 젖혀도 될까요?
B: 그럼요.

A: 저와 좌석을 바꾸실 수 있을까요?
B: 그럼요.

A: 제가 간식을 여기서 먹어도 되나요?
B: 그럼요, 어서 드세요.

Listen & Speak 2 Listen

1. G: Can I look _____ the stage?

   M: I'm sorry. I'm _____ you can't. It's _____ only for the actors.

2. B: Can I take _____ _____ the play?

   W: I'm sorry. I'm afraid you _____. It can _____ other people.

3. B: _____ I sit _____ I want?

   M: I'm afraid you can't. Your seat number is on your ticket.

1. G: 무대를 둘러봐도 되나요?
   M: 죄송하지만 안 됩니다. 무대는 배우들만 출입 가능합니다.
2. B: 연극 중에 사진 찍어도 되나요?
   W: 죄송하지만, 안됩니다. 다른 사람들을 방해할 수 있거든요.
3. B: 제가 앉고 싶은 곳에 앉아도 되나요?
   M: 죄송하지만 안 됩니다. 좌석 번호가 티켓에 쓰여 있습니다.

Listen & Speak 2 A-1

G: _____! This jacket is really cute. Let's _____ out this store.

B: Wait, I'm afraid we _____ take our drinks _____.

G: But I haven't _____ mine yet.

B: Let's finish our drinks _____. Then we _____ go inside.

G: 봐! 이 자켓 진짜 예쁘다. 이 가게 살펴보자.
B: 잠깐, 아쉽게도 음료는 내부 반입이 안 되네.
G: 하지만, 난 아직 다 못 마셨는데.
B: 우선 음료 먼저 다 마시자. 그러면 우리는 들어갈 수 있어.

Listen & Speak 2 A-2

G: Minho, can you _____ with us to the game expo this Sunday?

B: I'd love to, but I'm _____ I can't. I have an important test next week.

G: _____ too bad. They're having a _____ show of various games.

B: Yeah, I've _____ it's really great. What about _____ with me next Saturday _____?

G: Sure. Let's go _____ next Saturday.

G: 민호야, 이번 주 일요일에 우리와 함께 게임 엑스포에 갈래?
B: 그러고 싶은데, 안되겠다. 다음 주에 중요한 시험이 있거든.
G: 그것 참 안됐다. 다양한 게임들의 특별한 쇼가 있을 거야.
B: 응, 정말 좋다고 들었어. 그러면 나와 다음 주 토요일에 같이 가는 건 어때?
G: 그럼 좋지. 다음 주 토요일에 같이 가자.

Listen & Speak 2 B-1

A: Can I look _____ the stage?

B: I'm sorry. I'm afraid you can't. It's _____ only for the actors.

A: 무대를 둘러봐도 될까요?
B: 죄송하지만 안 됩니다. 배우들만 출입 가능합니다.

Listen & Speak 2 B-2

A: _____ I _____ this coupon?

B: I'm _____. I'm afraid you can't. The coupon is _____ for online orders.

A: 이 쿠폰을 사용해도 되나요?
B: 죄송하지만 안 됩니다. 쿠폰은 온라인 주문에만 사용 가능합니다.

Listen & Speak 2 B-3

A: _____ I seat anywhere I want?

B: I'm sorry. I'm afraid you _____. Your seat number is _____ your ticket.

해석

A: 제가 앉고 싶은 곳에 앉아도 되나요?

B: 죄송하지만, 안됩니다. 좌석 번호가 티켓에 쓰여 있습니다.

Real-Life Zone

Ben: Wow! This comic book is really hard _____ _____. Do you _____ if I take a look at it?

Dana: Not _____ _____. It's one of my _____. I've read it maybe a hundred times.

Ben: I've been _____ all _____ for it. Can you _____ it to me?

Dana: I'm _____ I can't. _____, it's not mine. It's my sister's. Sorry.

Ben: Oh, that's _____. I understand.

Dana: You know, if you really want it, you should check _____ bookstores _____.

Ben: Used bookstores online? I've never _____ of that. That's a good _____.

Dana: Let's look _____. Oh, here's one! It says it's "like new." What do you _____?

Ben: Great! And it's cheap! I'll _____ it. Thanks!

Ben: 와, 이 만화책 정말 찾기 힘든 건데. 내가 좀 봐도 되니?

Dana: 그럼. 이것은 내가 제일 좋아하는 것들 중 하나야. 아마 백 번 정도 읽었을 걸.

Ben: 난 이걸 찾아 샅샅이 살펴봤어. 나에게 빌려줄 수 있니?

Dana: 미안하지만 안 돼. 사실, 이게 내 것이 아니야. 언니 거야. 미안.

Ben: 어, 괜찮아. 이해해.

Dana: 있잖아, 네가 진짜 갖고 싶으면 인터넷 중고 서점을 확인해 봐.

Ben: 인터넷 중고 서점? 그건 생각해 보지 못했네. 좋은 생각이다.

Dana: 같이 찾아보자. 아, 여기 하나 있다! "거의 새 제품"이라고 하네. 어떻게 생각해?

Ben: 좋아! 그리고 저렴하네! 이거 살게. 고마워!

Wrap Up 1-2

B: The toy on your desk is so cute. Do you _____ if I take _____ _____ at it?

G: _____ at all. It's _____ a *maneki-neko*, or a good luck cat. My friend _____ it for me when she went to Japan.

B: Why is it _____ its hand up?

G: That _____ it is _____ you money.

B: Really? That's _____. Could you ask your friend _____ she got it? I'm going to Japan next week and I'd like to _____ one.

G: I'm sorry. I'm _____ I can't. I lost _____ with her.

B: 네 책상에 있는 장난감 너무 귀엽다. 내가 좀 봐도 되겠니?

G: 그럼. 마네키네코, 즉 행운의 고양이라고 불려. 내 친구가 일본에 갔을 때 사줬어.

B: 저건 왜 손을 올리고 있는 거니?

G: 그건 너에게 돈을 가져다준다는 의미야.

B: 정말? 흥미롭다. 네 친구한테 어디서 샀는지 물어봐 줄 수 있니? 나 다음 주에 일본 가는데 하나 사고 싶어서.

G: 미안하지만 안 되겠어. 연락이 끊어졌거든.

Wrap Up 3

B: I want to buy _____ traditional Korean gifts for my friends. Where's a good _____ to buy them?

G: Have you _____ to Insa-dong? They have lots of traditional Korean things there.

B: No, I've _____ been there.

G: How _____ I take you there this Friday afternoon?

B: Oh, I'm _____ I can't. I have other plans. _____ about Saturday?

G: That's _____ with me.

B: 나 친구들을 위해 한국 전통 선물을 좀 사고 싶어. 그것을 살 수 있는 좋은 장소가 어디니?

G: 인사동에 가봤니? 그곳에 한국 전통 물건들이 매우 많아.

B: 아니, 거기 가 본 적이 없어.

G: 이번 주 금요일 오후에 내가 널 거기 데려가는 건 어때?

B: 미안하지만 안 되겠어. 다른 계획이 있거든. 토요일은 어때?

G: 난 좋아.

[01~02] 다음 대화를 읽고 물음에 답하시오.

> B: Excuse me. I want ⓐto return these sneakers.
>
> W: Okay. Can I ask ⓑwhy do you want to return them?
>
> B: ⓒThere's dirt on them and ⓓI haven't even worn them yet.
>
> W: Do you mind ⓔif I have a look?
>
> B: Not at all. Here.

01 위 대화의 ⓐ~ⓔ 중 흐름상 어색한 부분을 찾아 바르게 고치시오.

➡ _____

02 위 대화를 읽고 대답할 수 <u>없는</u> 것은?

① When did B buy the sneakers?

② Who is B talking to?

③ Why does B want to return the sneakers?

④ Where are B and W having a conversation?

⑤ Who is going to take a look at the sneakers?

[03~04] 다음 대화를 읽고 물음에 답하시오.

> G: Look! This jacket is really cute. Let's check out this store.
>
> B: Wait, (A)유감이지만 음료를 내부로 갖고 들어갈 수 없어. (afraid, our drinks, inside)
>
> G: But I haven't finished (B)mine yet.
>
> B: Let's finish our drinks first. Then we can go inside.

03 위 대화의 밑줄 친 (A)의 우리말을 주어진 어구를 이용하여 영작하시오. (8 words)

➡ _____

04 위 대화의 밑줄 친 (B)mine이 가리키는 것을 찾아 쓰시오. (2 words)

➡ _____

[01~03] 다음 대화를 읽고 물음에 답하시오.

Ben: Wow! This comic book is really hard to find. (A)Do you mind if I take a look at it?

Dana: Not at all. It's one of my favorites. I've ___(a)___ it maybe a hundred times. ①

Ben: I've been looking all over for it. ②

Dana: I'm afraid I can't. Actually, it's not mine. It's my sister's. Sorry.

Ben: Oh, that's okay. I understand. ③

Dana: You know, if you really want it, you should check used bookstores online. ④

Ben: Used bookstores online? I've never ___(b)___ of that. That's a good idea. ⑤

Dana: Let's look together. Oh, here's one! It says it's "like new." What do you think?

Ben: Great! And it's cheap! I'll get it. Thanks!

01 위 대화의 밑줄 친 (A)와 바꿔 쓸 수 있는 것은?

① Do I take a look at it?

② Will I take a look at it?

③ Can you take look at it?

④ Would you mind if I take a look at it?

⑤ Would you mind taking a look at it?

02 위 대화의 빈칸 (a)와 (b)에 들어갈 말이 바르게 짝지어진 것은?

① read – thought
② read – think
③ to read – thought
④ reading – thought
⑤ reading – think

03 위 대화의 ①~⑤ 중 주어진 문장이 들어가기에 가장 적절한 곳은?

Can you lend it to me?

①　　②　　③　　④　　⑤

[04~05] 다음 대화를 읽고 물음에 답하시오.

M: What can I help you with?

G: I'd like to open a bank account. What should I do?

M: First, you need to fill out this form.

G: Sure. (A)제가 펜을 써도 될까요?

M: (B)Not at all.

서답형

04 위 대화의 밑줄 친 (A)를 Do로 시작하는 문장으로 영작하시오. (8 words)

➡ _____

05 위 대화의 밑줄 친 (B)와 바꿔 쓰기에 어색한 것은?

① No, I don't.
② No problem.
③ Yes, I'm sorry.
④ Of course not.
⑤ No, go ahead.

06 다음 중 짝지어진 대화가 어색한 것을 고르시오.

① A: Do you mind if I shut the blinds?
　 B: No, go ahead.

② A: Would you mind if I use your smart phone?
　 B: No, I do mind.

③ A: Do you mind if I have a look?
　 B: Not at all. Here.

④ A: Do you mind if I lean my seat back?
　 B: No, not at all.

⑤ A: Can I look around the stage?
　 B: I'm sorry. I'm afraid you can't.

[07~09] 다음 대화를 읽고 물음에 답하시오.

> G: Minho, can you (A)[come / go] with us to the game expo this Sunday?
>
> B: I (B)[would / should] love to, but (a)I'm afraid I can't. I have an important test next week.
>
> G: That's too bad. They're having a special show of various games.
>
> B: Yeah, I've heard it's really great. What about (C)[going / to go] with me next Saturday then?
>
> G: Sure. Let's go together next Saturday.

07 위 대화의 괄호 (A)~(C)에서 알맞은 것을 바르게 짝지은 것을 고르시오.

(A)	(B)	(C)

① come – would – to go

② come – should – going

③ come – would – going

④ go – should – going

⑤ go – would – to go

08 위 대화의 밑줄 친 (a)의 목적으로 가장 적절한 것은?

① 미안함 표현하기 ② 두려움 표현하기

③ 불가능 표현하기 ④ 요청 거절하기

⑤ 요청 승낙하기

09 위 대화의 내용과 일치하지 <u>않는</u> 것은?

① Minho wants to visit the game expo with G.

② Minho is going to take an important test next week.

③ Minho heard that there are going be various shows in the expo.

④ Minho and G are not going to the expo this Sunday.

⑤ Minho does not want to go to the game expo.

[10~11] 다음 대화를 읽고 물음에 답하시오.

> B: The toy on your desk is so cute. Do you mind if I take a look at it?
>
> G: Not at all. It's called a *maneki-neko*, or a good luck cat. My friend bought it for me when she went to Japan.
>
> B: Why is it putting its hand up?
>
> G: That means it is bringing you money.
>
> B: Really? That's interesting. (A)<u>네 친구가 그 걸 어디서 샀는지 친구한테 물어봐 줄래?</u>(could, got) I'm going to Japan next week and I'd like to get one.
>
> G: I'm sorry. I'm afraid I can't. I lost contact with her.

10 위 대화의 밑줄 친 (A)의 우리말을 주어진 단어를 이용해 영작하시오. (9 words)

➡ _____

11 위 대화를 읽고 대답할 수 <u>없는</u> 것은?

① What is the toy called?

② Who gave the toy to G?

③ Why is the toy putting its hand up?

④ Why did G lose contact with her friend?

⑤ Where is B going to go to next week?

[01~04] 다음 대화를 읽고 물음에 답하시오.

B: I want to buy some traditional Korean gifts for my friends. Where's a good place (a)buy them?
(A) No, I've never been there.
(B) Oh, I'm afraid I can't. I have other plans. What about Saturday?
(C) How about I (b)take you there this Friday afternoon?
(D) Have you been to Insa-dong? They have lots of traditional Korean things there.
G: (c)나는 그 날 괜찮아.

01 위 대화가 자연스럽게 이어지도록 순서대로 배열하시오.

➡ _____

02 위 대화의 밑줄 친 (a)buy와 (b)take를 문법상 적절한 형태로 바꾸시오.

(a) _____ (b) _____

03 위 대화의 밑줄 친 (c)의 우리말을 영작하시오. (4 words)

➡ _____

04 What does B want to buy for his friends? Answer in English with 11 words.

➡ _____
_____

[05~07] 다음 대화를 읽고 물음에 답하시오.

B: Excuse me. I want to return these sneakers.
W: Okay. (A)왜 반품하려는지 물어봐도 될까요? (ask / can / want / I / why / them / you / to return)
B: There's dirt on them and I haven't even worn them yet.
W: Do you mind if I have a look?
B: Not at all. Here.

05 위 대화의 밑줄 친 (A)의 우리말에 맞게 배열하시오.

➡ _____

06 다음 영영풀이에 맞는 단어를 위 대화에서 찾아 쓰시오.

to send, take, give, put, etc. something back to where it came from

➡ _____

07 위 대화의 내용과 일치하도록 빈칸에 알맞은 말을 쓰시오.

Today I went to the shoes store to (a)_____ the sneakers I had bought last time. I told the shop assistant that there (b)_____ dirt on them and I haven't worn them, not even once. She (c)_____ to have a look at them. I didn't mind her (d)_____ it.

Grammar

1 동등비교: as + 형용사/부사의 원급 + as

- **My old bike is almost as good as a new one.** 내 오래된 자전거는 거의 새것과 다름없이 좋아.

- 'as+형용사/부사의 원급+as'는 동등비교의 의미로, 서로 다른 두 개를 대등한 수준에서 비교할 때 사용한다.
  - Minho can jump **as** high **as** I can. 민호는 내가 뛸 수 있는 만큼 높이 뛸 수 있다.

- 'as+형용사/부사의 원급+as'의 형태로 쓰이고 해석은 '…만큼 ~한/하게'라고 해석한다.
  - My candy bar is **as** big **as** yours. 〈big → 형용사의 원급〉 내 초코바는 너의 것만큼 크다.
  - I sang **as** loudly **as** an opera singer. 〈loudly → 부사의 원급〉 나는 오페라 가수만큼 크게 노래를 불렀다.

- 'as … as' 앞에 'not'을 붙여 부정하면 대등하지 않은 두 개를 비교할 수 있다. 'not as[so] … as'의 형태이고, as는 'so'로 바꿔 쓸 수 있다.
  - Dogs are **not as[so]** fast **as** cheetahs. 개는 치타만큼 빠르지 않다.
  - = Cheetahs are **faster than** dogs. 치타는 개보다 빠르다.

- 'no/not A(부정 주어) so 원급 as B(B만큼 A하지 않다)'나 'as 형용사 as any 명사(누구 못지않게 형용사 한)'로 최상급의 의미를 표현할 수 있다.
  - **No** country has **as** many people **as** China. 어떤 나라도 중국만큼 인구가 많지 않다.
  - **Nothing** is **so** precious **as** time. 시간만큼 소중한 것은 없다.
  - He is **as** diligent **as any other** boy. 그는 다른 어떤 소년 못지 않게 부지런하다.

- 원급을 이용하여 배수를 표현할 수 있다. '배수사(twice, three times, one third, etc.)+as+형용사/부사+as'의 형태로 '~보다 몇 배 …하다'로 해석한다.
  - Building a new house will cost you **three times as** much money **as** renovating one.
    새로운 집을 짓는 것은 수리하는 것보다 돈이 세 배만큼 든다.

- 주의해야 할 원급, 동등비교 구문
  - Please send your response **as soon as possible**.
  - = Please send your response **as soon as you could**. 가능한 한 빨리 답장 부탁드립니다.
    〈as … as possible = as … as S+can[could] 될 수 있는 한 …하게〉

핵심 Check

1. 다음 괄호 안에서 알맞은 말을 고르시오.
   (1) He studied as (hard / harder) as you did.
   (2) She is not speaking as loudly (as / than) you are.

② 과거완료

> • He realized that he **had done** wrong. 그는 자신이 잘못했다는 것을 깨달았습니다.

■ 과거완료(had+p.p.)의 형태로 과거의 어떤 시점보다 앞서 일어난 일에 대해 말할 때 사용한다.
  • When I arrived at the café, he **had** already **gone**. 내가 카페에 도착했을 때, 그는 이미 가버렸다.

■ 과거완료는 '대과거, 완료, 결과, 경험, 계속'의 의미가 있다.
  • She **had** already **left** when her mom got there. 〈대과거〉 그녀는 어머니가 그곳에 왔을 때 이미 자리를 떠났다.
  • Diane was about to leave for work when she realized that she **had forgotten** to pick up her keys.
    Diane이 막 출근하려는데 열쇠를 가져오는 것을 잊은 것을 깨달았다.
  • They **had arrived** at the house before night fell. 〈완료: 막 ~하였다〉 그들은 밤이 찾아오기 전에 집에 도착했다.
  • Spring **had come** by the time she was well again. 〈결과: ~했다, ~해 버렸다〉
    그녀가 건강을 회복했을 때쯤 봄이 찾아왔다.
  • I **had** never **enjoyed** learning English before I found his lectures. 〈경험: ~해 본 적이 있었다〉
    나는 그의 강의를 찾기 전에는 영어 공부를 즐겨본 적이 없었다.
  • He **had wanted** to see me perform in a school play, but he couldn't leave his work. 〈계속: 계속 ~했다〉
    그는 내가 학교 연극에서 공연하는 것을 보고 싶었지만 회사에서 나올 수가 없었다.

■ 과거의 어떤 때를 기준으로 하여 그 이전부터 상태가 계속되는 것을 말한다. 즉, (과거 이전의) 대과거 시점으로부터 (기준이 되는) 과거 시점까지의 연속선상에 걸쳐있는 시제를 말한다.
  • Kate and Jimmy **had been married** for two years. Kate와 Jimmy는 결혼한지 2년이 되었다.

■ 시간 접속사 before, after 등과 함께 쓰일 경우 주절에 과거시제 동사를 쓸 수 있다.
  • He **got** up before the sun **rose**. 그는 해뜨기 전에 일어났다.

핵심 Check

2. 다음 괄호 안에서 알맞은 말을 고르시오.
  (1) No one (saw / had seen) the buildings until someone from France rediscovered them in 1861.
  (2) I (had not finished / had finished not) my homework when the teacher entered the classroom.

Grammar 시험대비 기본평가

01 다음 문장에서 어법상 <u>어색한</u> 부분을 찾아 바르게 고쳐 쓰시오.

(1) Try to exercise as hardly as possible.

_____ ➡ _____

(2) My grades weren't as well as I thought.

_____ ➡ _____

(3) When he arrived, the meeting has already finished.

_____ ➡ _____ .

02 다음 〈보기〉의 단어를 이용하여 빈칸에 올바른 어형을 쓰시오.

┌─ 보기 ├─
buy   start   see   late

(1) When we got to the hall, the concert _____ already _____ .
(2) I lost the cellular phone which I _____ the day before.
(3) She lets her children stay up as _____ as they like.
(4) I recognized him at once, for I _____ him several times before.

03 다음 우리말에 맞게 주어진 단어를 활용하여 영작하시오.

(1) 이 상자의 크기는 저 상자의 반이다. (as, big)

➡ _____

(2) 나는 영어를 한국어처럼 유창하게 말할 수 있다. (as, fluent)

➡ _____

(3) 전날 비가 와서 그라운드 컨디션이 좋지 않았다. (rain, because, field, the day before)   *be in bad condition 컨디션이 좋지 않다

➡ _____

서답형

01 다음 문장에서 어법상 틀린 부분을 찾아 바르게 고쳐 쓰시오.

> As she has booked a table in advance, she went to the restaurant.

———————— ➡ ————————

[02~03] 다음 글을 읽고 물음에 답하시오.

> Sarah ⓐ<u>go</u> to a party last week. Paul ⓑ<u>go</u> to the party too, but they didn't see each other. Paul ⓒ<u>leave</u> the party at 10:30 and Sarah ⓓ<u>arrive</u> at 11:00. So, when Sarah arrived at the party, Paul wasn't there. [have, home, go, he].

서답형

02 밑줄 친 단어 ⓐ~ⓓ를 알맞은 형태로 쓰시오.

➡ _____

_____

서답형

03 괄호 안에 있는 단어들을 활용하여 알맞은 순서대로 배열하시오. (어형 변화 가능)

➡ _____

04 다음 문장과 가장 가까운 뜻을 지닌 문장을 고르시오.

> Sleeping is just as important as eating and exercising.

① Sleeping is more important than eating and exercising.
② Eating and exercising are the most important things.
③ Eating and exercising are less important than sleeping.

④ Sleeping as well as eating and exercising is important.
⑤ Sleeping is the most important of all things.

05 다음 중 어법상 어색한 문장을 고르시오.

① Buy as much fruit as you want.
② She doesn't play as good as her sister.
③ It's past eight, but it's still as bright as day.
④ The growth in the economy has not been as great as predicted.
⑤ We can stay here for as long as our supplies hold out.

06 다음 빈칸에 들어갈 말끼리 알맞게 짝지어진 것을 고르시오.

> When I _____ the classroom, the math lesson _____.

① entered – had already begun
② had entered – already began
③ enter – had already begun
④ enter – already begin
⑤ had entered – had already begun

서답형

07 괄호 안의 단어를 활용하여 동등비교 문장을 완성하시오.

> You are _____ Suzy. (pretty)

➡ _____

08 다음 중 빈칸에 들어갈 단어가 나머지와 <u>다른</u> 것을 고르시오.

① I _____ already eaten lunch when he called me.

② He couldn't open the door because he _____ lost his key.

③ I _____ watched TV before I helped Mom.

④ I was glad my dad _____ made me a doll.

⑤ This milk _____ gone bad. It is sour.

09 다음 빈칸에 들어갈 말로 알맞은 것을 <u>모두</u> 고르시오.

> I didn't want to go out. I _____.

① had been tired ② would be tired

③ have been tired ④ was tired

⑤ am tired

★ 중요

10 다음 빈칸에 들어갈 말로 적절한 것을 고르시오.

> Yesterday Miju rode a horse for the first time. She had never _____ a horse before.

① ride ② rode

③ ridden ④ been ridden

⑤ be ridden

11 문맥상 빈칸에 들어갈 말로 알맞은 것을 고르시오.

> He was surprised that he _____ the door.

① has locked ② not had locked

③ hadn't locked ④ had locked not

⑤ haven't locked

12 다음 우리말을 영어로 바르게 옮긴 것을 <u>모두</u> 고르시오.

> 나는 물을 끓이고 난 다음에 라면을 냄비에 넣었다.

① I boiled the water then I put *ramen* into the pot.

② The water boiled, when I put *ramen* into the pot.

③ After the water boiled, I put *ramen* into the pot.

④ The water boiled, after I put *ramen* into the pot.

⑤ I put *ramen* into the pot, before the water boiled.

★ 중요

13 다음 우리말에 맞게 영작할 경우 어법상 <u>어색한</u> 것을 고르시오.

① 나는 평생을 포도농장에서 일해 온 한 늙은 농부를 만났다.
  ➡ I met an old farmer who had worked in his vineyard all his life.

② 그가 도착했을 때 그녀는 이미 떠났다.
  ➡ She had already left when he arrived.

③ 그녀는 수업 시간에 배운 이론을 적용해서 전지를 만들었다.
  ➡ She applied the theory she had learned in class to create an electoric battery.

④ 그는 내가 전화를 걸었을 때 소파에서 잠이 들었었다.
  ➡ He had fallen asleep on the sofa when I called him.

⑤ 그는 평생 몸담았던 강단을 떠났다.
  ➡ He retired from the university he worked for all his life.

14 다음 중 어법상 <u>어색한</u> 것을 고르시오.

① The referee declared that the ball touched a player before it went out.

② I had just had pizza. So I wasn't hungry at that time.

③ Paul went to England last year. It was her second time there. She'd been there once before.

④ What they needed was just water.

⑤ The girl is watching a movie that makes her excited.

15 <u>중요</u>

다음 빈칸에 들어갈 말로 바르게 짝지어진 것을 고르시오.

> I _____ (go) to the library to meet Jason, but I _____ (meet) her. He _____ _____ (go) home.

① go – meet – gone
② go – met – gone
③ went – didn't meet – had gone
④ went – didn't meet – has gone
⑤ went – met – had gone

16 다음 중 어법상 <u>어색한</u> 것을 고르시오.

① When Suzi has known Jay for a year, she walked arm in arm with him.

② She had been sick for two weeks, so she couldn't take part in the concert.

③ I recognized him at once, for I had seen him before.

④ Until then, your kimchi had tasted great.

⑤ He was very poor before.

17 <u>서답형</u>

우리말에 맞게 괄호 안의 단어를 활용하여 빈칸을 채우시오.

> When my mother came home, I _____ _____ (already, clean) the room.

➡ _____

18 <u>서답형</u>

우리말에 맞게 괄호 안의 어휘들을 배열하여 영작할 때, 3번째 단어를 쓰시오.

(1) 내가 그 재킷 값을 지불하자마자 재킷에 조그만 구멍이 있는 것을 보았다. (sooner, I, paid, had, for, the, no, that, than, it, in, a, small, hole, it, I, saw, jacket, had)

➡ _____

(2) 그는 나만큼 천천히 이야기를 한다.
(speaks, do, I, he, as, as, slowly)

➡ _____

19 <u>중요</u>

다음 중 어법상 <u>어색한</u> 것을 고르시오.

① I was very happy when I saw my daughter. I hadn't seen her for two years.

② He returned the book to where it is after he finished reading it.

③ My friend Minho had lived in the country till he moved to Seoul.

④ I got to the concert late. I found that the show that I wanted to see had finished.

⑤ When I heard the announcement, I realized that I'd gotten on the wrong train.

01 우리말에 맞게 괄호 안의 단어를 활용하여 빈칸을 채우시오.

> 나는 작년에 상한 음식을 먹고 식중독에 걸렸었다.
> (get, poisoning, after, that, go bad)

➡ _____

_____

02 다음 문장의 과거완료의 용법이 대과거이면 (대), 계속이면 (계), 경험이면 (경), 완료이면 (완), 결과이면 (결)을 괄호 안에 쓰시오.

(1) I had already taken the medical exam in January.

➡ _____

(2) I found that I had lost my camera in the zoo.

➡ _____

(3) I had lived there for two years when the war broke out.

➡ _____

(4) I had never seen such an amazing building until I visited the Taj Mahal.

➡ _____

(5) I had barely recovered from a cold when I caught the flu.

➡ _____

중요

03 다음 우리말에 맞게 괄호 안의 단어를 활용하여 빈칸을 채우시오.

(1) 그 고양이는 오랫동안 아팠는데 회복의 징조를 보였다. (be)

➡ The cat, which _____ _____ for a long time, showed signs of recovery.

(2) John은 독서 클럽에 가입할 때까지는 친구가 별로 없었다. (have)

➡ John _____ _____ few friends until he joined the reading club.

(3) 나는 한국 밖으로는 여행을 해 본 적이 없었다. (never, travel)

➡ I _____ _____ _____ outside of Korea.

(4) 독수리들은 도시에서 수년간 볼 수 없었는데 어제 목격되었다. (be, see)

➡ Eagles, which _____ _____ _____ in the city for years, were spotted yesterday.

(5) 일을 끝낸 후 나는 너희 집에 들렀다. (finish)

➡ I stopped by your house after I _____ _____ work.

(6) 내가 불어 공부를 그만두려고 한 것이 아니었다. 나는 그때 막 불어를 알아듣기 시작했었다. (only, start)

➡ I wasn't going to quit studying French. I _____ _____ _____ _____ to understand it.

(7) 신문에 폭풍이 우리 마을에서 가장 큰 나무를 부러뜨렸다고 쓰여 있었다. (break)

➡ In the newspaper, it said that the storm _____ _____ the biggest tree in our village.

(8) 내가 기차에서 내렸을 때 가방이 없어진 것을 발견했다. (lose)

➡ I found I _____ _____ my bag when I got off the train.

(9) 시합이 이미 시작된 후에 그들은 한 팀에 선수가 하나 빠졌다는 것을 발견했다. (begin)

➡ After the match _____ _____ _____, they discovered one of the teams was missing a player.

(10) 우리가 만나기 전에 그는 점심 식사를 했다. (have)

➡ He _____ _____ lunch before we met.

04 우리말에 맞게 괄호 안의 단어를 활용하여 빈칸을 채우시오.

> 그녀는 Lee 선생님만큼 키가 크다. (tall)

➡ _____

05 다음 글의 빈칸에 주어진 철자로 시작하는 어휘를 어법에 맞게 써 넣으시오.

> A burglar b_____ into my house last night. When I returned home from work, I f_____ that all my jewelery h_____ b_____ s_____. I wondered who had left the dresser drawer open. The next day the police caught the burglar. But he h_____ already s_____ off all my jewelery.
>
> *burglar: 밤도둑

06 다음 우리말에 맞게 빈칸에 들어갈 알맞은 말을 return을 이용하여 쓰시오.

> 나는 네가 벌써 돌아왔는지 몰랐어, Jason. Sally는 네가 샌프란시스코에 있다고 말했거든.
> ➡ I didn't know you _____ _____ already, Jason. Sally said you were in San Fransisco.

07 괄호 안의 단어를 활용하여 영작하시오.

> 나는 다이어트를 계속해 왔는데 뚱뚱하긴 마찬가지야.
> ➡ I've been dieting but I'm still _____ _____ (fat) ever.

08 다음 우리말에 맞게 괄호 안의 단어를 활용하여 빈칸을 채우시오.

(1) 그는 그가 전날 구입한 카메라 렌즈를 잃어버렸다. (buy)
➡ He lost the camera lense that he _____ _____ the day before.

(2) 그 영화배우는 내 여동생만큼 예쁘지 않다. (pretty)
➡ The actress is _____ _____ _____ _____ my sister.

(3) 될 수 있는 한 빨리 그 일을 끝내세요. (soon, possible)
➡ Please finish the work _____ _____ _____ _____.

(4) 올해 수입은 작년의 세 배이다. (much)
➡ This year's revenue is _____ _____ _____ _____ _____ last year's.

09 괄호 안의 단어를 바르고 써 넣어 문장을 완성하시오.

(1) I couldn't remember _____ _____ _____ _____ _____ _____. (had, the, where, I, book, put)

(2) She _____ _____ _____ _____ _____ with him for years. (secret, had, a, relationship, had)

(3) I thought _____ _____ _____ _____. (been, they, had, caught)

(4) When I visited Vietnam to report their life, I saw that _____ _____ _____ _____ on the wall. (graffiti, painted, had, been)

Seyun's First Online Sale

Seyun rides his bike to school every day. He likes his bike, but he is taller and stronger this year. His bike has become too small for him, so he wants to buy a bigger, faster one. However, he does not have enough money in his savings account. What can he do?

Suddenly, Seyun had an idea. "My old bike is almost as good as a new one. Maybe I can sell it and add the money to buy a new one."

He acted fast. He took a photo of his bike with his smartphone and posted the picture, with a short comment, on an online market: "Used bike in excellent condition. Only 100,000 won. Please text me." He was excited, thinking about the bike he planned to buy. He could see himself riding the shiny new bike. He could not wait to get a reply to his online advertisement. Every few minutes he checked the number of hits. As the number of hits went up, his expectations went up too. One hour passed, then two, and finally a whole day, but he received no texts. Nobody seemed to want his bike. New postings by other people pushed his post down the list. His heart began to sink.

account (은행) 계좌
suddenly 갑자기
sell 팔다
add 더하다
act 행동하다
post (안내문 등을) 게시하다, 공고하다
comment 언급
shiny 빛나는, 반짝거리는
advertisement 광고
sink 가라앉다, 빠지다

📎 **확인문제**

● 다음 문장이 본문의 내용과 일치하면 T, 일치하지 <u>않으면</u> F를 쓰시오.

1 Seyun goes to school by bike every day. ☐

2 Seyun has enough money in his savings account. ☐

3 Seyun took a photo of his bike with his smartphone and posted the picture, with a short comment, on an online market. ☐

4 Seyun didn't expect to get a reply to his online advertisement. ☐

5 Every few minutes Seyun checked the number of hits. ☐

6 New postings by other people pushed his post up the list. ☐

"What's wrong with my posting? Is my bike not attractive enough?"
= the matter 　　　　　　　　　　　　　　　　　　　형용사 뒤에 위치

He searched on the Internet for tips on how to sell online. Then he
　　인터넷을 검색했다　　　　　　　~에 대하여

realized what he had done wrong. He had been too hasty and too
선행사를 포함하는 관계대명사　　　과거완료 시제로, 과거의 어떤 시점보다 더 이전에 일어난 일을 표현할 때 사용

greedy. He had not given enough information to the possible buyers.

Also, when compared to other bicycles, his price was too high. He
부사절 'when his price was compared to other bicycles.'에서 '주어+be동사'가 생략된 분사구문

wrote a new posting with a longer description of the bike. He added

more photos to show his bike from different angles. "Twenty-four inch
　　　　　　to부정사의 부사적 용법(목적)

bicycle. Excellent condition. Always kept indoors. Rides just like new.

Very few scratches. Good for someone 12-14 years old. 80,000 won."
거의 없는, 복수명사와 함께 쓰임.　　　　someone과 '12-14 years old' 사이에 '주격 관계대명사+be동사(who[that] is)' 생략

This time he got several texts. Sadly, they all asked for a lower price.
　　　　　　　　　　　　　　　　　　　　　　　　　~을 요구했다

It was hard to accept at first, but finally he sold his bike for 70,000
가주어　　　　진주어

won. He met the buyer, handed over his bike, and got the money he
　　　　V1　　　　　　V2　　　　　　　　　　V3

needed. Now he could get a new bike. He felt both happy and sad. He
'the money'와 'he needed' 사이에 목적격 관계대명사 'that[which]'이 생략

was sad to see his old bike go, but he was happy with himself because
　　부사적 용법의 to부정사(감정의 원인)

he had learned a lot and grown up a bit through the experience.

---

attractive 매력적인

search 찾다. 검색하다

hasty 성급한

greedy 욕심 많은

description 묘사

angle 각도

scratch 긁힌 자국

accept 받아들이다

through ~을 통해

experience 경험

ask for ~을 요청하다

hand over 건네주다

grow up 성장하다

📎 **확인문제**

● 다음 문장이 본문의 내용과 일치하면 T, 일치하지 않으면 F를 쓰시오.

1　Seyun searched on the Internet for tips on how to sell online. ☐

2　Seyun had given sufficient information to the possible buyers. ☐

3　When compared to other bicycles, Seyun's price was too low. ☐

4　Seyun added a longer description of the bike to his earlier posting. ☐

5　This time Seyun got several texts, all of which asked for a lower price. ☐

6　Seyun didn't feel happy at all when he sold his bike. ☐

● 우리말을 참고하여 빈칸에 알맞은 말을 쓰시오.

1 Seyun's First _____ _____.

2 Seyun _____ _____ _____ to school every day.

3 He likes his bike, but he is _____ _____ _____ this year.

4 His bike has become _____ _____ _____ _____, so he wants to buy a bigger, faster one.

5 However, he does not have enough money in his _____ _____.

6 _____ can he do?

7 Suddenly, Seyun _____ _____ _____.

8 "My old bike is almost _____ _____ a new one.

9 Maybe I can sell it and _____ _____ to buy a new one."

10 He _____ _____.

11 He took a photo of his bike with his smartphone and _____ the picture, _____ _____ _____ _____, on an online market: "Used bike in excellent condition. Only 100,000 won. Please text me."

12 He was excited, _____ _____ the bike he planned to buy.

13 He could see _____ _____ the shiny new bike.

14 He _____ _____ _____ to get a reply to his online advertisement.

15 _____ _____ _____ he checked the number of hits.

16 _____ the number of hits _____ _____, his expectations went up too.

17 One hour passed, then two, and finally a whole day, but he _____ _____ _____.

18 _____ _____ to want his bike.

1 세윤이의 첫 온라인 판매

2 세윤이는 매일 학교에 자전거를 타고 갑니다.

3 세윤이는 자신의 자전거를 좋아하지만, 그는 올해 키가 더 크고 힘도 더 세졌습니다.

4 그의 자전거는 그에게 너무 작아져서, 그는 더 크고 더 빠른 자전거를 사기를 원합니다.

5 하지만, 그는 자신의 예금 계좌에 충분한 돈을 가지고 있지 않습니다.

6 그가 무엇을 할 수 있을까요?

7 갑자기, 세윤이는 아이디어가 떠올랐습니다.

8 "내 오래된 자전거는 거의 새것과 다름없이 좋아.

9 아마 나는 그것을 팔고 새것을 사기 위한 돈에 보탤 수 있을 거야."

10 그는 빠르게 행동했습니다.

11 그는 스마트폰으로 자신의 자전거 사진을 찍었고, 짧은 설명과 함께 온라인 장터에 사진을 게시했습니다. "훌륭한 상태의 중고 자전거. 겨우 십만 원. 문자 주세요."

12 세윤이는 자신이 구입하려고 계획한 자전거에 대해 생각하며 신이 났습니다.

13 그는 자신이 빛나는 새 자전거를 타고 있는 것을 상상할 수 있었습니다.

14 세윤이는 자신의 온라인 광고에 대한 대답이 오는 것을 무척 기다렸습니다.

15 몇 분마다 그는 조회 수를 체크했습니다.

16 숫자가 올라갈수록 그의 기대도 덩달아 올라갔습니다.

17 한 시간이 지나고, 두 시간이 지나고, 마침내 하루가 지났지만 세윤이는 문자를 받지 못했습니다.

18 아무도 그의 자전거를 원하지 않는 것처럼 보였습니다.

19 New postings by other people _____ _____ _____ _____ the list.

20 His heart began _____ _____.

21 "What's _____ _____ my posting?

22 Is my bike not _____ _____?"

23 He searched on the Internet _____ _____ _____ how to sell online.

24 Then he realized _____ _____ _____ _____ _____.

25 He had been too _____ and too _____.

26 He had not given enough information to the _____ _____.

27 Also, when _____ _____ other bicycles, his price was too _____.

28 He wrote a new posting _____ _____ _____ _____ of the bike.

29 He added more photos to show his bike _____ _____ _____.

30 "Twenty-four inch bicycle. Excellent condition. Always _____ _____. Rides just like new. Very few scratches. Good for someone 12-14 years old. 80,000 won."

31 This time he got _____ _____.

32 Sadly, they all _____ _____ a lower price.

33 It was hard _____ _____ at first, but finally he sold his bike _____ 70,000 won.

34 He met the buyer, _____ _____ his bike, and got the money he needed.

35 Now he _____ _____ a new bike.

36 He felt _____ _____ _____ _____.

37 He was sad to see his old bike _____, but he was happy with _____ because he had learned a lot and grown up a bit _____ _____ _____.

---

19 다른 사람들의 새 게시물이 그의 게시물을 리스트에서 밀어냈습니다.

20 세윤이의 가슴이 내려앉기 시작했습니다.

21 '내 포스팅에 무슨 문제가 있지?

22 내 자전거가 충분히 매력적이지 못한가?'

23 세윤이는 온라인에서 판매하는 방법에 대한 조언을 찾기 위해 인터넷을 검색했습니다.

24 곧 그는 자신의 잘못을 깨달았습니다.

25 세윤이는 너무 성급했고 너무 욕심이 많았습니다.

26 그는 구매 가능성이 있는 사람들에게 충분한 정보를 주지 않았습니다.

27 또한, 다른 자전거들과 비교했을 때 그의 가격은 너무 높았습니다.

28 세윤이는 자신의 자전거에 대한 더 긴 묘사가 있는 새 게시물을 작성했습니다.

29 그는 자신의 자전거를 다른 각도에서 보여 주기 위해서 더 많은 사진들을 첨부했습니다.

30 "24인치 자전거, 훌륭한 상태. 항상 실내에 보관했음. 새것처럼 탐. 스크래치 매우 적음. 12-14세에게 좋음. 8만 원."

31 이번에 그는 여러 통의 문자 메시지를 받았습니다.

32 애석하게도, 그들은 모두 더 낮은 가격을 요청했습니다.

33 처음에는 받아들이기 어려웠지만, 마침내 그는 자신의 자전거를 칠만 원에 팔았습니다.

34 세윤이는 구매자를 만나 자전거를 건네주고, 그가 필요했던 돈을 받았습니다.

35 이제 세윤이는 새 자전거를 살 수 있습니다.

36 그는 기쁘고 슬픈 감정을 동시에 느꼈습니다.

37 세윤이는 자신의 오래된 자전거가 떠나는 것을 봐서 슬펐지만, 이 경험을 통해 자신이 많은 것을 배우고 조금 더 성장한 것이 기뻤습니다.

● 우리말을 참고하여 본문을 영작하시오.

1 세윤이의 첫 온라인 판매
➡ _____

2 세윤이는 매일 학교에 자전거를 타고 갑니다.
➡ _____

3 세윤이는 자신의 자전거를 좋아하지만, 그는 올해 키가 더 크고 힘도 더 세졌습니다.
➡ _____

4 그의 자전거는 그에게 너무 작아져서, 그는 더 크고 더 빠른 자전거를 사기를 원합니다.
➡ _____

5 하지만, 그는 자신의 예금 계좌에 충분한 돈을 가지고 있지 않습니다.
➡ _____

6 그가 무엇을 할 수 있을까요?
➡ _____

7 갑자기, 세윤이는 아이디어가 떠올랐습니다.
➡ _____

8 "내 오래된 자전거는 거의 새것과 다름없이 좋아.
➡ _____

9 아마 나는 그것을 팔고 새것을 사기 위한 돈에 보탤 수 있을 거야."
➡ _____

10 그는 빠르게 행동했습니다.
➡ _____

11 그는 스마트폰으로 자신의 자전거 사진을 찍었고, 짧은 설명과 함께 온라인 장터에 사진을 게시했습니다. "훌륭한 상태의 중고 자전거. 겨우 십만 원. 문자 주세요."
➡ _____
_____

12 세윤이는 자신이 구입하려고 계획한 자전거에 대해 생각하며 신이 났습니다.
➡ _____

13 그는 자신이 빛나는 새 자전거를 타고 있는 것을 상상할 수 있었습니다.
➡ _____

14 세윤이는 자신의 온라인 광고에 대한 대답이 오는 것을 무척 기다렸습니다.
➡ _____

15 몇 분마다 그는 조회 수를 체크했습니다.
➡ _____

16 숫자가 올라갈수록 그의 기대도 덩달아 올라갔습니다.
➡ _____

17 한 시간이 지나고, 두 시간이 지나고, 마침내 하루가 지났지만 세윤이는 문자를 받지 못했습니다.
➡ _____

18 아무도 그의 자전거를 원하지 않는 것처럼 보였습니다.
➡ _____

19 다른 사람들의 새 게시물이 그의 게시물을 리스트에서 밀어냈습니다.
➡ _____

20 세윤이의 가슴이 내려앉기 시작했습니다.
➡ _____

21 '내 포스팅에 무슨 문제가 있지?
➡ _____

22 내 자전거가 충분히 매력적이지 못한가?'
➡ _____

23 세윤이는 온라인에서 판매하는 방법에 대한 조언을 찾기 위해 인터넷을 검색했습니다.
➡ _____

24 곧 그는 자신의 잘못을 깨달았습니다.
➡ _____

25 세윤이는 너무 성급했고 너무 욕심이 많았습니다.
➡ _____

26 그는 구매 가능성이 있는 사람들에게 충분한 정보를 주지 않았습니다.
➡ _____

27 또한, 다른 자전거들과 비교했을 때 그의 가격은 너무 높았습니다.
➡ _____

28 세윤이는 자신의 자전거에 대한 더 긴 묘사가 있는 새 게시물을 작성했습니다.
➡ _____

29 그는 자신의 자전거를 다른 각도에서 보여 주기 위해서 더 많은 사진들을 첨부했습니다.
➡ _____

30 "24인치 자전거, 훌륭한 상태. 항상 실내에 보관했음. 새것처럼 탐. 스크래치 매우 적음. 12–14세에게 좋음. 8만 원."
➡ _____
_____

31 이번에 그는 여러 통의 문자 메시지를 받았습니다.
➡ _____

32 애석하게도, 그들은 모두 더 낮은 가격을 요청했습니다.
➡ _____

33 처음에는 받아들이기 어려웠지만, 마침내 그는 자신의 자전거를 칠만 원에 팔았습니다.
➡ _____

34 세윤이는 구매자를 만나 자전거를 건네주고, 그가 필요했던 돈을 받았습니다.
➡ _____

35 이제 세윤이는 새 자전거를 살 수 있습니다.
➡ _____

36 그는 기쁘고 슬픈 감정을 동시에 느꼈습니다.
➡ _____

37 세윤이는 자신의 오래된 자전거가 떠나는 것을 봐서 슬펐지만, 이 경험을 통해 자신이 많은 것을 배우고 조금 더 성장한 것이 기뻤습니다.
➡ _____
_____

[01~03] 다음 글을 읽고 물음에 답하시오.

Seyun rides his bike to school every day. (①) He likes his bike, but he is taller and stronger this year. (②) His bike has become too small ___ⓐ___ him, so he wants to buy a bigger, faster one. (③) However, he does not have enough money ___ⓑ___ his savings account. (④)

Suddenly, Seyun had an idea. (⑤) "My old bike is almost as good as a new one. Maybe I can sell it and add the money to buy a new one."

01 위 글의 빈칸 ⓐ와 ⓑ에 들어갈 전치사가 바르게 짝지어진 것은?

	ⓐ	ⓑ		ⓐ	ⓑ		ⓐ	ⓑ
①	for – in		②	in – at		③	on – to

| ④ | for – to | | ⑤ | on – in |

02 위 글의 흐름으로 보아, 주어진 문장이 들어가기에 가장 적절한 곳은?

> What can he do?

①   ②   ③   ④   ⑤

03 According to the passage, which is NOT true?

① Seyun goes to school by bike every day.
② Seyun is tired of his bike.
③ Seyun wants to buy a bigger and faster bike.
④ Seyun's old bike is almost as good as a new one.
⑤ Seyun thinks he can sell his old bike and add the money to buy a new one.

04 주어진 글 다음에 이어질 글의 순서로 가장 적절한 것은?

He acted fast. He took a photo of his bike with his smartphone and posted the picture, with a short comment, on an online market: "Used bike in excellent condition. Only 100,000 won. Please text me."

(A) Nobody seemed to want his bike. New postings by other people pushed his post down the list. His heart began to sink.
(B) Every few minutes he checked the number of hits. As the number of hits went up, his expectations went up too. One hour passed, then two, and finally a whole day, but he received no texts.
(C) He was excited, thinking about the bike he planned to buy. He could see himself riding the shiny new bike. He could not wait to get a reply to his online advertisement.

① (A) – (C) – (B)   ② (B) – (A) – (C)
③ (B) – (C) – (A)   ④ (C) – (A) – (B)
⑤ (C) – (B) – (A)

[05~07] 다음 글을 읽고 물음에 답하시오.

"What's wrong with my posting? Is my bike not attractive enough?" He searched on the Internet for tips on how to sell online. Then he realized what he had done wrong. He had been too hasty and too greedy. ⓐHe had not given enough information to the existing buyers. Also, ⓑwhen compared to other bicycles, his price was too high. He wrote a new posting with a longer description of the bike. He added more photos to show his bike from different angles. "Twenty-four inch bicycle. Excellent condition. Always kept indoors. Rides just like new. Very few scratches. Good for someone 12-14 years old. 80,000 won."

서답형

05 위 글의 밑줄 친 ⓐ에서 흐름상 어색한 부분을 찾아 고치시오.

_____ ➡ _____

서답형

06 위 글의 밑줄 친 ⓑ에 생략된 말을 넣어 문장을 다시 쓰시오.

➡ _____

07 위 글의 주제로 알맞은 것을 고르시오.

① tips on how to sell online
② the importance of a low price
③ the necessity of more photos to sell online
④ to write a new posting which gives enough information
⑤ the feeling about the old bike

[08~10] 다음 글을 읽고 물음에 답하시오.

This time he got several texts. Sadly, they all asked for a (A)[higher / lower] price. It was hard to accept at first, but finally he sold his bike for 70,000 won. He met the buyer, handed over his bike, and got the money he needed. Now he could get a new bike. He felt (B)[both happy and sad / both happily and sadly]. He was sad ⓐto see his old bike (C)[go / to go], but he was happy with himself because he had learned a lot and grown up a bit through the experience.

서답형

08 위 글의 괄호 (A)~(C)에서 문맥이나 어법상 알맞은 낱말을 골라 쓰시오.

(A) _____
(B) _____
(C) _____

09 다음 〈보기〉에서 위 글의 밑줄 친 ⓐto see와 to부정사의 용법이 같은 것의 개수를 고르시오.

┌─── 보기 ───┐
① His job is to sing songs.
② She went to the store to buy some fruit.
③ He worked hard only to fail.
④ I don't have any friends to talk with.
⑤ She must be a fool to say like that.
└────────────┘

① 1개   ② 2개   ③ 3개   ④ 4개   ⑤ 5개

서답형

10 Why was he happy with himself though he was sad to sell his old bike? Answer in English beginning with "Because".

➡ _____
_____

[11~13] 다음 글을 읽고 물음에 답하시오.

Seyun rides his bike to school every day. He likes his bike, but he is taller and stronger this year. His bike has become too small for him, so he wants to buy a bigger, faster (A)one. ⓐ , he does not have enough money in his savings account. What can he do?

Suddenly, Seyun had an idea. "My old bike is almost as good as a new one. Maybe I can sell (B)it and add the money to buy a new one."

11 위 글의 빈칸 ⓐ에 들어갈 알맞은 말을 고르시오.

① That is   ② In addition
③ However   ④ Therefore
⑤ For example

12 위 글의 밑줄 친 (A)one과 문법적 쓰임이 같은 것을 고르시오.

① They all went off in one direction.
② One of my friends lost his camera.
③ One must observe the rules.
④ One man's meat is another man's poison.
⑤ Our car's always breaking down, so we're getting a new one soon.

서답형
13 위 글의 밑줄 친 (B)it이 가리키는 것을 본문에서 찾아 쓰시오.

➡ _____

[14~16] 다음 글을 읽고 물음에 답하시오.

"What's wrong with my posting? ①Is my bike not attractive enough?" He searched on the Internet for tips on how to sell online. ② Then he realized what he had done wrong. He had been too ___ⓐ___ and too ___ⓑ___. He had not given enough information to the possible buyers. ③Also, when compared to other bicycles, his price was too high. He wrote a new posting with a longer description of the bike. He added more photos to show his bike from different angles. "Twenty-four inch bicycle. Excellent condition. ④Always kept indoors. Rides just like new. ⑤Very few scratch. Good for someone 12-14 years old. 80,000 won."   <He: Seyun>

서답형
14 위 글의 빈칸 ⓐ와 ⓑ에 haste와 greed를 각각 알맞은 형태로 쓰시오.

(A) _____   (B) _____

서답형
15 위 글의 밑줄 친 ①~⑤ 중 어법상 틀린 것을 찾아 고치시오.

➡ _____

16 Which question CANNOT be answered after reading the passage?

① What did Seyun do wrong when he posted his bike online?
② Compared to other bicycles, was the price of Seyun's bike low?
③ What did Seyun add to his new posting?
④ Why did Seyun always keep his bike indoors?
⑤ To whom did Seyun recommend his bike?

[17~19] 다음 글을 읽고 물음에 답하시오.

He acted fast. He took a photo of his bike with his smartphone and posted the picture, with a short comment, on an online market: "Used bike ___ⓐ___ excellent condition. Only 100,000 won. Please text me." He was excited, (A)thinking about the bike he planned to buy. He could see himself riding the shiny new bike. He could not wait to get a reply to his online advertisement. Every few minutes he checked the number of hits. As the number of hits went up, his expectations went up too. One hour passed, then two, and finally a whole day, but he received no texts. Nobody seemed to want his bike. New postings ___ⓑ___ other people pushed his post down the list. His heart began to sink.

17 위 글의 빈칸 ⓐ와 ⓑ에 들어갈 전치사가 바르게 짝지어진 것은?

ⓐ ⓑ	ⓐ ⓑ
① on – for	② in – from
③ in – by	④ at – by
⑤ on – from	

18 위 글의 밑줄 친 (A)thinking과 문법적 쓰임이 같은 것을 모두 고르시오.

① Do you know that boy playing the piano?
② Be careful in crossing the street.
③ Her dream is being a scientist.
④ They sat talking for a long time.
⑤ He left the baby crying.

19 위 글에 어울리는 속담으로 가장 알맞은 것을 고르시오.

① Two heads are better than one.
② Don't count your chickens before they are hatched.
③ Strike while the iron is hot.
④ Too many cooks spoil the broth.
⑤ Every cloud has a silver lining.

[20~22] 다음 글을 읽고 물음에 답하시오.

This time he got several texts. Sadly, they all asked ____ⓐ____ a lower price. It was hard to accept at first, but finally he sold his bike ____ⓑ____ 70,000 won. He met the buyer, handed over his bike, and ⓒgot the money he needed. Now he could get a new bike. He felt both happy and sad. He was sad to see his old bike go, but he was happy with himself because he had learned a lot and grown up a bit through the experience.

<He: Seyun>

20 위 글의 빈칸 ⓐ와 ⓑ에 공통으로 들어갈 알맞은 전치사를 고르시오.

① to	② on	③ at
④ in	⑤ for	

서답형

21 위 글의 밑줄 친 ⓒ에 생략된 말을 넣어 다시 쓰시오.

➡ _____

22 Which question CANNOT be answered after reading the passage?

① How many texts did Seyun get this time?
② What did people ask Seyun for in their texts?
③ Was Seyun willing to accept people's demand at first?
④ How much did Seyun earn by selling his old bike?
⑤ Did Seyun deliver his old bike to the buyer by delivery service?

[01~03] 다음 글을 읽고 물음에 답하시오.

Seyun rides his bike to school every day. He likes his bike, but he is taller and stronger this year. His bike has become too small for him, so he wants to buy a bigger, faster ___ⓐ___ . However, he does not have enough money in his savings account. What can he do?

Suddenly, Seyun had an idea. "(A)내 오래된 자전거는 거의 새것과 다름없이 좋아. Maybe I can sell it and add the money to buy a new ___ⓑ___ ."

01 위 글의 빈칸 ⓐ와 ⓑ에 공통으로 들어갈 알맞은 말을 쓰시오.

➡ _____

02 위 글의 밑줄 친 (A)의 우리말에 맞게 주어진 어휘를 이용하여 11 단어로 영작하시오.

almost, good

➡ _____

03 본문의 내용과 일치하도록 다음 빈칸 (A)와 (B)에 알맞은 단어를 쓰시오.

Seyun's bike has become (A)_____ _____ for him, so he plans to sell it and add the money to buy a (B)_____ bike.

[04~07] 다음 글을 읽고 물음에 답하시오.

He acted fast. He took a photo of his bike with his smartphone and posted the picture, with a short comment, on an online market: "(A)[Using / Used] bike in excellent condition. Only ⓐ100,000 won. Please text me." He was excited, ⓑthinking about the bike he planned to buy. He could see himself (B)[riding / to ride] the shiny new bike. He could not wait to get a reply to his online advertisement. Every few (C)[minute / minutes] he checked the number of hits. As the number of hits went up, his expectations went up too. One hour passed, then two, and finally a whole day, but he received no texts. Nobody seemed to want his bike. New postings by other people pushed his post down the list. His heart began to sink.

04 위 글의 괄호 (A)~(C)에서 문맥이나 어법상 알맞은 낱말을 골라 쓰시오.

(A) _____ (B) _____ (C) _____

05 위 글의 밑줄 친 ⓐ100,000을 영어로 읽는 법을 쓰시오.

➡ _____

06 위 글의 밑줄 친 ⓑ를 부사절로 고치시오.

➡ _____
_____

07 주어진 영영풀이에 해당하는 단어를 본문에서 찾아 쓰시오.

visits to a website

➡ _____

[08~10] 다음 글을 읽고 물음에 답하시오.

This time he got several texts. Sadly, (A) they all asked for a lower price. It was hard to accept at first, but finally he sold his bike for 70,000 won. He ___ⓐ___ the buyer, ___ⓑ___ over his bike, and ___ⓒ___ the money he needed. Now he could get a new bike. He felt both happy and sad. He was sad to see his old bike go, but he was happy with himself because he had learned a lot and grown up a bit through the experience.

<He: Seyun>

08 위 글의 빈칸 ⓐ~ⓒ에 meet, hand, get을 각각 알맞은 형태로 쓰시오.

ⓐ _____ ⓑ _____ ⓒ _____

09 위 글의 밑줄 친 (A)they가 가리키는 것을 본문에서 찾아 쓰시오.

➡ _____

10 How did Seyun feel when he sold his old bike? Answer in English in a full sentence.

➡ _____

[11~13] 다음 글을 읽고 물음에 답하시오.

"What's wrong with my posting? Is my bike not attractive enough?" (A)He searched on the Internet for tips on how to sell online. Then he realized what he ___ⓐ___ wrong. He had been too hasty and too greedy. He had not given enough information to the possible buyers. Also, when compared to other bicycles, his price was too high. He wrote a new posting with a longer description of the bike. He added more photos to show his bike from different angles. "Twenty-four inch bicycle. Excellent condition. Always kept indoors. Rides just like new. Very few scratches. Good for someone 12-14 years old. 80,000 won."

<He: Seyun>

11 위 글의 빈칸 ⓐ에 do를 알맞은 형태로 쓰시오.

➡ _____

12 위 글의 밑줄 친 (A)를 다음과 같이 바꿔 쓸 때 빈칸에 들어갈 알맞은 말을 두 단어로 쓰시오.

He searched on the Internet for tips on how _____ _____ sell online.

13 다음 빈칸 (A)와 (B)에 알맞은 단어를 넣어 세윤이가 자신의 게시물을 바꾼 방법을 완성하시오.

Seyun wrote a new posting with a (A)_____ _____ of a bike, and added (B)_____ _____ to show his bike from different angles.

해석

After You Read B

Buyer: Hello? Are you the one who posted a bike for sale?
<small>주격 관계대명사</small>

Seyun: Yes, that's me.

Buyer: Can I check your bike to see if it's in good condition as you wrote?
<small>간접의문문을 이끌어 …인지 (아닌지) (whether)</small>

Seyun: Sure. It has very few scratches but nothing ugly.
<small>극소주의   nothing을 수식</small>

Buyer: Let me check.... Yeah, it seems good enough.

Seyun: Perfect!

Buyer: By the way, can I ask why you want to sell this bike?
<small>간접 의문문(의문사+주어+동사)</small>

Seyun: I've grown more than 10 cm this year, so it's too small for me now.
<small>~에 비해</small>

Buyer: Oh, I see.

<small>구문해설</small> • condition: 상태 • ugly: 추한 • by the way: 그런데

구매자: 안녕하세요? 자전거를 팔려고 게시한 분이신가요?

세윤: 네, 저예요.

구매자: 당신이 쓰신 것처럼 좋은 상태인지 보기 위하여 당신의 자전거를 좀 살펴봐도 될까요?

세윤: 물론이죠. 스크래치가 아주 조금 있지만 추하지는 않아요.

구매자: 한 번 볼게요.... 네, 충분히 좋은 것 같아요.

세윤: 정말 좋군요!

구매자: 그런데, 왜 이 자전거를 파시려고 하는지 물어봐도 될까요?

세윤: 올해 제 키가 10 cm 이상 커져서, 이제 이 자전거는 저에게 너무 작기 때문이에요.

구매자: 오, 알겠습니다.

Writing Workshop

If you are looking for a new swimming suit, this one would be perfect. It is
<small>현재진행형   = this one</small>
beautiful. Also, it is as cheap as the one that is on sale. I bought one, and I
<small>= this one   = swimming suit   = a swimming suit</small>
really like it. However, I would advise you to buy a bigger size than what you
<small>대조의 접속부사   비교급+than</small>
usually buy. Even though I had ordered the same size as what I normally wear,
<small>양보의 접속사   과거완료   관계대명사</small>
it was too small for me.

<small>구문해설</small> • swimming suit: 수영복 • perfect: 완전히, 완벽히 • normally: 평소, 보통

만약 당신이 새 수영복을 찾고 있다면, 이 수영복이 완벽할 것입니다. 이것은 예뻐요. 또한 이것은 세일 중에 있는 수영복만큼 저렴합니다. 나는 이 새 수영복을 구매했고, 지금 완전 맘에 듭니다. 그러나 나는 평소 당신이 사는 사이즈보다 큰 사이즈를 살 것을 권합니다. 나는 평소 내가 입는 사이즈와 같은 것을 주문했는데 이것은 나에게 너무 작습니다.

Wrap Up 7

September 8th, Monday

Last spring, I planted some potatoes with my grandfather in his garden. I

visited the garden and watered the potatoes often. I had never planted potatoes
<small>과거완료: had+p.p.</small>
before. It was fun. Today, my grandfather and I dug some of the potatoes.

They looked as good as the ones you see in the market, and there were so
<small>= the potatoes   as+형용사+as: ~만큼 …한   there+복수 명사</small>
many of them. My grandfather says we can take some of them to the market

and sell them! That will be really exciting.
<small>= the potatoes</small>

<small>구문해설</small> • plant: (나무 • 씨앗 등을) 심다 • water: 물을 주다 • dig: (땅에서) 캐다

9월 8일, 월요일
지난 봄, 나는 할아버지와 함께 그의 정원에서 감자를 심었다. 나는 종종 정원을 방문하여 감자에 물을 주었다. 나는 그 전에는 감자를 심어 본 적이 없었다. 그것은 재미있었다. 오늘, 할아버지와 나는 감자를 좀 캤다. 그것들은 시장에서 보는 것만큼 상태가 좋았고, 양도 많았다. 할아버지께서는 우리가 그것들 일부를 시장에 가져가서 팔수도 있다고 말씀하셨다! 그것은 정말 신날 것이다.

영역별 핵심문제

01 다음 짝지어진 단어의 관계가 같도록 빈칸에 알맞은 말을 쓰시오.

> maybe : probably = hasty : _____

02 다음 영영풀이에 해당하는 단어로 알맞은 것은?

> the feeling that good things are going to happen in the future

① scratch   ② regret

③ experience   ④ expectation

⑤ posting

03 다음 중 밑줄 친 부분의 뜻풀이가 바르지 않은 것은?

① I refuse to make any hasty decisions. (성급한)

② The artworks were in an excellent state of preservation. (탁월한, 훌륭한)

③ We had over 200 replies to our advertisement. (광고)

④ It is believed that oil does not mix with water. (섞이다, 섞다)

⑤ I don't feel I can comment on my brother's decision. (언급)

04 다음 주어진 문장의 밑줄 친 reply와 같은 의미로 쓰인 것은?

> I asked her what her name was but she made no reply.

① Reply by no later than 21 July.

② Nine times out of ten she doesn't reply.

③ You should receive a reply within seven days.

④ Susan was unsure how to reply to this question.

⑤ Mike didn't reply to my question.

05 다음 우리말에 맞게 주어진 어구를 배열하시오.

(1) 그 프로젝트 작업을 하면서 Emily는 값진 경험을 얻었다.
(gained / Emily / on the project / valuable / working / experience / while).

➡ _____

(2) 어떤 종류의 식물은 실내에서 기를 수 있다.
(some / indoors / grown / kinds of / can / be / plants)

➡ _____

(3) 모든 비행기들이 혹시 있을 수 있는 금 때문에 검사를 받고 있다.
(inspected / all / possible / are being / cracking / for / planes).

➡ _____

06 다음 우리말을 주어진 어구를 이용하여 영작하시오.

(1) 우리는 당신이 비행 편을 일찍 예약하는 것을 권장하고 싶습니다. (book, flight, recommend)

➡ _____

(2) 해커들은 장치에 저장된 귀중한 정보를 훔칠 수 있다. (valuable, store, steal)

➡ _____

(3) 그 소설가는 그녀의 묘사력으로 잘 알려져 있다. (description, well-known, her powers)

➡ _____

Conversation

[07~09] 다음 대화를 읽고 물음에 답하시오.

Ben: Wow! This comic book is really hard to find. (a)내가 한 번 봐도 될까?(take / it / do / if / a look / mind / you / I / at)

Dana: Not at all. It's one of my favorites. I've read it maybe a hundred times.

Ben: I've been (A)[to look / looking] all over for it. Can you lend it to me?

Dana: I'm afraid I can't. Actually, it's not mine. It's my sister's. Sorry.

Ben: Oh, that's okay. I understand.

Dana: You know, if you really (B)[want / wanted] it, you should check used bookstores online.

Ben: Used bookstores online? I've never (C)[thinking / thought] of that. That's a good idea.

Dana: Let's look together. Oh, here's one! It says it's "like new." What do you think?

Ben: Great! And it's cheap! I'll get it. Thanks!

07 위 대화의 괄호 (A)∼(C)에서 알맞은 말이 바르게 짝지어진 것은?

         (A)   (B)   (C)
① to look – want – thinking
② looking – want – thought
③ to look – want – thought
④ looking – wanted – thought
⑤ to look – wanted – thinking

08 위 대화의 밑줄 친 (a)의 우리말에 맞게 주어진 단어를 바르게 나열하시오.

➡ _____

09 위 대화의 내용으로 보아 알 수 <u>없는</u> 것은?

① Ben would like to borrow the comic book from Dana.
② Dana has read the comic book about a hundred times.
③ Dana can't lend the comic book because it's her sister's.
④ Ben and Dana are searching for the comic book online.
⑤ The comic book Ben and Dana found is not cheaper than Dana's.

10 다음 대화가 자연스럽게 이어지도록 순서에 맞게 나열하시오.

M: What can I help you with?
(A) Not at all.
(B) Sure. Do you mind if I use your pen?
(C) I'd like to open a bank account. What should I do?
(D) First, you need to fill out this form.

➡ _____

11 어법상 빈칸에 들어갈 말로 적절한 것을 <u>모두</u> 고르시오.

> Yunji had a straw three times as long as _____.

① mine ② I ③ my
④ me ⑤ my straw

12 다음 우리말에 맞게 괄호 안의 단어를 활용하여 빈칸을 채우시오.

> 내 가방은 네 가방보다 두 배 정도 크다.
> ➡ My backpack is about _____
> _____ _____ _____ yours. (big)

13 다음 중 어법상 <u>어색한</u> 문장을 고르시오.

① The movie had started before my friend showed up.
② When I got to the bakery, my favorite chocolate cake is sold out.
③ My hands are as cold as ice.
④ I had never planted potatoes before.
⑤ He was very happy because he had found missing pocket money.

14 우리말과 같은 뜻이 되도록 괄호 안의 어휘를 배열하여 영작하시오.

> 과학자들은 이 재앙을 예상하지 못했다.
> (predict, scientists, not, had, disaster, been, this, able, to)

➡ _____

15 다음 우리말에 맞게 괄호 안의 단어를 활용하여 빈칸을 5 단어로 채우시오.

> 나는 내가 할 수 있는 한 빨리 그곳에 갈 것이다.
> ➡ I will go there _____ _____
> _____ _____ _____. (soon)

16 우리말에 맞게 괄호 안의 어휘들을 배열하여 영작할 때, 4번째 단어를 쓰시오.

> 강도는 경찰이 도착하기 전에 도망갔다.
> (away, robber, before, had, the, run, police, the, arrived)

➡ _____

17 다음 우리말에 맞게 괄호 안의 단어를 활용하여 영작하시오.

(1) 그는 자기 형보다 용감하지 않다. (brave)
➡ He _____ his brother.

(2) 네가 생각하는 것만큼 모스크바의 겨울은 춥지 않다. (cold)
➡ Winter in Moscow _____ you think.

(3) 나는 그 일을 가능한 한 경제적으로 할 것이다. (economical)
➡ I'll do the job _____ possible.

(4) 이 가방은 내 것보다 4배 더 비싸다. (expensive)
➡ This bag _____ mine.

(5) 이 바나나는 저 바나나보다 두 배 더 무겁다. (heavy)
➡ This banana _____ that banana.

(6) 그녀는 자기 언니처럼 일찍 일어나지 않는다. (early)
➡ She _____ her sister.

[18~19] 다음 글을 읽고 물음에 답하시오.

Seyun rides his bike to school every day. He likes his bike, but he is taller and stronger this year. His bike ⓐhas become too small for him, so he wants to buy a bigger, faster one. However, he does not have enough money in his savings account. What can he do?

Suddenly, Seyun had an idea. "My old bike is almost as good as a new one. Maybe I can sell it and add the money to buy a new one."

18 위 글의 밑줄 친 ⓐhas become과 현재완료의 용법이 같은 것을 고르시오.

① Have you seen the movie yet?
② He has gone to New York.
③ How long have you been ill in bed?
④ I have just finished it.
⑤ How many times has she read the book?

19 Which question CANNOT be answered after reading the passage?

① How does Seyun go to school every day?
② Does Seyun have enough money to buy a new bike in his savings account?
③ What's the condition of Seyun's old bike?
④ How much money does Seyun have to add to buy a new bike?
⑤ How can Seyun add money to buy a new bike?

[20~22] 다음 글을 읽고 물음에 답하시오.

He acted fast. He took a photo of his bike with his smartphone and posted the picture, with a short comment, on an online market: "Used bike in excellent condition. Only 100,000 won. Please text me." He was excited, thinking about the bike he planned to buy. He could see himself riding the shiny new bike. He could not wait to get a reply to his online advertisement. ⓐ몇 분마다 그는 조회 수를 체크했습니다. As the number of hits went up, his expectations went up too. One hour passed, then two, and finally a whole day, but he received no texts. Nobody seemed to want his bike. New postings by other people pushed his post down the list. His heart began to sink. <He: Seyun>

20 위 글의 밑줄 친 ⓐ의 우리말에 맞게 주어진 어휘를 이용하여 9 단어로 영작하시오.

few

➡ _____

21 위 글의 제목으로 알맞은 것을 고르시오.

① Your Dream Will Come True
② Tips for a Wonderful Posting
③ Fruitless Online Advertisement
④ How to Increase the Hits
⑤ Hey! No News Is Good News!

22 According to the passage, which is NOT true?

① Seyun took a photo of his bike with his smartphone and posted the picture.
② Seyun was excited, thinking about the bike he planned to buy.

③ Seyun didn't wait to get a reply to his online advertisement.

④ As the number of hits went up, Seyun's expectations went up too.

⑤ New postings by other people pushed Seyun's post down the list.

[23~25] 다음 글을 읽고 물음에 답하시오.

"What's wrong with my posting? (①) Is my bike not attractive enough?" (②) He searched on the Internet for tips on how to sell online. (③) He had been too hasty and too greedy. (④) He had not given enough information to the possible buyers. (⑤) Also, when compared to other bicycles, his price was too high. He wrote a new posting with a longer description of the bike. He added more photos to show his bike from different angles. "Twenty-four inch bicycle. Excellent condition. Always kept indoors. Rides just like new. Very few scratches. Good for someone 12-14 years old. ⓐ80,000 won."

<He: Seyun>

23 위 글의 흐름으로 보아, 주어진 문장이 들어가기에 가장 적절한 곳은?

Then he realized what he had done wrong.

①   ②   ③   ④   ⑤

24 다음 중 자신의 자전거에 대해 세윤이가 바꿔 쓴 게시물에 포함되지 <u>않은</u> 사항을 고르시오.

① 크기   ② 상태
③ 보관 장소   ④ 추천 연령
⑤ 구매 가격

25 위 글의 밑줄 친 ⓐ80,000을 영어로 읽는 법을 쓰시오.

➡ _____

[26~27] 다음 글을 읽고 물음에 답하시오.

Customer Reviews

★★★★★

If you are looking for (A)a new swimming suit, this one would be perfect. It is beautiful. Also, it is as cheap as the one that is on sale. I bought one, and I really like it. However, I would advise you _____ⓐ_____ a bigger size than what you usually buy. Even though I had ordered the same size as what I normally wear, it was too small for me.

26 위 글의 빈칸 ⓐ에 buy를 알맞은 형태로 쓰시오.

➡ _____

27 다음 빈칸 (A)와 (B)에 알맞은 단어를 넣어 위 글의 밑줄 친 (A)에 대한 소개를 완성하시오.

It is beautiful and as cheap as the one that is (A)_____ _____. However, it would be better for you to buy a (B)_____ size than what you usually buy.

단원별 예상문제

출제율 95%

01 다음 영영풀이가 가리키는 것을 고르시오.

> the process of getting knowledge or skill from doing, seeing, or feeling things

① action   ② movement   ③ account
④ experience   ⑤ excuse

출제율 100%

02 〈보기〉에서 알맞은 단어를 골라 문장을 완성하시오.

┌─── 보기 ───
shiny / sadly / pass /
however / contact / sell
└─────────

(1) 6개월이 지났는데도 우리는 아직 부모님으로부터 어떤 소식도 듣지 못했다.
➡ Six months _____ and we still had no news of our parents.

(2) 그 바이러스는 우연한 접촉으로 감염된다고 알려져 있다.
➡ It is believed that the virus is spread by casual _____.

(3) Bobby는 갑자기 숲 속에서 무언가 빛나는 것을 보았다.
➡ Suddenly Bobby saw something _____ in the forest.

(4) 미성년자에게 담배를 파는 것은 불법이다.
➡ It is illegal to _____ cigarettes to children who are under age.

[03~05] 다음 대화를 읽고 물음에 답하시오.

B: I want to buy some traditional Korean gifts for my friends. Where's a good place ⓐto buy them?
G: Have you ⓑgone to Insa-dong? They have ⓒlots of traditional Korean things there.
B: (A)아니, 그곳에 가 본 적 없어.

G: How about I ⓓtake you there this Friday afternoon?
B: Oh, I'm afraid I ⓔcan't. I have other plans. What about Saturday?
G: (B)That is fine with me.

출제율 95%

03 위 대화의 ⓐ~ⓔ 중 어법상 어색한 것을 하나 찾아 바르게 고치시오.

_____ ➡ _____

출제율 90%

04 위 대화의 밑줄 친 (A)의 우리말을 영작하시오. (5 words)

➡ _____

출제율 90%

05 위 대화의 밑줄 친 (B)That이 가리키는 것을 찾아 우리말로 쓰시오.

➡ _____

[06~07] 다음 대화를 읽고 물음에 답하시오.

G: Minho, can you come with us to the game expo this Sunday?
B: I'd love to, but I'm afraid I can't. I have an important test next week.
G: That's too bad. They're having a special show of various games.
B: Yeah, I've heard it's really great. (A)그럼 다음 주 토요일에 나랑 같이 가는 건 어때? (about / then / with / next / me / what / going / Saturday)
G: Sure. Let's go together next Saturday.

06 위 대화의 밑줄 친 (A)의 우리말을 주어진 단어를 이용해 영작하시오.

➡ _____

07 위 대화에 나타난 G의 심정으로 가장 적절한 것을 고르시오.

① depressed　　② excited
③ confused　　④ angry
⑤ disappointed

08 〈보기〉에서 알맞은 단어를 골라 빈칸을 채우시오.

┌─ 보기 ─┐
as　　　had

(1) He is not _____ friendly as she is.
(2) When we got home last night, we saw that somebody _____ broken into our neighbor's house.

09 괄호 안의 단어를 사용하여 우리말에 맞게 동등비교 문장을 쓰시오.

그 여배우는 아이유(IU)만큼 유명하지 않다.
(famous)

➡ _____

10 다음 중 어색한 문장을 고르시오.

① Ted is as thin as a stick.
② Though it was early fall, it was as hot as the middle of summer.
③ Make some cheese cake as small as she can.
④ I'm trying to be as kind as possible.
⑤ I'll do as much as ever I can.

11 괄호 안의 단어를 활용하여 우리말에 맞게 빈칸을 채우시오.

(1) 너는 네 사무실만큼 큰 장소를 찾고 있니?
(look for, large)

➡ _____
_____

(2) 나는 소민이를 만나기 전에는 그토록 아름다운 소녀를 만난 적이 없었다. (never, before, girl)

➡ _____

(3) 내 여동생이 내 옷을 더럽힌 것을 알았을 때 동생과 싸웠다.(find, make)

➡ _____
_____

12 다음 주어진 단어를 활용하여 우리말에 맞게 영작하시오.

나는 나의 형보다 키가 크지 않다. (as, elder)

➡ _____

13 다음 우리말에 맞게 영작한 문장을 고르시오.

그녀는 겉보기만큼 젊지 않다.

① She is not so young as she looks.
② She is young as she looks.
③ She is not young as she looks.
④ She is not old as she looks.
⑤ She is not so old as she looks.

14 다음 우리말에 맞게 괄호 안의 단어를 활용하여 영작하시오.

출제율 95%

> 그녀는 비명을 있는 대로 질러댔다.
> (scream, loudly, can)

➡ _____

[15~17] 다음 글을 읽고 물음에 답하시오.

(①) He took a photo of his bike with his smartphone and posted the picture, with a short comment, on an online market: "Used bike in excellent condition. (②) Only 100,000 won. (③) Please text me." (④) He was excited, thinking about the bike he planned to buy. (⑤) He could see ⓐhimself riding the shiny new bike. He could not wait to get a reply to his online advertisement. Every few minutes he checked the number of hits. As the number of hits went up, his expectations went up too. One hour passed, then two, and finally a whole day, but he received no texts. Nobody seemed to want his bike. New postings by other people pushed his post down the list. His heart began to sink.

15 위 글의 흐름으로 보아, 주어진 문장이 들어가기에 가장 적절한 곳은?

출제율 95%

> He acted fast.

①   ②   ③   ④   ⑤

16 위 글의 밑줄 친 ⓐhimself와 재귀대명사의 용법이 같은 것을 모두 고르시오.

출제율 90%

① He himself made the chair.
② He looked at himself in the mirror.
③ He carried the suitcase himself.
④ He himself had to do his homework.
⑤ John killed himself last night.

17 위 글에서 알 수 있는 세윤이의 심경 변화로 가장 알맞은 것을 고르시오.

출제율 100%

① hopeful → amazed
② nervous → satisfied
③ excited → disappointed
④ bored → puzzled
⑤ satisfied → bored

[18~20] 다음 글을 읽고 물음에 답하시오.

"What's wrong with my posting? Is my bike not attractive enough?" He searched on the Internet for tips on how to sell online. Then he realized what he ⓐhad done wrong. He had been too hasty and too greedy. He had not given enough information to the possible buyers. Also, when compared to other bicycles, his price was too high. ⓑ그는 그 자전거에 대한 더 긴 묘사가 있는 새 게시물을 작성했습니다. He added more photos to show his bike from different angles. "Twenty-four inch bicycle. Excellent condition. Always kept indoors. Rides just like new. Very few scratches. Good for someone 12-14 years old. 80,000 won."

<He: Seyun>

18 위 글의 밑줄 친 @had done과 과거완료의 용법이 같은 것을 고르시오.

① I recognized him well because I had often seen him before.

② When I reached the station, the train had already started.

③ I lost the book which I had bought the day before.

④ He had lived there for ten years when his father died.

⑤ I had just finished my breakfast when he came.

출제율 90%

19 위 글의 밑줄 친 ⓑ의 우리말에 맞게 주어진 어휘를 알맞게 배열하시오.

> of the bike / wrote / a longer description / a new posting / with / he

➡ _____

_____

출제율 95%

20 According to the passage, which is NOT true?

① Seyun searched on the Internet for tips on how to sell online.

② Seyun was too hasty and too greedy.

③ Seyun didn't give enough information to the possible buyers.

④ When compared to other bicycles, Seyun's price wasn't too high.

⑤ Seyun added more photos to show his bike from different angles.

[21~22] 다음 대화를 읽고 물음에 답하시오.

> Buyer: Hello? Are you the one who posted a bike for sale?
>
> Seyun: Yes, that's me.
>
> Buyer: Can I check your bike to see @if it's in good condition as you wrote?
>
> Seyun: Sure. It has very few scratches but nothing ugly.
>
> Buyer: Let me check.... Yeah, it seems good enough.
>
> Seyun: Perfect!
>
> Buyer: By the way, can I ask why you want to sell this bike?
>
> Seyun: I've grown more than 10 cm this year, so it's too small for me now.
>
> Buyer: Oh, I see.

출제율 95%

21 위 글의 밑줄 친 @if와 같은 의미로 쓰인 것을 모두 고르시오.

① I will tell him if he comes.

② I wonder if he is at home.

③ If you speak too fast, they will not understand you.

④ If it's warm tomorrow, we'll drive in the country.

⑤ Ask him if it is true.

출제율 90%

22 Why does Seyun want to sell the bike? Answer in English beginning with "Because".

➡ _____

_____

[01~02] 다음 대화를 읽고 물음에 답하시오.

B: The toy on your desk is so cute. Do you mind if I take a look at it?

G: Not at all. It's called a *maneki-neko*, or a good luck cat. My friend bought it for me when she went to Japan.

B: Why is it putting its hand up?

G: That means it is bringing you money.

B: Really? That's interesting. Could you ask your friend where she got it? I'm going to Japan next week and I'd like to get one.

G: I'm sorry. I'm afraid I can't. I lost contact with her.

01 Where does the toy come from? (Answer in English with 4 words.)

➡ _____

02 Can the girl ask her friend where she got the toy?

➡ _____

[03~04] 다음 대화를 읽고 물음에 답하시오.

G: Look! This jacket is really cute. Let's check out this store.

B: Wait, I'm afraid we can't take our drinks inside.

G: But I haven't finished mine yet.

B: Let's finish our drinks first. Then we can go inside.

03 Why can the boy and the girl not enter the store? (Answer in English with 7 words beginning with "Because".)

➡ _____

04 What did the boy suggest the girl in order to go inside? (Answer in English with 11 words.)

➡ _____
_____

05 괄호 안의 단어를 활용하여 빈칸을 완성하시오.

(1) 내가 방에 들어왔을 때 창문으로 새 한 마리가 날아 들어와 있었다. (fly)

➡ _____ in through the window when I came into the room.

(2) 그녀는 그가 자기를 보았는지 확신이 서지 않았다. (see)

➡ She wasn't certain that _____.

(3) Jay는 12살이 될 때까지 5곡의 교향곡을 작곡했다. (write)   *symphony: 교향곡

➡ By the time he was 12, _____
_____.

(4) 난 잠시 동안 내가 들은 것을 믿을 수 없었다. (hear)

➡ I couldn't believe what _____
for a moment.

(5) 그들은 그때까지 동등한 권리를 위해 열심히 싸웠다. (fight)

➡ They _____ hard for equal rights until that time.

06 다음 우리말에 맞게 괄호 안의 단어를 활용하여 영작하시오.

(1) 고양이는 잠을 사람보다 두 배 더 많이 잔다. (twice, as)

➡ _____

(2) 우리 학교는 네 학교보다 컴퓨터가 5배나 많다. (as)

➡ _____

_____

07 다음 우리말에 맞게 괄호 안의 단어를 어법에 맞게 배열하시오.

보름달은 반달보다 2배 밝을까?
(bright, moon, full, moon, twice, is, as, the, as, half, the)

➡ _____

08 다음 문장에서 비교 대상을 쓰고 동등비교 내용이 무엇인지 쓰시오.

People who have a lot of friends are twice as happy as those with only a few friends.

(1) 비교 대상 ➡ _____

_____

(2) 동등비교 내용 ➡ _____

09 다음 우리말에 맞게 괄호 안의 단어를 활용하여 빈칸을 채우시오.

그녀는 피부가 비단결같이 매끄러웠다. (smooth)
➡ Her skin was _____ _____ _____ silk.

[10~11] 다음 글을 읽고 물음에 답하시오.

He acted fast. He took a photo of his bike with his smartphone and posted the picture, with a short comment, on an online market: "Used bike in excellent condition. Only 100,000 won. Please text me." ⓐ그는 자신이 구입하려고 계획한 자전거에 대해 생각하며 신이 났습니다. He could see himself riding the shiny new bike. He could not wait to get a reply to his online advertisement. Every few minutes he checked the number of hits. As the number of hits went up, his expectations went up too. One hour passed, then two, and finally a whole day, but he received no texts. Nobody seemed to want his bike.

10 위 글의 밑줄 친 ⓐ의 우리말에 맞게 주어진 어휘를 알맞게 배열하시오.

to buy / the bike / planned / about / he / excited / thinking / was / he / , /

➡ _____

_____

11 본문의 내용과 일치하도록 다음 빈칸 (A)와 (B)에 알맞은 단어를 쓰시오.

He was eager to get a reply to his online advertisement, and at first, the number of (A)_____ went up. But he received no texts, and (B)_____ _____ by other people pushed his post down the list.

01 다음은 상점의 광고 글이다. 밑줄 친 우리말을 괄호 안에 주어진 어휘를 이용하여 영작하시오.

> If you (A)찾고 있는 중이다(look for) a new cell phone, this one would be perfect. It (B)아주 멋진 카메라를 가지고 있다(really wonderful). It will (C)두 배만큼 좋다(good) our previous model. How about battery? This phone (D)세 배만큼 지속된다(endure, much) our previous model.

02 주어진 표현을 이용하여 다음 대화의 빈칸에 알맞은 말을 쓰시오.

> A: _____ I use this coupon?
> (Do you mind if / Would you mind if / Do you mind / Would you mind)
> B: _____ The coupon is only for online orders.
> (No, I don't. / Not at all. / No, go ahead. / No problem. / I'm sorry, but I'm afraid you can't.)

03 다음 내용을 바탕으로 물건의 구매 후기를 쓰시오.

> **What I bought recently: a swimming suit**
> • It is beautiful.
> • Also, it is as cheap as the one that is on sale.
> • It would be better for you to buy a bigger size than what you usually buy.
> • Even though it was the same size as what the purchaser normally wears, it was too small for the purchaser.

> If you are looking for a new (A)_____, this one would be perfect. It is (B)_____. Also, it is as (C)_____ as the one that is on sale. I bought one, and I really like it. However, I would advise you to buy a (D)_____ than what you usually buy. Even though I had ordered the same size as what I normally wear, it was (E)_____ for me.

단원별 모의고사

01 다음 영영풀이가 가리키는 것은?

> to look somewhere carefully in order to find something

① search　　　　② research
③ include　　　　④ investigate
⑤ comment

02 다음 중 단어들의 관계가 나머지와 <u>다른</u> 하나는?

① shut – open
② hasty – slow
③ thin – thick
④ greedy – avaricious
⑤ ahead – behind

03 다음 우리말에 맞게 빈칸에 알맞은 말을 쓰시오.

(1) 우리는 3시 지나 도착할 계획이다.
➡ We _____ _____ arrive some time after three.

(2) 노숙자들의 수가 빠르게 증가해 왔다.
➡ _____ _____ _____ homeless people has increased dramatically.

(3) Shelley는 퇴직해서 자리를 젊은 동료 한 명에게 넘겨주었다.
➡ Shelley resigned and _____ _____ her job to one of her younger colleagues.

(4) 물가가 작년에 비해 3 퍼센트 증가했다.
➡ The price has increased by three percent _____ _____ the year before.

[04~05] 다음 대화를 읽고 물음에 답하시오.

> M: What can I help you with?
> G: I'd like to open a bank account. What should I do?
> M: First, you need to fill out this form.
> G: Sure. (A)제가 펜을 사용해도 될까요? (mind / do / if / your pen / I / use / you)?
> M: Not at all.

04 위 대화의 밑줄 친 (A)의 우리말에 맞게 주어진 어구를 바르게 배열하시오.

➡ _____

05 Why did G visit the bank? (Answer in English with 9 words.)

➡ _____

[06~08] 다음 대화를 읽고 물음에 답하시오.

> B: Excuse me. I want to return these sneakers.
> W: Okay. Can I ask why you want to return them?
> B: There's dirt on them and I haven't even worn (A)them yet.
> W: (B)Do you mind if I have a look?
> B: Not at all. Here.

06 What is the purpose of the conversation?

① to try on the sneakers
② to have a look at the sneakers
③ to return the sneakers
④ to ask about the sneakers
⑤ to complain about the sneakers

07 위 대화에서 밑줄 친 (A)them이 가리키는 것을 영어로 쓰시오. (2 words)

➡ _____

08 다음 중 밑줄 친 (B)와 바꿔 쓸 수 <u>없는</u> 것은? (2개)

① Would you mind if I have a look?
② Would you mind my having a look?
③ Do you mind my having a look?
④ Would I have a look?
⑤ Why can I have a look?

09 주어진 대화가 자연스럽게 이어지도록 순서대로 배열하시오.

> G: Look! This jacket is really cute. Let's check out this store.
> (A) But I haven't finished mine yet.
> (B) Wait, I'm afraid we can't take our drinks inside.
> (C) Let's finish our drinks first. Then we can go inside.

➡ _____

[10~12] 다음 대화를 읽고 물음에 답하시오.

> B: I want to buy some traditional Korean gifts for my friends. ① Where's a good place to buy them?
> G: Have you been to Insa-dong? ②
> B: No, I've never been there. ③
> G: How about I take you there this Friday afternoon? ④
> B: Oh, I'm afraid I can't. I have other plans. ⑤ What about Saturday?
> G: That's fine with me.

10 위 대화의 ①~⑤ 중에서 주어진 문장이 들어가기에 가장 적절한 곳은?

> They have lots of traditional Korean things there.

①   ②   ③   ④   ⑤

11 When are G and B going to Insa-dong? (7 words)

➡ _____

12 위 대화에서 주어진 영영풀이에 맞는 단어를 찾아 쓰시오.

> following or belonging to customs, beliefs, or methods that have existed for a long time without changing

➡ _____

13 다음 대화의 밑줄 친 부분의 의도로 가장 적절한 것은?

> A: Do you mind if I lean my seat back?
> B: No, not at all.

① 허락 요청하기   ② 선호 물어보기
③ 요청 거절하기   ④ 요청 승낙하기
⑤ 설명 요구하기

14 다음 문장에서 어법상 어색한 부분을 찾아 고치시오. 어색하지 <u>않은</u> 것은 '없음'이라고 쓰시오.

(1) Jane is not so creative as her brother.

_____ ➡ _____

(2) He hadn't saw a good movie in several weeks.

_____ ➡ _____

15 다음 빈칸에 들어갈 말로 적절하지 <u>않은</u> 것을 고르시오.

> St. Basil's Cathedral is a tourist site as _____ as the Red Square and the Kremlin.

① famous   ② popular
③ beautiful   ④ romantic
⑤ popularity

16 다음 중 어법상 어색한 것은?

① For three years in a row, about 8.5 million people had visited the museum.
② She had never studied French before she went to Paris.
③ For years he fought a running battle with the authorities over the land.
④ When I went to the flower shop, a man had bought all the flowers.
⑤ When I went to the fish store, a cat steels a fish.

*running: 연속적인, 계속하는 **authorities: 당국

17 다음 우리말에 맞게 괄호 안의 단어를 활용하여 영작하시오.

> 그녀는 그들이 자신의 충고를 따랐다는 것을 알고 만족했다. (satisfy, follow)

➡ _____

_____

18 빈칸에 들어갈 말로 적절한 것을 고르시오.

> I ate as _____ as I could.

① much   ② many
③ better   ④ best
⑤ good

19 우리말에 맞게 괄호 안의 단어를 배열하시오.

> 너는 여전히 아름답다.
> (ever, you, beautiful, are, as, as)

➡ _____

20 다음 우리말에 맞게 괄호 안의 어구를 활용하여 배열하시오.

> 그들이 내가 그 직장에 취직이 되었다고 비공식적으로 말해 주었다.
> (the job, I, that, got, informally)

➡ _____

[21~22] 다음 글을 읽고 물음에 답하시오.

Seyun rides his bike to school every day. He likes his bike, but he is taller and stronger this year. His bike has become too small for him, so he wants to buy a bigger, faster one. However, he does not have enough money in his savings account. What can he do?

Suddenly, Seyun had an idea. "My old bike is almost as good as a new one. Maybe I can sell it and add the money ⓐto buy a new one."

21 위 글의 밑줄 친 ⓐto buy와 to부정사의 용법이 <u>다른</u> 것을 <u>모두</u> 고르시오.

① It's not necessary to buy a new one.
② I would be happy to buy a new one.
③ Tell me the reason to buy a new one.
④ Why do you want to buy a new one?
⑤ What did you do to buy a new one?

22 Why does Seyun want to buy a new bike though his old bike is almost as good as a new one? Fill in the blanks (A) and (B) with suitable words.

> Because he is (A)_____ _____ _____ this year, and his bike has become (B)_____ _____ for him.

[23~24] 다음 글을 읽고 물음에 답하시오.

He acted fast. He took a photo of his bike with his smartphone and posted the picture, with a short comment, on an online market: "Used bike in excellent condition. Only 100,000 won. Please text me." He was excited, thinking about the bike he planned to buy. He could see himself riding the shiny new bike. He could not wait to get a reply to his online advertisement. Every few minutes he checked the number of hits. As the number of hits went up, his expectations went up too. One hour passed, then two, and ⓐfinally a whole day, but he received no texts. Nobody seemed to want his bike. New postings by other people pushed his post down the list. His heart began to sink.

<He: Seyun>

23 위 글의 밑줄 친 ⓐfinally와 바꿔 쓸 수 <u>없는</u> 말을 고르시오.

① eventually   ② at last
③ in the end   ④ in the long run
⑤ to the end

24 Which question CANNOT be answered after reading the passage?

① With what did Seyun take a photo of his bike?
② How much moeny did Seyun want to get for his bike?
③ How many hits did Seyun get for a day?
④ Did Seyun receive any texts?
⑤ What pushed Seyun's post down the list?

[25~26] 다음 글을 읽고 물음에 답하시오.

"What's wrong with my posting? Is my bike not attractive enough?" He searched ⓐ the Internet for tips ⓑ how to sell online. Then he realized ⓒwhat he had done wrong. He had been too hasty and too greedy. He had not given enough information to the possible buyers. Also, when compared to other bicycles, his price was too high. He wrote a new posting with a longer description of the bike. He added more photos to show his bike from different angles. "Twenty-four inch bicycle. Excellent condition. Always kept indoors. Rides just like new. Very few scratches. Good for someone 12-14 years old. 80,000 won."

25 위 글의 빈칸 ⓐ와 ⓑ에 공통으로 들어갈 알맞은 전치사를 고르시오.

① from   ② at   ③ in

④ on   ⑤ for

26 다음 중 위 글의 밑줄 친 ⓒ에 해당하지 <u>않는</u> 것을 고르시오.

① He had been in a hurry.
② He had wanted to have more money than was reasonable.
③ He had given insufficient information to the possible buyers.
④ When compared to other bicycles, his bicycle was too expensive.
⑤ He wrote a posting with a too long description of the bike.

[27~28] 다음 글을 읽고 물음에 답하시오.

This time he got several texts. (①) It was hard to accept at first, but finally he sold his bike for 70,000 won. (②) He met the buyer, handed over his bike, and got the money he needed. (③) Now he could get a new bike. (④) He felt both happy and sad. (⑤) He was sad to see his old bike go, but he was happy with himself because he had learned a lot and grown up a bit through the experience. <He: Seyun>

27 위 글의 흐름으로 보아, 주어진 문장이 들어가기에 가장 적절한 곳은?

> Sadly, they all asked for a lower price.

①   ②   ③   ④   ⑤

28 According to the passage, which is NOT true?

① Several texts that Seyun got all asked for a lower price.
② From the beginning, Seyun gladly accepted the possible buyers' demand.
③ Seyun handed over his bike to the buyer, and got the money he needed.
④ Seyun was sad to see his old bike go.
⑤ Seyun was happy with himself because he had learned a lot and grown up a bit through the experience.

MEMO

Lesson 7

Small Ideas, Big Differences

🐋 의사소통 기능

- 궁금증 표현하기
  A: I wonder who those men are.
  B: They're the Wright brothers.

- 생각할 시간 요청하기
  A: What can we do with these VR glasses?
  B: Let me see.... Maybe we can play soccer.

🐋 언어 형식

- 가정법 과거
  The water inside **would** quickly **boil** over **if** the lid **did not have** that hole.

- so that 주어 can 동사원형
  The hole also prevents the window from fogging up **so that** you **can** enjoy that fantastic view.

Words & Expressions

Key Words

- **amount**[əmáunt] 명 양, 총계
- **balance**[bǽləns] 명 균형 동 균형을 잡다
- **boil**[bɔil] 명 끓기 동 끓이다
- **breathing**[bríːðiŋ] 명 호흡, 숨
- **careful**[kɛ́ərfəl] 형 주의 깊은, 조심스러운, 세심한
- **carefully**[kɛ́ərfəli] 부 주의 깊게, 조심스럽게
- **cause**[kɔːz] 동 ~을 야기하다 명 원인
- **company**[kʌ́mpəni] 명 회사, 동료
- **cook**[kuk] 동 요리하다
- **couch**[kautʃ] 명 소파, 긴 의자
- **cracker**[krǽkər] 명 크래커
- **crispy**[kríspi] 형 바삭한
- **death**[deθ] 명 죽음
- **emergency**[imə́ːrdʒənsi] 명 비상사태
- **especially**[ispéʃəli] 부 특히
- **fantastic**[fæntǽstik] 형 환상적인
- **fog**[fɔːg] 명 안개 동 수증기가 서리다
- **helpful**[hélpfəl] 형 유용한, 도움이 되는
- **hide**[haid] 동 숨기다, 숨다
- **hidden**[hídn] 형 숨겨져 있는
- **hill**[hil] 명 언덕
- **lid**[lid] 명 뚜껑

- **mirror**[mírə] 명 거울
- **necessary**[nésəsèri] 형 필수적인
- **north**[nɔːrθ] 형 북쪽의, 북부의
- **notice**[nóutis] 동 알아채다, 의식하다
- **pane**[pein] 명 판유리
- **perhaps**[pərhǽps] 부 아마, 어쩌면
- **pressure**[préʃər] 명 압력
- **prevent**[privént] 동 막다
- **product**[prádʌkt] 명 생산물, 상품
- **quickly**[kwíkli] 부 빨리
- **recently**[ríːsntli] 부 최근에
- **repair**[ripɛ́ər] 동 수리하다
- **result**[rizʌ́lt] 명 결과
- **roof**[ruːf] 명 지붕
- **rope**[roup] 명 밧줄
- **shaped**[ʃeipt] 형 ~ 모양의
- **sometimes**[sʌ́mtàimz] 부 때로, 때때로
- **steam**[stiːm] 명 수증기, 김
- **stick**[stik] 명 막대 모양의 물건
- **surprisingly**[sərpráiziŋli] 부 놀랍게도
- **swallow**[swálou] 동 삼키다
- **twist**[twist] 동 비틀다, 돌리다

Key Expressions

- **be made up of** ~로 구성되다
- **be on an airplane** 비행기를 타다
- **boil over** 끓어 넘치다
- **build up** 점점 커지다
- **cause death** 죽음을 야기하다
- **come out** 나오다
- **fog up** 안개로 흐려지다, 김이 서리다
- **in an emergency** 비상 상황에서
- **in the future** 미래에
- **keep A from -ing** A가 ~하는 것을 막다

- **let A B(동사원형)** A가 B하게 하다
- **let out** 내보내다
- **look around** 주위를 둘러보다
- **look at** ~을 보다
- **look out** 밖을 내다보다
- **pass through** 거쳐 지나가다, 통과하다
- **play a helpful role** 도움을 주는 역할을 하다
- **prevent A from -ing** A가 ~하는 것을 방지하다
- **the result of ~** ~의 결과
- **think about** ~에 대해 생각하다

Word Power

※ 서로 비슷한 뜻을 가진 어휘

- ☐ **careful** 주의 깊은, 조심스러운 – **cautious** 조심성 있는
- ☐ **cause** ~을 야기하다 – **bring about** 야기하다
- ☐ **hide** 숨기다, 숨다 – **conceal** 숨기다, 감추다
- ☐ **perhaps** 아마, 어쩌면 – **probably** 아마도

- ☐ **carefully** 주의 깊게, 조심스럽게 – **cautiously** 신중하게
- ☐ **helpful** 유용한, 도움이 되는 – **useful** 도움이 되는
- ☐ **necessary** 필수적인 – **essential** 필수적인, 가장 중요한
- ☐ **repair** 수리하다 – **mend** 수선하다, 고치다

※ 서로 반대의 뜻을 가진 어휘

- ☐ **careful** 주의 깊은, 조심스러운, 세심한 ↔ **careless** 부주의한, 조심성 없는
- ☐ **cause** 원인 ↔ **result** 결과
- ☐ **helpful** 유용한, 도움이 되는 ↔ **unhelpful** 도움이 되지 않는

- ☐ **carefully** 주의 깊게, 조심스럽게 ↔ **carelessly** 부주의하게
- ☐ **death** 죽음 ↔ **birth** 탄생
- ☐ **necessary** 필수적인 ↔ **unnecessary** 불필요한, 쓸데없는

※ 과거분사 ❶ 동사원형 +-ed

- ☐ **advertise** 광고하다 → **advertised**
- ☐ **cry** 울다 → **cried**
- ☐ **damage** 피해를 입다 → **damaged**
- ☐ **prevent** 막다, 예방하다 → **prevented**
- ☐ **stop** 막다 → **stopped**

- ☐ **balance** 균형을 잡다 → **balanced**
- ☐ **clean** 청소하다 → **cleaned**
- ☐ **plan** 계획하다 → **planned**
- ☐ **provide** 제공하다 → **provided**
- ☐ **study** 공부하다, 연구하다 → **studied**

※ 과거분사 ❷ 불규칙 변화형

- ☐ **am/is/are** 이다/있다 → **been**
- ☐ **begin** 시작하다 → **begun**
- ☐ **cost** (비용, 대가가) 들다 → **cost**
- ☐ **draw** 그리다 → **drawn**

- ☐ **fly** 날다, 비행하다 → **flown**
- ☐ **lead** 이끌다 → **led**
- ☐ **lie** 눕다, 놓여 있다 → **lain**
- ☐ **light** 불을 비추다 → **lit**

- ☐ **take** 가져가다, 차지하다 → **taken**
- ☐ **seek** 찾다, 구하다 → **sought**
- ☐ **understand** 이해하다 → **understood**
- ☐ **wear** 입다 → **worn**

English Dictionary

- ☐ **amount** 양, 총계
  - → the degree to which something is a lot or a little; how much something is
  - 어떤 것이 많은가 적은가의 정도; 어떤 것이 얼마나 있는지의 정도

- ☐ **balanc** 균형을 잡다
  - → to be in a position where you will stand without falling to either side, or to put something in this position
  - 어느 쪽으로도 치우치지 않는 위치에 있거나 혹은 어떤 것을 이 위치에 놓다

- ☐ **breathing** 호흡, 숨
  - → the process to take air into the lungs and let it out again
  - 공기를 폐 속으로 들여마시고 내뱉는 과정

- ☐ **emergency** 비상사태
  - → an unexpected and dangerous situation
  - 예상치 못한 위험한 상황

- ☐ **especially** 특히, 특별히
  - → very much; more than usual or more than other people or things
  - 매우 많이; 다른 사람이나 사물 이상으로, 흔히 있는 것 이상으로

- ☐ **helpful** 유용한, 도움이 되는
  - → willing to help, or useful
  - 기꺼이 도와주려고 하는; 유용한

- ☐ **necessary** 필수적인
  - → needed in order to achieve a particular result
  - 어떤 특정한 결과를 얻기 위해 필요한

- ☐ **notice** 알아채다, 의식하다
  - → to become aware of 알게 되다

- ☐ **normally** 보통, 보통 때는
  - → in the usual or expected way 보통의 혹은 예상되는 방식으로

- ☐ **prevent** 막다
  - → to stop something from happening or someone from doing something
  - 어떤 것이 일어나는 것을 막거나 혹은 어떤 사람이 어떤 것을 하는 것을 막다

- ☐ **product** 생산물, 상품
  - → something that is made to be sold, usually something that is produced by an industrial process
  - 팔기 위해 만든 어떤 것, 보통 산업적 과정을 통해 만들어진 어떤 것

- ☐ **recently** 최근에
  - → not long ago 오래 전이 아닌

- ☐ **repair** 수리하다
  - → to put something damaged back into good condition
  - 어떤 망가진 것을 다시 좋은 상태로 만들다

- ☐ **swallow** 삼키다
  - → to make food go down the throat
  - 음식을 목 안으로 내려가게 하다

서답형

01 다음 짝지어진 단어의 관계가 같도록 빈칸에 알맞은 말을 쓰시오.

careful : cautious = helpful : _____

02 다음 영영풀이가 가리키는 것을 고르시오.

to stop something from happening or someone from doing something

① advise
② help
③ provide
④ prevent
⑤ discourage

중요

03 다음 중 밑줄 친 부분의 뜻풀이가 바르지 않은 것은?

① The hotel is currently under repair. (수리하다)
② The result is entirely unpredictable. (결과)
③ My hobby is to collect round-shaped piece of stone. (형태의)
④ Who's going to cook supper? (요리하다)
⑤ He struggled to hide his disappointment. (숨기다)

04 다음 주어진 문장의 빈칸에 공통으로 들어갈 말로 가장 적절한 것은?

• Employees should be fully aware of _____ procedures.
• The pilot was forced to make a/an _____ landing.

① breathing
② fantastic
③ necessary
④ dangerous
⑤ emergency

서답형

05 다음 문장의 빈칸에 들어갈 말을 〈보기〉에서 골라 쓰시오.

┤ 보기 ├
be made up of / cause death / look around / think about / pass through

(1) The typhoon is expected to _____ _____ the East Sea between Sunday and Monday.
(2) In some places like Africa, diarrhea can _____ _____ due to dehydration and lack of medicine. *diarrhea: 설사
(3) Some theorists _____ _____ culture and cultural diversity in different ways.

중요

06 다음 문장의 (A)와 (B)에 각각 공통으로 들어갈 말이 바르게 짝지어진 것은?

• Can you look ___(A)___ the window and see whether she is coming?
• Everyone let ___(A)___ a sigh of relief.
• All the pressure built ___(B)___ and he was off work for weeks.
• Dokdo is made ___(B)___ of 89 islets and reefs. *islet: 작은 섬

① out – out
② out – up
③ at – out
④ at – up
⑤ around – up

01 다음 짝지어진 단어의 관계가 같도록 빈칸에 알맞은 말을 쓰시오.

> death : birth = necessary : _____

02 다음 주어진 영영풀이에 맞는 단어를 쓰시오.

> to become aware of

➡ _____

03 다음 문장의 빈칸에 들어갈 말을 〈보기〉에서 골라 쓰시오.

┌─ 보기 ─┐
twist / rope / pane / lid / hill

(1) The thief broke the _____ in order to unlock the door.
(2) We climbed to the very top of the _____.
(3) I saw her _____ the ring on her finger.

04 다음 우리말에 맞게 빈칸에 알맞은 말을 쓰시오.

(1) 놀랍게도 그것은 한국에서보다 외국에서 훨씬 더 저렴하다.
➡ _____ it's much cheaper abroad than in Korea.
(2) 그 남자 아이돌 그룹은 최근에 재결성되었다.
➡ The boy-band has _____ been re-formed.
(3) Paul은 그의 차를 조심스럽게 차고에 주차했다.
➡ Paul parked his car _____ into the garage.

05 다음 우리말에 맞게 주어진 단어를 사용하여 영작하시오.

(1) 잘 마무리된 지붕은 수년 간 비바람에 잘 견뎌야 한다. (weatherproof, the well-finished, roof, years)
➡ _____
_____

(2) 얼마나 빨리 서류를 준비할 수 있으신가요? (quickly, paperwork)
➡ _____

(3) 그는 막대기로 모래 위에 동그라미 하나를 그렸다. (stick, circle)
➡ _____
_____

06 다음 우리말과 일치하도록 주어진 어구를 바르게 나열하시오.

(1) 그의 얼굴이 거울에 비쳤다.
(his / reflected / was / in the mirror / face)
➡ _____

(2) 나는 목이 아파서 삼키기 힘들었다.
(hurt / had / swallow / a sore throat / it / and / to / I)
➡ _____

(3) 수증기에 다치지 않도록 조심하렴.
(the steam / be / to / hurt / careful / yourself / with / not)
➡ _____

Conversation

교과서

1 궁금증 표현하기

> **A** I wonder who those men are. 저 남자들이 누군지 궁금해.
>
> **B** They're the Wright brothers. 그들은 라이트 형제들이야.

- 대화 상대방에게 궁금한 점을 물을 때 "I wonder ~." 또는 "I am wondering ~.", "I was wondering ~." 등과 같은 표현을 쓸 수 있다.

- 이때 wonder와 함께 의문사(what/when/where/why/how)를 이용한 간접의문문을 사용하거나 혹은 if 절을 사용하기도 한다.
  - I wonder why I get tired so much. 난 내가 왜 이리 피곤한지 모르겠어.
  - If I ate less, I wonder how much weight I would lose. 내가 적게 먹으면 얼마나 살이 빠질지 궁금해.
  - I wonder if I should wear a coat or not. 코트를 입어야 할지 말지 모르겠어.
  - I wonder if you are going to attend the meeting at 2 p.m. 2시에 회의에 참석하실 건지 궁금합니다.

- "I wonder if you ~."라는 표현은 상대방에게 부탁할 경우에도 쓰일 수 있다.
  - I wonder if you could tell me the right direction to the subway station.
    제게 지하철역에 가는 정확한 방향을 가르쳐 주실 수 있나요?
  - I wonder if you could give me a discount a little bit. 할인을 조금 해주실 수 있나요?

핵심 Check

1. 다음 대화의 밑줄 친 우리말에 맞게 주어진 단어를 바르게 배열하시오.

   A: <u>난 최초의 비행기가 어떻게 생겼는지 궁금해.</u>

   (looked / I / plane / what / like / wonder / the / first).

   B: Look! There is a model. It looked like a big bird.

   ➡ _____

2 생각할 시간 요청하기

> **A** What can we do with these VR glasses? 이 VR 안경으로 뭘 할 수 있을까?
>
> **B** Let me see.... Maybe we can play soccer. 어디 보자… 아마 우리 축구할 수 있을 거야.

■ "Let me see."는 '잠깐만.', '어디 보자.'의 뜻으로 어떤 것을 기억해 내거나 잠시 생각을 정리할 시간이 필요할 때 사용하는 표현이다. 같은 표현인 "Let me think." 또는 "Just a moment." 등을 사용하여 생각할 시간을 요청할 수 있다.

생각할 시간 요청하기

- Let me see. 어디 보자.
- Let me think. 생각 좀 해보자.
- Just a moment. 잠깐만.
- Just a second. 잠깐만.
- Wait a moment. 잠깐만.

■ let은 동사원형을 목적격보어로 취하는 점에 유의한다.

- Let me think about it. (○)
- Let me thinking about it. (✕)
- Let me to think about it. (✕)

핵심 Check

2. 다음 대화의 빈칸에 들어갈 말로 적절하지 <u>않은</u> 것은?

A: What can we do with this VR glasses?

B: _____ .... We can play soccer.

① Let me see　　　　　　② Let me think

③ Just a moment　　　　　④ Just a second

⑤ Let me see what I can do

Real-Life Zone

G: I like these crackers. They're really good.

B: Yeah, me, too. ❶I wonder why crackers have these little holes in them.

G: I don't know. ❷Let me think…. Um … well … maybe it's because the holes ❸make the crackers look tastier.

B: That's ❹possible, but there must be some other reasons.

G: Let's ❺look up crackers on the Internet and see what it says.

B: Okay. Oh, look at this.

G: It says during baking, steam ❻comes out through the holes and that makes the crackers thin.

B: It also says that the holes make the crackers crispy.

G: Wow! So ❼that's why they have holes!

G: 난 이 크래커가 좋아. 정말 맛있어.

B: 응, 나도 좋아해. 나는 크래커에 왜 이 작은 구멍들이 있는지 궁금해.

G: 잘 모르겠어. 생각해 보자…. 음… 아마 그 구멍들이 크래커를 더욱 맛있게 보이도록 해 주기 때문이 아닐까.

B: 그럴 수도 있겠네. 하지만 다른 이유들이 있을 거야.

G: 크래커에 관해 인터넷에 찾아보고 뭐라고 하는지 알아보자.

B: 좋아. 오, 이것 봐.

G: 굽는 동안, 그 구멍들을 통해 수증기가 빠져나와서 크래커를 얇게 만드는 거래.

B: 또한 구멍들은 크래커를 바삭하게 만드는 거래.

G: 와! 크래커에 구멍들이 있는 거구나!

❶ 'I wonder ∼.'는 궁금증을 나타내는 표현으로, "I am wondering ∼.", 'I was wondering ∼.'과 같은 표현으로 대체할 수 있다. ❷ '잠깐만.', '어디 보자.'의 뜻으로 어떤 것을 기억해 내거나 잠시 생각을 정리할 시간이 필요할 때 사용하는 표현이다. ❸ make+목적어+목적보어(동사원형): 목적어를 목적보어하게 만들다 ❹ possible: 가능성 있는, 있을 수 있는 ❺ look up: (정보를) 찾아 보다 ❻ come out: 나오다 ❼ 'that is the reason why they have holes!'의 줄임말이다.

Check(√) True or False

(1) Both G and B did not know why crackers have little holes in them. T ☐ F ☐

(2) According to the Internet, the little holes in crackers make them thin and crispy. T ☐ F ☐

Wrap Up 1-2

B: Hi, Kate. Today's Saturday, so ❶what about going to the Einstein Science Park today?

G: ❷That sounds like a good idea. I heard that they have special programs on Saturdays. ❸I wonder what they are.

B: ❹Let me see…. I saw an advertisement in the newspaper. ❺ Here it is.

G: What does it say?

B: It says that today they have two shows: the Smart Design Show and the International Drone Show in Einstein Hall 101.

G: ❻They both sound fantastic.

B: I'll call them and ask what time they start.

B: 안녕, 케이트. 오늘은 토요일이야. 그래서 말인데, 오늘 아인슈타인 과학 공원에 가는 건 어때?

G: 좋은 생각이야. 나는 토요일마다 특별한 프로그램들이 있다고 들었어. 나는 그것들이 무엇인지 궁금해.

B: 어디 보자…. 내가 신문에서 광고를 봤어. 여기 있어.

G: 뭐라고 쓰여 있니?

B: 여기에 따르면 오늘 두 가지 공연이 있대. 아이슈타인 홀 101호에서 있는 스마트 디자인 쇼와 국제 드론 쇼야.

G: 둘 다 환상적일 것 같아.

B: 내가 전화해서 그것들이 몇 시에 시작하는지 물어볼게.

❶ 상대방에게 무언가를 제안하는 표현으로, 'How about ∼?'으로 바꿔 쓸 수 있다. ❷ 상대방의 제안을 승낙하는 표현으로, 'That sounds good.'으로 바꿔 쓸 수 있다. ❸ wonder와 함께 의문사(what/when/where/why/how)를 이용한 간접의문문을 사용하기도 한다. ❹ '잠깐만.', '어디 보자.'의 뜻으로 어떤 것을 기억해 내거나 잠시 생각을 정리할 시간이 필요할 때 사용하는 표현이다. ❺ '여기 있습니다.'라는 표현으로 단어나 어구가 정해진 위치를 벗어난 도치 문장이다. ❻ 이때 They는 앞서 언급된 'two shows'를 가리킨다.

Check(√) True or False

(3) There are going to be more than two shows on weekdays. T ☐ F ☐

(4) Both G and B are going to visit the Einstein Science Park today. T ☐ F ☐

Listen & Speak 1 Listen

1. **G:** Look at this picture. I wonder who ❶ those men are.
   B: They're the Wright brothers. They ❷ invented the airplane.
2. **G:** I wonder why they are standing ❸in front of the bicycle shop.
   B: They had a bicycle shop. They sold and repaired bicycles.
3. **G:** I wonder ❹what the first plane looked like.
   B: Look! There is a model. It looked like a big bird.
4. **G:** I wonder ❺where they first tried to fly their airplane.
   B: They tested their airplane on a hill in North Carolina.

❶ that의 복수형으로 지시형용사로 쓰였다.
❷ invent : 발명하다
❸ in front of ~: ~의 앞에
❹ 의문사 what을 사용한 간접의문문으로, '최초의 비행기가 어떻게 생겼는지'라고 해석한다.
❺ 의문사 where가 사용된 간접의문문으로, '그들이 어디서 최초로 비행을 시도했는지'라고 해석한다.

 Listen & Speak 1 A-1

B: Look at this invention. It can ❶help us cook without electricity.
G: Is that possible? ❷I wonder how it works.
B: It uses sunlight to cook food.
G: Wow. ❸That would be really helpful when you go camping.

❶ help는 목적보어로 동사원형이나 to부정사를 취한다.
❷ 'I wonder ~.'는 목적어로 의문사를 이용한 간접의문문을 취하기도 한다.
❸ That은 음식을 요리하기 위해 햇빛을 이용하는 것(using sunlight to cook food)을 가리킨다.

 Listen & Speak 1 A-2

B: Hi, class. ❶Have you ever heard about the Moai? They are tall, human-shaped stones in Chile. ❷Most of the stones are four meters tall, but the tallest one is 20 meters tall. I was wondering ❸how people moved them long ago. So I searched the Internet and learned that they used ropes. Isn't ❹that amazing?

❶ 'Have you ever ~?'는 상대방에게 어떤 일을 해 본 적이 있냐고 묻는 표현이다.
❷ Most of ~: ~의 대부분
❸ 의문사 how가 쓰인 간접의문문으로, '어떻게 사람들이 그것을 오래 전에 옮겼는지'라고 해석한다.
❹ 이때 that은 돌을 옮기기 위해 밧줄을 사용한 것(using ropes to move the stones)을 가리킨다.

 Listen & Speak 1 B-1

A: I wonder ❶who those men are.
B: They're the Wright brothers. ❷They invented the airplane.

❶ 의문사 who가 쓰인 간접의문문으로, '그 남자들이 누군지'라고 해석한다.
❷ 이때 they는 앞서 언급한 the Wright brothers를 가리킨다.

 Listen & Speak 1 B-2

A: I wonder ❶what the first plane looked like.
B: Look! There is a model. ❷It looked like a big bird.

❶ 의문사 what이 쓰인 간접의문문으로, '최초의 비행기는 어떻게 생겼는지'라고 해석한다.
❷ 이때 It은 'the first plane'을 가리킨다.

 Listen & Speak 1 B-3

A: I wonder ❶what country they're from.
B: They're from the U.S.

❶ 의문사 what이 쓰인 간접의문문으로, '그들이 어느 나라에서 왔는지'라고 해석한다.

 Listen & Speak 2 Listen

1. **G:** ❶What can we do with these VR glasses?
   B: Let me see.... ❷Maybe we can play soccer.
2. **B:** How does the ball float in the air?
   G: Let me see.... I think air ❸pushes the ball up.
3. **G:** How does this train start to move?
   B: ❹Let me see.... I think you can move it with a smartphone app.
4. **G:** What can we do with this drone?
   B: Well, let me see.... Maybe we can ❺take pictures from the sky.

❶ 의문사 what이 쓰인 직접의문으로, 'VR 안경으로 뭘 할 수 있지?'라고 해석한다.
❷ maybe: 아마도 (= probably)
❸ push up: ~을 밀어 올리다
❹ '잠깐만.', '어디 보자.'의 뜻으로 어떤 것을 기억해 내거나 잠시 생각을 정리할 시간이 필요할 때 사용하는 표현으로 "Let me think." 또는 "Just a moment." 등으로 대체할 수 있다.
❺ take a picture of ~: ~의 사진을 찍다 (= take a photo of ~)

Listen & Speak 2 A-1

G: Look at the number. It's ❶going up quickly.

B: When people ❷pass by, the number increases.

G: Oh, you're right. ❸What does the number mean?

B: Let me see.... Oh, when people ❹step on the floor, energy is made. It shows ❺the amount of energy that is made.

G: Wow, that's amazing!

❶ go up: 올라가다, 증가하다
❷ pass by: 지나가다
❸ 의문사 what이 쓰인 의문문으로, '그 숫자들이 뭘 의미하지?'라고 해석한다.
❹ step on: ~을 밟다
❺ the amount of ~: ~의 양

Listen & Speak 2 A-2

G: ❶We're going on a field trip tomorrow to the Invention Museum.

B: I've heard that ❷it has a lot of creative inventions.

G: ❸That's why I'm so excited. ❹How about planning the tour before we go?

B: Good idea. Let me see.... I have the school letter and a map of the museum.

G: Perfect. ❺Let's get started.

❶ 현재진행형 문장이지만 의미는 미래에 무엇을 할 것이라고 해석한다.
❷ 대명사 it은 'the Invention Museum'을 가리킨다.
❸ 'That's the reason why I'm so excited.'의 줄임말이다.
❹ 상대방에게 무언가를 제안할 때 쓸 수 있는 표현으로, 'What about ~?'으로 대체할 수 있다.
❺ '시작하자'라고 해석한다.

Listen & Speak 2 B-1

A: What can we do with this VR glasses?

B: ❶Let me see... We can play soccer.

❶ 이와 같은 표현인 "Let me think." 또는 "Just a moment." 등을 사용하여 생각할 시간을 요청할 수 있다.

Listen & Speak 2 B-2

A: What can we do with this drone?

B: Let me see... ❶We can take pictures from the sky.

❶ take pictures from the sky: 하늘에서 사진을 찍다

Listen & Speak 2 B-3

A: What can we do with the smart watch?

B: Let me see... We can ❶send text messages.

❶ send: ~을 보내다

Wrap Up 3~4

G: John, look. The school ❶is having an invention competition.

B: Really? ❷That sounds interesting.

G: Yeah. ❸You should enter that. You always have great ideas.

B: Does it say ❹when the competition is?

G: Let me see.... It says it's November 11. That's two weeks from today.

B: I wonder what I have to do to enter the competition.

G: It says here you should talk to Mr. Harrison, the science teacher.

❶ 현재진행형 문장이지만 의미는 미래에 무엇을 할 것이라고 해석한다.
❷ 대명사 That은 'an invention competition'을 가리킨다.
❸ 이때 should는 강한 강요의 의미가 아니라 부드럽게 권유하는 의미로 해석한다.
❹ 의문사 when이 사용된 간접의문문으로, '언제 그 대회가 시작하는지'라고 해석한다.

Conversation 교과서 확인학습

● 다음 우리말과 일치하도록 빈칸에 알맞은 말을 쓰시오.

Listen & Speak 1 Listen

1. **G:** Look at this _____. I wonder who _____ men are.
   B: They're the Wright brothers. They _____ the airplane.
2. **G:** I wonder _____ they are standing in _____ of the bicycle shop.
   B: They had a bicycle shop. They sold and _____ bicycles.
3. **G:** I wonder _____ the first plane _____ like.
   B: Look! There is a model. It looked _____ a big bird.
4. **G:** I _____ where they first _____ to fly their airplane.
   B: They _____ their airplane on a hill in North Carolina.

Listen & Speak 1 A-1

B: Look at this _____. It can help us _____ without _____.
G: Is that _____? I wonder how it _____.
B: It uses _____ to cook food.
G: Wow. That would be really _____ when you go camping.

Listen & Speak 1 A-2

B: Hi, class. Have you ever _____ about the Moai? They are tall, human-_____ stones in Chile. _____ of the stones are four meters _____, but the tallest one is 20 meters tall. I was _____ how people _____ them long ago. So I _____ the Internet and _____ that they used _____. Isn't that _____?

Listen & Speak 1 B-1

A: I wonder _____ those men are.
B: They're the Wright brothers. They _____ the airplane.

Listen & Speak 1 B-2

A: I wonder what the first plane _____ like.
B: Look! There is a _____. It looked _____ a big bird.

Listen & Speak 1 B-3

A: I _____ what _____ they're from.
B: They're _____ the U.S.

1. G: 이 사진을 봐. 나는 그 남자들이 누구인지 궁금해.
   B: 그들은 라이트 형제야. 그들은 비행기를 발명했어.
2. G: 나는 그들이 왜 자전거 가게 앞에 서 있는지 궁금해.
   B: 그들은 자전거 가게를 가지고 있었어. 그들은 자전거를 팔고 수리했어.
3. G: 나는 최초의 비행기가 어떻게 생겼는지 궁금해.
   B: 봐! 저기 모형이 있어. 그것은 큰 새처럼 생겼네.
4. G: 나는 그들이 어디에서 처음으로 비행을 시도했는지 궁금해.
   B: 그들은 노스캐롤라이나주의 한 언덕에서 그들의 비행기를 시험했어.

B: 이 발명품들을 봐. 이것은 우리가 전기 없이도 요리할 수 있도록 도와줘.
G: 그게 가능해? 나는 그것이 어떻게 작용하는지 궁금해.
B: 이것은 음식을 조리하기 위해 태양광을 사용해.
G: 와. 그것은 캠핑을 갈 때 정말 유용할 것 같아.

B: 안녕하세요, 여러분. 여러분은 모아이에 대해 들어 본 적이 있나요? 그것들은 칠레에 있는 크고 사람 모양을 한 돌입니다. 대부분의 돌들은 높이가 4미터이지만, 가장 큰 것은 높이가 20미터입니다. 저는 오래 전에 사람들이 어떻게 그것들을 옮겼는지 궁금했습니다. 그래서 저는 인터넷을 검색했고 그들이 밧줄을 이용했다는 것을 알게 되었습니다. 그 사실이 놀랍지 않나요?

A: 나는 그 남자들의 누구인지 궁금해.
B: 그들은 라이트 형제야. 그들은 비행기를 발명했어.

A: 나는 최초의 비행기가 어떻게 생겼는지 궁금해.
B: 봐! 저기 모형이 있어. 그것은 큰 새처럼 생겼었네.

A: 나는 그들이 어느 나라 출신인지 궁금해.
B: 그들은 미국 출신이야.

해석

Listen & Speak 2 Listen

1. **G:** _____ can we do with these VR glasses?

   B: _____ me see.... _____ we can play soccer.

2. **B:** _____ does the ball _____ in the air?

   G: Let me see.... I think air _____ the ball up.

3. **G:** How does this train start to _____?

   B: Let me _____.... I think you can move it _____ a smartphone app.

4. **G:** What can we do with this drone?

   B: Well, let me see.... Maybe we can take _____ from the sky.

1. G: 우리가 이 VR 안경으로 무엇을 할 수 있을까?
   B: 어디 보자.... 아마 우리는 축구를 할 수 있을 거야.
2. B: 어떻게 그 공이 공중에 뜰까?
   G: 어디 보자.... 내 생각에는 공기가 공을 위로 밀어 올리는 것 같아.
3. G: 이 기차는 어떻게 움직이기 시작할까?
   B: 어디 보자.... 내 생각에는 네가 스마트폰 앱으로 그것을 움직일 수 있을 것 같아.
4. G: 우리가 이 드론으로 무엇을 할 수 있을까?
   B: 음, 어디 보자.... 아마 우리는 하늘에서 사진을 찍을 수 있을 거야.

Listen & Speak 2 A-1

G: _____ at the number. It's going up _____.

B: When people _____ by, the number _____.

G: Oh, you're right. What does the number mean?

B: _____ me see.... Oh, when people _____ on the floor, energy is _____. It shows the amount of energy that is made.

G: Wow, that's _____!

G: 저 숫자를 봐. 빠르게 올라가고 있어.
B: 사람들이 지나갈 때, 그 숫자가 증가해.
G: 오, 네 말이 맞아. 그 숫자는 무엇을 의미할까?
B: 어디 보자.... 오, 사람들이 바닥을 밟을 때 에너지가 만들어져. 그것은 만들어지는 에너지의 양을 보여 줘.
G: 와, 놀라워!

Listen & Speak 2 A- 2

G: We're going on a _____ trip tomorrow to the _____ Museum.

B: I've heard that it has a lot of _____ inventions.

G: That's why I'm so _____. How about _____ the tour before we go?

B: _____ idea. Let me see.... I have the school letter and a map of the _____.

G: Perfect. Let's get _____.

G: 우리는 내일 '발명 박물관'으로 현장학습을 가.
B: 나는 그곳에 창의적인 발명품들이 많이 있다고 들었어.
G: 그것이 내가 들뜬 이유야. 우리 가기 전에 관람 계획을 짜는 것은 어때?
B: 좋은 생각이야. 어디 보자.... 나는 학교에서 받은 안내서와 박물관 지도가 있어.
G: 완벽해. 시작하자.

Listen & Speak 2 B-1

A: _____ can we do with this VR glasses?

B: Let me see... We can _____ soccer.

A: 우리가 이 VR 안경으로 무엇을 할 수 있을까?
B: 어디 보자.... 우리는 축구를 할 수 있어.

Listen & Speak 2 B-2

A: What can we do _____ this drone?

B: Let me _____... We can take pictures _____ the sky.

A: 우리가 이 드론으로 무엇을 할 수 있을까?
B: 어디 보자.... 우리는 하늘에서 사진을 찍을 수 있어.

Listen & Speak 2 B-3

A: _____ can we do with the smart watch?

B: Let me see… We can _____ text messages.

해석

A: 우리가 이 스마트워치로 무엇을 할 수 있을까?

B: 어디 보자…. 우리는 문자 메시지를 보낼 수 있어.

Real-Life Zone

G: I like _____ crackers. They're really good.

B: Yeah, me, too. I wonder _____ crackers have these little _____ in them.

G: I don't know. Let me _____…. Um … well … _____ it's because the holes make the crackers _____ tastier.

B: That's _____, but there _____ be some other _____.

G: Let's _____ up crackers on the Internet and see _____ it says.

B: Okay. Oh, look at this.

G: It _____ _____ baking, steam comes out _____ the holes and that makes the crackers _____.

B: It also says that the holes make the crackers _____.

G: Wow! So that's _____ they have holes!

G: 난 이 크래커가 좋아. 정말 맛있어.

B: 응, 나도 좋아해. 나는 크래커에 왜 이 작은 구멍들이 있는지 궁금해.

G: 잘 모르겠어. 생각해 보자…. 음… 아마 그 구멍들이 크래커를 더욱 맛있게 보이도록 해 주기 때문이 아닐까.

B: 그럴 수도 있겠네. 하지만 다른 이유들이 있을 거야.

G: 크래커에 관해 인터넷에 찾아보고 뭐라고 하는지 알아보자.

B: 좋아. 오, 이것 봐.

G: 굽는 동안, 그 구멍들을 통해 수증기가 빠져나와서 크래커를 얇게 만드는 거래.

B: 또한 구멍들은 크래커를 바삭하게 만드는 거래.

G: 와! 크래커에 구멍들이 있는 거구나!

Wrap Up 1-2

B: Hi, Kate. Today's Saturday, so _____ about _____ to the Einstein Science Park today?

G: That _____ like a good idea. I heard _____ they have special programs on _____. I wonder _____ they are.

B: Let me see…. I saw an _____ in the newspaper. _____ it is.

G: What does it _____?

B: It _____ that today they have two shows: the Smart Design Show and the International Drone Show in Einstein Hall 101.

G: They _____ sound _____.

B: I'll call them and ask _____ time they start.

B: 안녕, 케이트. 오늘은 토요일이야. 그래서 말인데, 오늘 아인슈타인 과학 공원에 가는 건 어때?

G: 좋은 생각이야. 나는 토요일마다 특별한 프로그램들이 있다고 들었어. 나는 그것들이 무엇인지 궁금해.

B: 어디 보자…. 내가 신문에서 광고를 봤어. 여기 있어.

G: 뭐라고 쓰여 있니?

B: 여기에 따르면 오늘 두 가지 공연이 있대. 아인슈타인 홀 101호에서 있는 스마트 디자인 쇼와 국제 드론 쇼야.

G: 둘 다 환상적일 것 같아.

B: 내가 전화해서 그것들이 몇 시에 시작하는지 물어볼게.

Wrap Up 3~4

G: John, look. The school is having an invention _____.

B: Really? That _____ interesting.

G: Yeah. You should _____ that. You always have great _____.

B: Does it say _____ the competition is?

G: Let me see…. It says it's November 11. That's two weeks _____ today.

B: I _____ what I _____ to do to enter the competition.

G: It says here you should _____ to Mr. Harrison, the _____ teacher.

G: 존, 봐. 학교에서 발명대회가 열린대.

B: 정말? 흥미로울 것 같아.

G: 응. 너는 참가해야 해. 너는 항상 아이디어가 훌륭하잖아.

B: 대회가 언제인지 나와 있니?

G: 어디 보자…. 11월 11일이래. 오늘로부터 2주 뒤야.

B: 대회에 참가하기 위해 내가 무엇을 해야 하는지 궁금해.

G: 여기에 따르면 너는 과학 선생님이신 해리슨 선생님께 말씀드려야 해.

[01~02] 다음 대화를 읽고 물음에 답하시오.

> B: Look at this invention. It can help us cook without electricity.
> G: Is that possible? (A)난 그게 어떻게 작동하는지 궁금해.
> B: (B)It uses sunlight to cook food.
> G: Wow. That would be really helpful when you go camping.

01 위 대화의 밑줄 친 (A)의 우리말을 바르게 영작하시오. (5 words)

➡ _____

02 위 대화의 밑줄 친 (B)가 가리키는 것을 찾아 쓰시오. (2 words)

➡ _____

[03~04] 다음 대화를 읽고 물음에 답하시오.

> G: Look at the number. It's going up quickly.
> B: When people pass by, the number increases.
> G: Oh, you're right. What does the number mean?
> B: (A)Let me see.... Oh, when people step on the floor, energy is made. It shows the amount of energy that is made.
> G: Wow, that's amazing!

03 위 대화의 밑줄 친 (A)와 바꿔 쓸 수 있는 것은?

① Let me see what I can do
② Let me see if it's right
③ Let me think what the number is
④ Let me think why people pass by
⑤ Let me think

04 How is the energy made? Answer in English with 9 words.

➡ _____

[01~03] 다음 대화를 읽고 물음에 답하시오.

G: I like these crackers. They're really good.

B: Yeah, me, too. I wonder why crackers ⓐ have these little holes in them.

G: I don't know. Let me ⓑthinking.... Um ... well ... maybe it's because the holes make the crackers look tastier.

B: That's possible, but there ⓒmust be some other reasons.

G: Let's look up crackers on the Internet and see ___(A)___ it says.

B: Okay. Oh, look at this.

G: It says during ⓓbaking, steam comes out through the holes and that makes the crackers thin.

B: It also ⓔsays that the holes make the crackers crispy.

G: Wow! So that's ___(B)___ they have holes!

서답형

01 위 대화의 밑줄 친 ⓐ~ⓔ 중 어색한 것을 찾아 바르게 고치시오.

_____ ➡ _____

02 위 대화의 빈칸 (A)와 (B)에 들어갈 말이 바르게 짝지어진 것은?

① what – why 　② what – how
③ how – what 　④ how – why
⑤ when – why

서답형

03 위 대화에서 주어진 영영풀이가 가리키는 단어를 찾아 쓰시오.

> the hot gas that is produced when water boils

➡ _____

[04~06] 다음 대화를 읽고 물음에 답하시오.

B: Hi, Kate. Today's Saturday, so what about going to the Einstein Science Park today?

G: That sounds like a good idea. ① I heard that they have special programs on Saturdays. (A)난 그 프로그램들이 뭔지 궁금해.

B: Let me see.... I saw an advertisement in the newspaper. ②

G: What does it say? ③

B: It says that today they have two shows: the Smart Design Show and the International Drone Show in Einstein Hall 101. ④

G: They both sound fantastic.

B: ⑤ I'll call them and ask what time they start.

04 위 대화의 ①~⑤ 중 주어진 문장이 들어가기에 가장 적절한 곳은?

Here it is.

①　　　　②　　　　③　　　　④　　　　⑤

서답형

05 위 대화의 밑줄 친 (A)의 우리말을 바르게 영작하시오. (5 words)

➡ _____

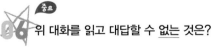

06 위 대화를 읽고 대답할 수 없는 것은?

① When are Kate and her friend going to the park?
② What kind of programs do the park have?
③ How many times do the programs take place on Saturdays?
④ Where are the programs taking place?
⑤ Who will call the park for the information?

[07~08] 다음 글을 읽고 물음에 답하시오.

> B: Hi, class. Have you ever (A)[hear / heard] about the Moai? They are tall, human-shaped stones in Chile. (B)[Most / Most of] the stones are four meters tall, but the (C)[taller/tallest] one is 20 meters tall. I was wondering how people moved them long ago. So I searched the Internet and learned that they used ropes. Isn't that amazing?

07 위 글의 괄호 (A)~(C)에서 알맞은 것을 바르게 짝지은 것을 고르시오.

    (A)   (B)   (C)

① hear – Most – tallest

② hear – Most of – taller

③ heard – Most of – tallest

④ heard – Most of – taller

⑤ heard – Most – tallest

08 위 글의 내용과 일치하는 것은?

① The Moai is the tallest stone in Chile.

② The tallest Moai is twenty meters tall.

③ The Moai is made up of stones only from Chile.

④ The average Moai is less than four meters tall.

⑤ It is not scientifically proved whether people used ropes.

09 다음 중 짝지어진 대화가 어색한 것을 고르시오.

① A: Look at this invention. It can help us cook without electricity.

   B: Sounds amazing! I wonder how it works.

② A: I wonder what the first train looked like.

   B: Look! There is a miniature model over there.

③ A: I wonder why they are standing in front of the bicycle shop.

   B: They had a bicycle shop. They sold and repaired bicycles.

④ A: I wonder what country they're from.

   B: They're from France.

⑤ A: I wonder where they first tried to fly their airplane.

   B: They tested their airplane 100 years ago.

[10~11] 다음 대화를 읽고 물음에 답하시오.

> G: We're going on a field trip tomorrow to the Invention Museum.
> B: I've heard that it has a lot of creative inventions.
> G: That's why I'm so excited. How about planning the tour before we go?
> B: Good idea. (A)Let me see... I have the school letter and a map of the museum.
> G: Perfect. Let's get started.

10 위 대화를 읽고 대답할 수 없는 것을 모두 고르시오. (2개)

① When are G and B going on a field trip?

② Who is going on a field trip with them?

③ How does G feel about the field trip?

④ What did G suggest B to do before the field trip?

⑤ What is the plan for the field trip?

11 What are G and B going to do afterwards?

① to find where the letter and the map are

② to search what kind of inventions there are in the museum

③ to hand over the school letter to parents

④ to make a plan for the field trip

⑤ to find out who is going to be on the same group

[01~02] 다음 대화를 읽고 물음에 답하시오.

G: John, look. The school is having an invention competition.

B: Really? That sounds interesting.

G: Yeah. You should enter that. You always have great ideas.

B: Does it say ___(A)___ the competition is?

G: Let me see.... It says it's November 11. That's two weeks from today.

B: I wonder ___(B)___ I have to do to enter the competition.

G: It says here you should talk to Mr. Harrison, the science teacher.

01 위 대화의 빈칸 (A)와 (B)에 들어갈 말을 쓰시오.

(A) _____ (B) _____

02 What does John have to do to enter the invention competition? (7 words)

➡ _____

[03~04] 다음 대화를 읽고 물음에 답하시오.

B: Look at this invention. It can help us cook without electricity.

(A) Wow. That would be really helpful when you go camping.

(B) Is that possible? I wonder how it works.

(C) It uses sunlight to cook food.

03 위 대화가 자연스럽게 이어지도록 순서대로 배열하시오.

➡ _____

04 What does the invention employ to cook? (6 words)

➡ _____

[05~07] 다음 글을 읽고 물음에 답하시오.

B: Hi, class. Have you ever heard about the Moai? They are tall, human-shaped stones in Chile. Most of the stones are four meters tall, but the tallest one is 20 meters tall. (A)저는 어떻게 사람들이 오래 전에 그것들을 옮겼는지 궁금했어요. (how / wondering / I / people / was / moved / long ago / them) So I searched the Internet and learned that they used ropes. Isn't that amazing?

05 위 글의 밑줄 친 (A)를 우리말에 맞게 나열하시오.

➡ _____

_____

06 다음 주어진 영영풀이에 맞는 단어를 위 글에서 찾아 쓰시오.

to look somewhere carefully in order to find something

➡ _____

07 According to the speaker, how did people in Chile move the stones? (7 words)

➡ _____

Grammar

1 가정법 과거: if + 주어 + 동사(과거형), 주어 + would + 동사원형

> • The water inside **would** quickly boil over **if** the lid **did** not have that hole.
> 만약 뚜껑에 저 구멍이 없다면, 안에 있는 물은 금방 끓어 넘칠 것이다.

■ 가정법 과거는 'If+주어+동사(과거형), 주어+would/should/could/might+동사원형'으로 쓰고 '만일 ~라면 …할 텐데.'로 해석하며, 현재 사실과 반대되는 일이나 상황을 가정한다.
   • **If** I **had** his phone number, I **would** call him. 만일 내가 그의 전화번호를 안다면 그에게 전화할 텐데.

■ If절의 동사(과거형)가 be동사일 경우 were를 쓰지만, 주어가 'I'나 '3인칭 단수'일 때는 구어체에서 was를 쓰기도 한다.
   • **If** I **were[was]** you, I **would** tell the truth. 만일 내가 너라면 진실을 말할 텐데.

■ 가정법 과거 표현에 as if를 활용한 것이 있는데 주절 동사의 시제에서 반대되는 상황이나 일을 표현하고자 할 때 사용하며 'S+V+as if+S+과거동사 ~'로 쓰고 '마치 ~인 것처럼'으로 해석한다.
   • He talks **as if** he **were[was]** rich. (= In fact, he is not rich.) 그는 마치 그가 부자인 것처럼 말한다.
   • He talked **as if** he **were** rich. (= In fact, he was not rich.) 그는 마치 그가 부자인 것처럼 말했다.

■ S+V+as if+S+had p.p./조동사 have p.p. ~: 마치 ~였던 것처럼
   • He talks **as if** he **had been** rich. 그는 마치 그가 부자였던 것처럼 말한다.
     (과거에 부자가 아니었는데 부자였던 것처럼 현재 말함.) (= In fact, he was not rich.)
   • He talked **as if** he **had been** rich. 그는 마치 그가 부자였던 것처럼 말했다.
     (말하는 과거 시점 이전에 부자가 아니었는데 부자였던 것처럼 말함.) (= In fact, he had not been rich.)

*가정법 과거완료: 과거 사실에 대한 반대되는 상황이나 일 표현

■ 가정법 과거완료는 'If+S+had p.p. ~, S+would/should/could/might+have p.p.'로 쓰고 '만일 ~했었다면, …했을 텐데.'로 해석하며, 과거 사실과 반대되는 일이나 상황을 가정한다.
   • **If** I **had studied** harder, I **could have passed** the test. 내가 공부를 열심히 했었더라면 시험에 통과했을 텐데.

핵심 Check

1. 다음 괄호 안에서 알맞은 말을 고르시오.
   (1) If I (get / got) up earlier, I would not be late for school.
   (2) I (would / will) be very glad if my son studied harder.

2 so that 주어 can

> • The hole also prevents the window from fogging up **so that** you **can** enjoy that fantastic view. 그 구멍은 또한, 당신이 멋진 경치를 즐길 수 있도록 창문에 김이 서리는 것을 막아 준다.

■ '주어 동사 so that 주어 can[could]'로 쓰고 '~ 할 수 있도록, ~하기 위해서'라고 해석한다. can 대신에 may를 쓰기도 하다.

 • I go to bed early **so that** I **can** wake up early. 나는 일찍 일어날 수 있도록 일찍 잔다.

■ '~하기 위해서'는 'so that 주어 can' 뿐만 아니라 'to', 'so as to', 'in order to', 'in order that S V'로도 표현할 수 있다.

 • She goes jogging every morning **so that** she **can[may]** stay healthy.
 그녀는 건강을 유지하기 위해 매일 아침 조깅을 한다.

 = She goes jogging every morning **to stay** healthy.

 = She goes jogging every morning **so as to stay** healthy.

 = She goes jogging every morning **in order to stay** healthy.

 = She goes jogging every morning **in order that** she **can[may]** stay healthy.

■ 그밖의 so that 용법

 1) ~, so that S V: (결과) 그래서 ~하다

 • It was freezing last weekend, **so that** I stayed at home all day.
 지난 주말에 너무 추워서 나는 하루 종일 집에 있었다.

 • There was a car accident on my way to work, **so that** I was late for the meeting.
 출근길에 차 사고가 있어서, 나는 회의에 늦었다.

 2) so 형용사/부사 that S V = such a 형용사+명사 that S V

 • He is **so** wealthy **that** he can purchase a building in Gangnam.
 그는 너무 돈이 많아서 강남에 있는 빌딩을 살 수 있다.

 • He is **such** a wealthy man **that** he can purchase a building in Gangnam.

 • She is **so** kind **that** everyone likes her. 그녀는 너무 친절해서 모두가 그녀를 좋아한다.

 • The grocery store near my house was **so** crowded **that** I had to go another store.
 집 근처에 있는 마트가 너무 사람이 많아서 나는 다른 마트에 가야 했다.

 • He drank **so** much last night **that** he's suffering from a hangover today.
 어젯밤에 술을 너무 마셔서 그는 오늘 숙취로 고생하고 있다.

핵심 Check

2. 다음 괄호 안에서 알맞은 말을 고르시오.

 ⑴ I study English hard (such / so) that I can speak English well.

 ⑵ I will buy toys so (that / what) I can give them to my brother.

01 다음 문장에서 어법상 <u>어색한</u> 부분을 바르게 고쳐 쓰시오.

(1) If she has a pretty dress like yours, she wouldn't cry.

_____ ➡ _____

(2) If I were the President, I will support that policy.

_____ ➡ _____

(3) I study hard so what I can get a good grade.

_____ ➡ _____

(4) She practices the violin so that she can't play the violin without mistakes.

_____ ➡ _____ .

02 다음 주어진 두 문장을 so that을 활용하여 한 문장으로 쓰시오.

(1) Jack is very tall. He can touch the ceiling.

➡ _____

(2) We worked hard. Everything will be ready in time.

➡ _____

(3) I got up early. I could catch the first bus.

➡ _____

(4) She works very hard. She deserves a vacation.

➡ _____

03 다음 우리말에 맞게 주어진 단어를 활용하여 영작하시오.

(1) 더 긴 팔을 가지고 있다면, 저 사과를 잡을 수 있을 텐데. (have, grab)

➡ _____

(2) 내가 만일 영국에 있다면, 영어를 더 잘 말할 수 있을 텐데. (be)

➡ _____

서답형

01 다음 문장에서 어법상 틀린 부분을 찾아 바르게 고쳐 쓰시오.

> If I had had time, I could gone there with you.

_____ ➡ _____

서답형

02 다음 문장과 같은 뜻이 되도록 As를 활용하여 바꿔 쓰시오.

> If he were rich, he would buy that car.

➡ _____

서답형

03 우리말에 맞게 괄호 안의 단어들을 알맞은 순서로 배열하시오.

> 얘기를 하게 좀 더 가까이 앉아라. (so, sit, little, we, closer, a, that, talk, a, have, can)

➡ _____

04 다음 문장과 같은 뜻을 지닌 문장을 고르시오.

> I gave her my phone number so that she could contact me.

① I gave her my phone number in order that she could contact me.
② I gave her my phone number if she could contact me.
③ I gave her my phone number that she doesn't know.
④ I gave her my phone number because she could contact me.
⑤ I gave her my phone number though she wanted to keep in touch with me.

중요

05 다음 중 어법상 <u>어색한</u> 문장을 고르시오.

① If Peter asked Karen out, she would say yes.
② If I had known, I would not done the work.
③ If I had a million dollars, I could buy my own helicopter.
④ If Diane was here right now, she would agree.
⑤ If I were not sick, I could go to the party.

06 다음 문맥상 빈칸에 들어갈 말로 알맞은 것을 고르시오.

> _____, I would tell you.

① If I knew her name
② If I had known her name
③ If I know her name
④ As I know her name
⑤ As I knew her name

서답형

07 빈칸에 들어갈 적절한 단어를 쓰시오.

> If I were you, I _____ not go there alone.

➡ _____

08 다음 중 빈칸에 들어갈 단어가 나머지와 <u>다른</u> 것을 고르시오.

① I need to study hard _____ I can get a full scholarship next semester.
② Turn it _____ I can see it.
③ We need the break _____ recharge.
④ Please bring him forward _____ we can have a closer look.
⑤ He has made a new plan _____ they can do that.

09 다음 빈칸에 들어갈 말로 알맞은 것을 고르시오.

> If the weather were fine, _____.

① I would have gone on a picnic
② I will go on a picnic
③ I have to go on a picnic
④ I would go on a picnic
⑤ I go on a picnic

10 (중요) 다음 빈칸에 들어갈 말로 적절한 것을 고르시오.

> He works hard _____ support his family.

① in order   ② in order to
③ in order that   ④ in as to
⑤ so as

11 다음 빈칸에 들어갈 말끼리 알맞게 짝지어진 것을 고르시오.

> Can you move aside _____ I _____ pass?

① so that – can   ② so that – can't
③ so what – can   ④ so what – can't
⑤ so what – couldn't

12 다음 우리말을 영작한 것으로 어법상 알맞은 것을 고르시오.

> 내가 형이 있다면, 그와 함께 놀 텐데.

① If I had a brother, I would hang out with him.
② If I have a brother, I would hang out with him.
③ If I had a brother, I will hang out with him.
④ If I have a brother, I hang out with him.
⑤ If I had a brother, I hang out with him.

서답형

13 다음 우리말에 맞게 괄호 안의 표현을 활용하여 영작하시오.

> 그 여자는 추운 듯 팔짱을 꼈다.
> (as if, fold one's arm)

➡ _____

14 다음 중 어법상 <u>어색한</u> 것을 고르시오.

① She talked as if she were the queen.
② She ate them all as if she hungered for weeks.
③ She said it as if she had read my thought.
④ She looks as if she had seen a ghost.
⑤ She felt as if she is flying.

15 다음 문장과 같은 뜻을 지닌 문장을 <u>모두</u> 고르시오.

> He slept earlier than usual so that he could get up early the next day.

① He slept earlier than usual but he got up early the next day.
② He slept earlier than usual in order that he could get up early the next day.
③ He slept earlier than usual for he could get up early the next day.
④ He slept earlier than usual in order to get up early the next day.
⑤ He slept earlier than usual in order not to get up early the next day.

서답형

16 우리말에 맞게 괄호 안의 단어를 활용하여 빈칸을 채우시오.

> We went early _____(so) get good seats.

➡ _____

서답형

17 다음 우리말에 맞게 괄호 안의 단어를 이용하여 영작하시오.

> 난 첫 기차를 놓치지 않으려고 일찍 일어났다. (in order to)

➡ _____

서답형

18 우리말에 맞게 괄호 안의 어휘들을 배열하여 영작할 때, 3번째 단어를 쓰시오. (If로 문장을 시작할 것.)

(1) 그가 더 열심히 운동한다면, 그는 좋은 운동선수가 될 텐데. (harder, be, if, he, he, would, exercised, good, athlete, a)

➡ _____

(2) 가령 네가 내 입장이라면 어떻게 하겠니? (me, you, do, you, if, what, were, would)

➡ _____

(3) 만약 내가 아프지 않았더라면, 어제 함께 여행을 갔을 텐데. (been, had, if, would, gone, on, trip, a, I, not, sick, I, have, yesterday, together)

➡ _____

19 다음 빈칸에 공통으로 들어갈 말을 고르시오.

> • He then attended Johns Hopkins University _____ earn his doctorate.
> • We studied last night _____ pass the test.
>
> *doctorate 박사학위

① so that   ② so
③ in order that   ④ that
⑤ so as to

01 괄호 안의 단어를 활용하여 우리말을 영작하시오.

> 내가 그의 전화번호를 안다면 그에게 전화를 할 텐데. (phone number, call)

➡ _____

02 다음 문장과 같은 뜻이 되도록 as if를 활용하여 빈칸을 채우시오.

> In fact, I am not her younger brother.
> ➡ She helps me _____
> _____.

03 다음과 같은 뜻의 문장을 각 조건에 맞춰 영작하시오.

> She goes jogging every morning so that she can stay healthy.

(to부정사 사용)
➡ _____

(so as to 사용)
➡ _____
_____

(in order to 사용)
➡ _____
_____

(in order that 사용)
➡ _____
_____

04 다음 두 문장을 활용하여 가정법 과거문장으로 영작하시오.

> • She studies harder.
> • She can pass the test.

➡ _____

 05 다음을 읽고 가정법 과거 문장으로 쓰시오.

> She wants to visit her friend's house, but she doesn't feel well.

➡ _____

06 다음 밑줄 친 부분과 같은 의미를 가진 3 단어를 쓰시오.

> I asked him out in order to know whether he had any interest in me.
> ➡ I asked him out _____ _____ _____ know whether he had any interest in me.

07 다음 빈칸에 공통으로 들어갈 말을 쓰시오.

> • I waited for an hour _____ _____ I could meet her.
> • My baby was born _____ small _____ he spent two weeks in an incubator.

08 다음 문장에서 <u>어색한</u> 곳을 바르게 고쳐 다시 쓰시오.

> In order to oversleep, I set the alarm for six o'clock.

➡ _____

_____

09 ⭐중요 다음 우리말에 맞게 괄호 안의 단어를 참고하여 각 조건에 맞게 영작하시오.

> 그들은 시간을 낭비하지 않기 위해 택시를 탔다. (take, waste)

(to부정사 사용)
➡ _____

(in order to 사용)
➡ _____

(so as to 사용)
➡ _____

10 다음 우리말에 맞게 괄호 안의 단어를 활용하여 영작하시오.

> 만약 Bob이 그 팀에서 일한다면, 그렇게 스트레스를 받지 않을 것이다. (work, be, so)

➡ _____

_____

11 🏠고난이도 우리말에 맞게 다음 각 문장의 빈칸에 들어갈 말을 괄호 안의 단어를 활용하여 쓰시오.

(1) 내가 휴대 전화를 가지고 있다면 도움을 요청할 텐데. (call for)
➡ If I had a cell phone, _____
_____ _____ _____ .

(2) 만약 내가 배를 갖고 있다면 타고 갈 텐데. (boat)
➡ _____ _____ _____ _____
_____ , I would sail away.

(3) 따라서, 만약 당신이 그 날 화성을 향해 빛을 쏘았다면, 그것은 186초 만에 화성에 도달하였을 것이다. (reach)
➡ Thus, if you had turned a light toward Mars that day, _____ _____
_____ _____ _____ in 186 seconds.

(4) 내가 새라면 날아갈 텐데. (be)
➡ _____ _____ _____ _____
_____ , I would fly away.

12 괄호 안의 단어를 활용하여 우리말에 맞게 영작하시오.

> 만약 내가 오늘 수업이 없다면, 놀이공원에 갈텐데. (have, go)

➡ _____
_____ (14 단어)

13 ⭐중요 괄호 안의 단어를 활용하여 다음 우리말에 맞게 빈칸을 알맞게 채우시오.

(1) 라면이 불기 전에 가스렌지 불을 껐다. (overcook, order to)
➡ I turned the range off _____
_____ _____ _____ the ramyon.

(2) 많은 시간을 가지려면 일찍 오너라. (have, order to)
➡ Come early _____ _____
_____ plenty of time.

Reading

교과서

Hidden Holes

Think about a hole that you have seen recently. Was it a good hole or
a bad hole? If it was a hole in your sock, it was bad. If it was a hole in
your shirt for a button, it was good. There are holes everywhere. Some
are so small you may not even notice them. They are well hidden, but
many of these small holes are very important and make your life safe.

Take a pen. Look at it carefully. Do you see a small hole in the cap?
Do you know why it is there? The hole in a pen cap can help save
lives. People, especially children, often put small things like pen caps
in their mouths. Sometimes they even swallow them. This can stop
their breathing and cause death. A famous pen company started putting
a small hole in their pen caps. The hole in the cap lets air pass through
and has saved lives.

recently 최근에
notice 알아채다, 의식하다
hide 숨기다, 숨다
especially 특히
swallow 삼키다
breathing 숨, 호흡
cause ~을 야기하다, 초래하다
death 죽음
pass through 거쳐 지나가다, 통과하다

확인문제

● 다음 문장이 본문의 내용과 일치하면 T, 일치하지 <u>않으면</u> F를 쓰시오.

1   If there is a hole in your sock, it is a bad hole. ☐

2   Many of the holes are so small that they aren't important. ☐

3   The hole in a pen cap can help save lives. ☐

4   Sometimes children even swallow large things. ☐

5   What children swallow can stop their breathing and cause death. ☐

6   Air can't pass through the hole in the cap. ☐

If you look around, you will see other holes that play a helpful role in
<u>주격 관계대명사</u>　　<u>play a role</u>: 역할을 하다
your life. If you <u>have</u> ever <u>cooked</u> anything in a pot with a lid, perhaps
현재완료 경험 용법
you noticed a small hole in the lid. This hole, too, is there for safety.

When cooking something in a pot with a lid, the pressure inside the
= When you cook, 접속사가 있는 분사구문　　　　　　　　'the pressure'를 수식하는 형용사구
pot builds up. The water inside would quickly boil over if the lid did
가정법 과거: if+주어+동사(과거형), 주어+조동사(과거형)+동사원형, 현재 사실에 반대되는 상황을 가정하는 문장
not have that hole. The hole lets steam out and <u>keeps</u> the water <u>from</u>
　　　　　　　　　　　　　　　　　keep A from -ing: A가 ~하는 것을 막다
coming out.

Have you ever been on an airplane? <u>Wasn't it exciting to look out the</u>
수사의문문: 수사의문문은 강한 반어적 표현으로 부정형 수사의문문은 강한 긍정의 뜻을 포함한다.
<u>window and see the world below?</u> <u>Surprisingly</u>, there was a small hole
문장 전체를 수식하는 부사
in your window. Airplane windows <u>are made up of</u> three panes. There
~로 이루어지다
is a hole in the middle pane. It balances the air pressure. <u>Without this</u>
가주어　　　　　　　　　　　　without+명사구, 주어+조동사(과거형)+동사원형: 가정법 과거
<u>little hole, airplane windows might break in an emergency.</u> The hole
also <u>prevents</u> the window <u>from fogging</u> up <u>so that</u> you <u>can</u> enjoy that
　　　prevent A from -ing: A가 ~하지 않게 막다　　　so that … can ~: …가 ~할 수 있도록(목적)
fantastic view.

There are many more products that have small hidden holes. In the
future, when you see a little hole in something, ask yourself why it is
there. Maybe it is the result of a careful design to <u>make</u> your life safer.
　　　　　　　　　　　　　　　　　　　　to부정사의 형용사적 용법

lid 뚜껑	
perhaps 아마, 어쩌면	
pressure 압력	
quickly 빨리, 빠르게	
boil 끓다, 끓이다	
steam 증기, 김	
build up 점점 커지다	
surprisingly 놀랍게도	
pane 판유리	
balance 균형을 유지하다	
emergency 비상(사태)	
prevent (~가 …하는 것을) 막다, 예방하다	
fantastic 환상적인	
product 생산물, 상품	
fog up 김이 서리다	

📎 **확인문제**

● 다음 문장이 본문의 내용과 일치하면 T, 일치하지 <u>않으면</u> F를 쓰시오.

1　All around you, there are other holes that play a helpful role in your life. ☐

2　When you cook something in a pot without a lid, the pressure inside the pot builds up. ☐

3　Thanks to a hole in the lid of a pot, steam can escape through it. ☐

4　There is a hole in the inner pane of airplane windows. ☐

5　The hole in the pane balances the air pressure. ☐

6　The hole in the airplane windows is too small to prevent the airplane windows from breaking in an emergency. ☐

● 우리말을 참고하여 빈칸에 알맞은 말을 쓰시오.

1 _____ Holes

2 Think about a hole that you _____ _____ _____.

3 Was it a _____ hole or a _____ hole?

4 If it was a hole _____ _____ _____, it was bad.

5 If it was a hole in your shirt _____ _____ _____, it was good.

6 There are holes _____.

7 Some are _____ _____ you may not even notice them.

8 They are _____ _____, but many of these small holes are very important and _____ _____ _____ _____.

9 _____ a pen.

10 _____ _____ it carefully.

11 Do you see _____ _____ _____ in the cap?

12 Do you know _____ _____ _____ _____?

13 The hole in a pen cap can _____ _____ _____.

14 People, especially children, often _____ small things like pen caps _____ their mouths.

15 Sometimes they even _____ _____.

16 This can _____ _____ _____ and cause death.

17 A famous pen company started _____ _____ _____ in their pen caps.

18 The hole in the cap lets air _____ _____ and has saved lives.

1	숨겨진 구멍들
2	여러분이 최근에 본 구멍에 대해 생각해 보라.
3	그것은 좋은 구멍이었는가, 아니면 나쁜 구멍이었는가?
4	만약 그것이 여러분의 양말에 있는 구멍이었다면, 그것은 좋지 않은 것이었다.
5	만약 그것이 단추를 위해 셔츠에 있는 구멍이었다면, 그것은 좋은 것이었다.
6	구멍은 어디에나 있다.
7	어떤 것들은 너무 작아서 인지하지 못할 수도 있다.
8	그것들은 잘 숨겨져 있지만, 이 작은 구멍들 중 많은 것들이 매우 중요하고 여러분의 삶을 안전하게 해 준다.
9	펜을 꺼내라.
10	그것을 자세히 관찰해 보라.
11	뚜껑에 작은 구멍이 보이는가?
12	여러분은 왜 거기에 구멍이 있는지 아는가?
13	펜 뚜껑에 있는 구멍이 생명을 구하는 데 도움을 줄 수 있기 때문이다.
14	사람들, 특히 아이들은 종종 펜 뚜껑 같은 작은 것들을 그들의 입에 넣는다.
15	때때로 그들은 심지어 그것들을 삼키기도 한다.
16	이것은 그들의 호흡을 막고 죽음을 초래할 수도 있다.
17	유명한 펜 회사가 자사의 펜 뚜껑에 작은 구멍을 넣기 시작했다.
18	뚜껑에 있는 그 구멍은 공기를 통하게 해 주고 생명들을 구했다.

19 If you look around, you will see other holes that _____ _____ _____ _____ in your life.

20 If you have ever cooked anything in a pot _____ _____ _____, perhaps you _____ a small hole in the lid.

21 This hole, too, is there _____ _____.

22 _____ _____ something in a pot with a lid, the pressure inside the pot _____ _____.

23 The water inside would quickly _____ _____ if the lid did not have that hole.

24 The hole lets steam out and _____ the water _____ _____ out.

25 _____ you ever _____ on an airplane?

26 _____ _____ _____ to look out the window and see the world below?

27 _____, there was a small hole in your window.

28 Airplane windows _____ _____ _____ _____ three panes.

29 There is a hole _____ _____ _____ _____.

30 It _____ the air pressure.

31 _____ this little hole, airplane windows might break _____ _____ _____.

32 The hole also _____ the window _____ _____ _____ so that you can enjoy that fantastic view.

33 There are many more products _____ _____ small hidden holes.

34 In the future, when you see a little hole in something, ask yourself _____ _____ _____ _____.

35 Maybe it is the result of a careful design _____ _____ _____ _____.

19 여러분이 주위를 둘러본다면, 여러분의 생활에 도움을 주는 다른 구멍들을 보게 될 것이다.

20 만약 여러분이 뚜껑 있는 냄비에 어떤 것을 요리해 본 적이 있다면, 아마도 여러분은 뚜껑에 작은 구멍이 있다는 것을 알아챘을 수도 있다.

21 이 구멍 역시 안전을 위해 존재한다.

22 뚜껑이 있는 냄비에 무언가를 요리할 때, 냄비 안쪽의 압력이 상승한다.

23 만약 뚜껑에 그 구멍이 없다면, 그 안의 물은 금방 끓어 넘칠 것이다.

24 그 구멍이 수증기를 나가게 해 주고 물이 밖으로 넘치는 것을 막아 준다.

25 비행기를 타 본 적이 있는가?

26 창밖을 내다보고 아래에 있는 세상을 보는 것이 신나지 않았는가?

27 놀랍게도, 여러분의 창문에는 작은 구멍이 하나 있었다.

28 비행기 창문은 세 개의 유리판으로 구성되어 있다.

29 그 중간 유리판에 구멍이 있다.

30 그것은 기압의 균형을 맞춰 준다.

31 이 작은 구멍이 없다면, 비행기 창문은 비상시에 깨질 수 있다.

32 그 구멍은 또한, 멋진 경치를 즐길 수 있도록 창문에 김이 서리는 것을 막아 준다.

33 숨겨진 작은 구멍들이 있는 더 많은 제품들이 있다.

34 앞으로, 여러분이 어떤 물건에서 작은 구멍을 본다면, 왜 그것이 거기에 있는지 자신에게 물어보라.

35 아마도 그것은 여러분의 삶을 더 안전하게 만들려는 사려 깊은 디자인의 결과일 것이다.

● 우리말을 참고하여 본문을 영작하시오.

1 숨겨진 구멍들
➡ _____

2 여러분이 최근에 본 구멍에 대해 생각해 보라.
➡ _____

3 그것은 좋은 구멍이었는가, 아니면 나쁜 구멍이었는가?
➡ _____

4 만약 그것이 여러분의 양말에 있는 구멍이었다면, 그것은 좋지 않은 것이었다.
➡ _____

5 만약 그것이 단추를 위해 셔츠에 있는 구멍이었다면, 그것은 좋은 것이었다.
➡ _____

6 구멍은 어디에나 있다.
➡ _____

7 어떤 것들은 너무 작아서 인지하지 못할 수도 있다.
➡ _____

8 그것들은 잘 숨겨져 있지만, 이 작은 구멍들 중 많은 것들이 매우 중요하고 여러분의 삶을 안전하게 해 준다.
➡ _____

9 펜을 꺼내라.
➡ _____

10 그것을 자세히 관찰해 보라.
➡ _____

11 뚜껑에 작은 구멍이 보이는가?
➡ _____

12 여러분은 왜 거기에 구멍이 있는지 아는가?
➡ _____

13 펜 뚜껑에 있는 구멍이 생명을 구하는 데 도움을 줄 수 있기 때문이다.
➡ _____

14 사람들, 특히 아이들은 종종 펜 뚜껑 같은 작은 것들을 그들의 입에 넣는다.
➡ _____

15 때때로 그들은 심지어 그것들을 삼키기도 한다.
➡ _____

16 이것은 그들의 호흡을 막고 죽음을 초래할 수도 있다.
➡ _____

17 유명한 펜 회사가 자사의 펜 뚜껑에 작은 구멍을 넣기 시작했다.
➡ _____

18 뚜껑에 있는 그 구멍은 공기를 통하게 해 주고 생명들을 구했다.
➡ _____

19 여러분이 주위를 둘러본다면, 여러분의 생활에 도움을 주는 다른 구멍들을 보게 될 것이다.

➡ _____

20 만약 여러분이 뚜껑 있는 냄비에 어떤 것을 요리해 본 적이 있다면, 아마도 여러분은 뚜껑에 작은 구멍이 있다는 것을 알아챘을 수도 있다.

➡ _____

21 이 구멍 역시 안전을 위해 존재한다.

➡ _____

22 뚜껑이 있는 냄비에 무언가를 요리할 때, 냄비 안쪽의 압력이 상승한다.

➡ _____

23 만약 뚜껑에 그 구멍이 없다면, 그 안의 물은 금방 끓어 넘칠 것이다.

➡ _____

24 그 구멍이 수증기를 나가게 해 주고 물이 밖으로 넘치는 것을 막아 준다.

➡ _____

25 비행기를 타 본 적이 있는가?

➡ _____

26 창밖을 내다보고 아래에 있는 세상을 보는 것이 신나지 않았는가?

➡ _____

27 놀랍게도, 여러분의 창문에는 작은 구멍이 하나 있었다.

➡ _____

28 비행기 창문은 세 개의 유리판으로 구성되어 있다.

➡ _____

29 그 중간 유리판에 구멍이 있다.

➡ _____

30 그것은 기압의 균형을 맞춰 준다.

➡ _____

31 이 작은 구멍이 없다면, 비행기 창문은 비상시에 깨질 수 있다.

➡ _____

32 그 구멍은 또한, 멋진 경치를 즐길 수 있도록 창문에 김이 서리는 것을 막아 준다.

➡ _____

33 숨겨진 작은 구멍들이 있는 더 많은 제품들이 있다.

➡ _____

34 앞으로, 여러분이 어떤 물건에서 작은 구멍을 본다면, 왜 그것이 거기에 있는지 자신에게 물어보라.

➡ _____

35 아마도 그것은 여러분의 삶을 더 안전하게 만들려는 사려 깊은 디자인의 결과일 것이다.

➡ _____

[01~03] 다음 글을 읽고 물음에 답하시오.

Think about a hole that you have seen recently. (①) Was it a good hole or a bad hole? (②) If it was a hole in your sock, it was bad. (③) If it was a hole in your shirt for a button, it was good. (④) Some are so small you may not even notice them. (⑤) They are well hidden, but many of these small holes are very important and make your life safe.

01 위 글의 흐름으로 보아, 주어진 문장이 들어가기에 가장 적절한 곳은?

> There are holes everywhere.

①   ②   ③   ④   ⑤

02 위 글의 제목으로 알맞은 것을 고르시오.

① Have You Ever Seen a Hole?
② Hidden but Important Holes
③ A Good Hole VS a Bad Hole
④ Oops, a Hole in the Sock
⑤ The Various Functions of Holes

03 According to the passage, which is NOT true?

① A hole in your sock is a bad hole.
② A hole in your shirt for a button is a good hole.
③ You can find holes everywhere.
④ Some holes are so small that you may not even notice them.
⑤ Many of the holes are so small that it can't keep your life safe.

[04~06] 다음 글을 읽고 물음에 답하시오.

Take a pen. Look at it carefully. Do you see a small hole in the cap? Do you know why it is there? The hole in a pen cap can help save lives. People, especially ①children, often put small things like pen caps in ②their mouths. ⓐSometimes ③they even swallow them. This can stop ④their breathing and cause death. A famous pen company started putting a small hole in ⑤their pen caps. The hole in the cap lets air pass through and has saved lives.

04 밑줄 친 ①~⑤ 중에서 가리키는 대상이 나머지 넷과 다른 것은?

①   ②   ③   ④   ⑤

05 위 글의 밑줄 친 ⓐSometimes와 바꿔 쓸 수 없는 말을 고르시오.

① Once in a while   ② Occasionally
③ From time to time   ④ Frequently
⑤ Now and then

06 위 글의 주제로 알맞은 것을 고르시오.

① the size of the hole in the cap
② the role of the hole in the cap
③ the dangerous habit of children
④ the reason people stop their breathing
⑤ the strange sound of the air passing through the hole

[07~09] 다음 글을 읽고 물음에 답하시오.

If you look around, you will see other holes (A)that play a helpful role in your life. If you have ever cooked anything in a pot with a lid, perhaps you noticed a small hole in the lid. This hole, too, is there for ⓐ . When cooking something in a pot with a lid, the pressure inside the pot builds up. The water inside would quickly boil over if the lid did not have that hole. The hole lets steam out and (B)keeps the water from coming out.

서답형

07 주어진 영영풀이를 참고하여 빈칸 ⓐ에 철자 s로 시작하는 단어를 쓰시오.

a state of being safe from harm or danger

➡ _____

08 위 글의 밑줄 친 (A)that과 문법적 쓰임이 같은 것을 모두 고르시오.

① He is the greatest novelist that has ever lived.
② It's true that we were a little late.
③ Are you sure she's that young?
④ There was no hope that she would recover her health.
⑤ This is the watch that I bought yesterday.

중요

09 위 글의 밑줄 친 (B)keeps와 바꿔 쓸 수 있는 말을 모두 고르시오.

① protects   ② stops
③ prevents   ④ denies
⑤ damages

[10~12] 다음 글을 읽고 물음에 답하시오.

ⓐHave you ever been on an airplane? Wasn't it exciting to look out the window and see the world below? Surprisingly, there was a small hole in your window. Airplane windows ⓑare made up of three panes. There is a hole in the middle pane. It balances the air pressure. Without this little hole, airplane windows might break in an emergency. The hole also prevents the window from fogging up so that you can enjoy that fantastic view.

There are many more products that have small hidden holes. ⓒIn the future, when you will see a little hole in something, ask yourself why it is there. Maybe it is the result of a careful design to make your life safer.

10 아래 〈보기〉에서 위 글의 밑줄 친 문장 ⓐ의 현재완료와 용법이 다른 것의 개수를 고르시오.

┌─── 보기 ───┐
① She has already left for Paris.
② I have heard about the project before.
③ Mr. Smith has just bought this sweater.
④ I have known him for three years.
⑤ We have sold out all the tickets, so there are no more tickets available.
└──────────┘

① 1개   ② 2개   ③ 3개   ④ 4개   ⑤ 5개

11 위 글의 밑줄 친 ⓑare made up of와 바꿔 쓸 수 있는 말을 모두 고르시오.

① are composed of   ② consist of
③ consist in   ④ deal with
⑤ are consisted of

서답형

12 위 글의 밑줄 친 ⓒ에서 어법상 틀린 부분을 찾아 고치시오.

_____ ➡ _____

[13~15] 다음 글을 읽고 물음에 답하시오.

If you look around, you will see (A)[another / other] holes that play a helpful ⓐrole in your life. If you have ever cooked anything in a pot with a lid, perhaps you noticed a small hole in the lid. This hole, too, is there for safety. When (B)[cooking / cooked] something in a pot with a lid, the pressure ____ⓑ____ the pot builds up. The water inside would quickly boil over if the lid did not have that hole. The hole lets steam (C)[in / out] and keeps the water ____ⓒ____ coming out.

서답형

13 위 글의 괄호 (A)~(C)에서 문맥이나 어법상 알맞은 낱말을 골라 쓰시오.

(A) _____ (B) _____ (C) _____

서답형

14 위 글의 밑줄 친 ⓐrole과 바꿔 쓸 수 있는 한 단어를 쓰시오.

➡ _____

15 위 글의 빈칸 ⓑ와 ⓒ에 들어갈 전치사가 바르게 짝지어진 것은?

	ⓑ	ⓒ		ⓑ	ⓒ
①	inside	on	②	outside	to
③	on	to	④	inside	from
⑤	outside	from			

16 주어진 글 다음에 이어질 글의 순서로 가장 적절한 것은?

Take a pen. Look at it carefully. Do you see a small hole in the cap?

(A) This can stop their breathing and cause death. A famous pen company started putting a small hole in their pen caps. The hole in the cap lets air pass through and has saved lives.
(B) Do you know why it is there? The hole in a pen cap can help save lives.
(C) People, especially children, often put small things like pen caps in their mouths. Sometimes they even swallow them.

① (A) – (C) – (B) ② (B) – (A) – (C)
③ (B) – (C) – (A) ④ (C) – (A) – (B)
⑤ (C) – (B) – (A)

[17~19] 다음 글을 읽고 물음에 답하시오.

Think about a hole that you have seen recently. Was it a good hole or a bad hole? If it was a hole in your sock, it was bad. If it was a hole in your shirt for a button, it was good. There are holes everywhere. ⓐ어떤 것들은 너무 작아서 인지하지 못할 수도 있다. They are well hidden, but ⓑmany of these small holes are very important and make your life safely.

서답형

17 위 글의 밑줄 친 ⓐ의 우리말에 맞게 주어진 어휘를 알맞게 배열하시오.

notice / small / may / are / them / not / you / even / some / so

➡ _____

서답형

18 위 글의 밑줄 친 ⓑ에서 어법상 **틀린** 부분을 찾아 고치시오.

_____ ➡ _____

19 Which question CANNOT be answered after reading the passage?

① If a hole is in your sock, is it a good hole?

② If a hole is in your shirt for a button, is it a good hole?

③ Where can we find holes?

④ Are the holes that we see around us all hidden?

⑤ How many kinds of holes are there in the world?

[20~21] 다음 글을 읽고 물음에 답하시오.

Take a pen. Look ____ⓐ____ it carefully. Do you see a small hole in the cap? Do you know why it is there? The hole in a pen cap can help (A)save lives. People, especially children, often put small things like pen caps ____ⓑ____ their mouths. Sometimes they even swallow them. This can stop their breathing and cause death. A famous pen company started putting a small hole in their pen caps. The hole in the cap lets air pass through and has saved lives.

20 위 글의 빈칸 ⓐ와 ⓑ에 들어갈 전치사가 바르게 짝지어진 것은?

	ⓐ	ⓑ		ⓐ	ⓑ
①	for	to	②	at	on
③	at	in	④	for	on
⑤	on	in			

21 위 글의 밑줄 친 (A)save와 같은 의미로 쓰인 것을 고르시오.

① We'll eat some now and save some for tomorrow.

② You should save a little each week.

③ Doctors were unable to save her.

④ We should try to save water.

⑤ Save data frequently.

[22~23] 다음 글을 읽고 물음에 답하시오.

Have you ever been on an airplane? Wasn't ⓐit exciting to look out the window and see the world below? Surprisingly, there was a small hole in your window. Airplane windows are made up of three panes. There is a hole in the middle pane. ⓑIt balances the air pressure. Without this little hole, airplane windows might break in an emergency. The hole also prevents the window from fogging up so that you can enjoy that fantastic view.

22 위 글의 밑줄 친 ⓐit과 문법적 쓰임이 같은 것을 고르시오.

① I think it strange that she doesn't want to go.

② It's two miles from here to the beach.

③ It is not easy to climb the mountain.

④ When the factory closes, it will mean 500 people losing their jobs.

⑤ It was she that told me the story.

서답형

23 위 글의 밑줄 친 ⓑIt이 가리키는 것을 영어로 쓰시오.

➡ _____

[01~04] 다음 글을 읽고 물음에 답하시오.

Think about a hole that you have seen recently. Was (A)it a good hole or a bad hole? If it was a hole in your sock, it was bad. If it was a hole in your shirt for a button, it was good. There are holes everywhere. (B) Some are so small you may not even notice them. They are well ___ⓐ___, but many of these small holes are very important and make your life safe.

중요

01 위 글의 빈칸 ⓐ에 hide를 알맞은 형태로 쓰시오.

➡ _____

02 위 글의 밑줄 친 (A)it이 가리키는 것을 본문에서 찾아 쓰시오.

➡ _____

03 위 글의 밑줄 친 문장 (B)에 생략된 접속사를 넣어 문장을 다시 쓰시오.

➡ _____

_____

고난이도

04 위 글의 내용을 다음과 같이 정리하고자 한다. 빈칸 (A)~(C)에 들어갈 알맞은 단어를 본문에서 찾아 쓰시오.

Everywhere you can find holes. Some of which are too (A)_____ to notice. But many of these small holes are very (B)_____ ones and thanks to them, your life becomes (C)_____.

[05~07] 다음 글을 읽고 물음에 답하시오.

If you look around, you will see other holes that play a helpful role in your life. If you have ever cooked anything in a pot with a lid, perhaps you noticed a small hole in the lid. This hole, too, is there for safety. ⓐ When cooking something in a pot with a lid, the pressure inside the pot builds up. ⓑThe water inside would quickly boil over if the lid did not have that hole. The hole lets steam out and keeps the water from coming out.

05 위 글의 밑줄 친 분사구문 ⓐ를 다음과 같이 바꿔 쓸 때 빈칸에 들어갈 알맞은 말을 두 단어로 쓰시오.

When _____ _____ something in a pot with a lid

고난이도

06 위 글의 밑줄 친 ⓑ를 접속사 as를 사용하여 직설법으로 고치시오.

➡ _____

_____

중요

07 다음 빈칸 (A)와 (B)에 알맞은 단어를 넣어 '냄비 뚜껑에 있는 작은 구멍의 역할'을 완성하시오.

When you cook something in a pot with a lid, the water inside doesn't quickly boil over thanks to the (A)_____ _____ in the lid. It lets (B)_____ _____ and keeps the water from coming out.

[08~11] 다음 글을 읽고 물음에 답하시오.

Take a pen. Look at it carefully. Do you see a small hole in the cap? Do you know why ⓐit is there? ⓑ펜 뚜껑에 있는 구멍이 생명을 구하는 데 도움을 줄 수 있기 때문이다. People, especially children, often put small things like pen caps in their mouths. Sometimes they even swallow them. This can stop their breathing and cause death. A famous pen company started putting a small hole in their pen caps. ⓒThe hole in the cap lets air pass through and has saved lives.

08 위 글의 밑줄 친 ⓐit이 가리키는 것을 본문에서 찾아 쓰시오.

➡ _____

09 위 글의 밑줄 친 ⓑ의 우리말에 맞게 주어진 어휘를 알맞게 배열하시오.

can / in a pen cap / help / lives / the hole / save

➡ _____

10 위 글의 밑줄 친 ⓒ를 다음과 같이 바꿔 쓸 때 빈칸에 들어갈 알맞은 말을 두 단어로 쓰시오.

The hole in the cap allows air _____ _____ through and has saved lives.

11 How can the hole in the pen cap save a life if someone swallows a pen cap? Fill in the blanks (A) and (B) with suitable words.

If someone swallows a pen cap, it can stop the person's (A)_____ and cause death. If there is a hole in the pen cap, however, it lets (B)_____ pass through and can save a life.

[12~14] 다음 글을 읽고 물음에 답하시오.

Have you ever been on an airplane? Wasn't it exciting to look out the window and (A)[saw / see] the world below? Surprisingly, there was a small hole in your window. Airplane windows are made up of three panes. There is a hole in the middle pane. It balances the air (B)[pleasure / pressure]. ⓐWithout this little hole, airplane windows might break in an (C)[emergence / emergency]. The hole also prevents the window from fogging up so that you can enjoy that fantastic view.

There are many more products that have small hidden holes. In the future, when you see a little hole in something, ask yourself why it is there. Maybe it is the result of a careful design to make your life safer.

12 위 글의 괄호 (A)~(C)에서 문맥이나 어법상 알맞은 낱말을 골라 쓰시오.

(A) _____ (B) _____ (C) _____

13 위 글의 밑줄 친 ⓐ를 If로 시작하여 고칠 때, 빈칸에 들어갈 알맞은 말을 쓰시오.

If _____ _____ _____ _____ this little hole,

14 다음 빈칸 (A)와 (B)에 알맞은 단어를 넣어 '비행기 창문'에 대한 소개를 완성하시오.

Airplane windows consist of (A)_____ _____ and a hole in the middle pane balances the (B)_____ _____.

After You Read B

1. It lets the air pass through even when people swallow the pen cap.
사역동사 'let'의 목적격 보어 자리에 동사원형만 올 수 있다.

2. It balances the air pressures.
기압

3. It lets steam out and prevents the water in the pot from boiling over.
prevent A from -ing: A가 ~하는 것을 막다

구문해설 · swallow: 삼키다 · pass through: 거쳐 지나가다, 통과하다 · balance: 균형을 유지하다
· steam: 증기, 김 · boil: 끓다, 끓이다

Work Together

Sweet Dream Helmet

This invention helps people dream sweet dreams. If you use the Sweet Dream
사역동사+목적어+목적격보어   단순 조건문 If S 현재시제 동사, S will 동사원형
Helmet, you will have a sweet dream every night. You can even select the type

of dream you want to dream so that you can have different experiences while
dream (that) you   so that S can 동사원형 ~: ~하기 위해서   ~하는 동안
you are sleeping.

구문해설 · invention: 발명(품) · select: 고르다, 선택하다 · so that: ~하도록 · experience: 경험
· while: ~하는 동안

Writing Workshop

A Refrigerator

Can you imagine without a refrigerator. We use it every day so that we can
= a refrigerator   ~할 수 있도록, ~하기 위해
keep food cool and fresh. In 1755, William Cullen invented the first form of
keep+목적어+형용사: ~을 …하게 유지하다
the refrigerator. After that, it developed through the years and has become a
수년에 걸쳐   현재완료
necessary part of modern life. If we did not have refrigerators in today's world,
가정법 과거: If+주어+동사의 과거형 ~, 주어+조동사의 과거형+동사원형 …
we would not be able to enjoy ice cream on hot summer days.

구문해설 · imagine: 상상하다 · invent: 발명하다 · develop: 발전하다 · necessary: 필요한
· modern: 현대의 · be able to: ~할 수 있다

해석

1. 사람들이 펜 뚜껑을 삼킬 때도 그것은 공기를 통하게 해 준다.
2. 그것은 기압의 균형을 맞춰 준다.
3. 그것은 수증기를 나가게 해 주고 냄비 안의 물이 끓어 넘치는 것을 막아 준다.

단 잠 헬멧
이 발명품은 사람들이 단 잠을 잘 수 있도록 돕는다. 만약 단 잠 헬멧을 사용한다면, 당신은 매일 밤 행복한 꿈을 꿀 것입니다. 당신이 잠든 동안 다양한 경험을 할 수 있기 위해 당신은 심지어 당신이 꿈꾸고 싶은 꿈의 형태를 고를 수 있습니다.

냉장고
여러분은 냉장고가 없는 세상을 상상할 수 있나요? 우리는 음식을 차갑고 신선하게 보관하기 위해 이것을 매일 사용합니다. 1755년, 윌리엄 컬런이 초기 형태의 냉장고를 발명했습니다. 그 이후, 이것은 수년 동안 발전했고, 현대의 생활에서 필수적인 부분이 되었습니다. 만약 우리에게 오늘날 냉장고가 없다면, 더운 여름날 아이스크림을 즐겨 먹을 수 없을 것입니다.

Words & Expressions

01 다음 짝지어진 단어의 관계가 같도록 빈칸에 알맞은 말을 쓰시오.

> repair : mend ＝ perhaps : _____

02 다음 중 밑줄 친 부분의 뜻풀이가 바르지 <u>않은</u> 것은?

① Watch the pot! The soup is about to <u>boil over</u> soon. (끓어 넘치다)
② The temperature difference makes the windows <u>fog up</u>. (김이 서리다)
③ You should <u>look out</u> for yourself from now on. (내다보다)
④ The fire extinguisher should only be used <u>in an emergency</u>. (비상 상황에서)
⑤ There will be a chance for parents to <u>look around</u> the school. (주위를 둘러보다)

03 다음 주어진 영영풀이가 가리키는 단어는?

> something that is made to be sold, usually something that is produced by an industrial process

① clothes ② product ③ present
④ pressure ⑤ invention

04 다음 우리말을 주어진 단어를 이용하여 영작하시오.

(1) 그것을 파손되지 않게 세심하게 포장하십시오. (wrap, protect, carefully, against breakage)
➡ _____

(2) 우리들 중 몇몇은 우리의 재능을 잘 숨기라는 말을 종종 듣는다. (often, keep, well hidden)
➡ _____
_____

05 다음 주어진 문장의 밑줄 친 notice와 같은 의미로 쓰인 것은?

> The first thing you will <u>notice</u> about the room is the smell.

① Don't take any <u>notice</u> of his words.
② Prices may be changed without any <u>notice</u>.
③ You may <u>notice</u> redness and swelling after the injection.
④ There is a <u>notice</u> on the board saying the class is cancelled.
⑤ You must give one month's <u>notice</u>.

06 다음 빈칸에 들어갈 말로 가장 적절한 것은?

> The study suggests that salt may _____ in childhood obesity.

① be known for ② play a role
③ be made up of ④ think about
⑤ look at

Conversation

[07~09] 다음 대화를 읽고 물음에 답하시오.

B: Hi, Kate. Today's Saturday, so what about (A)[to go / going] to the Einstein Science Park today?

G: That sounds like a good idea. I heard that they (B)[have / had] special programs on Saturdays. I wonder what they are.

B: Let me see.... I saw an advertisement in the newspaper. Here it is.

G: What (C)[did / does] it say?

B: It says that today they have two shows: the Smart Design Show and the International Drone Show in Einstein Hall 101.

G: They both sound fantastic.

B: I'll call them and ask what time they start.

07 위 대화의 괄호 (A)~(C)에 들어갈 말이 바르게 짝지어진 것은?

(A)　(B)　　(C)

① to go – had – did

② going – have – did

③ to go – have – did

④ going – have – does

⑤ to go – had – does

08 What will B do afterwards? (13 words)

➡ _____

_____

09 Where does the two shows take place? (7 words)

➡ _____

10 다음 대화의 밑줄 친 부분의 의도로 가장 적절한 것은?

A: I wonder what the first plane looked like.

B: Look! There is a model. It looked like a big bird.

① 묘사하기　　　　　② 조사하기

③ 감정 표현하기　　　④ 선호 표현하기

⑤ 궁금증 표현하기

[11~13] 다음 대화를 읽고 물음에 답하시오.

G: We're going on a field trip tomorrow to the Invention Museum.

B: ① I've heard that (A)it has a lot of creative inventions. ②

G: ③ That's why I'm so excited. How about planning the tour before we go?

B: ④ Let me see.... I have the school letter and a map of the museum.

G: ⑤ Perfect. Let's get started.

11 위 대화의 ①~⑤ 중에서 주어진 문장이 들어가기에 가장 적절한 곳은?

Good idea.

①　　　　②　　　　③　　　　④　　　　⑤

12 위 대화를 읽고 G의 심정으로 가장 적절한 것은?

① exhausted　　　② terrified

③ disappointed　　④ touched

⑤ excited

13 위 대화의 밑줄 친 (A)it이 가리키는 것을 쓰시오.

➡ _____

Grammar

14 어법상 빈칸에 들어갈 말로 적절한 것을 고르시오.

If today's top rock singer released his or her next piece on the Internet, it would _____ like playing in a theater with 20 million seats.

① have been   ② had been

③ was   ④ were

⑤ be

15 다음 우리말에 맞게 괄호 안의 단어를 활용하여 빈칸을 채우시오.

나는 오늘 아침 피곤하지 않기 위해서 일찍 잠자리에 들었다. (so)

➡ _____ I wouldn't be tired this morning.

16 다음 중 so that 구문이 어법상 나머지와 다른 것을 고르시오.

① I stood the little girl on a chair <u>so that</u> she could see well.

② I was excited, <u>so that</u> I couldn't get to sleep.

③ The criminal went off <u>so that</u> no one could find him.

④ We have two ears and one mouth <u>so that</u> we can listen twice as much as we speak.

⑤ Jane has come here <u>so that</u> she can see what happened with her own eyes.

17 우리말과 같은 뜻이 되도록 괄호 안의 어휘를 배열하여 영작하시오.

내가 Robinson Crusoe라면 낚시를 하러 가기 위해 보트를 만들 거야. (were, would, I, Robinson Crusoe, If, I, make, go, boat, a, to, fishing)

➡ _____

_____

18 다음 우리말에 맞게 괄호 안의 단어를 활용하여 영작하시오.

그녀는 자기의 개들을 마치 자기의 아이들인 것처럼 사랑한다. (be, as if, kids)

➡ _____

19 우리말에 맞게 괄호 안의 어휘들을 배열하여 영작할 때, 5번째 단어를 쓰시오.

내 친구는 그의 어머니가 노년을 즐길 수 있도록 열심히 일했다. (worked, that, my, his, mother, friend, hard, so, her, might, enjoy, old, age)

➡ _____

Reading

[20~22] 다음 글을 읽고 물음에 답하시오.

Think about a hole that you ⓐhave seen recently. Was it a good hole or a bad hole? If it was a hole in your sock, it was bad. If it was a hole in your shirt for a button, it was good. There are holes everywhere. Some are so small you may not even notice them. They are well hidden, but many of these small holes are very important and make your life safe.

20 위 글의 밑줄 친 ⓐhave seen과 현재완료의 용법이 같은 것을 모두 고르시오.

① I have never visited Paris.
② I have studied English since the third grade of elementary school.
③ Have the children finished their lunch yet?
④ She has watched the movie twice.
⑤ It has just stopped snowing.

21 다음 빈칸에 알맞은 단어를 넣어 '좋은 구멍'의 한 예를 완성하시오.

If a hole is in your shirt for _____ _____, it is a good hole.

➡ _____

22 What's the reason why you may not even notice holes? Fill in the blank with a suitable word.

Because some of the holes are too _____ for you to notice.

➡ _____

[23~24] 다음 글을 읽고 물음에 답하시오.

If you look around, you will see other holes that play a helpful role in your life. If you have ever cooked anything in a pot with a lid, perhaps you noticed a small hole in the lid. This hole, too, is ⓐthere for safety. When cooking something in a pot with a lid, the pressure inside the pot builds up. The water inside would quickly boil over if the lid did not have that hole. The hole lets steam out and keeps the water from coming out.

23 위 글의 밑줄 친 ⓐthere가 지칭하는 것을 본문에서 찾아 쓰시오.

➡ _____

24 According to the passage, which is NOT true?

① All around you, there are other holes that play a helpful role in your life.
② A small hole in the lid of a pot is also there for safety.
③ When you cook something in a pot without a lid, the pressure inside the pot builds up.
④ The water inside the pot doesn't quickly boil over as the lid has a hole.
⑤ Thanks to a hole in the lid of a pot, steam can escape through it.

[25~27] 다음 글을 읽고 물음에 답하시오.

Have you ever been on an airplane? (①) Wasn't it exciting to look out the window and see the world below? (②) Surprisingly, there was a small hole in your window. (③) Airplane windows are made up of three panes. (④) It balances the air pressure. (⑤) Without this little hole, airplane windows might break in an emergency. The hole also prevents the window from fogging up so that you can enjoy that fantastic view.

25 위 글의 흐름으로 보아, 주어진 문장이 들어가기에 가장 적절한 곳은?

> There is a hole in the middle pane.

①   ②   ③   ④   ⑤

26 위 글의 제목으로 알맞은 것을 고르시오.

① Have You Ever Been on an Airplane?
② The Exciting View from the Airplane
③ What Does the Hole in the Middle Pane Do?
④ Wow! Airplane Windows Are Made Up of Three Panes!
⑤ Many Products That Have Small Hidden Holes

27 Which question CANNOT be answered after reading the passage?

① How many panes do airplane windows consist of?
② Why are airplane windows made up of three panes?
③ Where is a small hole in the three panes of airplane windows?
④ If it were not for a small hole in the airplane windows, would it be possible to balance the air pressure in an emergency?
⑤ What prevents the window from fogging up in an airplane?

[28~29] 다음 글을 읽고 물음에 답하시오.

A Refrigerator

Can you imagine life without a refrigerator? We use it every day so that we can keep food cool and fresh. In 1755, William Cullen invented the first form of the refrigerator. After ⓐthat, it developed through the years and has become a necessary part of modern life. ⓑIf we did not have refrigerators in today's world, we will not be able to enjoy ice cream on hot summer days.

28 위 글의 밑줄 친 ⓐthat이 가리키는 것을 본문에서 찾아 쓰시오.

➡ _____

_____

29 위 글의 밑줄 친 ⓑ에서 어법상 틀린 부분을 찾아 고치시오.

_____ ➡ _____

출제율 90%

01 다음 영영풀이가 가리키는 것을 고르시오.

> the process to take air into the lungs and let it out again

① death　　② steam　　③ swallow
④ breathing　　⑤ pressure

출제율 95%

02 주어진 문장에 들어갈 단어로 가장 알맞은 것은?

> Doctors say that back pains can be _____ bad posture.

① in front of　　② built up
③ came out　　④ prevented from
⑤ the result of

[03~05] 다음 대화를 읽고 물음에 답하시오.

G: I like these crackers. They're really good.

B: Yeah, me, too. I wonder why crackers have these little holes in them.

G: I don't know. Let me think.... Um... well... maybe it's because the holes make the crackers look tastier.

B: That's possible, but there (A)must be some other reasons.

G: Let's look up crackers on the Internet and see what it says.

B: Okay. Oh, look at this.

G: It says during baking, steam comes out through the holes and (B)that makes the crackers thin.

B: It also says that the holes make the crackers crispy.

G: Wow! (C)그래서 그게 구멍을 갖고 있는 이유구나!

출제율 90%

03 위 대화의 밑줄 친 (A)must와 같은 의미로 쓰인 것은?

① You must finish this work toady.
② I must go to the bank and get some money.
③ You must be hungry after all that walking.
④ Cars must not park in front of the entrance.
⑤ You must not say things like that.

출제율 95%

04 위 대화의 밑줄 친 (B)that이 가리키는 것을 찾아 쓰시오. (6 words)

➡ _____

출제율 90%

05 위 대화의 밑줄 친 (C)의 우리말을 바르게 영작하시오. (6 words)

➡ _____

[06~07] 다음 대화를 읽고 물음에 답하시오.

B: Look at ⓐthis invention. ⓑIt can help us cook without electricity.

G: Is ⓒthat possible? I wonder how ⓓit works.

B: ⓔIt uses sunlight to cook food.

G: Wow. (A)캠핑을 갈 때 그건 정말 도움이 될 것 같아. (when / would / really / that / helpful / you / be / go camping)

06 위 대화의 밑줄 친 (A)의 우리말에 맞게 주어진 어구를 바르게 나열하시오.

➡ _____

07 위 대화의 밑줄 친 @~@ 중 가리키는 것이 <u>다른</u> 하나는?

① @   ② ⓑ   ③ ⓒ   ④ ⓓ   ⑤ ⓔ

[08~10] 다음 대화를 읽고 물음에 답하시오.

G: John, look. The school is having an invention competition.
B: Really? That sounds interesting.
G: Yeah. You should enter that. You always have great ideas.
B: Does it say when the competition is?
G: (A)Let me see.... It says it's November 11. That's two weeks from today.
B: (B)그 대회에 참가하기 위해 내가 뭘 해야 하는지 궁금해. (have, enter)
G: It says here you should talk to Mr. Harrison, the science teacher.

08 위 대화의 밑줄 친 (A)의 의도로 가장 적절한 것은?

① 생각할 시간 요청하기
② 아이디어 요청하기
③ 발명품 살펴보기
④ 지도 살펴보기
⑤ 계획 제안하기

09 위 대화의 밑줄 친 (B)의 우리말을 주어진 단어를 이용해 바르게 영작하시오. (11 words)

➡ _____

10 위 대화를 읽고 답할 수 <u>없는</u> 질문은?

① When will the invention competition take place?
② Why did G encourage B to enter the competition?
③ What is the prize for the winner of the competition?
④ What is Mr. Harrison?
⑤ What will B do afterwards?

11 다음 빈칸에 공통으로 들어갈 말을 쓰시오.

> • I'll go by car _____ I can take more luggage.
> • We left a message with his neighbor _____ he would know we'd called.

➡ _____

12 다음 우리말에 맞게 괄호 안의 단어를 활용하여 as if 구문으로 영작하시오.

> (millionaire)

(1) 그는 백만장자인 듯이 말한다.
➡ _____

(2) 그는 백만장자인 듯이 말했다.
➡ _____

13 다음 밑줄 친 부분이 나머지 넷과 다른 의미를 지닌 것을 고르시오.

① I wrote a report correctly so that you could understand it.

② Teamwork is required in order to achieve these aims.

③ The grocery store near my house was so crowded that I had to go to another store.

④ I signed up for the fitness club so as to get into shape.

⑤ In order that training should be effective, it must be planned systematically.

14 괄호 안의 단어를 활용하여 우리말에 맞게 빈칸을 채우시오.

(1) 만약 내가 UFO를 본다면 그것을 사진 찍을 텐데. (take)

➡ If I saw a UFO, I _____ of it.

(2) 만약 하나라도 깨지지 않은 화병이 있다면 그것을 송도로 가져갈 수 있을 텐데. (one, have)

➡ _____, I could take it to Songdo.

15 다음 주어진 단어를 활용하여 우리말에 맞게 영작하시오.

나는 그녀가 나에게 연락할 수 있도록 그녀에게 나의 전화번호를 주었다. (so that, contact)

➡ _____

_____

[16~18] 다음 글을 읽고 물음에 답하시오.

Take a pen. Look at it carefully. (①) Do you see a small hole in the cap? (②) The hole in a pen cap can help save lives. (③) People, especially children, often put small things like pen caps in their mouths. (④) Sometimes they even swallow them. (⑤) This can stop their breathing and cause death. A famous pen company started ⓐputting a small hole in their pen caps. The hole in the cap lets air pass through and has saved lives.

16 위 글의 흐름으로 보아, 주어진 문장이 들어가기에 가장 적절한 곳은?

Do you know why it is there?

① ② ③ ④ ⑤

17 위 글의 밑줄 친 ⓐputting과 문법적 쓰임이 같은 것을 모두 고르시오.

① Would you mind opening the window?

② His job is selling cars.

③ I found Tom crying.

④ He is good at playing tennis.

⑤ The man working in the garden is my father.

18 위 글을 읽고 알 수 없는 것을 고르시오.

① the reason why a small hole is in the cap of a pen

② the thing people often put in their mouths

③ who started putting a small hole in their pen caps

④ the common material used to make the pen cap

⑤ the function of the hole in the cap

[19~20] 다음 글을 읽고 물음에 답하시오.

If you look around, you will see other holes that play a helpful role in your life. If you have ever cooked anything in a pot with a lid, perhaps you noticed a small hole in the lid. This hole, too, is there for safety. When cooking something in a pot with a lid, the pressure inside the pot builds up. The water inside would quickly boil over if the lid did not have that hole. ⓐ그 구멍이 수증기를 나가게 해 주고 물이 밖으로 넘치는 것을 막아 준다.

출제율 90%

19 위 글의 밑줄 친 ⓐ의 우리말에 맞게 주어진 어휘를 이용하여 12 단어로 영작하시오.

> lets, keeps, coming

➡ _____

_____

출제율 100%

20 위 글의 주제로 알맞은 것을 고르시오.

① other holes that play a helpful role in your life

② the role of a small hole in the lid of a pot

③ how to cook something in a pot with a lid

④ the increasing pressure inside the pot

⑤ the importance of preventing the water inside the pot from boiling over

[21~23] 다음 글을 읽고 물음에 답하시오.

Have you ever been on an airplane? Wasn't it exciting to look out the window and see the world below? Surprisingly, there was a small hole in your window. Airplane windows are made up of three panes. There is a hole in the middle pane. It balances the air pressure. ⓐ With this little hole, airplane windows might break in an emergency. The hole also prevents the window from fogging up so that you can enjoy that fantastic view.

출제율 95%

21 위 글의 밑줄 친 ⓐ에서 흐름상 어색한 부분을 찾아 고치시오.

_____ ➡ _____

출제율 90%

22 본문의 내용과 일치하도록 다음 빈칸 (A)와 (B)에 알맞은 단어를 쓰시오.

> Were it not for (A)_____ _____ in the middle pane of airplane windows, you could not enjoy the fantastic view from an airplane because the window would (B)_____ _____.

출제율 100%

23 According to the passage, which is NOT true?

① There is a small hole in an airplane window.

② Airplane windows consist of three panes.

③ There is a hole in the inner pane of airplane windows.

④ The hole in the pane balances the air pressure.

⑤ A small hole in the airplane windows can prevent the airplane windows from breaking in an emergency.

[01~02] 다음 대화를 읽고 물음에 답하시오.

G: We're going on a field trip tomorrow to the Invention Museum.

B: I've heard that it has a lot of creative inventions.

G: That's why I'm so excited. How about planning the tour before we go?

B: Good idea. Let me see.... I have the school letter and a map of the museum.

G: Perfect. Let's get started.

01 What is the relationship between the speakers? (3 words)

➡ _____

02 What did B hear about the Invention Museum? (10 words)

➡ _____

[03~04] 다음 글을 읽고 물음에 답하시오.

B: Hi, class. Have you ever heard about the Moai? They are tall, human-shaped stones in Chile. Most of the stones are four meters tall, but the tallest one is 20 meters tall. I was wondering how people moved them long ago. So I searched the Internet and learned that they used ropes. Isn't that amazing?

03 Describe what the tallest Moai looks like. (Include two different features.)

➡ _____

_____

04 How did the speaker find out how people moved the stones?

➡ _____

05 다음 문장의 단어들을 활용하여 예상 가능한 가정법 과거 문장을 쓰시오.

> I'd like to lose weight by exercising every day. But It's not easy to practice every day.

➡ _____

06 다음 문장의 단어들을 활용하여 가능한 가정법 과거 문장을 〈조건〉에 맞게 쓰시오.

┌─── 조건 ───┐
1. 명령문으로 시작할 것.
2. as if와 in one's place(~의 입장에서)를 이용할 것.
└──────────┘

> I agree that "The rich have to help the poor." But my friend Joel doesn't agree to my thought. In this case, I could say to Joel, "_____"

➡ _____

07 괄호 안의 단어를 활용하여 두 문장 중 한 문장이 목적의 의미를 나타내도록 한 문장으로 바꿔 쓰시오.

> • I worked hard. • I could succeed.

➡ (so) _____

_____

➡ (in) _____

_____

08 다음 우리말에 맞게 괄호 안의 단어를 어법에 맞게 배열하시오.

> 그는 마치 지난밤에 귀신을 봤던 것처럼 말했다.
> (talked, seen, he, if, ghost, a, as, he, had, last, night)

➡ _____

[09~11] 다음 글을 읽고 물음에 답하시오.

> Take a pen. Look at it carefully. Do you see a small hole in the cap? ⓐ여러분은 왜 거기에 구멍이 있는지 아는가? The hole in a pen cap can help save lives. People, especially children, often put small things like pen caps in their mouths. Sometimes they even swallow them. This can stop their breathing and cause death. A famous pen company started putting a small hole in ⓑtheir pen caps. The hole in the cap lets air pass through and has saved lives.

09 위 글의 밑줄 친 ⓐ의 우리말에 맞게 주어진 어휘를 이용하여 7 단어로 영작하시오.

> it, there

➡ _____

10 위 글의 밑줄 친 ⓑ가 가리키는 것을 본문에서 찾아 쓰시오.

➡ _____

11 Why is there a small hole in the pen cap? Fill in the blanks (A) and (B) with suitable words.

> There is a small hole in the pen cap to let air (A)_____ _____ and (B)_____ a life if someone swallows it.

[12~13] 다음 글을 읽고 물음에 답하시오.

> Have you ever been (A)[on / to] an airplane? Wasn't it exciting to look out the window and see the world below? Surprisingly, there was a small hole in your window. Airplane windows are made up of three panes. There is a hole in the middle pane. It balances the air pressure. Without this little hole, airplane windows might break in an emergency. The hole also prevents the window from fogging up ⓐso that you can enjoy that fantastic view.
>
> There are many more products that have small hidden holes. In the future, when you see (B)[a few / a little] hole in something, ask yourself why it is there. Maybe it is the result of a careful design to make your life (C)[more safely / safer].

12 위 글의 괄호 (A)~(C)에서 문맥이나 어법상 알맞은 낱말을 골라 쓰시오.

(A) _____ (B) _____ (C) _____

13 위 글의 밑줄 친 ⓐ를 다음과 같이 바꿔 쓸 때 빈칸에 들어갈 알맞은 말을 두 단어로 쓰시오.

> for you _____ _____ that fantastic view

창의사고력 서술형 문제

01 다음은 아래 그림의 발명품에 대한 글이다. 다음 정보를 활용하여 빈칸을 채우시오.

> • The Role
> - We use a telephone every day.
> - We can talk to people who are far away from us.
> • The Information
> - In 1876, Alexander Bell invented the first practical form of the telephone.
> - Without telephones, we wouldn't be able to have a chat with friends living in another city.

Can you imagine life without a telephone? _____.

In 1876, _____.

After that, it developed quickly through the years and has become a necessary part of modern life. _____ in today's world, _____.

02 다음 내용을 바탕으로 발명품을 소개하는 글을 쓰시오.

> **A Refrigerator**
> • The Role: We use a refrigerator every day so that we can keep food cool and fresh.
> • The Information: In 1755, William Cullen invented the first form of the refrigerator. After the invention, it developed through the years and has become a necessary part of modern life. As we have refrigerators in today's world, we are able to enjoy ice cream on hot summer days.

> **A Refrigerator**
> Can you imagine life without a refrigerator? We use it every day so that we can keep food (A)_____. In 1755, (B)_____ invented the first form of the refrigerator. After that, it developed through the years and has become (C)_____. If we did not have refrigerators in today's world, we would not be able to enjoy (D)_____ on hot summer days.

단원별 모의고사

01 다음 영영풀이가 가리키는 것은?

> to be in a position where you will stand without falling to either side, or to put something in this position

① weigh　② expect　③ balance
④ stand　⑤ calculate

02 다음 주어진 문장의 빈칸에 가장 알맞은 단어는?

> _____ it would be better if you came back at once.

① Even though　② Although
③ Despite　④ Perhaps
⑤ Not only

03 다음 주어진 문장의 빈칸에 알맞은 말을 쓰시오.

(1) 우리는 독감이 퍼지는 것을 막기 위해 손을 최대한 자주 씻어야 한다.
　➡ We need to wash hands as often as possible to _____ the flu _____ spreading.

(2) 우리가 지금 취하는 결정은 미래의 사태에 영향을 미칠 수도 있다.
　➡ The decisions we take now may influence events _____ _____ _____.

[04~05] 다음 대화를 읽고 물음에 답하시오.

> G: Look at the number. It's going up quickly.
> B: (A)사람들이 지나갈 때 그 숫자가 증가해.
> G: Oh, you're right. What does the number mean?
> B: Let me see.... Oh, when people step on the floor, energy is made. It shows the amount of energy that is made.
> G: Wow, that's amazing!

04 위 대화의 밑줄 친 (A)의 우리말을 주어진 단어를 사용하여 영작하시오. (7 words)

➡ _____

05 위 대화에서 주어진 영영풀이에 맞는 단어를 찾아 쓰시오.

> the degree to which something is a lot or a little; how much something is

➡ _____

[06~08] 다음 대화를 읽고 물음에 답하시오.

> G: I like these crackers. They're really good.
> B: Yeah, me, too. I wonder why crackers have these little holes in them.
> G: I don't know. (A)어디 보자... Um... well... maybe it's because the holes make the crackers look tastier.
> B: That's possible, but there must be some other reasons.
> G: Let's look up crackers on the Internet and see what it says.
> B: Okay. Oh, look at this.

G: It says during baking, steam comes out through the holes and that makes the crackers thin.

B: It also says that the holes make the crackers crispy.

G: Wow! So that's why they have holes!

06 위 글의 밑줄 친 (A)를 영작한 표현으로 적절하지 <u>않은</u> 것은?

① Let me think   ② Let me see

③ Let me check   ④ Just a second

⑤ Just a minute

07 위 대화에 드러난 B와 G의 심경 변화로 가장 적절한 것은?

① excited → worried

② surprised → relieved

③ curious → stressed

④ excited → disappointed

⑤ curious → satisfied

08 Explain the reason why crackers have little holes in them. (11 words)

➡ _____

_____

09 주어진 대화가 자연스럽게 이어지도록 순서대로 배열하시오.

G: We're going on a field trip tomorrow to the Invention Museum.

(A) Good idea. Let me see.... I have the school letter and a map of the museum.

(B) That's why I'm so excited. How about planning the tour before we go?

(C) I've heard that it has a lot of creative inventions.

G: Perfect. Let's get started.

➡ _____

[10~11] 다음 대화를 읽고 물음에 답하시오.

B: Hi, Kate. Today's Saturday, so what about going to the Einstein Science Park today?

G: That sounds like a good idea. I heard that they have special programs on Saturdays. I wonder what they are.

B: Let me see…. I saw an advertisement in the newspaper. Here it is.

G: What does (A)it say?

B: It says that today they have two shows: the Smart Design Show and the International Drone Show in Einstein Hall 101.

G: They both sound fantastic.

B: I'll call them and ask what time they start.

10 위 대화의 밑줄 친 (A)it이 가리키는 것을 쓰시오. (5 words)

➡ _____

11 What kind of programs does the park have? (11 words)

➡ _____

_____

12 다음 중 짝지어진 대화가 <u>어색한</u> 것을 고르시오.

① A: What can we do with this drone?

B: Well, let me see.... Maybe we can take pictures from the sky.

② A: How does this train start to move?

B: Just a moment.... I think you can take it.

③ A: What can we do with this VR glasses?

B: Just a minute.... We can play soccer.

④ A: What can we do with the smart watch?

B: Let me think.... We can send text messages.

⑤ A: What do I have to do to enter the competition?

B: Let me see.... You should talk to Ann.

13 다음 문장에서 어법상 <u>어색한</u> 부분을 고치시오. 어색하지 않은 것은 '없음'이라고 쓰시오.

(1) Olivia exercises every day so that she can stay healthy.

_____ ➡ _____

(2) Joel is working hard so that he can't finish the project on time.

_____ ➡ _____

(3) I moved my legs out of the way such that she could get past.

_____ ➡ _____

(4) She hurried up so what she could get there on time.

_____ ➡ _____

14 다음 빈칸에 들어갈 말로 알맞은 것을 고르시오.

> She acts as if she had known everybody.
> ➡ In fact, she _____ everybody.

① didn't know   ② hasn't known

③ knew   ④ doesn't know

⑤ knows

15 다음 중 어법상 <u>어색한</u> 것은?

① If I took some time off, I could have a rest on weekdays.

② If he had done the assignment, he would have gotten A⁺.

③ If I had a time machine, I will go back to the 6th grade.

④ If I met a famous singer, I would take a picture with him.

⑤ If you had contacted me, you could have understood it.

16 다음 우리말에 맞게 괄호 안의 단어를 활용하여 영작하시오.

> 당신이 제 입장이라면 기분이 어떻겠어요? (in my situation)

➡ _____, how would you feel?

17 빈칸에 들어갈 말로 적절한 것을 쓰시오.

> Although Britney Spears makes much of her money through her worldwide tours, she recently said she wanted to stop traveling for a while _____ _____ she could take care of her new baby.

➡ _____

18 우리말에 맞게 괄호 안의 단어를 배열하시오.

> 나는 보기 위해 눈을 감는다. – Paul Gauguin
> (in, I, my, see, shut, order, eyes, to)

➡ _____

19 다음 우리말에 맞게 괄호 안의 단어를 이용하여 빈칸을 채우시오.

> Steve는 신선한 공기를 좀 마시기 위해 창문을 열었다. (so, some)
> ➡ Steve opened the window _____
> _____.
> ➡ Steve opened the window _____
> _____.

20 우리말에 맞게 괄호 안의 단어를 활용하여 빈칸에 들어갈 알맞은 말을 쓰시오.

(1) 만약 Jane이 노래를 잘 부른다면 노래 경연 대회에 출전할 텐데. (be, singing)

➡ _____,

Jane would enter the singing contest.

(2) 만약 아이돌 그룹이 학교에 온다면 나는 행복할 텐데. (come)

➡ _____,

I would be happy.

21 빈칸에 들어갈 말로 바르게 짝지어진 것끼리 고르시오.

> She decided to run for a parliamentary job _____ _____ she _____ help other North Korea defectors struggling to adjust to South Korean society.
> *run for: ~에 출마하다 *parliamentary job: 국회의원 *defector: 이탈자, 망명자

[22~23] 다음 글을 읽고 물음에 답하시오.

> Think about a hole that you have seen ⓐ <u>recently</u>. Was it a good hole or a bad hole? If it was a hole in your sock, it was bad. If it was a hole in your shirt for a button, it was good. There are holes everywhere. Some are so small you may not even notice them. They are well hidden, but many of these small holes are very important and make your life safe.

22 위 글의 밑줄 친 ⓐrecently와 바꿔 쓸 수 있는 말을 모두 고르시오.

① those days ② lately
③ previously ④ of late
⑤ of the other day

23 Are the holes that we see around us all good holes? If not, give an example beginning with "If".

➡ _____
_____
_____

[24~25] 다음 글을 읽고 물음에 답하시오.

> Take a pen. Look at it carefully. Do you see a small hole in the cap? Do you know why it is ⓐ<u>there</u>? The hole in a pen cap can help save lives. People, especially children, often put small things like pen caps in their mouths. Sometimes they even swallow them. This can stop their breathing and cause death. A famous pen company started putting a small hole in their pen caps. The hole in the cap lets air pass through and has saved lives.

24 위 글의 밑줄 친 @there가 지칭하는 것을 본문에서 찾아 쓰시오.

➡ _____

25 According to the passage, which is NOT true?

① The hole in a pen cap can help save lives.
② Children often put pen caps in their mouths.
③ Sometimes children even swallow large things.
④ What children swallow can stop their breathing and cause death.
⑤ Air can pass through the hole in the cap.

[26~27] 다음 글을 읽고 물음에 답하시오.

If you look around, you will see other holes that play a helpful role in your life. (①) If you have ever cooked anything in a pot with a lid, perhaps you noticed a small hole in the lid. (②) When cooking something in a pot with a lid, the pressure inside the pot builds up. (③) The water inside would quickly boil over if the lid did not have that hole. (④) The hole lets steam out and keeps the water from coming out. (⑤)

26 위 글의 흐름으로 보아, 주어진 문장이 들어가기에 가장 적절한 곳은?

This hole, too, is there for safety.

① ② ③ ④ ⑤

27 Which question CANNOT be answered after reading the passage?

① Why is there a hole in the lid of a pot?
② When you cook something in a pot with a lid, what happens?
③ If there were no hole in the lid of a pot, what would happen?
④ What does the hole in the lid of a pot do?
⑤ How long does it take for the hole to let steam out?

[28~29] 다음 글을 읽고 물음에 답하시오.

There are many more products that have small hidden holes. In the future, when you see a little hole in something, @왜 그것이 거기에 있는지 자신에게 물어보라. Maybe it is the result of a careful design ⓑto make your life safer.

28 위 글의 밑줄 친 @의 우리말에 맞게 한 단어를 보충하여, 주어진 어휘를 알맞게 배열하시오.

why / ask / is / there / it

➡ _____

29 위 글의 밑줄 친 ⓑto make와 to부정사의 용법이 같은 것을 모두 고르시오.

① He was the first man to land on the moon.
② I went to his house to fix the radio.
③ There are interesting activities to play outdoors.
④ They decided to go there.
⑤ He is too young to travel alone.

MEMO

Lesson 8

Healthy Food Around the World

의사소통 기능

- 반복 요청하기

  A: Have you ever tried *Rasmalai*?

  B: Sorry, could you say that again?

  A: *Rasmalai.*

- 추천하기

  A: Could you recommend a good traditional dish?

  B: Try Samgyetang. It'll give you energy.

언어 형식

- not only A but also B

  Gogol-mogol is **not only** good for people with a cold **but also** popular as a dessert for healthy people.

- 접속사 While

  While people in Korea and Finland look for drinks when sick, many people in America want a bowl of chicken soup.

Key Words

- □ **add** [æd] 동 더하다, 첨가하다
- □ **blend** [blend] 동 섞다
- □ **boil** [bɔil] 동 끓다, 끓이다
- □ **cell phone** 휴대폰
- □ **chop** [tʃɑp] 동 잘게 썰다
- □ **cool** [ku:l] 동 식히다
- □ **dessert** [dizə́:rt] 명 후식
- □ **dish** [diʃ] 명 요리
- □ **eastern** [í:stərn] 형 동쪽에 위치한
- □ **ginger** [dʒíndʒər] 명 생강
- □ **heat** [hi:t] 명 온도, 열
- □ **hold** [hould] 동 열다, 개최하다
- □ **honey** [hʌ́ni] 명 꿀
- □ **hurt** [hə:rt] 동 아프다
- □ **lamb** [læm] 명 양고기
- □ **little sister** 여동생
- □ **local** [lóukəl] 형 지역의, 현지의
- □ **low** [lou] 형 낮은
- □ **medicine** [médisn] 명 약
- □ **melt** [melt] 동 녹다
- □ **mix** [miks] 동 섞다
- □ **mixture** [míkstʃər] 명 혼합물
- □ **often** [ɔ́:fən] 부 자주
- □ **over** [óuvər] 전 ～ 위에
- □ **pain** [pein] 명 아픔, 통증
- □ **pepper** [pépər] 명 후추, 고추

- □ **pour** [pɔ:r] 동 붓다, 따르다
- □ **recipe** [résəpi] 명 요리법
- □ **recommend** [rèkəménd] 동 추천하다
- □ **reduce** [ridjú:s] 동 줄이다
- □ **refrigerator** [rifrídʒərèitər] 명 냉장고
- □ **room temperature** 상온, 실온
- □ **seafood** [sí:fud] 명 해산물
- □ **serve** [sə:rv] 동 제공하다
- □ **smooth** [smu:ð] 형 매끄러운, 고루 잘 섞인
- □ **sore** [sɔ:r] 형 아픈, 따가운
- □ **stay** [stei] 동 그대로 있다
- □ **stir** [stə:r] 동 휘젓다
- □ **stuffy** [stʌ́fi] 형 코가 막힌, 답답한
- □ **taste** [teist] 명 맛
- □ **temperature** [témpərətʃər] 명 온도, 기온
- □ **thick** [θik] 형 두꺼운, 걸쭉한
- □ **throat** [θrout] 명 목구멍, 목
- □ **touching** [tʌ́tʃiŋ] 형 감동적인
- □ **treasure** [tréʒər] 명 보물
- □ **vegetable** [védʒətəbl] 명 채소
- □ **warm** [wɔ:rm] 동 따뜻하게 하다 형 따뜻한
- □ **wear** [wɛər] 동 입다
- □ **weather** [wéðər] 명 날씨
- □ **while** [hwail] 접 반면에, ～하는 동안에
- □ **yogurt** [jóugərt] 명 요구르트

Key Expressions

- □ **a bottle of** ～ 한 병
- □ **a bowl of** ～ 한 그릇
- □ **a cup of** ～ 한 컵
- □ **a plate of** ～ 한 접시
- □ **as well as** ～에 더하여, 게다가
- □ **be different from** ～와 다르다
- □ **be good for** ～에 좋다
- □ **be made with** ～로 만들어지다
- □ **breathe through** ～를 통해서 숨쉬다
- □ **catch a cold** 감기에 걸리다
- □ **find out** 알아내다, 발견하다
- □ **for the first time** 처음으로
- □ **get sick** 병에 걸리다

- □ **half an hour** 30분
- □ **have a runny nose** 콧물이 흐르다
- □ **look for** 찾다, 기대하다
- □ **look like** ～처럼 보이다
- □ **not only A but also B** A뿐만 아니라 B도
- □ **of course** 당연히
- □ **put on** 몸에 걸치다
- □ **show A around B** A에게 B를 둘러보도록 안내하다
- □ **such as A** A와 같은
- □ **take a picture** 사진을 찍다
- □ **take a walk** 산책하다
- □ **turn off** 끄다

Word Power

※ 서로 비슷한 뜻을 가진 어휘

- ☐ **blend** 섞다 – **compound** 혼합하다, 섞어서 만들다
- ☐ **medicine** 약 – **medication** 약제, 약물
- ☐ **pain** 아픔, 통증 – **ache** 아픔, 쑤심
- ☐ **touching** 감동적인 – **moving** 감동시키는, 심금을 울리는

- ☐ **local** 지역의, 현지의 – **regional** 지방의, 지방적인
- ☐ **often** 자주 – **frequently** 종종, 빈번히
- ☐ **stay** 그대로 있다 – **remain** 계속 ~이다
- ☐ **while** 반면에 – **whereas** 반면에

※ 서로 반대의 뜻을 가진 어휘

- ☐ **add** 더하다, 첨가하다 ↔ **remove** 제거하다, 줄이다
- ☐ **low** 낮은 ↔ **high** 높은
- ☐ **smooth** 매끄러운 ↔ **rough** 거칠거칠한

- ☐ **cool** 식히다 ↔ **warm** 따뜻하게 하다
- ☐ **reduce** 줄이다 ↔ **increase** 증가하다, 늘다
- ☐ **thick** 두꺼운, 걸쭉한 ↔ **thin** 얇은, 가는

※ 접두사 re + 동사

- ☐ **re + consider → reconsider** 재고하다
- ☐ **re + form → reform** 개혁하다
- ☐ **re + generate → regenerate** 재건하다
- ☐ **re + make → remake** 새로 만들다, 리메이크하다
- ☐ **re + organize → reorganize** 재조직하다
- ☐ **re + touch → retouch** 수정하다

- ☐ **re + focus → refocus** 다시 집중하다
- ☐ **re + gain → regain** 되찾다
- ☐ **re + join → rejoin** 다시 합류하다
- ☐ **re + order → reorder** 재주문하다
- ☐ **re + produce → reproduce** 다시 만들어 내다
- ☐ **re + use → reuse** 재사용하다

English Dictionary

- ☐ **boil** 끓다, 끓이다
  - → to change from a liquid to a gas as a result of heat
    열의 결과로 액체에서 기체로 변하다
- ☐ **chop** 잘게 썰다
  - → to cut into smaller pieces
    더 작은 조각들로 자르다
- ☐ **ginger** 생강
  - → a reed-like plant originally from Southeast Asia but now grown in most warm countries, having a strong-smelling and spicy root used in cookery and medicine
    동남 아시아에서 왔지만 현재 대부분의 따뜻한 나라에서 자라는 갈대 모양의 식물로, 요리와 의학에 사용되고 강한 향과 매운 뿌리를 가지고 있는 식물
- ☐ **local** 지역의, 현지의
  - → relating to a city, town or small district rather than an entire state or country
    전체 주 또는 국가가 아닌 도시, 마을 또는 작은 구역에 관련된
- ☐ **pain** 아픔, 통증
  - → physical suffering
    육체적 고통
- ☐ **pour** 붓다, 따르다
  - → to flow, as from one container to another, or into, over, or on something
    어떤 것 안에 혹은 위에, 혹은 하나의 용기에서 다른 용기로 흐르다
- ☐ **recommend** 추천하다
  - → to urge or suggest as proper, useful or beneficial
    적절하거나 유용하거나 혹은 유익하다고 제안하거나 권고하다
- ☐ **stay** 그대로 있다
  - → to remain over a length of time, as in a place or situation
    한 장소나 상황에서 오랜 시간 동안 머무르다
- ☐ **temperature** 온도, 기온
  - → a measure of the warmth of an object with reference to a standard scale
    표준 척도를 기준으로 한 물체의 온기 측정
- ☐ **thick** 두꺼운
  - → having a great distance from one surface to the opposite
    한 표면에서 반대편까지 큰 거리가 있는
- ☐ **touching** 감동적인
  - → causing strong emotion
    강한 감동을 유발하는
- ☐ **treasure** 보물
  - → anything or person greatly valued
    매우 가치가 있는 것 또는 사람

서답형

01 다음 짝지어진 단어의 관계가 같도록 빈칸에 알맞은 말을 쓰시오.

> low : high = reduce : _____

02 다음 영영풀이가 가리키는 것을 고르시오.

> causing strong emotion

① injured   ② touching
③ stuffy   ④ painful
⑤ hurting

03 다음 중 밑줄 친 부분의 뜻풀이가 바르지 <u>않은</u> 것은?

① The <u>heat</u> and the wine made her sleepy. (열, 열기)
② The doctor has given me some <u>medicine</u> to take. (약)
③ The back <u>pain</u> got progressively worse. (통증)
④ How did this <u>dish</u> get broken? (요리)
⑤ I experimented until I got the <u>recipe</u> just right. (요리법)

서답형

04 다음 우리말을 주어진 어휘를 이용하여 영작하시오.

(1) 당신의 사무실 근처에 있는 호텔을 추천해 주시겠어요? (recommend)
➡ _____

(2) Sam의 식당은 훌륭한 프랑스 요리를 제공한다. (good, French cuisine)
➡ _____

(3) 눈은 언제 녹기 시작할까요? (start, melt)
➡ _____

서답형

05 다음 문장의 빈칸에 들어갈 말을 〈보기〉에서 골라 쓰시오. (필요하면 어형 변화를 할 것.)

> ┤ 보기 ├
> put on / get sick / find out /
> be different from

(1) American English _____ significantly _____ British English.
(2) It would be better to _____ my sweater in weather like today.
(3) The children were malnourished and _____ often. ※malnourished: 영양실조의

중요

06 다음 문장의 빈칸 (A)와 (B)에 각각 공통으로 들어갈 말이 바르게 짝지어진 것은?

> • She speaks French as well ___(A)___ English.
> • Organizations such ___(A)___ schools and clubs bind a community together.
> • The accident happened as the airplane was about to take ___(B)___.
> • Please turn ___(B)___ your cellphones during the meeting.

① on – up   ② on – off
③ as – up   ④ as – off
⑤ like – on

01 다음 짝지어진 단어의 관계가 같도록 빈칸에 알맞은 말을 쓰시오.

> pain : ache = touching : _____

02 다음 주어진 영영풀이에 맞는 단어를 쓰시오.

(1) having a great distance from one surface to the opposite

➡ _____

(2) anything or person greatly valued

➡ _____

03 다음 문장의 빈칸에 들어갈 말을 〈보기〉에서 골라 쓰시오. (필요하면 어형 변화를 할 것.)

> ┤ 보기 ├
> look like / show around / of course / for the first time

(1) She slept well _____ in a long time.
(2) New employees will be _____ by the HR manager.
(3) He may not _____ it, but he's a big eater.

04 우리말과 일치하도록 주어진 어구를 <u>모두</u> 배열하여 영작하시오.

(1) 그들은 산책을 하기 위해 공원에 갔다.
   (went / a walk / they / to / to / the park / take)

   ➡ _____

(2) 난 콧물이 나고 목이 아프다.
   (I / and / a sore throat / a runny nose / have)

   ➡ _____

05 다음 우리말에 맞게 주어진 단어를 사용하여 영작하시오.

(1) 우리는 기온 차이를 먼저 측정했다.
   (temperature, measure)

   ➡ _____

(2) 그 껍데기는 안쪽 면이 매끄럽다.
   (smooth, the shell, on)

   ➡ _____

06 다음 우리말에 맞게 빈칸에 알맞은 말을 쓰시오.

> Smith 부부는 책임이 있을 뿐만 아니라 고학력자이다.
> ➡ Mr. and Mrs. Smith are _____ responsible _____ highly educated.

Conversation

교과서

① 반복 요청하기

A Have you ever tried *Rasmalai*? 라스말라이 먹어 봤니?
B Sorry, could you say that again? 미안, 다시 말해 줄래?
A *Rasmalai*. 라스말라이.

- 'Could you say that again?'은 '다시 말해 줄래요?'라는 뜻으로 상대방에게 했던 말을 반복해 달라고 요청할 때 사용하는 표현이다.

- 비슷한 표현으로는 'Pardon?', 'I beg your pardon?', 'Pardon me?', 'Excuse me?', 'I'm sorry?', 'What did you say?', 'Say that again, please?', 'I can't hear you.', 'Could you speak a little louder, please?' 등이 있다.

- 반복을 요청할 때 정중한 표현과 덜 정중한 표현이 있으므로 사용에 유의한다. 'Pardon?', 'I beg your pardon?', 'Pardon me?', 'Excuse me?' 등은 상대적으로 정중한 표현이다. 'I'm sorry?', 'What did you say?', 'Say that again, please?', 'I can't hear you.', 'Could you speak a little louder, please?' 등은 앞의 표현들보다는 덜 정중한 표현이다.

핵심 Check

1. 다음 대화에서 밑줄 친 부분과 바꿔 쓸 수 <u>없는</u> 것은?

A: Have you ever tried *macaron*?
B: Sorry, <u>could you say that again</u>?
A: *Macaron*. It's a traditional dessert in France.

① I beg your pardon? ② Excuse me?
③ I'm sorry? ④ What did you say?
⑤ I can hear you.

2 추천하기

> **A** Could you recommend a good traditional dish? 괜찮은 전통 음식을 추천해 주시겠어요?
>
> **B** Try Samgyetang. It'll give you energy. 삼계탕을 드셔 보세요. 기운을 북돋아 줄 겁니다.

■ 'Could you recommend ~?'는 '~를 추천해 주시겠어요?'라는 뜻으로 상대방에게 추천해달라고 요청할 때 사용하는 표현이다.

■ 이와 같은 표현으로는, 'Can you recommend ~?', 또는 'Can/Could you give me a recommendation for ~?' 등이 있다. 반대로 상대방에게 추천해 줘도 되냐고 물어볼 때는 'Can I recommend something for you?', 'Can I make a recommendation?' 등의 표현을 쓸 수 있다.

■ 따라서 상대방에게 추천해 줄 때 'How about ~?', 'What about ~?', 'I recommend ~.', 'I'd recommend ~.', 'Try ~.'라고 말할 수 있다.

- How about ~? ~은 어때요?
- What about ~? ~은 어때요?
- I recommend ~. 전 ~를 추천합니다.
- I'd recommend ~. 전 ~를 추천할게요.
- Try ~. ~를 시도해 보세요.

핵심 Check

2. 다음 대화에서 밑줄 친 부분을 영작하시오.

A: 제 여동생을 위해 좋은 책을 추천해 주시겠어요?

B: I recommend this one. The story is touching.

➡ _____

Real-Life Zone

M: Good afternoon. ❶A table for two?

B: Yes.

M: ❷This way please. Here is the menu. I'll be back in a few minutes and ❸take your order.

B: Okay. Thank you.

G: I don't know ❹much about Korean food. ❺Could you recommend something?

B: Well, I'd recommend the Bibimbap.

G: I'm sorry. ❻Could you say that again, please?

B: This one. Bi-bim-bap. It's made with lots of vegetables, beef and an egg over rice. It's tasty and it's also ❼good for your health.

G: That sounds great. ❽I'll try it.

B: It's served with a spicy red pepper sauce. Is that okay?

G: No problem. I like spicy food.

M: 안녕하세요. 두 분이신가요?
B: 네.
M: 이쪽으로 오십시오. 메뉴는 여기 있습니다. 잠시 후에 와서 주문 받겠습니다.
B: 알겠습니다. 감사합니다.
G: 나 한국 음식에 대해서 잘 알지 못해. 네가 추천해 줄래?
B: 음, 나는 비빔밥을 추천할게.
G: 미안, 다시 한 번 말해 줄래?
B: 이거, 비-빔-밥. 그것은 밥 위에 많은 야채들과 소고기, 그리고 계란을 얹어 만들어. 맛있고 건강에도 좋아.
G: 굉장한데. 난 그거 먹어 볼래.
B: 매운 고추장 양념이랑 같이 나오는 거야. 괜찮겠니?
G: 문제 없어. 나 매운 음식을 좋아해.

❶ 직역하면 '두 사람을 위한 테이블이신가요?'라는 뜻으로 식당에 갔을 때 몇 사람이냐고 물을 때 사용하는 표현이다. ❷ '이쪽입니다'라는 뜻으로, 이 상황에선 웨이터가 손님에게 따라오라고 할 때 사용된다. ❸ take one's order 주문을 받다 ❹ much (셀 수 없는 명사 앞에 쓰여서) 많이 ❺ '~를 추천해 주시겠어요?라는 뜻으로 상대방에게 추천해달라고 요청할 때 사용하는 표현이다. ❻ '다시 말해 주세요.'라는 뜻으로 상대방에게 했던 말을 반복해 달라고 요청할 때 사용하는 표현이다. ❼ good for ~에 좋은 ❽ '그걸 시도해 볼게.'라는 뜻으로 이때 대명사 it은 앞서 말한 비빔밥을 가리킨다.

Check(√) True or False

(1) Both G and B have not tried Korean food before. T ☐ F ☐

(2) It's the first time G tries spicy Korean food because G does not like spicy food. T ☐ F ☐

Wrap Up 1-2

B: Tomorrow is my birthday.

G: I know. Are you going to ❶have a birthday party, Alex?

B: Yes. ❷Can you recommend a good place to have the party?

G: ❸I'd recommend the Happy Snack House. The food is really good and it'll be large enough.

B: ❹What dish would you recommend?

G: I'd recommend the onion rings. They're fantastic!

B: Oh, ❺just thinking about ❻them makes my mouth water.

B: 내일은 내 생일이야.
G: 알고 있어, Alex, 생일 파티할 거니?
B: 응. 파티 열기에 좋은 장소 추천해 줄래?
G: 나는 Happy Snack House를 추천할게. 음식이 정말 맛있고 장소도 충분히 넓어.
B: 넌 무슨 음식을 추천해 줄래?
G: 나는 양파 튀김을 추천할게. 정말 환상적이야!
B: 오, 그거 생각하는 것만으로도 침이 고인다.

❶ have a party 파티를 열다 ❷ '~를 추천해 주시겠어요?'라는 뜻으로 상대방에게 추천해달라고 요청할 때 사용하는 표현으로, 같은 표현으로는 'Can/Could you give me a recommendation for ~?' 등이 있다. ❸ 상대방에게 추천해 줄 때 사용할 수 있는 표현이다. ❹ '어떤 음식을 추천해 줄래?'라는 뜻으로 의문사 what이 쓰인 의문문이다. ❺ 동명사가 쓰인 구문으로 thinking about them 전체가 주어이다. ❻ 대명사 them은 앞서 언급한 음식 the onion rings를 가리킨다.

Check(√) True or False

(3) B is going to throw a birthday party. T ☐ F ☐

(4) The place that G recommends for the party is called the Happy Snack House. T ☐ F ☐

Listen & Speak 1 Listen 1

B: Hi, Grace. ❶Those are pretty. What are they called?

G: They're ❷called *dango*.

B: I'm sorry. ❸Could you say that again?

G: *Dan-go*. They're sweet and ❹made with rice cake powder. They're from Japan.

❶ Those는 대명사 that의 복수형이다.
❷ call ~라고 부르다
❸ '다시 말해 주겠니?'의 뜻이다.
❹ made with ~로 만들어진

Listen & Speak 1 Listen 2

B: Alice, ❶what's that you're eating?

G: It's *rasmalai*.

B: *Ra*.... Could you say that again?

G: *Ras-ma-lai*. It's like a cheesecake in a sweet cream. It's a ❷traditional food in India.

❶ '네가 먹고 있는 그것은 뭐니?'라는 뜻이다.
❷ traditional 전통적인

Listen & Speak 1 Listen 3

G: What's that you're eating, David? It ❶looks like a chocolate ball.

B: It's *brigadeiro*.

G: ❷Sorry? Could you say that again?

B: *Bri-ga-dei-ro*. It's sweet and ❸tasty. It's popular in Brazil.

❶ look like ~처럼 보이다
❷ 이때 사용된 'Sorry?'는 미안하다는 뜻이 아니라 상대방이 했던 말을 반복해 주기를 요청하는 표현이다.
❸ tasty 맛있는

Listen & Speak 1 A-1

G: My ❶favorite Korean traditional drink is Maesil-tea. ❷What about you, Jinsu?

B: Well, my favorite traditional drink is Sikhye.

G: Sik.... Can you say that again?

B: Sik-hye. It's sweet and cool.

G: I want to ❸try it.

❶ favorite 가장 좋아하는
❷ '너는 어때?'라는 뜻으로, 'How about you?'와 바꿔 쓸 수 있다.
❸ try (좋은지 보려고) 먹어 보다, 써 보다, 해 보다

Listen & Speak 1 A-2

B: ❶Have you ever tried *poke*?

G: Sorry, could you say that again, please?

B: *Po-ke*. It's a salad ❷that is popular in Hawaii.

G: What's so special about it?

B: It's made with rice and fish. It's ❸not only delicious but also very healthy.

❶ 현재완료의 경험 용법이 사용된 문장으로, '~해 본 적 있니?'라고 해석한다.
❷ 이때 that은 대명사가 아니라 접속사로 사용되었다.
❸ not only A but also B A뿐만 아니라 B도

Listen & Speak 1 B

1. **A:** Have you ever ❶tried *rasmalai*?
   B: Sorry, ❷could you say that again?
   A: *Rasmalai*. It's a traditional dessert in India.

2. **A:** Have you ever tried *brigadeiro*?
   B: Sorry, could you say that again?
   A: *Brigadeiro*. It's a ❸traditional dessert in Brazil.

3. **A:** Have you ever tried *macaron*?
   B: Sorry, could you say that again?
   A: *Macaron*. It's a traditional ❹dessert in France.

❶ try 써 보다, 해 보다, 먹어 보다
❷ '다시 말해 주시겠어요?'라는 뜻이다.
❸ traditional 전통적인
❹ dessert 디저트, 후식 *cf.* desert 사막, 버리다

Listen & Speak 2 Listen

1. B: Could you recommend a good traditional ❶dish?

   W: ❷Try Samgyetang. It'll give you energy.

2. G: Could you recommend a good book for my little sister?

   M: ❸I recommend this one. The story is ❹touching.

3. B: Could you recommend a guitar for beginners?

   W: ❺How about this one? Many beginners play it.

4. G: Could you recommend a snack for my dog?

   M: Sure. How about this? Dogs really like it.

❶ dish 음식
❷ 상대방에게 추천해 줄 때 쓰는 표현으로, '먹어 보세요.'라고 해석한다.
❸ 이와 같은 표현으로 'How about ~?', 'What about ~?', 'I'd recommend ~.', 'Try ~.'라고 말할 수 있다.
❹ touching 감동적인
❺ 상대방에게 추천해 줄 때 사용하는 표현이다.

Listen & Speak 2 A-2

M: Welcome to the Sydney Information Center. Sydney has many places ❶you will want to visit. The Rocks Markets is one of ❷them. There you can buy art, clothing, books and many other things. You can also eat fresh, tasty local food. We ❸recommend visiting the Rocks Markets and enjoying the food and the fun there.

❶ 관계대명사 that이나 which가 생략된 문장으로 many places를 꾸며 준다.
❷ 대명사 them은 앞선 문장에서 언급된 many places in Sydney를 가리킨다.
❸ recommend는 목적어로 동명사(~ing)를 취한다.

Listen & Speak 2 A-1

B: Tomorrow is my dad's birthday. ❶I'd like to do something special for him.

G: ❷How about cooking something for him? He would really like that.

B: That sounds great. Can you recommend ❸something easy to cook?

G: Umm. How about Gimchijeon? It's ❹easy to make and it's delicious.

B: Oh, that's a good idea. He'll love ❺it.

❶ would like to ~하고 싶다
❷ 'How about ~?'는 상대방에게 무언가를 제안하거나 추천할 때 쓰는 표현으로 'What about ~?'과 바꿔 쓸 수 있다.
❸ something은 형용사가 뒤에서 수식하기 때문에 형용사 easy가 something 뒤에 위치한다.
❹ easy to ~ ~하기 쉬운
❺ 대명사 it은 B가 만들 김치전을 가리킨다.

Listen & Speak 2 B

1. A: ❶Could you recommend a good traditional dish?

   B: ❷Try Samgyetang. It'll give you energy.

2. A: Could you recommend a good book for my little sister?

   B: I recommend ❸this one. The story is touching.

3. A: Could you recommend ❹a cell phone for my grandmother?

   B: How about this phone? It's ❺easy to use.

❶ 'Can you recommend ~?', 또는 'Can/Could you give me a recommendation for ~?' 등의 표현으로 대체할 수 있다.
❷ '삼계탕을 드셔 보세요.'라는 뜻으로, 'Try ~.' 이외에도 상대방에게 추천해 줄 때 'How about ~?', 'What about ~?', 'I recommend ~.', 'I'd recommend ~.' 등을 쓸 수 있다.
❸ 이때 this one은 책을 가리킨다.
❹ cell phone 휴대폰
❺ easy to use 사용하기 쉬운

● 다음 우리말과 일치하도록 빈칸에 알맞은 말을 쓰시오.

해석

Listen & Speak 1 Listen 1

B: Hi, Grace. Those are pretty. What are _____ called?

G: They're _____ *dango*.

B: I'm sorry. _____ you say that _____?

G: *Dan-go*. They're sweet and _____ with rice cake powder. They're _____ Japan.

B: Grace, 안녕. 그거 예쁘다. 그거 뭐라고 불리니?
G: 당고라고 불러.
B: 미안, 다시 말해 줄래?
G: 당-고. 달고 쌀가루로 만들어진 거야. 일본에서 온 거야.

Listen & Speak 1 Listen 2

B: Alice, what's that you're _____?

G: It's *rasmalai*.

B: *Ra*.... Could you _____ that again?

G: *Ras-ma-lai*. It's _____ a cheesecake in a sweet cream. It's a traditional _____ in India.

B: Alice, 네가 먹고 있는 것은 무엇이니?
G: 라스말라이야.
B: 라… 다시 한 번 말해 줄래?
G: 라스-마-라이. 달콤한 크림 안에 있는 치즈케이크 같은 거야. 인도의 전통 음식이지.

Listen & Speak 1 Listen 3

G: What's _____ you're eating, David? It _____ like a chocolate ball.

B: It's *brigadeiro*.

G: _____? Could you say that _____?

B: B*ri-ga-dei-ro*. It's sweet and tasty. It's _____ in Brazil.

G: David, 뭐 먹고 있니? 그거 초콜릿 볼처럼 생겼다.
B: 브리가데이로야.
G: 뭐라고? 다시 한 번 말해 줄래?
B: 브리-가-데이-로. 달고 맛있어. 브라질에서 인기 많아.

Listen & Speak 1 A-1

G: My _____ Korean traditional drink is Maesil-tea. _____ about you, Jinsu?

B: Well, my favorite _____ drink is Sikhye.

G: Sik.... Can you _____ that _____?

B: Sik-hye. It's _____ and cool.

G: I want to _____ it.

G: 내가 제일 좋아하는 한국 전통 음료는 매실차야. 진수, 너는 뭐니?
B: 음, 내가 제일 좋아하는 음료는 식혜야.
G: 식… 다시 말해 줄래?
B: 식-혜. 달고 시원해.
G: 먹어 보고 싶다.

Listen & Speak 1 A-2

B: Have you ever _____ *poke*?

G: Sorry, _____ you say that again, please?

B: *Po-ke*. It's a _____ that is _____ in Hawaii.

G: What's so _____ about it?

B: It's made _____ rice and fish. It's not _____ delicious _____ also very _____.

B: 너 포케 먹어 본 적 있니?
G: 미안, 다시 한 번 말해 줄래?
G: 포-케. 하와이에서 인기 많은 샐러드야.
G: 그게 뭐가 그렇게 특별한데?
G: 쌀이랑 생선으로 만들어. 맛도 있고 매우 건강한 음식이야.

Listen & Speak 1 B

1. **A:** _____ you ever tried *rasmalai*?
   B: _____, could you say that again?
   A: *Rasmalai*. It's a traditional _____ in India.
2. **A:** Have you ever _____ *brigadeiro*?
   B: Sorry, could you say that again?
   A: *Brigadeiro*. It's a _____ dessert in Brazil.
3. **A:** Have you _____ tried *macaron*?
   B: Sorry, could you say _____ again?
   A: *Macaron*. It's a traditional dessert _____ France.

1. A: 너 라스말라이 먹어 본 적 있니?
   B: 미안, 다시 말해 줄래?
   A: 라스말라이. 그건 인도의 전통 디저트야.
2. A: 너 브리가데이로 먹어 본 적 있니?
   B: 미안, 다시 말해 줄래?
   A: 브리가데이로. 그건 브라질의 전통 디저트야.
3. A: 너 마카롱 먹어 본 적 있니?
   B: 미안, 다시 말해 줄래?
   A: 마카롱. 그건 프랑스 전통 디저트야.

Listen & Speak 2 Listen

1. **B:** Could you _____ a good traditional dish?
   W: _____ Samgyetang. It'll give you energy.
2. **G:** _____ you recommend a good book _____ my little sister?
   M: I recommend this one. The story is _____.
3. **B:** Could you recommend a guitar for _____?
   W: How _____ this one? Many beginners play it.
4. **G:** Could you recommend a _____ for my dog?
   M: Sure. _____ about this? Dogs really like it.

1. B: 좋은 전통 음식 추천해 줄 수 있니?
   W: 삼계탕을 먹어봐. 너에게 에너지를 줄 거야.
2. G: 내 여동생에게 좋은 책을 추천해 줄 수 있니?
   M: 이것을 추천해. 이야기가 감동적이야.
3. B: 초보자를 위한 기타를 추천해 줄 수 있니?
   W: 이거 어때? 많은 초보자들이 그걸 연주해.
4. G: 내 개를 위한 간식을 추천해 줄래?
   M: 물론, 이거 어때? 개들이 그걸 정말 좋아해.

Listen & Speak 2 A-1

B: Tomorrow is my dad's birthday. I'd like to do something _____ for him.

G: _____ about _____ something for him? He _____ really like that.

B: That sounds great. Can you _____ something _____ to cook?

G: Umm. How _____ Gimchijeon? It's _____ to make and it's delicious.

B: Oh, that's a good _____. He'll love it.

B: 내일은 우리 아빠의 생신이야. 난 아빠를 위해 좀 특별한 것을 하고 싶어.
G: 아버지를 위해 무언가를 요리하는 건 어때? 정말 좋아하실 거야.
B: 그거 좋겠다. 요리하기 쉬운 것을 추천해 줄래?
G: 음, 김치전 어때? 만들기 쉽고 맛있어.
B: 오, 좋은 생각이다. 아빠가 좋아하실 거야.

Listen & Speak 2 B-2

M: _____ to the Sydney Information Center. Sydney has _____ places you will want to _____. The Rocks Markets is one of them. _____ you can buy art, clothing, books and many _____ things. You can also eat fresh, _____ _____ food. We _____ visiting the Rocks Markets and _____ the food and the fun there.

Real-Life Zone

M: Good afternoon. A table _____ two?

B: Yes.

M: This way please. _____ is the menu. I'll be _____ in a few minutes and _____ your order.

B: Okay. Thank you.

G: I don't know _____ about Korean food. Could you _____ something?

B: Well, I'd _____ the Bibimbap.

G: I'm sorry. _____ you say that again, please?

B: This one. Bi-bim-bap. It's _____ with lots of vegetables, beef and an egg over rice. It's tasty and it's also _____ for your _____.

G: That sounds great. I'll _____ it.

B: It's _____ with a spicy red pepper sauce. Is that _____?

G: No _____. I like spicy food.

Wrap Up 1-2

B: Tomorrow is my birthday.

G: I know. _____ you going to _____ a birthday party, Alex?

B: Yes. _____ you recommend a good _____ to have the party?

G: I'd _____ the Happy Snack House. The food is really good and it'll be large _____.

B: What dish _____ you _____?

G: I'd recommend the onion rings. They're _____!

B: Oh, just _____ about them makes my mouth _____.

해석

M: 시드니 여행 정보 센터에 오신 걸 환영합니다. 시드니는 여러분께서 방문하시고 싶으실 만한 장소들이 많습니다. Rocks Markets은 그 중의 하나죠. 그곳에선 예술 작품과 의류, 책 그리고 다른 많은 것들을 사실 수 있습니다. 또한 신선하고 맛있는 지역 음식도 드실 수 있습니다. 저희는 Rocks Markets에 가시는 것을 추천해 드리며 그곳에서 음식과 재미를 즐기시기를 추천합니다.

M: 안녕하세요. 두 분이신가요?
B: 네.
M: 이쪽으로 오십시오. 메뉴는 여기 있습니다. 잠시 후에 와서 주문 받겠습니다.
B: 알겠습니다. 감사합니다.
G: 나 한국 음식에 대해서 잘 알지 못해. 네가 추천해 줄래?
B: 음, 나는 비빔밥을 추천할게.
G: 미안, 다시 한 번 말해 줄래?
B: 이거. 비-빔-밥. 그것은 밥 위에 많은 야채들과 소고기, 그리고 계란을 얹어 만들어. 맛있고 건강에도 좋아.
G: 굉장한데. 난 그거 먹어 볼래.
B: 매운 고추장 양념이랑 같이 나오는 거야. 괜찮겠니?
G: 문제 없어. 나 매운 음식을 좋아해.

B: 내일은 내 생일이야.
G: 알고 있어. Alex, 생일 파티할 거니?
B: 응. 파티 열기에 좋은 장소 추천해 줄래?
G: 나는 Happy Snack House를 추천할게. 음식이 정말 맛있고 장소도 충분히 넓어.
B: 넌 무슨 음식을 추천해 줄래?
G: 나는 양파 튀김을 추천할게. 정말 환상적이야!
B: 오, 그거 생각하는 것만으로도 침이 고인다.

[01~02] 다음 대화를 읽고 물음에 답하시오.

> B: Hi, Grace. Those are pretty. What are they called?
> G: They're called *dango*.
> B: I'm sorry. _____(A)_____
> G: *Dan-go*. They're sweet and (B)make with rice cake powder. They're from Japan

01 위 대화의 빈칸 (A)에 알맞지 <u>않은</u> 것은?

① Can you say that again?
② Could you say that again?
③ Why did you say that again?
④ Excuse me?
⑤ Pardon me?

02 위 대화의 밑줄 친 (B)를 알맞은 형으로 고치시오.

➡ _____

[03~04] 다음 대화를 읽고 물음에 답하시오.

> B: Tomorrow is my dad's birthday. I'd like to do ⓐspecial something for him.
> G: How about ⓑcooking something for him? He ⓒwould really like that.
> B: That sounds ⓓgreat. (A)요리하기 쉬운 것을 추천해 줄래?(can, something)
> G: Umm. How about Gimchijeon? It's easy ⓔto make and it's delicious.
> B: Oh, that's a good idea. He'll love it.

03 위 대화의 밑줄 친 ⓐ~ⓔ 중에서 <u>어색한</u> 부분을 찾아 바르게 고치시오.

_____ ➡ _____

04 위 대화의 밑줄 친 (A)의 우리말을 주어진 단어를 이용해 영작하시오. (7 words)

➡ _____

[01~03] 다음 대화를 읽고 물음에 답하시오.

M: Good afternoon. A table for two?

B: Yes.

M: This way please. Here is the menu. I'll be back in (A)[few / a few] minutes and take your order.

B: Okay. Thank you.

G: I don't know much about Korean food. Could you recommend something?

B: Well, I'd recommend the Bibimbap.

G: I'm sorry. Could you say that again, please?

B: This one. Bi-bim-bap. It (B)[made / is made] with lots of vegetables, beef and an egg over rice. It's tasty and it's also good for your health.

G: That sounds great. I'll try it.

B: It (C)[served / is served] with a spicy red pepper sauce. Is that okay?

G: No problem. I like spicy food.

01 위 대화의 (A)~(C)에 알맞은 말이 바르게 짝지어진 것은?

① few – made – is served

② few – is made – served

③ a few – made – served

④ a few – is made – served

⑤ a few – is made – is served

02 위 대화에 나오는 M과 B의 관계로 적절한 것은?

① chef – critic　　② waiter – guest

③ chef – owner　　④ waiter – owner

⑤ critic – guest

서답형

03 According to B, describe what the Bibimbap is like. (8 words)

➡ _____

[04~05] 다음 대화를 읽고 물음에 답하시오.

B: Tomorrow is my birthday.

G: I know. Are you going to ⓐhave a birthday party, Alex?

B: Yes. Can you recommend a good place ⓑto have the party?

G: I'd recommend the Happy Snack House. The food is really good and (A)it'll be ⓒlarge enough.

B: What dish ⓓwould you recommend?

G: I'd recommend the onion rings. They're fantastic!

B: Oh, just ⓔthink about them makes my mouth water.

04 위 대화의 밑줄 친 ⓐ~ⓔ 중 어법상 어색한 것은?

① ⓐ　　② ⓑ　　③ ⓒ　　④ ⓓ　　⑤ ⓔ

서답형

05 위 대화의 밑줄 친 (A)it이 가리키는 것을 찾아 쓰시오. (4 words)

➡ _____

[06~08] 다음 대화를 읽고 물음에 답하시오.

G: My favorite Korean traditional drink is Maesil-tea. What about you, Jinsu?

B: Well, my favorite traditional drink is Sikhye.

G: Sik.... (A)Can you say that again?

B: Sik-hye. It's sweet and cool.

G: I want to try (B)it.

06 위 대화의 밑줄 친 (A)와 바꾸어 쓰기에 어색한 것은?

① Pardon? ② Excuse me?
③ Sorry for that. ④ I can't hear you.
⑤ What did you say?

서답형
07 위 대화에서 주어진 영영풀이가 가리키는 것을 찾아 쓰시오.

following or belonging to the ways of behaving or beliefs that have been established for a long time

➡ _____

서답형
08 위 대화에서 밑줄 친 (B)it이 가리키는 것을 찾아 쓰시오.

➡ _____

[09~11] 다음 글을 읽고 물음에 답하시오.

M: Welcome to the Sydney Information Center. Sydney has (A)[many / much] places you will want to visit. The Rocks Markets is one of them. There you can buy art, clothing, books and many other things. You can also eat fresh, tasty local food. We recommend (B)[to visit / visiting] the Rocks Markets and enjoying the food and the fun there.

서답형
09 위 글의 (A)와 (B)에서 적절한 것을 골라 쓰시오.

(A) _____ (B) _____

서답형
10 위 글에서 다음 영영풀이가 뜻하는 것을 찾아 쓰시오.

relating to a city, town or small district rather than an entire state or country

➡ _____

중요
11 위 글의 목적으로 가장 적절한 것은?

① to recommend ② to criticize
③ to demonstrate ④ to approve
⑤ to greet

[01~03] 다음 대화를 읽고 물음에 답하시오.

B: Have you ever tried *poke*?
(A) *Po-ke*. It's a salad that is popular in Hawaii.
(B) Sorry, could you say that again, please?
(C) What's so special about (a)it?
B: It's made with rice and fish. It's not only delicious but also very healthy.

01 주어진 두 문장 사이의 대화가 자연스럽게 이어지도록 순서 대로 배열하시오.

➡ _____

02 위 대화의 밑줄 친 (a)it이 가리키는 것을 쓰시오.

➡ _____

03 Why is *poke* so special and popular in Hawaii? (9 words)

➡ _____
_____

04 다음 대화의 밑줄 친 부분을 주어진 단어를 이용해 영작하 시오. (9 words)

A: 제 할머니를 위한 휴대폰을 추천해 주시겠어요?
(could, cell phone)
B: How about this phone? It's easy to use.

➡ _____
_____

[05~07] 다음 대화를 읽고 물음에 답하시오.

B: Tomorrow is my birthday.
G: I know. Are you going to have a birthday party, Alex?
B: Yes. (A)파티를 열 수 있는 좋은 장소를 추천해 줄래?
G: I'd recommend the Happy Snack House. The food is really good and it'll be large enough.
B: What dish would you recommend?
G: I'd recommend the onion rings. (B)They're fantastic!
B: Oh, just thinking about them makes my mouth water.

05 위 대화의 밑줄 친 (A)의 우리말을 주어진 단어를 이용해 바르게 영작하시오. (10 words) (can, have)

➡ _____
_____

06 위 대화의 밑줄 친 (B)가 가리키는 것을 영어로 쓰시오.

➡ _____

07 Why does G recommend the restaurant for B's birthday party? (11 words)

➡ _____
_____

Grammar

1 상관접속사 not only ~ but also ...

> • *Gogol-mogol* is **not only** good for people with a cold **but also** popular as a dessert for healthy people.
> 고골모골은 감기에 걸린 사람들에게 좋을 뿐 아니라 건강한 사람들의 후식으로도 인기가 있다.
>
> • John can speak **not only** English **but also** Chinese.
> John은 영어뿐 아니라 중국어도 말할 수 있다.

■ 상관접속사 'not only A but also B'는 'A뿐만 아니라 B도 또한'이라는 뜻이며, 'B as well as A'로 바꿀 수 있다. 접속사이므로 A와 B 자리에 명사 뿐 아니라 동사, 형용사, 준동사 등 어떤 것이든 올 수 있으나 A와 B에는 같은 품사가 와야 한다.

  • Eric is **not only** a singer **but also** an actor.
  = Eric is an actor **as well as** a singer. Eric은 가수일 뿐 아니라 배우이기도 하다.
  • Sunny **not only** sings **but also** plays the piano. Sunny는 노래뿐 아니라 피아노도 친다.

■ 상관접속사의 종류와 주어로 쓰일 때의 수의 일치

  (1) not only A but also B(= B as well as A): A뿐만 아니라 B도 또한 (B에 일치)
    • **Not only** you **but also** he sees the girl. 너뿐만 아니라 그도 소녀를 본다.
    = He **as well as** you **sees** the girl.

  (2) not A but B: A가 아니라 B (B에 일치)
    • **Not** you **but** he **sees** the girl. 당신이 아니라 그가 소녀를 본다.

  (3) both A and B: A와 B 둘 다 (복수 주어)
    • **Both** you **and** he **see** the girl. 당신과 그 (사람) 둘 다 소녀를 본다.

  (4) either A or B: A 또는 B 둘 중 하나 (동사와 가까운 주어에 일치)
    • **Either** you **or** he **sees** the girl. 당신 또는 그 (사람) 둘 중 하나는 소녀를 본다.

  (5) neither A nor B: A도 B도 아닌 (동사와 가까운 주어에 일치)
    • **Neither** you **nor** he **sees** the girl. 당신도 그도 소녀를 보지 않는다.

■ not only가 문두에 올 경우, 의문문 형식의 도치가 일어난다.
  • **Not only** is she smart, **but also** she is strong. 그녀는 똑똑할 뿐만 아니라 힘이 세다.

  • **Not only** did he join the club, **but also** he helped the children.
    그는 그 클럽에 가입했을 뿐만 아니라, 그 아이들을 돕기도 했다.

■ not only에서 only 대신 just, simply도 가능하고, but 뒤의 also는 생략해서 쓰기도 한다.
  • She bought **not just** his CDs **but** his posters. 그녀는 그의 CD뿐 아니라 포스터도 샀다.

핵심 Check

1. 다음 문장에서 어법상 **틀린** 곳을 찾아 바르게 고쳐 쓰시오.
  (1) Alex not only loves Jane but also respect her. _____ ➡ _____
  (2) Not only you but also she are going on the field trip. _____ ➡ _____

❷ 접속사 while

> • **While** people in Korea and Finland look for drinks when sick, many people in America want a bowl of chicken soup.
> 한국 사람들과 핀란드 사람들이 아플 때 음료를 찾는 반면, 미국의 많은 사람들은 닭고기 수프를 원한다.
>
> • My sister enjoys going out, **while** I enjoy staying home.
> 내 여동생은 나가는 것을 좋아하는데, 반면에 나는 집에 있는 것을 좋아한다.

■ 접속사 'while'은 부사절을 이끌며, 두 가지 뜻으로 사용된다.

(1) 다른 대상이나 상황을 비교 · 대조: '~인 반면에'

• **While** she is very good at science, she is so bad at literature.
그녀는 과학을 매우 잘하는 반면에, 문학은 아주 못 한다.

• My younger sister is very tall, **while** I am very short.
내 여동생은 매우 키가 크다, 반면에 나는 매우 작다.

(2) 시간: '~하는 동안에'

• Clean your room **while** your mom is preparing for dinner.
너의 엄마가 저녁 식사를 준비하시는 동안에 너의 방을 청소해라.

• Don't bother him **while** he's studying. 그가 공부하는 동안에 그를 귀찮게 하지 마라.
(주의) 전치사 during으로 바꿀 수 없다. Don't bother him ~~during~~ he's studying. (X)

■ while과 유사한 의미의 문장들을 다양하게 표현할 수 있다.

• **While** it is raining here, it is snowing in Daejeon. 여기는 비가 오는 반면에, 대전에는 눈이 온다.

= It is raining here, **but** it is snowing in Daejeon. (등위접속사 but으로 연결)

= It is raining here. **However**, it is snowing in Daejeon. (접속부사 however로 연결)

= **Though[Although]** it is raining here, it is snowing in Daejeon. (종속접속사 though로 연결)

핵심 Check

2. 다음 괄호 안에서 알맞은 말을 고르시오.

(1) He was watching TV (while / however) she was taking a shower.

(2) I am a late riser, (so / while) my brother is an early riser.

01 다음 빈칸에 들어갈 말로 알맞은 것은?

> Ginger tea not only warms your body but also _____.

① comforting your sore throat
② simple and easy to drink at a time
③ good for a cold in winter
④ different from a family to another
⑤ helps reduce the pain in your throat

02 다음 두 문장을 한 문장으로 바꿔 쓸 때, 빈칸에 들어갈 말로 가장 적절한 것은?

> • People in Korea and Finland look for drinks when sick.
> • But many people in America want a bowl of chicken soup.
> ➡ _____ people in Korea and Finland look for drinks when sick, many people in America want a bowl of chicken soup.

① Since   ② As   ③ While
④ Until   ⑤ Like

03 다음 중 어법상 어색한 것을 고르시오.

① The kids are interested either in swimming or in fishing.
② Sana has not only the character figure but also its house.
③ Doris' sisters not only dance well but sing well.
④ The gentleman is both generous and intelligent.
⑤ Mr. Kim not only speaks English but also handsome.

04 다음 빈칸에 공통으로 들어갈 말로 가장 적절한 것은? (대 · 소문자 무시.)

> • Drink the soup _____ it is still hot.
> • My sister enjoys going out _____ I enjoy reading books.
> • _____ many Koreans eat Samgyetang when they are sick, many people in India eat tomato soup.

① as   ② because   ③ though
④ before   ⑤ while

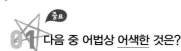
01 다음 중 어법상 <u>어색한</u> 것은?

① Not only his instruments but also my violin have that kind of problems.

② Jessy ate not only the bread but also the cookies that her brother had bought.

③ The cellist was not only kind to the young musicians but also influential to the members on the orchestra.

④ Not only the athletes but also the coach is working on the field.

⑤ My uncle has lived not only in Egypt but also in Italy.

[02~03] 다음 중 어법상 옳은 것을 고르시오.

02 ① The actor doesn't have neither a car nor a bike.

② Not only she was hungry but also couldn't walk any longer.

③ Both the animals and their owner is happy with the result.

④ Not only the girls but also the goose have lived in the farm since last year.

⑤ Mina bought her brother not only the books but also the bag.

03 ① Peter not only imagines but also making the plan of his holidays.

② Tell her not only what you like but also you want to buy.

③ Not only the employees but also the employer know what the product is.

④ Johnson not only teaches skiing but also sells a lot of ski boots.

⑤ Not only you but also Smith speak French well.

[04~05] 다음 우리말을 어법상 알맞게 영작한 것을 고르시오.

04
> 서양의 팬 케이크는 밀가루로 만들어지는 반면에, 녹두전은 간 녹두콩과 많은 다른 채소들로 만들어진다.

① While Nokdujeon is made with ground nokdu beans with many different vegetables, a western pancake is made with flour.

② Even though Nokdujeon is made with ground nokdu beans with many different vegetables, a western pancake is made with flour.

③ Since a western pancake is made with flour, Nokdujeon is made with ground nokdu beans with many different vegetables.

④ Whether a western pancake is made with flour, Nokdujeon is made with ground nokdu beans with many different vegetables.

⑤ While a western pancake is made with flour, Nokdujeon is made with ground nokdu beans with many different vegetables.

05 녹두전은 맛있을 뿐 아니라 영양가도 좋다.

① Nokdujeon is not delicious but nutritious.
② Nokdujeon not only is delicious but turns nutritious.
③ Nokdujeon is either delicious or also nutritious.
④ Nokdujeon is not only delicious but also nutritious.
⑤ Nokdujeon is delicious as well as nutritious.

06 다음 대화의 빈칸에 들어갈 말로 가장 적절한 것은?

> A: What is Dave doing outside?
> B: He is practicing basketball _____ it is raining.

① though   ② during   ③ like
④ since   ⑤ because

07 다음 두 문장을 한 문장으로 바꿔 쓸 때 적절하지 <u>않은</u> 것은?

① Susan can make a paper plane. + Or Jenny can make a paper plane.
➡ Either Susan or Jenny can make a paper plane.
② Michelle could grow fruits. + Michelle could make the juice as well.
➡ Not only could Michelle grow fruits but also make the juice.
③ Ellen likes the movie. + Yujin likes the movie, too.
➡ Not only Ellen but also Yujin likes the movie.

④ Cathy watches the TV program. + Mina watches the program, too.
➡ Both Cathy and Mina watches the TV program.
⑤ Bentley doesn't know the way to the supermarket. + His brothers don't know the way to the supermarket, either.
➡ Neither Bentley nor his brothers know the way to the supermarket.

08 다음 빈칸 (A)~(C)에 들어갈 알맞은 말이 바르게 짝지어진 것은?

> • (A)_____ Hyejin wears glasses, Yuna does not.
> • He wasn't late for class (B)_____ he got up late.
> • Soyeon has long hair, (C)_____ Yeji has short hair.

　　(A)　　　(B)　　　(C)
① Since – though – while
② Since – since – until
③ While – before – as
④ While – though – while
⑤ After – since – as

09 다음 〈보기〉의 문장과 가장 가까운 뜻을 가진 문장을 고르시오.

> ┤ 보기 ├
> Not only Grace but also Ken doesn't like swimming as well as running.

① Neither Grace nor Ken doesn't like swimming but also running.
② Neither Grace nor Ken likes both swimming and running.
③ Either Grace or Ken doesn't like swimming nor running.

④ Both Grace and Ken like not swimming but running.

⑤ Both Grace and Ken don't like swimming but running.

서답형

10 다음 두 문장을 한 문장으로 표현할 때, 빈칸에 들어갈 알맞은 말을 쓰시오.

> • Sean began to work out at the gym two weeks ago.
>
> • Sean's classmates started working out at the gym two weeks ago as well.
>
> ➡ _____ _____ _____ _____
>
> _____ his classmates have been working out at the gym for two weeks.

11 다음 두 문장을 접속사를 이용하여 한 문장으로 만들 때 가장 적절한 것은?

> • The virus came from China.
> • But some Chinese politicians blamed other countries.

① Since the virus came from China, some Chinese politicians blamed other countries.

② As some Chinese politicians blamed other countries, the virus came from China.

③ If the virus didn't come from China, some Chinese politicians would not blame other countries.

④ When some Chinese politicians blamed other countries, the virus came from China.

⑤ While the virus came from China, some Chinese politicians blamed other countries.

[12~13] 다음 중 어법상 옳은 문장은?

12 ① Not only the audience were surprised but also impressed.

② They can not only meet the Santa Clause but also sees the Rudolph in Finland.

③ Shakespeare only liked to write the plays but also acted himself.

④ Hermione had lost not only her husband's watch and also his ties.

⑤ The participants of the experiment not only arrived on time but also worked hard.

13 ① Charlotte liked not only Wilson but also Tylor.

② Can either you nor the doctor explain to me what made his condition worse?

③ Both Mina or her friend, Sana, watched the movie directed by the professor.

④ I think either Jade or her sister know how the problems were solved.

⑤ Not only Jessie but also Nadia wonder if the speaker is lying.

서답형

14 우리말과 일치하도록 (1)과 (2)에 공통으로 알맞은 접속사를 추가하여, 주어진 단어들을 바르게 배열하시오.

(1) 내가 샤워를 하는 동안에 전화가 울렸다.

(a shower, was, I, taking), the phone rang.

➡ _____

(2) 그녀는 지하철을 타고 출근하는 것을 선호하는 반면에, 나는 버스를 타는 것을 좋아한다.

(the subway, take, work, prefers, to, to, she), I like taking the bus.

➡ _____

01 다음 우리말과 일치하도록 괄호 안에 주어진 단어들을 바르게 배열하여 빈칸을 채우시오.

(1) 따뜻한 차가 감기에 걸린 사람들에게 좋을 뿐 아니라 건강한 사람들에게도 디저트로서 인기가 있다. (for, with, only, also, popular, good, but, not, people, colds)

➡ Warm tea is _____

_____ as a dessert

for healthy people.

(2) 고골모골은 달걀뿐만 아니라 꿀을 가지고도 만들어진다. (with, eggs, but, only, honey, not, made, also)

➡ *Gogol-mogol* is _____

_____.

(3) 당신뿐만 아니라 그들도 나에게 모두 친절했다. (they, you, but, not, were, only, also)

➡ _____

all kind to me.

(4) 민주와 예나 둘 다 그 문제에 책임이 있다. (Minju, Yena, responsible, and, are, for, both)

➡ _____

the problem.

02 다음은 고골모골을 만드는 방법이다. 각 빈칸에 아래 〈보기〉의 단어들 중에서 알맞은 것을 넣으시오.

┌─ 보기 ─┐
while   until   as   and   how
└────────┘

• (1)_____ to Make *Gogol-mogol*

1. Put the egg and the honey in a large cup (2)_____ mix them.

2. Pour half a cup of milk in a pan. Add the butter. Warm it (3)_____ the butter melts.

3. Pour the hot milk and butter into the cup with the egg and the honey. Stir (4)_____ you pour.

4. Drink (5)_____ it is hot.

[03~05] 다음에 소개하는 각각의 음료를 주어로 하여, 'not only ~ but also 구문'을 포함하는 완전한 한 문장을 영작하시오. (단, 소개에 나오는 and를 제외한 모든 단어를 사용할 것.)

03
┌────────────────────────────┐
│ A chicken soup: great for a sore throat │
│ and a stuffy nose   │
└────────────────────────────┘

➡ _____

_____

04
┌────────────────────────────┐
│ Samgyetang: warms your body and helps │
│ reduce the pain in your throat   │
└────────────────────────────┘

➡ _____

_____

05
┌────────────────────────────┐
│ The onion milk: a drink that is boiled │
│ with milk and chopped onion   │
└────────────────────────────┘

➡ _____

_____

[06~09] 다음 두 문장을 접속사 While로 시작하는 완전한 하나의 문장으로 쓰시오.

06
• Steve was born into a super rich family.
• Bob's parents were very poor.

➡ _____

_____

07

- Linda left my room to watch TV.
- I was doing my homework at that time.

➡ _____

_____

08

- Marco sets the alarm to wake up early in the morning.
- Marco's wife doesn't use the alarm.

➡ _____

_____

09

- I could hear so many kinds of birds singing in the woods.
- I was taking a walk along the lake park.

➡ _____

_____

_____

10 주어진 우리말을 〈조건〉에 맞게 영작하시오.

┌─ 조건 ┐

1. 'not only A but also B'를 사용할 것.
2. 주어진 단어를 괄호 안의 글자 수 조건에 맞추어 어법에 맞게 활용할 것.

(1) Ms. Elena, good teacher, great artist.
   (12 단어, Ms. Elena는 한 단어로 간주할 것.)
(2) can, Jenny, sing well, rap fast in English (12 단어)
(3) Dahyun, pretty, very smart (9 단어)
(4) Anna, her sisters, rich (9 단어)

(1) _____

_____

(2) _____

_____

(3) _____

_____

(4) _____

_____

11 다음 그림을 보고 괄호 안의 단어를 배열하여 빈칸을 알맞게 채우시오.

(1)

Samgyetang _____
_____ yummy.
(but, promotes, not, is, health, only, your)

(2)

VS

Andy enjoys pizza, _____
_____.
(the rest, love, while, members, his family, of, chicken)

Foods That Fight Colds

What do you do when you catch a cold? Of course, you want to stay
〜할 때'(접속사)   stay: 머물다. 특정 상태를 유지하다. stay warm: 따뜻함을 유지하다
warm, so maybe you put on more clothes. Some people like to drink
                    put on: 〜을 입다
hot tea. Ginger tea is something people in Korea often drink. With its
                    something 다음에 목적격 관계대명사 'that'이 생략되었음.
special taste, it warms your body and helps reduce the pain in your
throat. What do people drink or eat in other countries when they catch
a cold? Let's find out.

In Finland, where it is very cold in winter, people have a special
               문장에 삽입된 절로, 'Finland'를 보충 설명
drink when they catch a cold. It is a cup of onion milk. They put
chopped onion in milk and boil it over low heat for half an hour. This
다진 양파. 과거분사 chopped가 onion을 앞에서 수식
simple drink is said to be good for a cold.
              〜라고 한다   〜에 좋다
While people in Korea and Finland look for drinks when sick, many
〜인 반면에(대조를 나타내는 접속사)
people in America want a bowl of chicken soup. It is usually made
                           닭고기 수프 be made with: 〜으로 만들어지다.
with chicken and vegetables, but the recipe is different from one family
'with' 다음에는 재료가 나옴.
to another. Salt and pepper can be added before eating. People in
America believe that a bowl of warm chicken soup is great for a sore
throat and a stuffy nose.

ginger 생강
taste 맛
reduce 줄이다
pain 아픔, 통증
throat 목구멍, 목
catch a cold 감기에 걸리다
find out 알아내다, 발견하다
chop 다지다, 잘게 썰다
boil 끓다, 끓이다
recipe 요리법, 조리법
pepper 후추
sore 아픈, 따가운
stuffy (코가) 막힌

확인문제

● 다음 문장이 본문의 내용과 일치하면 T, 일치하지 않으면 F를 쓰시오.

1 Ginger tea is what people in Korea often drink. ☐

2 Ginger tea warms your body and helps reduce a fever. ☐

3 In Finland, people have a cup of onion milk when they catch a cold. ☐

4 To make onion milk, you need to put chopped onion in milk and boil it over high
   heat for an hour. ☐

5 Many people in America want a bowl of chicken soup when sick. ☐

6 The recipe for chicken soup is alike everywhere. ☐

In Russia and in Eastern Europe, when people get sick, they eat a dessert called *gogol-mogol*. It is made with eggs and honey.
고골모골이라고 불리는 후식. a dessert 다음에 'which is'가 생략

Some people add chocolate, butter, lemon juice, or milk to make it taste better. It looks like thick yogurt. People often drink a cup of warm *gogol-mogol* when they have a sore throat. *Gogol-mogol* is not only good for people with a cold but also popular as a dessert for healthy people. When served as a dessert, it is usually served cold or at room temperature.

to make: 부사적 용법(목적). make(사역동사)+목적어+동사원형
taste+형용사: ~한 맛이 나다
not only A but also B = B as well as A: A뿐만 아니라 B도

Why not try making one of the foods you have found out about? It will be fun and good for your health.
제안하는 표현, '~하는 게 어때?'

How to Make *Gogol-mogol* (Serves one)
~하는 방법   (음식의 양이) 돌아가다

You need: 1 egg, 1/2 cup of milk, honey (5 g), butter (15 g)

1. Put the egg and the honey in a large cup and mix them.

2. Pour half a cup of milk in a pan. Add the butter. Warm it until the butter melts.

3. Pour the hot milk and butter into the cup with the egg and the honey. Stir as you pour.
~하는 동안에(접속사)

4. Drink while it is hot.

---

eastern 동쪽의

honey 꿀

thick 진한, 걸쭉한

yogurt 요구르트

serve 제공하다

temperature 온도, 체온

mix 섞다

pour 붓다

melt 녹다

stir 젓다

확인문제

● 다음 문장이 본문의 내용과 일치하면 T, 일치하지 않으면 F를 쓰시오.

1 In Russia and in Eastern Europe, people eat a dessert called *gogol-mogol* when they get sick. ☐

2 *Gogol-mogol* is made with mainly chocolate, butter, lemon juice, or milk. ☐

3 *Gogol-mogol* is popular as a dessert for healthy people as well as good for people with a cold. ☐

4 When served as a dessert, *gogol-mogol* is usually served hot or at room temperature. ☐

5 To make one portion of *gogol-mogol*, 1/2 cup of milk is needed. ☐

6 When you make *gogol-mogol*, pepper is added to the milk before warming it. ☐

우리말을 참고하여 빈칸에 알맞은 말을 쓰시오.

1 Foods That _____ _____

2 What do you do when you _____ _____ _____?

3 Of course, you want to _____ _____, so maybe you put on more clothes.

4 Some people like _____ _____ _____ _____.

5 Ginger tea is _____ people in Korea _____ _____.

6 With its special taste, it warms your body and _____ _____ _____ _____ in your throat.

7 _____ _____ _____ _____ _____ _____ in other countries when they catch a cold?

8 Let's _____ _____.

9 In Finland, where it is very cold in winter, people _____ _____ _____ _____ when they catch a cold.

10 It is _____ _____ _____ _____ _____.

11 They put _____ _____ in milk and boil it _____ _____ _____ for half an hour.

12 This simple drink _____ _____ _____ _____ for a cold.

13 _____ people in Korea and Finland look for drinks when sick, many people in America want _____ _____ _____ _____ _____.

14 It is usually made with chicken and vegetables, but the recipe is different _____ _____ _____ _____.

15 Salt and pepper _____ _____ _____ before eating.

16 People in America believe that a bowl of warm chicken soup is _____ _____ _____ _____ _____ _____ _____.

1 감기와 싸우는 음식들

2 여러분은 감기에 걸리면 어떻게 하는가?

3 당연히, 따뜻함을 유지하고자 할 것이고, 아마도 옷을 더 입을 것이다.

4 몇몇 사람들은 따뜻한 차를 마시는 것을 좋아한다.

5 생강차는 한국인들이 자주 마시는 것이다.

6 특별한 맛과 함께, 그것은 여러분의 몸을 따뜻하게 하고 목 통증을 완화하는 데 도움을 준다.

7 다른 나라에서는 사람들이 감기에 걸렸을 때 무엇을 마시거나 먹을까?

8 함께 알아보자.

9 겨울이 매우 추운 핀란드에서는 사람들이 감기에 걸리면 특별한 음료를 마신다.

10 그것은 양파 우유이다.

11 그들은 우유에 잘게 썬 양파를 넣고 30분 동안 약한 불에서 끓인다.

12 이 단순한 음료는 감기에 좋다고 한다.

13 한국 사람들과 핀란드 사람들이 아플 때 음료를 찾는 반면, 미국의 많은 사람들은 닭고기 수프를 원한다.

14 그것은 보통 닭고기와 야채로 만들어지는데, 요리법은 가정마다 다르다.

15 소금과 후추를 먹기 전에 넣기도 한다.

16 미국인들은 따뜻한 닭고기 수프 한 그릇이 부은 목과 막힌 코에 좋다고 믿는다.

17 In Russia and in Eastern Europe, when people get sick, they eat a dessert _____ gogol-mogol.

18 It _____ _____ _____ eggs and honey.

19 Some people add chocolate, butter, lemon juice, or milk _____ _____ _____ _____ _____.

20 It _____ _____ thick yogurt.

21 People often drink a cup of warm gogol-mogol when they _____ _____ _____ _____.

22 Gogol-mogol is _____ _____ good for people with a cold _____ _____ popular as a dessert for healthy people.

23 When _____ as a dessert, it is usually served cold or _____ _____ _____.

24 _____ _____ try making one of the foods you have found out _____ ?

25 It will be fun and _____ _____ your health.

26 _____ _____ _____ Gogol-mogol (Serves one)

27 _____ _____ : 1 egg, 1/2 cup of milk, honey (5 g), butter (15 g)

28 1. Put the egg and the honey in a large cup and _____ _____.

29 2. _____ half a cup of milk in a pan.

30 _____ the butter.

31 _____ it until the butter _____.

32 3. _____ the hot milk and butter _____ the cup _____ the egg and the honey.

33 _____ _____ you pour.

34 4. Drink _____ it is hot.

17 러시아와 동유럽에서는 사람들이 아플 때, 고골모골이라는 후식을 먹는다.

18 그것은 달걀과 꿀로 만든다.

19 어떤 사람들은 그것을 더 맛있게 하기 위해 초콜릿, 버터, 레몬주스, 또는 우유를 첨가한다.

20 그것은 진한 요구르트처럼 보인다.

21 사람들은 목이 아플 때 종종 따뜻한 고골모골 한 잔을 마신다.

22 고골모골은 감기에 걸린 사람들에게 좋을 뿐만 아니라 건강한 사람들의 후식으로도 인기가 있다.

23 후식으로 제공될 때에는 보통 차갑게 또는 실온으로 제공된다.

24 여러분이 알아본 음식들 중 하나를 만들어 보는 것은 어떨까?

25 그것은 재미있고 여러분의 건강에 좋을 것이다.

26 고골모골 만드는 방법 (1인분)

27 필요한 것: 달걀 1개, 우유 1/2 컵, 꿀 5g, 버터 15g

28 1. 달걀과 꿀을 큰 컵에 넣고 섞는다.

29 2. 우유 반 컵을 팬에 붓는다.

30 버터를 추가한다.

31 버터가 녹을 때까지 데운다.

32 3. 뜨거운 우유와 버터를 달걀과 꿀이 있는 컵에 붓는다.

33 부으면서 젓는다.

34 4. 뜨거울 때 마신다.

● 우리말을 참고하여 본문을 영작하시오.

1 감기와 싸우는 음식들

➡ _____

2 여러분은 감기에 걸리면 어떻게 하는가?

➡ _____

3 당연히, 따뜻함을 유지하고자 할 것이고, 아마도 옷을 더 입을 것이다.

➡ _____

4 몇몇 사람들은 따뜻한 차를 마시는 것을 좋아한다.

➡ _____

5 생강차는 한국인들이 자주 마시는 것이다.

➡ _____

6 특별한 맛과 함께, 그것은 여러분의 몸을 따뜻하게 하고 목 통증을 완화하는 데 도움을 준다.

➡ _____

7 다른 나라에서는 사람들이 감기에 걸렸을 때 무엇을 마시거나 먹을까?

➡ _____

8 함께 알아보자.

➡ _____

9 겨울이 매우 추운 핀란드에서는 사람들이 감기에 걸리면 특별한 음료를 마신다.

➡ _____

10 그것은 양파 우유이다.

➡ _____

11 그들은 우유에 잘게 썬 양파를 넣고 30분 동안 약한 불에서 끓인다.

➡ _____

12 이 단순한 음료는 감기에 좋다고 한다.

➡ _____

13 한국 사람들과 핀란드 사람들이 아플 때 음료를 찾는 반면, 미국의 많은 사람들은 닭고기 수프를 원한다.

➡ _____

14 그것은 보통 닭고기와 야채로 만들어지는데, 요리법은 가정마다 다르다.

➡ _____

15 소금과 후추를 먹기 전에 넣기도 한다.

➡ _____

16 미국인들은 따뜻한 닭고기 수프 한 그릇이 부은 목과 막힌 코에 좋다고 믿는다.

➡ _____

17 러시아와 동유럽에서는 사람들이 아플 때, 고골모골이라는 후식을 먹는다.

➡ _____

18 그것은 달걀과 꿀로 만든다.

➡ _____

19 어떤 사람들은 그것을 더 맛있게 하기 위해 초콜릿, 버터, 레몬주스, 또는 우유를 첨가한다.

➡ _____

20 그것은 진한 요구르트처럼 보인다.

➡ _____

21 사람들은 목이 아플 때 종종 따뜻한 고골모골 한 잔을 마신다.

➡ _____

22 고골모골은 감기에 걸린 사람들에게 좋을 뿐만 아니라 건강한 사람들의 후식으로도 인기가 있다.

➡ _____

23 후식으로 제공될 때에는 보통 차갑게 또는 실온으로 제공된다.

➡ _____

24 여러분이 알아본 음식들 중 하나를 만들어 보는 것은 어떨까?

➡ _____

25 그것은 재미있고 여러분의 건강에 좋을 것이다.

➡ _____

26 고골모골 만드는 방법 (1인분)

➡ _____

27 필요한 것: 달걀 1개, 우유 1/2컵, 꿀 5g, 버터 15g

➡ _____

28 1. 달걀과 꿀을 큰 컵에 넣고 섞는다.

➡ _____

29 2. 우유 반 컵을 팬에 붓는다.

➡ _____

30 버터를 추가한다.

➡ _____

31 버터가 녹을 때까지 데운다.

➡ _____

32 3. 뜨거운 우유와 버터를 달걀과 꿀이 있는 컵에 붓는다.

➡ _____

33 부으면서 젓는다.

➡ _____

34 4. 뜨거울 때 마신다.

➡ _____

[01~03] 다음 글을 읽고 물음에 답하시오.

What do you do when you catch a cold? (①) Of course, ⓐyou want to stay warmly, so maybe you put on more clothes. (②) Some people like to drink hot tea. (③) Ginger tea is something people in Korea often drink. (④) What do people drink or eat in other countries when they catch a cold? (⑤) Let's find out.

01 위 글의 흐름으로 보아, 주어진 문장이 들어가기에 가장 적절한 곳은?

With its special taste, it warms your body and helps reduce the pain in your throat.

①   ②   ③   ④   ⑤

서답형

02 위 글의 밑줄 친 ⓐ에서 어법상 틀린 부분을 찾아 고치시오.

_____ ➡ _____

중요

03 위 글의 뒤에 올 내용으로 가장 알맞은 것을 고르시오.

① the various ways to stay warm when people catch a cold

② the clothes people like to wear when they catch a cold

③ what people in other countries drink or eat as a dessert

④ the simple way to reduce the pain in the throat

⑤ the things people around the world drink or eat to fight colds

[04~06] 다음 글을 읽고 물음에 답하시오.

ⓐWhile people in Korea and Finland look for drinks when sick, many people in America want a bowl of chicken soup. It is usually made with chicken and vegetables, but the recipe is different from one family to another. Salt and pepper can be added before eating. People in America believe that a bowl of warm chicken soup is great for a sore throat and a stuffy nose.

04 위 글의 밑줄 친 ⓐWhile과 같은 의미로 쓰인 것을 모두 고르시오.

① Did anyone call while I was away?

② While Tom's very good at science, his brother is absolutely hopeless.

③ It took him a while to calm down.

④ Strike while the iron is hot.

⑤ The walls are green, while the ceiling is white.

서답형

05 다음 문장에서 위 글의 내용과 다른 부분을 찾아 고치시오.

Many people in America look for drinks when sick.

➡ _____

_____

_____

서답형

06 What can be added to chicken soup before eating it? Answer in English in a full sentence. (6 words)

➡ _____

[07~09] 다음 글을 읽고 물음에 답하시오.

In Finland, where it is very cold in winter, people have a special drink when they catch a cold. ⓐIt is a cup of onion milk. They put _____ⓑ_____ onion in milk and boil it (A)[above / over] low heat (B)[during / for] half an hour. This simple drink is said to be good (C)[at / for] a cold.

서답형

07 다음 빈칸에 알맞은 단어를 넣어 위 글의 밑줄 친 ⓐ이 가리키는 것을 완성하시오.

_____ people have in Finland when they catch a cold

서답형

08 위 글의 빈칸 ⓑ에 chop을 알맞은 형태로 쓰시오.

➡ _____

서답형

09 위 글의 괄호 (A)~(C)에서 문맥이나 어법상 알맞은 낱말을 골라 쓰시오.

(A) _____ (B) _____ (C) _____

[10~12] 다음 글을 읽고 물음에 답하시오.

In Russia and in Eastern Europe, when people get sick, they eat a dessert called *gogol-mogol*. (①) Some people add chocolate, butter, lemon juice, or milk to make it taste better. (②) It looks like thick yogurt. (③) People often drink a cup of warm *gogol-mogol* when they have a sore throat. (④) *Gogol-mogol* is ⓐ<u>not only</u> good for people with a cold but also popular as a dessert for healthy people. (⑤) When served as a dessert, it is usually served cold or at room temperature.

10 위 글의 흐름으로 보아, 주어진 문장이 들어가기에 가장 적절한 곳은?

It is made with eggs and honey.

①   ②   ③   ④   ⑤

11 위 글의 밑줄 친 ⓐnot only와 바꿔 쓸 수 있는 말을 모두 고르시오.

① as well as   ② not just
③ not   ④ not simply
⑤ not merely

12 Which question CANNOT be answered after reading the passage?

① In Russia and in Eastern Europe, when people get sick, what do they eat?
② What is *gogol-mogol* made with?
③ To make *gogol-mogol* taste better, what do some people add?
④ How long does it take to make *gogol-mogol*?
⑤ Do people eat *gogol-mogol* only when they're sick?

[13~15] 다음 글을 읽고 물음에 답하시오.

While people in Korea and Finland look for drinks when sick, many people in America want ___ⓐ___ chicken soup. It is usually made with chicken and vegetables, but ⓑ요리법은 가정마다 다르다. Salt and pepper can be added before eating. People in America believe that a bowl of warm chicken soup is great for a sore throat and a stuffy nose.

13 위 글의 빈칸 ⓐ에 들어갈 알맞은 말을 고르시오.

① a glass of   ② a bottle of

③ a piece of   ④ a bowl of

⑤ a plate of

서답형

14 위 글의 밑줄 친 ⓑ의 우리말에 맞게 주어진 어휘를 이용하여 9 단어로 영작하시오.

the recipe, from, another

➡ _____

중요

15 Which question CANNOT be answered after reading the passage?

① What do people in Korea and Finland look for when sick?

② What do many people in America want when sick?

③ How long does chicken soup have to be boiled?

④ What is chicken soup usually made with?

⑤ What do people in America believe warm chicken soup is great for?

16 주어진 문장 다음에 이어질 글의 순서로 가장 적절한 것은?

What do you do when you catch a cold?

(A) Ginger tea is something people in Korea often drink. With its special taste, it warms your body and helps reduce the pain in your throat.
(B) Of course, you want to stay warm, so maybe you put on more clothes. Some people like to drink hot tea.
(C) What do people drink or eat in other countries when they catch a cold? Let's find out.

① (A) – (C) – (B)   ② (B) – (A) – (C)

③ (B) – (C) – (A)   ④ (C) – (A) – (B)

⑤ (C) – (B) – (A)

[17~18] 다음 글을 읽고 물음에 답하시오.

In Russia and in Eastern Europe, when people get sick, they eat a dessert called ① *gogol-mogol*. It is made with eggs and honey. Some people add chocolate, butter, lemon juice, or milk to make ②it taste better. ③It looks like thick ④yogurt. People often drink a cup of warm *gogol-mogol* when they have a sore throat. *Gogol-mogol* is not only good for people with a cold but also popular as a dessert for healthy people. When served as a dessert, ⑤it is usually served cold or at room temperature.

17 밑줄 친 ①~⑤ 중에서 가리키는 대상이 나머지 넷과 <u>다른</u> 것은?

①   ②   ③   ④   ⑤

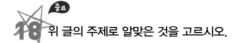 위 글의 주제로 알맞은 것을 고르시오.

① the ingredients for *gogol-mogol*, a popular dessert in Russia and in Eastern Europe

② the best way to relieve the symptoms of a cold

③ *gogol-mogol*, a popular dessert in sickness and in health in Russia and in Eastern Europe

④ the recipe for *gogol-mogol*, a popular dessert in sickness and in health

⑤ the effective therapy to treat disease

[19~20] 다음 글을 읽고 물음에 답하시오.

What do you do when you catch a cold? Of course, you want to stay warm, so maybe you put on more clothes. Some people like to drink hot tea. Ginger tea is something people in Korea often drink. With its special taste, it warms your body and helps reduce the pain in your throat. What do people drink or eat in other countries when they catch a cold? Let's find out.

19 위 글의 제목으로 알맞은 것을 고르시오.

① Put on More Clothes to Stay Warm

② The Best Hot Tea to Drink When You Feel Cold

③ What Do You Drink or Eat When You Catch a Cold?

④ The Way You Can Avoid Catching a Cold

⑤ How to Reduce the Pain in Your Throat

20 According to the passage, which is NOT true?

① Some people put on more clothes when they catch a cold.

② Some people like to drink hot tea when they catch a cold.

③ Koreans often drink ginger tea when they catch a cold.

④ Ginger tea has a special smell.

⑤ Ginger tea warms your body and helps reduce the pain in your throat.

[21~22] 다음 글을 읽고 물음에 답하시오.

Why not try ⓐmake one of the foods you have found out about? It will be fun and good for your health.

_____ⓑ_____ (Serves one)

You need: 1 egg, 1/2 cup of milk, honey (5 g), butter (15 g)

1. Put the egg and the honey in a large cup and mix them.

2. Pour half a cup of milk in a pan. Add the butter. Warm it until the butter melts.

3. Pour the hot milk and butter into the cup with the egg and the honey. Stir as you pour.

4. Drink while it is hot.

21 위 글의 밑줄 친 ⓐmake를 알맞은 형으로 고치시오.

➡ _____

22 위 글의 빈칸 ⓑ에 들어갈 제목으로 알맞은 것을 고르시오.

① What Is Good for Your Health?

② How to Make *Gogol-mogol*

③ What Is *Gogol-mogol* Made with?

④ The Reason *Gogol-mogol* Tastes Good

⑤ What Does *Gogol-mogol* Look Like?

[01~03] 다음 글을 읽고 물음에 답하시오.

What do you do when you catch a cold? Of course, ⓐyou want to stay warm, so maybe you take off more clothes. Some people like to drink hot tea. ⓑ생강차는 한국인들이 자주 마시는 것이다. With its special taste, it warms your body and helps reduce the pain in your throat. What do people drink or eat in other countries when they catch a cold? Let's find out.

01 위 글의 밑줄 친 ⓐ에서 흐름상 어색한 부분을 찾아 고치시오.

⟶ _____ ⟹ _____

02 위 글의 밑줄 친 ⓑ의 우리말에 맞게 주어진 어휘를 알맞게 배열하시오.

> often / people in Korea / something / is / drink / ginger tea

➡ _____

_____

03 다음 빈칸 (A)와 (B)에 알맞은 단어를 넣어 '생강차의 효능'을 완성하시오.

> It (A)_____ your body and helps to reduce the pain in your (B)_____.

[04~06] 다음 글을 읽고 물음에 답하시오.

In Finland, ___ⓐ___ it is very cold in winter, people have a special drink when they catch a cold. It is a cup of onion milk. They put chopped onion in milk and boil ⓑit over low heat for half an hour. ⓒThis simple drink is said to be good for a cold.

04 위 글의 빈칸 ⓐ에 들어갈 알맞은 한 단어를 쓰시오.

➡ _____

05 위 글의 밑줄 친 ⓑit이 가리키는 것을 본문에서 찾아 쓰시오.

➡ _____

06 위 글의 밑줄 친 ⓒ를 다음과 같이 바꿔 쓸 때 빈칸에 들어갈 알맞은 말을 4 단어로 쓰시오.

> It is said that _____ _____ _____
> _____ good for a cold.

[07~09] 다음 글을 읽고 물음에 답하시오.

(A)While people in Korea and Finland look for drinks when sick, many people in America want a bowl of chicken soup. (B)It is usually made with chicken and vegetables, but the recipe is different from one family to another. Salt and pepper can ___ⓐ___ before eating. People in America believe that a bowl of warm chicken soup is great for a sore throat and a stuffy nose.

07 위 글의 빈칸 ⓐ에 add를 알맞은 형태로 쓰시오.

➡ _____

08 위 글의 밑줄 친 문장 (A)에 생략된 말을 넣어 문장을 다시 쓰시오.

➡ _____

_____

중요

09 위 글의 밑줄 친 (B)를 능동태로 고치시오.

➡ _____

[10~12] 다음 글을 읽고 물음에 답하시오.

ⓐWhy not try making one of the foods you have found out about? It will be fun and good for your health.
How to Make *Gogol-mogol* (Serves one)
ⓑYou need: 1 egg, 1/2 cup of milk, honey (5 g), butter (15 g)
1. Put the egg and the honey in a large cup and mix ⓒthem.
2. Pour half a cup of milk in a pan. Add the butter. Warm it until the butter melts.
3. Pour the hot milk and butter into the cup with the egg and the honey. Stir as you pour.
4. Drink while it is hot.

10 위 글의 밑줄 친 ⓐ를 다음과 같이 바꿔 쓸 때 빈칸에 들어갈 알맞은 단어를 쓰시오.

(1) How about _____ making one of the foods you have found out about?

(2) _____ _____ _____ try making one of the foods you have found out about?

고 난이도

11 위 글의 밑줄 친 ⓑYou need와 바꿔 쓸 수 있는 한 단어를 철자 l로 시작하여 쓰시오.

➡ _____

12 위 글의 밑줄 친 ⓒthem이 가리키는 것을 본문에서 찾아 쓰시오.

➡ _____

[13~14] 다음 글을 읽고 물음에 답하시오.

In Russia and in Eastern Europe, when people get sick, they eat a dessert called *gogol-mogol*. It is made with eggs and honey. ⓐSome people add chocolate, butter, lemon juice, or milk to make it tasting better. It looks like thick yogurt. People often drink a cup of warm *gogol-mogol* when they have a sore throat. ⓑGogol-mogol is not only good for people with a cold but also popular as a dessert for healthy people. When served as a dessert, it is usually served cold or at room temperature.

중요

13 위 글의 밑줄 친 ⓐ에서 어법상 틀린 부분을 찾아 고치시오.

_____ ➡ _____

고 난이도

14 위 글의 밑줄 친 ⓑ를 as well as를 사용하여 고쳐 쓰시오.

➡ _____

_____

해석

After You Read B

Look! I've made *gogol-mogol*.

Happy07: What is *gogol-mogol*?

└, Bora: It's a dessert that people in Russia and in Eastern Europe eat when
　　　　　　　　목적격 관계대명사

　　they are sick.

Yumyum: It looks delicious. What is it made with?
　　　　　　　　　　　　　　　~으로 만들어지다

└, Bora: It's made with eggs and honey.
　　　　　　　with 다음에는 재료가 온다.

Yumyum: What's that you put on top of it?
　　　　　　　　　　　　　　　　↓ taste+형용사: ~한 맛이 나다

└, Bora: I put chocolate on top to make it taste better.
　　　　　　　　　　　　부사적 용법(목적),　사역동사 make+목적어+동사원형.

Happy07: Do people also eat it when they're not sick?
　　　　　　　　　　　　　　　gogol-mogol

└, Bora: Sure. It's a popular dessert. When served as a dessert, it's usually
　　　　　　　　　　　　　　　　When과 served 사이에 it is가 생략됨.

　　served cold or at room temperature.

구문해설 · **eastern**: 동쪽의 · **honey**: 꿀 · **serve**: 제공하다 · **temperature**: 온도, 체온

봐! 나는 고골모골을 만들었어.

Happy07: 고골모골이 뭐야?

보라: 그것은 러시아와 동유럽에서 사람들이 아플 때 먹는 후식이야.

Yumyum: 그것은 맛있어 보여. 그것은 무엇으로 만들어지니?

보라: 그것은 달걀과 꿀로 만들어져.

Yumyum: 그것 꼭대기에 올린 것이 뭐니?

보라: 나는 그것을 더 맛있게 하기 위해 꼭대기에 초콜릿을 올렸어.

Happy07: 사람들이 아프지 않을 때도 그것을 먹니?

보라: 물론이야. 그것은 인기 있는 후식이야. 후식으로 제공될 때에는 보통 차갑게 또는 실온으로 제공돼.

Writing Workshop

While many Koreans eat Samgyetang when they are sick, many people in
'대조'의 접속사 ~인 반면에

India eat tomato soup. Here is how to make it.
　　　　　　　　　　유도부사(도치)　의문사+to부정사(명사구)

You need: 1 tomato, some water, black pepper, salt

First, chop one fresh tomato. Then put the chopped tomato in a pan and pour
　　　　　　　　　　　　　　　　　　　　　　과거분사(수동)

some water over it. Next, boil the mixture for ten minutes. Then turn off the

heat and leave it to cool down. Next, blend it until it is smooth. Finally, add
　　　　　　자동사: to be cooled(×)　　　　　'시간'의 접속사 will be(×)

some black pepper and salt. Now you can enjoy the tomato soup. This tomato

soup is not only healthy but also delicious.
　　　　　　not only 형용사 but also 형용사

구문해설 · **black pepper**: 후추 · **chop**: (잘게) 썰다, 다지다 · **blend**: 섞다, 혼합하다

많은 한국인들이 아플 때 삼계탕을 먹는 반면에, 인도의 많은 사람들은 토마토 수프를 먹는다. 여기 그것을 만드는 방법이 있다.

필요한 것: 토마토 한 개, 물 약간, 후추, 소금

첫 번째로, 신선한 토마토 한 개를 다진다. 그 후, 다진 토마토를 팬 위에 놓고 그 위에 물을 조금 붓는다. 다음으로, 그 혼합물을 10분간 끓인다. 불을 끄고 식도록 둔다. 다음, 부드러워질 때까지 그것을 섞는다. 마지막으로, 후추와 소금을 약간 넣는다. 이제 토마토 수프를 즐길 수 있다. 이 토마토 수프는 건강에 좋을 뿐 아니라 맛있다.

영역별 핵심문제

01 다음 짝지어진 단어의 관계가 같도록 빈칸에 알맞은 말을 쓰시오.

> blend : compound = while : _____

02 다음 중 밑줄 친 부분의 뜻풀이가 바르지 <u>않은</u> 것은?

① <u>Blend</u> the flour with the milk to make a smooth paste. (혼합하다)
② The stage is covered with sand for the <u>desert</u> scenes. (후식)
③ Jasmine was <u>hurt</u> by the coldness in his voice. (아프다, 아프게 하다)
④ <u>Local</u> entertainments are listed in the newspaper. (지역의)
⑤ This <u>recipe</u> will be enough for ten servings. (요리법)

03 다음 주어진 문장의 밑줄 친 <u>warm</u>과 같은 의미로 쓰인 것은?

> The <u>warm</u> climate favours many types of tropical plants.

① Take a <u>warm</u> bath to soothe tense, tired muscles.
② It'll <u>warm</u> up in the day time in the spring.
③ <u>Warm</u> up before lifting heavy weights.
④ The room was decorated in <u>warm</u> shades of red and orange.
⑤ I wish it would <u>warm</u> up soon. It's been so cold.

04 다음 우리말을 주어진 단어를 이용하여 영작하시오.

> 너는 입을 통해서가 아니라, 코를 통해서 호흡해야 한다. (breathe through)

➡ _____

05 다음 영영풀이에 해당하는 단어로 알맞은 것은?

> to flow, as from one container to another, or into, over, or on something

① wear ② pour ③ stir
④ reduce ⑤ melt

[06~07] 다음 대화를 읽고 물음에 답하시오.

B: Alice, what's that you're eating?
G: It's *rasmalai*.
B: Ra.... (A)<u>Could you say that again?</u>
G: *Ras-ma-lai*. It's like a cheesecake in a sweet cream. It's a traditional food in India.

06 위 대화의 밑줄 친 (A)와 바꿔 쓸 수 있는 표현을 두 개 이상 쓰시오.

➡ _____

07 Where is *rasmalai* from? (4 words)

➡ _____

08 다음 대화의 밑줄 친 부분과 바꿔 쓸 수 없는 것은?

> A: Have you ever tried *macaron*?
> B: <u>Could you say that again?</u>
> A: *Macaron*. It's a traditional dessert in France.

① Sorry?
② Pardon?
③ I beg your pardon?
④ Can you lower your voice down?
⑤ Say that again, please?

09 다음 대화의 빈칸에 들어갈 수 없는 것은?

> A: _____ a good traditional dish?
> B: Try Samgyetang. It'll give you energy.

① Can you recommend
② Could you recommend
③ Can you give me a recommendation for
④ Could you give me a recommendation for
⑤ Can I make a recommendation for

[10~12] 다음 대화를 읽고 물음에 답하시오.

> M: Good afternoon. A table for two?
> B: Yes.
> M: This way please. Here is the menu. ① I'll be back in a few minutes and take your order.
> B: Okay. Thank you.
> G: ② Could you recommend something?
> B: ③ Well, I'd recommend the Bibimbap.
> G: I'm sorry. Could you say that again, please? ④
> B: This one. Bi-bim-bap. It's made with lots of vegetables, beef and an egg over rice. It's tasty and it's also good for your health.
> G: That sounds great. ⑤ I'll try it.
> B: It's served with a spicy red pepper sauce. Is that okay?
> G: No problem. I like spicy food.

10 위 대화의 ①~⑤ 중에서 주어진 문장이 들어가기에 가장 적절한 곳은?

> I don't know much about Korean food.

①   ②   ③   ④   ⑤

11 다음 중 위 대화를 읽고 대답할 수 없는 질문은?

① What did M say to B and G?
② What kind of food did B recommend G?
③ Has G ever tried any Korean food before?
④ What is the Bibimbap made with?
⑤ What is the Bibimbap good for?

12 위 대화에 나타난 G의 심경으로 가장 적절한 것을 고르시오.

① concerned   ② bored
③ shocked   ④ scared
⑤ excited

[13~14] 다음 중 어법상 어색한 문장을 모두 고르시오.

13
① April not only lent me her house for a week but also offered me a job.
② Not only Karen but also Tylor had the courage to fight against the disease.
③ My mom made not only those candies but also very yummy.
④ The people were already aware of not only the event but also the rumors.
⑤ Not only Victor was good at running, but also he played soccer well.

14
① Both the owners or the borrowers of the houses were disappointed with the government policy.
② Neither Jordan nor his basketball team members were happy with the scores.
③ Either Minsu and his friends are coming this evening.
④ Not only can the villagers imagine the story but they also guess the ending.
⑤ Not only you but also your teacher was at the meeting.

[15~16] 다음 주어진 두 문장을 같은 의미의 한 문장으로 알맞게 바꾼 것은?

15
• Sarah believed the news.
• Her daughter didn't believe it.

① Sarah believed the news as her daughter didn't.
② Since Sarah believed the news, her daughter didn't believe it.
③ Sarah believed the news before her daughter didn't.
④ Sarah believed the news while her daughter didn't.
⑤ Sarah believed the news whether her daughter didn't believe it or not.

16
• Harrison was fired from the company.
• Others had a job and could make a living.

① Because Harrison was fired from the company, others had a job and could make a living.
② While Harrison was fired from the company, others had a job and could make a living.
③ Harrison was fired from the company, and thus others had a job and could make a living.
④ If Harrison was fired from the company, others had a job and could make a living.
⑤ During Harrison was fired from the company, others had a job and could make a living.

Reading

[17~18] 다음 글을 읽고 물음에 답하시오.

In Finland, ⓐwhere it is very cold in winter, people have a special drink when they catch a cold. It is a cup of onion milk. They put chopped onion in milk and boil it over low heat for half an hour. This simple drink is said to be good for a cold.

17 위 글의 밑줄 친 ⓐwhere와 문법적 쓰임이 같은 것을 고르시오.

① Where do you live?
② This is the house where I was born.
③ Where there's a will, there's a way.
④ Where are you going?
⑤ I don't know where to go.

18 According to the passage, which is NOT true?

① In Finland, it is very cold in winter.
② In Finland, people have a cup of onion milk when they catch a cold.
③ To make the onion milk, it is necessary to put chopped onion in milk.
④ You should boil the chopped onion in milk over low heat for thirty minutes.
⑤ The onion milk is too simple to be good for a cold.

[19~20] 다음 글을 읽고 물음에 답하시오.

While people in Korea and Finland look for drinks when sick, many people in America want a bowl of chicken soup. ⓐIt is usually made with chicken and vegetables, but the recipe is different from one family to another. Salt and pepper can be added before eating. People in America believe that a bowl of warm chicken soup is great for a sore throat and a stuffy nose.

19 위 글의 밑줄 친 ⓐIt이 가리키는 것을 본문에서 찾아 쓰시오.

➡ _____

20 본문의 내용과 일치하도록 다음 빈칸에 알맞은 단어를 쓰시오.

Unlike people in Korea and Finland, many people in America look for _____ _____ _____ _____ _____ when sick.

[21~23] 다음 글을 읽고 물음에 답하시오.

In Russia and in Eastern Europe, when people get sick, they eat a dessert called *gogol-mogol*. It is made ____ⓐ____ eggs and honey. Some people add chocolate, butter, lemon juice, or milk (A)그것을 더 맛있게 하기 위해. It looks like thick yogurt. People often drink a cup of warm *gogol-mogol* when they have a sore throat. *Gogol-mogol* is not only good for people with a cold but also popular ____ⓑ____ a dessert for healthy people. When ____ⓒ____ as a dessert, it is usually served cold or at room temperature.

21 위 글의 빈칸 ⓐ와 ⓑ에 들어갈 전치사가 바르게 짝지어진 것은?

	ⓐ	ⓑ		ⓐ	ⓑ
①	with	as	②	from	at
③	of	for	④	from	as
⑤	with	for			

22 위 글의 빈칸 ⓒ에 serve를 알맞은 형태로 쓰시오.

➡ _____

23 위 글의 밑줄 친 (A)의 우리말에 맞게 주어진 어휘를 이용하여 5 단어로 영작하시오.

make

➡ _____

[24~26] 다음 글을 읽고 물음에 답하시오.

While many Koreans eat Samgyetang when they are sick, many people in India eat tomato soup. Here is how to make it.

You need: 1 tomato, some water, black pepper, salt

First, chop one fresh tomato. Then put the chopped tomato in a pan and pour some water over it. Next, boil the mixture for ten minutes. Then turn off the heat and leave it to cool down. Next, blend it until it is smooth. Finally, add some black pepper and salt. Now you can enjoy the tomato soup. ⓐThis tomato soup is not only healthy but also delicious.

24 다음 중 인도의 토마토 수프를 만드는 재료가 아닌 것을 고르시오.

① 토마토　　② 물　　③ 쌀
④ 후추　　⑤ 소금

25 What should be mixed in a pan first? Answer in English in a full sentence.

➡ _____
_____

26 위 글의 밑줄 친 ⓐ와 같은 뜻이 아닌 문장을 고르시오.

① This tomato soup is not only healthy but delicious as well.
② This tomato soup is not just healthy but also delicious.
③ This tomato soup is delicious as well as healthy.
④ This tomato soup is not healthy but delicious.
⑤ Besides being healthy, this tomato soup is delicious.

01 다음 영영풀이가 가리키는 것을 고르시오. 출제율 90%

> to change from a liquid to a gas as a result of heat

① boil　　② chop　　③ soup
④ stir　　⑤ taste

02 〈보기〉에서 알맞은 단어를 골라 문장을 완성하시오. 출제율 100%

> ── 보기 ──
> a bottle of / a cup of / as well as / be different from / is good for

(1) I bought _____ wine for her housewarming party.
(2) Exercising every day _____ your health.
(3) The mind _____ the body needs exercise.

[03~05] 다음 글을 읽고 물음에 답하시오.

M: Welcome to the Sydney Information Center. Sydney has many places you will want to visit. The Rocks Markets is one of (A)them. There you can buy art, clothing, books and many other things. You can also eat fresh, tasty local food. (B)저희는 the Rocks Markets에 방문하실 것을 추천합니다, and enjoying the food and the fun there.

03 위 글의 밑줄 친 (A)them이 가리키는 것을 찾아 쓰시오. (8 words) 출제율 90%

➡ _____

04 위 글의 밑줄 친 (B)를 주어진 우리말을 이용하여 영작하시오. 출제율 95%

➡ _____

05 위 글에서 언급된 the Rocks Markets에서 찾을 수 없는 것은? 출제율 100%

① paintings　② clothes　③ hotels
④ books　　⑤ local food

[06~08] 다음 대화를 읽고 물음에 답하시오.

B: Tomorrow is my dad's birthday. I'd like to do something special for him.
G: (A)How about cooking something for him? He would really like that.
B: That sounds great. Can you recommend something easy to cook?
G: Umm. How about Gimchijeon? (B)그건 만들기 쉽고 맛있어.
B: Oh, that's a good idea. He'll love it.

06 위 대화의 밑줄 친 (A)를 'I would'로 시작하는 문장으로 바꿔 쓰시오. (7 words) 출제율 95%

➡ _____

07 위 대화의 밑줄 친 (B)를 영작하시오. (7 words) 출제율 90%

➡ _____

08 위 대화를 읽고 답할 수 <u>없는</u> 질문을 고르시오.

① When is B's dad's birthday?
② What kind of birthday gift is B preparing for his dad?
③ What did G recommend B for B's dad's birthday?
④ What kind of food does B's dad like most?
⑤ What did G say about the Korean food she recommended?

[09~10] 다음 대화를 읽고 물음에 답하시오.

A: Have you ever (A)<u>tried</u> *brigadeiro*?
B: Sorry, could you say that again?
A: *Brigadeiro*. It's a (B)<u>tradition</u> dessert in Brazil.

출제율 95%

09 다음 중 위 대화의 밑줄 친 (A)tried와 같은 의미로 쓰이지 <u>않은</u> 것은?

① This is delicious. You ought to <u>try</u> some.
② Harry isn't here. <u>Try</u> phoning his home number.
③ <u>Try</u> this new dish, created by our head chef.
④ You should <u>try</u> the shoes on before you buy them.
⑤ <u>Try</u> not to excite your baby too much before bedtime.

출제율 90%

10 위 대화의 밑줄 친 (B)를 알맞은 형으로 고치시오.

➡ _____

출제율 95%

11 다음 대화의 밑줄 친 부분의 목적으로 가장 적절한 것은?

> B: <u>Could you recommend a good traditional dish?</u>
> W: Try Samgyetang. It'll give you energy.

① to request a recommendation
② to make a recommendation
③ to request a treat
④ to give W energy
⑤ to ask to cook

[12~13] 다음 중 빈칸에 들어갈 수 <u>없는</u> 말을 고르시오.

출제율 95%

12

> Rachel of the volunteer organization was not only _____ but also generous.

① smart　　② friendly　　③ lovely
④ kind　　⑤ truly

출제율 100%

13

> *Gogol-mogol* is not only good for people with a cold but also _____.

① widely known as a cold-prevention effect for healthy people
② effective in healing people with other diseases
③ acts as a refreshing drink for the nervous people.
④ considered to be helpful in lowering body temperature
⑤ popular as a dessert for healthy people

14 다음 문장의 빈칸 (A), (B), (C)에 들어갈 말로 가장 적절하게 짝지어진 것은?

> • (A)_____ she took a long walk, Sumi felt so tired.
> • (B)_____ I was watching the show, I could hear something crying behind the stage.
> • (C)_____ he liked to go fishing, his wife hated fishing very much.

    (A)   (B)   (C)
① Since – While – While
② As – Before – While
③ Though – Until – Although
④ As – While – As
⑤ Though – Until – As

15 다음 중 밑줄 친 부분이 흐름상 어색한 것은?

① My daughter never takes off her life jacket <u>while</u> she is on the boat.
② <u>While</u> climbing the mountain, they saw a huge bear between the trees.
③ <u>While</u> my baby son was brushing his teeth, one of them came out.
④ <u>While</u> the girls were eating some snacks, they heard the news.
⑤ <u>While</u> you need anything at all, call me at any time.

[16~18] 다음 글을 읽고 물음에 답하시오.

What do you do when you ⓐ<u>catch a cold</u>? Of course, you want to stay warm, so maybe you put on more clothes. Some people like to drink hot tea. ⓑ<u>Ginger tea is something people in Korea often drink.</u> With its special taste, ⓒ<u>it</u> warms your body and helps reduce the pain in your throat. What do people drink or eat in other countries when they catch a cold? Let's find out.

16 위 글의 밑줄 친 ⓐcatch a cold와 바꿔 쓸 수 <u>없는</u> 말을 고르시오.

① come down with a cold
② get a cold
③ have a cough
④ take cold
⑤ have a cold

17 위 글의 밑줄 친 문장 ⓑ에 생략된 말을 넣어 문장을 다시 쓰시오.

➡ _____
_____

18 위 글의 밑줄 친 ⓒit이 가리키는 것을 본문에서 찾아 쓰시오.

➡ _____

[19~21] 다음 글을 읽고 물음에 답하시오.

While people in Korea and Finland look for drinks when sick, many people in America want a bowl of chicken soup. It is usually made with chicken and vegetables, but the ___ⓐ___ is different from one family to another. Salt and pepper can be added before eating. People in America believe that a bowl of warm chicken soup is great for a sore throat and a stuffy nose.

19 주어진 영영풀이를 참고하여 빈칸 ⓐ에 철자 r로 시작하는 단어를 쓰시오.

> a list of ingredients and a set of instructions that tell you how to cook something

➡ _____

20 위 글의 제목으로 알맞은 것을 고르시오.

① What Do People in Finland Look for When They Catch a Cold?
② What Do Americans Want When Sick?
③ Special Ingredients for Chicken Soup
④ The Reason Salt and Pepper Are Added Before Eating
⑤ What Is Good for a Sore Throat and a Stuffy Nose?

21 According to the passage, which is NOT true?

① People in Korea and Finland look for drinks when sick.
② Many people in America want a bowl of chicken soup when sick.
③ Chicken soup is usually made with chicken and vegetables.
④ People add salt and pepper while cooking chicken soup.
⑤ In America, a bowl of warm chicken soup is believed to be great for a sore throat and a stuffy nose.

[22~24] 다음 글을 읽고 물음에 답하시오.

In Russia and in Eastern Europe, when people get sick, they eat a dessert ____ⓐ____ *gogol-mogol*. It is made with eggs and honey. Some people add chocolate, butter, lemon juice, or milk (A)[makes / to make] it taste better. It looks like (B)[huge / thick] yogurt. People often drink a cup of warm *gogol-mogol* when they have a sore throat. *Gogol-mogol* is not only good for people with a cold but also popular as a dessert for (C)[healthful / healthy] people. When served as a dessert, ⓑ그것은 보통 차갑게 또는 실온으로 제공된다.

22 위 글의 빈칸 ⓐ에 call을 알맞은 형태로 쓰시오.

➡ _____

23 위 글의 괄호 (A)~(C)에서 문맥이나 어법상 알맞은 낱말을 골라 쓰시오.

(A) _____ (B) _____ (C) _____

24 위 글의 밑줄 친 ⓑ의 우리말에 맞게 주어진 어휘를 알맞게 배열하시오.

> served / usually / room temperature / it / cold / at / is / or

➡ _____

[01~02] 다음 대화를 읽고 물음에 답하시오.

> G: My favorite Korean traditional drink is Maesil-tea. What about you, Jinsu?
> B: Well, my favorite traditional drink is Sik-hye.
> G: Sik.... Can you say that again?
> B: Sik-hye. It's sweet and cool.
> G: I want to try it.

01 What is G's favorite Korean traditional drink? (7 words)

➡ _____

02 How does B describe his favorite drink? Include two features. (10 words)

➡ _____

_____

[03~04] 다음 대화를 읽고 물음에 답하시오.

> B: Have you ever tried *poke*?
> G: Sorry, could you say that again, please?
> B: *Po-ke*. It's a salad who is popular in Hawaii.
> G: What's so special about it?
> B: It's made with rice and fish. It's ___(a)___ delicious ___(b)___ very healthy.

03 위 대화에서 어법상 어색한 것을 하나 찾아 바르게 고치시오.

_____ ➡ _____

04 위 대화의 빈칸 (a)와 (b)에 들어갈 말을 각각 두 단어로 쓰시오.

(A) _____ (B) _____

05 다음 문장에서 어법상 어색한 단어를 하나씩만 찾아 바르게 고치시오.

(1) Not only Angela but also Julie believe that they have to get a perfect score on the final exam so that they can graduate.

➡ _____ ➡ _____

(2) Both your uncle and my teacher is the fan of the baseball team.

➡ _____ ➡ _____

(3) Either you or Charlie have to stay here monitoring the market situation.

➡ _____ ➡ _____

(4) The new song the composer made yesterday was not only easy to remember but also very excited.

➡ _____ ➡ _____

(5) I wonder why not only the restaurant but also the stores in my neighborhood is crowded with clients recently.

➡ _____ ➡ _____

06 다음 우리말과 같은 뜻이 되도록 접속사 while과 주어진 어구를 활용하여, 제시된 글자 수와 어법에 맞게 영작하시오.

(1) 그는 말을 많이 하는 반면에, 행동은 거의 하지 않는다. (act, talk, little, a lot, 8 단어)

➡ _____

_____

(2) Paula가 요리를 하고 있는 동안, 그녀의 삼촌이 집에 찾아오셨다. (visit, cook, uncle, 9 단어)

➡ _____

_____

[07~09] 다음 글을 읽고 물음에 답하시오.

What do you do when you catch a cold? Of course, you want to stay warm, so maybe you put on more (A)[cloths / clothes]. Some people like to drink hot tea. Ginger tea is something people in Korea often drink. (B)[With / Without] its special taste, it warms your body and ⓐhelps reduce the pain in your throat. What do people drink or eat in (C)[another / other] countries when they catch a cold? Let's find out.

07 위 글의 괄호 (A)~(C)에서 문맥이나 어법상 알맞은 낱말을 골라 쓰시오.

(A) _____ (B) _____ (C) _____

08 위 글의 밑줄 친 ⓐ를 다음과 같이 바꿔 쓸 때 빈칸에 들어갈 알맞은 말을 두 단어로 쓰시오.

| helps _____ _____ the pain in your throat |

09 본문의 내용과 일치하도록 다음 빈칸 (A)와 (B)에 알맞은 단어를 쓰시오.

| When people catch a cold, some of them like to drink (A)_____ _____ like ginger tea. It has special taste, warms the body and helps (B)_____ _____ _____ in the throat. |

[10~12] 다음 글을 읽고 물음에 답하시오.

In Russia and in Eastern Europe, when people get sick, they eat a dessert called *gogol-mogol*. It is made with eggs and honey. Some people add chocolate, butter, lemon juice, or milk to make it taste better. ⓐIt looks thick yogurt. People often drink a cup of warm *gogol-mogol* when they have a sore throat. *Gogol-mogol* is not only good for people with a cold but also popular as a dessert for healthy people. ⓑWhen served as a dessert, it is usually served cold or at room temperature.

10 위 글의 밑줄 친 ⓐ에서 어법상 틀린 부분을 찾아 고치시오.

_____ ➡ _____

11 위 글의 밑줄 친 ⓑ를 능동태로 고칠 때 다음 빈칸 (A)와 (B)에 공통으로 들어갈 알맞은 단어를 쓰시오.

| When people (A)_____ it as a dessert, they usually (B)_____ it cold or at room temperature. |

➡ _____

12 In Russia and in Eastern Europe, what do people often drink when they have a sore throat? Answer in English in a full sentence. (8 words)

➡ _____
_____

01 다음 그림과 표를 보고, 〈보기〉와 같이 접속사 while을 사용하여 Hana와 Duna의 대조적인 특징을 나타내는 문장을 자유롭게 3문장 이상 영작하시오.

	Hana	Duna
hair	short	long
clothes	jeans	skirt
glasses	yes	no
favorite food	ice cream	waffle
math test result	A	C
like	singing	dancing
pet	no	yes

보기

While Duna has a pet, Hana doesn't.

---

(1) _____

(2) _____

(3) _____

02 다음 내용을 바탕으로 인도식 토마토 수프 요리법을 완성하시오.

---

1. Chop one fresh tomato.
2. Put the chopped tomato in a pan and pour some water over it.
3. Boil for ten minutes.
4. Leave it to cool down.
5. Blend it until it is smooth.
6. Add some black pepper and salt.

While many Koreans eat Samgyetang when they are sick, many people in India eat tomato soup. Here is how to make it.

You need: 1 tomato, some water, black pepper, salt

First, (A)_____ one fresh tomato. Then put the chopped tomato in a pan and (B)_____ over it. Next, boil the mixture (C)_____. Then turn off the heat and leave it (D)_____. Next, (E)_____ until it is smooth. Finally, add (F)_____. Now you can enjoy the tomato soup. This tomato soup is not only healthy but also delicious.

01 다음 영영풀이가 가리키는 것은?

> a measure of the warmth of an object with reference to a standard scale

① weather   ② medicine

③ temperature   ④ taste

⑤ climate

02 다음 빈칸에 알맞은 단어를 고르시오.

> Thieves had broken in _____ we were away.

① while   ② even though

③ as if   ④ despite

⑤ where

03 다음 우리말에 맞게 빈칸에 알맞은 말을 쓰시오.

(1) 계산서에는 10프로의 서비스 비용이 추가되었다.

➡ A service charge of 10% was _____ on to the bill.

(2) 그 공동체 회의는 커뮤니티 센터에서 열릴 것이다.

➡ The community meeting will be _____ in the community center.

(3) 우리는 실험을 통해 기름과 물이 섞이지 않을 것이라는 것을 배울 수 있다.

➡ We can learn by experiment that oil and water will not _____.

[04~05] 다음 대화를 읽고 물음에 답하시오.

> B: Hi, Grace. Those are pretty. What are they called?
>
> G: They're called *dango*.
>
> B: I'm sorry. (A)Could you say that again?
>
> G: *Dan-go*. (B)그것들은 달콤하고 쌀가루로 만들어져. They're from Japan.

04 위 대화의 밑줄 친 (A)의 목적으로 가장 적절한 것은?

① to ask how to pronounce it

② to ask what she is eating

③ to ask what it's from

④ to ask about the dessert

⑤ to ask G to repeat what she said

05 위 대화의 밑줄 친 (B)를 주어진 우리말을 이용하여 영작하시오. (make, powder) (8 words)

➡ _____

[06~08] 다음 대화를 읽고 물음에 답하시오.

> M: Good afternoon. A table for two?
>
> B: Yes.
>
> M: This way please. Here is the menu. I'll be back in a few minutes and take your order.
>
> B: Okay. Thank you.
>
> G: I don't know much about Korean food. (A)무언가 추천해 주겠니?
>
> B: Well, I'd recommend the Bibimbap.
>
> G: I'm sorry. Could you say that again, please?
>
> B: This one. Bi-bim-bap. (B)그건 밥 위에 많은 야채들과 소고기, 그리고 계란을 얹어 만들어진다. (vegetables / beef and an egg / lots of / made with / over rice / it's) It's tasty and it's also good for your health.

G: That sounds great. I'll try it.

B: It's served with a spicy red pepper sauce. Is that okay?

G: No problem. I like spicy food.

06 위 대화의 밑줄 친 (A)를 주어진 단어를 이용해 영작하시오. (could, something) (4 words)

➡ _____

07 위 대화의 밑줄 친 (B)의 우리말에 맞게 주어진 어구를 나열하시오.

➡ _____

_____

08 위 대화의 내용과 일치하지 않는 것은? (2개)

① G does not know much about Korean food.

② G asks B to try Korean food.

③ The Bibimbap is good for your health.

④ The Bibimbap is served with spicy sauce.

⑤ G does not like spicy food.

09 다음 대화가 자연스럽게 이어지도록 순서대로 배열하시오.

(A) *Rasmalai*. It's a traditional dessert in India.

(B) Sorry, could you say that again?

(C) Have you ever tried *rasmalai*?

➡ _____

[10~11] 다음 대화를 읽고 물음에 답하시오.

B: Tomorrow is my birthday.

G: I know. Are you going to have a birthday party, Alex? ①

B: Yes. Can you recommend a good place to have the party? ②

G: I'd recommend the Happy Snack House. The food is really good and it'll be large enough. ③

B: What dish would you recommend? ④

G: I'd recommend the onion rings. ⑤

B: Oh, just thinking about them makes my mouth water.

10 위 대화의 ①~⑤ 중에서 주어진 문장이 들어가기에 가장 적절한 곳은?

They're fantastic!

①   ②   ③   ④   ⑤

11 위 대화를 읽고 대답할 수 없는 질문을 고르시오.

① Who is going to throw a birthday party?

② Who is going to be invited to the party?

③ Where is the party going to take place?

④ What kind of food does G recommend?

⑤ Does B like the onion rings?

12 다음 중 짝지어진 대화가 어색한 것을 고르시오.

① A: Could you recommend a good book for my little sister?

B: I'd recommend this one. The story is touching.

② A: Could you recommend a cell phone for my grandmother?

B: How about this phone? It's easy to use.

③ A: Could you recommend a guitar for beginners?

B: Try this one. Many beginners play it.

④ A: Could you recommend a good book for my sister?

B: Pardon me? The story is touching.

⑤ A: Could you recommend a snack for my dog?

B: Sure. How about this? Dogs really like it.

[13~14] 다음 주어진 우리말을 영작한 것으로 옳은 것을 고르면?

13

해피 분식집의 음식은 정말 맛있을 뿐 아니라, 혼자 먹기에 양도 너무 많다.

① The food at Happy Snack is not only delicious, but also too much to eat alone.

② The food at Happy Snack not only is delicious, but also eats too much alone.

③ Not only the food at Happy Snack is delicious, but also much to eat alone.

④ Not only is the food at Happy Snack delicious, but also too much is to eat alone.

⑤ The food at Happy Snack is not only too delicious, but also much to eat alone.

14

Henry는 바이올린을 연주할 수 있을 뿐만 아니라, 퍼즐도 빠르게 풀 수 있다.

① Henry can not only play the violin, but also solves puzzles quickly.

② Henry can play not only the violin, but also solve puzzles quickly.

③ Not only can Henry play the violin, but also solve puzzles quickly.

④ Not only Henry can play the violin, but also can he solve puzzles quickly.

⑤ Not only can Henry play the violin, but also he solve puzzles quickly.

[15~16] 다음 중 밑줄 친 while의 의미가 나머지와 다른 것은?

15 ① Dave likes playing soccer while his brother likes playing the computer soccer game.

② While Elisabeth is good at music, her boyfriend is poor at it.

③ Minju wants to go out while her brother insists staying home.

④ Someone named Ryan called you while you were walking the dogs along the park.

⑤ While the girl has short hair, Tom, the only son of the family, has long hair.

16 ① While Sarah was waiting for the bus, she saw a lady coming to her.

② While you are in Busan, try Busan fish cake and the soup of pork and rice.

③ You had better prepare the sauce while you are cooking the chicken salad.

④ While his girl friend Celine likes the Korean history very much, Walter doesn't like it.

⑤ Those who started late arrived while we were having dinner.

17 다음 그림의 내용에 알맞게, 주어진 어구를 배열하여 빈칸을 채우시오.

(1)

> but, made, broke, the speed limit, also, an, illegal

➡ The car not only _____

_____ lane change.

(2)

> while, in, I, a guitar, interested, was

➡ She tried to sell me _____

_____ other instruments.

[18~19] 다음 글을 읽고 물음에 답하시오.

In Finland, where it is very cold in winter, people have a special drink when they catch a cold. It is a cup of onion milk. They put chopped onion in milk and boil it over low heat for half an hour. ⓐThis simple drink is said to be good for a cold.

18 위 글의 밑줄 친 ⓐThis simple drink가 가리키는 것을 본문에서 찾아 쓰시오.

➡ _____

19 위 글을 읽고 알 수 없는 것을 고르시오.

① How is the weather in Finland in winter?
② What do people in Finland drink when they catch a cold?
③ What ingredients do you need to make the onion milk?
④ What's the recipe for the onion milk?
⑤ Why is the onion milk good for a cold?

[20~21] 다음 글을 읽고 물음에 답하시오.

_____ ⓐ _____ people in Korea and Finland look for drinks when sick, many people in America want a bowl of chicken soup. It is usually made with chicken and vegetables, but the recipe is different from one family to another. ⓑSalt and pepper can be added before eating. People in America believe that a bowl of warm chicken soup is great for a sore throat and a stuffy nose.

20 위 글의 빈칸 ⓐ에 알맞은 말을 고르시오.

① However   ② While
③ Otherwise   ④ Unless
⑤ As long as

21 위 글의 밑줄 친 ⓑ를 능동태로 고치시오.

➡ _____

[22~23] 다음 글을 읽고 물음에 답하시오.

In Russia and in Eastern Europe, when people get sick, they eat a dessert called *gogol-mogol*. It is made with eggs and honey. Some people add chocolate, butter, lemon juice, or milk ⓐto make it taste better. It looks like thick yogurt. People often drink a cup of warm *gogol-mogol* when they have a sore throat. *Gogol-mogol* is not only good for people with a cold but also popular as a dessert for healthy people. When served as a dessert, it is usually served cold or at room temperature.

22 아래 〈보기〉에서 위 글의 밑줄 친 ⓐto make와 to부정사의 용법이 같은 것의 개수를 고르시오.

┌─ 보기 ┐
① He was glad to make it taste better.
② My dream is to make it taste better.
③ Tell me the way to make it taste better.
④ She tried to make it taste better.
⑤ It was hard to make it taste better.
└────────┘

① 1개   ② 2개   ③ 3개   ④ 4개   ⑤ 5개

23 According to the passage, which is NOT true?

① In Russia and in Eastern Europe, people eat *gogol-mogol* when sick.
② *Gogol-mogol* is made with eggs and honey.
③ Chocolate, butter, lemon juice, or milk can make *gogol-mogol* taste better.
④ *Gogol-mogol* looks like thick yogurt.
⑤ In Russia and in Eastern Europe, people eat *gogol-mogol* only when they're sick.

[24~25] 다음 글을 읽고 물음에 답하시오.

Why not try making one of the foods you have found out ___ⓐ___ ? It will be fun and good for your health.

How to Make *Gogol-mogol* ((A)Serves one)
You need: 1 egg, 1/2 cup of milk, honey (5 g), butter (15 g)
1. Put the egg and the honey in a large cup and mix them.
2. Pour half a cup of milk in a pan. Add the butter. Warm it until the butter melts.
3. Pour the hot milk and butter ___ⓑ___ the cup with the egg and the honey. Stir as you pour.
4. Drink while it is hot.

24 위 글의 빈칸 ⓐ와 ⓑ에 들어갈 전치사가 바르게 짝지어진 것은?

	ⓐ	ⓑ		ⓐ	ⓑ
①	for	into	②	for	on
③	on	for	④	about	into
⑤	about	on			

25 위 글의 밑줄 친 (A)Serves와 같은 의미로 쓰인 것을 고르시오.

① The sofa serves as a bed for a night or two.
② He serves God.
③ This dish serves four hungry people.
④ She serves in the medical corps.
⑤ He serves behind a counter.

MEMO

Lesson

Special

A Christmas Miracle

Words & Expressions

Key Words

- **actually** [ǽktʃuəli] 부 사실은
- **address** [ədrés] 명 주소
- **aim** [eim] 명 목표
- **along** [əlɔ́:ŋ] 전 ~를 따라
- **although** [ɔ:lðóu] 접 비록 ~이긴 하지만
- **baseball** [béisbɔ̀l] 명 야구
- **begin** [bigín] 동 시작하다
- **boldly** [bóuldli] 부 대담하게
- **carol** [kǽrəl] 명 캐럴
- **either** [í:ðər] 부 ~도, ~ 또한
- **enemy** [énəmi] 명 적군, 적
- **English** [íŋgliʃ] 형 영국의 명 영어
- **entire** [intáiər] 형 전체의
- **example** [igzǽmpl] 명 예시, 본보기
- **exchange** [ikstʃéindʒ] 동 교환하다
- **expect** [ikspékt] 동 예상하다
- **face** [feis] 동 마주하다
- **familiar** [fəmíljər] 형 익숙한, 친숙한
- **few** [fju:] 형 많지 않은
- **fight** [fait] 동 싸우다
- **follow** [fálou] 동 따라가다
- **front line** 최전선, 최전방
- **German** [dʒɔ́:rmən] 형 독일의
- **greeting** [grí:tiŋ] 명 인사, 안부의 말
- **happen** [hǽpən] 동 일어나다
- **human** [hjú:mən] 명 인간, 사람
- **keep** [ki:p] 동 유지하다, 계속 있다
- **lantern** [lǽntərn] 명 조명

- **learn** [lə:rn] 동 ~을 알게 되다
- **light** [lait] 동 빛나다, 비추다
- **might** [mait] 조 ~일지도 모른다
- **mind** [maind] 명 마음, 정신
- **miracle** [mírəkl] 명 기적
- **miss** [mis] 동 그리워하다
- **month** [mʌnθ] 명 달, 월, 개월
- **move** [mu:v] 동 움직이다
- **peace** [pi:s] 명 평화
- **race** [reis] 명 경주, 시합
- **several** [sévərəl] 형 몇의, 수개의
- **share** [ʃɛər] 동 공유하다, 나누다
- **sheep** [ʃi:p] 명 양
- **shoot** [ʃu:t] 동 쏘다
- **shout** [ʃaut] 명 외침, 고함
- **sight** [sait] 명 광경
- **silent** [sáilənt] 형 고요한
- **soldier** [sóuldʒər] 명 군인, 병사
- **suddenly** [sʌ́dnli] 부 갑자기
- **surprise** [sərpráiz] 동 놀라게 하다
- **tired** [taiərd] 형 피곤한
- **trench** [trentʃ] 명 참호
- **trick** [trik] 명 속임수
- **truly** [trú:li] 부 정말로, 진심으로
- **unbelievable** [ənbəlívəbəl] 형 믿기 힘든
- **weapon** [wépən] 명 무기
- **wet** [wet] 형 젖은
- **World War I** 1차 세계 대전

Key Expressions

- **all the more** 더욱 더
- **at war** 전쟁 중인
- **be able to** ~할 수 있다
- **by ~ing** ~함으로써
- **come from** ~에서 오다
- **come out** 나오다
- **each other** 서로
- **follow one's example** ~의 사례를 따르다, 모범으로 삼다
- **for the first time** 처음으로
- **go on** (일, 상황이) 돌아가다
- **have a talk** 이야기하다

- **in peace** 평화 속에서
- **look out of** ~ 밖을 내다보다
- **no man's land** 황무지, 중간 지대
- **one after another** 잇따라서
- **one by one** 차례로
- **on the front line** 최전선에
- **pass away** 사망하다
- **put down** 내려놓다
- **shake hands** 악수하다
- **such as** ~와 같은

Word Power

※ 서로 비슷한 뜻을 가진 어휘

□ **actually** 사실은 – **in fact** 사실은
□ **aim** 목표 – **purpose** 목적, 의도
□ **begin** 시작하다 – **initiate** 시작하다
□ **entire** 전체의 – **whole** 전체의, 모든
□ **expect** 예상하다 – **predict** 예측하다

□ **happen** 일어나다 – **occur** 일어나다, 발생하다
□ **silent** 고요한 – **quiet** 조용한, 고요한
□ **suddenly** 갑자기 – **unexpectedly** 예상 외로, 갑자기
□ **truly** 정말로, 진심으로 – **really** 정말로

※ 서로 반대의 뜻을 가진 어휘

□ **begin** 시작하다 ↔ **end** 끝나다
□ **face** 마주하다 ↔ **avoid** 피하다
□ **familiar** 익숙한, 친숙한 ↔ **unfamiliar** 익숙치 못한
□ **keep** 유지하다 ↔ **lose** 잃다, 상실하다
□ **peace** 평화 ↔ **war** 전쟁, 무력 충돌

□ **silent** 고요한 ↔ **noisy** 떠들썩한, 시끄러운
□ **truly** 정말로, 진심으로 ↔ **falsely** 거짓으로, 속여서
□ **unbelievable** 믿기 힘든 ↔ **credible** 믿을 수 있는
□ **wet** 젖은 ↔ **dry** 마른, 물기 없는

※ 접두사 un-+ 형용사

□ **un + believable → unbelievable** 믿기 힘든
□ **un + known → unknown** 알려지지 않은
□ **un + grateful → ungrateful** 감사할 줄 모르는
□ **un + healthy → unhealthy** 건강하지 못한
□ **un + necessary → unnecessary** 불필요한

□ **un + clean → unclean** 더러운
□ **un + fortunate → unfortunate** 운이 없는, 불운한
□ **un + happy → unhappy** 불행한
□ **un + important → unimportant** 중요하지 않은
□ **un + usual → unusual** 특이한

English Dictionary

□ **boldly** 대담하게
→ in a brave and confident way, without showing any fear
용기 있고 자신감 있는 방식으로, 어떠한 두려움도 보이지 않고

□ **carol** 캐럴
→ Christmas song or hymn
크리스마스 노래 또는 찬송가

□ **exchange** 교환하다
→ to give and receive reciprocally; interchange
상호적으로 주고 받다; 교환하다

□ **greeting** 인사, 안부의 말
→ an act or words of welcoming
환영의 행위 또는 말

□ **peace** 평화
→ freedom from war; absence of fighting between nations
전쟁이 없는 상태; 국가 간 충돌의 부재

□ **race** 경주, 시합
→ a contest of speed, such as running, riding, driving or sailing
달리기, 라이딩, 운전 혹은 항해와 같은 속도 경쟁

□ **share** 공유하다, 나누다
→ to divide and distribute something in shares
무언가를 나누거나 분배하다

□ **shoot** 쏘다
→ to hit with a bullet, shell, or other missile fired from a weapon
총알, 포탄 혹은 무기에서 발사된 미사일로 타격하다

□ **shout** 외침, 고함
→ a loud call or cry
큰 소리로 부르거나 외침

□ **sight** 광경
→ something seen or worth seeing
보이는 어떤 것이나 볼 가치가 있는 것

□ **soldier** 군인, 병사
→ a person who is in an army and wears its uniform, especially someone who fights when there is a war
군대에 있어서 제복을 입는 사람, 특히 전쟁에서 싸우는 사람

□ **surprise** 놀라게 하다
→ to strike with a sudden feeling of wonder or astonishment especially by being unexpected
놀라움이나 깜짝 놀라는 감정, 특히 예상하지 못한 감정에 치이다

□ **trick** 속임수
→ a sneaky scheme to deceive or cheat
속이거나 사기를 치려는 교활한 계획

Reading

교과서

A Christmas Miracle

It was Christmas Eve in 1914, the first year of World War I. English
비인칭 주어로 시간, 날씨, 요일, 날짜, 무게 등을 나타낸다.

soldiers were facing German soldiers from their trenches as they had
~처럼, ~와 같이(접속사)

done for the last few months. The trenches were cold and wet. The
과거에 일어났던 일보다 더 앞서 일어난 일에 대해 언급하기 위해서 과거완료를 사용

soldiers were tired and missed their home, all the more so because it
더욱 더

was Christmas.

Suddenly, a familiar song was heard coming from the German
주어가 동작을 받는 대상이므로 동사가 'was heard'라는 수동태로 쓰였음.

trenches. It was a Christmas carol! What's going on? It might be a trick
확실하지 않은 일을 추측할 때 사용

to make them come out of the trenches. A few English soldiers boldly
명사 'trick'을 수식하는 to부정사의 형용사적 용법

looked out of their trenches. One by one, other soldiers followed their
차례차례, 하나씩 하나씩

example.

What they saw was a sight they never expected. Along the German
선행사를 포함하고 있는 관계대명사   'a sight'와 'they' 사이에 목적격 관계대명사 'which[that]'가 생략   along: ~을 따라(전치사)

trenches, Christmas trees were standing lit with lanterns! The German
수동형 분사구문

soldiers sang one Christmas song after another. The English soldiers

began to answer by also singing Christmas songs. The warm lights and

the Christmas carols made them forget they were on the front line.
사역동사 make+목적어+목적격 보어(동사원형)

soldier 군인, 병사
face 마주하다
trench 참호
wet 젖은
all the more 더욱 더
carol 캐럴 (전통적으로 크리스마스 기간에 불리는 노래)
trick 속임수, 마술
boldly 용감하게
sight 광경

📎 **확인문제**

● 다음 문장이 본문의 내용과 일치하면 T, 일치하지 않으면 F를 쓰시오.

1 On Christmas Eve in 1914, the first year of World War I, English soldiers were facing
   German soldiers from their trenches as they had done for the last few months. ☐

2 Suddenly, a familiar song was heard coming from the English trenches. ☐

3 Along the German trenches, Christmas trees were standing lit with lanterns. ☐

4 Even the warm lights and the Christmas carols couldn't make them forget they were
   on the front line. ☐

Then a shout came out from the German side: "Happy Christmas! You no shoot, we no shoot!" Soon, soldiers whose aim had been to kill
소유격 관계대명사, 사람 또는 사물을 선행사로 취하며 생략할 수 없다.
each other just a few hours before began to exchange greetings. For the first time in several months, the soldiers were able to spend a night in
가능의 의미를 가진 조동사 'could'로 바꿔 쓸 수 있다.
peace. It truly was a silent night.

Christmas morning came. Soldiers on both sides put down their
주어   V1
weapons and came out of their trenches. They met in the no man's
V2
land between their trenches and shook hands. They exchanged small
악수했다
gifts such as wine and cake. They sang carols together. Some even
~와 같은, 예를 들어(예를 들 때 사용)   몇몇, 어떤 사람들(부정대명사)
exchanged addresses and played football.
V1   V2

This unbelievable Christmas Day was written about in letters English
'letters'와 'English soldiers' 사이에 목적격 관계대명사 'which[that]'가 생략
soldiers sent home. One soldier wrote, "On Christmas Day, English and German soldiers met between the two lines and had talks. We also had bike races." Another wrote, "We didn't think that we were at
현재분사구로 앞의 명사 'enemy'를 수식
war. Here we were, enemy talking to enemy. They were like us, with
장소나 방향을 뜻하는 부사가 문장 앞으로 올 때 주어가 대명사인 경우 주어와 동사를 도치하지 않는다.   ~와 같은, ~처럼(전치사)
mothers, with friends, with wives who were waiting to welcome their
'who were'는 '주격 관계대명사+be동사'로 생략 가능
men home again."

aim 목적, 목표
exchange 교환하다
peace 평화
silent 고요한
weapon 무기
address 주소
put down 내려놓다
enemy 적군, 적

확인문제

● 다음 문장이 본문의 내용과 일치하면 T, 일치하지 않으면 F를 쓰시오.

1   For the first time in several months, the soldiers were able to spend a night peacefully. ☐

2   Soldiers met in their trenches and shook hands. ☐

3   Soldiers exchanged small gifts such as wine and cake. ☐

4   Soldiers even exchanged addresses and played basketball. ☐

5   This unbelievable Christmas Day was written about in letters English soldiers sent home. ☐

6   On Christmas Day, English and German soldiers met between the two lines and fought with each other. ☐

● 우리말을 참고하여 빈칸에 알맞은 말을 쓰시오.

1 A Christmas _____

2 It was Christmas Eve in 1914, _____ _____ _____ of World War I.

3 English soldiers _____ _____ German soldiers from their trenches as they _____ _____ for the last few months.

4 The trenches were _____ _____ _____.

5 The soldiers were tired and missed their home, _____ _____ _____ _____ because it was Christmas.

6 Suddenly, a familiar song _____ _____ _____ from the German trenches.

7 It was a Christmas _____!

8 What's _____ _____?

9 It _____ _____ _____ _____ to make them come out of the trenches.

10 A few English soldiers _____ _____ _____ _____ their trenches.

11 _____ _____ _____, other soldiers followed their example.

12 _____ they saw was a sight they never expected.

13 Along the German trenches, Christmas trees were standing _____ _____ _____!

14 The German soldiers sang _____ _____ _____ _____ _____.

15 The English soldiers began to answer _____ _____ Christmas songs.

16 The warm lights and the Christmas carols _____ _____ _____ they were on the front line.

1 크리스마스의 기적

2 제일차 세계 대전의 첫해였던 1914년의 크리스마스이브였습니다.

3 영국 군인들은 지난 몇 달 동안 그래왔듯이 그들의 참호에서 독일 군인들과 대치하고 있었어요.

4 참호는 춥고 축축했습니다.

5 군인들은 지쳤고 자신들의 집을 그리워했는데, 크리스마스라는 이유로 더욱 더 그랬습니다.

6 갑자기 익숙한 노래가 독일 군인들의 참호로부터 들려왔습니다.

7 그것은 크리스마스 캐럴이었어요!

8 무슨 일이 벌어지고 있는 걸까요?

9 어쩌면 그들을 참호 밖으로 유인하고자 하는 속임수일지도 모릅니다.

10 몇몇 영국 군인들이 용감하게 자신들의 참호 밖을 내다보았어요.

11 차례차례 다른 군인들도 앞사람을 따랐습니다.

12 영국 군인들이 본 것은 그들이 절대 예상하지 못한 광경이었어요.

13 독일 군인들의 참호를 따라, 크리스마스트리들이 랜턴으로 밝혀진 채 있었습니다!

14 독일 군인들은 크리스마스 캐럴을 연이어 불렀어요.

15 영국 군인들도 크리스마스 캐럴을 부르며 화답하기 시작했습니다.

16 따뜻한 불빛과 크리스마스 캐럴은 그들이 최전선에 있다는 것을 잊게 만들었어요.

17 Then a shout _____ _____ _____ the German side: "Happy Christmas! You no shoot, we no shoot!"

18 Soon, soldiers _____ _____ had been to kill each other just a few hours before began to _____ _____.

19 For the first time _____ _____ _____, the soldiers were able to spend a night in peace.

20 _____ _____ _____ a silent night.

21 Christmas morning _____.

22 Soldiers _____ _____ _____ put down their weapons and came out of their trenches.

23 They met _____ _____ _____ _____ _____ between their trenches and shook hands.

24 They exchanged small gifts _____ _____ wine and cake.

25 They _____ _____ together.

26 Some even _____ _____ and played football.

27 This _____ Christmas Day was written _____ in letters English soldiers sent home.

28 One soldier wrote, "On Christmas Day, English and German soldiers met _____ _____ _____ _____ and had talks.

29 We also _____ _____ _____."

30 Another wrote, "We didn't think that we _____ _____ _____.

31 _____ _____ _____, enemy talking to enemy.

32 They were _____ _____, with mothers, with friends, with wives who were _____ _____ _____ their men home again."

17 그리고 독일 군인들 쪽에서 고함이 터져 나왔습니다. "행복한 크리스마스예요! 당신들이 쏘지 않는다면, 우리도 쏘지 않을게요!"

18 곧, 단지 몇 시간 전까지만 해도 서로를 죽이는 것이 목적이었던 군인들은 인사를 나누기 시작했습니다.

19 몇 달 만에 처음으로, 군인들은 평화롭게 밤을 지낼 수 있었어요.

20 그날은 정말로 조용한 밤이었습니다.

21 크리스마스 아침이 밝았습니다.

22 양편의 군인들은 자신들의 무기를 내려놓고 참호 밖으로 나왔어요.

23 그들은 무인 지대에서 만났고 악수를 했습니다.

24 그들은 와인과 케이크 같은 작은 선물도 교환했어요.

25 그들은 캐럴을 함께 불렀습니다.

26 몇몇은 심지어 주소를 교환하기도 했고 함께 축구를 했습니다.

27 이 믿을 수 없는 크리스마스는 영국 군인들이 집으로 보낸 편지에 적혀 있었습니다.

28 한 군인은 "크리스마스에 영국 군인들과 독일 군인들은 두 경계선 사이에서 만났고 대화를 나눴어.

29 우리는 자전거 시합도 했어."라고 적었어요.

30 다른 군인은 "우리는 전쟁 중이라는 생각이 들지 않았어.

31 여기서 우리는 적대 관계인 서로와 대화를 나누고 있는 상황이었어.

32 그들은 우리와 마찬가지로, 그들의 남자들이 집으로 다시 돌아오기를 고대하는 어머니와, 친구들, 부인이 있는 사람들이었어."라고 썼습니다.

● 우리말을 참고하여 본문을 영작하시오.

1 크리스마스의 기적
➡ _____

2 제일차 세계 대전의 첫해였던 1914년의 크리스마스이브였습니다.
➡ _____

3 영국 군인들은 지난 몇 달 동안 그래왔듯이 그들의 참호에서 독일 군인들과 대치하고 있었어요.
➡ _____
_____

4 참호는 춥고 축축했습니다.
➡ _____

5 군인들은 지쳤고 자신들의 집을 그리워했는데, 크리스마스라는 이유로 더욱 더 그랬습니다.
➡ _____

6 갑자기 익숙한 노래가 독일 군인들의 참호로부터 들려왔습니다.
➡ _____

7 그것은 크리스마스 캐럴이었어요!
➡ _____

8 무슨 일이 벌어지고 있는 걸까요?
➡ _____

9 어쩌면 그들을 참호 밖으로 유인하고자 하는 속임수일지도 모릅니다.
➡ _____

10 몇몇 영국 군인들이 용감하게 자신들의 참호 밖을 내다보았어요.
➡ _____

11 차례차례 다른 군인들도 앞사람을 따랐습니다.
➡ _____

12 영국 군인들이 본 것은 그들이 절대 예상하지 못한 광경이었어요.
➡ _____

13 독일 군인들의 참호를 따라, 크리스마스트리들이 랜턴으로 밝혀진 채 있었습니다!
➡ _____

14 독일 군인들은 크리스마스 캐럴을 연이어 불렀어요.
➡ _____

15 영국 군인들도 크리스마스 캐럴을 부르며 화답하기 시작했습니다.
➡ _____

16 따뜻한 불빛과 크리스마스 캐럴은 그들이 최전선에 있다는 것을 잊게 만들었어요.
➡ _____

17 그리고 독일 군인들 쪽에서 고함이 터져 나왔습니다. "행복한 크리스마스예요! 당신들이 쏘지 않는다면, 우리도 쏘지 않을게요!"
➡ _____

18 곧, 단지 몇 시간 전까지만 해도 서로를 죽이는 것이 목적이었던 군인들은 인사를 나누기 시작했습니다.
➡ _____
_____

19 몇 달 만에 처음으로, 군인들은 평화롭게 밤을 지낼 수 있었어요.
➡ _____

20 그날은 정말로 조용한 밤이었습니다.
➡ _____

21 크리스마스 아침이 밝았습니다.
➡ _____

22 양편의 군인들은 자신들의 무기를 내려놓고 참호 밖으로 나왔어요.
➡ _____

23 그들은 무인 지대에서 만났고 악수를 했습니다.
➡ _____

24 그들은 와인과 케이크 같은 작은 선물도 교환했어요.
➡ _____

25 그들은 캐럴을 함께 불렀습니다.
➡ _____

26 몇몇은 심지어 주소를 교환하기도 했고 함께 축구를 했습니다.
➡ _____

27 이 믿을 수 없는 크리스마스는 영국 군인들이 집으로 보낸 편지에 적혀 있었습니다.
➡ _____

28 한 군인은 "크리스마스에 영국 군인들과 독일 군인들은 두 경계선 사이에서 만났고 대화를 나눴어.
➡ _____
_____

29 우리는 자전거 시합도 했어."라고 적었어요.
➡ _____

30 다른 군인은 "우리는 전쟁 중이라는 생각이 들지 않았어.
➡ _____

31 여기서 우리는 적대 관계인 서로와 대화를 나누고 있는 상황이었어.
➡ _____

32 그들은 우리와 마찬가지로, 그들의 남자들이 집으로 다시 돌아오기를 고대하는 어머니와, 친구들, 부인이 있는 사람들이었어."라고 썼습니다.
➡ _____
_____

01 다음 짝지어진 단어의 관계가 같도록 빈칸에 알맞은 말을 쓰시오.

> begin : end = familiar : _____

02 다음 빈칸에 알맞은 말을 쓰시오.

> 난 처음으로 유럽에 갈 것이다.
> ➡ I will go to Europe _____ .

03 다음 문장의 빈칸에 들어갈 말을 〈보기〉에서 골라 쓰시오.

> ┌─ 보기 ─┐
> come from / have a talk / for the first
> time / one by one / come out

(1) Will the colors _____ if I wash it?

(2) We solved the problems _____ .

(3) My parents and I _____ every evening.

04 우리말과 일치하도록 주어진 어구를 배열하여 영작하시오.

(1) 그들은 선생님을 지나가기 위해 속임수를 생각해내야 했다. (get past / they / a trick / to / think of / the teacher / had to)

➡ _____

(2) 이른 아침의 길거리는 고요했다. (morning / the / street / silent / was / early)

➡ _____
_____

(3) Lana는 다른 세 명의 다른 학생들과 집을 함께 쓴다. (three / shares / students / Lana / with / other / a house)

➡ _____
_____

05 다음 우리말에 맞게 주어진 어구를 이용하여 영작하시오.

(1) 그들은 서로 사랑하게 되었다.
(each other, fall in love)

➡ _____

(2) 너는 훌륭한 과학자들을 모범으로 삼아야 한다.
(have, follow the example)

➡ _____
_____

(3) 마라톤 선수들이 결승선에 잇따라 도착했다.
(one after another, the finish line)

➡ _____
_____

It was Christmas Eve in 1914, the first year of (A)World War I. English soldiers were facing German soldiers from their trenches as they ___ⓐ___ for the last few months. The trenches were cold and wet. The soldiers were tired and missed their home, all the more so because it was Christmas.

06 위 글의 밑줄 친 (A)World War I을 영어로 읽는 법을 쓰시오.

➡ _____

07 위 글의 빈칸 ⓐ에 do를 알맞은 형태로 쓰시오.

➡ _____

08 Why were the soldiers tired and missed their home all the more? Answer in English beginning with "Because". (4 words)

➡ _____

[09~11] 다음 글을 읽고 물음에 답하시오.

What they saw was a sight they never expected. Along the German trenches, Christmas trees were standing lit with lanterns! The German soldiers sang one Christmas song after another. The English soldiers began to answer by also singing Christmas songs. (A)The warm lights and the Christmas carols made them forgetting they were on the front line. Then a shout came out from the German side: "Happy Christmas! You no shoot, we no shoot!" Soon, soldiers ___ⓐ___ aim had been to kill each other just a few hours before began to exchange greetings. For the first time in several months, the soldiers were able to spend a night in peace. It truly was a silent night.

09 위 글의 밑줄 친 (A)에서 어법상 틀린 부분을 찾아 고치시오.

_____ ➡ _____

10 위 글의 빈칸 ⓐ에 들어갈 알맞은 관계대명사를 쓰시오.

➡ _____

11 본문의 내용과 일치하도록 다음 빈칸 (A)와 (B)에 알맞은 단어를 쓰시오.

When the German soldiers sang one Christmas song after another, the English soldiers began to answer by also (A)_____ _____ _____. For the first time in several months, the soldiers were able to spend a night (B)_____.

출제율 90%

01 다음 짝지어진 단어의 관계가 같도록 빈칸에 알맞은 말을 쓰시오.

> entire : whole = silent : _____

출제율 95%

02 다음 중 밑줄 친 부분의 뜻풀이가 바르지 <u>않은</u> 것은?

① <u>Follow</u> the path through the woods. (따라가다)
② We huddled together to <u>keep</u> warm. (유지하다, 계속 있다)
③ The book is <u>aimed</u> at very young children. (목표)
④ We will <u>miss</u> her when she leaves. (그리워하다)
⑤ He has a lot of <u>enemies</u> in the company. (적군들, 적들)

출제율 95%

03 다음 우리말을 주어진 단어를 이용하여 영작하시오.

> 그 부엌은 비록 작지만, 설계가 잘 되어 있다. (Although)

➡ _____

출제율 90%

04 다음 주어진 문장의 밑줄 친 light와 같은 의미로 쓰인 것은?

> Ann wanted to <u>light</u> the candles.

① Flashes of <u>light</u> were followed by an explosion.
② He was about to <u>light</u> a cigarette.
③ A solitary <u>light</u> burned dimly in the hall.
④ <u>Light</u> refreshments will be served during the break.
⑤ After the accident he was moved to <u>light</u> work.

출제율 95%

05 다음 빈칸에 공통으로 들어갈 단어로 알맞은 것을 쓰시오.

> • I like tropical fruits _____ bananas and pineapples.
> • People need essential services _____ gas, water and electricity.

출제율 90%

06 다음 영영 풀이에 해당하는 단어로 알맞은 것은?

> something seen or worth seeing

① soldier   ② peace
③ miracle   ④ trick
⑤ sight

[07~09] 다음 글을 읽고 물음에 답하시오.

It was Christmas Eve in 1914, the first year of World War I. English soldiers were facing German soldiers from ⓐtheir trenches as they ⓑhad done for the last few months. The trenches were cold and wet. The soldiers were tired and missed their home, all the more so because it was Christmas.

✏ 출제율 90%

07 위 글의 밑줄 친 ⓐtheir가 가리키는 것을 본문에서 찾아 쓰시오.

➡ _____

✏ 출제율 95%

08 위 글의 밑줄 친 ⓑhad done과 과거완료의 용법이 같은 것을 모두 고르시오.

① I had never seen such a strange animal before.
② How long had he worked here before he quit?
③ When I reached the station, the train had already started.
④ He had been sick for days before he went to the hospital.
⑤ I knew him well, for I had often met him before.

✏ 출제율 95%

09 On Christmas Eve in 1914, whom were the English soldiers facing from their trenches? Answer in English in a full sentence. (6 words)

➡ _____

✏ 출제율 95%

10 주어진 글 다음에 이어질 글의 순서로 가장 적절한 것은?

Christmas morning came. Soldiers on both sides put down their weapons and came out of their trenches.

(A) They exchanged small gifts such as wine and cake. They sang carols together.
(B) They met in the no man's land between their trenches and shook hands.
(C) Some even exchanged addresses and played football.

① (A)–(C)–(B)
② (B)–(A)–(C)
③ (B)–(C)–(A)
④ (C)–(A)–(B)
⑤ (C)–(B)–(A)

[11~14] 다음 글을 읽고 물음에 답하시오.

_____ ⓐ _____ they saw was a sight they never expected. (①) Along the German trenches, Christmas trees were standing lit with lanterns! (②) The German soldiers sang one Christmas song after another. (③) The warm lights and the Christmas carols made them forget they were on the front line. (④) Then a shout came out from the German side: "Happy Christmas! (⑤) You no shoot, we no shoot!" Soon, ⓑ단지 몇 시간 전까지만 해도 서로를 죽이는 것이 목적이었던 군인들은 인사를 나누기 시작했습니다. For the first time in several months, the soldiers were able to spend a night in peace. It truly was a silent night.

11 위 글의 빈칸 ⓐ에 들어갈 알맞은 말을 고르시오.
출제율 95%

① Which ② That
③ What ④ Who
⑤ Where

12 위 글의 흐름으로 보아, 주어진 문장이 들어가기에 가장 적절한 곳은?
출제율 100%

> The English soldiers began to answer by also singing Christmas songs.

① ② ③ ④ ⑤

13 위 글의 밑줄 친 ⓑ의 우리말에 맞게 주어진 어휘를 알맞게 배열하시오.
출제율 95%

> had been / aim / each other / greetings / soldiers / before / to exchange / whose / to kill / just a few hours / began

➡ _____
_____
_____

14 According to the passage, which is NOT true?
출제율 100%

① Christmas trees were standing lit with lanterns along the German trenches.
② The German soldiers sang one Christmas song after another.
③ The English soldiers began to answer by also singing Christmas songs.
④ Thanks to the warm lights and the Christmas carols, the soldiers forgot they were on the front line.
⑤ For several months, the soldiers were able to spend a night in peace.

[15~16] 다음 글을 읽고 물음에 답하시오.

Christmas morning came. Soldiers on both sides put down their weapons and came out of their trenches. They met in the no man's land between their trenches and shook hands. They exchanged small gifts such as wine and cake. They sang carols together. ⓐSome even changed addresses and played football.

15 위 글의 밑줄 친 ⓐ에서 흐름상 어색한 부분을 찾아 고치시오.
출제율 95%

_____ ➡ _____

16 Which question CANNOT be answered after reading the passage?
출제율 100%

① When did the English and German soldiers meet?
② What did the English and German soldiers do?
③ Where did the English and German soldiers meet?
④ What did the English and German soldiers exchange?
⑤ How long did the English and German soldiers play football?

[17~19] 다음 글을 읽고 물음에 답하시오.

This (A)[believable / unbelievable] Christmas Day was written about in letters English soldiers sent home. One soldier wrote, "___ⓐ___ Christmas Day, English and German soldiers met (B)[among / between] the two lines and had talks. We also had bike races." Another wrote, "We didn't think that we were ___ⓑ___ war. Here we were, enemy talking to enemy. They were (C)[alike / like] us, with mothers, with friends, with wives who were waiting to welcome their men home again."

17 위 글의 빈칸 ⓐ와 ⓑ에 들어갈 전치사가 바르게 짝지어진 것은?

	ⓐ	ⓑ			ⓐ	ⓑ
①	For	in		②	On	at
③	In	at		④	For	on
⑤	On	in				

18 위 글의 괄호 (A)~(C)에서 문맥이나 어법상 알맞은 낱말을 골라 쓰시오.

(A) _____ (B) _____ (C) _____

19 위 글을 읽고 알 수 <u>없는</u> 것을 고르시오.

① How did people know about this story?
② According to the letters, where did the English and German soldiers meet?
③ What did the English and German soldiers do when they met between the two lines?
④ How did the English and German soldiers feel when they fought again after Christmas Day?
⑤ What did the English soldiers think of the German soldiers?

[20~22] 다음 글을 읽고 물음에 답하시오.

Suddenly, ⓐa familiar song was heard coming from the German trenches. It was a Christmas carol! What's going on? It might be a trick to make ⓑthem come out of the trenches. A few English soldiers boldly looked out of their trenches. ⓒOne by one, other soldiers followed their example.

20 위 글의 밑줄 친 ⓐ를 English soldiers를 주어로 하여 능동태로 고치시오.

➡ _____

_____

21 위 글의 밑줄 친 ⓑthem이 가리키는 것을 본문에서 찾아 쓰시오.

➡ _____

22 다음 빈칸에 알맞은 단어를 넣어 위 글의 밑줄 친 ⓒ가 의미하는 것을 완성하시오. (5 단어)

One after another, other soldiers _____ _____ _____ _____ _____ , too.

MEMO

Middle School 3-2
학교시험 완벽 대비

2학기 전과정
적중100 plus
영어 기출문제집

영어 중 3

시사 | 송미정

Best Collection

내용문의 중등영어발전소 적중100 편집부 TEL 070-4416-3636

INSIGHT
on the textbook

교과서 파헤치기

영어 기출 문제집

적중100 plus
2학기 전과정

영어 중 3

시사 | 송미정

INSIGHT
on the textbook
교과서 파헤치기

※ 다음 영어를 우리말로 쓰시오.

01 means _____

02 attention _____

03 below _____

04 meaning _____

05 relax _____

06 closely _____

07 magazine _____

08 bright _____

09 drop _____

10 emotion _____

11 cheerful _____

12 independent _____

13 article _____

14 relate _____

15 personality _____

16 protection _____

17 reasonable _____

18 difference _____

19 dependent _____

20 curious _____

21 delay _____

22 annoyed _____

23 useful _____

24 various _____

25 comfortable _____

26 popular _____

27 detail _____

28 realistic _____

29 imagination _____

30 calm _____

31 careful _____

32 loudly _____

33 peaceful _____

34 reduce _____

35 sold out _____

36 deal with _____

37 get along _____

38 at the same time _____

39 in other words _____

40 be related to _____

41 have to do with _____

42 according to _____

43 on the other hand _____

※ 다음 우리말을 영어로 쓰시오.

01 기사 _____

02 상황, 환경 _____

03 다름, 차이점 _____

04 (긴장을) 늦추다,
   휴식을 취하다 _____

05 잡지 _____

06 창의적인 _____

07 감정 _____

08 방울 _____

09 ~을 관련[연결]시키다 _____

10 독립적인, 자립심이 강한 _____

11 발랄한, 쾌활한 _____

12 편한, 편안한 _____

13 조리[요리]법 _____

14 호기심이 있는 _____

15 합리적인 _____

16 의존적인 _____

17 성격 _____

18 여러 가지의, 다양한 _____

19 보호 _____

20 상상, 상상력 _____

21 차분한 _____

22 줄이다 _____

23 인기 있는 _____

24 세부 사항 _____

25 현실적인 _____

26 주의 깊은 _____

27 평화로운 _____

28 미루다, 연기하다 _____

29 표현하다 _____

30 면밀히, 밀접하게 _____

31 짜증이 난 _____

32 의미 _____

33 수단, 방법 _____

34 의견 _____

35 다시 말하면 _____

36 ~을 다루다, ~을 처리하다 _____

37 (사람들과) 잘 어울리다 _____

38 ~와 연관되다 _____

39 ~에 따르면, ~에 따라 _____

40 ~와 관련되다 _____

41 동시에, 함께 _____

42 반면에, 한편으로는 _____

43 자신에게 관심을 끌다 _____

※ 다음 영영풀이에 알맞은 단어를 <보기>에서 골라 쓴 후, 우리말 뜻을 쓰시오.

1 _____ : fair and sensible: _____

2 _____ : feeling or showing fear: _____

3 _____ : a set of instructions for making food: _____

4 _____ : to wait until later to do something: _____

5 _____ : not excited, nervous, or upset: _____

6 _____ : not causing any physically unpleasant feelings: _____

7 _____ : a place where you can sit, for example a chair: _____

8 _____ : to direct your attention or effort at something specific: _____

9 _____ : to make something smaller in size, amount, number, etc.: _____

10 _____ : believing that something you want will happen: _____

11 _____ : the way you think and feel about someone or something: _____

12 _____ : not requiring or relying on other people for help or support:

_____

13 _____ : to show or make known a feeling, an opinion, etc. by words, looks or

actions: _____

14 _____ : something that makes one thing or person not the same as another thing

or person: _____

15 _____ : a piece of writing about a particular subject that is included in a magazine,

newspaper, etc.: _____

16 _____ : the set of emotional qualities, ways of behaving, etc., that makes a

person different from other people: _____

보기			
article	comfortable	focus	seat
independent	frightened	reduce	reasonable
express	calm	difference	recipe
attitude	delay	hopeful	personality

※ 다음 우리말과 일치하도록 빈칸에 알맞은 말을 쓰시오.

Listen & Speak 1 Listen

1. G: What _____ "be in a cold sweat" _____?
   B: It means "to be _____ or _____ before _____ something."
2. B: What _____ "feel blue" _____?
   G: It means "to _____ _____."
3. G: What _____ "have a long face" _____?
   B: It _____ "to _____ _____."
4. B: What _____ "throw up one's hands" _____?
   G: It _____ "to _____ _____."

Listen & Speak 1 A

1. G: Hi, Jack! _____ are you _____?
   B: I'm on cloud nine! I got a concert ticket _____ my favorite band.
   G: What _____ "on cloud nine" _____?
   B: It _____ I'm really _____ and _____.
2. G: I took a _____ _____ today. I _____ _____ _____ a house.
   B: A house?
   G: Yeah. _____ _____ the test, you can tell _____ _____ about a person _____ their drawing. Here's _____.
   B: Interesting. So what _____ these big windows _____?
   G: They _____ I'm _____ to _____ people.

Listen & Speak 2 Listen

1. M: Sorry. The tickets for the blue zone are all _____.
   G: _____ _____ any _____ _____?
   M: Yes, we have _____ _____ for the red zone.
2. W: What would you like on your hot dog? We have _____ sauce and _____ sauce.
   B: Are there any _____ _____?
   W: Sorry. Those are the _____ _____ we have.
3. M: What _____ you _____ _____ drink? A soft drink _____?
   G: Are there _____ _____ drinks? Soft drinks have _____ _____ _____ in them.
   M: We have apple juice _____.
4. W: This is _____ _____ _____ cap in our store.
   B: Are there any _____ _____?
   W: Sure, we have _____ more. They're _____ _____. I'll show you.

해석

1. G: 'be in a cold sweat'가 무엇을 의미하니?
   B: 그것은 '무언가 하기 전에 긴장하거나 겁을 먹는 것'을 의미해.
2. B: 'feel blue'가 무엇을 의미하니?
   G: 그것은 '슬프게 느끼는 것'을 의미해.
3. G: 'have a long face'가 무엇을 의미하니?
   B: 그것은 '슬퍼 보이는 것'을 의미해.
4. B: 'throw up one's hands'가 무엇을 의미하니?
   G: 그것은 '포기하는 것'을 의미해.

1. G: 안녕, 잭! 어떻게 지내니?
   B: 나는 날아갈 것 같아! 내가 가장 좋아하는 밴드의 콘서트 티켓을 얻었어.
   G: 'on cloud nine'이 무엇을 의미하니?
   B: 그것은 내가 아주 기쁘고 들떠 있다는 뜻이야.
2. G: 나 오늘 성격검사를 했어. 나는 집을 그려야 했어.
   B: 집?
   G: 응, 그 시험에 따르면 그림을 통해서 사람의 많은 것을 알 수 있대. 여기 내 것이 있어.
   B: 흥미롭구나. 그러면 이 큰 창문들은 무엇을 의미하니?
   G: 그들은 내가 타인에게 열려 있다는 것을 의미해.

1. M: 죄송합니다. 파란 구역의 표는 매진입니다.
   G: 다른 자리가 있나요?
   M: 네, 빨간 구역의 표가 좀 있습니다.
2. W: 핫도그에 무엇을 올릴까요? 저희에겐 매운 소스와 달콤한 소스가 있습니다.
   B: 다른 소스들도 있나요?
   W: 죄송합니다. 이것들이 저희가 가진 오직 두 가지입니다.
3. M: 무엇을 마시겠습니까? 혹시 탄산음료를 마시겠어요?
   G: 다른 음료가 있나요? 탄산음료에는 지나치게 많은 설탕이 들어 있어요.
   M: 사과 주스도 있습니다.
4. W: 이것은 우리 가게에서 가장 인기 있는 모자예요.
   B: 다른 색도 있나요?
   W: 물론이죠. 우리는 더 많이 가지고 있어요. 그것들은 이쪽에 있어요. 제가 보여드릴게요.

Listen & Speak 2 A

1. **B:** Jane, what are you _____?

   G: I'm reading an interesting magazine. It _____ colors can _____ _____ _____.

   B: That's _____.

   G: Yes. _____ _____, the color red can _____ _____ better.

   B: Are there any other _____ _____?

   G: Yes. The color blue _____ people _____.

2. **M:** EDPI Test Center. Do you want to learn _____ about _____? We have many _____ _____ personality tests. If there are any _____ _____ you want to learn more about, we are here to help you.

   B: Hi, I'm _____ _____ _____ a personality _____. Can I do one this afternoon?

   M: Sure, you can come _____ _____ _____ 5 o'clock.

Real-Life Zone

Hajun: Look! I found this test on an app that tells _____ _____ _____ person you are. Do you want _____ _____ it?

Emma: Sure. Sounds _____ _____.

Hajun: Okay, listen. What are you _____ _____? Choose _____ _____ these: crowds, _____, or dark places.

Emma: I hate _____ _____. I cannot sleep _____ a night light _____. What does that _____?

Hajun: It _____ you are _____ _____ imagination. _____ you _____ dark places _____ all kinds of _____ _____.

Emma: That's very interesting. What _____ you? Is there _____ you are _____ _____?

Hajun: I chose dark places too. But I don't think I have a _____ _____.

Emma: This is fun. I want to do some more. Are there _____ _____ we can _____?

Hajun: Sure. This app has _____ _____ _____ them.

Wrap Up 1~2

B: What's your _____ _____?

G: Type A. Why?

B: I'm reading _____ _____. It _____ that blood type tells something about _____ _____.

G: Wow. Then what does _____ _____ mean?

B: People _____ blood type A are _____. They are good _____, _____.

---

1. **B:** 제인, 무엇을 읽고 있니?
   G: 나는 흥미로운 잡지를 읽고 있어. 이것이 말하길 색깔은 사람들의 기분을 바꿀 수 있대.
   B: 그거 놀랍네.
   G: 응. 예를 들어, 빨간색은 우리가 집중을 더 잘하도록 도와준대.
   B: 다른 유용한 색깔들도 있니?
   G: 응. 파란색은 사람들이 편안하도록 도와줘.
2. **M:** EDPI 검사 센터입니다. 자신에 대해 더 알고 싶으신가요? 우리는 여러 종류의 성격검사를 가지고 있습니다. 당신이 더 알아보고 싶은 검사가 있다면 우리는 이곳에서 당신을 도와드리겠습니다.
   B: 안녕하세요. 성격검사를 받기 위해 전화드렸습니다. 오늘 오후에 하나 해 볼 수 있을까요?
   M: 물론입니다. 5시 전에 아무 때나 오시면 됩니다.

하준: 봐! 네가 어떤 종류의 사람인지 말해주는 앱에서 이 검사를 발견했어. 한 번 해볼래?
Emma: 물론이지. 재미있겠다.
하준: 응, 들어봐. 당신이 두려워하는 것은 무엇입니까? 이들 중 하나를 고르세요. 군중, 거미, 또는 어두운 곳.
Emma: 나는 어두운 곳을 싫어해. 나는 야간등을 켜놓지 않고는 잘 수 없어. 그것은 무엇을 의미하니?
하준: 그것은 네가 상상력이 풍부하다는 것을 말해줘. 그것이 네가 어두운 곳을 온갖 종류의 무서운 것들로 채우는 이유야.
Emma: 매우 흥미롭구나. 너는 어때? 너는 두려워하는 것이 있니?
하준: 나도 어두운 곳을 골랐어. 그렇지만 나는 내가 상상력이 풍부하다고 생각하지 않아.
Emma: 이거 재미있다. 더 하고 싶어. 우리가 할 수 있는 다른 검사들이 있니?
하준: 물론이지. 이 앱에는 많은 검사가 있어.

B: 너의 혈액형은 무엇이니?
G: A형이야. 왜?
B: 내가 기사 하나를 읽고 있어. 거기에서 말하길 혈액형이 너의 성격에 대해 무언가 말해준대.
G: 와. 그러면 A형은 무엇을 의미하니?
B: 혈액형이 A형인 사람들은 차분해. 그들은 또한 남의 말을 잘 들어주는 사람이기도 해.

※ 다음 우리말에 맞도록 대화를 영어로 쓰시오.

해석

Listen & Speak 1 Listen

1. G: _____
   B: _____
2. B: _____
   G: _____
3. G: _____
   B: _____
4. B: _____
   G: _____

Listen & Speak 1 A

1. G: _____
   B: _____
   G: _____
   B: _____
2. G: _____
   B: _____
   G: _____
   _____
   B: _____
   G: _____

Listen & Speak 2 Listen

1. M: _____
   G: _____
   M: _____
2. W: _____
   _____
   B: _____
   W: _____
3. M: _____
   G: _____
   M: _____
4. W: _____
   B: _____
   W: _____

1. G: 'be in a cold sweat'가 무엇을 의미하니?
   B: 그것은 '무언가 하기 전에 긴장하거나 겁을 먹는 것'을 의미해.
2. B: 'feel blue'가 무엇을 의미하니?
   G: 그것은 '슬프게 느끼는 것'을 의미해.
3. G: 'have a long face'가 무엇을 의미하니?
   B: 그것은 '슬퍼 보이는 것'을 의미해.
4. B: 'throw up one's hands'가 무엇을 의미하니?
   G: 그것은 '포기하는 것'을 의미해.

1. G: 안녕, 잭! 어떻게 지내니?
   B: 나는 날아갈 것 같아! 내가 가장 좋아하는 밴드의 콘서트 티켓을 얻었어.
   G: 'on cloud nine'이 무엇을 의미하니?
   B: 그것은 내가 아주 기쁘고 들떠 있다는 뜻이야.
2. G: 나 오늘 성격검사를 했어. 나는 집을 그려야 했어.
   B: 집?
   G: 응, 그 시험에 따르면 그림을 통해서 사람의 많은 것을 알 수 있대. 여기 내 것이 있어.
   B: 흥미롭구나. 그러면 이 큰 창문들은 무엇을 의미하니?
   G: 그들은 내가 타인에게 열려 있다는 것을 의미해.

1. M: 죄송합니다. 파란 구역의 표는 매진입니다.
   G: 다른 자리가 있나요?
   M: 네, 빨간 구역의 표가 좀 있습니다.
2. W: 핫도그에 무엇을 올릴까요? 저희에겐 매운 소스와 달콤한 소스가 있습니다.
   B: 다른 소스들도 있나요?
   W: 죄송합니다. 이것들이 저희가 가진 오직 두 가지입니다.
3. M: 무엇을 마시겠습니까? 혹시 탄산음료를 마시겠어요?
   G: 다른 음료가 있나요? 탄산음료에는 지나치게 많은 설탕이 들어 있어요.
   M: 사과 주스도 있습니다.
4. W: 이것은 우리 가게에서 가장 인기 있는 모자예요.
   B: 다른 색도 있나요?
   W: 물론이죠. 우리는 더 많이 가지고 있어요. 그것들은 이쪽에 있어요. 제가 보여드릴게요.

Listen & Speak 2 A

1. B: _____

   G: _____

   _____

   B: _____

   G: _____

   B: _____

   G: _____

2. M: _____

   _____

   _____

   B: _____

   M: _____

Real-Life Zone

Hajun: _____

_____

Emma: _____

Hajun: _____

_____

Emma: _____

_____

Hajun: _____

_____

Emma: _____

_____

Hajun: _____

Emma: _____

Hajun: _____

Wrap Up 1~2

B: _____

G: _____

B: _____

_____

G: _____

B: _____

---

1. B: 제인, 무엇을 읽고 있니?
   G: 나는 흥미로운 잡지를 읽고 있어. 이것이 말하길 색깔은 사람들의 기분을 바꿀 수 있대.
   B: 그거 놀랍네.
   G: 응. 예를 들어, 빨간색은 우리가 집중을 더 잘하도록 도와준대.
   B: 다른 유용한 색깔들도 있니?
   G: 응. 파란색은 사람들이 편안하도록 도와줘.
2. M: EDPI 검사 센터입니다. 자신에 대해 더 알고 싶으신가요? 우리는 여러 종류의 성격검사를 가지고 있습니다. 당신이 더 알아보고 싶은 검사가 있다면 우리는 이곳에서 당신을 도와드리겠습니다.
   B: 안녕하세요. 성격검사를 받기 위해 전화드렸습니다. 오늘 오후에 하나 해 볼 수 있을까요?
   M: 물론입니다. 5시 전에 아무 때나 오시면 됩니다.

하준: 봐! 네가 어떤 종류의 사람인지 말해주는 앱에서 이 검사를 발견했어. 한 번 해볼래?
Emma: 물론이지. 재미있겠다.
하준: 응, 들어봐. 당신이 두려워하는 것은 무엇입니까? 이들 중 하나를 고르세요. 군중, 거미, 또는 어두운 곳.
Emma: 나는 어두운 곳을 싫어해. 나는 야간등을 켜놓지 않고는 잘 수 없어. 그것은 무엇을 의미하니?
하준: 그것은 네가 상상력이 풍부하다는 것을 말해줘. 그것이 네가 어두운 곳을 온갖 종류의 무서운 것들로 채우는 이유야.
Emma: 매우 흥미롭구나. 너는 어때? 너는 두려워하는 것이 있니?
하준: 나도 어두운 곳을 골랐어. 그렇지만 나는 내가 상상력이 풍부하다고 생각하지 않아.
Emma: 이거 재미있다. 더 하고 싶어. 우리가 할 수 있는 다른 검사들이 있니?
하준: 물론이지. 이 앱에는 많은 검사가 있어.

B: 너의 혈액형은 무엇이니?
G: A형이야. 왜?
B: 내가 기사 하나를 읽고 있어. 거기에서 말하길 혈액형이 너의 성격에 대해 무언가 말해준대.
G: 와. 그러면 A형은 무엇을 의미하니?
B: 혈액형이 A형인 사람들은 차분해. 그들은 또한 남의 말을 잘 들어주는 사람이기도 해.

※ 다음 우리말과 일치하도록 빈칸에 알맞은 것을 골라 쓰시오.

Drawing the Mind

1 _____ you _____ _____ _____ about you.
　　A. something　　B. everything　　C. says　　D. do

2 The language you use, the clothes you _____, and _____ the pets you _____ somehow show what _____ of person you are.
　　A. raise　　B. wear　　C. kind　　D. even

3 The _____ you _____ are not _____ _____.
　　A. much　　B. things　　C. draw　　D. different

4 _____ you draw and _____ you draw it are _____ to your _____.
　　A. personality　　B. how　　C. related　　D. what

5 Doctors have been _____ _____ drawing tests to _____ _____ people.
　　A. better　　B. various　　C. understand　　D. using

6 _____ of _____ _____ is the Draw-a-Person-in-the-Rain (DAPR) _____.
　　A. tests　　B. test　　C. those　　D. one

7 _____ the pictures _____.
　　A. below　　B. study

8 The _____ in Drawing A is _____ an umbrella in a _____ _____.
　　A. light　　B. holding　　C. person　　D. rain

9 On the _____ _____, the person in Drawing B is in a _____ rain and has _____ umbrella.
　　A. heavy　　B. no　　C. hand　　D. other

10 Also, _____ are _____ clouds _____ the _____ in Drawing B.
　　A. above　　B. dark　　C. person　　D. there

11 _____ can these _____ _____?
　　A. differences　　B. what　　C. mean

12 First, the _____ shows the _____ the person _____ drew the picture is _____.
　　A. under　　B. stress　　C. rain　　D. who

13 The _____ the _____ are or the more _____ the rain is _____, the bigger the stress is.
　　A. heavily　　B. bigger　　C. drops　　D. falling

14 The clouds mean problems _____ to _____, so a big cloud shows the drawer is not very _____ about the _____.
　　A. happen　　B. future　　C. waiting　　D. hopeful

마음 그리기

1 당신이 하는 모든 행동은 당신에 대해 말해 줍니다.

2 당신이 사용하는 언어, 당신이 입는 옷, 그리고 당신이 기르는 애완동물까지도 당신이 어떤 종류의 사람인지 보여 줍니다.

3 당신이 그리는 그림도 마찬가지입니다.

4 당신이 무엇을 그리는지 그리고 그것을 어떻게 그리는지는 당신의 성격과 관련이 있습니다.

5 의사들은 사람들을 더 잘 이해하기 위해 다양한 그림 그리기 검사를 사용해 오고 있습니다.

6 이런 검사들 중 하나는 빗속의 사람 그리기 검사입니다.

7 아래의 그림들을 연구해 봅시다.

8 A 그림 속의 사람은 가벼운 빗속에서 우산을 들고 있습니다.

9 반면에, B 그림 속의 사람은 거센 빗속에서 우산을 가지고 있지 않습니다.

10 또한, 검은 구름들이 B 그림의 사람 머리 위에 있습니다.

11 이런 차이는 무엇을 의미하는 걸까요?

12 첫 번째, 비는 그림을 그린 사람이 받고 있는 스트레스를 보여 줍니다.

13 빗방울의 크기가 크면 클수록, 혹은 비가 더 세게 내리면 내릴수록 스트레스는 더 큽니다.

14 구름은 앞으로 벌어질 문제를 의미하기 때문에, 큰 구름은 그림을 그린 사람이 미래에 대해 그다지 희망적이지 않다는 것을 나타냅니다.

15 _____, the umbrella means the _____ the person has in a
_____ _____.

    A. stressful   B. second   C. situation   D. protection

16 A _____ umbrella _____ that the drawer has a lot of _____
or _____.

    A. plans   B. big   C. protection   D. shows

17 If there's no umbrella in the _____, the drawer does not have
any _____ to _____ _____ difficult situations.

    A. drawing   B. with   C. means   D. deal

18 Third, the _____ in the drawing of the person _____ to
do _____ the drawer's _____ under stress.

    A. attitude   B. details   C. have   D. with

19 For _____, someone who _____ a person _____ a face
does not want to draw people's _____ to himself or herself.

    A. attention   B. without   C. example   D. draws

20 Someone who draws the person on the _____ _____ of the
paper is _____ _____ meet the future.

    A. right   B. ready   C. side   D. to

21 On the other _____, someone who draws the person on the
left side _____ be _____ about things that have _____
in the past.

    A. happened   B. may   C. hand   D. worried

22 These are some of the _____ _____ of each _____ of
the _____.

    A. meanings   B. part   C. possible   D. drawings

23 Now, _____ _____ and _____ _____ the two drawings.

    A. at   B. back   C. look   D. go

24 _____ _____ them _____.

    A. yourself   B. reading   C. try

25 Can you understand _____ _____ of person drew _____
_____?

    A. one   B. kind   C. each   D. what

26 What's _____ _____?

    A. opinion   B. your

---

15 두 번째, 우산은 스트레스를 받는 상황에서 그 사람이 가지고 있는 보호 기제를 의미합니다.

16 큰 우산은 그림을 그린 사람이 많은 계획이나 보호 기제를 가지고 있음을 보여 줍니다.

17 만약 그림에 우산이 없다면, 그 그림을 그린 사람은 어려운 상황을 헤쳐 나갈 어떤 방법도 가지고 있지 않습니다.

18 세 번째, 그림 속 사람의 세부적인 것들은 그 그림을 그린 사람이 스트레스를 받을 때의 태도와 관련이 있습니다.

19 예를 들어, 얼굴이 없는 사람을 그린 사람은 사람들의 관심을 끌기를 원하지 않습니다.

20 사람을 종이의 오른쪽에 그린 사람은 미래를 맞이할 준비가 되어 있습니다.

21 반면에, 사람을 왼쪽에 그린 사람은 과거에 일어났던 일에 대해 걱정하고 있을 수도 있습니다.

22 이것들은 그림 각 부분의 가능한 의미 풀이 중 일부입니다.

23 이제, 돌아가서 두 그림을 보세요.

24 그 그림들을 스스로 읽으려고 시도해 보세요.

25 당신은 각 그림을 그린 사람이 어떤 사람인지 알 수 있나요?

26 당신의 의견은 어떤가요?

※ 다음 우리말과 일치하도록 빈칸에 알맞은 것을 골라 쓰시오.

Drawing the Mind

1 _____ you do _____ _____ about you.

2 The language you _____, the clothes you _____, and _____ the pets you _____ somehow show _____ _____ _____ _____ _____ _____.

3 The things you _____ are not _____ different.

4 _____ you draw and _____ you draw it _____ _____ _____ your _____.

5 Doctors _____ _____ _____ _____ various drawing tests _____ _____ _____ people.

6 _____ of _____ _____ is the Draw-a-Person-in-the-Rain (DAPR) test.

7 _____ the pictures _____.

8 The person in Drawing A is _____ an umbrella in a _____ rain.

9 _____ _____ _____ _____, the person in Drawing B is in a _____ rain and has _____ umbrella.

10 Also, _____ _____ dark clouds _____ the person in Drawing B.

11 What can these _____ _____?

12 First, the rain shows the _____ the person _____ drew the picture is _____.

13 _____ the drops are or _____ _____ _____ the rain is falling, _____ _____ the stress is.

14 The clouds mean problems _____ to _____, so a big cloud shows the drawer is not very _____ about the _____.

1 당신이 하는 모든 행동은 당신에 대해 말해 줍니다.

2 당신이 사용하는 언어, 당신이 입는 옷, 그리고 당신이 기르는 애완동물까지도 당신이 어떤 종류의 사람인지 보여 줍니다.

3 당신이 그리는 그림도 마찬가지입니다.

4 당신이 무엇을 그리는지 그리고 그것을 어떻게 그리는지는 당신의 성격과 관련이 있습니다.

5 의사들은 사람들을 더 잘 이해하기 위해 다양한 그림 그리기 검사를 사용해 오고 있습니다.

6 이런 검사들 중 하나는 빗속의 사람 그리기 검사입니다.

7 아래의 그림들을 연구해 봅시다.

8 A 그림 속의 사람은 가벼운 빗속에서 우산을 들고 있습니다.

9 반면에, B 그림 속의 사람은 거센 빗속에서 우산을 가지고 있지 않습니다.

10 또한, 검은 구름들이 B 그림의 사람 머리 위에 있습니다.

11 이런 차이는 무엇을 의미하는 걸까요?

12 첫 번째, 비는 그림을 그린 사람이 받고 있는 스트레스를 보여 줍니다.

13 빗방울의 크기가 크면 클수록, 혹은 비가 더 세게 내리면 내릴수록 스트레스는 더 큽니다.

14 구름은 앞으로 벌어질 문제를 의미하기 때문에, 큰 구름은 그림을 그린 사람이 미래에 대해 그다지 희망적이지 않다는 것을 나타냅니다.

15 _____, the umbrella means the _____ the person has in a _____ _____.

16 A _____ umbrella _____ that the drawer has _____ _____ _____ _____ or _____.

17 If there's no umbrella in the _____, the drawer does not have any _____ to _____ _____ _____ _____.

18 _____, the _____ in the drawing of the person _____ _____ _____ with the drawer's _____ under stress.

19 For _____, someone _____ draws a person _____ a face does not want to draw people's _____ to _____ or _____.

20 Someone _____ draws the person on the _____ side of the paper _____ _____ _____ _____ the future.

21 On the other _____, someone who draws the person on the left side _____ be _____ about things that have _____ in the past.

22 These are some of the _____ _____ of each _____ of the _____.

23 Now, go _____ and _____ the two drawings.

24 Try _____ them _____.

25 Can you understand _____ _____ of person _____ _____ _____?

26 What's your _____?

---

15 두 번째, 우산은 스트레스를 받는 상황에서 그 사람이 가지고 있는 보호 기제를 의미합니다.

16 큰 우산은 그림을 그린 사람이 많은 계획이나 보호 기제를 가지고 있음을 보여 줍니다.

17 만약 그림에 우산이 없다면, 그 그림을 그린 사람은 어려운 상황을 헤쳐 나갈 어떤 방법도 가지고 있지 않습니다.

18 세 번째, 그림 속 사람의 세부적인 것들은 그 그림을 그린 사람이 스트레스를 받을 때의 태도와 관련이 있습니다.

19 예를 들어, 얼굴이 없는 사람을 그린 사람은 사람들의 관심을 끌기를 원하지 않습니다.

20 사람을 종이의 오른쪽에 그린 사람은 미래를 맞이할 준비가 되어 있습니다.

21 반면에, 사람을 왼쪽에 그린 사람은 과거에 일어났던 일에 대해 걱정하고 있을 수도 있습니다.

22 이것들은 그림 각 부분의 가능한 의미 풀이 중 일부입니다.

23 이제, 돌아가서 두 그림을 보세요.

24 그 그림들을 스스로 읽으려고 시도해 보세요.

25 당신은 각 그림을 그린 사람이 어떤 사람인지 알 수 있나요?

26 당신의 의견은 어떤가요?

※ 다음 문장을 우리말로 쓰시오.

Drawing the Mind

1 Everything you do says something about you.

➡ _____

2 The language you use, the clothes you wear, and even the pets you raise somehow show what kind of person you are.

➡ _____

3 The things you draw are not much different.

➡ _____

4 What you draw and how you draw it are related to your personality.

➡ _____

5 Doctors have been using various drawing tests to better understand people.

➡ _____

6 One of those tests is the Draw-a-Person-in-the-Rain (DAPR) test.

➡ _____

7 Study the pictures below.

➡ _____

8 The person in Drawing A is holding an umbrella in a light rain.

➡ _____

9 On the other hand, the person in Drawing B is in a heavy rain and has no umbrella.

➡ _____

10 Also, there are dark clouds above the person in Drawing B.

➡ _____

11 What can these differences mean?

➡ _____

12 First, the rain shows the stress the person who drew the picture is under.

➡ _____

13 The bigger the drops are or the more heavily the rain is falling, the bigger the stress is.

➡ _____

14 The clouds mean problems waiting to happen, so a big cloud shows the drawer is not very hopeful about the future.

➡ _____
_____

15 Second, the umbrella means the protection the person has in a stressful situation.

➡ _____

16 A big umbrella shows that the drawer has a lot of plans or protection.

➡ _____

17 If there's no umbrella in the drawing, the drawer does not have any means to deal with difficult situations.

➡ _____

18 Third, the details in the drawing of the person have to do with the drawer's attitude under stress.

➡ _____

19 For example, someone who draws a person without a face does not want to draw people's attention to himself or herself.

➡ _____

20 Someone who draws the person on the right side of the paper is ready to meet the future.

➡ _____

21 On the other hand, someone who draws the person on the left side may be worried about things that have happened in the past.

➡ _____

22 These are some of the possible meanings of each part of the drawings.

➡ _____

23 Now, go back and look at the two drawings.

➡ _____

24 Try reading them yourself.

➡ _____

25 Can you understand what kind of person drew each one?

➡ _____

26 What's your opinion?

➡ _____

※ 다음 괄호 안의 단어들을 우리말에 맞도록 바르게 배열하시오.

Drawing the Mind

1 (you / everything / do / something / says / you. / about)
➡ _____

2 (language / the / use, / you / clothes / the / wear, / you / even / and / the / you / pets / somehow / raise / what / show / of / kind / person / are. / you)
➡ _____
_____

3 (things / the / draw / you / not / are / different. / much)
➡ _____

4 (you / what / and / draw / you / how / draw / are / it / to / related / personality. / your)
➡ _____

5 (have / doctors / using / been / drawing / various / tests / better / to / people. / understand)
➡ _____

6 (of / one / tests / those / the / is / / test. / Draw-a-Person-in-the-Rain (DAPR))
➡ _____

7 (the / study / below. / pictures)
➡ _____

8 (person / the / Drawing / in / A / holding / is / an / umbrella / in / light / a / rain.)
➡ _____

9 (the / on / hand, / other / person / the / Drawing / in / B / in / is / heavy / a / rain / and / no / has / umbrella.)
➡ _____

10 (there / also, / are / clouds / dark / the / above / in / person / B. / Drawing)
➡ _____

11 (can / what / differences / these / mean?)
➡ _____

12 (the / first, / rain / the / shows / the / stress / person / drew / who / picture / the / under. / is)
➡ _____

13 (bigger / the / drops / the / or / are / more / the / the / heavily / rain / falling, / is / bigger / the / stress / the / is.)
➡ _____

14 (clouds / the / problems / mean / to / waiting / happen, / a / so / cloud / big / the / shows / drawer / not / is / hopeful / very / the / about / future.)
➡ _____
_____

마음 그리기

1 당신이 하는 모든 행동은 당신에 대해 말해 줍니다.

2 당신이 사용하는 언어, 당신이 입는 옷, 그리고 당신이 기르는 애완동물까지도 당신이 어떤 종류의 사람인지 보여 줍니다.

3 당신이 그리는 그림도 마찬가지입니다.

4 당신이 무엇을 그리는지 그리고 그것을 어떻게 그리는지는 당신의 성격과 관련이 있습니다.

5 의사들은 사람들을 더 잘 이해하기 위해 다양한 그림 그리기 검사를 사용해 오고 있습니다.

6 이런 검사들 중 하나는 빗속의 사람 그리기 검사입니다.

7 아래의 그림들을 연구해 봅시다.

8 A 그림 속의 사람은 가벼운 빗속에서 우산을 들고 있습니다.

9 반면에, B 그림 속의 사람은 거센 빗속에서 우산을 가지고 있지 않습니다.

10 또한, 검은 구름들이 B 그림의 사람 머리 위에 있습니다.

11 이런 차이는 무엇을 의미하는 걸까요?

12 첫 번째, 비는 그림을 그린 사람이 받고 있는 스트레스를 보여 줍니다.

13 빗방울의 크기가 크면 클수록, 혹은 비가 더 세게 내리면 내릴수록 스트레스는 더 큽니다.

14 구름은 앞으로 벌어질 문제를 의미하기 때문에, 큰 구름은 그림을 그린 사람이 미래에 대해 그다지 희망적이지 않다는 것을 나타냅니다.

15 (the / second, / umbrella / the / means / the / protection / person / has / a / in / situation. / stressful)

➡ _____

_____

16 (big / a / shows / umbrella / the / that / has / drawer / a / of / lot / or / plans / protection.)

➡ _____

17 (there's / if / umbrella / no / the / in / drawing, / drawer / the / does / have / not / any / means / to / deal / difficult / with / situations.)

➡ _____

18 (the / third, / details / the / in / drawing / of / person / the / to / have / with / do / drawer's / the / attitude / stress. / under)

➡ _____

19 (example, / for / who / someone / a / draws / without / person / face / a / does / want / not / draw / to / attention / people's / himself / to / herself. / or)

➡ _____

_____

20 (who / someone / the / draws / person / the / on / side / right / of / paper / the / ready / is / meet / to / future. / the)

➡ _____

_____

21 (the / on / hand, / other / who / someone / draws / person / the / on / left / the / may / side / be / worried / things / about / have / that / in / happened / past. / the)

➡ _____

_____

22 (are / these / of / some / possible / the / of / meanings / part / each / the / of / drawings.)

➡ _____

23 (go / now, / back / look / and / the / at / drawings. / two)

➡ _____

24 (reading / try / yourself. / them)

➡ _____

25 (you / can / what / understand / of / kind / drew / person / one? / each)

➡ _____

26 (your / what's / opinion?)

➡ _____

15 두 번째, 우산은 스트레스를 받는 상황에서 그 사람이 가지고 있는 보호 기제를 의미합니다.

16 큰 우산은 그림을 그린 사람이 많은 계획이나 보호 기제를 가지고 있음을 보여 줍니다.

17 만약 그림에 우산이 없다면, 그 그림을 그린 사람은 어려운 상황을 헤쳐 나갈 어떤 방법도 가지고 있지 않습니다.

18 세 번째, 그림 속 사람의 세부적인 것들은 그 그림을 그린 사람이 스트레스를 받을 때의 태도와 관련이 있습니다.

19 예를 들어, 얼굴이 없는 사람을 그린 사람은 사람들의 관심을 끌기를 원하지 않습니다.

20 사람을 종이의 오른쪽에 그린 사람은 미래를 맞이할 준비가 되어 있습니다.

21 반면에, 사람을 왼쪽에 그린 사람은 과거에 일어났던 일에 대해 걱정하고 있을 수도 있습니다.

22 이것들은 그림 각 부분의 가능한 의미 풀이 중 일부입니다.

23 이제, 돌아가서 두 그림을 보세요.

24 그 그림들을 스스로 읽으려고 시도해 보세요.

25 당신은 각 그림을 그린 사람이 어떤 사람인지 알 수 있나요?

26 당신의 의견은 어떤가요?

※ 다음 우리말을 영어로 쓰시오.

Drawing the Mind

1 당신이 하는 모든 행동은 당신에 대해 말해 줍니다.

➡ _____

2 당신이 사용하는 언어, 당신이 입는 옷, 그리고 당신이 기르는 애완동물까지도 당신이 어떤 종류의 사람인지 보여 줍니다.

➡ _____

_____

3 당신이 그리는 그림도 마찬가지입니다.

➡ _____

4 당신이 무엇을 그리는지 그리고 그것을 어떻게 그리는지는 당신의 성격과 관련이 있습니다.

➡ _____

5 의사들은 사람들을 더 잘 이해하기 위해 다양한 그림 그리기 검사를 사용해 오고 있습니다.

➡ _____

6 이런 검사들 중 하나는 빗속의 사람 그리기 검사입니다.

➡ _____

7 아래의 그림들을 연구해 봅시다.

➡ _____

8 A 그림 속의 사람은 가벼운 빗속에서 우산을 들고 있습니다.

➡ _____

9 반면에, B 그림 속의 사람은 거센 빗속에서 우산을 가지고 있지 않습니다.

➡ _____

10 또한, 검은 구름들이 B 그림의 사람 머리 위에 있습니다.

➡ _____

11 이런 차이는 무엇을 의미하는 걸까요?

➡ _____

12 첫 번째, 비는 그림을 그린 사람이 받고 있는 스트레스를 보여줍니다.

➡ _____

13 빗방울의 크기가 크면 클수록, 혹은 비가 더 세게 내리면 내릴수록 스트레스는 더 큽니다.

➡ _____

14 구름은 앞으로 벌어질 문제를 의미하기 때문에, 큰 구름은 그림을 그린 사람이 미래에 대해 그다지 희망적이지 않다는 것을 나타냅니다.

➡ _____

_____

15 두 번째, 우산은 스트레스를 받는 상황에서 그 사람이 가지고 있는 보호 기제를 의미합니다.

➡ _____

16 큰 우산은 그림을 그린 사람이 많은 계획이나 보호 기제를 가지고 있음을 보여 줍니다.

➡ _____

17 만약 그림에 우산이 없다면, 그 그림을 그린 사람은 어려운 상황을 헤쳐 나갈 어떤 방법도 가지고 있지 않습니다.

➡ _____

18 세 번째, 그림 속 사람의 세부적인 것들은 그 그림을 그린 사람이 스트레스를 받을 때의 태도와 관련이 있습니다.

➡ _____

19 예를 들어, 얼굴이 없는 사람을 그린 사람은 사람들의 관심을 끌기를 원하지 않습니다.

➡ _____
_____

20 사람을 종이의 오른쪽에 그린 사람은 미래를 맞이할 준비가 되어 있습니다.

➡ _____

21 반면에, 사람을 왼쪽에 그린 사람은 과거에 일어났던 일에 대해 걱정하고 있을 수도 있습니다.

➡ _____
_____

22 이것들은 그림 각 부분의 가능한 의미 풀이 중 일부입니다.

➡ _____

23 이제, 돌아가서 두 그림을 보세요.

➡ _____

24 그 그림들을 스스로 읽으려고 시도해 보세요.

➡ _____

25 당신은 각 그림을 그린 사람이 어떤 사람인지 알 수 있나요?

➡ _____

26 당신의 의견은 어떤가요?

➡ _____

※ 다음 우리말과 일치하도록 빈칸에 알맞은 말을 쓰시오.

Before You Read

1. A picture is often _____ _____ _____ _____ you're feeling in your mind.

2. _____ you _____ a picture, it _____ _____ _____.

3. _____ _____ _____, your various feelings _____ _____ _____ through pictures.

4. _____, you can _____ _____ other people's feelings if you _____ _____ _____ _____ their drawings.

1. 그림은 네 마음속에 느끼고 있는 것과 밀접한 관계가 있다.
2. 네가 그림을 그릴 때, 그것은 너의 감정들을 나타낸다.
3. 다시 말해서, 너의 다양한 감정들은 그림을 통해 표현될 수 있다.
4. 그러므로 너는 다른 사람들의 그림에 주의 깊게 관심을 기울인다면 그들의 감정을 이해할 수 있다.

Writing Workshop

1. This year, we _____ _____ _____ a lot of _____ _____ _____ activities at school.

2. Today, we _____ _____ _____ _____ our _____ _____ and then talk about a friend's personality.

3. I _____ _____ as _____ and _____.

4. _____ my friend _____ about me was _____ _____.

5. She said I am _____ and _____ because I _____ _____ _____ others and am in _____ _____ _____.

1. 올해, 우리는 학교에서 많은 다양한 종류의 활동들을 해 오고 있다.
2. 오늘 우리는 우리 자신의 성격과 친구의 성격에 대해 말해야 했다.
3. 나는 내 자신이 수줍음이 많고 친절하다고 생각했다.
4. 나에 대해 내 친구가 말한 것은 매우 달랐다.
5. 그녀는 내가 활동적이고 호기심이 많다고 말했는데, 그 이유는 내가 다른 사람들과 잘 지내고 많은 동아리에 속해 있기 때문이라고 했다.

Wrap Up 3~4

1. G: I _____ _____ _____ to Daegu today, but there are _____ _____ _____ _____.

2. Are there _____ _____ _____ to get there?

3. B: You can _____ _____ _____. It's fast and _____.

4. G: That's a great idea. I'll _____ _____.

1. G: 나는 오늘 대구에 가야 하지만 남아 있는 기차표가 없어.
2. 거기로 가는 다른 방법이 있을까?
3. B: 버스를 탈 수 있어. 그것은 빠르고 편해.
4. G: 좋은 생각이야. 그렇게 할게.

※ 다음 우리말을 영어로 쓰시오.

Before You Read

1. 그림은 네 마음속에 느끼고 있는 것과 밀접한 관계가 있다.

   ➡ _____

2. 네가 그림을 그릴 때, 그것은 너의 감정들을 나타낸다.

   ➡ _____

3. 다시 말해서, 너의 다양한 감정들은 그림을 통해 표현될 수 있다.

   ➡ _____

4. 그러므로 너는 다른 사람들의 그림에 주의 깊게 관심을 기울인다면 그들의 감정을 이해할 수 있다.

   ➡ _____

Writing Workshop

1. 올해, 우리는 학교에서 많은 다양한 종류의 활동들을 해 오고 있다.

   ➡ _____

2. 오늘 우리는 우리 자신의 성격과 친구의 성격에 대해 말해야 했다.

   ➡ _____

3. 나는 내 자신이 수줍음이 많고 친절하다고 생각했다.

   ➡ _____

4. 나에 대해 내 친구가 말한 것은 매우 달랐다.

   ➡ _____

5. 그녀는 내가 활동적이고 호기심이 많다고 말했는데, 그 이유는 내가 다른 사람들과 잘 지내고 많은 동아리에 속해 있기 때문이라고 했다.

   ➡ _____

Wrap Up 3~4

1. G: 나는 오늘 대구에 가야 하지만 남아 있는 기차표가 없어.

   ➡ _____

2. 거기로 가는 다른 방법이 있을까?

   ➡ _____

3. B: 버스를 탈 수 있어. 그것은 빠르고 편해.

   ➡ _____

4. G: 좋은 생각이야. 그렇게 할게.

   ➡ _____

※ 다음 영어를 우리말로 쓰시오.

01 advertisement	22 expectation
02 hasty	23 normally
03 several	24 grocery
04 category	25 description
05 ahead	26 greedy
06 however	27 realize
07 suddenly	28 sale
08 comment	29 excellent
09 through	30 lend
10 scratch	31 excuse
11 contact	32 angle
12 recommend	33 indoors
13 seem	34 used
14 buyer	35 as good as ~
15 customer	36 compared to ~
16 finally	37 push down
17 deliver	38 a whole day
18 savings	39 hand over
19 account	40 the number of ~
20 maybe	41 ask for
21 attractive	42 from different angles
	43 good for ~

※ 다음 우리말을 영어로 쓰시오.

01 은행 계좌	
02 긁힌 자국	
03 아마도	
04 예금	
05 보통, 보통 때는	
06 받아들이다	
07 게시 글	
08 욕심 많은	
09 언급	
10 ~을 통해	
11 중고의	
12 ~처럼 보이다, ~인 것 같다	
13 광고	
14 추천하다	
15 앞으로	
16 묘사	
17 각도	
18 갑자기	
19 깨닫다	
20 구매자	
21 식료품, 식료품점	

22 범주, 부류	
23 배달하다	
24 (무례나 실수 등을) 용서하다	
25 연락, 접촉	
26 성급한	
27 고객	
28 매력적인	
29 기대	
30 결국에	
31 실내의	
32 섞다	
33 몇몇의	
34 (안내문 등을) 게시하다	
35 성장하다	
36 ~을 요청하다	
37 답장을 받다, 댓글이 달리다	
38 ~만큼 좋은	
39 ~을 건네주다	
40 ~에 좋은	
41 하루 종일	
42 밀어 내리다	
43 ~에 비교해서	

※ 다음 영영풀이에 알맞은 단어를 <보기>에서 골라 쓴 후, 우리말 뜻을 쓰시오.

1 _____ : not new: _____

2 _____ : to forgive someone: _____

3 _____ : unpleasant to look at; not attractive: _____

4 _____ : in the usual or expected way: _____

5 _____ : something that you say or write to express your opinion: _____

6 _____ : to look somewhere carefully in order to find something: _____

7 _____ : to agree to take something; to say yes to an offer or invitation: _____

8 _____ : the feeling that good things are going to happen in the future: _____

9 _____ : communication with someone, especially by speaking or writing to them regularly: _____

10 _____ : to give something to someone to be used for a period of time and then returned: _____

11 _____ : to go down below the surface or towards the bottom of a liquid or soft substance: _____

12 _____ : the amount of money that you have saved especially in a bank over a period of time: _____

13 _____ : to behave in the stated way; to do something for a particular purpose or to solve a problem: _____

14 _____ : the process of getting knowledge or skill from doing, seeing, or feeling things: _____

15 _____ : an arrangement with a bank to keep your money there and to allow you to take it out when you need to: _____

16 _____ : a line or mark in the surface of something that is caused by something rough or sharp rubbing against it: _____

보기			
scratch	normally	act	accept
lend	comment	contact	ugly
account	search	experience	expectation
sink	excuse	savings	used

※ 다음 우리말과 일치하도록 빈칸에 알맞은 말을 쓰시오.

Listen & Speak 1 Listen

1. **M:** Do you _____ if I _____ my seat back?
   G: No, not _____ _____.
2. **B:** Mom, do you _____ if I use your smartphone?
   W: No, I _____ mind.
3. **G:** Do you mind if I _____ _____ with you?
   B: I'm sorry. I'm _____ my friend.
4. **B:** Do you mind if I _____ the blinds?
   G: No, go _____.

Listen & Speak 1 A-1

B: _____ me. I want to _____ these sneakers.
W: Okay. Can I ask _____ you want _____ _____ them?
B: There's _____ on them and I _____ even _____ them yet.
W: Do you _____ if I have _____ _____?
B: Not at _____. _____.

Listen & Speak 1 A-2

M: _____ can I help you with?
G: I'd like to _____ a bank account. What _____ I do?
M: First, you need to _____ _____ this _____.
G: Sure. Do you mind if I _____ your pen?
M: Not _____ _____.

Listen & Speak 1 B-1

A: Do you mind if I _____ my seat back?
B: No, not _____ _____.

Listen & Speak 1 B-2

A: _____ you _____ if I change _____ with you?
B: No, not at all.

Listen & Speak 1 B-3

A: _____ you mind if I _____ this snack here?
B: No, go _____.

해석

1. **M:** 제가 좌석을 뒤로 젖혀도 될까요?
   G: 네, 그럼요.
2. **B:** 엄마, 제가 이 스마트폰을 사용해도 될까요?
   W: 그래, 그러렴.
3. **G:** 저랑 좌석을 바꾸실 수 있을까요?
   B: 죄송하지만, 친구랑 같이 있어서요.
4. **B:** 제가 블라인드를 쳐도 될까요?
   G: 그럼요, 하세요.

B: 실례합니다. 이 운동화 반품하고 싶은데요.
W: 알겠습니다. 왜 반품하고 싶으신지 물어봐도 될까요?
B: 먼지가 묻어 있고요, 저는 아직 안 신어 봤어요.
W: 제가 좀 봐도 될까요?
B: 그럼요. 여기 있습니다.

M: 무엇을 도와 드릴까요?
G: 은행 계좌를 열고 싶은데요. 뭘 하면 될까요?
M: 우선, 이 양식을 작성해 주세요.
G: 그럼요. 제가 펜을 써도 될까요?
M: 그럼요.

A: 제가 좌석을 뒤로 젖혀도 될까요?
B: 그럼요.

A: 저와 좌석을 바꾸실 수 있을까요?
B: 그럼요.

A: 제가 간식을 여기서 먹어도 되나요?
B: 그럼요, 어서 드세요.

Listen & Speak 2 Listen

1. **G:** Can I _____ _____ the stage?

   M: I'm sorry. I'm _____ you can't. It's _____ only for the actors.

2. **B:** Can I take _____ _____ the play?

   W: I'm sorry. I'm _____ you _____. It can _____ _____ people.

3. **B:** _____ I sit _____ I want?

   M: I'm _____ you can't. Your seat number is on your ticket.

1. **G:** 무대를 둘러봐도 되나요?
   M: 죄송하지만 안 됩니다. 무대는 배우들만 출입 가능합니다.
2. **B:** 연극 중에 사진 찍어도 되나요?
   W: 죄송하지만, 안됩니다. 다른 사람들을 방해할 수 있거든요.
3. **B:** 제가 앉고 싶은 곳에 앉아도 되나요?
   M: 죄송하지만 안 됩니다. 좌석 번호가 티켓에 쓰여 있습니다.

Listen & Speak 2 A-1

G: _____! This jacket is really cute. _____ _____ out this store.

B: Wait, I'm afraid we _____ take our drinks _____.

G: But I _____ _____ mine _____.

B: Let's finish our drinks _____. Then we _____ go inside.

G: 봐! 이 자켓 진짜 예쁘다. 이 가게 살펴보자.
B: 잠깐, 아쉽게도 음료는 내부 반입이 안 되네.
G: 하지만, 난 아직 다 못 마셨는데.
B: 우선 음료 먼저 다 마시자. 그러면 우리는 들어갈 수 있어.

Listen & Speak 2 A-2

G: Minho, can you _____ with us to the game expo this Sunday?

B: I'd love to, but I'm _____ I can't. I have an important test next week.

G: _____ too bad. They're having a _____ show of _____ _____.

B: Yeah, I've _____ it's really great. What about _____ with me next Saturday _____?

G: Sure. _____ go _____ next Saturday.

G: 민호야, 이번 주 일요일에 우리와 함께 게임 엑스포에 갈래?
B: 그러고 싶은데, 안되겠다. 다음 주에 중요한 시험이 있거든.
G: 그것 참 안됐다. 다양한 게임들의 특별한 쇼가 있을 거야.
B: 응, 정말 좋다고 들었어. 그러면 나와 다음 주 토요일에 같이 가는 건 어때?
G: 그럼 좋지. 다음 주 토요일에 같이 가자.

Listen & Speak 2 B-1

A: Can I look _____ the stage?

B: I'm sorry. I'm afraid you can't. It's _____ _____ for the actors.

A: 무대를 둘러봐도 될까요?
B: 죄송하지만 안 됩니다. 배우들만 출입 가능합니다.

Listen & Speak 2 B-2

A: _____ I _____ this coupon?

B: I'm _____. I'm afraid you can't. The coupon is _____ for _____ _____.

A: 이 쿠폰을 사용해도 되나요?
B: 죄송하지만 안 됩니다. 쿠폰은 온라인 주문에만 사용 가능합니다.

Listen & Speak 2 B-3

A: _____ I seat anywhere I want?

B: I'm sorry. I'm afraid you _____. Your seat number is _____ your ticket.

A: 제가 앉고 싶은 곳에 앉아도 되나요?

B: 죄송하지만, 안됩니다. 좌석 번호가 티켓에 쓰여 있습니다.

Real-Life Zone

Ben: Wow! This comic book is really hard _____ _____. Do you _____ if I _____ a look at it?

Dana: Not _____ _____. It's one of my _____. I've read it maybe a hundred times.

Ben: I've been _____ all _____ for it. Can you _____ it to me?

Dana: I'm _____ I can't. _____, it's not mine. It's my sister's. Sorry.

Ben: Oh, that's _____. I understand.

Dana: You know, if you really want it, you should check _____ bookstores _____.

Ben: _____ _____ online? I've never _____ of that. That's a good _____.

Dana: Let's look _____. Oh, here's one! It says it's "like new." What do you _____?

Ben: Great! And it's _____! I'll _____ it. Thanks!

Ben: 와, 이 만화책 정말 찾기 힘든 건데. 내가 좀 봐도 되니?

Dana: 그럼. 이것은 내가 제일 좋아하는 것들 중 하나야. 아마 백 번 정도 읽었을 걸.

Ben: 난 이걸 찾아 샅샅이 살펴봤어. 나에게 빌려줄 수 있니?

Dana: 미안하지만 안 돼. 사실, 이게 내 것이 아니야. 언니 거야. 미안.

Ben: 어, 괜찮아. 이해해.

Dana: 있잖아, 네가 진짜 갖고 싶으면 인터넷 중고 서점을 확인해 봐.

Ben: 인터넷 중고 서점? 그건 생각해 보지 못했네. 좋은 생각이다.

Dana: 같이 찾아보자. 아, 여기 하나 있다! "거의 새 제품"이라고 하네. 어떻게 생각해?

Ben: 좋아! 그리고 저렴하네! 이거 살게. 고마워!

Wrap Up 1-2

B: The toy on your desk is so cute. Do you _____ if I take _____ _____ at it?

G: _____ at all. It's _____ a *maneki-neko*, or a good luck cat. My friend _____ it for me when she went to Japan.

B: Why is it _____ its hand up?

G: That _____ it is _____ you money.

B: Really? That's _____. Could you ask your friend _____ she got it? I'm going to Japan next week and I'd like to _____ one.

G: I'm sorry. I'm _____ I can't. I lost _____ _____ her.

B: 네 책상에 있는 장난감 너무 귀엽다. 내가 좀 봐도 되겠니?

G: 그럼. 마네키네코, 즉 행운의 고양이라고 불려. 내 친구가 일본에 갔을 때 사줬어.

B: 저건 왜 손을 올리고 있는 거니?

G: 그건 너에게 돈을 가져다준다는 의미야.

B: 정말? 흥미롭다. 네 친구한테 어디서 샀는지 물어봐 줄 수 있니? 나 다음 주에 일본 가는데 하나 사고 싶어서.

G: 미안하지만 안 되겠어. 연락이 끊어졌거든.

Wrap Up 3~4

B: I want to buy _____ traditional Korean gifts for my friends. Where's a good _____ _____ _____ them?

G: Have you _____ to Insa-dong? They have _____ _____ traditional Korean things there.

B: No, I've _____ _____ there.

G: How _____ I take you there this Friday afternoon?

B: Oh, I'm _____ I can't. I have other plans. _____ about Saturday?

G: That's _____ with me.

B: 나 친구들을 위해 한국 전통 선물을 좀 사고 싶어. 그것을 살 수 있는 좋은 장소가 어디니?

G: 인사동에 가봤니? 그곳에 한국 전통 물건들이 매우 많아.

B: 아니, 거기 가 본 적이 없어.

G: 이번 주 금요일 오후에 내가 널 거기 데려가는 건 어때?

B: 미안하지만 안 되겠어. 다른 계획이 있거든. 토요일은 어때?

G: 난 좋아.

※ 다음 우리말에 맞도록 대화를 영어로 쓰시오.

Listen & Speak 1 Listen

1. M: _____
   G: _____
2. B: _____
   W: _____
3. G: _____
   B: _____
4. B: _____
   G: _____

Listen & Speak 1 A-1

B: _____
W: _____
B: _____
W: _____
B: _____

Listen & Speak 1 A-2

M: _____
G: _____
M: _____
G: _____
M: _____

Listen & Speak 1 B-1

A: _____
B: _____

Listen & Speak 1 B-2

A: _____
B: _____

Listen & Speak 1 B-3

A: _____
B: _____

해석

1. M: 제가 좌석을 뒤로 젖혀도 될까요?
   G: 네, 그럼요.
2. B: 엄마, 제가 이 스마트폰을 사용해도 될까요?
   W: 그래, 그러렴.
3. G: 저랑 좌석을 바꾸실 수 있을까요?
   B: 죄송하지만, 친구랑 같이 있어서요.
4. B: 제가 블라인드를 쳐도 될까요?
   G: 그럼요, 하세요.

B: 실례합니다. 이 운동화 반품하고 싶은데요.
W: 알겠습니다. 왜 반품하고 싶으신지 물어봐도 될까요?
B: 먼지가 묻어 있고요, 저는 아직 안 신어 봤어요.
W: 제가 좀 봐도 될까요?
B: 그럼요. 여기 있습니다.

M: 무엇을 도와 드릴까요?
G: 은행 계좌를 열고 싶은데요. 뭘 하면 될까요?
M: 우선, 이 양식을 작성해 주세요.
G: 그럼요. 제가 펜을 써도 될까요?
M: 그럼요.

A: 제가 좌석을 뒤로 젖혀도 될까요?
B: 그럼요.

A: 저와 좌석을 바꾸실 수 있을까요?
B: 그럼요.

A: 제가 간식을 여기서 먹어도 되나요?
B: 그럼요, 어서 드세요.

Listen & Speak 2 Listen

1. G: _____
   M: _____

2. B: _____
   W: _____

3. B: _____
   M: _____

Listen & Speak 2 A-1

G: _____
B: _____
G: _____
B: _____

Listen & Speak 2 A-2

G: _____
B: _____
G: _____
B: _____
G: _____

Listen & Speak 2 B-1

A: _____
B: _____

Listen & Speak 2 B-2

A: _____
B: _____

1. G: 무대를 둘러봐도 되나요?
   M: 죄송하지만 안 됩니다. 무대는 배우들만 출입 가능합니다.
2. B: 연극 중에 사진 찍어도 되나요?
   W: 죄송하지만, 안됩니다. 다른 사람들을 방해할 수 있거든요.
3. B: 제가 앉고 싶은 곳에 앉아도 되나요?
   M: 죄송하지만 안 됩니다. 좌석 번호가 티켓에 쓰여 있습니다.

G: 봐! 이 자켓 진짜 예쁘다. 이 가게 살펴보자.
B: 잠깐, 아쉽게도 음료는 내부 반입이 안 되네.
G: 하지만, 난 아직 다 못 마셨는데.
B: 우선 음료 먼저 다 마시자. 그러면 우리는 들어갈 수 있어.

G: 민호야, 이번 주 일요일에 우리와 함께 게임 엑스포에 갈래?
B: 그러고 싶은데, 안되겠다. 다음 주에 중요한 시험이 있거든.
G: 그것 참 안됐다. 다양한 게임들의 특별한 쇼가 있을 거래.
B: 응, 정말 좋다고 들었어. 그러면 나와 다음 주 토요일에 같이 가는 건 어때?
G: 그럼 좋지. 다음 주 토요일에 같이 가자.

A: 무대를 둘러봐도 될까요?
B: 죄송하지만 안 됩니다. 배우들만 출입 가능합니다.

A: 이 쿠폰을 사용해도 되나요?
B: 죄송하지만 안 됩니다. 쿠폰은 온라인 주문에만 사용 가능합니다.

Listen & Speak 2 B-3

A: _____

B: _____

Real-Life Zone

Ben: _____

Dana: _____

Ben: _____

Dana: _____

Ben: _____

Dana: _____

Ben: _____

Dana: _____

Ben: _____

Wrap Up 1-2

B: _____

G: _____

_____

B: _____

G: _____

B: _____

G: _____

Wrap Up 3~4

B: _____

G: _____

B: _____

G: _____

B: _____

G: _____

A: 제가 앉고 싶은 곳에 앉아도 되나요?
B: 죄송하지만, 안됩니다. 좌석 번호가 티켓에 쓰여 있습니다.

Ben: 와, 이 만화책 정말 찾기 힘든 건데. 내가 좀 봐도 되니?
Dana: 그럼. 이것은 내가 제일 좋아하는 것들 중 하나야. 아마 백 번 정도 읽었을 걸.
Ben: 난 이걸 찾아 샅샅이 살펴봤어. 나에게 빌려줄 수 있니?
Dana: 미안하지만 안 돼. 사실, 이게 내 것이 아니야. 언니 거야. 미안.
Ben: 어, 괜찮아. 이해해.
Dana: 있잖아, 네가 진짜 갖고 싶으면 인터넷 중고 서점을 확인해 봐.
Ben: 인터넷 중고 서점? 그건 생각해 보지 못했네. 좋은 생각이다.
Dana: 같이 찾아보자. 아, 여기 하나 있다! "거의 새 제품"이라고 하네. 어떻게 생각해?
Ben: 좋아! 그리고 저렴하네! 이거 살게. 고마워!

B: 네 책상에 있는 장난감 너무 귀엽다. 내가 좀 봐도 되겠니?
G: 그럼. 마네키네코, 즉 행운의 고양이라고 불려. 내 친구가 일본에 갔을 때 사줬어.
B: 저건 왜 손을 올리고 있는 거니?
G: 그건 너에게 돈을 가져다준다는 의미야.
B: 정말? 흥미롭다. 네 친구한테 어디서 샀는지 물어봐 줄 수 있니? 나 다음 주에 일본 가는데 하나 사고 싶어서.
G: 미안하지만 안 되겠어. 연락이 끊어졌거든.

B: 나 친구들을 위해 한국 전통 선물을 좀 사고 싶어. 그것을 살 수 있는 좋은 장소가 어디니?
G: 인사동에 가봤니? 그곳에 한국 전통 물건들이 매우 많아.
B: 아니, 거기 가 본 적이 없어.
G: 이번 주 금요일 오후에 내가 널 거기 데려가는 건 어때?
B: 미안하지만 안 되겠어. 다른 계획이 있거든. 토요일은 어때?
G: 난 좋아.

※ 다음 우리말과 일치하도록 빈칸에 알맞은 것을 골라 쓰시오.

1 Seyun's _____ _____ _____.
A. Sale   B. First   C. Online

2 Seyun _____ his _____ to school _____ _____.
A. bike   B day   C. rides   D. every

3 He likes his bike, but he is _____ _____ _____ this _____.
A. taller   B. year   C. stronger   D. and

4 His bike has _____ small _____ him, so he wants to buy a bigger, faster _____.
A. too   B. one   C. become   D. for

5 _____, he does not have _____ money in his _____.
A. enough   B. account   C. however   D. savings

6 _____ _____ he _____?
A. can   B. do   C. what

7 _____, Seyun _____ _____ _____.
A. an   B. had   C. suddenly   D. idea

8 "My old bike is _____ _____ _____ a new _____.
A. one   B. almost   C. as   D. good

9 _____ I can _____ it and _____ the _____ to buy a new one."
A. add   B. maybe   C. money   D. sell

10 He _____ _____.
A. fast   B. acted

11 He took a photo of his bike with his smartphone and _____ the picture, _____ a short _____, on an online market: "Used bike in _____ condition. Only 100,000 won. Please text me."
A. comment   B. excellent   C. posted   D. with

12 He was _____, _____ about the bike he _____ to _____.
A. planned   B. buy   C. thinking   D. excited

13 He could see _____ _____ the _____ _____ bike.
A. shiny   B. himself   C. new   D. riding

14 He _____ not _____ to get a _____ to his online _____.
A. reply   B. wait   C. advertisement   D. could

15 _____ few _____ he _____ the number of _____.
A. minutes   B. hits   C. every   D. checked

16 _____ the number of hits _____ _____, his _____ went up too.
A. expectations   B. went   C. as   D. up

17 One hour _____, then two, and finally a _____ day, but he _____ no _____.
A. whole   B. passed   C. texts   D. received

18 _____ _____ to want his _____.
A. seemed   B. nobody   C. bike

---

1 세윤이의 첫 온라인 판매

2 세윤이는 매일 학교에 자전거를 타고 갑니다.

3 세윤이는 자신의 자전거를 좋아하지만, 그는 올해 키가 더 크고 힘도 더 세졌습니다.

4 그의 자전거는 그에게 너무 작아져서, 그는 더 크고 더 빠른 자전거를 사기를 원합니다.

5 하지만, 그는 자신의 예금 계좌에 충분한 돈을 가지고 있지 않습니다.

6 그가 무엇을 할 수 있을까요?

7 갑자기, 세윤이는 아이디어가 떠올랐습니다.

8 "내 오래된 자전거는 거의 새것과 다름없이 좋아.

9 아마 나는 그것을 팔고 새것을 사기 위한 돈에 보탤 수 있을 거야."

10 그는 빠르게 행동했습니다.

11 그는 스마트폰으로 자신의 자전거 사진을 찍었고, 짧은 설명과 함께 온라인 장터에 사진을 게시했습니다. "훌륭한 상태의 중고 자전거. 겨우 십만 원. 문자 주세요."

12 세윤이는 자신이 구입하려고 계획한 자전거에 대해 생각하며 신이 났습니다.

13 그는 자신이 빛나는 새 자전거를 타고 있는 것을 상상할 수 있었습니다.

14 세윤이는 자신의 온라인 광고에 대한 대답이 오는 것을 무척 기다렸습니다.

15 몇 분마다 그는 조회 수를 체크했습니다.

16 숫자가 올라갈수록 그의 기대도 덩달아 올라갔습니다.

17 한 시간이 지나고, 두 시간이 지나고, 마침내 하루가 지났지만 세윤이는 문자를 받지 못했습니다.

18 아무도 그의 자전거를 원하지 않는 것처럼 보였습니다.

19 New _____ by other people _____ his _____ the list.

    A. pushed   B. postings   C. down   D. post

20 His _____ began _____ _____ .

    A. to   B. heart   C. sink

21 "What's _____ my _____ ?"

    A. posting   B. wrong   C. with

22 Is my _____ not _____ ?"

    A. attractive   B. bike   C. enough

23 He _____ the Internet for _____ on how to _____ online.

    A. tips   B. searched   C. sell   D. on

24 Then he _____ _____ he had _____ .

    A. done   B. realized   C. wrong   D. what

25 He had _____ too _____ and too _____ .

    A. greedy   B. been   C. hasty

26 He had not given _____ _____ to the _____ .

    A. enough   B. buyers   C. information   D. possible

27 Also, when _____ _____ other bicycles, his _____ was too _____ .

    A. price   B. compared   C. high   D. to

28 He _____ a new _____ with a _____ _____ of the bike.

    A. description   B. wrote   C. posting   D. longer

29 He _____ more photos to show his bike _____ _____ .

    A. different   B. added   C. from   D. angles

30 "Twenty-four inch bicycle. Excellent condition. Always _____ _____ . Rides just _____ new. Very few _____ . Good for someone 12-14 years old. 80,000 won."

    A. kept   B. scratches   C. indoors   D. like

31 This time he _____ _____ .

    A. several   B. got   C. texts

32 _____ , they all _____ for a _____ .

    A. price   B. sadly   C. lower   D. asked

33 It was hard _____ at first, but finally he _____ his bike _____ 70,000 won.

    A. for   B. accept   C. sold   D. to

34 He met the _____ , _____ his bike, and got the money he _____ .

    A. over   B. needed   C. buyer   D. handed

35 Now he _____ a _____ .

    A. get   B. could   C. bike   D. new

36 He _____ _____ and _____ .

    A. happy   B. felt   C. sad   D. both

37 He was sad to see his old bike go, but he was happy with _____ because he had learned a lot and _____ up a bit _____ the _____ .

    A. himself   B. grown   C. experience   D. through

19 다른 사람들의 새 게시물이 그의 게시물을 리스트에서 밀어냈습니다.

20 세윤이의 가슴이 내려앉기 시작했습니다.

21 '내 포스팅에 무슨 문제가 있지?

22 내 자전거가 충분히 매력적이지 못한가?'

23 세윤이는 온라인에서 판매하는 방법에 대한 조언을 찾기 위해 인터넷을 검색했습니다.

24 곧 그는 자신의 잘못을 깨달았습니다.

25 세윤이는 너무 성급했고 너무 욕심이 많았습니다.

26 그는 구매 가능성이 있는 사람들에게 충분한 정보를 주지 않았습니다.

27 또한, 다른 자전거들과 비교했을 때 그의 가격은 너무 높았습니다.

28 세윤이는 자신의 자전거에 대한 더 긴 묘사가 있는 새 게시물을 작성했습니다.

29 그는 자신의 자전거를 다른 각도에서 보여 주기 위해서 더 많은 사진들을 첨부했습니다.

30 "24인치 자전거. 훌륭한 상태. 항상 실내에 보관했음. 새것처럼 탐. 스크래치 매우 적음. 12-14세에게 좋음. 8만 원."

31 이번에 그는 여러 통의 문자 메시지를 받았습니다.

32 애석하게도, 그들은 모두 더 낮은 가격을 요청했습니다.

33 처음에는 받아들이기 어려웠지만, 마침내 그는 자신의 자전거를 칠만 원에 팔았습니다.

34 세윤이는 구매자를 만나 자전거를 건네주고, 그가 필요했던 돈을 받았습니다.

35 이제 세윤이는 새 자전거를 살 수 있습니다.

36 그는 기쁘고 슬픈 감정을 동시에 느꼈습니다.

37 세윤이는 자신의 오래된 자전거가 떠나는 것을 봐서 슬펐지만, 이 경험을 통해 자신이 많은 것을 배우고 조금 더 성장한 것이 기뻤습니다.

※ 다음 우리말과 일치하도록 빈칸에 알맞은 말을 쓰시오.

1　Seyun's First _____ _____.

2　Seyun _____ _____ _____ to school _____ _____.

3　He likes his bike, but he is _____ _____ _____ this year.

4　His bike has become _____ _____ _____ _____, so he wants to buy a _____, _____ one.

5　However, he does not have _____ _____ in his _____ _____.

6　_____ can he do?

7　_____, Seyun _____ _____ _____.

8　"My old bike is _____ _____ _____ _____ a new one.

9　Maybe I can sell it and _____ _____ to buy a new one."

10　He _____ _____.

11　He took a photo of his bike with his smartphone and _____ the picture, _____ _____ _____ _____, on an online market: "_____ _____ in excellent condition. Only 100,000 won. Please _____ me."

12　He was excited, _____ _____ the bike he planned to buy.

13　He could see _____ _____ the _____ new bike.

14　He _____ _____ _____ to get a reply to his online _____.

15　_____ _____ _____ _____ he checked the number of hits.

16　_____ the number of hits _____ _____, his expectations _____ _____ too.

17　One hour passed, then two, and _____ a _____ _____, but he _____ _____ _____.

18　_____ _____ to want his bike.

1　세윤이의 첫 온라인 판매

2　세윤이는 매일 학교에 자전거를 타고 갑니다.

3　세윤이는 자신의 자전거를 좋아 하지만, 그는 올해 키가 더 크고 힘도 더 세졌습니다.

4　그의 자전거는 그에게 너무 작 아져서, 그는 더 크고 더 빠른 자전거를 사기를 원합니다.

5　하지만, 그는 자신의 예금 계좌 에 충분한 돈을 가지고 있지 않 습니다.

6　그가 무엇을 할 수 있을까요?

7　갑자기, 세윤이는 아이디어가 떠올랐습니다.

8　"내 오래된 자전거는 거의 새것 과 다름없이 좋아.

9　아마 나는 그것을 팔고 새것을 사 기 위한 돈에 보탤 수 있을 거야."

10　그는 빠르게 행동했습니다.

11　그는 스마트폰으로 자신의 자전 거 사진을 찍었고, 짧은 설명과 함께 온라인 장터에 사진을 게 시했습니다. "훌륭한 상태의 중 고 자전거. 겨우 십만 원. 문자 주세요."

12　세윤이는 자신이 구입하려고 계 획한 자전거에 대해 생각하며 신이 났습니다.

13　그는 자신이 빛나는 새 자전거 를 타고 있는 것을 상상할 수 있었습니다.

14　세윤이는 자신의 온라인 광고에 대한 대답이 오는 것을 무척 기 다렸습니다.

15　몇 분마다 그는 조회 수를 체크 했습니다.

16　숫자가 올라갈수록 그의 기대도 덩달아 올라갔습니다.

17　한 시간이 지나고, 두 시간이 지 나고, 마침내 하루가 지났지만 세 윤이는 문자를 받지 못했습니다.

18　아무도 그의 자전거를 원하지 않 는 것처럼 보였습니다.

19 New _____ by other people _____ _____ _____ _____ the list.

20 His heart began _____ _____.

21 "What's _____ _____ my posting?

22 Is my bike not _____ _____?"

23 He searched on the Internet _____ _____ _____ _____ _____ _____ online.

24 Then he realized _____ _____ _____ _____ _____ _____ _____ _____.

25 He had been too _____ and too _____.

26 He had not given enough information to the _____ _____.

27 Also, when _____ _____ other bicycles, his _____ was too _____.

28 He wrote a new posting _____ _____ _____ _____ of the bike.

29 He _____ more photos to show his bike _____ _____ _____.

30 "Twenty-four inch bicycle. Excellent condition. Always _____ _____. Rides just like new. Very few _____. Good for someone 12-14 years old. 80,000 won."

31 This time he got _____ _____.

32 Sadly, they all _____ a _____ _____.

33 It was hard _____ _____ at first, but _____ he sold his bike _____ 70,000 won.

34 He met the buyer, _____ _____ his bike, and got the money he needed.

35 Now he _____ _____ a new bike.

36 He felt _____ _____ _____ _____.

37 He was sad to see his old bike _____, but he was happy with _____ because he had learned a lot and _____ _____ a bit _____ _____ _____.

19 다른 사람들의 새 게시물이 그의 게시물을 리스트에서 밀어냈습니다.

20 세윤이의 가슴이 내려앉기 시작했습니다.

21 '내 포스팅에 무슨 문제가 있지?

22 내 자전거가 충분히 매력적이지 못한가?'

23 세윤이는 온라인에서 판매하는 방법에 대한 조언을 찾기 위해 인터넷을 검색했습니다.

24 곧 그는 자신의 잘못을 깨달았습니다.

25 세윤이는 너무 성급했고 너무 욕심이 많았습니다.

26 그는 구매 가능성이 있는 사람들에게 충분한 정보를 주지 않았습니다.

27 또한, 다른 자전거들과 비교했을 때 그의 가격은 너무 높았습니다.

28 세윤이는 자신의 자전거에 대한 더 긴 묘사가 있는 새 게시물을 작성했습니다.

29 그는 자신의 자전거를 다른 각도에서 보여 주기 위해서 더 많은 사진들을 첨부했습니다.

30 "24인치 자전거. 훌륭한 상태. 항상 실내에 보관했음. 새것처럼 탐. 스크래치 매우 적음. 12-14세에게 좋음. 8만 원."

31 이번에 그는 여러 통의 문자 메시지를 받았습니다.

32 애석하게도, 그들은 모두 더 낮은 가격을 요청했습니다.

33 처음에는 받아들이기 어려웠지만. 마침내 그는 자신의 자전거를 칠만 원에 팔았습니다.

34 세윤이는 구매자를 만나 자전거를 건네주고, 그가 필요했던 돈을 받았습니다.

35 이제 세윤이는 새 자전거를 살 수 있습니다.

36 그는 기쁘고 슬픈 감정을 동시에 느꼈습니다.

37 세윤이는 자신의 오래된 자전거가 떠나는 것을 봐서 슬펐지만, 이 경험을 통해 자신이 많은 것을 배우고 조금 더 성장한 것이 기뻤습니다.

※ 다음 문장을 우리말로 쓰시오.

1 ▶ Seyun's First Online Sale
➡ _____

2 ▶ Seyun rides his bike to school every day.
➡ _____

3 ▶ He likes his bike, but he is taller and stronger this year.
➡ _____

4 ▶ His bike has become too small for him, so he wants to buy a bigger, faster one.
➡ _____

5 ▶ However, he does not have enough money in his savings account.
➡ _____

6 ▶ What can he do?
➡ _____

7 ▶ Suddenly, Seyun had an idea.
➡ _____

8 ▶ "My old bike is almost as good as a new one.
➡ _____

9 ▶ Maybe I can sell it and add the money to buy a new one."
➡ _____

10 ▶ He acted fast.
➡ _____

11 ▶ He took a photo of his bike with his smartphone and posted the picture, with a short comment, on an online market: "Used bike in excellent condition. Only 100,000 won. Please text me."
➡ _____
_____

12 ▶ He was excited, thinking about the bike he planned to buy.
➡ _____

13 ▶ He could see himself riding the shiny new bike.
➡ _____

14 ▶ He could not wait to get a reply to his online advertisement.
➡ _____

15 ▶ Every few minutes he checked the number of hits.
➡ _____

16 ▶ As the number of hits went up, his expectations went up too.
➡ _____

17 ▶ One hour passed, then two, and finally a whole day, but he received no texts.
➡ _____

18 ▶ Nobody seemed to want his bike.
➡ _____

19 ▶ New postings by other people pushed his post down the list.
➡ _____

20 ▶ His heart began to sink.
➡ _____

21 ▶ "What's wrong with my posting?
➡ _____

22 ▶ Is my bike not attractive enough?"
➡ _____

23 ▶ He searched on the Internet for tips on how to sell online.
➡ _____

24 ▶ Then he realized what he had done wrong.
➡ _____

25 ▶ He had been too hasty and too greedy.
➡ _____

26 ▶ He had not given enough information to the possible buyers.
➡ _____

27 ▶ Also, when compared to other bicycles, his price was too high.
➡ _____

28 ▶ He wrote a new posting with a longer description of the bike.
➡ _____

29 ▶ He added more photos to show his bike from different angles.
➡ _____

30 ▶ "Twenty-four inch bicycle. Excellent condition. Always kept indoors. Rides just like new. Very few scratches. Good for someone 12-14 years old. 80,000 won."
➡ _____

31 ▶ This time he got several texts.
➡ _____

32 ▶ Sadly, they all asked for a lower price.
➡ _____

33 ▶ It was hard to accept at first, but finally he sold his bike for 70,000 won.
➡ _____

34 ▶ He met the buyer, handed over his bike, and got the money he needed.
➡ _____

35 ▶ Now he could get a new bike.
➡ _____

36 ▶ He felt both happy and sad.
➡ _____

37 ▶ He was sad to see his old bike go, but he was happy with himself because he had learned a lot and grown up a bit through the experience.
➡ _____
_____

※ 다음 괄호 안의 단어들을 우리말에 맞도록 바르게 배열하시오.

1 (First / Seyun's / Sale / Online)
➡ _____

2 (rides / Seyun / bike / his / school / to / day. / every)
➡ _____

3 (likes / he / bike, / his / he / but / taller / is / and / this / stronger / year.)
➡ _____

4 (bike / his / become / has / small / too / him, / for / he / so / to / wants / buy / bigger, / a / one. / faster)
➡ _____

5 (he / however, / not / does / enough / have / in / money / his / account. / savings)
➡ _____

6 (can / what / do? / he)
➡ _____

7 (Seyun / suddenly, / an / had / idea.)
➡ _____

8 (old / "my / bike / almost / is / good / as / a / as / one. / new)
➡ _____

9 (I / maybe / sell / can / and / it / the / add / money / to / a / buy / one." / new)
➡ _____

10 (acted / he / fast.)
➡ _____

11 (took / he / photo / a / his / of / with / bike / smartphone / his / posted / and / picture, / the / with / short / a / comment, / an / on / market: / online / bike / "used / excellent / in / condition. // 100,000 won. / only // text / please / me.")
➡ _____
_____

12 (was / he / excited, / about / thinking / bike / the / planned / he / buy. / to)
➡ _____

13 (could / he / himself / see / the / riding / new / shiny / bike.)
➡ _____

14 (could / he / wait / not / get / to / a / reply / to / his / advertisement. / online)
➡ _____

15 (few / every / he / minutes / checked / number / the / hits. / of)
➡ _____

16 (the / as / of / number / hits / up, / went / expectations / his / up / went / too.)
➡ _____

17 (hour / one / passed, / two, / then / finally / and / a / day, / whole / he / but / no / received / texts.)
➡ _____

18 (seemed / nobody / want / to / bike. / his)
➡ _____

1 세윤이의 첫 온라인 판매

2 세윤이는 매일 학교에 자전거를 타고 갑니다.

3 세윤이는 자신의 자전거를 좋아하지만, 그는 올해 키가 더 크고 힘도 더 세졌습니다.

4 그의 자전거는 그에게 너무 작아져서, 그는 더 크고 더 빠른 자전거를 사기를 원합니다.

5 하지만, 그는 자신의 예금 계좌에 충분한 돈을 가지고 있지 않습니다.

6 그가 무엇을 할 수 있을까요?

7 갑자기, 세윤이는 아이디어가 떠올랐습니다.

8 "내 오래된 자전거는 거의 새것과 다름없이 좋아.

9 아마 나는 그것을 팔고 새것을 사기 위한 돈에 보탤 수 있을 거야."

10 그는 빠르게 행동했습니다.

11 그는 스마트폰으로 자신의 자전거 사진을 찍었고, 짧은 설명과 함께 온라인 장터에 사진을 게시했습니다. "훌륭한 상태의 중고 자전거. 겨우 십만 원. 문자 주세요."

12 세윤이는 자신이 구입하려고 계획한 자전거에 대해 생각하며 신이 났습니다.

13 그는 자신이 빛나는 새 자전거를 타고 있는 것을 상상할 수 있었습니다.

14 세윤이는 자신의 온라인 광고에 대한 대답이 오는 것을 무척 기다렸습니다.

15 몇 분마다 그는 조회 수를 체크했습니다.

16 숫자가 올라갈수록 그의 기대도 덩달아 올라갔습니다.

17 한 시간이 지나고, 두 시간이 지나고, 마침내 하루가 지났지만 세윤이는 문자를 받지 못했습니다.

18 아무도 그의 자전거를 원하지 않는 것처럼 보였습니다.

19 (postings / new / other / by / pushed / people / post / his / the / down / list.)

➡ _____

20 (heart / his / to / began / sink.)

➡ _____

21 (wrong / "what's / my / with / posting?)

➡ _____

22 (my / is / bike / attracitve / not / enough?"

➡ _____

23 (searched / he / the / on / for / Internet / on / tips / to / how / online. / sell)

➡ _____

24 (he / then / what / realized / had / he / wrong. / done)

➡ _____

25 (had / he / too / been / and / hasty / greedy. / too)

➡ _____

26 (had / he / given / not / information / enough / the / to / buyers. / possible)

➡ _____

27 (when / also / to / compared / bicycles, / other / price / his / too / was / high.)

➡ _____

28 (wrote / he / new / a / posting / a / with / longer / of / description / bike. / the)

➡ _____

29 (added / he / photos / more / show / to / bike / his / different / from / angles.)

➡ _____

30 (inch / "twenty-four / bicycle. // condition. / excellent // kept / always / indoors. // just / rides / new. / like // few / vry / scratches. // for / good / 12-14 / someone / old. / years // won." / 80,000)

➡ _____

➡ _____

➡ _____

31 (time / this / got / he / texts. / several)

➡ _____

32 (they / sadly, / asked / all / a / for / price. / lower)

➡ _____

33 (was / it / to / hard / at / accept / first, / finally / but / sold / he / bike / his / for / won. / 70,000)

➡ _____

34 (met / he / buyer, / the / over / handed / bike, / his / got / and / money / the / needed. / he)

➡ _____

35 (he / now / get / could / new / bike. / a)

➡ _____

36 (felt / he / happy / both / sad. / and)

➡ _____

37 (was / he / to / sad / his / see / bike / old / go, / he / but / happy / was / himself / with / he / because / learned / had / lot / a / and / up / grown / bit / a / the / through / experience.)

➡ _____

---

19 다른 사람들의 새 게시물이 그의 게시물을 리스트에서 밀어냈습니다.

20 세윤이의 가슴이 내려앉기 시작했습니다.

21 '내 포스팅에 무슨 문제가 있지?

22 내 자전거가 충분히 매력적이지 못한가?'

23 세윤이는 온라인에서 판매하는 방법에 대한 조언을 찾기 위해 인터넷을 검색했습니다.

24 곧 그는 자신의 잘못을 깨달았습니다.

25 세윤이는 너무 성급했고 너무 욕심이 많았습니다.

26 그는 구매 가능성이 있는 사람들에게 충분한 정보를 주지 않았습니다.

27 또한, 다른 자전거들과 비교했을 때 그의 가격은 너무 높았습니다.

28 세윤이는 자신의 자전거에 대한 더 긴 묘사가 있는 새 게시물을 작성했습니다.

29 그는 자신의 자전거를 다른 각도에서 보여 주기 위해서 더 많은 사진들을 첨부했습니다.

30 "24인치 자전거. 훌륭한 상태. 항상 실내에 보관함. 새것처럼 탐. 스크래치 매우 적음. 12–14세에게 좋음. 8만 원."

31 이번에 그는 여러 통의 문자 메시지를 받았습니다.

32 애석하게도, 그들은 모두 더 낮은 가격을 요청했습니다.

33 처음에는 받아들이기 어려웠지만, 마침내 그는 자신의 자전거를 칠만 원에 팔았습니다.

34 세윤이는 구매자를 만나 자전거를 건네주고, 그가 필요했던 돈을 받았습니다.

35 이제 세윤이는 새 자전거를 살 수 있습니다.

36 그는 기쁘고 슬픈 감정을 동시에 느꼈습니다.

37 세윤이는 자신의 오래된 자전거가 떠나는 것을 봐서 슬펐지만, 이 경험을 통해 자신이 많은 것을 배우고 조금 더 성장한 것이 기뻤습니다.

※ 다음 우리말을 영어로 쓰시오.

1 세윤이의 첫 온라인 판매
➡ _____

2 세윤이는 매일 학교에 자전거를 타고 갑니다.
➡ _____

3 세윤이는 자신의 자전거를 좋아하지만, 그는 올해 키가 더 크고 힘도 더 세졌습니다.
➡ _____

4 그의 자전거는 그에게 너무 작아져서, 그는 더 크고 더 빠른 자전거를 사기를 원합니다.
➡ _____

5 하지만, 그는 자신의 예금 계좌에 충분한 돈을 가지고 있지 않습니다.
➡ _____

6 그가 무엇을 할 수 있을까요?
➡ _____

7 갑자기, 세윤이는 아이디어가 떠올랐습니다.
➡ _____

8 "내 오래된 자전거는 거의 새것과 다름없이 좋아.
➡ _____

9 아마 나는 그것을 팔고 새것을 사기 위한 돈에 보탤 수 있을 거야."
➡ _____

10 그는 빠르게 행동했습니다.
➡ _____

11 그는 스마트폰으로 자신의 자전거 사진을 찍었고, 짧은 설명과 함께 온라인 장터에 사진을 게시했습니다. "훌륭한 상태의 중고 자전거. 겨우 십만 원. 문자 주세요."
➡ _____
_____

12 세윤이는 자신이 구입하려고 계획한 자전거에 대해 생각하며 신이 났습니다.
➡ _____

13 그는 자신이 빛나는 새 자전거를 타고 있는 것을 상상할 수 있었습니다.
➡ _____

14 세윤이는 자신의 온라인 광고에 대한 대답이 오는 것을 무척 기다렸습니다.
➡ _____

15 몇 분마다 그는 조회 수를 체크했습니다.
➡ _____

16 숫자가 올라갈수록 그의 기대도 덩달아 올라갔습니다.
➡ _____

17 한 시간이 지나고, 두 시간이 지나고, 마침내 하루가 지났지만 세윤이는 문자를 받지 못했습니다.
➡ _____

18 아무도 그의 자전거를 원하지 않는 것처럼 보였습니다.
➡ _____

19 다른 사람들의 새 게시물이 그의 게시물을 리스트에서 밀어냈습니다.

➡ _____

20 세윤이의 가슴이 내려앉기 시작했습니다.

➡ _____

21 '내 포스팅에 무슨 문제가 있지?

➡ _____

22 내 자전거가 충분히 매력적이지 못한가?'

➡ _____

23 세윤이는 온라인에서 판매하는 방법에 대한 조언을 찾기 위해 인터넷을 검색했습니다.

➡ _____

24 곧 그는 자신의 잘못을 깨달았습니다.

➡ _____

25 세윤이는 너무 성급했고 너무 욕심이 많았습니다.

➡ _____

26 그는 구매 가능성이 있는 사람들에게 충분한 정보를 주지 않았습니다.

➡ _____

27 또한, 다른 자전거들과 비교했을 때 그의 가격은 너무 높았습니다.

➡ _____

28 세윤이는 자신의 자전거에 대한 더 긴 묘사가 있는 새 게시물을 작성했습니다.

➡ _____

29 그는 자신의 자전거를 다른 각도에서 보여 주기 위해서 더 많은 사진들을 첨부했습니다.

➡ _____

30 "24인치 자전거. 훌륭한 상태. 항상 실내에 보관했음. 새것처럼 탐. 스크래치 매우 적음. 12-14세에게 좋음. 8만 원."

➡ _____

31 이번에 그는 여러 통의 문자 메시지를 받았습니다.

➡ _____

32 애석하게도, 그들은 모두 더 낮은 가격을 요청했습니다.

➡ _____

33 처음에는 받아들이기 어려웠지만, 마침내 그는 자신의 자전거를 칠만 원에 팔았습니다.

➡ _____

34 세윤이는 구매자를 만나 자전거를 건네주고, 그가 필요했던 돈을 받았습니다.

➡ _____

35 이제 세윤이는 새 자전거를 살 수 있습니다.

➡ _____

36 그는 기쁘고 슬픈 감정을 동시에 느꼈습니다.

➡ _____

37 세윤이는 자신의 오래된 자전거가 떠나는 것을 봐서 슬펐지만, 이 경험을 통해 자신이 많은 것을 배우고 조금 더 성장한 것이 기뻤습니다.

➡ _____

_____

※ 다음 우리말과 일치하도록 빈칸에 알맞은 말을 쓰시오.

After You Read B

1. Buyer: Hello? Are you the one _____ _____ _____ _____ _____?

2. Seyun: Yes, that's _____.

3. Buyer: Can I _____ your bike _____ _____ if it's in good condition _____ _____ _____?

4. Seyun: Sure. It _____ very _____ _____ but nothing _____.

5. Buyer: _____ me _____.... Yeah, it _____ _____ _____.

6. Seyun: _____!

7. Buyer: _____ _____ _____, can I ask _____ _____ _____ _____ this bike?

8. Seyun: I've _____ _____ _____ 10 cm _____ _____, so it's _____ _____ _____ _____ now.

9. Buyer: Oh, I _____.

1. 구매자: 안녕하세요? 자전거를 팔려고 게시한 분이신가요?
2. 세윤: 네, 저예요.
3. 구매자: 당신이 쓰신 것처럼 좋은 상태 인지 보기 위하여 당신의 자전 거를 좀 살펴봐도 될까요?
4. 세윤: 물론이죠. 스크래치가 아주 조금 있지만 추하지는 않아요.
5. 구매자: 한 번 볼게요…. 네, 충분히 좋은 것 같아요.
6. 세윤: 정말 좋군요!
7. 구매자: 그런데, 왜 이 자전거를 파시려 고 하는지 물어봐도 될까요?
8. 세윤: 올해 제 키가 10 cm 이상 커져 서, 이제 이 자전거는 저에게 너 무 작기 때문이에요.
9. 구매자: 오, 알겠습니다.

Writing Workshop

1. _____ you _____ _____ _____ a new swimming suit, this one _____ _____ _____. It is beautiful.

2. Also, it is _____ _____ _____ the one that is _____ _____.

3. I _____ _____, and I really like _____.

4. However, I _____ _____ you _____ _____ _____ than _____ _____ _____ _____ _____.

5. _____ _____ I had ordered _____ _____ size _____ _____ I _____ _____, it was _____ _____ _____ me.

1. 만약 당신이 새 수영복을 찾고 있다면, 이 수영복이 완벽 할 것입니다. 이것은 예뻐요.
2. 또한 이것은 세일 중에 있는 수영복만 큼 저렴합니다.
3. 나는 이 새 수영복을 구매했고, 지금 완전 맘에 듭니다.
4. 그러나 나는 평소 당신이 사는 사이즈 보다 큰 것을 살 것을 권합니다.
5. 나는 평소 내가 입는 사이즈와 같은 것을 주문했는데 이것은 나에게 너무 작습니다.

Wrap Up 7

1. _____ _____, Monday

2. _____ _____, I planted some potatoes _____ _____ _____ in his garden.

3. I _____ the garden and _____ _____ _____ _____ _____.

4. I _____ _____ _____ potatoes _____. It was fun.

5. Today, my grandfather and I _____ _____ _____ the potatoes.

6. They _____ _____ _____ _____ the ones you see in the market, and _____ _____ so many of them.

7. My grandfather says we _____ _____ _____ _____ them _____ _____ _____ and _____ them!

8. That _____ _____ _____.

1. 9월 8일, 월요일
2. 지난 봄, 나는 할아버지와 함께 그의 정원에서 감자를 심었다.
3. 나는 종종 정원을 방문하여 감자에 물 을 주었다.
4. 나는 그 전에는 감자를 심어 본 적이 없었다. 그것은 재미있었다.
5. 오늘, 할아버지와 나는 감자를 좀 캤다.
6. 그것들은 시장에서 보는 것만큼 상태 가 좋았고, 양도 많았다.
7. 할아버지께서는 우리가 그것들 일부를 시장에 가져가서 팔 수도 있다고 말씀 하셨다!
8. 그것은 정말 신날 것이다.

※ **다음 우리말을 영어로 쓰시오.**

After You Read B

1. 구매자: 안녕하세요? 자전거를 팔려고 게시한 분이신가요?
➡ _____

2. 세윤: 네, 저에요.
➡ _____

3. 구매자: 당신이 쓰신 것처럼 좋은 상태인지 보기 위하여 당신의 자전거를 좀 살펴봐도 될까요?
➡ _____

4. 세윤: 물론이죠. 스크래치가 아주 조금 있지만 추하지는 않아요.
➡ _____

5. 구매자: 한 번 볼게요…. 네, 충분히 좋은 것 같아요.
➡ _____

6. 세윤: 정말 좋군요!
➡ _____

7. 구매자: 그런데, 왜 이 자전거를 파시려고 하는지 물어봐도 될까요?
➡ _____

8. 세윤: 올해 제 키가 10 cm 이상 커져서, 이제 이 자전거는 저에게 너무 작기 때문이에요.
➡ _____

9. 구매자: 오, 알겠습니다.
➡ _____

Writing Workshop

1. 만약 당신이 새 수영복을 찾고 있다면, 이 수영복이 완벽 할 것입니다. 이것은 예뻐요.
➡ _____

2. 또한 이것은 세일 중에 있는 수영복만큼 저렴합니다.
➡ _____

3. 나는 이 새 수영복을 구매했고, 지금 완전 맘에 듭니다.
➡ _____

4. 그러나 나는 평소 당신이 사는 사이즈보다 큰 사이즈를 살 것을 권합니다.
➡ _____

5. 나는 평소 내가 입는 사이즈와 같은 것을 주문했는데 이것은 나에게 너무 작습니다.
➡ _____

Wrap Up 7

1. 9월 8일, 월요일
➡ _____

2. 지난 봄, 나는 할아버지와 함께 그의 정원에서 감자를 심었다.
➡ _____

3. 나는 종종 정원을 방문하여 감자에 물을 주었다.
➡ _____

4. 나는 그 전에는 감자를 심어 본 적이 없었다. 그것은 재미있었다.
➡ _____

5. 오늘, 할아버지와 나는 감자를 좀 캤다.
➡ _____

6. 그것들은 시장에서 보는 것만큼 상태가 좋았고, 양도 많았다.
➡ _____

7. 할아버지께서는 우리가 그것들 일부를 시장에 가져가서 팔 수도 있다고 말씀하셨다.
➡ _____

8. 그것은 정말 신날 것이다.
➡ _____

※ 다음 영어를 우리말로 쓰시오.

01 careful	_____
02 pane	_____
03 surprisingly	_____
04 crispy	_____
05 perhaps	_____
06 swallow	_____
07 result	_____
08 twist	_____
09 prevent	_____
10 fantastic	_____
11 repair	_____
12 pressure	_____
13 notice	_____
14 steam	_____
15 boil	_____
16 carefully	_____
17 death	_____
18 emergency	_____
19 amount	_____
20 roof	_____
21 balance	_____

22 breathing	_____
23 especially	_____
24 couch	_____
25 necessary	_____
26 recently	_____
27 shaped	_____
28 hide	_____
29 lid	_____
30 fog	_____
31 company	_____
32 cause	_____
33 product	_____
34 helpful	_____
35 build up	_____
36 prevent A from -ing	_____
37 boil over	_____
38 fog up	_____
39 let out	_____
40 look around	_____
41 be made up of	_____
42 the result of ~	_____
43 pass through	_____

※ 다음 우리말을 영어로 쓰시오.

01	놀랍게도	
02	비틀다, 돌리다	
03	숨기다, 숨다	
04	바삭한	
05	알아채다, 의식하다	
06	판유리	
07	숨겨져 있는	
08	호흡, 숨	
09	삼키다	
10	소파, 긴 의자	
11	유용한, 도움이 되는	
12	수리하다	
13	죽음	
14	최근에	
15	~ 모양의	
16	생산물, 상품	
17	비상사태	
18	양, 총계	
19	압력	
20	뚜껑	
21	주의 깊게, 조심스럽게	

22	끓기; 끓이다	
23	특히	
24	막다	
25	균형; 균형을 잡다	
26	안개; 수증기가 서리다	
27	주의 깊은, 조심스러운	
28	필수적인	
29	표현하다	
30	아마, 어쩌면	
31	~을 야기하다; 원인	
32	회사, 동료	
33	지붕	
34	수증기, 김	
35	끓어 넘치다	
36	내보내다	
37	~의 결과	
38	밖을 내다보다	
39	거쳐 지나가다, 통과하다	
40	주위를 둘러보다	
41	A가 ~하는 것을 막다	
42	~로 구성되다	
43	비상 상황에서	

※ 다음 영영풀이에 알맞은 단어를 <보기>에서 골라 쓴 후, 우리말 뜻을 쓰시오.

1 _____ : not long ago: _____

2 _____ : to make food go down the throat: _____

3 _____ : willing to help, or useful: _____

4 _____ : to become aware of: _____

5 _____ : in the usual or expected way: _____

6 _____ : an unexpected and dangerous situation: _____

7 _____ : needed in order to achieve a particular result: _____

8 _____ : a long comfortable seat for two or more people to sit on: _____

9 _____ : to put something damaged back into good condition: _____

10 _____ : the structure that covers or forms the top of a building or vehicle: _____

11 _____ : the process to take air into the lungs and let it out again: _____

12 _____ : very much; more than usual or more than other people or things: _____

13 _____ : to stop something from happening or someone from doing something: _____

14 _____ : the degree to which something is a lot or a little; how much something is: _____

15 _____ : something that is made to be sold, usually something that is produced by an industrial process: _____

16 _____ : to be in a position where you will stand without falling to either side, or to put something in this position: _____

보기

amount	emergency	prevent	couch
roof	notice	repair	swallow
balance	necessary	product	normally
especially	recently	breathing	helpful

Step1

※ 다음 우리말과 일치하도록 빈칸에 알맞은 말을 쓰시오.

Listen & Speak 1 Listen

1. G: Look at this _____. I wonder who _____ men are.
   B: They're the Wright brothers. They _____ the airplane.
2. G: I wonder _____ they are standing in _____ of the bicycle shop.
   B: They had a bicycle shop. They _____ and _____ bicycles.
3. G: I wonder _____ the first plane _____ like.
   B: Look! There is a model. It _____ _____ a big bird.
4. G: I _____ where they first _____ to fly their airplane.
   B: They _____ their airplane on a hill in North Carolina.

Listen & Speak 1 A-1

B: Look at this _____. It can help us _____ _____ _____.
G: Is that _____? I wonder _____ _____ _____.
B: It uses _____ to cook food.
G: Wow. That would be really _____ when you go camping.

Listen & Speak 1 A-2

B: Hi, class. _____ you ever _____ about the Moai? They are tall, human-_____ stones in Chile. _____ of the stones are four meters _____, but the tallest one is 20 meters tall. I was _____ _____ _____ _____ them long ago. So I _____ the Internet and _____ that they used _____. Isn't that _____?

Listen & Speak 1 B-1

A: I wonder _____ those men are.
B: They're the Wright brothers. They _____ the airplane.

Listen & Speak 1 B-2

A: I wonder what the first plane _____ _____.
B: Look! There is a _____. It looked _____ a big bird.

Listen & Speak 1 B-3

A: I _____ what _____ they're _____.
B: They're _____ the U.S.

해석

1. G: 이 사진을 봐. 나는 그 남자들이 누구인지 궁금해.
   B: 그들은 라이트 형제야. 그들은 비행기를 발명했어.
2. G: 나는 그들이 왜 자전거 가게 앞에 서 있는지 궁금해.
   B: 그들은 자전거 가게를 가지고 있었어. 그들은 자전거를 팔고 수리했어.
3. G: 나는 최초의 비행기가 어떻게 생겼는지 궁금해.
   B: 봐! 저기 모형이 있어. 그것은 큰 새처럼 생겼었네.
4. G: 나는 그들이 어디에서 처음으로 비행을 시도했는지 궁금해.
   B: 그들은 노스캐롤라이나주의 한 언덕에서 그들의 비행기를 시험했어.

B: 이 발명품들을 봐. 이것은 우리가 전기 없이도 요리할 수 있도록 도와줘.
G: 그게 가능해? 나는 그것이 어떻게 작용하는지 궁금해.
B: 이것은 음식을 조리하기 위해 태양광을 사용해.
G: 와. 그것은 캠핑을 갈 때 정말 유용할 것 같아.

B: 안녕하세요, 여러분. 여러분은 모아이에 대해 들어 본 적이 있나요? 그것들은 칠레에 있는 크고 사람 모양을 한 돌입니다. 대부분의 돌들은 높이가 4미터이지만, 가장 큰 것은 높이가 20미터입니다. 저는 오래 전에 사람들이 어떻게 그것들을 옮겼는지 궁금했습니다. 그래서 저는 인터넷을 검색했고 그들이 밧줄을 이용했다는 것을 알게 되었습니다. 그 사실이 놀랍지 않나요?

A: 나는 그 남자들의 누구인지 궁금해.
B: 그들은 라이트 형제야. 그들은 비행기를 발명했어.

A: 나는 최조의 비행기가 어떻게 생겼는지 궁금해.
B: 봐! 저기 모형이 있어. 그것은 큰 새처럼 생겼었네.

A: 나는 그들이 어느 나라 출신인지 궁금해.
B: 그들은 미국 출신이야.

Listen & Speak 2 Listen

1. **G:** _____ can we do _____ these VR glasses?
   B: _____ me see.... _____ we can play soccer.

2. **B:** _____ does the ball _____ in the air?
   G: Let me see.... I think air _____ the ball _____.

3. **G:** How does this train start to _____?
   B: Let me _____.... I think you can move it _____ a smartphone app.

4. **B:** What can we do _____ this drone?
   G: Well, let me see.... Maybe we can take _____ from the sky.

Listen & Speak 2 A-1

G: _____ at the number. It's _____ _____ _____.
B: When people _____ by, the number _____.
G: Oh, you're right. What does the number _____?
B: _____ me see.... Oh, when people _____ on the floor, energy is _____. It shows the _____ of energy that is made.
G: Wow, that's _____!

Listen & Speak 2 A- 2

G: We're going on a _____ trip tomorrow to the _____ Museum.
B: I've heard that it has a lot of _____ _____.
G: That's why I'm so _____. How about _____ the tour before we go?
B: _____ idea. _____ me see.... I have the school letter and a map of the _____.
G: Perfect. _____ get _____.

Listen & Speak 2 B-1

A: _____ can we do _____ this VR glasses?
B: _____ me _____ … We can _____ soccer.

Listen & Speak 2 B-2

A: What can we do _____ this drone?
B: Let me _____ … We can take pictures _____ the sky.

1. **G:** 우리가 이 VR 안경으로 무엇을 할 수 있을까?
   B: 어디 보자.... 아마 우리는 축구를 할 수 있을 거야.
2. **G:** 어떻게 그 공이 공중에 뜰까?
   B: 어디 보자.... 내 생각에는 공기가 공을 위로 밀어 올리는 것 같아.
3. **G:** 이 기차는 어떻게 움직이기 시작할까?
   B: 어디 보자.... 내 생각에는 네가 스마트폰 앱으로 그것을 움직일 수 있을 것 같아.
4. **G:** 우리가 이 드론으로 무엇을 할 수 있을까?
   B: 음, 어디 보자.... 아마 우리는 하늘에서 사진을 찍을 수 있을 거야.

G: 저 숫자를 봐. 빠르게 올라가고 있어.
B: 사람들이 지나갈 때, 그 숫자가 증가해.
G: 오, 네 말이 맞아. 그 숫자는 무엇을 의미할까?
B: 어디 보자.... 오, 사람들이 바닥을 밟을 때 에너지가 만들어져. 그것은 만들어지는 에너지의 양을 보여 줘.
G: 와, 놀라워!

G: 우리는 내일 '발명 박물관'으로 현장 학습을 가.
B: 나는 그곳에 창의적인 발명품들이 많이 있다고 들었어.
G: 그것이 내가 들뜬 이유야. 우리 가기 전에 관람 계획을 짜는 것은 어때?
B: 좋은 생각이야. 어디 보자.... 나는 학교에서 받은 안내서와 박물관 지도가 있어.
G: 완벽해. 시작하자.

A: 우리가 이 VR 안경으로 무엇을 할 수 있을까?
B: 어디 보자.... 우리는 축구를 할 수 있어.

A: 우리가 이 드론으로 무엇을 할 수 있을까?
B: 어디 보자.... 우리는 하늘에서 사진을 찍을 수 있어.

Listen & Speak 2 B-3

A: _____ can we do _____ the smart watch?

B: Let me see… We can _____ _____ _____.

A: 우리가 이 스마트워치로 무엇을 할 수 있을까?

B: 어디 보자…. 우리는 문자 메시지를 보낼 수 있어.

Real-Life Zone

G: I like _____ crackers. They're really good.

B: Yeah, me, too. I wonder _____ crackers have these _____ _____ in them.

G: I don't know. Let me _____…. Um … well … _____ it's because the holes _____ the crackers _____ _____.

B: That's _____, but there _____ be some other _____.

G: Let's _____ up crackers on the Internet and see _____ it says.

B: Okay. Oh, look at this.

G: It _____ _____ baking, steam comes out _____ the holes and that makes the crackers _____.

B: It also says that the holes _____ the crackers _____.

G: Wow! So that's _____ they have holes!

G: 난 이 크래커가 좋아. 정말 맛있어.

B: 응, 나도 좋아해. 나는 크래커에 왜 이 작은 구멍이 있는지 궁금해.

G: 잘 모르겠어. 생각해 보자…. 음… 아마 그 구멍들이 크래커를 더욱 맛있게 보이도록 해 주기 때문이 아닐까.

B: 그럴 수도 있겠네. 하지만 다른 이유들이 있을 거야.

G: 크래커에 관해 인터넷에 찾아보고 뭐라고 하는지 알아보자.

B: 좋아. 오, 이것 봐.

G: 굽는 동안, 그 구멍들을 통해 수증기가 빠져나와서 크래커를 얇게 만드는 거래.

B: 또한 구멍들은 크래커를 바삭하게 만드는 거래.

G: 와! 크래커에 구멍들이 있는 거구나!

Wrap Up 1~2

B: Hi, Kate. Today's Saturday, so _____ about _____ to the Einstein Science Park today?

G: That _____ like a good idea. I heard _____ they have special programs on _____. I wonder _____ _____ _____.

B: Let me see…. I saw an _____ in the newspaper. _____ it is.

G: What does it _____?

B: It _____ that today they have two shows: the Smart Design Show and the International Drone Show in Einstein Hall 101.

G: They _____ sound _____.

B: I'll _____ them and ask _____ time they start.

B: 안녕, 케이트. 오늘은 토요일이야. 그래서 말인데, 오늘 아인슈타인 과학 공원에 가는 건 어때?

G: 좋은 생각이야. 나는 토요일마다 특별한 프로그램들이 있다고 들었어. 나는 그것들이 무엇인지 궁금해.

B: 어디 보자…. 내가 신문에서 광고를 봤어. 여기 있어.

G: 뭐라고 쓰여 있니?

B: 여기에 따르면 오늘 두 가지 공연이 있대. 아인슈타인 홀 101호에서 있는 스마트 디자인 쇼와 국제 드론 쇼야.

G: 둘 다 환상적일 것 같아.

B: 내가 전화해서 그것들이 몇 시에 시작하는지 물어볼게.

Wrap Up 3~4

G: John, look. The school is having an _____ _____.

B: Really? That _____ interesting.

G: Yeah. You should _____ that. You always have great _____.

B: Does it say _____ the _____ _____?

G: Let me see…. It says it's November 11. That's two weeks _____ today.

B: I _____ what I _____ to do to enter the competition.

G: It says here you should _____ to Mr. Harrison, the _____ teacher.

G: 존, 봐. 학교에서 발명대회가 열린대.

B: 정말? 흥미로울 것 같아.

G: 응. 너는 참가해야 해. 너는 항상 아이디어가 훌륭하잖아.

B: 대회가 언제인지 나와 있니?

G: 어디 보자…. 11월 11일이래. 오늘로부터 2주 뒤야.

B: 대회에 참가하기 위해 내가 무엇을 해야 하는지 궁금해.

G: 여기에 따르면 너는 과학 선생님이신 해리슨 선생님께 말씀드려야 해.

※ 다음 우리말에 맞도록 대화를 영어로 쓰시오.

Listen & Speak 1 Listen

1. G: _____
   B: _____

2. G: _____
   B: _____

3. G: _____
   B: _____

4. G: _____
   B: _____

Listen & Speak 1 A-1

B: _____
G: _____
B: _____
G: _____

Listen & Speak 1 A-2

B: _____
   _____
   _____
   _____

Listen & Speak 1 B-1

A: _____
B: _____

Listen & Speak 1 B-2

A: _____
B: _____

Listen & Speak 1 B-3

A: _____
B: _____

해석

1. G: 이 사진을 봐. 나는 그 남자들이 누구인지 궁금해.
   B: 그들은 라이트 형제야. 그들은 비행기를 발명했어.
2. G: 나는 그들이 왜 자전거 가게 앞에 서 있는지 궁금해.
   B: 그들은 자전거 가게를 가지고 있었어. 그들은 자전거를 팔고 수리했어.
3. G: 나는 최초의 비행기가 어떻게 생겼는지 궁금해.
   B: 봐! 저기 모형이 있어. 그것은 큰 새처럼 생겼었네.
4. G: 나는 그들이 어디에서 처음으로 비행을 시도했는지 궁금해.
   B: 그들은 노스캐롤라이나주의 한 언덕에서 그들의 비행기를 시험했어.

B: 이 발명품들을 봐. 이것은 우리가 전기 없이도 요리할 수 있도록 도와줘.
G: 그게 가능해? 나는 그것이 어떻게 작용하는지 궁금해.
B: 이것은 음식을 조리하기 위해 태양광을 사용해.
G: 와. 그것은 캠핑을 갈 때 정말 유용할 것 같아.

B: 안녕하세요, 여러분. 여러분은 모아이에 대해 들어 본 적이 있나요? 그것들은 칠레에 있는 크고 사람 모양을 한 돌입니다. 대부분의 돌들은 높이가 4미터이지만, 가장 큰 것은 높이가 20미터입니다. 저는 오래 전에 사람들이 어떻게 그것들을 옮겼는지 궁금했습니다. 그래서 저는 인터넷을 검색했고 그들이 밧줄을 이용했다는 것을 알게 되었습니다. 그 사실이 놀랍지 않나요?
A: 나는 그 남자들의 누구인지 궁금해.
B: 그들은 라이트 형제야. 그들은 비행기를 발명했어.

A: 나는 최초의 비행기가 어떻게 생겼는지 궁금해.
B: 봐! 저기 모형이 있어. 그것은 큰 새처럼 생겼었네.

A: 나는 그들이 어느 나라 출신인지 궁금해.
B: 그들은 미국 출신이야.

Listen & Speak 2 Listen

1. G: _____

   B: _____

2. B: _____

   G: _____

3. G: _____

   B: _____

4. B: _____

   G: _____

Listen & Speak 2 A-1

G: _____

B: _____

G: _____

B: _____

G: _____

Listen & Speak 2 A- 2

G: _____

B: _____

G: _____

B: _____

G: _____

Listen & Speak 2 B-1

A: _____

B: _____

Listen & Speak 2 B-2

A: _____

B: _____

1. G: 우리가 이 VR 안경으로 무엇을 할 수 있을까?
   B: 어디 보자.... 아마 우리는 축구를 할 수 있을 거야.
2. G: 어떻게 그 공이 공중에 뜰까?
   B: 어디 보자.... 내 생각에는 공기가 공을 위로 밀어 올리는 것 같아.
3. G: 이 기차는 어떻게 움직이기 시작할까?
   B: 어디 보자.... 내 생각에는 네가 스마트폰 앱으로 그것을 움직일 수 있을 것 같아.
4. G: 우리가 이 드론으로 무엇을 할 수 있을까?
   B: 음, 어디 보자.... 아마 우리는 하늘에서 사진을 찍을 수 있을 거야.

G: 저 숫자를 봐. 빠르게 올라가고 있어.
B: 사람들이 지나갈 때, 그 숫자가 증가해.
G: 오, 네 말이 맞아. 그 숫자는 무엇을 의미할까?
B: 어디 보자.... 오, 사람들이 바닥을 밟을 때 에너지가 만들어져. 그것은 만들어지는 에너지의 양을 보여 줘.
G: 와, 놀라워!

G: 우리는 내일 '발명 박물관'으로 현장 학습을 가.
B: 나는 그곳에 창의적인 발명품들이 많이 있다고 들었어.
G: 그것이 내가 들뜬 이유야. 우리 가기 전에 관람 계획을 짜는 것은 어때?
B: 좋은 생각이야. 어디 보자.... 나는 학교에서 받은 안내서와 박물관 지도가 있어.
G: 완벽해. 시작하자.

A: 우리가 이 VR 안경으로 무엇을 할 수 있을까?
B: 어디 보자.... 우리는 축구를 할 수 있어.

A: 우리가 이 드론으로 무엇을 할 수 있을까?
B: 어디 보자.... 우리는 하늘에서 사진을 찍을 수 있어.

Listen & Speak 2 B-3

A: _____

B: _____

Real-Life Zone

G: _____

B: _____

G: _____

_____

B: _____

G: _____

B: _____

G: _____

B: _____

G: _____

Wrap Up 1~2

B: _____

G: _____

B: _____

G: _____

B: _____

G: _____

B: _____

Wrap Up 3~4

G: _____

B: _____

G: _____

B: _____

G: _____

B: _____

G: _____

A: 우리가 이 스마트워치로 무엇을 할 수 있을까?
B: 어디 보자.... 우리는 문자 메시지를 보낼 수 있어.

G: 난 이 크래커가 좋아. 정말 맛있어.
B: 응, 나도 좋아해. 나는 크래커에 왜 이 작은 구멍들이 있는지 궁금해.
G: 잘 모르겠어. 생각해 보자.... 음... 아마 그 구멍들이 크래커를 더욱 맛있게 보이도록 해 주기 때문이 아닐까.
B: 그럴 수도 있겠네, 하지만 다른 이유들이 있을 거야.
G: 크래커에 관해 인터넷에 찾아보고 뭐라고 하는지 알아보자.
B: 좋아. 오, 이것 봐.
G: 굽는 동안, 그 구멍들을 통해 수증기가 빠져나와서 크래커를 얇게 만드는 거래.
B: 또한 구멍들은 크래커를 바삭하게 만드는 거래.
G: 와! 크래커에 구멍들이 있는 거구나!

B: 안녕, 케이트. 오늘은 토요일이야. 그래서 말인데, 오늘 아인슈타인 과학 공원에 가는 건 어때?
G: 좋은 생각이야. 나는 토요일마다 특별한 프로그램들이 있다고 들었어. 나는 그것들이 무엇인지 궁금해.
B: 어디 보자.... 내가 신문에서 광고를 봤어. 여기 있어.
G: 뭐라고 쓰여 있니?
B: 여기에 따르면 오늘 두 가지 공연이 있대. 아이슈타인 홀 101호에서 있는 스마트 디자인 쇼와 국제 드론 쇼야.
G: 둘 다 환상적일 것 같아.
B: 내가 전화해서 그것들이 몇 시에 시작하는지 물어볼게.

G: 존, 봐. 학교에서 발명대회가 열린대.
B: 정말? 흥미로울 것 같아.
G: 응. 너는 참가해야 해. 너는 항상 아이디어가 훌륭하잖아.
B: 대회가 언제인지 나와 있니?
G: 어디 보자.... 11월 11일이래. 오늘로부터 2주 뒤야.
B: 대회에 참가하기 위해 내가 무엇을 해야 하는지 궁금해.
G: 여기에 따르면 너는 과학 선생님이신 해리슨 선생님께 말씀드려야 해.

※ 다음 우리말과 일치하도록 빈칸에 알맞은 것을 골라 쓰시오.

1 _____ _____
A. Holes   B. Hidden

2 _____ about a _____ that you have _____ _____.
A. hole   B. seen   C. think   D. recently

3 _____ it a _____ hole _____ a _____ hole?
A. bad   B. or   C. good   D. was

4 _____ it was a _____ in your _____, it was _____.
A. sock   B. if   C. bad   D. hole

5 If it was a _____ in your shirt _____ a _____, it was _____.
A. button   B. for   C. hole   D. good

6 _____ are _____ _____.
A. everywhere   B. there   C. holes

7 Some are _____ small you _____ not _____ _____ them.
A. even   B. so   C. notice   D. may

8 They are well _____, but many of these small holes are very important and _____ your _____ _____.
A. make   B. hidden   C. safe   D. life

9 _____ a _____.
A. pen   B. take

10 _____ _____ it _____.
A. at   B. look   C. carefully

11 Do you see a _____ _____ in the _____?
A. hole   B. small   C. cap

12 Do you know _____ _____ _____ _____?
A. it   B. there   C. is   D. why

13 The _____ in a pen cap can _____ _____ _____.
A. help   B. hole   C. lives   D. save

14 People, _____ children, often _____ small things _____ pen caps _____ their mouths.
A. like   B. especially   C. in   D. put

15 _____ they _____ them.
A. even   B. sometimes   C. swallow

16 This can _____ their _____ and _____.
A. breathing   B. stop   C. death   D. cause

17 A _____ pen _____ started _____ a small _____ in their pen caps.
A. company   B. hole   C. famous   D. putting

18 The hole in the cap _____ air _____ _____ and has saved _____.
A. pass   B. lives   C. lets   D. through

1 숨겨진 구멍들

2 여러분이 최근에 본 구멍에 대해 생각해 보라.

3 그것은 좋은 구멍이었는가, 아니면 나쁜 구멍이었는가?

4 만약 그것이 여러분의 양말에 있는 구멍이었다면, 그것은 좋지 않은 것이었다.

5 만약 그것이 단추를 위해 셔츠에 있는 구멍이었다면, 그것은 좋은 것이었다.

6 구멍은 어디에나 있다.

7 어떤 것들은 너무 작아서 인지하지 못할 수도 있다.

8 그것들은 잘 숨겨져 있지만, 이 작은 구멍들 중 많은 것들이 매우 중요하고 여러분의 삶을 안전하게 해 준다.

9 펜을 꺼내라.

10 그것을 자세히 관찰해 보라.

11 뚜껑에 작은 구멍이 보이는가?

12 여러분은 왜 거기에 구멍이 있는지 아는가?

13 펜 뚜껑에 있는 구멍이 생명을 구하는 데 도움을 줄 수 있기 때문이다.

14 사람들, 특히 아이들은 종종 펜 뚜껑 같은 작은 것들을 그들의 입에 넣는다.

15 때때로 그들은 심지어 그것들을 삼키기도 한다.

16 이것은 그들의 호흡을 막고 죽음을 초래할 수도 있다.

17 유명한 펜 회사가 자사의 펜 뚜껑에 작은 구멍을 넣기 시작했다.

18 뚜껑에 있는 그 구멍은 공기를 통하게 해 주고 생명들을 구했다.

19 If you _____ _____, you will see other holes that play a _____ _____ in your life.

    A. around   B. role   C. look   D. helpful

20 If you have ever cooked anything in a pot _____ a _____, _____ you _____ a small hole in the lid.

    A. perhaps   B. with   C. noticed   D. lid

21 This _____, _____, is there for _____.

    A. safety   B. too   C. hole

22 When _____ something in a pot with a lid, the _____ inside the pot _____ _____.

    A. pressure   B. up   C. cooking   D. builds

23 The water _____ would quickly _____ _____ if the lid did not have that _____.

    A. hole   B. boil   C. inside   D. over

24 The hole lets steam _____ and _____ the water _____ out.

    A. from   B. out   C. coming   D. keeps

25 _____ you _____ _____ _____ an airplane?

    A. ever   B. have   C. on   D. been

26 _____ _____ _____ to look out the window and see the world _____?

    A. exciting   B. it   C. below   D. wasn't

27 _____, _____ _____ a small hole _____ your window.

    A. was   B. surprisingly   C. in   D. there

28 Airplane windows _____ _____ _____ _____ three panes.

    A. made   B. of   C. are   D. up

29 There is a hole _____ _____ _____ _____.

    A. the   B. pane   C. in   D. middle

30 It _____ the _____ _____.

    A. air   B. balances   C. pressure

31 _____ this _____ hole, airplane windows might _____ in an _____.

    A. little   B. emergency   C. without   D. break

32 The hole also _____ the window _____ _____ so that you can enjoy that fantastic view.

    A. from   B. up   C. prevents   D. fogging

33 There are many _____ _____ that have small _____ _____.

    A. hidden   B. products   C. more   D. holes

34 In the future, when you see a little hole in something, ask yourself _____ _____ _____ _____.

    A. is   B. why   C. there   D. it

35 Maybe it is the _____ of a _____ design to make your _____ _____.

    A. careful   B. safer   C. result   D. life

---

19 여러분이 주위를 둘러본다면, 여러분의 생활에 도움을 주는 다른 구멍들을 보게 될 것이다.

20 만약 여러분이 뚜껑 있는 냄비에 어떤 것을 요리해 본 적이 있다면, 아마도 여러분은 뚜껑에 작은 구멍이 있다는 것을 알아챘을 수도 있다.

21 이 구멍 역시 안전을 위해 존재한다.

22 뚜껑이 있는 냄비에 무언가를 요리할 때, 냄비 안쪽의 압력이 상승한다.

23 만약 뚜껑에 그 구멍이 없다면, 그 안의 물은 금방 끓어 넘칠 것이다.

24 그 구멍이 수증기를 나가게 해 주고 물이 밖으로 넘치는 것을 막아 준다.

25 비행기를 타 본 적이 있는가?

26 창밖을 내다보고 아래에 있는 세상을 보는 것이 신나지 않았는가?

27 놀랍게도, 여러분의 창문에는 작은 구멍이 하나 있었다.

28 비행기 창문은 세 개의 유리판으로 구성되어 있다.

29 그 중간 유리판에 구멍이 있다.

30 그것은 기압의 균형을 맞춰 준다.

31 이 작은 구멍이 없다면, 비행기 창문은 비상시에 깨질 수 있다.

32 그 구멍은 또한, 멋진 경치를 즐길 수 있도록 창문에 김이 서리는 것을 막아 준다.

33 숨겨진 작은 구멍들이 있는 더 많은 제품들이 있다.

34 앞으로, 여러분이 어떤 물건에서 작은 구멍을 본다면, 왜 그것이 거기에 있는지 자신에게 물어보라.

35 아마도 그것은 여러분의 삶을 더 안전하게 만들려는 사려 깊은 디자인의 결과일 것이다.

※ 다음 우리말과 일치하도록 빈칸에 알맞은 것을 골라 쓰시오.

1 _____ Holes

2 Think about a hole that you _____ _____ _____ .

3 Was it a _____ hole or a _____ hole?

4 If it was a hole _____ _____ _____ , it was bad.

5 If it was a hole in your shirt _____ _____ _____ , it was good.

6 _____ are holes _____ .

7 Some are _____ _____ you may not even _____ them.

8 They are _____ _____ , but many of these small holes are very important and _____ _____ _____ _____ .

9 _____ a pen.

10 _____ _____ it _____ .

11 Do you see _____ _____ _____ in the cap?

12 Do you know _____ _____ _____ _____ ?

13 The hole in a pen cap can _____ _____ _____ .

14 People, especially children, often _____ small things _____ pen caps _____ their mouths.

15 _____ they even _____ _____ .

16 This can _____ _____ _____ and _____ _____ .

17 A famous pen company started _____ _____ _____ in their pen caps.

18 The hole in the cap _____ air _____ _____ and has _____ _____ .

1 숨겨진 구멍들

2 여러분이 최근에 본 구멍에 대해 생각해 보라.

3 그것은 좋은 구멍이었는가, 아니면 나쁜 구멍이었는가?

4 만약 그것이 여러분의 양말에 있는 구멍이었다면, 그것은 좋지 않은 것이었다.

5 만약 그것이 단추를 위해 셔츠에 있는 구멍이었다면, 그것은 좋은 것이었다.

6 구멍은 어디에나 있다.

7 어떤 것들은 너무 작아서 인지하지 못할 수도 있다.

8 그것들은 잘 숨겨져 있지만, 이 작은 구멍들 중 많은 것들이 매우 중요하고 여러분의 삶을 안전하게 해 준다.

9 펜을 꺼내라.

10 그것을 자세히 관찰해 보라.

11 뚜껑에 작은 구멍이 보이는가?

12 여러분은 왜 거기에 구멍이 있는지 아는가?

13 펜 뚜껑에 있는 구멍이 생명을 구하는 데 도움을 줄 수 있기 때문이다.

14 사람들, 특히 아이들은 종종 펜 뚜껑 같은 작은 것들을 그들의 입에 넣는다.

15 때때로 그들은 심지어 그것들을 삼키기도 한다.

16 이것은 그들의 호흡을 막고 죽음을 초래할 수도 있다.

17 유명한 펜 회사가 자사의 펜 뚜껑에 작은 구멍을 넣기 시작했다.

18 뚜껑에 있는 그 구멍은 공기를 통하게 해 주고 생명들을 구했다.

19 If you _____ _____, you will see other holes that _____ _____ _____ _____ in your life.

20 If you have ever cooked anything in a pot _____ _____ _____, perhaps you _____ a small hole in the _____.

21 This hole, too, is there _____ _____.

22 _____ _____ something in a pot with a lid, the _____ inside the pot _____ _____.

23 The water inside would quickly _____ _____ if the lid did not have that hole.

24 The hole lets _____ _____ and _____ the water _____ _____ out.

25 _____ you ever _____ on an airplane?

26 _____ _____ _____ to _____ _____ the window and see the world below?

27 _____, there was a small hole in your window.

28 Airplane windows _____ _____ _____ _____ three panes.

29 There is a hole _____ _____ _____ _____.

30 It _____ the _____ _____.

31 _____ this _____ _____, airplane windows might break _____ _____ _____.

32 The hole also _____ the window _____ _____ _____ so that you can enjoy that _____ _____.

33 There are many more products _____ _____ small _____ _____.

34 In the future, when you see a little hole in something, ask yourself _____ _____ _____ _____.

35 Maybe it is _____ _____ of a careful design _____ _____ _____ _____.

---

19 여러분이 주위를 둘러본다면, 여러분의 생활에 도움을 주는 다른 구멍들을 보게 될 것이다.

20 만약 여러분이 뚜껑 있는 냄비에 어떤 것을 요리해 본 적이 있다면, 아마도 여러분은 뚜껑에 작은 구멍이 있다는 것을 알아챘을 수도 있다.

21 이 구멍 역시 안전을 위해 존재한다.

22 뚜껑이 있는 냄비에 무언가를 요리할 때, 냄비 안쪽의 압력이 상승한다.

23 만약 뚜껑에 그 구멍이 없다면, 그 안의 물은 금방 끓어 넘칠 것이다.

24 그 구멍이 수증기를 나가게 해주고 물이 밖으로 넘치는 것을 막아 준다.

25 비행기를 타 본 적이 있는가?

26 창밖을 내다보고 아래에 있는 세상을 보는 것이 신나지 않았는가?

27 놀랍게도, 여러분의 창문에는 작은 구멍이 하나 있었다.

28 비행기 창문은 세 개의 유리판으로 구성되어 있다.

29 그 중간 유리판에 구멍이 있다.

30 그것은 기압의 균형을 맞춰 준다.

31 이 작은 구멍이 없다면, 비행기 창문은 비상시에 깨질 수 있다.

32 그 구멍은 또한, 멋진 경치를 즐길 수 있도록 창문에 김이 서리는 것을 막아 준다.

33 숨겨진 작은 구멍들이 있는 더 많은 제품들이 있다.

34 앞으로, 여러분이 어떤 물건에서 작은 구멍을 본다면, 왜 그것이 거기에 있는지 자신에게 물어보라.

35 아마도 그것은 여러분의 삶을 더 안전하게 만들려는 사려 깊은 디자인의 결과일 것이다.

※ 다음 문장을 우리말로 쓰시오.

1 Hidden Holes
➡ _____

2 Think about a hole that you have seen recently.
➡ _____

3 Was it a good hole or a bad hole?
➡ _____

4 If it was a hole in your sock, it was bad.
➡ _____

5 If it was a hole in your shirt for a button, it was good.
➡ _____

6 There are holes everywhere.
➡ _____

7 Some are so small you may not even notice them.
➡ _____

8 They are well hidden, but many of these small holes are very important and make your life safe.
➡ _____

9 Take a pen.
➡ _____

10 Look at it carefully.
➡ _____

11 Do you see a small hole in the cap?
➡ _____

12 Do you know why it is there?
➡ _____

13 The hole in a pen cap can help save lives.
➡ _____

14 People, especially children, often put small things like pen caps in their mouths.
➡ _____

15 Sometimes they even swallow them.
➡ _____

16 This can stop their breathing and cause death.
➡ _____

17 A famous pen company started putting a small hole in their pen caps.
➡ _____

18 The hole in the cap lets air pass through and has saved lives.
➡ _____

19 If you look around, you will see other holes that play a helpful role in your life.

➡ _____

20 If you have ever cooked anything in a pot with a lid, perhaps you noticed a small hole in the lid.

➡ _____

_____

21 This hole, too, is there for safety.

➡ _____

22 When cooking something in a pot with a lid, the pressure inside the pot builds up.

➡ _____

23 The water inside would quickly boil over if the lid did not have that hole.

➡ _____

24 The hole lets steam out and keeps the water from coming out.

➡ _____

25 Have you ever been on an airplane?

➡ _____

26 Wasn't it exciting to look out the window and see the world below?

➡ _____

27 Surprisingly, there was a small hole in your window.

➡ _____

28 Airplane windows are made up of three panes.

➡ _____

29 There is a hole in the middle pane.

➡ _____

30 It balances the air pressure.

➡ _____

31 Without this little hole, airplane windows might break in an emergency.

➡ _____

32 The hole also prevents the window from fogging up so that you can enjoy that fantastic view.

➡ _____

33 There are many more products that have small hidden holes.

➡ _____

34 In the future, when you see a little hole in something, ask yourself why it is there.

➡ _____

35 Maybe it is the result of a careful design to make your life safer.

➡ _____

※ 다음 괄호 안의 단어들을 우리말에 맞도록 바르게 배열하시오.

1 (Holes / Hidden)
➡ _____

2 (about / think / hole / a / you / that / seen / have / recently.)
➡ _____

3 (it / was / good / a / hole / or / bad / a / hole?)
➡ _____

4 (it / if / a / was / hole / your / in / sock, / was / it / bad.)
➡ _____

5 (it / if / was / hole / a / your / in / shirt / for / button, / a / was / it / good.)
➡ _____

6 (are / there / everywhere. / holes)
➡ _____

7 (are / some / small / so / may / you / even / not / them. / notice)
➡ _____

8 (are / they / hidden, / well / many / but / these / of / holes / small / are / important / very / and / your / make / safe. / life)
➡ _____

9 (a / pen. / take)
➡ _____

10 (at / look / carefully. / it)
➡ _____

11 (you / do / a / see / hole / small / the / in / cap?)
➡ _____

12 (you / do / why / know / is / it / there?)
➡ _____

13 (hole / the / a / in / cap / pen / help / can / lives. / save)
➡ _____

14 (especially / people, / often / children, / put / things / small / pen / like / in / caps / mouths. / their)
➡ _____

15 (they / sometimes / swallow / even / them.)
➡ _____

16 (can / this / their / stop / and / breathing / death. / cause)
➡ _____

17 (famous / a / company / pen / putting / started / small / a / hole / their / in / caps. / pen)
➡ _____

18 (hole / the / the / in / lets / cap / pass / air / and / through / saved / has / lives.)
➡ _____

1 숨겨진 구멍들

2 여러분이 최근에 본 구멍에 대해 생각해 보라.

3 그것은 좋은 구멍이었는가, 아니면 나쁜 구멍이었는가?

4 만약 그것이 여러분의 양말에 있는 구멍이었다면, 그것은 좋지 않은 것이었다.

5 만약 그것이 단추를 위해 셔츠에 있는 구멍이었다면, 그것은 좋은 것이었다.

6 구멍은 어디에나 있다.

7 어떤 것들은 너무 작아서 인지하지 못할 수도 있다.

8 그것들은 잘 숨겨져 있지만, 이 작은 구멍들 중 많은 것들이 매우 중요하고 여러분의 삶을 안전하게 해 준다.

9 펜을 꺼내라.

10 그것을 자세히 관찰해 보라.

11 뚜껑에 작은 구멍이 보이는가?

12 여러분은 왜 거기에 구멍이 있는지 아는가?

13 펜 뚜껑에 있는 구멍이 생명을 구하는 데 도움을 줄 수 있기 때문이다.

14 사람들, 특히 아이들은 종종 펜 뚜껑 같은 작은 것들을 그들의 입에 넣는다.

15 때때로 그들은 심지어 그것들을 삼키기도 한다.

16 이것은 그들의 호흡을 막고 죽음을 초래할 수도 있다.

17 유명한 펜 회사가 자사의 펜 뚜껑에 작은 구멍을 넣기 시작했다.

18 뚜껑에 있는 그 구멍은 공기를 통하게 해 주고 생명들을 구했다.

19 (you / if / around, / look / will / you / see / holes / other / play / that / role / a / helpful / in / life. / your)
➡ _____

20 (you / if / ever / have / anything / cooked / in / pot / a / with / lid, / a / perhaps / noticed / you / hole / a / small / the / in / lid.)
➡ _____

21 (hole, / this / is / too, / for / there / safety.)
➡ _____

22 (cooking / when / something / a / in / with / pot / lid, / a / the / inside / pressure / the / up. / builds)
➡ _____

23 (water / the / would / inside / boil / quickly / if / over / lid / the / did / have / not / hole. / that)
➡ _____

24 (hole / the / steam / lets / out / and / the / keeps / from / water / out. / coming)
➡ _____

25 (you / have / been / ever / an / on / airplane?)
➡ _____

26 (it / wasn't / exciting / look / to / out / window / the / and / the / see / below? / world)
➡ _____

27 (there / surprisingly, / was / small / a / hole / your / in / window.)
➡ _____

28 (windows / airplane / made / are / of / up / panes. / three)
➡ _____

29 (is / there / hole / a / the / in / pane. / middle)
➡ _____

30 (balances / it / air / the / pressure.)
➡ _____

31 (this / without / hole, / little / windows / airplane / break / might / an / in / emergency.)
➡ _____

32 (hole / the / prevents / also / window / the / fogging / from / so / up / that / can / you / that / enjoy / view. / fantastic)
➡ _____

33 (are / there / more / many / that / products / have / hidden / small / holes.)
➡ _____

34 (the / in / when / future, / see / you / little / a / hole / something, / in / yourself / ask / it / why / there. / is)
➡ _____

35 (it / maybe / the / is / of / result / a / design / careful / make / to / life / your / safer.)
➡ _____

19 여러분이 주위를 둘러본다면, 여러분의 생활에 도움을 주는 다른 구멍들을 보게 될 것이다.
20 만약 여러분이 뚜껑 있는 냄비에 어떤 것을 요리해 본 적이 있다면, 아마도 여러분은 뚜껑에 작은 구멍이 있다는 것을 알아챘을 수도 있다.
21 이 구멍 역시 안전을 위해 존재한다.
22 뚜껑이 있는 냄비에 무언가를 요리할 때, 냄비 안쪽의 압력이 상승한다.
23 만약 뚜껑에 그 구멍이 없다면, 그 안의 물은 금방 끓어 넘칠 것이다.
24 그 구멍이 수증기를 나가게 해 주고 물이 밖으로 넘치는 것을 막아 준다.
25 비행기를 타 본 적이 있는가?
26 창밖을 내다보고 아래에 있는 세상을 보는 것이 신나지 않았는가?
27 놀랍게도, 여러분의 창문에는 작은 구멍이 하나 있었다.
28 비행기 창문은 세 개의 유리판으로 구성되어 있다.
29 그 중간 유리판에 구멍이 있다.
30 그것은 기압의 균형을 맞춰 준다.
31 이 작은 구멍이 없다면, 비행기 창문은 비상시에 깨질 수 있다.
32 그 구멍은 또한, 멋진 경치를 즐길 수 있도록 창문에 김이 서리는 것을 막아 준다.
33 숨겨진 작은 구멍들이 있는 더 많은 제품들이 있다.
34 앞으로, 여러분이 어떤 물건에서 작은 구멍을 본다면, 왜 그것이 거기에 있는지 자신에게 물어보라.
35 아마도 그것은 여러분의 삶을 더 안전하게 만들려는 사려 깊은 디자인의 결과일 것이다.

※ 다음 우리말을 영어로 쓰시오.

1 숨겨진 구멍들

➡ _____

2 여러분이 최근에 본 구멍에 대해 생각해 보라.

➡ _____

3 그것은 좋은 구멍이었는가, 아니면 나쁜 구멍이었는가?

➡ _____

4 만약 그것이 여러분의 양말에 있는 구멍이었다면, 그것은 좋지 않은 것이었다.

➡ _____

5 만약 그것이 단추를 위해 셔츠에 있는 구멍이었다면, 그것은 좋은 것이었다.

➡ _____

6 구멍은 어디에나 있다.

➡ _____

7 어떤 것들은 너무 작아서 인지하지 못할 수도 있다.

➡ _____

8 그것들은 잘 숨겨져 있지만, 이 작은 구멍들 중 많은 것들이 매우 중요하고 여러분의 삶을 안전하게 해 준다.

➡ _____

9 펜을 꺼내라.

➡ _____

10 그것을 자세히 관찰해 보라.

➡ _____

11 뚜껑에 작은 구멍이 보이는가?

➡ _____

12 여러분은 왜 거기에 구멍이 있는지 아는가?

➡ _____

13 펜 뚜껑에 있는 구멍이 생명을 구하는 데 도움을 줄 수 있기 때문이다.

➡ _____

14 사람들, 특히 아이들은 종종 펜 뚜껑 같은 작은 것들을 그들의 입에 넣는다.

➡ _____

15 때때로 그들은 심지어 그것들을 삼키기도 한다.

➡ _____

16 이것은 그들의 호흡을 막고 죽음을 초래할 수도 있다.

➡ _____

17 유명한 펜 회사가 자사의 펜 뚜껑에 작은 구멍을 넣기 시작했다.

➡ _____

18 뚜껑에 있는 그 구멍은 공기를 통하게 해 주고 생명들을 구했다.

➡ _____

19 여러분이 주위를 둘러본다면, 여러분의 생활에 도움을 주는 다른 구멍들을 보게 될 것이다.
➡ _____

20 만약 여러분이 뚜껑 있는 냄비에 어떤 것을 요리해 본 적이 있다면, 아마도 여러분은 뚜껑에 작은 구멍이 있다는 것을 알아챘을 수도 있다.
➡ _____

21 이 구멍 역시 안전을 위해 존재한다.
➡ _____

22 뚜껑이 있는 냄비에 무언가를 요리할 때, 냄비 안쪽의 압력이 상승한다.
➡ _____

23 만약 뚜껑에 그 구멍이 없다면, 그 안의 물은 금방 끓어 넘칠 것이다.
➡ _____

24 그 구멍이 수증기를 나가게 해 주고 물이 밖으로 넘치는 것을 막아 준다.
➡ _____

25 비행기를 타 본 적이 있는가?
➡ _____

26 창밖을 내다보고 아래에 있는 세상을 보는 것이 신나지 않았는가?
➡ _____

27 놀랍게도, 여러분의 창문에는 작은 구멍이 하나 있었다.
➡ _____

28 비행기 창문은 세 개의 유리판으로 구성되어 있다.
➡ _____

29 그 중간 유리판에 구멍이 있다.
➡ _____

30 그것은 기압의 균형을 맞춰 준다.
➡ _____

31 이 작은 구멍이 없다면, 비행기 창문은 비상시에 깨질 수 있다.
➡ _____

32 그 구멍은 또한, 멋진 경치를 즐길 수 있도록 창문에 김이 서리는 것을 막아 준다.
➡ _____

33 숨겨진 작은 구멍들이 있는 더 많은 제품들이 있다.
➡ _____

34 앞으로, 여러분이 어떤 물건에서 작은 구멍을 본다면, 왜 그것이 거기에 있는지 자신에게 물어보라.
➡ _____

35 아마도 그것은 여러분의 삶을 더 안전하게 만들려는 사려 깊은 디자인의 결과일 것이다.
➡ _____

※ 다음 우리말과 일치하도록 빈칸에 알맞은 말을 쓰시오.

After You Read B

1. It _____ _____ _____ _____ _____ even when people _____ the pen cap.

2. It _____ _____ _____ _____.

3. It _____ _____ _____ and _____ the water in the pot _____ _____ _____.

1. 사람들이 펜 뚜껑을 삼킬 때도 그것은 공기를 통하게 해준다.
2. 그것은 기압의 균형을 맞춰 준다.
3. 그것은 수증기를 나가게 해 주고 냄비의 물이 끓어 넘치는 것을 막아 준다.

Work Together

1. _____ _____ Helmet

2. This invention _____ _____ _____ _____ _____ _____.

3. If you use the Sweet Dream Helmet, you will _____ _____ _____ _____ _____.

4. You can even _____ _____ _____ _____ _____ you want to dream _____ _____ you can have different experiences _____ _____ _____.

1. 단 잠 헬멧
2. 이 발명품은 사람들이 단 잠을 잘 수 있도록 돕는다..
3. 만약 단 잠 헬멧을 사용한다면, 당신은 매일 밤 행복한 꿈을 꿀 것입니다.
4. 당신이 잠든 동안 다양한 경험을 할 수 있기 위해 당신은 심지어 당신이 꿈꾸고 싶은 꿈의 형태를 고를 수 있습니다.

Writing Workshop

1. A _____

2. _____ you _____ _____ a refrigerator?

3. We use it every day _____ _____ we can _____ _____ _____ and _____.

4. In 1755, William Cullen _____ the first _____ _____ _____ _____.

5. After that, it _____ _____ the years and _____ _____ _____ _____ _____ _____ _____ _____.

6. _____ we _____ _____ _____ refrigerators in today's world, we _____ _____ _____ _____ _____ _____ ice cream on hot summer days.

1. 냉장고
2. 여러분은 냉장고가 없는 세상을 상상할 수 있나요?
3. 우리는 음식을 차갑고 신선하게 보관하기 위해 이것을 매일 사용합니다.
4. 1755년, 윌리엄 컬런이 초기 형태의 냉장고를 발명했습니다.
5. 그 이후, 이것을 수년 동안 발전했고, 현대의 생활에서 필수적인 부분이 되었습니다.
6. 만약 우리에게 오늘날 냉장고가 없다면, 더운 여름날 아이스크림을 즐겨 먹을 수 없을 것입니다.

※ 다음 우리말을 영어로 쓰시오.

After You Read B

1. 사람들이 펜 뚜껑을 삼킬 때도 그것은 공기를 통하게 해준다.
   ➡ _____

2. 그것은 기압의 균형을 맞춰 준다.
   ➡ _____

3. 그것은 수증기를 나가게 해 주고 냄비의 물이 끓어 넘치는 것을 막아 준다.
   ➡ _____

Work Together

1. 단 잠 헬멧
   ➡ _____

2. 이 발명품은 사람들이 단 잠을 잘 수 있도록 돕는다.
   ➡ _____

3. 만약 단 잠 헬멧을 사용한다면, 당신은 매일 밤 행복한 꿈을 꿀 것입니다.
   ➡ _____

4. 당신이 잠든 동안 다양한 경험을 할 수 있기 위해 당신은 심지어 당신이 꿈꾸고 싶은 꿈의 형태를 고를 수 있습니다.
   ➡ _____
   _____

Writing Workshop

1. 냉장고
   ➡ _____

2. 여러분은 냉장고가 없는 세상을 상상할 수 있나요?
   ➡ _____

3. 우리는 음식을 차갑고 신선하게 보관하기 위해 이것을 매일 사용합니다.
   ➡ _____

4. 1755년, 윌리엄 컬런이 초기 형태의 냉장고를 발명했습니다.
   ➡ _____

5. 그 이후, 이것을 수년 동안 발전했고, 현대의 생활에서 필수적인 부분이 되었습니다.
   ➡ _____

6. 만약 우리에게 오늘날 냉장고가 없다면, 더운 여름날 아이스크림을 즐겨 먹을 수 없을 것입니다.
   ➡ _____
   _____

※ 다음 영어를 우리말로 쓰시오.

01	boil	22	stuffy
02	touching	23	thick
03	warm	24	low
04	chop	25	stay
05	while	26	medicine
06	serve	27	seafood
07	add	28	recommend
08	blend	29	stir
09	ginger	30	mixture
10	cool	31	sore
11	treasure	32	pour
12	taste	33	mix
13	pain	34	recipe
14	smooth	35	such as A
15	hold	36	be made with
16	throat	37	find out
17	pepper	38	a bowl of
18	temperature	39	as well as
19	reduce	40	be different from
20	melt	41	show A around B
21	local	42	be good for
		43	not only A but also B

※ 다음 우리말을 영어로 쓰시오.

01 붓다, 따르다	
02 요리법	
03 식히다	
04 열다, 개최하다	
05 더하다, 첨가하다	
06 섞다	
07 추천하다	
08 잘게 썰다	
09 끓다, 끓이다	
10 약	
11 고루 잘 섞인	
12 동쪽에 위치한	
13 생강	
14 혼합물	
15 제공하다	
16 코가 막힌, 답답한	
17 맛	
18 반면에, ~하는 동안에	
19 아픔, 통증	
20 녹다	
21 후추, 고추	

22 온도, 기온	
23 두꺼운, 걸쭉한	
24 목구멍, 목	
25 휘젓다	
26 줄이다	
27 감동적인	
28 보물	
29 해산물	
30 지역의, 현지의	
31 섞다	
32 양고기	
33 그대로 있다	
34 아픈, 따가운	
35 ~와 다르다	
36 ~ 한 접시	
37 ~에 더하여, 게다가	
38 알아내다, 발견하다	
39 몸에 걸치다	
40 처음으로	
41 A와 같은	
42 A뿐만 아니라 B도	
43 ~로 만들어지다	

※ 다음 영영풀이에 알맞은 단어를 <보기>에서 골라 쓴 후, 우리말 뜻을 쓰시오.

1 _____ : physical suffering: _____

2 _____ : causing strong emotion: _____

3 _____ : to cut into smaller pieces: _____

4 _____ : anything or person greatly valued: _____

5 _____ : having a great distance from one surface to the opposite: _____

6 _____ : to make something smaller in size, amount, number, etc.: _____

7 _____ : to change from a liquid to a gas as a result of heat: _____

8 _____ : something made by combining two or more ingredients: _____

9 _____ : to urge or suggest as proper, useful or beneficial: _____

10 _____ : to flow, as from once container to another, or into, over, or on something: _____

11 _____ : to remain over a length of time, as in a place or situation: _____

12 _____ : to move a liquid or substance around, using a spoon or something similar: _____

13 _____ : a measure of the warmth of an object with reference to a standard scale: _____

14 _____ : to change or to cause something to change from a solid to a liquid usually because of heat: _____

15 _____ : relating to a city, town or small district rather than an entire state or country: _____

16 _____ : a reed-like plant originally from Southeast Asia but now grown in most warm countries, having a strong-smelling and spicy root used in cookery and medicine: _____

보기

pour	temperature	chop	thick
stir	local	mixture	treasure
recommend	stay	touching	pain
melt	ginger	reduce	boil

※ 다음 우리말과 일치하도록 빈칸에 알맞은 말을 쓰시오.

Listen & Speak 1 Listen 1

B: Hi, Grace. Those are pretty. What are _____ _____?

G: They're _____ *dango*.

B: I'm sorry. _____ you say that _____?

G: *Dan-go*. They're sweet and _____ _____ rice cake powder.

　　They're _____ Japan.

B: Grace, 안녕. 그거 예쁘다. 그거 뭐라고 불리니?
G: 당고라고 불러.
B: 미안, 다시 말해 줄래?
G: 당-고. 달고 쌀가루로 만들어진 거야. 일본에서 온 거야.

Listen & Speak 1 Listen 2

B: Alice, what's that you're _____?

G: It's *rasmalai*.

B: *Ra*.... Could you _____ that _____?

G: *Ras-ma-lai*. It's _____ a cheesecake in a sweet cream. It's a _____ _____ in India.

B: Alice, 네가 먹고 있는 것은 무엇이니?
G: 라스말라이야.
B: 라… 다시 한 번 말해 줄래?
G: 라스-마-라이. 달콤한 크림 안에 있는 치즈 케이크 같은 거야. 인도의 전통 음식이지.

Listen & Speak 1 Listen 3

G: What's _____ you're _____, David? It _____ _____ a chocolate ball.

B: It's *brigadeiro*.

G: _____? Could you say that _____?

B: B*ri-ga-dei-ro*. It's sweet and _____. It's _____ in Brazil.

G: David, 뭐 먹고 있니? 그거 초콜릿 볼처럼 생겼다.
B: 브리가데이로야.
G: 뭐라고? 다시 한 번 말해 줄래?
B: 브리-가-데이-로. 달고 맛있어. 브라질에서 인기 많아.

Listen & Speak 1 A-1

G: My _____ Korean traditional drink is Maesil-tea. _____ about you, Jinsu?

B: Well, my favorite _____ _____ is Sikhye.

G: Sik.... Can you _____ that _____?

B: Sik-hye. It's _____ and cool.

G: I want to _____ it.

G: 내가 제일 좋아하는 한국 전통 음료는 매실차야. 진수, 너는 뭐니?
B: 음, 내가 제일 좋아하는 음료는 식혜야.
G: 식… 다시 말해 줄래?
B: 식-혜. 달고 시원해.
G: 먹어 보고 싶다.

Listen & Speak 1 A-2

B: Have you ever _____ *poke*?

G: Sorry, _____ you say that again, please?

B: *Po-ke*. It's a _____ that is _____ in Hawaii.

G: What's so _____ about it?

B: It's made _____ _____ and _____. It's not _____ delicious _____ also very _____.

Listen & Speak 1 B

1. **A:** _____ you ever _____ *rasmalai*?

   B: _____, could you say that again?

   A: *Rasmalai*. It's a _____ _____ in India.

2. **A:** Have you ever _____ *brigadeiro*?

   B: Sorry, could you say that again?

   A: *Brigadeiro*. It's a _____ dessert in Brazil.

3. **A:** Have you _____ _____ *macaron*?

   B: Sorry, could you say _____ again?

   A: *Macaron*. It's a traditional dessert _____ France.

Listen & Speak 2 Listen

1. **B:** Could you _____ a good _____ dish?

   W: _____ Samgyetang. It'll give you energy.

2. **G:** _____ you recommend a good book _____ my little sister?

   M: I recommend this one. The story is _____.

3. **B:** Could you _____ a guitar for _____?

   W: How _____ this one? Many beginners play it.

4. **G:** Could you recommend a _____ for my dog?

   M: Sure. _____ about this? Dogs really like it.

Listen & Speak 2 A-1

B: Tomorrow is my dad's birthday. I'd like to do _____ _____ for him.

G: _____ about _____ something for him? He _____ really like that.

B: That sounds great. Can you _____ something _____ to cook?

G: Umm. How _____ Gimchijeon? It's _____ to make and it's _____.

B: Oh, that's a good _____. He'll love it.

B: 너 포케 먹어 본 적 있니?

G: 미안, 다시 한 번 말해 줄래?

G: 포-케. 하와이에서 인기 많은 샐러드야.

G: 그게 뭐가 그렇게 특별한데?

G: 쌀이랑 생선으로 만들어. 맛도 있고 매우 건강한 음식이야.

1. **A:** 너 라스말라이 먹어 본 적 있니?
   B: 미안, 다시 말해 줄래?
   A: 라스말라이. 그건 인도의 전통 디저트야.
2. **A:** 너 브리가데이로 먹어 본 적 있니?
   B: 미안, 다시 말해 줄래?
   A: 브리가데이로. 그건 브라질의 전통 디저트야.
3. **A:** 너 마카롱 먹어 본 적 있니?
   B: 미안, 다시 말해 줄래?
   A: 마카롱. 그건 프랑스 전통 디저트야.

1. **B:** 좋은 전통 음식 추천해 줄 수 있니?
   W: 삼계탕을 먹어봐. 너에게 에너지를 줄 거야.
2. **G:** 내 여동생에게 좋은 책을 추천해 줄 수 있니?
   M: 이것을 추천해. 이야기가 감동적이야.
3. **B:** 초보자를 위한 기타를 추천해 줄 수 있니?
   W: 이거 어때? 많은 초보자들이 그걸 연주해.
4. **G:** 내 개를 위한 간식을 추천해 줄래?
   M: 물론, 이거 어때? 개들이 그걸 정말 좋아해.

B: 내일은 우리 아빠의 생신이야. 난 아빠를 위해 좀 특별한 것을 하고 싶어.

G: 아버지를 위해 무언가를 요리하는 건 어때? 정말 좋아하실 거야.

B: 그거 좋겠다. 요리하기 쉬운 것을 추천해 줄래?

G: 음, 김치전 어때? 만들기 쉽고 맛있어.

B: 오, 좋은 생각이다. 아빠가 좋아하실 거야.

Listen & Speak 2 B-2

M: _____ to the Sydney Information Center. Sydney has _____ places you will want to _____. The Rocks Markets is one of them. _____ you can buy art, _____, books and many _____ things. You can also eat fresh, _____ _____ food. We _____ _____ the Rocks Markets and _____ the food and the fun there.

Real-Life Zone

M: Good afternoon. A table _____ two?

B: Yes.

M: This way please. _____ is the menu. I'll be _____ in a few minutes and _____ your order.

B: Okay. Thank you.

G: I don't know _____ about Korean food. Could you _____ something?

B: Well, I'd _____ the Bibimbap.

G: I'm sorry. _____ you say that again, please?

B: This one. Bi-bim-bap. It's _____ with lots of vegetables, beef and an egg _____ rice. It's tasty and it's also _____ for your _____.

G: That sounds great. I'll _____ it.

B: It's _____ with a _____ red _____ sauce. Is that _____?

G: No _____. I like spicy food.

Wrap Up 1-2

B: Tomorrow is my birthday.

G: I know. _____ you going to _____ a birthday party, Alex?

B: Yes. _____ you recommend a good _____ to have the party?

G: I'd _____ the Happy Snack House. The food is really good and it'll be large _____.

B: What dish _____ you _____?

G: I'd recommend the onion rings. They're _____!

B: Oh, just _____ about them _____ my mouth _____.

M: 시드니 여행 정보 센터에 오신 걸 환영합니다. 시드니는 여러분께서 방문하시고 싶으실 만한 장소들이 많습니다. Rocks Markets은 그 중의 하나죠. 그곳에선 예술 작품과 의류, 책 그리고 다른 많은 것들을 사실 수 있습니다. 또한 신선하고 맛있는 지역 음식도 드실 수 있습니다. 저희는 Rocks Markets에 가시는 것을 추천해 드리며 그곳에서 음식과 재미를 즐기시기를 추천합니다.

M: 안녕하세요. 두 분이신가요?
B: 네.
M: 이쪽으로 오십시오. 메뉴는 여기 있습니다. 잠시 후에 와서 주문 받겠습니다.
B: 알겠습니다. 감사합니다.
G: 나 한국 음식에 대해서 잘 알지 못해. 네가 추천해 줄래?
B: 음, 나는 비빔밥을 추천할게.
G: 미안, 다시 한 번 말해 줄래?
B: 이거. 비-빔-밥. 그것은 밥 위에 많은 야채들과 소고기, 그리고 계란을 얹어 만들어. 맛있고 건강에도 좋아.
G: 굉장한데. 난 그거 먹어 볼래.
B: 매운 고추장 양념이랑 같이 나오는 거야. 괜찮겠니?
G: 문제 없어. 나 매운 음식을 좋아해.

B: 내일은 내 생일이야.
G: 알고 있어. Alex, 생일 파티할 거니?
B: 응. 파티 열기에 좋은 장소 추천해 줄래?
G: 나는 Happy Snack House를 추천할게. 음식이 정말 맛있고 장소도 충분히 넓어.
B: 넌 무슨 음식을 추천해 줄래?
G: 나는 양파 튀김을 추천할게. 정말 환상적이야!
B: 오, 그거 생각하는 것만으로도 침이 고인다.

※ 다음 우리말에 맞도록 대화를 영어로 쓰시오.

해석

Listen & Speak 1 Listen 1

B: _____

G: _____

B: _____

G: _____

B: Grace, 안녕. 그거 예쁘다. 그거 뭐라고 불리니?
G: 당고라고 불러.
B: 미안, 다시 말해 줄래?
G: 당–고. 달고 쌀가루로 만들어진 거야. 일본에서 온 거야.

Listen & Speak 1 Listen 2

B: _____

G: _____

B: _____

G: _____
_____

B: Alice, 네가 먹고 있는 것은 무엇이니?
G: 라스말라이야.
B: 라… 다시 한 번 말해 줄래?
G: 라즈–마–라이. 달콤한 크림 안에 있는 치즈 케이크 같은 거야. 인도의 전통 음식이지.

Listen & Speak 1 Listen 3

G: _____

B: _____

G: _____

B: _____

G: David, 뭐 먹고 있니? 그거 초콜릿 볼처럼 생겼다.
B: 브리가데이로야.
G: 뭐라고? 다시 한 번 말해 줄래?
B: 브리–가–데이–로. 달고 맛있어. 브라질에서 인기 많아.

Listen & Speak 1 A-1

G: _____

B: _____

G: _____

B: _____

G: _____

G: 내가 제일 좋아하는 한국 전통 음료는 매실차야. 진수, 너는 뭐니?
B: 음, 내가 제일 좋아하는 음료는 식혜야.
G: 식… 다시 말해 줄래?
B: 식–혜. 달고 시원해.
G: 먹어 보고 싶다.

B: _____

G: _____

B: _____

G: _____

B: _____

B: 너 포케 먹어 본 적 있니?

G: 미안, 다시 한 번 말해 줄래?

G: 포-케. 하와이에서 인기 많은 샐러드야.

G: 그게 뭐가 그렇게 특별한데?

G: 쌀이랑 생선으로 만들어. 맛도 있고 매우 건강한 음식이야.

Listen & Speak 1 B

1. A: _____

   B: _____

   A: _____

2. A: _____

   B: _____

   A: _____

3. A: _____

   B: _____

   A: _____

1. A: 너 라스말라이 먹어 본 적 있니?
   B: 미안, 다시 말해 줄래?
   A: 라스말라이. 그건 인도의 전통 디저트야.
2. A: 너 브리가데이로 먹어 본 적 있니?
   B: 미안, 다시 말해 줄래?
   A: 브리가데이로. 그건 브라질의 전통 디저트야.
3. A: 너 마카롱 먹어 본 적 있니?
   B: 미안, 다시 말해 줄래?
   A: 마카롱. 그건 프랑스 전통 디저트야.

Listen & Speak 2 Listen

1. B: _____

   W: _____

2. G: _____

   M: _____

3. B: _____

   W: _____

4. G: _____

   M: _____

1. B: 좋은 전통 음식 추천해 줄 수 있니?
   W: 삼계탕을 먹어봐. 너에게 에너지를 줄 거야.
2. G: 내 여동생에게 좋은 책을 추천해 줄 수 있니?
   M: 이것을 추천해. 이야기가 감동적이야.
3. B: 초보자를 위한 기타를 추천해 줄 수 있니?
   W: 이거 어때? 많은 초보자들이 그걸 연주해.
4. G: 내 개를 위한 간식을 추천해 줄래?
   M: 물론, 이거 어때? 개들이 그걸 정말 좋아해.

Listen & Speak 2 A-1

B: _____

G: _____

B: _____

G: _____

B: _____

B: 내일은 우리 아빠의 생신이야. 난 아빠를 위해 좀 특별한 것을 하고 싶어.

G: 아버지를 위해 무언가를 요리하는 건 어때? 정말 좋아하실 거야.

B: 그거 좋겠다. 요리하기 쉬운 것을 추천해 줄래?

G: 음, 김치전 어때? 만들기 쉽고 맛있어.

B: 오, 좋은 생각이다. 아빠가 좋아하실 거야.

Listen & Speak 2 B-2

M: _____

_____

_____

_____

_____

M: 시드니 여행 정보 센터에 오신 걸 환영합니다. 시드니는 여러분께서 방문하시고 싶으실 만한 장소들이 많습니다. Rocks Markets은 그 중의 하나죠. 그곳에선 예술 작품과 의류, 책 그리고 다른 많은 것들을 사실 수 있습니다. 또한 신선하고 맛있는 지역 음식도 드실 수 있습니다. 저희는 Rocks Markets에 가시는 것을 추천해 드리며 그곳에서 음식과 재미를 즐기시기를 추천합니다.

Real-Life Zone

M: _____

B: _____

M: _____

_____

B: _____

G: _____

B: _____

G: _____

B: _____

_____

G: _____

B: _____

G: _____

M: 안녕하세요. 두 분이신가요?
B: 네.
M: 이쪽으로 오십시오. 메뉴는 여기 있습니다. 잠시 후에 와서 주문 받겠습니다.
B: 알겠습니다. 감사합니다.
G: 나 한국 음식에 대해서 잘 알지 못해. 네가 추천해 줄래?
B: 음, 나는 비빔밥을 추천할게.
G: 미안, 다시 한 번 말해 줄래?
B: 이거. 비-빔-밥. 그것은 밥 위에 많은 야채들과 소고기, 그리고 계란을 얹어 만들어. 맛있고 건강에도 좋아.
G: 굉장한데. 난 그거 먹어 볼래.
B: 매운 고추장 양념이랑 같이 나오는 거야. 괜찮겠니?
G: 문제 없어. 나 매운 음식을 좋아해.

Wrap Up 1-2

B: _____

G: _____

B: _____

G: _____

B: _____

G: _____

B: _____

B: 내일은 내 생일이야.
G: 알고 있어. Alex, 생일 파티할 거니?
B: 응. 파티 열기에 좋은 장소 추천해 줄래?
G: 나는 Happy Snack House를 추천할게. 음식이 정말 맛있고 장소도 충분히 넓어.
B: 넌 무슨 음식을 추천해 줄래?
G: 나는 양파 튀김을 추천할게. 정말 환상적이야!
B: 오, 그거 생각하는 것만으로도 침이 고인다.

※ 다음 우리말과 일치하도록 빈칸에 알맞은 것을 골라 쓰시오.

1 _____ That _____ _____
A. Fight   B. Foods   C. Colds

2 What do you do _____ you _____ a _____?
A. cold   B. when   C. catch

3 Of course, you want to _____ _____, so maybe you _____ on more _____.
A. warm   B. clothes   C. put   D. stay

4 _____ people like to _____ _____ _____.
A. drink   B. some   C. tea   D. hot

5 Ginger tea is _____ in Korea _____ _____.
A. often   B. something   C. drink   D. people

6 With its special _____, it _____ your body and helps _____ the _____ in your throat.
A. pain   B. taste   C. reduce   D. warms

7 _____ do people drink or eat in _____ _____ when they catch a _____?
A. other   B. cold   C. what   D. countries

8 _____ _____ _____ _____.
A. out   B. let's   C. find

9 In Finland, where it is very cold in winter, people _____ a _____ _____ _____ when they _____ a cold.
A. special   B. catch   C. drink   D. have

10 It is a _____ of _____ _____.
A. milk   B. cup   C. onion

11 They put _____ onion in milk and boil it _____ _____ heat for _____ an hour.
A. low   B. chopped   C. half   D. over

12 This _____ drink is _____ to _____ _____ for a cold.
A. said   B. simple   C. good   D. be

13 _____ people in Korea and Finland look for _____ when _____, many people in America want a _____ of chicken soup.
A. bowl   B. while   C. sick   D. drinks

14 It is usually made with chicken and vegetables, but the _____ is different from _____ family _____ _____.
A. recipe   B. one   C. another   D. to

15 Salt and pepper _____ _____ _____ before _____.
A. added   B. eating   C. be   D. can

16 People in America believe that a bowl of warm chicken soup is great for a _____ _____ and a _____ _____.
A. nose   B. sore   C. stuffy   D. throat

---

1 감기와 싸우는 음식들

2 여러분은 감기에 걸리면 어떻게 하는가?

3 당연히, 따뜻함을 유지하고자 할 것이고, 아마도 옷을 더 입을 것이다.

4 몇몇 사람들은 따뜻한 차를 마시는 것을 좋아한다.

5 생강차는 한국인이 자주 마시는 것이다.

6 특별한 맛과 함께, 그것은 여러분의 몸을 따뜻하게 하고 목 통증을 완화하는 데 도움을 준다.

7 다른 나라에서는 사람들이 감기에 걸렸을 때 무엇을 마시거나 먹을까?

8 함께 알아보자.

9 겨울이 매우 추운 핀란드에서는 사람들이 감기에 걸리면 특별한 음료를 마신다.

10 그것은 양파 우유이다.

11 그들은 우유에 잘게 썬 양파를 넣고 30분 동안 약한 불에서 끓인다.

12 이 단순한 음료는 감기에 좋다고 한다.

13 한국 사람들과 핀란드 사람들이 아플 때 음료를 찾는 반면, 미국의 많은 사람들은 닭고기 수프를 원한다.

14 그것은 보통 닭고기와 야채로 만들어지는데, 요리법은 가정마다 다르다.

15 소금과 후추를 먹기 전에 넣기도 한다.

16 미국인들은 따뜻한 닭고기 수프 한 그릇이 부은 목과 막힌 코에 좋다고 믿는다.

17 In Russia and in _____ Europe, when people _____
_____, they eat a dessert _____ *gogol-mogol*.
 A. called B. get C. Eastern D. sick

18 It _____ _____ _____ eggs and honey.
 A. with B. is C. made

19 Some people add chocolate, butter, lemon juice, or milk
_____ _____ it _____ _____.
 A. better B. to C. taste D. make

20 It _____ _____ _____ yogurt.
 A. thick B. looks C. like

21 People often drink a cup of _____ *gogol-mogol* when
they _____ a _____ _____.
 A. warm B. throat C. have D. sore

22 *Gogol-mogol* is not _____ good for people with a cold
_____ also _____ as a dessert for _____ people.
 A. healthy B. only C. popular D. but

23 When _____ as a dessert, it is _____ served _____ or
at room _____.
 A. temperature B. served C. cold D. usually

24 _____ _____ try making one of the foods you have
_____ out _____?
 A. about B. not C. found D. why

25 It will be _____ and _____ _____ your _____.
 A. for B. good C. fun D. health

26 _____ _____ _____ *Gogol-mogol* (Serves one)
 A. Make B. to C. How

27 _____ _____: 1 egg, 1/2 cup of milk, _____ (5 g), butter
(15 g)
 A. need B. you C. honey

28 1. _____ the egg and the honey _____ a large cup and
_____ _____.
 A. in B. them C. put D. mix

29 2. _____ a cup of milk _____ a _____.
 A. half B. in C. pour D. pan

30 _____ the _____.
 A. butter B. add

31 _____ it _____ the butter _____.
 A. melts B. warm C. until

32 3. _____ the _____ milk and butter _____ the cup
_____ the egg and the honey.
 A. into B. pour C. with D. hot

33 _____ _____ you _____.
 A. as B. pour C. stir

34 4. _____ _____ it is _____.
 A. while B. hot C. drink

17 러시아와 동유럽에서는 사람들이 아플 때, 고골모골이라는 후식을 먹는다.

18 그것은 달걀과 꿀로 만든다.

19 어떤 사람들은 그것을 더 맛있게 하기 위해 초콜릿, 버터, 레몬주스, 또는 우유를 첨가한다.

20 그것은 진한 요구르트처럼 보인다.

21 사람들은 목이 아플 때 종종 따뜻한 고골모골 한 잔을 마신다.

22 고골모골은 감기에 걸린 사람들에게 좋을 뿐만 아니라 건강한 사람들의 후식으로도 인기가 있다.

23 후식으로 제공될 때에는 보통 차갑게 또는 실온으로 제공된다.

24 여러분이 알아본 음식들 중 하나를 만들어 보는 것은 어떨까?

25 그것은 재미있고 여러분의 건강에 좋을 것이다.

26 고골모골 만드는 방법 (1인분)

27 필요한 것: 달걀 1개, 우유 1/2컵, 꿀 5g, 버터 15g

28 1. 달걀과 꿀을 큰 컵에 넣고 섞는다.

29 2. 우유 반 컵을 팬에 붓는다.

30 버터를 추가한다.

31 버터가 녹을 때까지 데운다.

32 3. 뜨거운 우유와 버터를 달걀과 꿀이 있는 컵에 붓는다.

33 부으면서 젓는다.

34 4. 뜨거울 때 마신다.

본문 Test **73**

※ 다음 우리말과 일치하도록 빈칸에 알맞은 말을 쓰시오.

1 Foods That _____ _____

2 What do you do when you _____ _____ _____ ?

3 Of course, you want to _____ _____ , so maybe you _____ _____ more clothes.

4 Some people like _____ _____ _____ _____ .

5 Ginger tea is _____ people in Korea _____ _____ .

6 With its special taste, it warms your body and _____ _____ _____ _____ _____ in your _____ .

7 _____ _____ _____ _____ _____ _____ in other countries when they catch a cold?

8 Let's _____ _____ .

9 In Finland, where it is very cold in winter, people _____ _____ _____ _____ when they catch a cold.

10 It is _____ _____ _____ _____ _____ .

11 They put _____ _____ in milk and boil it _____ _____ _____ for _____ _____ _____ .

12 This simple drink _____ _____ _____ _____ for a cold.

13 _____ people in Korea and Finland _____ _____ drinks when sick, many people in America want _____ _____ _____ _____ _____ .

14 It is usually made with chicken and vegetables, but the recipe is different _____ _____ _____ _____ _____ .

15 Salt and pepper _____ _____ _____ before _____ .

16 People in America believe that a bowl of warm chicken soup is _____ _____ _____ _____ _____ _____ _____ _____ _____ .

1 감기와 싸우는 음식들

2 여러분은 감기에 걸리면 어떻게 하는가?

3 당연히, 따뜻함을 유지하고자 할 것이고, 아마도 옷을 더 입을 것이다.

4 몇몇 사람들은 따뜻한 차를 마시는 것을 좋아한다.

5 생강차는 한국인들이 자주 마시는 것이다.

6 특별한 맛과 함께, 그것은 여러분의 몸을 따뜻하게 하고 목 통증을 완화하는 데 도움을 준다.

7 다른 나라에서는 사람들이 감기에 걸렸을 때 무엇을 마시거나 먹을까?

8 함께 알아보자.

9 겨울이 매우 추운 핀란드에서는 사람들이 감기에 걸리면 특별한 음료를 마신다.

10 그것은 양파 우유이다.

11 그들은 우유에 잘게 썬 양파를 넣고 30분 동안 약한 불에서 끓인다.

12 이 단순한 음료는 감기에 좋다고 한다.

13 한국 사람들과 핀란드 사람들이 아플 때 음료를 찾는 반면, 미국의 많은 사람들은 닭고기 수프를 원한다.

14 그것은 보통 닭고기와 야채로 만들어지는데, 요리법은 가정마다 다르다.

15 소금과 후추를 먹기 전에 넣기도 한다.

16 미국인들은 따뜻한 닭고기 수프 한 그릇이 부은 목과 막힌 코에 좋다고 믿는다.

17 In Russia and in Eastern Europe, when people get sick, they eat a dessert _____ *gogol-mogol*.

18 It _____ _____ _____ eggs and honey.

19 Some people _____ chocolate, butter, lemon juice, or milk _____ _____ _____ _____ _____ .

20 It _____ _____ yogurt.

21 People often drink a cup of warm *gogol-mogol* when they _____ _____ _____ _____ .

22 *Gogol-mogol* is _____ _____ good for people with a cold _____ _____ popular as a dessert for _____ people.

23 When _____ as a dessert, it is usually _____ cold or _____ _____ _____ .

24 _____ _____ try making one of the foods you have _____ _____ _____ ?

25 It will be fun and _____ _____ your health.

26 _____ _____ _____ *Gogol-mogol* (Serves one)

27 _____ _____ : 1 egg, 1/2 cup of milk, honey (5 g), butter (15 g)

28 1. _____ the egg and the honey _____ a large cup and _____ _____ .

29 2. _____ half a cup of milk in a pan.

30 _____ the butter.

31 _____ it _____ the butter _____ .

32 3. _____ the hot milk and butter _____ the cup _____ the egg and the honey.

33 _____ _____ you _____ .

34 4. Drink _____ it is hot.

17 러시아와 동유럽에서는 사람들이 아플 때, 고골모골이라는 후식을 먹는다.

18 그것은 달걀과 꿀로 만든다.

19 어떤 사람들은 그것을 더 맛있게 하기 위해 초콜릿, 버터, 레몬주스, 또는 우유를 첨가한다.

20 그것은 진한 요구르트처럼 보인다.

21 사람들은 목이 아플 때 종종 따뜻한 고골모골 한 잔을 마신다.

22 고골모골은 감기에 걸린 사람들에게 좋을 뿐만 아니라 건강한 사람들의 후식으로도 인기가 있다.

23 후식으로 제공될 때에는 보통 차갑게 또는 실온으로 제공된다.

24 여러분이 알아본 음식들 중 하나를 만들어 보는 것은 어떨까?

25 그것은 재미있고 여러분의 건강에 좋을 것이다.

26 고골모골 만드는 방법 (1인분)

27 필요한 것: 달걀 1개, 우유 1/2컵, 꿀 5g, 버터 15g

28 1. 달걀과 꿀을 큰 컵에 넣고 섞는다.

29 2. 우유 반 컵을 팬에 붓는다.

30 버터를 추가한다.

31 버터가 녹을 때까지 데운다.

32 3. 뜨거운 우유와 버터를 달걀과 꿀이 있는 컵에 붓는다.

33 부으면서 젓는다.

34 4. 뜨거울 때 마신다.

※ 다음 문장을 우리말로 쓰시오.

1 Foods That Fight Colds
➡ _____

2 What do you do when you catch a cold?
➡ _____

3 Of course, you want to stay warm, so maybe you put on more clothes.
➡ _____

4 Some people like to drink hot tea.
➡ _____

5 Ginger tea is something people in Korea often drink.
➡ _____

6 With its special taste, it warms your body and helps reduce the pain in your throat.
➡ _____

7 What do people drink or eat in other countries when they catch a cold?
➡ _____

8 Let's find out.
➡ _____

9 In Finland, where it is very cold in winter, people have a special drink when they catch a cold.
➡ _____

10 It is a cup of onion milk.
➡ _____

11 They put chopped onion in milk and boil it over low heat for half an hour.
➡ _____

12 This simple drink is said to be good for a cold.
➡ _____

13 While people in Korea and Finland look for drinks when sick, many people in America want a bowl of chicken soup.
➡ _____

14 It is usually made with chicken and vegetables, but the recipe is different from one family to another.
➡ _____

15 Salt and pepper can be added before eating.
➡ _____

16 People in America believe that a bowl of warm chicken soup is great for a sore throat and a stuffy nose.
➡ _____

17 In Russia and in Eastern Europe, when people get sick, they eat a dessert called *gogol-mogol*.

➡ _____

18 It is made with eggs and honey.

➡ _____

19 Some people add chocolate, butter, lemon juice, or milk to make it taste better.

➡ _____

20 It looks like thick yogurt.

➡ _____

21 People often drink a cup of warm *gogol-mogol* when they have a sore throat.

➡ _____

22 *Gogol-mogol* is not only good for people with a cold but also popular as a dessert for healthy people.

➡ _____

23 When served as a dessert, it is usually served cold or at room temperature.

➡ _____

24 Why not try making one of the foods you have found out about?

➡ _____

25 It will be fun and good for your health.

➡ _____

26 How to Make *Gogol-mogol* (Serves one)

➡ _____

27 You need: 1 egg, 1/2 cup of milk, honey (5 g), butter (15 g)

➡ _____

28 1. Put the egg and the honey in a large cup and mix them.

➡ _____

29 2. Pour half a cup of milk in a pan.

➡ _____

30 Add the butter.

➡ _____

31 Warm it until the butter melts.

➡ _____

32 3. Pour the hot milk and butter into the cup with the egg and the honey.

➡ _____

33 Stir as you pour.

➡ _____

34 4. Drink while it is hot.

➡ _____

※ 다음 괄호 안의 단어들을 우리말에 맞도록 바르게 배열하시오.

1 (That / Foods / Colds / Fight)
➡ _____

2 (do / what / do / you / when / catch / you / cold? / a)
➡ _____

3 (course, / of / want / you / stay / to / warm, / maybe / so / put / you / on / clothes. / more)
➡ _____

4 (people / some / to / like / hot / drink / tea.)
➡ _____

5 (tea / ginger / something / is / people / Korea / in / drink. / often)
➡ _____

6 (its / with / taste, / special / warms / it / body / your / and / reduce / helps / pain / the / in / throat. / your)
➡ _____
_____

7 (do / what / drink / people / or / in / eat / other / when / countries / catch / they / cold? / a)
➡ _____

8 (find / let's / out.)
➡ _____

9 (Finland, / in / it / where / is / cold / very / winter, / in / have / people / a / drink / special / they / when / catch / cold. / a)
➡ _____
_____

10 (is / it / cup / a / onion / of / milk.)
➡ _____

11 (put / they / onion / chopped / milk / in / and / it / boil / low / over / heat / half / for / hour. / an)
➡ _____
_____

12 (simple / this / is / drink / to / said / good / be / for / cold. / a)
➡ _____

13 (people / while / Korea / in / and / look / Finland / for / when / drinks / sick, / people / many / America / in / a / want / of / bowl / soup. / chicken)
➡ _____
_____

14 (is / it / made / usually / chicken / with / vegetables, / and / the / but / is / recipe / from / different / one / to / family / another.)
➡ _____
_____

15 (pepper / and / salt / be / can / before / added / eating.)
➡ _____

16 (in / people / Americia / that / believe / a / of / bowl / chicken / warm / is / soup / great / a / for / throat / sore / a / and / nose. / stuffy)
➡ _____
_____

---

1 감기와 싸우는 음식들

2 여러분은 감기에 걸리면 어떻게 하는가?

3 당연히, 따뜻함을 유지하고자 할 것이고, 아마도 옷을 더 입을 것이다.

4 몇몇 사람들은 따뜻한 차를 마시는 것을 좋아한다.

5 생강차는 한국인들이 자주 마시는 것이다.

6 특별한 맛과 함께, 그것은 여러분의 몸을 따뜻하게 하고 목 통증을 완화하는 데 도움을 준다.

7 다른 나라에서는 사람들이 감기에 걸렸을 때 무엇을 마시거나 먹을까?

8 함께 알아보자.

9 겨울이 매우 추운 핀란드에서는 사람들이 감기에 걸리면 특별한 음료를 마신다.

10 그것은 양파 우유이다.

11 그들은 우유에 잘게 썬 양파를 넣고 30분 동안 약한 불에서 끓인다.

12 이 단순한 음료는 감기에 좋다고 한다.

13 한국 사람들과 핀란드 사람들이 아플 때 음료를 찾는 반면, 미국의 많은 사람들은 닭고기 수프를 원한다.

14 그것은 보통 닭고기와 야채로 만들어지는데, 요리법은 가정마다 다르다.

15 소금과 후추를 먹기 전에 넣기도 한다.

16 미국인들은 따뜻한 닭고기 수프한 그릇이 부은 목과 막힌 코에 좋다고 믿는다.

17 (Russia / in / and / Eastern / in / when / Europe, / get / people / sick, / eat / they / dessert / a / called / *gogol-mogol.*)
➡ _____

_____

18 (is / it / with / made / hoeny. / and / eggs)
➡ _____

19 (people / some / add / butter, / chocolate, / juice, / lemon / or / to / milk / it / make / better. / taste)
➡ _____

20 (looks / it / thick / like / yogurt.)
➡ _____

21 (often / people / a / drink / cup / warm / of / when / *gogol-mogol* / have / they / sore / a / throat.)
➡ _____

22 (is / *gogol-mogol* / only / not / for / good / with / people / cold / a / also / but / as / popular / dessert / a / healthy / for / people.)
➡ _____

23 (served / when / a / as / dessert, / is / it / served / usually / cold / at / or / temperature. / room)
➡ _____

24 (not / why / making / try / of / one / foods / the / have / you / out / found / about?)
➡ _____

25 (will / it / fun / be / and / for / good / health. / your)
➡ _____

26 (to / How / *Gogol-mogol* / Make / one) / (serves)
➡ _____

27 (need: / you / egg, / 1 / cup / 1/2 / milk, / of / (5 g), / honey / (15 g) / butter)
➡ _____

28 (1. / the / put / and / egg / honey / the / a / in / large / and / cup / them. / mix)
➡ _____

29 (2. / half / pour / cup / a / of / in / milk / pan. / a)
➡ _____

30 (the / add / butter.)
➡ _____

31 (it / warm / the / until / melts. / butter)
➡ _____

32 (3. / the / pour / milk / hot / and / into / butter / cup / the / the / with / egg / the / and / honey.)
➡ _____

33 (as / stir / pour. / you)
➡ _____

34 (4. / while / drink / is / it / hot.)
➡ _____

17 러시아와 동유럽에서는 사람들이 아플 때, 고골모골이라는 후식을 먹는다.

18 그것은 달걀과 꿀로 만든다.

19 어떤 사람들은 그것을 더 맛있게 하기 위해 초콜릿, 버터, 레몬주스, 또는 우유를 첨가한다.

20 그것은 진한 요구르트처럼 보인다.

21 사람들은 목이 아플 때 종종 따뜻한 고골모골 한 잔을 마신다.

22 고골모골은 감기에 걸린 사람들에게 좋을 뿐만 아니라 건강한 사람들의 후식으로도 인기가 있다.

23 후식으로 제공될 때에는 보통 차갑게 또는 실온으로 제공된다.

24 여러분이 알아본 음식들 중 하나를 만들어 보는 것은 어떨까?

25 그것은 재미있고 여러분의 건강에 좋을 것이다.

26 고골모골 만드는 방법 (1인분)

27 필요한 것: 달걀 1개, 우유 1/2 컵, 꿀 5g, 버터 15g

28 1. 달걀과 꿀을 큰 컵에 넣고 섞는다.

29 2. 우유 반 컵을 팬에 붓는다.

30 버터를 추가한다.

31 버터가 녹을 때까지 데운다.

32 3. 뜨거운 우유와 버터를 달걀과 꿀이 있는 컵에 붓는다.

33 부으면서 젓는다.

34 4. 뜨거울 때 마신다.

※ 다음 우리말을 영어로 쓰시오.

1 감기와 싸우는 음식들

➡ _____

2 여러분은 감기에 걸리면 어떻게 하는가?

➡ _____

3 당연히, 따뜻함을 유지하고자 할 것이고, 아마도 옷을 더 입을 것이다.

➡ _____

4 몇몇 사람들은 따뜻한 차를 마시는 것을 좋아한다.

➡ _____

5 생강차는 한국인들이 자주 마시는 것이다.

➡ _____

6 특별한 맛과 함께, 그것은 여러분의 몸을 따뜻하게 하고 목 통증을 완화하는 데 도움을 준다.

➡ _____

7 다른 나라에서는 사람들이 감기에 걸렸을 때 무엇을 마시거나 먹을까?

➡ _____

8 함께 알아보자.

➡ _____

9 겨울이 매우 추운 핀란드에서는 사람들이 감기에 걸리면 특별한 음료를 마신다.

➡ _____

10 그것은 양파 우유이다.

➡ _____

11 그들은 우유에 잘게 썬 양파를 넣고 30분 동안 약한 불에서 끓인다.

➡ _____

12 이 단순한 음료는 감기에 좋다고 한다.

➡ _____

13 한국 사람들과 핀란드 사람들이 아플 때 음료를 찾는 반면, 미국의 많은 사람들은 닭고기 수프를 원한다.

➡ _____

14 그것은 보통 닭고기와 야채로 만들어지는데, 요리법은 가정마다 다르다.

➡ _____

15 소금과 후추를 먹기 전에 넣기도 한다.

➡ _____

16 미국인들은 따뜻한 닭고기 수프 한 그릇이 부은 목과 막힌 코에 좋다고 믿는다.

➡ _____

_____

17 러시아와 동유럽에서는 사람들이 아플 때, 고골모골이라는 후식을 먹는다.
➡ _____

18 그것은 달걀과 꿀로 만든다.
➡ _____

19 어떤 사람들은 그것을 더 맛있게 하기 위해 초콜릿, 버터, 레몬주스, 또는 우유를 첨가한다.
➡ _____

20 그것은 진한 요구르트처럼 보인다.
➡ _____

21 사람들은 목이 아플 때 종종 따뜻한 고골모골 한 잔을 마신다.
➡ _____

22 고골모골은 감기에 걸린 사람들에게 좋을 뿐만 아니라 건강한 사람들의 후식으로도 인기가 있다.
➡ _____
_____

23 후식으로 제공될 때에는 보통 차갑게 또는 실온으로 제공된다.
➡ _____

24 여러분이 알아본 음식들 중 하나를 만들어 보는 것은 어떨까?
➡ _____

25 그것은 재미있고 여러분의 건강에 좋을 것이다.
➡ _____

26 고골모골 만드는 방법 (1인분)
➡ _____

27 필요한 것: 달걀 1개, 우유 1/2컵, 꿀 5g, 버터 15g
➡ _____

28 1. 달걀과 꿀을 큰 컵에 넣고 섞는다.
➡ _____

29 2. 우유 반 컵을 팬에 붓는다.
➡ _____

30 버터를 추가한다.
➡ _____

31 버터가 녹을 때까지 데운다.
➡ _____

32 3. 뜨거운 우유와 버터를 달걀과 꿀이 있는 컵에 붓는다.
➡ _____

33 부으면서 젓는다.
➡ _____

34 4. 뜨거울 때 마신다.
➡ _____

※ 다음 우리말과 일치하도록 빈칸에 알맞은 말을 쓰시오.

After You Read B

1. Look! _____ _____ *gogol-mogol*.

2. Happy07: _____ _____ *gogol-mogol*?

3. Bora: It's a dessert _____ people in Russia and _____ _____ _____ eat _____ they _____ _____.

4. Yumyum: It _____ _____. What is it _____ _____?

5. Bora: It's _____ _____ _____ and honey.

6. Yumyum: What's that you _____ _____ _____ _____?

7. Bora: I put chocolate on top _____ _____ it _____ _____.

8. Happy07: Do people also eat it _____ _____ _____ _____?

9. Bora: Sure. It's a _____ _____. _____ _____ as a dessert, it's _____ _____ cold or _____ _____ _____.

1. 봐! 나는 고골모골을 만들었어.
2. Happy07: 고골모골이 뭐야?
3. 보라: 그것은 러시아와 동유럽에서 사람이 아플 때 먹는 후식이야.
4. Yumyum: 그것은 맛있어 보여. 그것은 무엇으로 만들어지니?
5. 보라: 그것은 달걀과 꿀로 만들어져.
6. Yumyum: 그것 꼭대기에 올린 것이 뭐니?
7. 보라: 나는 그것을 더 맛있게 하기 위해 꼭대기에 초콜릿을 올렸어.
8. Happy07: 사람들이 아프지 않을 때도 그것을 먹니?
9. 보라: 물론이야. 그것은 인기 있는 후식이야. 후식으로 제공될 때에는 보통 차갑게 또는 실온으로 제공돼.

Writing Workshop

1. _____ many Koreans eat Samgyetang _____ _____ _____ _____, _____ _____ _____ _____ _____ eat tomato soup.

2. Here is _____ _____ _____ it.

3. _____ _____: 1 tomato, some water, _____ _____, _____

4. First, _____ one fresh tomato. Then _____ the _____ tomato _____ a pan and _____ some water _____ it.

5. Next, _____ _____ _____ for ten minutes. Then _____ the heat and _____ it _____ _____ _____.

6. Next, _____ it _____ it _____ smooth. Finally, _____ some _____ _____ and _____.

7. Now you _____ _____ the tomato soup.

8. This tomato soup is _____ _____ _____ _____ _____.

1. 많은 한국인들이 아플 때 삼계탕을 먹는 반면에, 인도의 많은 사람들은 토마토 수프를 먹는다.
2. 여기 그것을 만드는 방법이 있다.
3. 필요한 것: 토마토 한 개, 물 약간, 후추, 소금
4. 첫 번째로, 신선한 토마토 한 개를 다진다. 그 후, 다진 토마토를 팬 위에 놓고 그 위에 물을 조금 붓는다.
5. 다음으로, 그 혼합물을 10분간 끓인다. 불을 끄고 식도록 둔다.
6. 다음, 부드러워질 때까지 그것을 섞는다. 마지막으로, 후추와 소금을 약간 넣는다.
7. 이제 토마토 수프를 즐길 수 있다.
8. 이 토마토 수프는 건강에 좋을 뿐 아니라 맛있다.

※ 다음 우리말을 영어로 쓰시오.

After You Read B

1. 봐! 나는 고골모골을 만들었어.

➡ _____

2. Happy07: 고골모골이 뭐야?

➡ _____

3. 보라: 그것은 러시아와 동유럽에서 사람들이 아플 때 먹는 후식이야.

➡ _____

4. Yumyum: 그것은 맛있어 보여. 그것은 무엇으로 만들어지니?

➡ _____

5. 보라: 그것은 달걀과 꿀로 만들어져.

➡ _____

6. Yumyum: 그것 꼭대기에 올린 것이 뭐니?

➡ _____

7. 보라: 나는 그것을 더 맛있게 하기 위해 꼭대기에 초콜릿을 올렸어.

➡ _____

8. Happy07: 사람들이 아프지 않을 때도 그것을 먹니?

➡ _____

9. 보라: 물론이야. 그것은 인기 있는 후식이야. 후식으로 제공될 때에는 보통 차갑게 또는 실온으로 제공돼.

➡ _____

Writing Workshop

1. 많은 한국인들이 아플 때 삼계탕을 먹는 반면에, 인도의 많은 사람들은 토마토 수프를 먹는다.

➡ _____

2. 여기 그것을 만드는 방법이 있다.

➡ _____

3. 필요한 것: 토마토 한 개, 물 약간, 후추, 소금

➡ _____

4. 첫 번째로, 신선한 토마토 한 개를 다진다. 그 후, 다진 토마토를 팬 위에 놓고 그 위에 물을 조금 붓는다.

➡ _____

5. 다음으로, 그 혼합물을 10분간 끓인다. 불을 끄고 식도록 둔다.

➡ _____

6. 다음, 부드러워질 때까지 그것을 섞는다. 마지막으로, 후추와 소금을 약간 넣는다.

➡ _____

7. 이제 토마토 수프를 즐길 수 있다.

➡ _____

8. 이 토마토 수프는 건강에 좋을 뿐 아니라 맛있다.

➡ _____

※ 다음 영어를 우리말로 쓰시오.

01 aim	
02 weapon	
03 along	
04 suddenly	
05 happen	
06 face	
07 human	
08 surprise	
09 miracle	
10 trench	
11 entire	
12 sight	
13 although	
14 wet	
15 might	
16 follow	
17 actually	
18 unbelievable	
19 soldier	
20 address	
21 front line	

22 greeting	
23 miss	
24 truly	
25 boldly	
26 exchange	
27 shout	
28 either	
29 enemy	
30 trick	
31 familiar	
32 share	
33 several	
34 keep	
35 look out of	
36 all the more	
37 each other	
38 in peace	
39 at war	
40 pass away	
41 such as	
42 put down	
43 one after another	

※ 다음 우리말을 영어로 쓰시오.

01 몇의, 수개의 _____

02 전체의 _____

03 속임수 _____

04 사실은 _____

05 그리워하다 _____

06 ~를 따라 _____

07 외침, 고함 _____

08 목표 _____

09 마주하다 _____

10 빛나다, 비추다 _____

11 주소 _____

12 정말로, 진심으로 _____

13 무기 _____

14 군인, 병사 _____

15 익숙한, 친숙한 _____

16 믿기 힘든 _____

17 기적 _____

18 대담하게 _____

19 광경 _____

20 젖은 _____

21 갑자기 _____

22 적군, 적 _____

23 교환하다 _____

24 놀라게 하다 _____

25 참호 _____

26 인사, 안부의 말 _____

27 인간, 사람 _____

28 예상하다 _____

29 조명 _____

30 비록 ~이긴 하지만 _____

31 일어나다 _____

32 공유하다, 나누다 _____

33 ~도, ~ 또한 _____

34 따라가다 _____

35 잇따라서 _____

36 전쟁 중인 _____

37 차례로 _____

38 내려놓다 _____

39 악수하다 _____

40 ~와 같은 _____

41 최전선에 _____

42 사망하다 _____

43 ~ 밖을 내다보다 _____

※ 다음 영영풀이에 알맞은 단어를 <보기>에서 골라 쓴 후, 우리말 뜻을 쓰시오.

1 _____ : Christmas song or hymn: _____

2 _____ : a loud call or cry: _____

3 _____ : an act or words of welcoming: _____

4 _____ : to divide and distribute something in shares: _____

5 _____ : something seen or worth seeing: _____

6 _____ : a sneaky scheme to deceive or cheat: _____

7 _____ : something you hope to achieve by doing something: _____

8 _____ : to give and receive reciprocally; interchange: _____

9 _____ : freedom from war; absence of fighting between nations: _____

10 _____ : a contest of speed, such as running, riding, driving or sailing:

   _____

11 _____ : to hit with a bullet, shell, or other missile fired from a weapon: _____

12 _____ : in a brave and confident way, without showing any fear: _____

13 _____ : details of where someone lives or works and where letters, etc. can be sent:

   _____

14 _____ : an object such as a knife, gun, bomb, etc. that is used for fighting or

   attacking somebody: _____

15 _____ : a person who is in an army and wears its uniform, especially someone

   who fights when there is a war: _____

16 _____ : to strike with a sudden feeling of wonder or astonishment especially by

   being unexpected: _____

보기			
trick	weapon	aim	exchange
greeting	boldly	shout	address
surprise	carol	soldier	shoot
peace	sight	race	share

Step1

※ 다음 우리말과 일치하도록 빈칸에 알맞은 것을 골라 쓰시오.

1 A _____ _____
A. Miracle   B. Christmas

2 _____ was Christmas Eve _____ 1914, the _____
_____ of World War I.
A. year   B. it   C. in   D. first

3 English soldiers were _____ German soldiers from their
trenches as they _____ _____ for the last _____ months.
A. done   B. facing   C. few   D. had

4 The _____ were _____ and _____.
A. wet   B. trenches   C. cold

5 The soldiers were _____ and _____ their home, all the
_____ _____ because it was Christmas.
A. more   B. tired   C. so   D. missed

6 _____, a _____ song was _____ from the
German trenches.
A. heard   B. suddenly   C. coming   D. familiar

7 _____ was a _____ _____!
A. Christmas   B. it   C. carol

8 What's _____ _____?
A. on   B. going

9 It _____ _____ a _____ to make them come _____ of
the trenches.
A. trick   B. might   C. out   D. be

10 A few English soldiers _____ _____ _____
their trenches.
A. out   B. boldly   C. of   D. looked

11 One _____ one, _____ soldiers _____ their _____.
A. followed   B. by   C. example   D. other

12 _____ they saw was a _____ they _____ _____.
A. sight   B. expected   C. never   D. what

13 _____ the German trenches, Christmas trees were _____
_____ _____ lanterns!
A. lit   B. along   C. with   D. standing

14 The German soldiers sang _____ Christmas _____ _____
_____.
A. after   B. one   C. another   D. song

15 The English soldiers began to _____ _____ _____
_____ Christmas songs.
A. by   B. answer   C. singing   D. also

16 The warm _____ and the Christmas carols _____ them
_____ they were on the _____ line.
A. forget   B. lights   C. front   D. made

1 크리스마스의 기적

2 제일차 세계 대전의 첫해였던 1914
년의 크리스마스이브였습니다.

3 영국 군인들은 지난 몇 달 동안
그래왔듯이 그들의 참호에서 독
일 군인들과 대치하고 있었어요.

4 참호는 춥고 축축했습니다.

5 군인들은 지쳤고 자신들의 집을
그리워했는데, 크리스마스라는
이유로 더욱 더 그랬습니다.

6 갑자기 익숙한 노래가 독일 군인
들의 참호로부터 들려왔습니다.

7 그것은 크리스마스 캐럴이었어요!

8 무슨 일이 벌어지고 있는 걸까요?

9 어쩌면 그들을 참호 밖으로 유
인하고자 하는 속임수일지도 모
릅니다.

10 몇몇 영국 군인들이 용감하게 자
신들의 참호 밖을 내다보았어요.

11 차례차례 다른 군인들도 앞사람
을 따랐습니다.

12 영국 군인들이 본 것은 그들이 절
대 예상하지 못한 광경이었어요.

13 독일 군인들의 참호를 따라, 크
리스마스트리들이 랜턴으로 밝
혀진 채 있었습니다!

14 독일 군인들은 크리스마스 캐럴
을 연이어 불렀어요.

15 영국 군인들도 크리스마스 캐럴을
부르며 화답하기 시작했습니다.

16 따뜻한 불빛과 크리스마스 캐럴
은 그들이 최전선에 있다는 것
을 잊게 만들었어요.

17 Then a shout _____ _____ _____ the German side: "Happy Christmas! You no _____, we no shoot!"

    A. out   B. shoot   C. came   D. from

18 Soon, soldiers _____ _____ had been to kill each other just a few hours before began to _____ _____.

    A. aim   B. greetings   C. whose   D. exchange

19 For the first time in _____ months, the soldiers were _____ to spend a night _____ _____.

    A. able   B. peace   C. several   D. in

20 It _____ was a _____ _____ _____.

    A. night   B. truly   C. silent

21 Christmas _____ _____.

    A. came   B. morning

22 Soldiers _____ _____ _____ put _____ their weapons and came out of their trenches.

    A. down   B. on   C. sides   D. both

23 They met in the no _____ _____ _____ their trenches _____ shook hands.

    A. between   B. man's   C. and   D. land

24 They _____ small _____ _____ _____ wine and cake.

    A. such   B. exchanged   C. as   D. gifts

25 They _____ _____ _____.

    A. together   B. sang   C. carols

26 _____ _____ _____ and played football.

    A. exchanged   B. some   C. addresses   D. even

27 This _____ Christmas Day was _____ about in English _____ sent home.

    A. soldiers   B. unbelievable   C. written   D. letters

28 One soldier _____, "On Christmas Day, English and German soldiers met _____ the two _____ and had _____.

    A. lines   B. wrote   C. between   D. talks

29 We _____ _____ bike _____."

    A. had   B. races   C. also

30 _____ wrote, "We didn't _____ that we were _____ _____.

    A. at   B. another   C. war   D. think

31 _____ we _____, enemy _____ to _____.

    A. enemy   B. here   C. talking   D. were

32 They were _____ us, with mothers, with friends, with _____ who were _____ to _____ their men home again."

    A. welcome   B. like   C. waiting   D. wives

17 그리고 독일 군인들 쪽에서 고함이 터져 나왔습니다. "행복한 크리스마스예요! 당신들이 쏘지 않는다면, 우리도 쏘지 않을게요!"

18 곧, 단지 몇 시간 전까지만 해도 서로를 죽이는 것이 목적이었던 군인들은 인사를 나누기 시작했습니다.

19 몇 달 만에 처음으로, 군인들은 평화롭게 밤을 지낼 수 있었어요.

20 그날은 정말로 조용한 밤이었습니다.

21 크리스마스 아침이 밝았습니다.

22 양편의 군인들은 자신들의 무기를 내려놓고 참호 밖으로 나왔어요.

23 그들은 무인 지대에서 만났고 악수를 했습니다.

24 그들은 와인과 케이크 같은 작은 선물도 교환했어요.

25 그들은 캐럴을 함께 불렀습니다.

26 몇몇은 심지어 주소를 교환하기도 했고 함께 축구를 했습니다.

27 이 믿을 수 없는 크리스마스는 영국 군인들이 집으로 보낸 편지에 적혀 있었습니다.

28 한 군인은 "크리스마스에 영국 군인들과 독일 군인들은 두 경계선 사이에서 만났고 대화를 나눴어.

29 우리는 자전거 시합도 했어."라고 적었어요.

30 다른 군인은 "우리는 전쟁 중이라는 생각이 들지 않았어.

31 여기서 우리는 적대 관계인 서로와 대화를 나누고 있는 상황이었어.

32 그들은 우리와 마찬가지로, 그들의 남자들이 집으로 다시 돌아오기를 고대하는 어머니와, 친구들, 부인이 있는 사람들이었어."라고 썼습니다.

※ 다음 우리말과 일치하도록 빈칸에 알맞은 것을 골라 쓰시오.

1 A Christmas _____

2 It was Christmas Eve in 1914, _____ _____ _____ of World War I.

3 English soldiers _____ _____ German soldiers from their trenches as they _____ _____ for the last _____ _____.

4 The trenches were _____ _____ _____.

5 The soldiers were tired and _____ their home, _____ _____ _____ _____ _____ it was Christmas.

6 _____, a familiar song _____ _____ _____ from the German trenches.

7 It was a Christmas _____!

8 What's _____ _____?

9 It _____ _____ _____ _____ to make them come out of the _____.

10 A few English soldiers _____ _____ _____ _____ their trenches.

11 _____ _____ _____, other soldiers _____ their example.

12 _____ they saw was a _____ they never _____.

13 Along the German trenches, Christmas trees were standing _____ _____ _____!

14 The German soldiers sang _____ _____ _____ _____.

15 The English soldiers began to answer _____ _____ Christmas songs.

16 The warm lights and the Christmas carols _____ _____ _____ they were on the _____ _____.

1 크리스마스의 기적

2 제일차 세계 대전의 첫해였던 1914년의 크리스마스이브였습니다.

3 영국 군인들은 지난 몇 달 동안 그래왔듯이 그들의 참호에서 독일 군인들과 대치하고 있었어요.

4 참호는 춥고 축축했습니다.

5 군인들은 지쳤고 자신들의 집을 그리워했는데, 크리스마스라는 이유로 더욱 더 그랬습니다.

6 갑자기 익숙한 노래가 독일 군인들의 참호로부터 들려왔습니다.

7 그것은 크리스마스 캐럴이었어요!

8 무슨 일이 벌어지고 있는 걸까요?

9 어쩌면 그들을 참호 밖으로 유인하고자 하는 속임수일지도 모릅니다.

10 몇몇 영국 군인들이 용감하게 자신들의 참호 밖을 내다보았어요.

11 차례차례 다른 군인들도 앞사람을 따랐습니다.

12 영국 군인들이 본 것은 그들이 절대 예상하지 못한 광경이었어요.

13 독일 군인들의 참호를 따라, 크리스마스트리들이 랜턴으로 밝혀진 채 있었습니다!

14 독일 군인들은 크리스마스 캐럴을 연이어 불렀어요.

15 영국 군인들도 크리스마스 캐럴을 부르며 화답하기 시작했습니다.

16 따뜻한 불빛과 크리스마스 캐럴은 그들이 최전선에 있다는 것을 잊게 만들었어요.

17 Then a shout _____ _____ _____ the German side: "Happy Christmas! You no _____, we no shoot!"

18 Soon, soldiers _____ _____ had been to kill _____ _____ just a few hours before began to _____ _____.

19 For the first time _____ _____ _____, the soldiers were able to spend a night _____ _____.

20 _____ _____ _____ a silent night.

21 Christmas morning _____.

22 Soldiers _____ _____ _____ put down their weapons and _____ _____ _____ their trenches.

23 They met _____ _____ _____ _____ _____ between their trenches and _____ _____.

24 They exchanged small gifts _____ _____ wine and cake.

25 They _____ _____ together.

26 Some even _____ _____ and played football.

27 This _____ Christmas Day was written _____ in letters English soldiers _____ home.

28 One soldier wrote, "On Christmas Day, English and German soldiers met _____ _____ _____ _____ and had talks.

29 We also _____ _____ _____."

30 Another wrote, "We didn't think that we _____ _____ _____.

31 _____ _____ _____, enemy talking to _____.

32 They were _____ _____, with mothers, with friends, with wives who were _____ _____ _____ their men home again."

17 그리고 독일 군인들 쪽에서 고함이 터져 나왔습니다. "행복한 크리스마스예요! 당신들이 쏘지 않는다면, 우리도 쏘지 않을게요!"

18 곧, 단지 몇 시간 전까지만 해도 서로를 죽이는 것이 목적이었던 군인들은 인사를 나누기 시작했습니다.

19 몇 달 만에 처음으로, 군인들은 평화롭게 밤을 지낼 수 있었어요.

20 그날은 정말로 조용한 밤이었습니다.

21 크리스마스 아침이 밝았습니다.

22 양편의 군인들은 자신들의 무기를 내려놓고 참호 밖으로 나왔어요.

23 그들은 무인 지대에서 만났고 악수를 했습니다.

24 그들은 와인과 케이크 같은 작은 선물도 교환했어요.

25 그들은 캐럴을 함께 불렀습니다.

26 몇몇은 심지어 주소를 교환하기도 했고 함께 축구를 했습니다.

27 이 믿을 수 없는 크리스마스는 영국 군인들이 집으로 보낸 편지에 적혀 있었습니다.

28 한 군인은 "크리스마스에 영국 군인들과 독일 군인들은 두 경계선 사이에서 만났고 대화를 나눴어.

29 우리는 자전거 시합도 했어."라고 적었어요.

30 다른 군인은 "우리는 전쟁 중이라는 생각이 들지 않았어.

31 여기서 우리는 적대 관계인 서로와 대화를 나누고 있는 상황이었어.

32 그들은 우리와 마찬가지로, 그들의 남자들이 집으로 다시 돌아오기를 고대하는 어머니와, 친구들, 부인이 있는 사람들이었어."라고 썼습니다.

※ 다음 문장을 우리말로 쓰시오.

1 ▶ A Christmas Miracle

➡ _____

2 ▶ It was Christmas Eve in 1914, the first year of World War I.

➡ _____

3 ▶ English soldiers were facing German soldiers from their trenches as they had done for the last few months.

➡ _____

4 ▶ The trenches were cold and wet.

➡ _____

5 ▶ The soldiers were tired and missed their home, all the more so because it was Christmas.

➡ _____

6 ▶ Suddenly, a familiar song was heard coming from the German trenches.

➡ _____

7 ▶ It was a Christmas carol!

➡ _____

8 ▶ What's going on?

➡ _____

9 ▶ It might be a trick to make them come out of the trenches.

➡ _____

10 ▶ A few English soldiers boldly looked out of their trenches.

➡ _____

11 ▶ One by one, other soldiers followed their example.

➡ _____

12 ▶ What they saw was a sight they never expected.

➡ _____

13 ▶ Along the German trenches, Christmas trees were standing lit with lanterns!

➡ _____

14 ▶ The German soldiers sang one Christmas song after another.

➡ _____

15 ▶ The English soldiers began to answer by also singing Christmas songs.

➡ _____

16 ▶ The warm lights and the Christmas carols made them forget they were on the front line.

➡ _____

17 Then a shout came out from the German side: "Happy Christmas! You no shoot, we no shoot!"

➡ _____

_____

18 Soon, soldiers whose aim had been to kill each other just a few hours before began to exchange greetings.

➡ _____

19 For the first time in several months, the soldiers were able to spend a night in peace.

➡ _____

20 It truly was a silent night.

➡ _____

21 Christmas morning came.

➡ _____

22 Soldiers on both sides put down their weapons and came out of their trenches.

➡ _____

23 They met in the no man's land between their trenches and shook hands.

➡ _____

24 They exchanged small gifts such as wine and cake.

➡ _____

25 They sang carols together.

➡ _____

26 Some even exchanged addresses and played football.

➡ _____

27 This unbelievable Christmas Day was written about in letters English soldiers sent home.

➡ _____

28 One soldier wrote, "On Christmas Day, English and German soldiers met between the two lines and had talks.

➡ _____

29 We also had bike races."

➡ _____

30 Another wrote, "We didn't think that we were at war.

➡ _____

31 Here we were, enemy talking to enemy.

➡ _____

32 They were like us, with mothers, with friends, with wives who were waiting to welcome their men home again."

➡ _____

_____

본문 Test

※ 다음 괄호 안의 단어들을 우리말에 맞도록 바르게 배열하시오.

1 (Christmas / A / Miracle)
➡ _____

2 (was / it / Eve / Christmas / 1914, / in / first / the / of / year / War / World / I.)
➡ _____

3 soldiers / English / facing / were / soldiers / German / their / from / as / trenches / had / they / for / done / last / the / months. / few)
➡ _____

4 (trenches / the / cold / were / wet. / and)
➡ _____

5 (soldiers / the / tired / were / and / their / missed / home, / the / all / so / more / it / because / Christmas. / was)
➡ _____

6 (a / suddenly, / familiar / was / song / coming / heard / the / from / trenches. / German)
➡ _____

7 (was / it / Christmas / a / carol!)
➡ _____

8 (going / what's / on?)
➡ _____

9 (might / it / a / be / to / trick / them / make / out / come / the / of / trenches.)
➡ _____

10 (few / a / soldiers / English / looked / boldly / of / out / trenches. / their)
➡ _____

11 (by / one / other / one, / soldiers / their / followed / example.)
➡ _____

12 (they / what / was / saw / sight / a / never / they / expected.)
➡ _____

13 (the / along / trenches, / German / trees / Christmas / standing / were / with / lit / lanterns!)
➡ _____

14 (German / the / sang / soldiers / Chrtistmas / one / after / another. / song)
➡ _____

15 (English / the / began / soldiers / answer / to / also / by / Christmas / singing / songs.)
➡ _____

16 (warm / the / and / lights / Christmas / the / made / carols / forget / them / were / they / the / on / line. / front)
➡ _____

1 크리스마스의 기적

2 제일차 세계 대전의 첫해였던 1914년의 크리스마스이브였습니다.

3 영국 군인들은 지난 몇 달 동안 그래왔듯이 그들의 참호에서 독일 군인들과 대치하고 있었어요.

4 참호는 춥고 축축했습니다.

5 군인들은 지쳤고 자신들의 집을 그리워했는데, 크리스마스라는 이유로 더욱 더 그랬습니다.

6 갑자기 익숙한 노래가 독일 군인들의 참호로부터 들려왔습니다.

7 그것은 크리스마스 캐럴이었어요!

8 무슨 일이 벌어지고 있는 걸까요?

9 어쩌면 그들을 참호 밖으로 유인하고자 하는 속임수일지도 모릅니다.

10 몇몇 영국 군인들이 용감하게 자신들의 참호 밖을 내다보았어요.

11 차례차례 다른 군인들도 앞사람을 따랐습니다.

12 영국 군인들이 본 것은 그들이 절대 예상하지 못한 광경이었어요.

13 독일 군인들의 참호를 따라, 크리스마스트리들이 랜턴으로 밝혀진 채 있었습니다!

14 독일 군인들은 크리스마스 캐럴을 연이어 불렀어요.

15 영국 군인들도 크리스마스 캐럴을 부르며 화답하기 시작했습니다.

16 따뜻한 불빛과 크리스마스 캐럴은 그들이 최전선에 있다는 것을 잊게 만들었어요.

17 ▸ (a / then / came / shout / out / the / from / side: / German / Christmas! / "happy // no / you / shoot, / no / we / shoot!")
➡ _____
_____

18 ▸ (soldiers / soon, / whose / had / aim / to / been / each / kill / other / a / just / hours / few / began / before / exchange / to / greetings.)
➡ _____

19 ▸ (the / for / time / first / several / in / months, / soldiers / the / able / were / spend / to / night / a / peace. / in)
➡ _____

20 ▸ (truly / it / a / was / night. / silent)
➡ _____

21 ▸ (morning / Christmas / came.)
➡ _____

22 ▸ (on / soldiers / sides / both / down / put / weapons / their / and / out / came / their / of / trenches.)
➡ _____

23 ▸ (met / they / the / in / no / land / man's / their / between / and / trenches / hands. / shook)
➡ _____

24 ▸ (exchanged / they / gifts / small / as / such / cake. / and / wine)
➡ _____

25 ▸ (sang / they / together. / carols)
➡ _____

26 ▸ (even / some / addresses / exchanged / and / football. / played)
➡ _____

27 ▸ (unbelievable / this / Day / Christmas / written / was / about / letters / in / soldiers / English / home. / sent)
➡ _____

28 ▸ (soldier / one / wrote, / Christmas / "on / Day, / German / and / English / met / soldiers / the / between / lines / two / and / talks. / had)
➡ _____

29 ▸ (also / we / bike / had / races.")
➡ _____

30 ▸ (wrote, / another / didn't / "we / that / think / were / we / war. / at)
➡ _____

31 ▸ (we / here / were, / talking / enemy / enemy. / to)
➡ _____

32 ▸ (were / they / us, / like / mothers, / with / friends, / with / wives / with / were / who / waiting / welcome / to / men / their / again." / home)
➡ _____
_____

17 그리고 독일 군인들 쪽에서 고함이 터져 나왔습니다. "행복한 크리스마스예요! 당신들이 쏘지 않는다면, 우리도 쏘지 않을게요!"

18 곧, 단지 몇 시간 전까지만 해도 서로를 죽이는 것이 목적이었던 군인들은 인사를 나누기 시작했습니다.

19 몇 달 만에 처음으로, 군인들은 평화롭게 밤을 지낼 수 있었어요.

20 그날은 정말로 조용한 밤이었습니다.

21 크리스마스 아침이 밝았습니다.

22 양편의 군인들은 자신들의 무기를 내려놓고 참호 밖으로 나왔어요.

23 그들은 무인 지대에서 만났고 악수를 했습니다.

24 그들은 와인과 케이크 같은 작은 선물도 교환했어요.

25 그들은 캐럴을 함께 불렀습니다.

26 몇몇은 심지어 주소를 교환하기도 했고 함께 축구를 했습니다.

27 이 믿을 수 없는 크리스마스는 영국 군인들이 집으로 보낸 편지에 적혀 있었습니다.

28 한 군인은 "크리스마스에 영국 군인들과 독일 군인들은 두 경계선 사이에서 만났고 대화를 나눴어.

29 우리는 자전거 시합도 했어."라고 적었어요.

30 다른 군인은 "우리는 전쟁 중이라는 생각이 들지 않았어.

31 여기서 우리는 적대 관계인 서로와 대화를 나누고 있는 상황이었어.

32 그들은 우리와 마찬가지로, 그들의 남자들이 집으로 다시 돌아오기를 고대하는 어머니와, 친구들, 부인이 있는 사람들이었어."라고 썼습니다.

※ 다음 우리말을 영어로 쓰시오.

1 크리스마스의 기적

➡ _____

2 제일차 세계 대전의 첫해였던 1914년의 크리스마스이브였습니다.

➡ _____

3 영국 군인들은 지난 몇 달 동안 그래왔듯이 그들의 참호에서 독일 군인들과 대치하고 있었어요.

➡ _____

_____

4 참호는 춥고 축축했습니다.

➡ _____

5 군인들은 지쳤고 자신들의 집을 그리워했는데, 크리스마스라는 이유로 더욱 더 그랬습니다.

➡ _____

6 갑자기 익숙한 노래가 독일 군인들의 참호로부터 들려왔습니다.

➡ _____

7 그것은 크리스마스 캐럴이었어요!

➡ _____

8 무슨 일이 벌어지고 있는 걸까요?

➡ _____

9 어쩌면 그들을 참호 밖으로 유인하고자 하는 속임수일지도 모릅니다.

➡ _____

10 몇몇 영국 군인들이 용감하게 자신들의 참호 밖을 내다보았어요.

➡ _____

11 차례차례 다른 군인들도 앞사람을 따랐습니다.

➡ _____

12 영국 군인들이 본 것은 그들이 절대 예상하지 못한 광경이었어요.

➡ _____

13 독일 군인들의 참호를 따라, 크리스마스트리들이 랜턴으로 밝혀진 채 있었습니다!

➡ _____

14 독일 군인들은 크리스마스 캐럴을 연이어 불렀어요.

➡ _____

15 영국 군인들도 크리스마스 캐럴을 부르며 화답하기 시작했습니다.

➡ _____

16 따뜻한 불빛과 크리스마스 캐럴은 그들이 최전선에 있다는 것을 잊게 만들었어요.

➡ _____

17 그리고 독일 군인들 쪽에서 고함이 터져 나왔습니다. "행복한 크리스마스예요! 당신들이 쏘지 않는다면, 우리도 쏘지 않을게요!"
➡

18 곧, 단지 몇 시간 전까지만 해도 서로를 죽이는 것이 목적이었던 군인들은 인사를 나누기 시작했습니다.
➡

19 몇 달 만에 처음으로, 군인들은 평화롭게 밤을 지낼 수 있었어요.
➡

20 그날은 정말로 조용한 밤이었습니다.
➡

21 크리스마스 아침이 밝았습니다.
➡

22 양편의 군인들은 자신들의 무기를 내려놓고 참호 밖으로 나왔어요.
➡

23 그들은 무인 지대에서 만났고 악수를 했습니다.
➡

24 그들은 와인과 케이크 같은 작은 선물도 교환했어요.
➡

25 그들은 캐럴을 함께 불렀습니다.
➡

26 몇몇은 심지어 주소를 교환하기도 했고 함께 축구를 했습니다.
➡

27 이 믿을 수 없는 크리스마스는 영국 군인들이 집으로 보낸 편지에 적혀 있었습니다.
➡

28 한 군인은 "크리스마스에 영국 군인들과 독일 군인들은 두 경계선 사이에서 만났고 대화를 나눴어.
➡

29 우리는 자전거 시합도 했어."라고 적었어요.
➡

30 다른 군인은 "우리는 전쟁 중이라는 생각이 들지 않았어.
➡

31 여기서 우리는 적대 관계인 서로와 대화를 나누고 있는 상황이었어.
➡

32 그들은 우리와 마찬가지로, 그들의 남자들이 집으로 다시 돌아오기를 고대하는 어머니와, 친구들, 부인이 있는 사람들이었어."라고 썼습니다.
➡

영어 기출 문제집

2학기

정답 및 해설

시사 | 송미정

중 3

영어 기출 문제집

2학기 전과정 적중 100 plus

2학기

정답 및 해설

시사 | 송미정

중 3

Lesson 5

Look Inside You

시험대비 실력평가 p.08

01 independent   02 ⑤   03 ④

04 sold out   05 (a)ttitude   06 ④

07 (1) protection   (2) situation   (3) difference

01 주어진 관계는 반의어 관계이다. dependent: 의존적인, independent: 독립적인

02 '어떤 사람을 다른 사람과 구별시켜 주는 일련의 감정적인 특성, 행동 방식 따위'를 가리키는 말은 personality(성격)이다.

03 ④번 문장에서 means는 '수단'을 의미한다.

04 sold out: 매진된, 다 팔린

05 '사람이나 사물에 대해 생각하거나 느끼는 방식'을 가리키는 단어는 attitude(태도)이다.

06 주어진 문장과 나머지는 '표현하다'를 나타내지만 ④번은 '급행'을 나타낸다.

서술형 시험대비 p.09

01 (s)imilarity

02 (1) details   (2) opinion   (3) raise   (4) focus

03 (1) at the same time   (2) According to

    (3) participate in

04 (r)easonable, (f)rightened, (r)educe

    (1) frightened   (2) reasonable   (3) reduce

05 various

06 (1) Jake is not ready to live on his own.

    (2) Jane knows how to deal with angry dogs.

    (3) It may have to do with culture.

01 주어진 관계는 반의어 관계이다. difference: 차이, 다름 / similarity: 유사, 비슷함

02 (1) detail: 세부 사항 / 그의 상사는 회의 전에 세부 사항들을 확인했다. (2) opinion: 의견 / 이 상황에서 내 개인적인 의견은 중요하지 않다. (3) raise: 기르다 / 너는 개를 키울 때 책임감을 가져야 한다. (4) focus: 집중하다 / 너는 공부에 더 집중하는 게 좋겠다.

03 (1) at the same time: 동시에 (2) according to: ~에 따르면 (3) participate in: ~에 참여하다

04 reasonable: 합리적인, 타당하고 분별 있는 / frightened: 겁 먹은, 두려워하는, 두려움을 느끼거나 드러내는 / reduce: 줄이

다, 어떤 것의 크기, 양, 수 등이 작아지게 하다 (1) Ellen은 대중 앞에서 말하는 것을 두려워했다. (2) 그는 아주 합리적인 사람이다. (3) 우리는 그 무게를 절반으로 줄여야 할 것이다.

05 various: 다양한, 여러 가지의 / 이제 환경 친화적인 다양한 자동차들이 있다.

06 (1) be ready to: ~할 준비가 되다 (2) deal with: ~을 다루다 (3) have to do with: ~와 관련이 있다

교과서

Conversation

핵심 Check p.10~11

1 (B) – (C) – (A)

2 ④

3 are there any other ways to get there?

교과서 대화문 익히기

Check(√) True or False p.12

1 F   2 T   3 T   4 F

교과서 확인학습 p.14~15

Listen and Speak 1 Listen

1. mean / nervous, frightened, doing
2. does, mean / feel sad
3. does, mean / means, look sad
4. does, mean / means, give up

Listen and Speak 1 A

1. How, doing / for / does, mean / means, happy, excited
2. personality test, had to / According to, a lot, by, mine / do, mean / mean, other

Listen and Speak 2 Listen

1. sold out / other seats / some tickets
2. spicy, sweet / other sauces / only
3. would, like to, maybe / too much sugar / too
4. the most popluar / other colors / lots, over here

Listen and Speak 2 A

1. reading, says, people's feelings / surprising / For example, help us focus / useful colors / helps,

relax

2. more, yourself, kinds of, other tests / take, test / before

Real-Life Zone

what kind of, to try / like / afraid of, one of / dark places, without, on, mean / says, full of, That's why, fill, with, scary things / about, anything, afraid of / big imagination / any other tests / a lot of

Wrap Up 1~2

blood type / an article, says / your personality / type A / with, calm, too

---

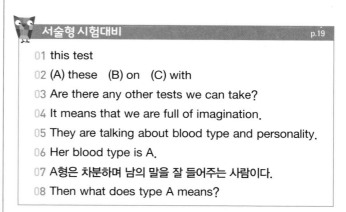

시험대비 기본평가 p.16

01 ②　　　　02 spicy sauce and sweet sauce
03 ③　　　　04 (D) – (B) – (E) – (C) – (A)

01 Are there any other ~?는 '다른 ~가 있나요?'라는 의미로 대안을 묻는 표현이다.

02 Those는 앞에 나온 것을 지칭하는 지시대명사로 spicy sauce and sweet sauce를 가리킨다.

03 What does ~ mean?은 의미를 설명해 달라고 요청하는 말이므로 그에 대한 대답은 It means ~.(그것은 ~을 의미해.)가 적절하다.

시험대비 실력평가 p.17~18

01 ④　　　　02 ②　　　　03 meaning
04 these big windows　　05 open　　06 ⑤
07 (A) → (D) → (C) → (B)　　08 ①
09 Are there any other useful colors?　　10 ③
11 ④　　　　12 a personality test　　13 ③

01 그것이 무슨 뜻인지 묻는 질문에 '그는 너를 이해하는 것 같아.'라는 대답은 어색하다.

02 by: ~에 따르면, ~로 보아

03 What does ~ mean?은 What is the meaning of ~?로 바꿔 쓸 수 있다.

04 인칭대명사 They는 앞에 나온 these big windows를 가리킨다.

05 '생각과 감정을 직접적이고 정직하게 표현하는'을 가리키는 말은 open(솔직한, 숨김없는)이다.

06 큰 창문들은 다른 사람에게 솔직하다는 것을 의미한다.

07 (A) 안부 묻기 → (D) 안부에 답하기 → (C) 'on cloud nine'의 의미 묻기 → (B) 의미 설명

08 주어진 문장의 It은 an interesting magazine을 가리키므로 ①번이 적절하다.

---

09 Are there any other ~?: 다른 어떤 ~가 있니?

10 Jane은 잡지를 통해서 색깔이 사람의 감정에 영향을 미치는 것을 알게 되었다.

11 (A) There are any other ~.: 다른 어떤 ~이 있습니다. (C) any time: 언제든지

12 부정대명사 one은 앞에 나온 a personality test를 가리킨다.

13 B는 적성검사를 받기 위해 전화를 했다.

서술형 시험대비 p.19

01 this test
02 (A) these　(B) on　(C) with
03 Are there any other tests we can take?
04 It means that we are full of imagination.
05 They are talking about blood type and personality.
06 Her blood type is A.
07 A형은 차분하며 남의 말을 잘 들어주는 사람이다.
08 Then what does type A means?

01 인칭대명사 it은 앞에 나온 this test를 가리킨다.

02 (A) one of+복수명사: ~ 중 하나 (B) 어두운 밤을 싫어한다고 했으므로 불을 켜야만 잠을 잘 수 있다는 내용이 자연스럽다. (C) fill A with B: A를 B로 채우다

03 Are there any other ~?: 다른 어떤 ~가 있니? / take a test: 검사를 받다

04 어두운 곳을 싫어한다면 상상력이 풍부한 사람이라는 의미이다.

05 그들은 혈액형과 성격에 관해 이야기하고 있다.

06 소녀의 혈액형은 무엇인가?

07 A형은 차분하며 남의 말을 잘 들어주는 사람이다.

08 what does ~ means?: ~은 무슨 뜻이니?

교과서

Grammar

핵심 Check p.20~21

1 (1) what　(2) What
2 (1) have been living　(2) has been drawing

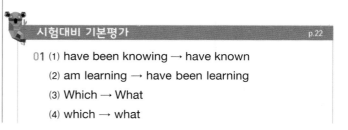

시험대비 기본평가 p.22

01 (1) have been knowing → have known
　(2) am learning → have been learning
　(3) Which → What
　(4) which → what

3

02 You can tell me what you need.

03 (1) It has been raining since lunch time.

(2) They have been running for one hour.

(3) What Paul cooked was a pizza.

(4) I bought my son what he really needed.

(5) Suji has been studying English for a year.

01 (1) 인식, 소유, 감정 등을 나타내는 동사는 현재완료진행형으로 쓰지 않는다. (2) 4개월째 공부해 온 것이므로 현재완료진행형으로 쓰는 것이 적절하다. (3) 관계대명사 what은 명사절을 이끌며 선행사를 포함한다. 주격 관계대명사로 쓰였다. (4) 관계대명사 what은 명사절을 이끌며 선행사를 포함한다. 목적격 관계대명사로 쓰였다.

02 관계대명사 what은 명사절을 이끌며 선행사를 포함한다.

03 (1) 점심시간 이후로 비가 쭉 내리고 있는 것이므로 현재완료진행형을 쓰는 것이 적절하다. (2) 그들이 한 시간 동안 계속 달리고 있는 것이므로 현재완료진행형으로 쓰는 것이 적절하다. (3) 관계대명사 what은 명사절을 이끌며 선행사를 포함한다. 주격 관계대명사로 쓰였다. (4) 관계대명사 what은 명사절을 이끌며 선행사를 포함한다. 목적격 관계대명사로 쓰였다. (5) 1년 동안 쭉 공부하고 있는 중이므로 현재완료진행형으로 쓰는 것이 적절하다.

시험대비 실력평가 p.23~25

01 has cooking → has been cooking 02 What

03 have been studying

04 ④   05 ②   06 ①

07 She bought a luxurious house that[which] has a huge pool.

08 ②   09 have been doing

10 It has been raining for three days.   11 ③

12 ⑤   13 ①, ③   14 ③   15 is

16 (1) have been doing   (2) What my friend said

(3) have been raising   (4) has been snowing

(5) What I want

(6) What Jane and Jay will see

17 ④   18 ②, ⑤   19 ①

20 has been playing

01 엄마는 두 시간 동안 부엌에서 소고기 스튜를 요리하고 계신다. 두 시간 동안 요리를 하고 있으므로 현재완료진행형을 쓰는 것이 적절하다.

02 done의 목적어와 is의 주어 역할을 할 수 있는 What이 적절하다.

03 하루에 적어도 1시간씩 지속적으로 해오고 있는 것이므로 현재완료진행형이 들어가는 것이 적절하고 have been studying으로 쓴다.

04 ④ 내가 아는 모든 것을 너에게 말했다. 선행사 everything이 있으므로 what이 아닌 that이 적절하다. ① 그는 내가 신뢰할 수 있는 유일한 사람이다. ② Sam과 Son은 물에 대한 저항을 최소화할 수 있는 수영복을 샀다. ③ 나는 사람들이 말하는 것에 신경 쓰지 않는다. ⑤ 그 미술가들은 그들이 보는 것을 그리고 있다.

05 그가 말한 것은 사실이다. The thing which를 What이 대신할 수 있으므로 ②가 적절하다.

06 Jay는 내가 가르친 가장 똑똑한 학생입니다. 선행사 the most brilliant student가 있고 빈칸 뒤에 taught의 목적어가 없으므로 that이 적절하다.

07 • 그녀는 호화로운 집을 샀다 • 그것은 큰 수영장을 가지고 있다. 두 문장을 한 문장으로 만들고자 할 때 중복된 단어는 a luxurious house이고 이것을 선행사로 하고 관계대명사는 that이나 which로 한다.

08 do의 목적어와 is의 주어 역할을 할 수 있는 What이 적절하다.

09 지난달 이후로 지금까지 사용한 방법이므로 현재완료진행형이 들어가야 적절하다.

10 3일 동안 지속해서 비가 오고 있으므로 현재완료진행형을 쓰는 것이 적절하다.

11 3시간 동안 계속해서 페인트칠을 하고 있는 중이므로 현재완료진행으로 쓰며 painted를 has been painting으로 고치는 것이 적절하다.

12 과거에 시작되어 현재도 지속되는 일을 표현할 때 쓰고, 기간을 나타내기 위해 'for, how long, since' 등을 함께 쓸 수 있다.

13 관계대명사 What은 The thing which로 쓸 수 있고 '내가 필요하다'라는 불완전한 절인 주절을 이끌기 위해 선행사를 포함한 what을 쓰는 것이 적절하다.

14 • 나를 기쁘게 만드는 것은 축구를 하는 것이다. • 그가 썼던 책은 큰 히트를 쳤다. 첫 번째 문장은 선행사를 포함하며 주절을 이끄는 관계대명사 What이 나오는 것이 적절하다. 두 번째 문장은 선행사가 있고 wrote의 목적어가 없으므로 that이 나오는 것이 적절하다.

15 어법에 맞게 배열하면 What John and Paul want to eat is fried chicken.

16 (1), (3), (4)는 현재완료진행형을 쓰는 문제이므로 'have[has]+been+~ing'로 쓰고, (2), (5), (6)은 선행사를 포함하고 명사절을 이끄는 관계대명사를 쓰는 문제이므로 관계대명사 what을 쓰는 것이 적절하다.

17 ④ 그녀는 최근에 매우 열심히 일을 하고 있었다. 부사 recently와 과거진행형과는 어울리지 않는다. ① 나는 내 친구들과 그 이후로 나무를 심고 있다. ② 나는 20년 동안 호주에서 살고 있다. ③ Jason은 오늘 아침부터 기분이 별로 좋지 않다. ⑤ 나는 이것을 찾고 있었다.

18 ② Harry는 30분째 버스를 기다리고 있다. ⑤ 그녀는 20살부터 운전을 했습니다. ①은 have planting을 have been

4 정답 및 해설

planting으로 쓰는 것이 적절하다. 우리는 거기에 정기적으로 꽃을 심고 있다. ③ since로 보아 2019년 이래로 쭉 프로젝트를 진행한 것이므로 worked를 has been working으로 쓰는 것이 적절하다. ④ since로 보아 그가 오늘 아침부터 계속해서 TV를 보고 있는 것이므로 has been watched를 has been watching으로 쓰는 것이 적절하다. since는 보통 완료형과 함께 쓰이는 것에 주의한다.

19 ① 내가 말했던 것을 잊지 마세요. that → what ② 그녀는 그녀가 해야 했던 것을 했다. ③ 나는 딸에게 먹고 싶어 하는 것을 요리해 줄 것이다. ④ 그들이 필요했던 것은 단지 한 병의 물이었다. ⑤ 그 소녀는 그녀를 흥미진진하게 하는 영화를 보고 있다.

20 현재완료진행 형태로 has been playing으로 쓰는 것이 적절하다.

서술형 시험대비
p.26~27

01 what you're feeling

02 What

03 (1) I know what you want.
   (2) This is what I mean.
   (3) Do what I do.
   (4) What Suji will take to the theater is a bus.

04 They have been eating chicken for thirty minutes.

05 I know what you did last summer.

06 (1) I don't care what people say.
   (2) I don't care the thing[things] which people say.

07 (1) John has been singing for two hours.
   (2) They have been playing darts for one[an] hour.
   (3) What they want is to talk and play.

08 (1) I know the thing which you're doing these days.
   (2) I know what you're doing these days.

09 What I have to finish, I have been writing

10 What John wants to do with Sally is to see a movie.

11 (1) have been doing
   (2) what the company will become

01 빈칸에 '당신이 느끼고 있는 것'이 들어가야 하므로 'what you're feeling'으로 쓰는 것이 적절하다.

02 내가 갖고 싶은 것은 컴퓨터이다. The thing which 대신 들어갈 수 있는 것으로 관계대명사 What이 적절하다.

03 (1) '나는 안다'의 의미로 I know가 오고 '네가 원하는 것'이라는 의미가 know 뒤에 이어져야 하므로 선행사를 포함한 what을 쓰는 것이 적절하다. 관계대명사 what절에서는 want에 대한 목적어를 what이 대신한다. (2) '이것은 ~이다'의 의미가 먼저 와야 하므로 This is로 시작하고 '바로 내가 의미하는 것이다'라는

의미가 뒤에 이어져야 하므로 is에 대한 보어로 선행사를 포함한 what을 쓰는 것이 적절하다. 관계대명사 절 안에서 mean의 목적어를 what이 대신한다. (3) 명령문 '~해 봐'의 의미를 쓰기 위해 do가 문장 맨 앞에 오고, '내가 하는 것'이란 의미가 뒤에 이어져야하므로 what I do를 쓰는 것이 적절하다. (4) 'Suji가 영화관에 타고 갈 것'이란 내용이 먼저 와야 하므로 'What Suji will take to the theater'를 쓰고 이어 '버스이다'가 와야 하므로 'is a bus'를 쓰는 것이 적절하다.

04 30분 동안 계속해서 먹고 있으므로 8 단어에 맞추어 현재완료진행형으로 쓰는 것이 적절하다.

05 '나는 알고 있다'+'네가 지난여름에 한 일'. 한 문장 안에 두 절이 있으므로 선행사를 포함하는 관계대명사 what으로 연결시키는 것이 적절하다.

06 관계대명사 what은 선행사를 포함하고 명사절을 이끄는 관계대명사이므로 'I don't care what people say.'로 쓰는 것이 적절하고, which는 선행사가 필요하므로 the thing[things]를 넣어 'I don't care the thing[things] which people say.'로 쓰는 것이 적절하다.

07 (1), (2)는 몇 시간 동안 계속해서 노래를 부르거나 게임을 하고 있는 것이므로 현재완료진행 시제를 쓰는 것이 적절하다. (3) 주어 자리에 쓰인 명사절로 관계대명사 what을 쓰는 것이 적절하고 what 뒤에는 주어가 빠진 불완전한 절이 이어져야 한다.

08 the thing which = what. what을 중심으로 '나는 안다'는 의미를 갖은 말이 앞에 오고 '요즘 네가 무엇을 하는지'라는 말이 what에 뒤이어 오는 것이 적절하다.

09 3시까지 내가 끝내야 하는 것은 에세이 숙제다. 그러나 나는 그것을 끝내기에 충분한 시간이 없다. 나는 한 시간 동안 에세이를 쓰고 있는데, 단지 두 문장밖에 적지 못했다. 나는 시간이 더 필요하다!

10 주어 자리에 쓰인 명사절로 관계대명사 What을 쓰는 것이 적절하다.

11 (1) 전치사 since가 힌트가 되어 아침부터 쭉 지금까지 숙제로 해오고 있는 중이므로 현재완료진행형을 쓰는 것이 적절하다.
   (2) 관계대명사 what은 know의 목적절을 이끄는 역할을 하면서, become의 보어 역할을 한다.

교과서
Reading

확인문제
p.28

1 T 2 F 3 F

확인문제
p.29

1 F 2 T 3 F 4 T

01 says something

02 use, wear, even, raise, what kind of

03 draw, much

04 What, how, are related to

05 to better understand   06 One, those tests

07 below   08 holding, light

09 other hand, heavy, no   10 above

11 differences mean   12 who, under

13 The bigger, the more heavily, the bigger

14 waiting, happen, hopeful, future

15 Second, protection, stressful

16 big, shows, plans, protection

17 drawing, means, deal with

18 Third, details, have to do, attitude

19 example, who, without, attention, himself, herself

20 who, right, is ready to

21 hand, may, worried, happened

22 possible meanings, part   23 back, at

24 reading, yourself   25 what kind, each one

26 opinion

1 Everything you do says something about you.

2 The language you use, the clothes you wear, and even the pets you raise somehow show what kind of person you are.

3 The things you draw are not much different.

4 What you draw and how you draw it are related to your personality.

5 Doctors have been using various drawing tests to better understand people.

6 One of those tests is the Draw-a-Person-in-the-Rain (DAPR) test.

7 Study the pictures below.

8 The person in Drawing A is holding an umbrella in a light rain.

9 On the other hand, the person in Drawing B is in a heavy rain and has no umbrella.

10 Also, there are dark clouds above the person in Drawing B.

11 What can these differences mean?

12 First, the rain shows the stress the person who drew the picture is under.

13 The bigger the drops are or the more heavily the rain is falling, the bigger the stress is.

14 The clouds mean problems waiting to happen, so a big cloud shows the drawer is not very hopeful about the future.

15 Second, the umbrella means the protection the person has in a stressful situation.

16 A big umbrella shows that the drawer has a lot of plans or protection.

17 If there's no umbrella in the drawing, the drawer does not have any means to deal with difficult situations.

18 Third, the details in the drawing of the person have to do with the drawer's attitude under stress.

19 For example, someone who draws a person without a face does not want to draw people's attention to himself or herself.

20 Someone who draws the person on the right side of the paper is ready to meet the future.

21 On the other hand, someone who draws the person on the left side may be worried about things that have happened in the past.

22 These are some of the possible meanings of each part of the drawings.

23 Now, go back and look at the two drawings.

24 Try reading them yourself.

25 Can you understand what kind of person drew each one?

26 What's your opinion?

01 ③   02 ⓐ What ⓑ how   03 ⑤

04 ⑤   05 ③   06 waiting   07 ⑤

08 stressful   09 ②

10 그림을 그린 사람이 많은 계획이나 보호 기제를 가지고 있음을 보여 준다.

11 ③

12 (A) For example (B) On the other hand

13 future   14 ③   15 ④

16 drawing   17 ②

18 what kind of person you are   19 ①

20 personality 21 ②

22 As, bigger or the rain is falling more heavily, the stress is bigger

23 ①   24 many   25 ⑤   26 ⑤

27 two drawings

28 당신은 어떤 종류의 사람이 각각의 그림을 그렸는지 이해할 수 있나요?

01 여러분이 그리는 그림이 성격과 관련이 있다는 문장 앞에 와야 한다.

02 글의 흐름상 '당신이 무엇을 그리는지 그리고 그것을 어떻게 그리는지'가 되어야 한다.

03 의사들이 사람들을 더 잘 이해하기 위해 그림 그리기 검사를 사용해 오고 있다고 언급되었으므로 ⑤가 알맞다.

04 문맥상 '반면에'의 뜻을 가진 On the other hand가 적절하다.

05 be under the stress: 스트레스를 받다

06 능동의 의미이므로 현재분사가 알맞다.

07 ⑤ 큰 구름은 그림을 그린 사람이 미래에 희망적이지 않다는 것을 보여준다고 언급되었다.

08 stressful: 스트레스를 주는 / stressed: 스트레스를 받는

09 ⓑ, ② 형용사적 용법 ①, ③, ④ 명사적 용법 ⑤ 부사적 용법

10 A big umbrella shows that the drawer has a lot of plans or protection.을 참고할 것.

11 draw one's attention to: ~에게 주의를 끌다

12 for example: 예를 들면 / on the other hand: 한편

13 future: 미래 / past: 과거

14 ⓑ와 ③의 may는 '~일지도 모르다'의 뜻으로 약한 추측을 나타낸다.

15 문맥상 '그 그림들을 스스로 읽으려고 시도해 보세요'가 알맞으므로 try+-ing 형이 되어야 한다.

16 one은 부정대명사로 앞에 나온 단수 명사를 받는다.

17 문맥상 '당신이 하는 모든 행동은 당신에 대해 무엇인가를 말해준다'가 알맞다.

18 what kind of: 어떤 종류의

19 문맥상 '당신이 그리는 것'이라는 뜻으로 draw의 목적어이므로 What이 알맞다. which는 특정하게 주어진 것 중에서 선택을 나타내므로 알맞지 않다.

20 personal: 개인의, 개인적인 / personality: 성격, 개성

21 선행사가 사람이고 주격이므로 who가 알맞다.

22 'the+비교급 ~, the+비교급 …' 구문은 접속사 as를 써서 바꿔 쓸 수 있다. as 구문에서는 비교급 앞에 정관사 the를 붙이지 않는다.

23 문맥상 '그래서'의 뜻을 가진 so가 알맞다.

24 a lot of 뒤에 셀 수 있는 명사의 복수형이 오므로 many가 알맞다.

25 deal with: ~을 처리하다, ~을 다루다

26 ⑤ 큰 우산은 그림을 그린 사람이 많은 계획을 가지고 있음을 보여 준다고 언급되었다.

27 them은 앞에 나온 복수 명사를 받는다.

28 what kind of person 이하는 간접의문문으로 understand의 목적어이다.

서술형 시험대비 p.38~39

01 hand　　02 heavy　　03 differences

04 There are dark clouds.

05 with　　06 himself or herself

07 have happened

08 미래를 맞이할 준비가 되었다.

09 Everything you do says something about you.

10 당신이 그리는 그림을 통해서 당신이 어떤 종류의 사람인지 알 수 있다.

11 당신이 그리는 것

12 They have been using various drawing tests to better understand people.

13 The bigger the drops are or the more heavily the rain is falling, the bigger the stress is.

14 waiting　　15 stressful

---

01 on the other hand: 반면에

02 문맥상 light의 반의어 heavy가 알맞다.

03 different의 명사형 difference의 복수형이 알맞다.

04 Also, there are dark clouds above the person in Drawing B.를 참고할 것

05 have to do with: ~와 관계가 있다

06 전치사 to의 목적어가 주어 자신이므로 재귀대명사로 고쳐야 한다.

07 happen은 자동사이므로 수동태로 쓸 수 없다.

09 you do 앞에 관계대명사 that이 생략되었다.

11 it은 인칭대명사로 앞에 나온 What you draw를 받는다.

13 'the+비교급 ~, the+비교급 …' 구문이므로 bigger the stress is 앞에도 the를 붙인다.

14 능동의 의미로 problems를 수식하므로 현재분사가 알맞다.

15 stressed: 스트레스를 받는 / stressful: 스트레스를 주는

영역별 핵심문제 p.41~45

01 below　　02 ⑤　　03 ⑤　　04 ⑤

05 ②　　06 ②

07 (1) gets along with

　(2) In other words

　(3) has to do with

08 ①

09 what is the meaning of / what do you mean by

10 Are there any other ways to get there?

11 She will take a bus.

12 ②　　13 is → are

14 He wants to take a personality test this afternoon.

15 (A) to help (B) to take

16 소년은 성격 검사 일정을 잡기 위해서 전화를 걸고 있다.

17 (1) have been using

7

(2) what makes me happy

(3) has been living

(4) what I can do

18 ①　　　　19 What they want is some food.

20 what I am going to say

21 (1) what they wanted

(2) have known

(3) have been working

(4) what I say

22 don't know

23 (1) what he says

(2) I knew what

24 Henry couldn't understand what the teacher said.

25 ③　　　26 light　　27 hopeful　　28 ⑤

29 ⑤　　　30 ④　　　31 past

32 He or she is ready to meet the future.　33 ③

34 ④　　　35 curious

---

01 주어진 관계는 반의어 관계이다. above: ～ 위에 : below: ～ 아래에

02 '다른 사람에게 도움이나 지원을 구하거나 의지하지 않는'을 뜻하는 말은 independent(독립적인)이다.

03 be covered with: ～로 덮여 있다 / deal with: ～을 다루다

04 against: ～에 반대하는, for: ～에 찬성하는

05 personality: 성격 / 내 친구는 잘생기고 성격도 좋다.

06 raise: 기르다, 들다 / • 나는 애완동물로 햄스터를 기른다. • 답을 알면 손을 드세요.

07 (1) get along with ～: ～와 잘 어울리다 (2) in other words: 다시 말하면 (3) have to do with: ～와 관련이 있다

08 소녀가 집을 그려야 했다고 말하자 소년이 A house?라고 묻고 있으므로 ①번이 적절하다.

09 what do ～ mean?은 what is the meaning of ～?, what do you mean by ～? 등으로 바꿔 쓸 수 있다.

10 Are there any other ～?: 다른 ～이 있나요?

11 소녀는 버스를 타고 갈 것이다.

12 혈액형이 무엇인지 묻자 - (B) 대답하고 이유 묻기 - (D) 이유 설명 - (A) A형에 대한 의미 묻기 (C) A형에 대한 특징 설명

13 주어가 People이므로 복수동사 are가 되어야 한다.

14 소년은 오늘 오후에 성격검사를 받고 싶어 한다.

15 목적을 나타내는 to부정사 형태가 되어야 한다.

17 (1) 사용하고 있는 중이므로 have been using이 적절하다. (2) 괄호 안의 what이 보어 자리에 '나를 행복하게 한다'는 명사절을 이끌어야 하므로 what makes me happy가 나오는 것이 적절하다. (3) 2010년 이후로 지금까지 쭉 서울에서 살고 있는 것이므로 현재완료진행형이 나오는 것이 적절하다. (4) '내가 할 수 있는 일'이란 의미가 들어가야 하므로 'what I can do'가

나오는 것이 적절하다.

18 ① 사람들이 보고 싶은 것은 고흐가 쓴 편지이다. ② what → who 또는 that ③ the thing 삭제 ④,⑤ that → what

19 괄호 안에 what이 있고 동사 want의 목적어가 없으므로 관계대명사 what절을 쓰는 것이 적절하다.

20 '내가 말하려고 하던 것'을 what을 이용하여 6 단어로 'what I am going to say'로 쓴다.

21 (1) 보어 자리에 들어갈 명사절이 와야 하므로 'what they wanted'가 나오는 것이 적절하다. (2) know, like, believe 동사는 진행형으로 쓰지 않으므로 현재완료로 쓰는 것이 적절하다. (3) 작년부터 지금까지 진행되어 온 것이므로 현재완료진행형을 쓰는 것이 적절하다. (4) 목적어 자리에 들어갈 명사절이 와야 하므로 'what I say'가 나오는 것이 적절하다.

22 내가 뭘 먼저 할 수 있을지 모르겠어.

23 (1) 나는 믿을 수 없다+그가 말했던 것 (2) 나는 알고 있었다+네가 발견했던 것

24 헨리는 선생님이 말씀하신 것을 이해하지 못했다. 문장에서 understand에 대한 목적어와 said에 대한 목적어가 없으므로 두 개의 목적어 대신 관계대명사 what을 써서 한 문장으로 만드는 것이 적절하다.

25 Also에 주목한다. 처음 그림 B에 있는 사람을 언급한 문장 다음인 ③에 와야 한다.

26 heavy: 무거운, 심한 / light: 가벼운

27 hope의 형용사형이 와야 한다.

28 큰 구름은 그림을 그린 사람이 미래에 대해 희망적이지 않다고 언급되었다.

29 under stress: 스트레스를 받을 때

30 for example: 예를 들면, on the other hand: 반면에

31 문맥상 future의 반의어인 past(과거)가 알맞다.

32 그림의 오른쪽에 있는 사람은 미래를 맞이할 준비가 되어 있다고 하였다.

33 나와 친구의 성격에 대해 말해야 했다는 문장 다음인 ③에 와야 한다.

34 선행사를 포함하는 관계대명사 what이 알맞다.

35 '어떤 것에 흥미를 가지고 그것에 관해 더 많이 알기를 원하는'은 curious(호기심이 있는)이다.

단원별 예상문제　p.46~49

01 ③　　02 ⑤　　03 (d)rops　04 ⑤

05 ①　　06 relax　　07 to look sad

08 ④　　09 According to

10 큰 창문들은 그녀가 타인에게 개방되어 있다는 것을 의미한다.

11 (1) that (2) what

12 It has been raining heavily for three hours.

13 ①

14 (1) that they wanted

  (2) what she needed

  (3) have been working

15 have been discussing

16 These are some of the possible meanings of each part of the drawings.

17 ⑤　　　18 ④　　　19 ③　　　20 ④

21 Because he gets along well with others and is in lots of clubs.

22 The bigger the drops are or the more heavily the rain is falling, the bigger the stress is.

23 ③　　　24 ②　　　25 ①　　　26 ⑤

27 큰 우산은 그림을 그린 사람이 많은 계획이나 보호 기제를 가지고 있음을 보여 준다.

01 ③은 동의어 관계이지만 나머지는 반의어 관계이다. ① heavy(무거운) - light(가벼운) ② future(미래) - past(과거) ③ various(다양한) - diverse(다양한) ④ calm(차분한) - excited(흥분한) ⑤ carefully: 조심스럽게 - carelessly: 부주의하게

02 see A as B: A를 B로 보다, 나는 내 자신이 수줍음이 많고 친절하다고 생각했다. / deal with: ~을 다루다, 난 다른 두 가지 문제를 다루고 싶다.

03 drop: 방울 / 하늘이 어두워지더니 비가 몇 방울 떨어졌다. / 둥그란 모양으로 떨어지는 매우 적은 양의 액체

04 at the same time: 동시에(=simultaneously)

05 주어진 문장은 잡지에 대한 보충 설명이므로 ①에 오는 것이 적절하다.

06 누군가 더 차분해지고 덜 걱정하게 되거나 되게 하다: relax(안심[진정]하다)

07 have a long face는 '슬퍼 보이는 것'을 의미한다.

08 (A) take a personality test: 성격 검사를 받다 (C) what does ~ mean?: ~는 무엇을 의미하니?

09 according to: ~에 따르면

11 (1) 내가 아는 모든 사람은 정직하고 친절하다. (2) 그는 내가 원하는 것을 주었다.

12 현재완료진행은 과거에서부터 지금까지 진행되고 있는 의미를 표현할 때 사용한다.

13 ① know, like, believe 등은 진행형으로 사용 불가하므로 I have known him since my childhood.가 적절하다. ② 그녀는 어젯밤부터 계속해서 울고 있다. ③ 난 5년 동안 스페인어를 공부하고 있다. ④ 나는 네가 빌려준 책을 읽고 있다. ⑤ 그

는 8살부터 우표를 모으는 중이다.

14 (1) 선행사 the house가 있으므로 관계대명사 that을 쓰는 것이 적절하다. (2) 선행사를 포함하는 관계대명사 what을 쓰는 것이 적절하다. (3) 지난해부터 여기에서 일하고 있으므로 현재완료진행을 쓰는 것이 적절하다.

15 우리는 1시간 동안 그 문제들에 대해 의논해 왔다.

16 these를 문장의 주어로 한다.

17 both 뒤에는 복수형이 오므로 each로 고쳐야 한다.

18 kinds가 복수 명사이므로 much는 쓸 수 없다.

19 필자의 성격에 대한 판단이 필자 본인과 친구가 각각 달랐다는 내용이 적절하므로 different가 들어가야 한다.

20 민수의 친구는 민수가 적극적이라고 말했다.

22 이때의 as는 '~함에 따라서'의 뜻으로 'the+비교급 ~, the+비교급 …' 구문을 써서 바꿔 쓸 수 있다.

23 구름들은 앞으로 벌어질 문제들을 의미하므로 큰 구름은 그림을 그린 사람이 미래에 대해 희망적이지 않다는 것이 문맥상 자연스럽다.

24 (C), ② 동사의 목적어가 되는 명사절을 이끄는 접속사이다. ① 진주어 ③, ⑤ 관계대명사 ④ It ... that 강조 구문

25 문맥상 조건을 나타내는 접속사 if가 알맞다.

26 우산이 없는 그림을 그리는 사람은 어려운 상황을 대처할 수단이 없다고 하였다.

서술형 실전문제
p.50~51

01 (1) to feel sad (2) to give up

02 It is about colors and people's feelings.

03 색깔이 사람들의 기분을 바꿀 수 있다는 것

04 (1) He is the very man that loves music.

  (2) pick what you want

  (3) It is the very music that he loves.

  (4) what you brought

05 I have been doing the course for six months.

06 He has been taking a bus for two hours.

07 ④번 → is　　08 clothes

09 여러분이 그리는 그림을 통해서 여러분이 어떤 종류의 사람 인지 알 수 있다.

10 그림 A의 인물은 가벼운 빗속에 우산을 가지고 있고, 그림 B의 인물은 심한 빗속에 우산도 없고 또한 그 인물의 위에 어두운 구름들이 있는 것

11 그 그림을 그린 사람이 스트레스를 받을 때의 태도를 알 수 있다.

12 worried

01 (1) feel blue는 to feel sad(슬프게 느끼는 것)을 의미한다.
　 (2) throw up one's hands는 to give up(포기하는 것)을 의미한다.

02 잡지는 색깔과 사람의 기분에 관한 내용이다.

04 (1)과 (3)은 선행사 the very man, the very music이 있으므로 관계대명사 that을 써서 문장을 완성하는 것이 적절하다.
　 (2)와 (4)는 선행사를 포함하고 각 동사의 목적어가 되는 명사절이 나와야 하므로 관계대명사 what을 써서 문장을 완성하는 것이 적절하다.

05 6개월 동안 지속되고 있는 것이므로 현재완료진행형이 오는 것이 적절하므로 have been doing으로 써야 한다.

06 그는 버스를 2시간 동안 타고 있는 것이므로 'he has been taking a bus'가 오고 2시간 동안이라는 정확한 숫자 표현이 나왔으므로 전치사 for를 사용하여 'for two hours'를 쓴다.

07 주어가 One이므로 단수로 받아야 한다.

08 셔츠, 상의, 바지, 드레스와 같이 사람들이 입는 것들: clothes(옷, 의복)

12 사람이 걱정하는 것이므로 과거분사형이 알맞다.

창의사고력 서술형 문제　　　　　　　　p.52

[모범답안]

01 (2) → (3) → (1)

02 (2) What I like to do is watching movies.
　 (3) What I have to do is (to) do my homework.
　 (4) What I have in my pocket is the doll.

03 (A) street dancing
　 (B) taking modern dance lessons for three months
　 (C) want is to post wonderful video clips of me
　　　 dancing someday

02 선행사를 쓰지 않고 '~하는 것'으로 해석되는 관계대명사 what을 쓴다.

단원별 모의고사　　　　　　　　　　p.53~56

01 ⑤　　　　02 ②　　　　03 (1) out　(2) in　(3) to
04 ④　　　　05 (1) detail　(2) attention　(3) attitude
06 ①, ③　　　07 ④
08 Is there anything you are afraid of?
09 (A) why (B) too (C) other
10 imagination　　　　　　　　11 ③

---

12 (1) This is what I like. /
　　 This is the thing which I like.
　 (2) The thing which she said is true. /
　　 What she said is true.
　 (3) I like the thing which is colorful. /
　　 I like what is colorful.

13 ②　　　　14 ④　　　　15 ④　　　　16 ①

17 The cook has been taking a vacation, so the restaurant is closed.

18 The thing which[that] I'm interested in is to learn how to play the guitar. / What I'm interested in is to learn how to play the guitar.

19 What　　20 have been playing, for

21 has been feeling sick since this morning

22 ⑤　　　　23 friendly　　24 ④

25 (1) 수줍다 (2) 친절하다 / (1) 능동적이다 (2) 호기심이 있다

26 ①　　　　27 ②　　　　28 ④　　　　29 ③

---

01 frightened: 두려워하는 scared: 무서워하는, 겁먹은

02 draw attention to oneself: 자신에게 관심을 끌다 / 그녀는 밝은 색의 옷을 입어 이목을 끌려고 한다.

03 (1) sold out: 매진된 / 모든 콘서트 표가 매진되었다. participate in: ~에 참가하다 / 그녀는 회의에 참가하지 않았다. (3) according to: ~에 따라 / 모든 것이 계획대로 되어 갔다.

04 '지원, 도움 등을 얻기 위해 다른 사람이나 사물이 필요한'을 뜻하는 단어는 dependent(의존하는)이다.

05 (1) detail: 세부 사항 (2) attention: 주의, 집중 (3) attitude: 태도

06 '어떻게 지내니?'라는 뜻으로 How have you been?, How's it going? 등으로 바꿔 쓸 수 있다.

07 on cloud nine은 더할 나위 없이 기분이 좋은 상태를 의미한다.

08 Is there ~?: ~이 있니? / be afraid of: ~을 두려워하다

09 (A) That why ~.: 그것이 ~한 이유이다. (B) 긍정문이므로 too를 쓴다. (C) Are there any other ~?: 다른 어떤 ~가 있니?

10 '보거나 경험해 보지 못한 것을 마음속으로 그려 볼 수 있는 능력'을 나타내는 단어는 imagination(상상력)이다.

11 ③ Emma는 불을 켜놓지 않고는 잠을 잘 수 없다고 했다.

12 what = the thing which

13 2012년 이후 현재까지 영어를 가르치고 있기 때문에 현재완료진행형이 나오는 것이 적절하다.

14 ④ 네가 하는 말을 못 알아듣겠어. that을 what으로 바꾸는 것이 적절하다. ① 이것이 너를 돕기 위해 내가 할 수 있는 것이다. ② 나는 내가 해야 하는 일을 잘하기를 원한다. ③ 그가 좋아하는 것

을 말해줄게. ⑤ 그녀가 그를 사랑한다는 것이 나를 놀라게 만들었다.

15 • 그들은 민수를 30분 동안 기다리고 있다. 30분 전부터 지금까지 계속 민수를 기다리고 있는 것이고 숫자 앞에 '~ 동안'이라는 의미를 담고 있는 전치사가 와야 하므로 for가 나오는 것이 적절하다.

16 know, like, believe 등의 동사는 진행형으로 쓰이지 않으므로 현재완료진행형이 아닌 현재완료가 적절하다.

17 요리사가 휴가 중이므로 'the cook has been taking a vacation'이 나오고 '그래서 음식점이 문을 닫았다'는 의미가 뒤에 이어져야 하므로 'so the restaurant is closed'를 쓴다.

18 the thing which[that] = what

19 내가 주문한 것은 사과 주스 한 잔이다.

20 2시간째 피구를 하고 있는 것이므로 현재완료진행형을 쓴다.

21 오늘 아침부터 쭉 몸이 안 좋았던 것이므로 has been feeling sick이 나오는 것이 적절하다.

22 문맥상 '다른 사람들'의 뜻이 되어야 하므로 others로 고쳐야 한다.

23 명사 friend의 형용사형으로 고친다.

24 get along well with: ~와 잘 지내다

26 ⓐ, ① …도[조차] ② 한층, 훨씬 ③ 짝수의 ④ 동일한 ⑤ 평평한

27 be related to: ~와 관계가 있다

28 ⓒ, ④ 부사적 용법 ①, ③, ⑤ 명사적 용법 ② 형용사적 용법

29 여러분이 먹는 음식은 언급되지 않았다.

Buy and Sell Wisely

시험대비 실력평가　　　　　　　　p.60

01 outdoors　　02 ①　　　　03 ①

04 (1) We would like to welcome you as a new customer.
  (2) Peter has shopped at the grocery for years.

05 (1) realize　(2) used　(3) several　(4) posted

06 ③

01 greedy(욕심 많은)와 generous(관대한, 후한)의 뜻은 반의어 관계이다. 따라서 indoors(실내의)의 반의어 관계에 있는 단어는 outdoors(외부의, 야외에서)이다.

02 '어떤 것을 취하기로 동의하다' 또는 '제안이나 초대에 응하다'라는 뜻을 가진 단어는 ① accept(받아들이다, 수용하다)이다.

03 ① '그의 설명은 일부러 모호했다.'라는 의미로, 여기서 account는 '은행 계좌'가 아니라 '설명'이라는 뜻으로 사용되었다.

04 (1) customer 고객 / welcome 환영하다, 맞이하다 (2) grocery 식료품점, 식료품 / shop 물건을 사다, 쇼핑하다

05 (1) 우리는 이 범죄의 심각성을 깨달아야 한다. realize 깨닫다 (2) 많은 중고 서점들이 일반 서점에서 찾기 힘든 책들을 갖고 있다. used 중고의 (3) 며칠 동안 그 스캔들은 헤드라인을 장식했다. several 몇몇의 (4) 시험 결과는 인터넷에 게시될 것입니다. post 게시하다

06 good for ~에 좋은 / ask for ~을 요청하다 / go up 오르다, 올라가다 / grow up 성장하다

서술형 시험대비　　　　　　　　p.61

01 more charming

02 (1) think about　(2) hand over　(3) this time

03 comment

04 (1) I suddenly found myself running down the street.
  (2) She found the job tiring at first but she soon got used to it.
  (3) The foundations of the building is starting to sink.

05 (1) take a photo of　(2) as good as
  (3) have an idea

06 (1) She stepped up to receive her prize in the Academy Awards.
  (2) Julia won the grand prize in the movie category.
  (3) Her eyes are the reason people find her attractive.

01 heavier(더 무거운)은 형용사 heavy의 비교급이다. 따라서 charming의 비교급은 more charming(더 매력적인)이다.

02 (1) think about ~에 대해 생각하다 (2) hand over ~을 건네 주다 (3) this time 이번에

03 '의견을 표현하기 위해 하는 어떤 말이나 글'은 comment(언급)를 가리킨다.

04 (1) suddenly 갑자기 (2) at first 처음에는 (3) sink 가라앉다

05 (1) 그 사진가는 어떤 종류의 차 사진도 찍고 그걸 팔아도 된다고 허락을 받았다. (2) 매일이 오늘 만큼 좋을 수 없다는 게 너무 아쉽다. (3) 나는 내 전 남자친구가 아직도 이 근처 어딘가에 살고 있다는 생각이 든다.

06 (1) receive 받다 (2) category 범주, 부류, 부문 (3) attractive 매력적인

교과서
Conversation

핵심 Check　　　　　　　　p.62~63

1 ④, ⑤　　　　2 I'm afraid you can't.

교과서 대화문 익히기

Check(√) True or False　　　　　　p.64

1 T　2 F　3 T　4 F

교과서 확인학습　　　　　　　　p.67~69

Listen and Speak 1 Listen

1. lean / at all
2. mind / don't
3. change seats
4. shut / ahead

Listen and Speak 1 A-1

Excuse, return / why / haven't, worn / mind, a look / all, Here

Listen and Speak 1 A-2

What / open, should / fill, form / use

Listen and Speak 1 B-1

at all

Listen and Speak 1 B-2

Do, mind

Listen and Speak 1 B-3

Do, eat / ahead

Listen and Speak 2 Listen

1. around / afraid, open
2. pictures during / can't, disturb
3. Can, anywhere

Listen & Speak 2 A-1

Look, check / can't, inside / finished / first, can

Listen & Speak 2 A-2

come / afraid / That's, special / heard, going, then / together

Listen & Speak 2 B-1

around / open

Listen & Speak 2 B-2

Can, use / sorry, only

Listen & Speak 2 B-3

Can / can't, on

Real-Life Zone

to find, mind / at all, favorites / looking, over, lend / afraid, Actually / okay / used, online / thought, idea / together, think / get

Wrap Up 1-2

mind, a look / Not, called, bought / putting / means, bringing / interesting, where, get / afraid, contact

Wrap Up 3~4

some, place / been / never / about / afraid, What / fine

---

01 ⓑwhy do you want → why you want

02 ①

03 I'm afraid we can't take our drinks inside.

04 my drink

01 위 문장은 의문사 why를 이용한 간접의문이 포함된 문장이다. 간접의문문은 '의문사+주어+ 동사' 순이며 이때 조동사는 생략된다. 따라서 조동사 do를 제거해야 한다.

02 B가 언제 신발을 샀는지는 알 수 없다.

03 '유감이지만 ~할 수 없다'라는 말을 쓸 때, "I'm afraid I can't ~.'의 표현을 쓴다.

04 대명사 m1ine은 '나의 것'이라는 뜻을 지닌다. 대화의 문맥상 G가 갖고 있는 것은 위에서 언급한 drink를 가리킨다.

---

01 ④   02 ①   03 ②

04 Do you mind if I use your pen?   05 ③

06 ②   07 ③   08 ④   09 ⑤

10 Could you ask your friend where she got it?

11 ④

01 허락을 요청하는 표현인 'Do you mind if I ~?'와 같은 표현은 "Do you mind ~ing?", "Would you mind if I ~?"와 같은 표현을 사용할 수 있다.

02 두 빈칸 모두 현재완료 용법의 시제가 들어가야 적절하다. 단, (a)는 과거부터 현재까지 이어져 온다는 의미의 현재완료의 계속적 용법이, (b)는 어떤 것을 해 본 적이 없다는 의미에서 현재완료의 경험적 용법으로 해석한다.

03 주어진 문장에서 it이 무엇을 가리키느냐에 따라 위치가 달라지는데, 대화의 문맥상 Ben이 찾고 있던 만화책을 Dana가 갖고 있고 따라서 Ben이 빌릴 수 있냐고 물어보는 위치에 주어진 문장이 들어가는 것이 가장 적절하다.

04 상대방에게 허락을 요구하는 표현으로 "Do you mind if I ~?", "Would you mind if I ~?"와 같은 표현이 있다.

05 G가 Do you mind if I ~?라고 물어봤고 M은 요청을 승낙('Not at all.')했다. 여기서 ③ Yes, I'm sorry.는 요청을 거절하는 표현이다.

06 ② A가 스마트폰을 써도 되겠냐고 물어보는데, B의 대답 No, I do mind.는 잘못된 표현이다. do를 don't로 고치면 올바르다.

07 can you come with us? 우리와 같이 갈래? I'd love to는 I would love to의 줄임말이다. 전치사 about가 쓰였으므로 목적어로 동명사 going를 써야 한다.

08 위 대화의 문맥상 (a) I'm afraid I can't.의 의도는 ④'요청을 거절하기'이다.

09 ⑤ '민호는 엑스포에 가고 싶어 하지 않는다' (Minho does not want to go to the game expo.)는 민호와 G가 다음 주 토요일에 같이 엑스포에 간다('Let's go together next Saturday.')는 말과 일치하지 않는다.

10 상대방에게 무언가를 요청할 때 쓰는 표현으로 'Can you ~?' 또는 'Coud you ~?'를 쓸 수 있다.

11 ④ '왜 G가 그녀의 친구와 연락이 끊겼는지'는 대화에서 언급되어 있지 않다.

---

01 (D) – (A) – (C) – (B)

02 (a) to buy   (b) take

03 That's fine with me.

04 He wants to buy some traditional Korean gifts for

13

his friends.

05 Can I ask why you want to return them?

06 return

07 (a) return (b) is (c) wanted (d) checking

01 B가 한국 전통 선물을 살 수 있는 곳을 물어봤고, 이에 (D)에서 인사동을 가 보았는지 물어보며 권하는 문장이 오는 것이 자연스럽다. 그 다음으로 (A)에서 가 보지 않았다고 대답하면서 (C) 같이 가자고 제안하고, (B)에서 함께 일정을 조율하며 따라서 맨 마지막에 G가 제안을 승낙하는 순서로 이어지는 것이 가장 적절하다.

02 (a)에는 a good place를 꾸며주는 to부정사의 형용사적 용법이, (b)에는 접속사 that이 생략된 명사절의 주어 I의 동사로 take가 가장 적절하다.

03 상대방이 어떤 제안을 했을 때 제안을 승낙할 때 쓸 수 있는 표현으로 'That's fine with me.' 또는 'That's alright.', 'Sounds good.' 등이 있다.

04 'B가 친구들을 위해 사기를 원하는 것이 무엇이냐'에 대한 대답은 대화를 시작하는 B의 말에서 찾을 수 있다.

05 상대방에게 승낙을 요구하는 표현 Can I ask ~?와 의문사 why가 쓰인 간접의문문이 결합된 문장이다.

06 '어떤 것을 원래 있던 자리로 돌려보내거나 돌려주거나 돌려놓다'라는 영영풀이에 맞는 단어는 return(반품하다, 반납하다)이다.

07 나는 오늘 내가 저번에 산 운동화를 반품하기 위해 신발 가게에 갔다. 나는 점원에게 운동화에 먼지가 묻어 있고 단 한 번도 신지 않았다고 말했다. 그 점원은 신발을 살펴보겠다고 요청했다. 나는 그녀가 그것을 살펴보는 것을 언짢아하지 않았다.

교과서
Grammar

핵심 Check
p.74~75

1 (1) hard (2) as
2 (1) had seen (2) had not finished

시험대비 기본평가
p.76

01 (1) hardly → hard
   (2) well → good
   (3) has → had
02 (1) had, started (2) had bought (3) late
   (4) had seen
03 (1) This box is half as big as that one.
   (2) I can speak English as fluently as Korean.

(3) The field was in bad condition because it had rained the day before.

01 (1) hard와 hardly는 둘 다 부사의 의미를 가지고 있지만 'hardly'는 '거의 ~않게'라는 뜻을 지니고 있다. 따라서 '열심히'라는 의미를 지닌 'hard'로 쓰는 것이 적절하다. (2) be동사 뒤에서 보어로 쓰이기 때문에 부사 'well'이 아니라 형용사 'good'으로 쓰는 것이 적절하다. 'well'이 형용사로 쓰일 경우에는 '건강한'이라는 의미를 갖는다. (3) 그가 도착했을 때 이미 회의가 끝난 상태이기 때문에 과거시제보다 앞선 대과거로 has를 had로 쓰는 것이 적절하다.

02 (1) 도착한 것보다 시작한 상황이 먼저 일어났으므로 'had started'로 쓰는 것이 적절하다. (2) 휴대폰을 산 것은 잃어버린 것보다 먼저 일어났으므로 'had bought'로 쓰는 것이 적절하다. (3) 'late'는 형용사와 부사의 뜻이 같으므로 부사의 형태 'late'를 쓰는 것이 적절하다. (참고) 'lately: 최근에' (4) 그를 알아보았다는 행위보다 이전에 여러 번 본 적이 있는 행위가 먼저 일어났으므로 'had seen'으로 쓰는 것이 적절하다.

03 (1), (2) 동등비교 문장으로 (1)은 '배수사+as+원급+as' 어순으로 쓰는 것이 적절하다. (2)는 '비교대상+as+원급+as+비교대상'으로 일반동사 play를 수식해 줄 수 있는 부사가 필요하기 때문에 fluently를 쓰는 것이 적절하다. (3) 비가 온 것이 과거보다 앞서므로 과거완료로 쓰는 것이 적절하다.

시험대비 실력평가
p.77~79

01 has booked → had booked
02 ⓐ go → went, ⓑ go → went, ⓒ leave → left,
   ⓓ arrive → arrived
03 He had gone home.   04 ④   05 ②
06 ①   07 as pretty as   08 ⑤
09 ①, ④   10 ③   11 ③   12 ①, ③
13 ⑤   14 ①   15 ③   16 ①
17 had already cleaned   18 (1) had (2) as
19 ②

01 과거완료인 had booked를 쓰는 것이 적절하다.

02 빈칸 모두 과거 시점에서 일어난 일들을 말하고 있는 것이므로 과거시제를 써준다.

03 폴이 집에 간 것은 과거의 특정한 시점보다 더 이전에 일어난 일이므로 과거완료시제로 쓰는 것이 적절하다.

04 잠자는 것은 먹는 것과 운동하는 것만큼 중요하므로 가까운 뜻을 갖고 있는 ④번이 적절하다.

05 ② 일반동사 play를 수식해 줄 수 있는 부사가 필요하기 때문에 good의 부사형인 well을 쓰는 것이 적절하다. ① 원하는 만큼 많은 과일을 사라. ③ 8시가 지났는데도 대낮같이 환하다. ④

경제의 성장은 예상했던 것만큼 대단하지 않았다. ⑤ 우리는 비축 물자가 떨어지지 않는 한 여기에 머물 수 있다. *hold out: (특히 어려운 상황에서) 지속되다[없어지지 않다]

06 내가 교실에 들어갔을 때, 수학 수업은 이미 시작되었다. 내가 교실에 들어간 것보다 수업이 시작된 것이 먼저이므로 entered - had begun이 들어가야 적절하다.

07 • 너는 수지만큼 예쁘다. 비교 대상은 you와 Suzy이다. be동사 뒤에 형용사가 와야 하므로 'as pretty as'로 쓰는 것이 적절하다.

08 ⑤ 이 우유는 상했다. 신맛이 난다. 빈칸에 has가 들어가는 것이 적절하다. 나머지는 모두 had가 들어간다. ① 그가 나를 불렀을 때 나는 이미 점심을 먹었다. ② 그는 열쇠를 잃어버렸기 때문에 문을 열 수 없었다. ③ 엄마를 도와드리기 전에 나는 TV를 보았다. ④ 아빠가 나에게 인형을 만들어 주셔서 기뻤다.

09 나는 밖에 나가고 싶지 않았다. 나는 피곤했다. 피곤한 상태였으므로 ①, ④ 모두 빈칸에 들어가는 것이 적절하다.

10 Miju는 어제 말을 처음 타 봤다. 전에는 타 본 적이 없었다.

11 그는 문을 잠그지 않아서 놀랐다. 놀란 시점보다 문을 잠그지 않은 시점이 더 앞선 시제이므로 과거완료시제를 쓰는 것이 적절하다.

12 시간 순서상 물을 끓인 것이 앞서므로 ① 물을 끓이고 나서 라면을 냄비에 넣었다고 표현한 것과 ③ 물이 끓고 나서 라면을 냄비에 넣었다고 표현하는 것이 적절하다.

13 퇴직할 때까지 계속 일해 왔던 것이므로 worked를 had worked로 쓰는 것이 적절하다.

14 ① 심판은 터치아웃을 선언했다. touched를 had touched로 쓰는 것이 적절하다. ② 나는 막 피자를 먹었었다. 그래서 그때 배가 고프지 않았다. ③ Paul은 작년에 영국에 갔다. 그것은 두 번째였다. 전에 한 번 가 봤었다. ④ 그들이 필요로 하는 것은 단지 물이었다. ⑤ 그 소녀는 그녀를 즐겁게 하는 영화를 보고 있다.

15 • Jason을 만나러 도서관에 갔지만 만나지 못했다. 그가 집으로 가 버렸다.

16 ① 수지는 Jay를 1년 동안 만났을 때 팔짱을 끼고 걸었다. has known → had known 또는 knew ② 그녀는 2주 동안 아파서 콘서트에 참여할 수 없었다. ③ 나는 전에 그를 본 적이 있기 때문에 그를 한 번에 알아봤다. ④ 그때까지는 네가 담근 김치가 굉장히 맛있었다. ⑤ 그는 전에는 아주 가난했다.

17 엄마가 집에 오셨을 때 나는 이미 방청소를 했다.

18 어법에 맞게 배열하면 (1) No sooner had I paid for the jacket than I saw that it had a small hole in it. (2) He speaks as slowly as I do.

19 ② 그는 책을 다 읽고 나서 제자리에 갖다 놓았다. where it is 를 where it had been으로 쓰는 것이 적절하다. ① 나는 딸을 보았을 때 매우 기뻤다. 2년 동안 그녀를 보지 못했다. ③ 내 친구 Minho는 서울로 이사 오기 전까지 시골에서 살았다. ④ 나는 콘서트에 늦게 도착했다. 보고 싶었던 쇼가 끝난 것을 알았다. ⑤ 나는 안내 방송을 들었을 때 기차를 잘못 탄 것을 알았다.

01 Last year, I got food poisoning after eating food that had gone bad.

02 (1) (완) (2) (결) (3) (계) (4) (경) (5) (대)

03 (1) had been sick　(2) had had
(3) had never traveled　(4) had not been seen
(5) had finished　(6) had only just started
(7) had broken　(8) had lost　(9) had already begun
(10) had had

04 She is as tall as Mr.[Ms.] Lee.

05 (b)roke, (f)ound, (h)ad, (b)een, (s)tolen, (h)ad, (s)old

06 had returned　　　　　07 as fat as

08 (1) had bought　(2) not as[so] pretty as
(3) as soon as possible
(4) three times as much as

09 (1) where I had put the book
(2) had had a secret relationship
(3) they had been caught
(4) graffiti had been painted

01 상한 음식을 먹고 식중독에 걸린 것보다 음식이 상한 것이 더 앞선 시제이므로 음식이 상한 것을 had gone bad로 쓰는 것이 적절하다.

02 (1) 나는 1월에 이미 의학시험을 쳤었다. (2) 나는 동물원에서 내 카메라를 잃어버린 것을 알았다. (3) 전쟁이 일어났을 때 나는 그곳에서 2년째 살고 있었다. (4) 나는 타지마할을 방문할 때까지 그토록 놀라운 건축물을 본 적이 없었다. (5) 감기가 채 떨어지기도 전에 독감에 걸렸다.

03 과거완료(had+p.p)의 형태로 과거의 어떤 시점보다 앞서 일어난 일에 대해 말할 때 사용한다. 과거완료시제는 'had+p.p.'로 쓰고 부정은 'had not+p.p.', 부사 또는 빈도부사는 'had+부사 또는 빈도부사+p.p.'로 쓴다. (5), (9), (10)의 경우는 시간 접속사 before, after 등과 함께 쓰일 경우 주절에 과거시제 동사를 쓸 수 있다.

04 비교 대상 as 원급 as 비교 대상. 주어의 키를 비교하는 것이므로 be동사의 보어로 형용사가 오는 것이 적절하다.

05 어젯밤에 도둑이 들었다. 직장에서 집으로 돌아왔을 때, 모든 패물을 도난당한 것을 알았다. 누가 옷장 서랍을 열어 놓고 갔는지 궁금했다. 그 다음날 경찰이 도둑을 잡았다. 하지만 도둑이 이미 모든 패물을 다 팔아 버린 뒤였다.

06 네가 이미 돌아와 있었던 상태이므로 had returned로 쓰는 것이 적절하다.

07 다이어트를 계속하고 있지만 예전과 마찬가지로 뚱뚱한 것이므로 as fat as 동등비교 표현을 쓰는 것이 적절하다.

08 (1) the day before: 전날 (2) 부정어 as[so] 원급 as (3) as soon as possible: 가능한 한 빨리 (4) 배수사 as 원급 as

15

09 (1) 나는 그 책을 어디에 두었는지 기억이 나지 않았다. (2) 그녀는 수년간 그와 밀회를 나누었다. (3) 난 걔네들이 잡힌 줄 알았다. (4) 베트남에 그들의 삶을 취재하러 갔을 때, 낙서가 벽에 쓰여 있던 것을 보았다.

Reading

확인문제 p.82

1 T 2 F 3 T 4 F 5 T 6 F

확인문제 p.83

1 T 2 F 3 F 4 T 5 T 6 F

교과서 확인학습 A p.84~85

01 Online Sale
02 rides his bike
03 taller and stronger
04 too small for him
05 savings account
06 What
07 had an idea
08 as good as
09 add the money
10 acted fast
11 posted, with a short comment
12 thinking about
13 himself riding
14 could not wait
15 Every few minutes
16 As, went up
17 received no texts
18 Nobody seemed
19 pushed his post down
20 to sink
21 wrong with
22 attractive enough
23 for tips on
24 what he had done wrong
25 hasty, greedy
26 possible buyers
27 compared to, high
28 with a longer description
29 from different angles
30 kept indoors
31 several texts
32 asked for
33 to accept, for
34 handed over
35 could get
36 both happy and sad
37 go, himself, through the experience

교과서 확인학습 B p.86~87

1 Seyun's First Online Sale.
2 Seyun rides his bike to school every day.
3 He likes his bike, but he is taller and stronger this year.

4 His bike has become too small for him, so he wants to buy a bigger, faster one.
5 However, he does not have enough money in his savings account.
6 What can he do?
7 Suddenly, Seyun had an idea.
8 "My old bike is almost as good as a new one.
9 Maybe I can sell it and add the money to buy a new one."
10 He acted fast.
11 He took a photo of his bike with his smartphone and posted the picture, with a short comment, on an online market: "Used bike in excellent condition. Only 100,000 won. Please text me."
12 He was excited, thinking about the bike he planned to buy.
13 He could see himself riding the shiny new bike.
14 He could not wait to get a reply to his online advertisement.
15 Every few minutes he checked the number of hits.
16 As the number of hits went up, his expectations went up too.
17 One hour passed, then two, and finally a whole day, but he received no texts.
18 Nobody seemed to want his bike.
19 New postings by other people pushed his post down the list.
20 His heart began to sink.
21 "What's wrong with my posting?
22 Is my bike not attractive enough?"
23 He searched on the Internet for tips on how to sell online.
24 Then he realized what he had done wrong.
25 He had been too hasty and too greedy.
26 He had not given enough information to the possible buyers.
27 Also, when compared to other bicycles, his price was too high.
28 He wrote a new posting with a longer description of the bike.
29 He added more photos to show his bike from different angles.
30 "Twenty-four inch bicycle. Excellent condition. Always kept indoors. Rides just like new. Very few scratches. Good for someone 12–14 years old. 80,000 won."
31 This time he got several texts.
32 Sadly, they all asked for a lower price.

33 It was hard to accept at first, but finally he sold his bike for 70,000 won.

34 He met the buyer, handed over his bike, and got the money he needed.

35 Now he could get a new bike.

36 He felt both happy and sad.

37 He was sad to see his old bike go, but he was happy with himself because he had learned a lot and grown up a bit through the experience.

시험대비 실력평가

p.88~91

01 ①　　　　02 ④　　　　03 ②　　　　04 ⑤

05 existing → possible

06 when his price was compared to other bicycles

07 ④

08 (A) lower　(B) both happy and sad　(C) go

09 ③

10 Because he had learned a lot and grown up a bit through the experience.

11 ③　　　　12 ⑤　　　　13 my old bike

14 (A) hasty　(B) greedy

15 ⑤번, scratch → scratches

16 ④　　　　17 ③　　　　18 ①, ④, ⑤　　19 ②

20 ⑤　　　　21 got the money that[which] he needed

22 ①

01 ⓐ for: ~에게, ⓑ in his savings account: 그의 예금 계좌에

02 ④번 뒤에 이어지는 문장의 내용에 주목한다. 주어진 문장에 대한 아이디어를 떠올린 것이므로 ④번이 적절하다.

03 세윤이는 자신의 자전거를 좋아한다. be tired of: 싫증이 나다

04 (B)는 (C)에서 올린 온라인 광고에 대한 대답이 오기를 기다리는 모습을 설명하는 것이므로 (C) 다음에 (B)가 이어지고 (A)는 (B)의 마지막 문장을 더 자세히 설명하는 것이므로 (B) 다음에 (A)가 와야 한다. 그러므로 (C)-(B)-(A)의 순서가 적절하다.

05 '구매 가능성이 있는' 사람들에게 충분한 정보를 주지 않았다고 해야 하므로, 'existing'을 'possible'로 고치는 것이 적절하다. existing: 기존의

06 'when compared to other bicycles'는 'when his price was compared to other bicycles,'에서 '주어+be동사'가 생략된 분사구문이다. 분사구문의 뜻을 명확히 하기 위해 접속사를 생략하지 않을 수 있다.

07 이 글은 '세윤이가 자신의 잘못을 깨닫고 충분한 정보를 주는 새 게시물을 작성하는 것'에 관한 글이므로, 주제로는 ④번 '충분한 정보를 주는 새 게시물을 작성하기'가 적절하다.

08 (A) 그들(구매 가능성이 있는 사람들)은 모두 '더 낮은' 가격을

요청했다고 해야 하므로 lower가 적절하다. 또한 'price'가 낮다고 할 때는 cheap보다 low를 쓰는 것이 적절하다. (B) felt 의 보어에 해당하므로 형용사 'both happy and sad'가 적절하다. (C) 지각동사 see의 목적격보어에 to부정사를 쓸 수 없고 동사원형이나 현재분사를 써야 하므로 go가 적절하다.

09 ⓐ와 ②, ③, ⑤: 부사적 용법, ①: 명사적 용법, ④: 형용사적 용법

10 이 경험을 통해 자신이 많은 것을 배우고 조금 더 성장했기 때문이다.

11 앞에 나오는 내용과 상반되는 내용이 뒤에 이어지므로 However가 가장 적절하다. ① 즉[말하자면], ② 게다가, 더욱이, ④ 그러므로

12 (A)와 ⑤: 앞에 이미 언급했거나 상대방이 알고 있는 사람·사물을 가리킬 때 명사의 반복을 피하기 위해 씀(대명사), ① 같은, 한(형용사), ② (특정한 사람·물건 중의) 하나(대명사), ③ [총칭 인칭으로서; 복수형 없음] (일반적으로) 사람(대명사), ④ [another, the other와 대조적으로] 한쪽의, 한편의(형용사)

13 '내 오래된 자전거'를 가리킨다.

14 각각 '형용사' 형태로 쓰는 것이 적절하다.

15 'few' 뒤에는 셀 수 있는 명사의 복수를 써야 하므로, 'scratches'로 고치는 것이 적절하다.

16 '세윤이가 왜 자전거를 항상 실내에 보관했는지'는 대답할 수 없다. ① He was too hasty and too greedy and didn't give enough information to the possible buyers. ② No, it was too high. ③ He added more photos to show his bike from different angles. ⑤ He recommended his bike to someone 12-14 years old.

17 ⓐ in excellent condition: 훌륭한 상태의, ⓑ by: ~가 한 [쓴/만든 등](행위자, 창작자, 유발자 등을 나타냄)

18 (A)와 ①, ④, ⑤: 현재분사, ②, ③ : 동명사

19 이 글은 '자전거를 팔려는 온라인 광고를 게시한 후 그 돈으로 새로 구입하려고 계획한 자전거에 대해 생각하며 신이 났지만, 아무도 문자를 보내지 않았고 다른 사람들의 새 게시물이 그의 게시물을 리스트에서 밀어내어 실망하는' 내용의 글이므로, 어울리는 속담으로는 ②번 '김칫국부터 마시지 말라'가 적절하다. ① 백지장도 맞들면 낫다[한 사람이 하는 것보다는 두 사람이 하는 것이 낫다], ③ 쇠가 달았을 때 두드려라(기회를 놓치지 말라는 뜻), ④ 사공이 많으면 배가 산으로 올라간다(어떤 일에 관여하는 사람이 너무 많으면 일을 망친다는 뜻). ⑤ 모든 구름의 뒤편은 은빛으로 빛난다.(괴로움 뒤에는 기쁨이 있다.)

20 ⓐ ask for: ~을 요구하다, ⓑ for: [교환] ~와 교환으로; ~에 대하여; ~의 금액[값]으로

21 'the money'와 'he needed' 사이에 목적격 관계대명사 'that[which]'이 생략되었다.

22 '이번에 세윤이가 얼마나 많은 문자 메시지를 받았는지'는 대답할 수 없다. ② They all asked for a lower price. ③ No, it

17

was hard to accept at first. ④ He earned 70,000 won. ⑤ No, he met the buyer directly and handed over his bike.

작성했고 자신의 자전거를 다른 각도에서 보여 주기 위해서 '더 많은 사진들'을 첨부했다.

01 hurried   02 ④   03 ⑤   04 ③

05 (1) Emily gained valuable experience while working on the project.
   (2) Some kinds of plants can be grown indoors.
   (3) All planes are being inspected for possible cracking.

06 (1) We would like to recommend you to book your flight early.
   (2) Hackers can steal the valuable information stored in the device.
   (3) The novelist is well-known for her powers of description.

07 ②   08 Do you mind if I take a look at it?

09 ⑤   10 (C) – (D) – (B) – (A)

11 ①, ⑤   12 twice as big as   13 ②

14 Scientists had not been able to predict this disaster.

15 as soon as I can   16 run

17 (1) is not so[as] brave as
   (2) is not so[as] cold as
   (3) as economically as
   (4) is four times as expensive as
   (5) is twice[two times] as heavy as
   (6) doesn't get up as early as

18 ②   19 ④

20 Every few minutes he checked the number of hits.

21 ③   22 ③   23 ③   24 ⑤

25 eighty thousand   26 to buy

27 (A) on sale (B) bigger

---

01 one

02 My old bike is almost as good as a new one.

03 (A) too small   (B) new

04 (A) Used   (B) riding   (C) minutes

05 one hundred thousand

06 as[while] he thought about the bike he planned to buy

07 hits

08 ⓐ met   ⓑ handed   ⓒ got

09 several texts

10 He felt both happy and sad.

11 had done

12 he should

13 (A) longer description   (B) more photos

01 앞에 이미 언급했거나 상대방이 알고 있는 사람·사물을 가리킬 때 명사의 반복을 피하기 위해 쓰는 부정대명사 one이 적절하다. ⓐ와 ⓑ 둘 다 bike를 대신한 것이다.

02 as+형용사/부사의 원급+as: ~와 같은 정도로, ~와 마찬가지로 (as ... as ~에서, 앞의 as는 지시부사, 뒤의 as는 접속사)

03 세윤이의 자전거는 그에게 '너무 작아져서', 그는 그것을 팔고 '새'것을 사기 위한 돈에 보탤 계획이다.

04 (A) '중고' 자전거라고 해야 하므로 Used가 적절하다. (B) 지각동사 see의 목적격보어이므로 현재분사 riding이 적절하다. (C) 몇 분'마다'라고 해야 하므로 minutes가 적절하다. every+기수+복수명사: ~마다

05 천의 자리에 thousand를 붙여 읽고, 콤마를 기준으로 끊어 읽는 것이 적절하다.

06 'thinking about ~'은 동시동작을 나타내는 분사구문으로, 접속사 as나 while 등을 사용해 부사절로 바꿔 쓸 수 있다.

07 hit: 인터넷 등에서의 사이트 방문, 검색 결과

08 문장의 동사가 'A, B, and C'의 병렬 구조로 연결되도록 과거형 'met,' 'handed,' 'got'으로 쓰는 것이 적절하다.

09 '여러 통의 문자 메시지'를 가리킨다.

10 그는 기쁘고 슬픈 감정을 동시에 느꼈다.

11 과거의 어떤 시점보다 더 이전에 일어난 일을 표현할 때 사용하는 과거완료 시제('had done')로 쓰는 것이 적절하다.

12 '의문사+to부정사'는 '의문사+주어+should+동사원형'으로 바꿔 쓸 수 있다.

13 세윤이는 자신의 자전거에 대한 '더 긴 묘사'가 있는 새 게시물을

01 maybe(아마도)와 probably(아마도)는 유의어 관계이다. 따라서 hasty(성급한)와 유의어 관계에 있는 단어는 hurried(서두르는)이다.

02 '좋은 일이 미래에 일어날 것이라는 느낌'이라는 영영풀이는 ④ expectation(기대)이다.

03 ⑤ '나는 내 오빠의 결정에 대해 논평할 수 없다고 느낀다.'라는 문장에서 comment는 '언급'이라는 명사가 아니라 동사로 '언급하다, 논평하다'라는 의미로 사용되었다.

04 주어진 문장에서 reply는 '답장, 답신'이라는 뜻으로 사용 되었다. ③ 당신은 7일 내에 답신을 받게 될 것이다(You should receive a reply within seven days.)에서 역시 reply는 '대답, 회신'이라는 뜻으로 쓰였다.

05 (1) experience 경험; 경험하다 / valuable 귀중한, 값진 (2) indoors 실내에서 / grow 기르다 (3) possible 발생 가능한, 있을 수 있는 / inspect 조사하다, 검사하다

06 (1) recommend 추천하다 (2) steal 훔치다 (3) description 묘사

07 ② (A) 과거에서부터 현재까지 이어져 오고 있는 일을 의미하는 현재완료진행형이므로 'have been ~ing'으로 쓴다. (B) 현재 사실에 대한 단순한 조건문이므로 현재형인 want가 들어가는 것이 적절하다. (C) 과거 또는 현재에 경험한 일에 대한 일을 의미하는 현재완료형의 경험 용법이 들어가야 한다. 따라서 thought 가 적절하다.

08 상대방에게 허락을 구하는 표현인 'Do you mind if I~?'가 사용된 문장으로, "Would you mind if I ~?"와 같은 표현으로 대체할 수 있다.

09 ⑤ 'Ben과 Dana가 찾은 만화책은 Dana의 책보다 더 저렴하지 않다.'는 말은 위 대화에서 언급되지 않았다.

10 M이 무엇을 도와줄까요?라고 물었으므로 (C)에서 은행 계좌를 열고 싶은데 무엇을 해야 하느냐고 되묻는 것이 자연스럽다. 그러면 은행원이 (D)에서 은행 계좌를 열기 위한 양식을 작성하라고 요청하고 (B)에서는 작성하기 위해 펜을 빌리려는 질문을 하는 것이 자연스럽다. 그리고 마지막으로 (A)에서 펜을 써도 된다는 승낙으로 이어지는 것이 문맥상 가장 적절하다.

11 윤지는 내 빨대보다 3배 더 긴 빨대를 갖고 있었다. 배수사+as 원급 as+비교 대상

12 배수사 as 원급 as

13 ② 빵집에 갔을 때, 내가 가장 좋아하는 초콜릿 케이크는 다 팔리고 없었다. 초콜릿이 다 팔린 상황은 내가 빵집에 갔을 때보다 먼저 일어난 상황이므로 과거완료 had sold out으로 쓰는 것이 적절하다. ① 내 친구가 도착하기 전에 영화는 시작했다. ③ 내 손은 얼음같이 차다. ④ 나는 전에 감자를 심어 본 적이 없었다. ⑤ 그는 잃어버린 용돈을 찾아서 매우 기뻤다.

14 had not p.p. 재앙이 발생한 원인을 미리 예측하지 못한 것이므로 과거완료로 쓰는 것이 적절하다.

15 as soon as I can: 내가 할 수 있는 한 빨리

16 어순대로 영작하면, The robber had run away before the police arrived.

17 (1), (2) be동사가 쓰인 동등비교 문장의 부정은 'be동사+부정어+so(또는 as)+원급+as' (3) 일반동사 do를 수식해 줄 수 있는 부사가 필요하기 때문에 'as economically as'로 쓰는 것이 적절하다. (4), (5)는 '배수사+as+원급+as' (6) 일반동사가 쓰인 동등비교 문장의 현재형 부정은 'don't[doesn't]+동사+as+원급+as'로 쓰고 일반동사 get up을 수식해 줄 수 있는 부사 early를 쓰는 것이 적절하다.

18 ⓐ와 ②: 결과 용법, ①과 ④: 완료 용법, ③ 계속 용법, ⑤ 경험 용법

19 '세윤이가 새 자전거를 사기 위해 얼마를 보태야 하는 지'는 대답할 수 없다. ① He rides his bike to school every day. ② No, he doesn't. ③ His old bike is almost as good as a new one. ⑤ He can add money by selling his old bike.

20 every+기수+복수명사: ~마다

21 이 글은 '자전거를 팔려는 온라인 광고를 게시한 후 그 돈으로 새로 구입하려고 계획한 자전거에 대해 생각하며 신이 났지만, 아무도 문자를 보내지 않았고 다른 사람들의 새 게시물이 그의 게시물을 리스트에서 밀어내어 실망하는' 내용의 글이므로, 제목으로는 ③번 '성과 없는 온라인 광고'가 적절하다. fruitless: 성과[결실] 없는

22 ③ cannot wait to+동사원형: ~이 기대된다, 몹시 기다려진다

23 주어진 문장의 Then에 주목한다. ③번 앞 문장의 내용에 이어지는 내용을 계속 설명하는 것이므로 ③번이 적절하다.

24 '판매 가격'은 포함되어 있지만, '구매 가격'은 포함되어 있지 않다.

25 천의 자리에 thousand를 붙여 읽고, 콤마를 기준으로 끊어 읽는 것이 적절하다.

26 advise는 목적격보어에 to부정사로 쓰는 것이 적절하다.

27 (A) '할인 중인' 물건만큼 값이 싸다. (B) 당신이 보통 사는 것보다 '더 큰' 사이즈를 사는 편이 좋을 것이다.

단원별 예상문제 p.100~103

01 ④ **02** (1) passed (2) contact (3) shiny
(4) sell **03** ⓑ gone → been
04 No, I've never been there.
05 금요일 대신 토요일에 인사동에 같이 방문하는 것
06 What about going with me next Saturday then?
07 ② **08** (1) as (2) had
09 The actress is not as[so] famous as IU.
10 ③
11 (1) Are you looking for a place as large as your office?
(2) I had never met such a beautiful girl before I met Somin.
(3) I fought with my sister when I found that she had made my clothes dirty.
12 I'm not as[so] tall as my elder brother. **13** ①
14 She screamed as loudly as she could.
15 ① **16** ②, ⑤ **17** ③ **18** ③
19 He wrote a new posting with a longer description of the bike.
20 ④ **21** ②, ⑤
22 Because he has grown more than 10 cm this year, so it's too small for him now.

19

01 '사물들을 행하거나 보거나 느낌으로써 오는 지식이나 기술을 얻는 과정'이라는 뜻을 가진 영영풀이는 ④experience(경험)를 가리킨다.

02 (1) pass (시간이) 지나가다, 흐르다 (2) contact 접촉, 연락 (3) shiny 빛나는 (4) sell 팔다

03 어디에 가 본 적이 있냐고 물을 때는 'Have you gone to ~?'가 아니라 'Have you been to ~?'라고 묻는다. 따라서 ⓑ gone을 been으로 고쳐야 한다.

04 상대방이 Have you been to ~? 라고 물었으므로, 이에 대해 대답할 때는 'Yes, I have.' 또는 'No, I haven't.'라고 대답한다. 이때, never를 써서 'No, I have never been there.'라고 대답할 수도 있다.

05 '그것은 난 좋아'라고 대답했을 때 '그것'이 의미하는 것은 앞선 문장에서 확인할 수 있다. 같이 인사동을 방문하는 계획을 이야기하다가 B가 '금요일 오후 대신 토요일은 어때?'라고 물었다. 따라서 (B)That이 가리키는 것은 '금요일 대신 토요일에 인사동을 같이 방문하는 것'이다.

06 '~하는 건 어때?'라고 제안할 때 쓸 수 있는 표현으로 'What about ~?' 외에 'How about ~?', 'Why don't we ~?' 등이 있다.

07 대화의 마지막 부분에 다음 주에 가고 싶었던 게임 엑스포에 친구와 같이 가게 되었으므로 ② excited(흥분된, 신난)가 가장 적절하다.

08 (1) 그는 그녀만큼 친절하지 않다. (2) 우리가 어젯밤에 집에 도착했을 때, 누군가가 우리 이웃집에 침입했던 것을 보았다.

09 동등비교의 부정문 표현이다.

10 ③ 가능한 한 치즈케이크를 작게 만들어 주세요. Make의 주어는 you이므로 she를 you로 고쳐주는 것이 적절하다. ① Ted는 꼬챙이처럼 말랐다. ② 초가을인데도 날씨가 한여름처럼 더웠다. ④ 나는 가능한 한 친절해지려고 노력하고 있다. ⑤ 제가 할 수 있는 데까지는 하겠습니다.

11 (1) 비교 대상 as 원급 as 비교 대상 (2) had+부정어+p.p.

12 비교 대상 부정어 as(so) 원급 as 비교 대상

13 '…만큼 ~하지 않다'라는 표현의 동등 비교는 'not so[as] 원급 as'로 쓴다. 그녀가 겉보기에는 젊어 보이지만 사실상 젊지는 않다는 의미이므로 ①처럼 쓰는 것이 적절하다.

14 그녀가 할 수 있는 한 크게 비명을 지른 것이므로 She screamed as loudly as she could.로 표현하는 것이 적절하다.

15 ①번 다음 문장의 내용이 주어진 문장의 내용을 자세히 설명하는 것이므로 ①번이 적절하다.

16 ⓐ와 ②, ⑤: 재귀 용법, ①, ③, ⑤: 강조 용법

17 전반부의 'He was excited, thinking about the bike he planned to buy.'를 통해 'excited'를, 하반부의 'His heart began to sink.'를 통해 'disappointed'를 찾을 수 있다. ① amazed: 놀란, ③ disappointed: 실망한, ④ bored: 지루한, puzzled: 어리둥절해하는

18 ⓐ와 ③: 대과거 용법, ① 경험 용법, ②와 ⑤: 완료 용법, ④ 계속 용법

19 'with a longer description of the bike'가 'a new posting'을 뒤에서 꾸며주도록 쓰는 것이 적절하다.

20 다른 자전거들과 비교했을 때 세윤이의 가격은 '너무 높았다.'

21 ⓐ와 ②와 ⑤: 간접의문문을 이끌어 ~인지 (아닌지) (whether), ①, ③, ④: 만약

22 그는 올해 키가 10 cm 이상 커져서, 이제 그의 자전거는 그에게 너무 작기 때문이다.

서술형 실전문제
p.104~105

01 It comes from Japan.

02 No, she can't. She lost contact with her.

03 Because they can't take their drinks inside.

04 He suggested her to finish their drinks first to go inside.

05 (1) A bird had flown (2) he had seen her
   (3) Jay had writtenfive symphonies
   (4) I had heard (5) had fought

06 (1) Cats sleep twice as much as people.
   (2) My school has five times as many computers as your school.

07 Is the full moon twice as bright as the half moon?

08 (1) people who have a lot of friends, those with only a few friends
   (2) are twice as happy as

09 as smooth as

10 He was excited, thinking about the bike he planned to buy.

11 (A) hits   (B) new postings

01 '그 장난감은 어디서 오는가?'라는 질문에 대한 답은 G의 말에서 찾을 수 있다. G에 따르면 친구가 일본에 갔을 때 사다 준 것("My friend bought it for me when she went to Japan.")이라고 말했다.

03 왜 B와 G가 상점에 들어갈 수 없는가?'라는 질문에 대한 답은 B의 말에 나와 있다. 음료를 내부로 반입할 수 없기 때문이다 ("Wait, I'm afraid we can't take our drinks inside.").

04 '상점에 들어가기 위해 B가 G에게 무엇을 제안했나?'라는 질문에 대한 답은 대화 후반부에서 찾아볼 수 있다. B는 음료를 먼저

다 마시자고 ("Let's finish our drinks first. Then we can go inside.") 제안했다.

05 과거완료는 'had+p.p.'로 쓴다.

06 비교 대상+배수사+as+원급+as+비교 대상. (1) 일반동사인 sleep을 수식해 주어야 하므로 원급에 much가 오는 것이 적절하다. (2) 비교 대상은 나의 학교와 네 학교에 있는 컴퓨터이므로 my school과 your school로 쓰는 것이 적절하고 5배나 많다는 표현은 five times as many computers as로 쓰는 것이 적절하다. 컴퓨터는 셀 수 있으므로 many로 쓴다.

07 '배수사+as+원급+as' 표현을 활용한 의문문으로 비교 대상은 the full moon과 the half moon이다. 평서문으로 쓰면, The full moon is twice as bright as the half moon.이므로 의문문으로 쓸 때는 be동사와 주어를 도치시켜 쓰는 것이 적절하다.

08 친구를 많이 가진 사람들은 친구가 적은 사람들보다 두 배나 행복하다.

09 비교 대상 as 원급 as 비교 대상

10 동시동작을 나타내는 분사구문 'thinking about ~'으로 쓰는 것이 적절하다.

11 그는 자신의 온라인 광고에 대한 대답이 오기를 갈망했고, 처음에는 '조회 수'가 올라갔다. 그러나 그는 문자를 받지 못했고 다른 사람들의 '새 게시물'이 그의 게시물을 리스트에서 밀어냈다.

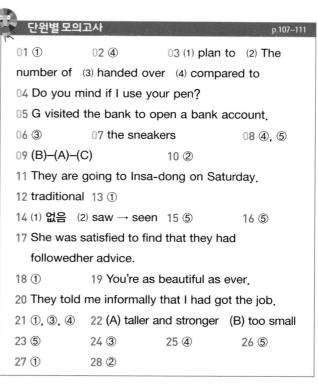

단원별 모의고사 p.107~111

01 ①　　　**02** ④　　　**03** (1) plan to　(2) The number of　(3) handed over　(4) compared to

04 Do you mind if I use your pen?

05 G visited the bank to open a bank account.

06 ③　　　**07** the sneakers　　　**08** ④, ⑤

09 (B)–(A)–(C)　　　**10** ②

11 They are going to Insa-dong on Saturday.

12 traditional　**13** ①

14 (1) 없음　(2) saw → seen　**15** ⑤　　　**16** ⑤

17 She was satisfied to find that they had followedher advice.

18 ①　　　　　　**19** You're as beautiful as ever.

20 They told me informally that I had got the job.

21 ①, ③, ④　**22** (A) taller and stronger　(B) too small

23 ⑤　　　**24** ③　　　**25** ④　　　**26** ⑤

27 ①　　　**28** ②

01 '무언가를 찾기 위해 주의 깊게 어느 곳을 찾다'는 뜻을 가진 영영풀이가 가리키는 것은 ① search(찾다, 검색하다)이다.

02 나머지는 모두 반의어 관계이지만, ④ greedy와 avaricious는 둘 다 '탐욕스러운'이라는 뜻을 갖는 동의어이다.

03 (1) plan to ~을 계획하다 (2) the number of ~의 숫자, 수 (3) hand over 넘겨주다 (4) compared to ~에 비해

04 '제가 펜을 사용해도 될까요?'라는 표현은 'Do you mind if I use your pen?' 이외에도 더 정중한 표현으로 'Would you mind if I use your pen?'으로 대체할 수 있다.

05 위 대화 초반에 G가 은행 계좌를 열고 싶다고 언급했다.

06 위 대화 초반에 ③ 운동화를 반품하기 위해서(To return the sneakers)라고 언급되어 있다.

07 인칭대명사 them은 the sneakers(운동화)를 가리킨다.

08 ④와 ⑤는 다른 표현들처럼 대화 상대방에게 허락을 요청하는 표현이 아니다.

09 주어진 대화에서 G는 자켓이 마음에 들어 상점에 들어가 보자고 제안한다. 그러나 (B)에서 음료를 갖고 있기 때문에 내부로 들어갈 수 없다고 말하고 따라서 (A)에서 음료수를 아직 다 마시지 않았다고 말하자 (C)에서 우선 음료수를 다 마시고 그 다음에 들어가자고 말하는 순서가 되는 것이 문맥상 가장 자연스럽다.

10 주어진 문장은 '거기에는 많은 한국 전통 물건들이 있어.'라는 뜻의 문장이다. 따라서 인사동을 먼저 언급한 다음에 오는 것이 가장 적절하다.

11 대화 후반부에 나와 있듯이, B와 G는 토요일에 인사동에 가기

창의사고력 서술형 문제 p.106

|모범답안|

01 (A) are looking for

　　(B) has a really wonderful camera

　　(C) be twice as good as

　　(D) endures three times as much as

02 (1) Do you mind if / Would you mind if

　　(2) I'm sorry, but I'm afraid you can't.

03 (A) swimming suit　(B) beautiful

　　(C) cheap　(D) bigger size　(E) too small

02 "Do you mind if I ~?"에서 'mind'는 '~하기를 꺼려하다, 언짢아하다'라는 뜻이다. 따라서 "Yes, I do."라고 답하면 꺼려한다는 의미이므로 상대방의 요청에 거절하는 의미이다. 그러나 실생활에서는 보통 정중하게 거절하는 표현인 'I'm sorry but I'm afraid I can't.'를 사용한다. 반면 "No, I don't." "Not at all."이라고 답하면 상대방의 요청을 허락한다는 의미이다.

로 결정했다.

12 '변화하지 않고 오랫동안 존재해 온 관습이나 믿음, 방법 등에 속하거나 그것을 따르는'이라는 말을 가리키는 것은 traditional(전통적인)이다.

13 주어진 문장은 '~해도 되겠습니까?'라고 묻는 문장으로 ①허락을 요청하는 표현이다.

14 (1) Jane은 그녀의 오빠만큼 창의적이지 않다. (2) 그는 몇 주 내에 좋은 영화를 본적이 없다. 과거완료는 had+p.p.로 표현한다.

15 성 바실리크 성당은 붉은 광장과 크렘린 궁 만큼 ~하다. 빈칸에는 형용사가 올 자리이므로 명사인 popularity는 부적절하다.

16 ⑤ 생선 가게에 갔을 때, 고양이는 생선을 훔쳐갔다. 내가 과거에 생선 가게에 갔을 때 고양이가 생선을 훔쳐간 것이므로 stole 또는 had stolen으로 쓰는 것이 적절하다. ① 연속적으로 3년간 약 850만 명의 사람들이 이 박물관을 방문했습니다. ② 그녀는 파리에 가기 전에 결코 불어를 공부한 적이 없었다. ③ 그는 그 땅을 두고 당국과 여러 해 동안 오랜 싸움을 벌였다. ④ 꽃 가게에 갔을 때, 한 남자가 모든 꽃을 다 샀다.

17 그들이 그녀의 충고를 따른 것이 더 앞선 상황이므로 that 뒤는 과거완료로 쓰는 것이 적절하다.

18 내가 할 수 있는 한 많이 먹었다. as+원급+as. 먹는 것은 양을 나타내므로 원급에 much가 오는 것이 적절하다.

19 'as+원급+as' 동등 비교 문장. be동사의 보어로 주어의 상태를 설명해 줄 수 있는 형용사 beautiful이 오는 것이 적절하다.

20 그들이 말해주는 시점보다 내가 취직이 된 시점이 더 앞선 시제이므로 과거완료로 나타낸다.

21 ⓐ와 ②, ⑤: 부사적 용법, ①, ④: 명사적 용법, ③: 형용사적 용법

22 그는 올해 '키가 더 크고 힘도 더 세졌고', 그의 자전거는 그에게 너무 '작아졌기' 때문이다.

23 finally / eventually / at last / in the end / in the long run: 마침내, ⑤ to the end: 마지막까지

24 ③ '세윤이가 하루에 몇 개의 조회를 기록했는지'는 대답할 수 없다. ① He took a photo of his bike with his smartphone. ② 100,000 won. ④ No, he didn't. ⑤ New postings by other people did.

25 ⓐ search on the Internet: 인터넷을 검색하다, ⓑ tips on ~: ~에 대한 조언

26 그가 자신의 자전거에 대한 긴 묘사가 있는 게시물을 작성한 것은 자신의 잘못을 깨달은 후에 한 일이었다. ② reasonable: 타당한, 사리에 맞는, ③ insufficient: 불충분한

27 주어진 문장의 they에 주목한다. ①번 앞 문장의 several texts 를 받고 있으므로 ①번이 적절하다.

28 처음에 세윤이는 구매 가능성이 있는 사람들의 요청을 받아들이기 어려웠다.

Small Ideas, Big Differences

시험대비 실력평가   p.116

01 useful   02 ④   03 ①   04 ⑤
05 (1) pass through (2) cause death (3) think about
06 ②

01 careful(주의 깊은, 조심스러운, 세심한)과 cautious(조심성 있는)는 동의어 관계이다. 따라서 helpful(유용한, 도움이 되는)과 동의어 관계에 있는 단어는 useful(도움이 되는)이다.

02 '어떤 것이 일어나는 것을 막거나 혹은 어떤 사람이 어떤 것을 하는 것을 막다'는 뜻을 가진 영영풀이가 가리키는 것은 ④ prevent(막다)이다.

03 ① repair는 '수리하다'라는 동사적 의미가 아닌 '수리'라는 명사적 의미로 사용되었다.

04 '직원들은 비상사태 절차를 충분히 알고 있어야 한다.', '그 파일럿은 어쩔 수 없이 비상 착륙을 해야 했다.'라는 문장에서 공통으로 들어갈 수 있는 단어는 ⑤ emergency(비상 상황, 비상 사태)이다.

05 (1) pass through ~을 지나가다 (2) cause death 죽음을 야기하다 (3) think about ~에 대해 생각하다

06 (A) look out 밖을 내다보다 / let out 내보내다 (B) build up 점점 커지다 / be made up of ~로 구성되다

서술형 시험대비   p.117

01 unnecessary   02 notice
03 (1) pane (2) hill (3) twist
04 (1) Surprisingly (2) recently (3) carefully
05 (1) The well-finished roof should be weatherproof for years.
   (2) How quickly can you prepare the paperwork?
   (3) He drew a circle in the sand with a stick.
06 (1) His face was reflected in the mirror.
   (2) I had a sore throat and it hurt to swallow.
   (3) Be careful not to hurt yourself with the steam.

01 death(죽음)와 birth(탄생)는 반의어 관계이다. 따라서 necessary(필수적인)와 반의어 관계에 있는 단어는 unnecessary(불필요한, 쓸데없는)이다.

02 '알게 되다'라는 영영풀이에 맞는 단어는 'notice'(알아채다, 의식하다)이다.

03 (1) pane 판유리 (2) hill 언덕, 산 (3) twist 돌리다

04 (1) surprisingly 놀랍게도 (2) recently 최근에 (3) carefully 조심스럽게

05 (1) roof 지붕 (2) quickly 빨리 (3) stick 막대기

06 (1) mirror 거울 (2) swallow 삼키다 (3) steam 수증기

[교과서]
Conversation

핵심 Check   p.118~119

1 I wonder what the first plane looked like.
2 ⑤

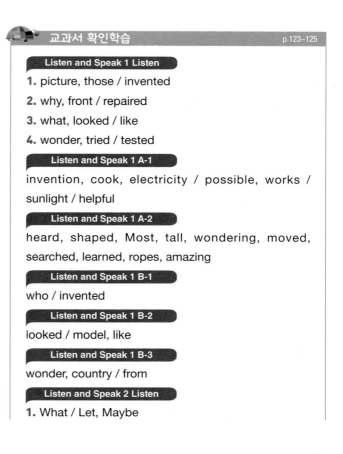

교과서 대화문 익히기

Check(√) True or False   p.120

1 T   2 T   3 F   4 T

교과서 확인학습   p.123~125

Listen and Speak 1 Listen
1. picture, those / invented
2. why, front / repaired
3. what, looked / like
4. wonder, tried / tested

Listen and Speak 1 A-1
invention, cook, electricity / possible, works / sunlight / helpful

Listen and Speak 1 A-2
heard, shaped, Most, tall, wondering, moved, searched, learned, ropes, amazing

Listen and Speak 1 B-1
who / invented

Listen and Speak 1 B-2
looked / model, like

Listen and Speak 1 B-3
wonder, country / from

Listen and Speak 2 Listen
1. What / Let, Maybe

2. How, float / pushes

3. move / see, with

4. pictures

Listen & Speak 2 A-1

Look, quickly / pass, increases / Let, step, made / amazing

Listen & Speak 2 A-2

field, Invention / creative / excited, planning / Good, museum / started

Listen & Speak 2 B-1

What / play

Listen & Speak 2 B-2

with / see, from

Listen & Speak 2 B-3

What / send

Real-Life Zone

these / why, holes / think, maybe, look / possible, must, reasons / look, what / says during, through, thin / crispy, why

Wrap Up 1-2

what, going / sounds, that, Saturdays, what / advertisement, Here / say / says / both, fantastic / what

Wrap Up 3~4

competition / sounds / enter, ideas / when / from / wonder, have / talk, science

---

시험대비 기본평가 p.126

01 I wonder how it works.

02 The invention   03 ⑤

04 It is made when people step on the floor.

01 상대방에게 궁금한 점을 물을 때 "I wonder ~." 또는 "I am wondering ~.", 'I was wondering ~."과 같은 표현을 쓸 수 있다. 이때 '어떻게 작동하는지'라는 목적어는 의문사 how를 이용한 간접의문문을 사용해서 만든다.

02 음식을 요리하기 위해 태양광을 사용하는 건 위 대화 전반에서 이야기하고 있는 'the invention'(그 발명품)이다.

03 "Let me see."는 '잠깐만.', '어디 보자.'의 뜻으로 어떤 것을 기억해 내거나 잠시 생각을 정리할 시간이 필요할 때 사용하는 표현이다. 같은 표현인 "Let me think."를 대신 사용할 수 있다.

04 위 대화의 후반에서 사람들이 바닥을 밟으면 에너지가 만들어진다고 언급되어 있다.

시험대비 실력평가 p.127~128

01 ⓑthinking → think   02 ①   03 steam

04 ②   05 I wonder what they are.   06 ③

07 ③   08 ②   09 ⑤   10 ②, ⑤

11 ④

01 동사 let은 목적보어로 동사원형을 취한다. 따라서 ⓑthinking을 think로 고쳐야 한다.

02 빈칸이 포함된 문장 모두 의문사가 포함된 간접의문문이 쓰였다. 대화의 문맥상 (A) '무엇을 말하는지'(what it says)와 (B) '그것들이 구멍을 가진 이유'(why they have holes)가 들어가는 것이 적절하다.

03 '물이 끓을 때 만들어지는 뜨거운 가스'는 'steam'(수증기)을 의미한다.

04 '여기 있어.'라는 표현은 어떤 것을 상대방에게 건네줄 때, 혹은 무언가가 여기 있다고 말할 때 쓸 수 있는 표현이다. 이 대화에서는 후자의 의미로 사용되었으며 신문에 있는 광고를 찾았다고 말하는 ②에 들어가는 것이 가장 적절하다.

05 대화 상대방에게 궁금한 점을 물을 때 "I wonder ~." 또는 "I am wondering ~."과 같은 표현을 쓸 수 있다. 이때 '그 프로그램들이 무엇인지'라는 목적어는 의문사 what와 대명사 they를 이용해 what they are로 쓸 수 있다.

06 ③ '토요일마다 몇 번 씩 프로그램이 진행되는가'는 위 대화에서 언급되어 있지 않다.

07 (A) 현재완료 구문으로 과거분사가 쓰여야 한다. (B) most는 일반적인 것을, most of는 특정한 것을 가리킬 때 사용한다. (C) 문맥상 가장 큰 Moai는 높이가 20미터라는 문장이 되어야 적절하다. 따라서 비교급이 아니라 최상급이 쓰여야 한다.

08 ② '가장 큰 모아이는 높이가 20미터'라고 언급되어 있다.

09 ⑤의 대화에서 A가 최초의 비행기가 어디서 비행을 시도했는지 궁금하다고 질문했는데, 이에 B는 실험 비행을 100년 전에 했다고 대답했다. 따라서 B의 대답은 문맥상 적절하지 않다.

10 ② 누가 그들과 같이 현장 학습을 가는지는 언급되어 있지 않으며, ⑤ '현장 학습의 계획이 무엇인지'는 역시 언급되지 않았다.

11 대화 후반에 G가 가기 전에 계획을 세우자고 제안했고 B가 승낙했으므로 ④ '현장 학습 계획 세우기'를 할 것으로 추정된다.

서술형 시험대비 p.129

01 (A) when   (B) what

02 He has to talk to Mr. Harrison.

03 (B) – (C) – (A)

04 It employs sunlight to cook food.

05 I was wondering how people moved them long ago.

06 search

07 They moved the stones by using ropes.

01 위 대화의 문맥상, (A) 대회가 언제인지(when), (B) 대회에 출전하기 위해 뭘 해야 하는지(what) 물어보는 질문이 들어가야 한다.

02 대회에 출전하기 위해 B가 무엇을 해야 하는지는 G의 마지막 말에 언급되어 있다.

03 전기를 쓰지 않고 요리를 할 수 있게 도와주는 발명품에 대해 소개하고 있는 B의 말에 상대방은 (B) 그것이 가능하냐고 묻고 어떻게 작동하는지 되묻는 것이 자연스럽다. 이에 (C) 태양광을 이용해 요리를 할 수 있게 만든다고 하자 (A) 캠핑을 갈 때 정말 유용하겠다고 하는 내용이 이어지는 것이 문맥상 가장 자연스럽다.

04 위 대화의 (C)에서 나와 있듯이, 그 발명품은 전기 없이 태양광을 이용해 음식을 요리할 수 있게 한다. employ: 사용하다, 쓰다

05 상대방에게 궁금한 점을 물을 때 "I wonder ~." 또는 "I am wondering ~.", 'I was wondering ~.'과 같은 표현을 쓸 수 있다. 또한 목적어 자리에는 의문사 how를 이용한 목적어 'how people moved them long ago'라고 나열할 수 있다.

06 '무언가를 찾기 위해 주의 깊게 어느 곳을 찾다'라는 영영풀이에 맞는 단어는 search(찾다, 검색하다)이다.

07 위 글의 마지막 문장에 나와 있듯이, 모아이를 만들기 위해 밧줄을 이용했다. by -ing: ~을 함으로써

교과서
Grammar

핵심 Check p.130~131

1 (1) got (2) would   **2** (1) so (2) that

시험대비 기본평가 p.132

01 (1) has → had (2) will → would
   (3) what → that (4) can't → can

02 (1) Jack is so tall that he can touch the ceiling.
   (2) We worked hard so that everything would be ready in time.
   (3) I got up early so that I could catch the first bus.
   (4) She works so hard that she deserves a vacation.

03 (1) If I had longer arms, I could grab that apple.
   (2) If I were[was] in the UK, I could speak English better.

01 (1) 가정법 과거. If S 동사의 과거형 ~, S would(should/could/might) 동사원형. 현재 사실과 반대되는 일이나 상황일

때 사용한다. 현재 그녀는 네 것과 같은 예쁜 드레스가 없어서 울고 있는 것을 의미한다. has를 had로 고치는 것이 적절하다. (2) 가정법 과거. 현재 나는 대통령이 아닌 상황을 묘사하고 있으며 주절의 will을 would로 고치는 것이 적절하다. (3) '~하기 위해서'라는 의미를 표현할 때 'so that S 조동사'를 사용하므로 what을 that으로 고치는 것이 적절하다. (4) 의미상 실수 없이 바이올린을 연주하기 위해 바이올린 연습을 하는 것이므로 can't를 can으로 쓰는 것이 적절하다.

02 (1)과 (4)는 'so 형/부 that S V'의 구문이다. (2)와 (3)은 'S V so that S V'로 'so that S V'는 '~하기 위해서, ~하도록'으로 해석한다.

03 가정법 과거는 현재 사실에 대한 반대를 표현할 때 사용하며 'If S 동사의 과거형 ~, S would/should/could/might 동사원형' 이다. (1) If 절의 동사는 had로 쓰는 것이 적절하고 주절에는 could grab으로 쓰는 것이 적절하다. (2)의 경우 가정법 과거에서 be동사의 과거형은 were로 쓰며 구어체에서는 was도 가능하다. 그러므로 If 절의 동사는 were 또는 was로 쓰고 주절은 could speak으로 쓰는 것이 적절하다.

시험대비 실력평가 p.133~135

01 could gone → could have gone

02 As he is not rich, he does not buy that car.

03 Sit a little closer so that we can have a talk.

04 ①   05 ②   06 ①   07 would

08 ③   09 ④   10 ②   11 ①

12 ①

13 She folded her arms as if she was[were] cold.

14 ⑤   15 ②, ④   16 so as to

17 I got up early in order not to miss the first train.

18 (1) exercised (2) were (3) had   19 ⑤

01 · 내가 시간이 있었더라면 너랑 갈 수 있었을 텐데. 가정법 과거 완료로 과거 사실에 대해 반대되는 상황이나 일을 가정할 때 쓰고 'If S had p.p. ~, S would/should/could/might have p.p.'이므로 could gone을 could have gone으로 쓰는 것이 적절하다.

02 만약 그가 부자라면 그 차를 살 텐데. 보기의 문장은 현재 사실에 대한 반대를 나타내고 있다. 부자가 아니어서 그 차를 사지 않는 것이므로 As를 활용하여 현재시제로 동사를 써야 한다.

03 'so that ~ can'을 활용한 명령문으로 주절 내용은 '좀 더 가까이 앉아라.'이고 부사절은 '이야기하기 위해서'이다.

04 나는 그녀가 나에게 연락할 수 있도록 나의 전화번호를 주었다. so that ~ can은 in order that과 같은 의미로 쓸 수 있으므로 ①처럼 바꿔 쓰는 것이 적절하다.

05 ② 만일 내가 알았더라면 그 일을 하지 않았을 것이다. 가정법

과거완료이므로 would not have done이 오는 것이 적절하다.
① Peter가 Karen에게 데이트 신청하면, 그녀가 승낙할 것이다. ③ 내가 백만 달러가 있다면, 나는 헬리콥터를 살 수 있을 텐데. ④ Diane이 지금 여기 있다면, 그녀는 동의할 텐데. ⑤ 내가 아프지 않다면, 나는 파티에 갈 수 있을 텐데.

06 • 내가 그녀의 이름을 안다면, 너에게 말할 텐데. 가정법 과거 문장으로 'If 주어 동사의 과거형 ~, S would/should/could/might 동사원형 ~'으로 쓰고 현재 사실에 대한 반대되는 일이나 상황을 가정할 때 사용한다.

07 • 내가 너라면, 나는 거기에 혼자 가지 않을 텐데. 가정법 과거는 현재 사실에 대한 반대되는 사실이나 일을 가정할 때 사용하며 빈칸에는 would가 들어가는 것이 적절하다.

08 ③ 우리는 재충전을 위해 휴식이 필요하다. 5개 문장 모두 빈칸 뒤를 '~하기 위해'로 해석한다. 하지만 ③은 to나 in order[so as] to가 들어가고 나머지 4개 문장은 so that이 들어가는 것이 적절하므로 답은 ③이다. ① 다음 학기에 전액 장학금 받으려면 열심히 공부해야 해, ② 내가 볼 수 있도록 그것을 돌려주세요. ④ 자세히 좀 보게 그를 앞으로 데려와 주세요. ⑤ 그는 그들이 그것을 할 수 있도록 새로운 계획을 세웠다.

09 날씨가 좋다면 소풍을 갈 텐데. 가정법 과거 문장으로 'If 주어 동사의 과거형 ~, S would/should/could/might 동사원형 ~'으로 쓰고 현재 사실에 대한 반대되는 일이나 상황을 가정할 때 사용한다. 가정법 과거에 맞춰 ④처럼 쓰는 것이 적절하다.

10 • 그는 가족을 부양하기 위해 열심히 일한다. '~하기 위해'라는 의미를 나타내는 'in order to, in order that'을 쓸 수 있다. ③은 빈칸에 that이 오면 빈칸 뒤에 'S+V'가 나와야 하므로 ②번이 들어가는 것이 적절하다.

11 '내가 지나가도록 옆으로 비켜주겠습니까?'의 의미로 'so that I can pass'는 '~하기 위해서'라고 해석하고 빈칸에 so that ~ can이 들어가는 것이 적절하다.

12 가정법 과거 문장으로 'If 주어 동사의 과거형 ~, S would/should/could/might 동사원형 ~'으로 쓰고 현재 사실에 대한 반대되는 일이나 상황을 가정할 때 사용하므로 ①처럼 쓰는 것이 적절하다.

13 as if를 활용한 가정법 과거 표현으로 주절의 시제에서 반대되는 상황이나 일을 표현할 때 쓴다. 'as if S be동사'에서 be동사는 주어가 3인칭 단수일 경우 was나 were 모두 사용 가능하므로 She folded her arms as if she was(또는 were)로 쓰는 것이 적절하다.

14 ⑤ 그녀는 마치 그녀가 날고 있는 것처럼 느꼈다. 'S V as if 가정법 과거'로 써야 하므로 'She felt as if she were flying.'으로 고치는 것이 적절하다. ① 그녀는 마치 여왕인 듯이 말했다.(as if 가정법 과거. 현재 사실과 반대되는 일이나 상황의 가정) ② 그녀는 몇 주 동안 굶었다는 듯이 다 먹어치웠다.(as if 가정법 과거. 현재 사실과 반대되는 일이나 상황의 가정) ③ 그녀는 내 생각을 읽은 것처럼 말했다.(가정법 과거완료. 과거 사실과 반

대되는 일이나 상황의 가정) ④ 그녀는 마치 유령이라도 봤던 것처럼 보인다.(as if 가정법 과거완료. 과거 사실에 대해 반대되는 일이나 상황의 가정)

15 • 그는 다음날 일찍 일어나기 위해 평소보다 더 일찍 갔다. 'S V so that S V'는 'S V in order that S V'와 'S V in order to 부정사'와 같은 뜻을 지니므로 ②와 ④처럼 쓰는 것이 적절하다.

16 우리는 좋은 자리를 잡기 위해서 일찍 갔다. '~하기 위해'라는 표현으로 'so that S V', 'in order to 동사원형', 'so as to 동사원형' 등이 있는데 괄호에 so를 사용하라고 나와 있고 빈칸 뒤에 동사원형이 있기 때문에 'so as to'가 빈칸에 오는 것이 적절하다.

17 괄호 안에 주어진 in order to를 이용하여 '~하기 위해'를 부정할 때 to 앞에 not을 써서 표현하므로 'I got up early in order not to miss the first train.'으로 영작하는 것이 적절하다.

18 어법에 맞게 배열하면 • If he exercised harder, he would be a good athlete. • If you were me, what would you do? • If I had not been sick, I would have gone on a trip together yesterday.

19 • 그 때 그는 박사 학위를 취득하기 위해 존스 홉킨스 대학에 입학했다. • 우리는 시험에 통과하기 위해 지난밤에 공부했다. 빈칸 뒤의 내용은 '~하기 위해'로 해석 되므로 'so that S V'와 같은 의미를 지닌 'in order to', 'in order that', 'so as to' 등이 올 수 있다. 빈칸 뒤에 바로 동사원형이 오기 때문에 ⑤가 오는 것이 적절하다.

서술형 시험대비
p.136~137

01 If I knew his phone number, I would call him.

02 as if I were[was] her younger brother

03 She goes jogging every morning to stay healthy. / She goes jogging every morning so as to stay healthy. / She goes jogging every morning in order to stay healthy. / She goes jogging every morning in order that she can[may] stay healthy.

04 If she studied harder, she could pass the test.

05 If she felt well, she would visit her friend's house.

06 so as to   07 so that

08 In order not to oversleep, I set the alarm for six o'clock.

09 They took a taxi not to waste time. / They took a taxi in order not to waste time. / They took a taxi so as not to waste time.

10 If Bob worked in the team, he wouldn't be so stressed.

11 (1) I would call for help   (2) If I had a boat
   (3) it would have reached Mars
   (4) If I were[was] a bird

12 If I didn't have any classes today, I would go to

01 가정법 과거는 현재 사실에 대해 반대되는 상황이나 일을 가정할 때 사용하고 'If S 동사의 과거형 ~, S would/should/could/might 동사원형'으로 쓴다.

02 그녀는 마치 내가 그녀의 남동생인 것처럼 나를 도와준다. 빈칸이 속한 문장은 가정법 과거 문장으로 현재 사실에 대해 반대되는 일이나 상황을 표현할 때 쓴다. 문제에서 as if를 활용하라고 했으므로 'S V as if 가정법 과거'에 맞춰 쓰면 'as if I were her younger brother.'라고 쓰는 것이 적절하다.

03 그녀는 건강을 유지하기 위해 매일 아침 조깅을 한다. '~하기 위해서'라는 표현은 'to 동사원형', 'so as to 동사원형', 'in order to 동사원형', 'in order that S V' 등이 있다.

04 • 그녀는 더 열심히 공부한다. • 그녀는 시험에 통과할 수 있다. • 만약 그녀가 더 열심히 공부한다면 시험에 통과할 텐데. 가정법 과거는 'If S 동사의 과거형 ~, S would/should/could/might 동사원형'이고 현재 사실에 대한 반대되는 상황이나 일을 가정할 때 사용한다.

05 • 그녀는 그녀의 친구 집에 방문하고 싶지만, 그녀는 몸 상태가 좋지 않다. 주어진 문장은 친구 집에 방문하고 싶지만 현재 몸 상태가 좋지 않아 가지 않는 것이므로 'If she felt well, she would visit her friend's house.'라는 가정법 과거 문장을 쓰는 것이 적절하다.

06 나는 그가 나에게 약간의 관심이라도 가지고 있는지를 알기 위해 그에게 데이트 신청을 했다. 'in order to'는 'in order that', 'so that', 'so as to'와 같고 빈칸 뒤에 know라는 동사가 있으므로 so as to를 쓰는 것이 적절하다.

07 • 그녀를 만나기 위해 나는 한 시간 동안 기다렸다. • 나의 아기는 너무 작게 태어나서 2주 동안 인큐베이터에서 지냈다. 첫 번째 문장은 'S V ~ so that S V'로 so that 종속절 문장은 '~하기 위해서'로 해석하고, 두 번째 문장은 'so 형용사 that S V'로 '너무 ~해서 …하다'로 해석한다. 그러므로 빈칸에는 so와 that이 들어가는 것이 적절하다.

08 • 늦잠을 자지 않기 위해, 나는 6시에 알람을 맞췄다. 주절의 행동에 대한 목적의 의미를 지닌 'in order to 동사원형'은 주절에서 '내'가 알람을 설정한 이유가 늦잠을 자지 않기 위해이므로 'In order not to oversleep'으로 고쳐 쓰는 것이 적절하다.

09 '~하지 않기 위해'를 표현할 때 'to부정사', 'in order to', 'so as to' 등을 쓸 수 있고 부정을 나타내기 위하여 to부정사 앞에 not을 붙여 쓰는 것이 적절하다.

10 가정법 과거는 'If S 동사의 과거형 ~, S would/should/could/might 동사원형'으로 쓰므로 'If Bob worked in the team, he wouldn't be so stressed.'로 쓰는 것이 적절하다.

11 가정법 과거로 현재 사실에 대한 반대되는 상황이나 일을 가정할 때 쓰는 표현이다. 그러므로 (1)은 'I would call you help', (2)는 'If I had a boat', (3)은 가정법 과거완료로 과

12 가정법 과거는 현재 사실에 대한 반대되는 상황이나 일을 가정할 때 사용하며 'If S 동사의 과거형 ~, S would/should/could/might 동사원형'으로 쓰므로 괄호 안의 단어를 활용하여 'If I didn't have any classes today, I would go to an amusement park.'로 영작하는 것이 적절하다.

13 '~하기 위해서'라는 표현으로 in order to를 쓰고 부정의 경우 to 앞에 not을 붙여 'in order not to 동사원형'으로 쓰는 것이 적절하다.

거 사실에 대한 반대되는 상황이나 일을 가정할 때 쓰는 표현이다. 'it would have reached Mars', (4)는 'If I were(또는 was) a bird'로 쓰는 것이 적절하다.

Reading 교과서

확인문제   p.138

1 T 2 F 3 T 4 F 5 T 6 F

확인문제   p.139

1 T 2 F 3 T 4 F 5 T 6 F

교과서 확인학습 A   p.140~141

01 Hidden	02 have seen recently
03 good, bad	04 in your sock
05 for a button	06 everywhere
07 so small	
08 well hidden, make your life safe	
09 Take	10 Look at
11 a small hole	12 why it is there
13 help save lives	14 put, in
15 swallow them	16 stop their breathing
17 putting a small hole	18 pass through
19 play a helpful role	20 with a lid, noticed
21 for safety	
22 When cooking, builds up	23 boil over
24 keeps, from coming	25 Have, been
26 Wasn't it exciting	27 Surprisingly
28 are made up of	29 in the middle pane
30 balances	
31 Without, in an emergency	
32 prevents, from fogging up	33 that have
34 why it is there	
35 to make your life safer	

1 Hidden Holes

2 Think about a hole that you have seen recently.

3 Was it a good hole or a bad hole?

4 If it was a hole in your sock, it was bad.

5 If it was a hole in your shirt for a button, it was good.

6 There are holes everywhere.

7 Some are so small you may not even notice them.

8 They are well hidden, but many of these small holes are very important and make your life safe.

9 Take a pen.

10 Look at it carefully.

11 Do you see a small hole in the cap?

12 Do you know why it is there?

13 The hole in a pen cap can help save lives.

14 People, especially children, often put small things like pen caps in their mouths.

15 Sometimes they even swallow them.

16 This can stop their breathing and cause death.

17 A famous pen company started putting a small hole in their pen caps.

18 The hole in the cap lets air pass through and has saved lives.

19 If you look around, you will see other holes that play a helpful role in your life.

20 If you have ever cooked anything in a pot with a lid, perhaps you noticed a small hole in the lid.

21 This hole, too, is there for safety.

22 When cooking something in a pot with a lid, the pressure inside the pot builds up.

23 The water inside would quickly boil over if the lid did not have that hole.

24 The hole lets steam out and keeps the water from coming out.

25 Have you ever been on an airplane?

26 Wasn't it exciting to look out the window and see the world below?

27 Surprisingly, there was a small hole in your window.

28 Airplane windows are made up of three panes.

29 There is a hole in the middle pane.

30 It balances the air pressure.

31 Without this little hole, airplane windows might break in an emergency.

32 The hole also prevents the window from fogging up so that you can enjoy that fantastic view.

33 There are many more products that have small hidden holes.

34 In the future, when you see a little hole in something, ask yourself why it is there.

35 Maybe it is the result of a careful design to make your life safer.

01 ④	02 ②	03 ⑤	04 ⑤
05 ④	06 ②	07 safety	08 ①, ⑤
09 ②, ③	10 ④	11 ①, ②	

12 will see → see

13 (A) other (B) cooking (C) out   14 part

15 ④   16 ③

17 Some are so small you may not even notice them.

18 safely → safe   19 ⑤

20 ③   21 ③   22 ③

23 The hole in the middle pane

01 ④번 다음 문장의 Some에 주목한다. 주어진 문장의 holes 중의 어떤 것들을 가리키는 것이므로 ④번이 적절하다.

02 이 글은 '구멍은 어디에나 있고, 작고 숨겨져 있어도 많은 구멍들이 매우 중요하다'는 내용의 글이므로, 제목으로는 ②번 '숨겨진 그러나 중요한 구멍들'이 적절하다.

03 이 작은 구멍들 중 많은 것들이 매우 중요하고 '여러분의 삶을 안전하게 해 준다.'

04 ⑤는 '유명한 펜 회사'를 가리키고, 나머지는 다 '아이들'을 가리킨다.

05 sometimes = occasionally = once in a while = from time to time = (every) now and then: 가끔, ④ frequently: 자주, 흔히

06 이 글은 '사람들, 특히 아이들은 종종 펜 뚜껑 같은 작은 것들을 그들의 입에 넣고 삼키기도 하는데 이것은 그들의 호흡을 막고 죽음을 초래할 수도 있기 때문에, 펜 뚜껑에 작은 구멍을 넣었고 그 구멍은 공기를 통하게 해 주고 생명들을 구했다'는 내용의 글이므로, 주제로는 ②번 '펜 뚜껑에 있는 구멍의 역할'이 적절하다.

07 safety: 안전(함), 당신이 해나 위험으로부터 안전한 상태

08 (A)와 ①, ⑤: 관계대명사, ② 명사절을 이끄는 접속사, ③ [수량·정도를 나타내는 말을 한정하여] 그만큼, 그렇게(so), 그 정도로(부사), ④ [동격절을 이끌어] ~이라는, ~하다는(접속사)

09 keep/stop/prevent A from -ing: A가 ~하는 것을 막다, ① 보호하다, ④ 부인하다 ⑤ 손상을 주다, 피해를 입히다

10 ⓐ와 ②: 경험 용법, ①과 ③ 완료 용법, ④ 계속 용법, ⑤ 결과 용법

11 be made up of = be composed of = consist of: ~로 구성되다, consist of는 수동태로 쓸 수 없다. ③ consist in: ~에

있다, ④ deal with: ~을 다루다

12 '때'를 나타내는 부사절에서는 현재시제가 미래시제를 대신하기 때문에, will see를 see로 고치는 것이 적절하다.

13 (A) 'another+단수명사'이므로 other가 적절하다. (B) 'when you cook ~'에서 주어가 일반인이므로 생략하고 동사를 분사로 바꾼 분사구문이므로 cooking이 적절하다. (C) 냄비 안쪽의 압력이 상승할 때 그 구멍이 수증기를 '나가게' 해 주는 것이므로 out이 적절하다.

14 play a role = play a part: 역할을 하다

15 ⓑ 냄비 '안쪽'의 압력이 상승한다고 해야 하므로 inside가 적절하다. ⓒ 물이 밖으로 넘치는 것을 '막아 준다'고 해야 하므로 from이 적절하다. keep A from -ing: A가 ~하는 것을 막다

16 (B)의 it이 주어진 글의 a small hole in the cap을 가리키므로 제일 먼저 오고 (C)는 (B)의 예에 해당하므로 (B) 다음에 (C)가 이어지고 (A)의 첫 문장은 (C)의 마지막 문장의 결과에 해당하므로 (C) 다음에 (A)가 와야 한다. 그러므로 (B)-(C)-(A)의 순서가 적절하다.

17 so ... that: 너무 …해서 ~하다, 'you' 앞에 접속사 'that'을 생략할 수 있다.

18 make의 목적격보어에 해당하므로 형용사 'safe'로 고치는 것이 적절하다.

19 '이 세상에 몇 종류의 구멍들이 있는지'는 대답할 수 없다. ① No, it isn't. ② Yes, it is. ③ We can find holes everywhere. ④ No, they aren't.

20 ⓐ look at: ~을 보다, look for: ~을 찾다, ⓑ put A in B: A를 B에 넣다

21 (A)와 ③: 구하다, ① (나중에 쓰거나 하려고) 남겨 두다[아끼다], ② (특히 무엇을 사거나 하기 위해) (돈을) 모으다, 저축하다, ④ 절약하다, (낭비하지 않고) 아끼다, ⑤ 저장하다

22 ⓐ와 ③: 가주어, ① 가목적어, ② 비인칭 주어, ④ (이미 알고 있거나 진행 중인 사실·상황을 가리켜) 그것, ⑤ It is ~ that의 구문으로, 문장의 어떤 부분을 강조할 때 쓰는 대명사

23 '중간 유리판에 있는 구멍'을 가리킨다.

🦉 서술형 시험대비
p.148~149

01 hidden

02 the hole that you have seen recently

03 Some are so small that you may not even notice them.

04 (A) small　(B) important　(C) safe

05 you cook

06 The water inside doesn't quickly boil over as the lid has that hole.

07 (A) small hole　(B) steam out

08 the small hole

09 The hole in a pen cap can help save lives.

10 to pass

11 (A) breathing　(B) air

12 (A) see　(B) pressure　(C) emergency

13 it were[was] not for

14 (A) three panes　(B) air pressure

---

01 그것들은 잘 '숨겨져 있다'고 해야 하므로, 수동태 문장을 나타내기 위해 과거분사 'hidden'으로 쓰는 것이 적절하다.

02 '여러분이 최근에 본 구멍'을 가리킨다.

03 so ~ that...: 너무 ~해서 그 결과 …하다, 'you' 앞에 접속사 'that'이 생략되었다.

04 여러분은 어디에서나 구멍을 발견할 수 있고 그것들 중의 어떤 것들은 너무 '작아서' 인지할 수 없다. 그러나 이 작은 구멍들 중 많은 것들이 매우 '중요한' 것들이고 그것들 덕분에 여러분의 삶이 '안전해'진다.

05 'When cooking ~'은 접속사를 그대로 유지한 분사구문으로 'When you cook ~'에서 주어가 일반인이므로 생략하고 동사를 분사로 바꾼 형태이다.

06 가정법 과거(if+주어+동사(과거형), 주어+과거형 조동사+동사원형)는 직설법 현재로 고치는 것이 적절하다.

07 여러분이 뚜껑 있는 냄비에 어떤 것을 요리할 때 뚜껑에 있는 작은 구멍이 '수증기를 나가게' 해 주고 물이 밖으로 넘치는 것을 막아 주기 때문에, 냄비 안의 물은 금방 끓어 넘치지 않는다.

08 '작은 구멍'을 가리킨다.

09 in a pen cap이 The hole을 수식하도록 쓰는 것이 적절하다. help 다음에는 원형부정사를 쓸 수 있다.

10 let+목적어+원형부정사 = allow+목적어+to부정사

11 어떤 사람이 펜 뚜껑을 삼키면, 그것은 그 사람의 '호흡'을 막고 죽음을 초래할 수도 있다. 그러나 만약 펜 뚜껑에 구멍이 있으면, 그것이 '공기'를 통하게 해 주어 생명을 구할 수 있다.

12 (A) 'to look'과 병렬구문을 이루도록 '(to) see'가 적절하다. (B) '기압'의 균형을 맞춰 준다고 해야 하므로, pressure로 쓰는 것이 적절하다. air pressure: 기압, pleasure: 기쁨, 즐거움, (C) 비행기 창문은 '비상시'에 깨질 수 있다고 해야 하므로 emergency가 적절하다. emergency: 비상(사태), emergence: 출현, 발생

13 Without = If it were[was] not for = But for: ~이 없다면

14 비행기 창문은 '세 개의 유리판'으로 구성되어 있고, 그 중간 유리판에 있는 구멍이 '기압'의 균형을 맞춰 준다.

01 probably　　**02** ③　　　　**03** ②

04 (1) Wrap it up carefully to protect against breakage.

(2) Some of us are often told to keep our talents well hidden.

05 ③　　　　**06** ②　　　　**07** ④

08 B will call the Einstein Science Park to ask what time they start.

09 It takes place in Einstein Hall 101.　　**10** ⑤

11 ④　　　　**12** ⑤　　　　**13** the Invention Museum

14 ⑤　　　　**15** I went to bed early so that

16 ②

17 If I were Robinson Crusoe, I would make a boat to go fishing.

18 She loves her dogs as if they were her kids.

19 so　　**20** ①, ④　　**21** a button　　**22** small

23 in the lid　　**24** ③　　　**25** ④　　　**26** ③

27 ②

28 In 1755, William Cullen invented the first form of the refrigerator.

29 will → would

---

01 repair(수리하다)와 mend(수선하다, 고치다)는 동의어 관계에 있는 단어들이다. 따라서 perhaps(아마도, 어쩌면)과 동의어 관계에 있는 단어는 probably(아마도)이다.

02 ③ look out은 '조심하다, 주의하다, 신경 쓰다'라는 뜻으로 사용되었다.

03 '팔기 위해 만든 어떤 것, 보통 산업적 과정을 통해 만들어진 어떤 것'이라는 뜻을 가진 영영풀이가 가리키는 것은 ② product(생산물, 상품)이다.

04 (1) carefully: 조심스럽게 / breakage: 파손 / wrap up: 포장하다 (2) well hidden: 잘 숨긴

05 주어진 문장에서 notice는 '알아채다, 인식하다'라는 뜻으로 사용되었다. ③ '주사 맞은 후에 붉어짐과 부풀어짐을 알아챌지도 모른다.'라는 문장에서 쓰임이 같다. ① take notice of: ~을 신경 쓰다 ② 통지 ④ 공고문 ⑤ 통지, 예고

06 주어진 문장은 '소금이 아동 비만에 역할을 할 수도 있다.'는 내용으로, ② play a role(역할을 하다)이 빈칸에 가장 적절하다.

07 (A) 전치사 about은 목적어로 명사형을 취한다. 따라서 동명사 going이 적절하다. (B) 특별한 프로그램이 과거가 아닌 현재에도 존재하는 것이므로 과거형이 아니라 현재형을 쓴다. (C) '신문에 나온 광고가 뭐라고 하니?'라는 문장이므로 현재형이 적절하다.

08 대화에서 B의 마지막 말에 언급되어 있듯이, 아인슈타인 과학 공원에 연락을 해서 몇 시에 프로그램이 시작하는지 물어볼 것이다.

09 대화에서 B의 말에서 언급되었듯이, 아인슈타인 홀 101(Einstein Hall 101)에서 진행된다고 한다.

10 ⑤ "I wonder ~." 또는 "I am wondering ~.", "I was wondering ~."과 같은 표현은 대화 상대방에게 궁금한 점을 물을 때 사용한다.

11 '좋은 생각이야.'라는 문장은 상대방이 어떤 의견을 냈을 때 동의하거나 승낙하는 표현이다. 따라서 G가 계획을 짜자고 제안한 문장 다음인 ④에 들어가는 것이 문맥상 가장 적절하다.

12 위 대화에서 내일 갈 현장 학습에 대해서 이야기하고 있고 같이 현장 학습 계획을 짜기로 했으므로, G의 심정으로 가장 적절한 것은 ⑤ excited(신난, 흥분한)이다.

13 '그것은 많은 창의적인 발명품을 갖고 있다고 들었어'라는 문장에서 그것이 가리키는 것은 앞서 언급한 'the Invention Museum'이다.

14 • 만약 현대의 최고의 록 가수가 그 혹은 그녀의 다음 곡을 인터넷상에 올리면, 그것은 2천만 객석을 갖춘 극장에서 연주되는 것처럼 연주될 수 있을 텐데. 가정법 과거는 현재 사실에 대한 반대되는 일 또는 상황을 가정할 때 사용하고 'If S 동사의 과거형 ~, S would/should/could/might 동사원형'으로 쓰므로 빈칸에는 be가 들어가는 것이 적절하다.

15 so가 들어가는 '~하기 위해서'라는 표현은 'so as to 동사원형'과 'so that S V'가 있다. 제시된 영어 문장은 'I wouldn't be tired this morning'이므로 빈칸에 so that이 나와야 하며 빈칸에 해당하는 곳에는 'I went to bed early'가 들어가는 것이 적절하다.

16 ② 나는 너무 즐거워서 잠을 잘 수 없었다. 'so that' 바로 앞에 '콤마(,)'가 있으면 보통 결과의 부사절을 이끈다. 그러므로 해석도 'S가 V해서 that절하다.'로 해석하므로 답으로 ②번이 적절하다. ① 나는 그 어린 여자애가 잘 볼 수 있도록 의자 위에 세웠다. ③ 그 범인은 아무도 그를 찾을 수 없도록 도망갔다. ④ 우리는 우리가 말하는 것보다 두 배만큼 들을 수 있기 위해서 두 개의 귀와 하나의 입을 가지고 있다. ⑤ 제인은 자신의 눈으로 무슨 일이 있었는지 보기 위해서 여기에 왔다.

17 가정법 과거는 'If S 동사의 과거형 ~, S would/should/could/might 동사원형'으로 현재 사실에 반대되는 상황이나 일을 가정할 때 사용한다. 그러므로 어법에 맞게 배열하면 If I were Robinson Crusoe, I would make a boat to go fishing.으로 쓰는 것이 적절하다.

18 as if를 활용한 가정법 과거는 'S V as if S 동사의 과거형 ~'이며 주절에 쓰인 동사의 시제에 반대되는 상황이나 일을 말하고자 할 때 사용한다. She loves her dogs as if they were her kids.로 쓰는 것이 적절하다.

19 영작하면, My friend worked hard so that his mother might enjoy her old age.

20 ⓐ와 ①과 ④: 경험 용법, ② 계속 용법, ③과 ⑤ 완료 용법

21 만약 구멍이 '단추'를 위해 셔츠에 있다면, 그것은 좋은 구멍이다.

22 어떤 구멍들은 여러분이 인지하기에는 너무 '작기' 때문이다.

23 there: 뚜껑에

24 뚜껑이 '있는' 냄비에 무언가를 요리할 때, 냄비 안쪽의 압력이 상승한다.

25 주어진 문장의 the middle pane에 주목한다. ④번 앞 문장의 three panes 중 '중간 유리판'을 가리키는 것이므로 ④번이 적절하다.

26 이 글은 '비행기 창문 중간 유리판에 있는 구멍이 기압의 균형을 맞춰 주고 그 구멍 또한, 멋진 경치를 즐길 수 있도록 창문에 김이 서리는 것을 막아 준다'는 내용의 글이므로, 제목으로는 ③번 '가운데 유리에 있는 구멍은 무엇을 하나요?'가 적절하다.

27 '비행기 창문이 왜 세 개의 유리판으로 구성되어 있는지'는 대답할 수 없다. ① They consist of three panes. ③ It is in the middle pane. ④ No. If it were not for a small hole in the airplane windows, airplane windows might break in an emergency. ⑤ A small hole in the middle pane does.

28 'William Cullen이 1755년에 냉장고의 최초 형태를 발명한 것'을 가리킨다.

29 가정법 과거(if+주어+동사(과거형), 주어+과거형 조동사+동사원형)이므로, 'will'을 'would'로 고치는 것이 적절하다.

01 ④　　02 ⑤　　03 ③

04 steam coming out through the holes

05 So that's why they have holes!

06 That would be really helpful when you go camping.

07 ③　　08 ①

09 I wonder what I have to do to enter the competition.

10 ③　　11 so that 또는 in order that

12 (1) He talks as if he were a millionaire.

　(2) He talked as if he were a millionaire.

13 ③

14 (1) would take a picture

　(2) If I had one unbroken vase

15 I gave her my phone number so that she could contact me.

16 ②　　17 ①, ②, ④　　18 ④

19 The hole lets steam out and keeps the water from coming out.

20 ②　　21 With → Without

22 (A) the hole　(B) fog up　23 ③

01 '공기를 폐 속으로 들여마시고 내뱉는 과정'이라는 영영풀이가 가리키는 것은 ④ breathing(호흡, 숨)이다.

02 '의사들은 허리 통증이 나쁜 자세의 결과라고 말한다.'라는 문장에 들어갈 단어는 ⑤ the result of(~의 결과)가 가장 적절하다.

03 (A)와 ③의 must는 '~임에 틀림없다'의 뜻으로 추측을 나타낸다.

04 (B)that은 앞에서 언급된 단수 명사, 구 또는 절을 가리킨다. 따라서 같은 문장 안에서 쓰인 steam coming out through the holes가 대명사 that이 가리키는 명사(구)이다.

05 의문사 why를 이용한 간접의문문을 사용해 쓸 수 있다. 이때 'that's why they have holes!'는 'that is the reason why they have holes!'의 줄임말이다.

06 helpful: 도움이 되는 / go camping: 캠핑을 가다

07 ③ ⓒthat이 가리키는 것은 앞 문장('It can help us cook without electricity.') 전체이다. 나머지는 모두 ⓐthis invention을 가리킨다.

08 (A)는 '어디 보자'라는 의미로, 의도하는 것은 ① '생각할 시간 요청하기'이다.

09 상대방에게 궁금한 점을 물을 때 "I wonder ~."를 쓰는데, 이때 wonder의 목적어로 의문사를 포함한 간접의문문을 취하기도 한다.

10 ③ '대회의 1등에게 주어지는 상은 무엇인가?'는 대화에서 언급되지 않았다.

11 • 나는 더 많은 짐을 가져가기 위해 차로 갈 것이다. • 우리는 우리가 전화했다는 것을 그가 알 수 있도록 그의 이웃에게 메시지를 남겼다. 두 문장 모두 빈칸 뒤에 목적의 의미를 나타내고, 뒤에 주어와 동사가 있으므로 절을 이끄는 so that이나 in order that을 쓰는 것이 적절하다.

12 as if를 활용한 가정법 과거는 'S V as if S 동사의 과거형 ~'이며 주절에 쓰인 동사의 시제에 반대되는 상황이나 일을 말하고자 할 때 사용한다. (1)은 우리말 해석에 현재시제로 되어 있으므로 'He talks as if he were a millionaire.'로 영작하는 것이 적절하다. (2) 우리말 해석에 과거 시제로 되어 있으므로 'He talked as if he were a millionaire.'로 영작하는 것이 적절하다.

13 ③ 집 근처에 있는 상점은 너무 사람이 많아서 나는 다른 상점에 가야 했다. 'so 형용사 that S V'는 '너무 ~해서 …하다'로 해석되므로 나머지 넷과 다른 의미를 지닌다. ① 나는 당신이 보고서를 이해할 수 있도록 정확히 썼다. ② 이들 목표를 달성하려면 팀워크가 요구된다. ④ 몸매를 가꾸기 위해 헬스 클럽에 등록했다. ⑤ 훈련이 효율적으로 되도록 하려면 체계적으로 계획을 세워야 한다.

14 가정법 과거는 현재 사실에 대한 반대되는 상황이나 일을 표현할 때 사용하고 'If S 동사의 과거형 ~, S would/should/could/

31

might 동사원형'이다.

15 주어진 so that을 활용하여 '~하기 위해서'라는 문장을 영작할 때 'S V so that S can/could V'로 쓴다. so that 뒤에는 목적의 내용이 나오므로 'I gave her my phone number so that she could contact me.'라고 영작하는 것이 적절하다.

16 주어진 문장의 it과 there에 주목한다. 각각 ②번 앞 문장의 a small hole과 in the cap을 받고 있으므로 ②번이 적절하다.

17 ⓐ와 ①, ②, ④: 동명사, ③, ⑤ 현재분사

18 '펜 뚜껑을 만들기 위해 사용되는 흔한 재료'는 알 수 없다. ① To help save lives. ② Small things like pen caps. ③ A famous pen company. ⑤ To let air pass through.

19 keep A from -ing: A가 ~하는 것을 막다

20 이 글은 '뚜껑이 있는 냄비에 무언가를 요리할 때 냄비 안쪽의 압력이 상승하는데, 만약 뚜껑에 구멍이 없다면 그 안의 물은 금방 끓어 넘칠 것이지만 그 구멍 덕분에 수증기는 나가고 물이 밖으로 넘치지 않는다.'는 내용의 글이므로, 주제로는 ②번 '냄비 뚜껑에 있는 작은 구멍의 역할'이 적절하다.

21 이 작은 구멍이 '없다면', 비행기 창문은 비상시에 깨질 수도 있다고 해야 하므로, With를 Without으로 고치는 것이 적절하다.

22 비행기 창문의 중간 유리판에 '구멍'이 없다면, 창문에 '김이 서려' 당신은 비행기에서 멋진 경치를 즐길 수 없을 것이다. fog up 김이 서리다(자동사 또는 타동사 둘 다로 쓰일 수 있다.)

23 비행기 창문은 세 개의 유리판으로 구성되어 있는데, 그 '중간 유리판'에 구멍이 있다.

서술형 실전문제 <small>p.160~161</small>

01 They are classmates.

02 B heard that it has a lot of creative inventions.

03 The tallest Moai is 20 meters tall, and is a human-shaped stone.

04 He (or She) found out by searching the Internet.

05 If I exercised every day, I could lose weight.

06 Think as if you were in their place.

07 I worked hard so that I could succeed. 또는 I worked hard so as to succeed. / I worked hard in order that I could succeed. 또는 I worked hard in order to succeed.

08 He talked as if he had seen a ghost last night.

09 Do you know why it is there?

10 a famous pen company

11 (A) pass through and (B) save

12 (A) on (B) a little (C) safer

13 to enjoy

---

01 대화의 내용으로 미루어 볼 때 두 화자는 학급 친구이다.

02 위 대화의 내용에 따르면, B는 발명 박물관에 많은 창의적인 발명품들이 있다고 들었다고 한다.

03 위 지문에 따르면 가장 큰 모아이는 높이가 20미터이고 인간 형태의 돌이라고 한다.

04 화자가 어떻게 모아이를 옮겼는지 찾은 방법은 지문의 후반부에 언급되어 있다.

05 나는 매일 운동하면서 살을 빼고 싶다. 그러나 매일 하기는 쉽지 않다. 바람과 달리 현재 매일 운동을 해서 살을 빼기 어려운 상태의 아쉬움을 나타내고 있으므로 가정법 과거 문장으로 표현할 수 있다.

06 나는 '부자가 가난한 사람을 도와주어야 한다.'는 의견에 동의해. 그러나 내 친구 Joel은 내 생각에 동의하지 않아. 이 경우, 나는 Joel에게 '입장을 바꿔 놓고 생각해 봐.'라고 말할 수 있다.

07 • 나는 열심히 일했다. • 나는 성공할 수 있었다. 목적의 의미를 나타내면서 so와 in을 활용하여 한 문장으로 만들 때 that과 to 부정사를 이용하여 쓸 수 있다. so that과 in order that을 쓸 때는 that 뒤에 목적의 의미를 나타내는 절을 써서 한 문장으로 만드는 것이 적절하고, so as to, in order to를 사용할 때는 to 부정사 뒤에 목적의 의미를 나타내는 동사원형을 써서 한 문장으로 만드는 것이 적절하다.

08 • 영작하면, He talked as if he had seen a ghost last night.

09 know의 목적어 자리에 간접의문문(의문사+주어+동사)인 'why it is there'의 어순으로 쓰는 것이 적절하다.

10 '유명한 펜 회사'를 가리킨다.

11 만약 어떤 사람이 펜 뚜껑을 삼키면 구멍이 공기를 '통하게' 해 주어 생명을 '구하게' 하려고 펜 뚜껑에 작은 구멍이 있다.

12 (A) '비행기를 타 본 적이 있는가?'라고 해야 하므로 on이 적절하다. have been to: ~에 가 본 적이 있다(경험 용법), ~에 다녀왔다(완료 용법) (B) '어떤 물건에서 작은 구멍을 본다면'이라고 해야 하므로 a little이 적절하다. a few+복수 명사: 약간의 ~, (C) make의 목적격보어에 '형용사'를 써야 하므로 safer가 적절하다.

13 목적(~할 수 있도록)을 나타내는 'so that ... can'을 부사적 용법(목적)의 to부정사로 고치는 것이 적절하다.

창의사고력 서술형 문제 <small>p.162</small>

|모범답안|

01 We use it every day so that we can talk to people who are far away from us. / Alexander Bell invented the first practical form of the telephone. / If we did not have telephones, / we would not be able to have a chat with friends living in another city.

02 (A) cool and fresh   (B) William Cullen
   (C) a necessary part of modern life   (D) ice cream

단원별 모의고사
p.163~167

01 ③   02 ④

03 (1) prevent, from   (2) in the future

04 When people pass by, the number increases.

05 amount   06 ③   07 ⑤

08 It's because the little holes make the crackersthin and crispy.

09 (C) – (B) – (A)

10 an advertisement in the newspaper

11 They have the Smart Design Show and the International Drone Show.

12 ②

13 (1) 없음   (2) can't → can
   (3) such → so   (4) what → that

14 ①   15 ③

16 If you were in my situation

17 so that   18 I shut my eyes in order to see.

19 so that he could get some fresh air / so as to get some fresh air

20 (1) If Jane were(또는 was) good at singing
   (2) If an idol group came to my school

21 so that, could   22 ②, ④

23 No, they aren't. If it is a hole in your sock, it is bad[a bad hole]. 또는 If a hole is in your sock, it is bad[a bad hole]. 또는 If there is a hole in your sock, it is bad[a bad hole].

24 in the cap 25 ③   26 ②   27 ⑤

28 ask yourself why it is there   29 ①, ③

01 '어느 쪽으로도 치우치지 않는 위치에 있거나 혹은 어떤 것을 이 위치에 놓다'라는 영영풀이가 가리키는 것은 ③ balance (균형을 잡다)이다.

02 주어진 문장은 '네가 즉시 돌아온다면 아마 더 좋을 것이다.'라는 의미로, 따라서 빈칸에는 ④ perhaps(아마도)가 가장 적절하다.

03 (1) prevent A from A가 ~하는 것을 막다 (2) in the future 미래에

04 pass by: 지나가다 / increase: 증가하다

05 '어떤 것이 많은가 적은가의 정도; 어떤 것이 얼마나 있는지의 정도'라는 뜻을 가진 영영풀이가 가리키는 것은 amount(양, 총량)이다.

06 나머지는 모두 생각할 시간을 요청하는 표현이지만 ③ Let me check은 '확인해 보자'라는 뜻을 갖는 문장이다.

07 위 대화에서 B와 G는 왜 크래커에 구멍이 있는지 궁금해서 인터넷 서치를 통해 이유를 찾다가 그 이유를 알게 되었다. 따라서 ⑤ curious(궁금한) → satisfied(만족스러운)가 B와 G의 심경 변화로 가장 적절하다.

08 왜 크래커가 작은 구멍을 갖고 있는지는 B와 G의 대화 후반에 직접 언급되어 있다.

09 대화 시작에 G는 내일 발명 박물관으로 현장 학습을 간다고 말한다. 상대방은 (C)에서 박물관을 그것이라고 가리키며 많은 창의적인 발명품이 있다고 들었다고 말한다. 이어서 다시 G는 신난다고 말하면서 내일 현장 학습을 위한 계획을 세우자고 제안하고, (A)에서 제안을 받아들이는 순서로 이어지는 것이 문맥상 가장 적절하다.

10 it은 단수 명사를 대신하는 인칭대명사로, 이 대화에서는 앞선 문장에서 언급된 'an advertisement in the newspaper'를 가리킨다.

11 '아인슈타인 과학 공원이 무슨 프로그램을 운영하느냐?'는 질문에 대한 답은 B의 대답에서 찾을 수 있다.

12 ②에서 A가 '어떻게 이 기차가 움직이기 시작할까?'라고 물었고 이에 B는 '잠시만, 넌 이거 탈 수 있어.'(Just a moment… I think you can take it.)라고 말하는데 이는 문맥상 어색한 대화가 된다.

13 (1) Olivia는 건강을 유지하기 위해 매일 운동을 한다. (2) 그 프로젝트를 제시간에 끝내기 위해 Joel은 열심히 일하는 중이다. so that 뒤의 내용은 주절의 내용을 위한 목적이 나와야 의미상 적절하므로 can't가 아닌 can이 적절하다. (3) 나는 그녀가 지나갈 수 있도록 다리를 비켜 주었다. '~하기 위해서'를 나타내는 표현은 'such that'이 아닌 'so that'이므로 such를 so로 고치는 것이 적절하다. (4) 그녀는 정각에 그곳에 도착하기 위해 서둘렀다. 'so that S V'가 '~하기 위해서'라는 뜻이므로 what을 that으로 고치는 것이 적절하다.

14 그녀는 마치 그녀가 모든 사람들을 알고 있었던 것처럼 행동한다. 사실 그녀는 모두를 알진 못했다. 'as if S 가정법 과거완료'가 쓰였고 acts로 현재이므로 현재보다 이전 시제인 ①이 오는 것이 적절하다.

15 ③ 만약 내가 타이머신을 갖고 있다면 6학년 때로 돌아갈 텐데. 가정법 과거로 현재 사실에 대해 이룰 수 없는 상황에 대한 가정으로 'If S 동사의 과거형 ~, S would/should/could/might 동사원형'이므로 어법에 맞게 고치면 'If I had a time machine, I would go back to the 6th grade.'가 되는 것이 적절하다.

33

16 가정법 과거는 현재 사실에 대한 이룰 수 없는 상황이나 일을 나타낼 때 사용하며 'If S 동사의 과거형 ~, S would/should/could/might 동사원형'이다.

17 비록 Britney Spears는 전 세계 공연을 통해 대부분의 돈을 벌지만 그녀는 그녀의 새로 태어난 아기를 돌볼 수 있게 한 동안 여행을 그만두고 싶다고 최근 말했다. 빈칸 뒤의 내용이 목적을 나타내므로 so that을 쓰는 것이 적절하다.

18 우리말에 맞게 배열하면 'I shut my eyes in order to see.'이다.

19 괄호 안의 단어 so를 활용한 목적의 의미를 나타내는 표현은 'so that S V ~'와 'so as to 동사원형'이 있으므로 so that he could get some fresh air'와 'so as to get some fresh air'로 쓰는 것이 적절하다.

20 가정법 과거는 현재 사실에 대한 반대되는 사실이나 일을 가정할 때 쓰고 'If S 동사의 과거형 ~, S would/should/could/might 동사원형'으로 쓴다.

21 그녀는 한국 사회에 적응하려고 애쓰고 있는 탈북자를 돕기 위해 국회의원에 출마하기로 결심했다.

22 recently = lately = of late: 최근에, ① those days: 그 당시에 그때, ③ previously: 이전에, 미리, ⑤ of the other day: 저번의

23 만약 여러분의 양말에 구멍이 있다면, 그것은 좋지 않은 것이다.

24 there: 뚜껑에

25 때때로 아이들은 심지어 '펜 뚜껑 같은 작은 것들'을 삼키기도 한다.

26 주어진 문장의 This hole에 주목한다. ②번 앞 문장의 a small hole을 받고 있으므로 ②번이 적절하다.

27 그 구멍이 수증기를 나가게 하는 데 얼마나 오래 걸리는지'는 대답할 수 없다. ① It is for safety. ② The pressure inside the pot builds up. ③ The water inside would quickly boil over. ④ It lets steam out and keeps the water from coming out.

28 'yourself'를 보충하면 된다. ask의 간접목적어로는 재귀대명사 'yourself'를, 직접목적어로는 간접의문문 'why it is there'를 쓰는 것이 적절하다.

29 ⓑ와 ①, ③: 형용사적 용법, ②, ⑤: 부사적 용법, ④: 명사적 용법

Healthy Food
Around the World

01 increase   02 ②   03 ④

04 (1) Could you recommend a hotel near your office?

    (2) Sam's restaurant serves good French cuisine.

    (3) When does the snow start to melt?

05 (1) is, different from   (2) put on   (3) got sick

06 ④

01 low(낮은)와 high(높은)는 반의어 관계에 있는 단어들이다. 따라서 reduce(줄이다)와 반의어 관계에 있는 단어는 increase(증가하다, 늘다)이다.

02 '강한 감동을 유발하는'이라는 의미를 가진 영영풀이가 의미하는 것은 ② touching(감동적인)이다.

03 ④에 쓰인 dish는 요리가 아니라 접시라는 뜻으로 사용되었다.

04 (1) recommend 추천하다 (2) serve 제공하다 (3) melt 녹다

05 (1) be different from ~와 다르다 (2) put on 입다 (3) get sick 병에 걸리다

06 A as well as B B 뿐만 아니라 A도 / such as ~ ~와 같은 / take off 이륙하다 / turn off 끄다

01 moving   02 (1) thick   (2) treasure

03 (1) for the first time   (2) shown around

    (3) look like

04 (1) They went to the park to take a walk.

    (2) I have a runny nose and a sore throat.

05 (1) We first measured the difference in temperature.

    (2) The shell is smooth on the inside.

06 not only, but also

01 pain(아픔)과 ache(아픔)는 비슷한 의미를 가진 단어들이다. 따라서 touching(감동적인)과 동의어 관계에 있는 단어는 moving(감동시키는)이다.

02 (1) '한 표면에서 반대편까지 큰 거리가 있는', thick 두꺼운 (2) '매우 가치가 있는 것 또는 사람', treasure 보물

03 (1) for the first time 처음으로 (2) show around 안내하다 (3) look like ~처럼 보이다

04 (1) take a walk 산책하다 (2) have a runny nose 콧물이 흐르다

05 (1) temperature 온도, 기온 (2) smooth 매끄러운

06 not only A but also B A뿐만 아니라 B도

1 ⑤

2 Could[Can] you recommend a good book for my sister?

1 F   2 F   3 T   4 T

Listen and Speak 1 Listen 1

they / called / Could, again / made, from

Listen and Speak 1 Listen 2

eating / say / like, food

Listen and Speak 1 Listen 3

that, looks / Sorry, again / popular

Listen and Speak 1 A-1

favorite, What / traditional / say, again / sweet / try

Listen and Speak 1 A-2

tried / could / salad, popular / special / with, only but, healthy

Listen and Speak 1 B

1. Have / Sorry / dessert

2. tried / traditional

3. ever / that / in

Listen and Speak 2 Listen

1. recommend / Try

2. Could, for / touching

3. beginners / about

4. snack / How

Listen & Speak 2 A-1

special / How, cooking, would / recommend, easy /
about, easy / idea

Listen & Speak 2 B-2

Welcome, many, visit, There, other, tasty local,
recommend, enjoying

Real-Life Zone

for / Here, back, take / much, recommend / recommend
/ Could / made, good, health / try / served, okay /
problem

Wrap Up 1-2

Are, have / Can, place / recommend, enough / would,
recommend / fantastic / thinking, water

시험대비 기본평가   p.182

01 ③   02 made
03 ⓐspecial something → something special
04 Can you recommend something easy to cook?

01 문맥상 (A)에는 상대방에게 했던 말을 다시 말해 달라고 요청
　 하는 표현이 들어가야 적절하다. 따라서 ③ 왜 그걸 다시 말했
　 니?(Why did you say that again?)라는 표현은 빈칸 (A)에
　 들어가기에 어색하다.

02 수동태가 되어야 하므로 과거분사 made로 고친다.

03 ⓐsomething은 형용사가 수식할 때 항상 뒤에서 수식한다. 따
　 라서 something special이 옳은 표현이다.

04 'Can you recommend ~?'는 상대방에게 추천해 달라고 요청
　 할 때 사용하는 표현이다.

시험대비 실력평가   p.183~184

01 ⑤   02 ②
03 It's tasty and also good for your health.
04 ⑤   05 the Happy Snack House 06 ③
07 traditional 08 Sikhye   09 (A) many (B) visiting
10 local   11 ①

01 (A) '몇분 후에'의 뜻이므로 a few가 알맞다. (B) be made
　 with ~로 만들어지다 (C) is served 제공되다

02 위 대화의 초반부는 식당에 입장할 때의 상황이므로 M과 B의
　 관계는 ② '웨이터 - 손님'이 적절하다.

03 위 대화에서 B의 말에 따르면, 비빔밥은 맛도 좋고 건강에 좋다
　 고 한다.

04 위 대화의 think가 포함된 문장에서 think는 주어의 역할을 하
　 기 때문에 동명사 thinking의 형태가 되어야 한다.

05 대명사 it이 가리키는 것은 문맥상 앞서 언급된 식당을 가리킨다.

06 'Can you say that again?'은 '다시 말해 주세요.'라는 뜻으로
　 상대방에게 했던 말을 반복해달라고 요청할 때 사용하는 표현이
　 다. ③은 '그것에 대해 미안해.'라는 뜻으로 상대방에게 반복을
　 요청하는 나머지와는 다른 뜻이다.

07 '오랫동안 만들어진 행동 방식이나 믿음에 속하거나 따르'라
　 는 뜻을 가진 단어는 traditional(전통적인)이다.

08 대명사 it이 가리키는 것은 대화의 문맥상 앞 문장에서 언급된
　 식혜이다.

09 (A) places라는 셀 수 있는 명사가 사용되었으므로 many가
　 오는 것이 적절하다. (B) 동사 recommend는 목적어로 동명
　 사(~ing)를 취한다.

10 '전체 주 또는 국가가 아닌 도시, 마을 또는 작은 구역에 관련된'
　 이라는 뜻이 의미하는 것은 local(지역의)이다.

11 위 글은 시드니의 the Rocks Markets를 소개하면서 글
　 을 읽는 사람에게 추천하고 있다. 따라서 ① 추천하기(to
　 recommend)가 글의 목적으로 가장 적절하다.

서술형 시험대비   p.185

01 (B) – (A) – (C)   02 poke
03 Because it's not only delicious but also very
　 healthy.
04 Could you recommend a cell phone for my
　 grandmother?
05 Can you recommend a good place to have the
　 party?
06 the onion rings
07 Because the food is really good and it'll be large
　 enough.

01 B가 poke를 먹어 봤냐고 묻자 이에 대한 대답으로 (B)에서 상
　 대방은 그게 무엇인지 다시 말해달라고 한다. B가 (A)에서 반
　 복해서 말해 주면서 하와이에서 유명한 샐러드라고 말을 해 주
　 고, (C)에서 상대방이 다시 그것이 그렇게 특별한 이유를 묻는
　 순서가 되어 마지막에 B가 맛도 좋고 건강하다고 대답하는 것이
　 가장 자연스럽다.

02 위 대화에서 A가 poke가 특별한 점이 무엇이냐고 물어 보고 B
　 가 poke에 대해 설명하고 있다.

03 위 대화에서 B의 마지막 말에 나와 있듯이, poke는 맛도 좋고 건
　 강에도 좋다고 한다.

04 상대방에게 추천해달라고 요청할 때 사용하는 표현으로는 'Can
　 you recommend ~?', 또는 'Can/Could you give me a
　 recommendation for ~?' 등이 있다.

05 상대방에게 추천해달라고 요청할 때 'Can[Could] you
　 recommend ~?', 또는 'Can/Could you give me a

recommendation for ~?' 등을 사용할 수 있다. have a party 파티를 열다, 파티를 하다

06 대명사 They는 바로 앞 문장에서 언급한 the onion rings를 가리킨다.

07 위 대화에서 G의 말에 따르면 그 식당이 음식도 정말 맛있고 충분히 크다고 생각한다고 말했다.

교과서
Grammar

핵심 Check   p.186~187

1 (1) respect → respects   (2) are → is
2 (1) while   (2) while

시험대비 기본평가   p.188

01 ⑤   02 ③   03 ⑤   04 ⑤

01 상관접속사 not only와 but also 뒤에는 문법적으로 대등한 것이 있어야 한다. 동사이면서 3인칭 단수 현재형인 helps가 적절하다.

02 보기의 두 문장이 서로 대조되는 내용이므로, 대조의 역할을 하는 종속접속사 While이 적절하다.

03 ⑤ 상관접속사 not only와 but also 뒤에는 문법적으로 대등한 것이 들어가야 한다. not only 뒤에 동사 speaks가 오면, but also 뒤에도 동사가 와야 하는데, handsome은 형용사이다.

04 첫 번째 빈칸은 '~하는 동안'이라는 뜻을 가진 접속사가 필요하고, 나머지 두 빈칸은 '~인 반면에'라는 뜻을 가진 접속사가 들어가는 것이 적절하다. 두 가지 의미를 동시에 전달하는 접속사는 while 뿐이다.

시험대비 실력평가   p.189~191

01 ①   02 ⑤   03 ④   04 ⑤
05 ④   06 ①   07 ④   08 ④
09 ②   10 Not only Sean but also   11 ⑤
12 ⑤   13 ①
14 (1) While I was taking a shower
     (2) While she prefers to take the subway to work

01 ① not only ~ but also에서는 but also 뒤의 명사에 동사의 수를 일치시킨다. have → has가 적절하다.

02 ① neither ~ nor는 부정문과 함께 사용할 수 없다.(doesn't have → has) ② '그녀는 배가 고팠을 뿐만 아니라 더 이상 걸

어갈 수 없었다.'는 문장이다. not only가 문두에 오면 주어와 동사를 도치시킨다.(she was → was she) ③ both는 복수 주어(is → are) ④ 'not only A but also B'는 B에 수의 일치를 한다.(have → has)

03 ① making → makes ② you want → what you want ③ know → knows ⑤ speak → speaks

04 '대조'의 부사절을 이끄는 접속사 'while'이 적절하게 쓰인 것을 고르는 문제이다. ①, ②는 어법상 문제가 없으나, 우리말과 반대로 '녹두전이 ~인 반면에'로 해석되며, ③, ④는 접속사의 성격이 다르다. *ground: 간, 갈린('갈다' grind의 과거분사)

05 오답들을 해석해 보면, ① '맛이 없지만 영양가가 있다.' ② '맛있을 뿐 아니라 영양가가 좋아진다.' ③ '맛이 있거나 또는 영양가가 좋다.' ⑤ '영양가가 좋을 뿐 아니라 맛있다.'가 되어 적절한 문장은 ④이다.

06 '비가 오고 있는 것'과 농구 연습을 하는 것은 대조적인 상황이므로 '역접'의 접속사가 필요하다.

07 ④ Both A and B는 복수 동사를 써야 한다. watches → watch가 적절하다.

08 (A) 혜진이는 안경을 쓰는 반면에, 유나는 아니다. (B) 그는 비록 늦게 일어났지만, 수업에 늦지 않았다. (C) 소연이는 머리가 길고, 반면에 예지는 머리가 짧다.

09 <보기>는 'Grace뿐만 아니라 Ken도 달리기만 아니라 수영하는 것도 좋아하지 않는다.'라는 문장이다. ① 문법적 오류 ③ '둘 중 하나는 수영도 달리기도 좋아하지 않는다.' ④ '둘 다 수영이 아닌 달리기를 좋아한다.' ⑤ '둘 다 달리기가 아닌 수영을 좋아하는 것은 아니다.'

10 Sean과 그의 학급 친구들이 2주 전에 체육관에서 운동을 시작했으므로, 5개의 빈칸에 알맞게 쓰려면 'not only A but also B'를 활용하는 것이 적절하다.

11 '바이러스가 중국에서 왔다.'는 문장과, '그러나 중국의 몇몇 정치인들은 타국을 비난했다.'는 문장은 대조된다. 그러므로 '대조'의 부사절을 이끄는 접속사 while 또는 Though 등이 적절하다.

12 ① the audience were → were the audience ② sees → see ③ only → not only ④ and also → but also

13 ② nor → or ③ or → and ④ know → knows ⑤ wonder → wonders

14 (1) '~하는 동안'의 의미를 가진 접속사를 추가하여, 단어를 적절하게 배열한다. (2) '~하는 반면에'의 의미를 가진 접속사를 추가한다. (1)과 (2)에 공통으로 들어가는 접속사로서 '~하는 동안'과 '~하는 반면에'의 의미를 모두 갖는 것은 While 뿐이다.

01 (1) not only good for people with colds, but also popular

   (2) made with not only eggs but also honey

   (3) Not only you but also they were

   (4) Both Minju and Yena are responsible for

02 (1) How   (2) and   (3) until   (4) as   (5) while

03 A chicken soup is great for not only a sore throat but also a stuffy nose.

04 Samgyetang not only warms your body but also helps reduce the pain in your throat.

05 The onion milk is a drink that is boiled with not only milk but also chopped onion.

06 While Steve was born into a super rich family, Bob's parents were very poor.

07 While I was doing my homework, Linda left my room to watch TV.

08 While Marco sets the alarm to wake up early in the morning, his wife doesn't use the alarm.

09 While I was taking a walk along the lake park, I could hear so many kinds of birds singing in the woods.

10 (1) Ms. Elena is not only a good teacher but also a great artist.

   (2) Jenny can not only sing well but also rap fast in English.

   (3) Dahyun is not only pretty but also very smart.

   (4) Not only Anna but also her sisters are rich.

11 (1) not only promotes your health but is

   (2) while the rest of his family members love chicken

01 (1), (2), (3)은 'not only A but also B'를, (4)는 'both A and B'를 활용하는 문제이다. 의미에 맞게 단어를 배열한다. *people with colds: 감기에 걸린 사람들 *be responsible for: ~에 대해 책임이 있다.

02 의문사 how를 제외하고는 모두 접속사들이다. 문장의 자연스런 연결상 알맞은 단어를 넣도록 한다. (1) 고골모골을 만드는 방법 (2) 그리고, 그것들을 섞으시오. (3) 버터가 녹을 때까지 (4) 부으면서 저으시오. (5) 뜨거울 때 마시세요.

03 닭고기 수프는 부은 목뿐만 아니라 막힌 코에도 좋다.

04 삼계탕은 당신의 몸을 따뜻하게 해줄 뿐만 아니라, 목의 통증을 줄이도록 도와준다.

05 양파 우유는 우유뿐만 아니라 잘게 썬 양파로 만들어지는 음료이다.

06 Steve가 엄청나게 부유한 가정에서 태어난 반면에, Bob의 부모님은 매우 가난했다.

07 내가 숙제를 하는 동안 Linda는 TV를 보기 위해서 내 방을 나

갔다.

08 Marco가 아침에 일찍 일어나기 위해 알람을 설정하는 반면에, 그의 아내는 알람을 사용하지 않는다.

09 호수 공원을 따라 산책을 하는 동안, 나는 아주 많은 종류의 새들이 숲속에서 노래하는 것을 들을 수 있었다.

10 (1) Ms. Elena는 좋은 선생님일 뿐 아니라 훌륭한 화가이다.

   (2) Jenny는 노래를 잘할 수 있을 뿐 아니라, 영어로 빠르게 랩을 할 수 있다. (3) 다현이는 예쁠 뿐만 아니라 매우 똑똑하다.

   (4) Anna뿐만 아니라 그녀의 언니들도 부유하다.

11 (1) 삼계탕은 당신의 건강을 증진시켜 줄 뿐만 아니라, 맛있다.

   (2) Andy는 피자를 즐기는 반면에, 그의 나머지 가족들은 치킨을 좋아한다.

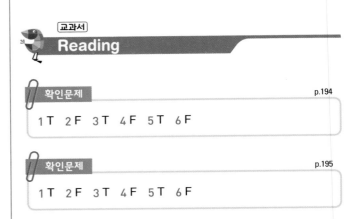

교과서 Reading

1 T   2 F   3 T   4 F   5 T   6 F

1 T   2 F   3 T   4 F   5 T   6 F

01 Fight Colds   02 catch a cold

03 stay warm   04 to drink hot tea

05 something, often drink

06 helps reduce the pain

07 What do people drink or eat

08 find out   09 have a special drink

10 a cup of onion milk

11 chopped onion, over low heat

12 is said to be good

13 While, a bowl of chicken soup

14 from one family to another

15 can be added

16 great for a sore throat and a stuffy nose

17 called   18 is made with

19 to make it taste better   20 looks like

21 have a sore throat   22 not only, but also

23 served, at room temperature

24 Why not, about   25 good for

26 How to Make   27 You need

28 mix them   29 Pour

30 Add
31 Warm, melts
32 Pour, into, with
33 Stir as
34 while

1 Foods That Fight Colds

2 What do you do when you catch a cold?

3 Of course, you want to stay warm, so maybe you put on more clothes.

4 Some people like to drink hot tea.

5 Ginger tea is something people in Korea often drink.

6 With its special taste, it warms your body and helps reduce the pain in your throat.

7 What do people drink or eat in other countries when they catch a cold?

8 Let's find out.

9 In Finland, where it is very cold in winter, people have a special drink when they catch a cold.

10 It is a cup of onion milk.

11 They put chopped onion in milk and boil it over low heat for half an hour.

12 This simple drink is said to be good for a cold.

13 While people in Korea and Finland look for drinks when sick, many people in America want a bowl of chicken soup.

14 It is usually made with chicken and vegetables, but the recipe is different from one family to another.

15 Salt and pepper can be added before eating.

16 People in America believe that a bowl of warm chicken soup is great for a sore throt and a suffy nose.

17 In Russia and in Eastern Europe, when people get sick, they eat a dessert called *gogol-mogol*.

18 It is made with eggs and honey.

19 Some people add chocolate, butter, lemon juice, or milk to make it taste better.

20 It looks like thick yogurt.

21 People often drink a cup of warm *gogol-mogol* when they have a sore throat.

22 *Gogol-mogol* is not only good for people with a cold but also popular as a dessert for healthy people.

23 When served as a dessert, it is usually served cold or at room temperature.

24 Why not try making one of the foods you have found out about?

25 It will be fun and good for your health.

26 How to make *Gogol-mogol* (Serves one)

27 You need: 1 egg, 1/2 cup of milk, honey (5 g), butter (15 g)

28 1. Put the egg and the honey in a large cup and mix them.

29 2. Pour half a cup of milk in a pan.

30 Add the butter.

31 Warm it until the butter melts.

32 3. Pour the hot milk and butter into the cup with the egg and the honey.

33 Stir as you pour.

34 4. Drink while it is hot.

01 ④　　02 warmly → warm　　03 ⑤

04 ②, ⑤

05 Many people in America → People in Korea and Finland 또는 look for drinks → want a bowl of chicken soup

06 Salt and pepper can be added.

07 a special drink　　08 chopped

09 (A) over　(B) for　(C) for　10 ①

11 ②, ④, ⑤　12 ④　　13 ④

14 the recipe is different from one family to another

15 ③　　16 ②　　17 ④　　18 ③

19 ③　　20 ④　　21 making　22 ②

01 주어진 문장의 its에 주목한다. ④번 앞 문장의 'Ginger tea'를 가리키므로 ④번이 적절하다.

02 stay의 '보어'에 해당하므로, warmly를 '형용사 warm'으로 고치는 것이 적절하다.

03 글의 마지막에서 '다른 나라에서는 사람들이 감기에 걸렸을 때 무엇을 마시거나 먹을까? 함께 알아보자.'라고 했으므로, 뒤에 올 내용으로는 '전 세계 사람들이 감기와 싸우기 위해서 마시고 먹는 것들'이 적절하다.

04 ⓐ와 ②, ⑤: ~인 반면에(대조를 나타내는 접속사), ①과 ④: ~하는 동안, ~하는 사이(접속사), ③ 시간, 일정 기간(명사)

05 '한국 사람들과 핀란드 사람들은' 아플 때 음료를 찾는다. 미국의 많은 사람들은 아플 때 '닭고기 수프를 원한다.'

06 닭고기 수프를 먹기 전에 '소금'과 '후추'를 넣기도 한다.

07 핀란드에서 사람들이 감기에 걸리면 마시는 '특별한 음료'를 가리킨다.

08 '잘게 썬 양파'라고 해야 하므로 'chopped(다져진, 잘게 썰린)'

09 (A) over low heat: 약한 불에서, (B) 'during+기간을 나타내는 명사, for+숫자'이므로 for가 적절하다. half an hour = thirty minutes, (C) '감기에 좋다'고 해야 하므로 for가 적절하다. be good at: ~을 잘하다, be good for: ~에 좋다

10 주어진 문장의 It에 주목한다. ①번 앞 문장의 gogol-mogol을 받고 있으므로 ①번이 적절하다.

11 not only/just/simply/merely A but (also) B = not only/just/simply/merely A but B as well = B as well as A: A뿐만 아니라 B도

12 '고골모골을 만드는 데 얼마나 오래 걸리는지'는 대답할 수 없다. ① They eat a dessert called *gogol-mogol*. ② It is made with eggs and honey. ③ They add chocolate, butter, lemon juice, or milk. ⑤ No. *Gogol-mogol* is not only good for people with a cold but also popular as a dessert for healthy people.

13 물질명사는 그 물질을 세는 단위나, 물질을 담고 있는 그릇(용기)의 단수, 복수형을 이용해서 수량을 표시한다. '닭고기 수프'는 보통 '그릇'에 담아 먹으므로 'a bowl of chicken soup'로 세는 것이 적절하다.

14 from one family to another: 가정마다

15 '닭고기 수프가 얼마나 오래 끓여져야 하는지'는 대답할 수 없다. ① They look for drinks. ② They want a bowl of chicken soup. ④ It is usually made with chicken and vegetables. ⑤ They believe that a bowl of warm chicken soup is great for a sore throat and a stuffy nose.

16 (B)가 주어진 글에 대한 답을 설명하는 것이므로 제일 먼저 오고 (A)의 'Ginger tea'가 (B)의 'hot tea'의 예에 해당하므로 (B) 다음에 (A)가 이어지고, (A)에서 '한국인들이 자주 마시는 것'을 소개한 다음에 (C)에서 '다른 나라 사람들은 감기에 걸렸을 때 무엇을 마시거나 먹을지 알아보자'고 해야 하므로 (A) 다음에 (C)가 와야 한다. 그러므로 (B)-(A)-(C)의 순서가 적절하다.

17 ①, ②, ③, ⑤: '고골모골'

18 이 글은 '러시아와 동유럽에서는 사람들이 아픈 사람들뿐만 아니라 건강한 사람들도 고골모골이라는 후식을 먹는다.'는 내용의 글이므로, 주제로는 ③번 '러시아와 동유럽에서 아플 때나 건강할 때나 인기 있는 후식인 고골모골'이 적절하다. ② relieve: 없애[덜어] 주다, ⑤ therapy: 치료, 요법

19 이 글은 '사람들이 감기에 걸렸을 때 무엇을 마시거나 먹는지'에 관해 알아보려는 글이므로, 제목으로는 ③번 '당신은 감기에 걸렸을 때 무엇을 마시거나 먹는가?'가 적절하다.

20 생강차는 '특별한 맛'을 가지고 있다.

21 try+동명사: ~해 보다, ~을 시도하다

22 이 글은 '고골모골을 만드는 방법'에 관한 글이므로, 제목으로는 ②번 '고골모골을 만드는 방법'이 적절하다.

로 쓰는 것이 적절하다. chop 다지다, 잘게 썰다

---

01 take off → put on

02 Ginger tea is something people in Korea often drink

03 (A) warms (B) throat   **04** where

05 chopped onion in milk   **06** this simple drink is

07 be added

08 While people in Korea and Finland look for drinks when they are sick

09 They usually make it with chicken and vegetables

10 (1) trying (2) Why don't you

11 Ingredients

12 the egg and the honey

13 tasting → taste

14 *Gogol-mogol* is popular as a dessert for healthy people as well as good for people with a cold.

---

01 감기에 걸리면 따뜻함을 유지하려고 아마도 옷을 '더 입을 것'이라고 하는 것이 적절하다. 그러므로 take off(옷을 벗다)를 put on(옷을 입다)으로 바꾸는 것이 적절하다.

02 'something' 다음에 목적격 관계대명사 'that'이 생략되었다.

03 그것은 여러분의 몸을 '따뜻하게 하고' '목' 통증을 완화하는 데 도움을 준다.

04 선행사가 'Finland'이므로, 장소를 나타내는 관계부사 'where'를 쓰는 것이 적절하다.

05 '우유에 넣은 잘게 썬 양파'를 가리킨다.

06 This simple drink를 '종속절의 주어'로 쓰고, to부정사는 시제에 맞춰 '종속절의 동사'로 바꿔 쓰는 것이 적절하다.

07 먹기 전에 소금과 후추가 '넣어지는' 것이므로 수동태로 쓰는 것이 적절하다.

08 when 다음에 'they[people in Korea and Finland]are'가 생략되어 있다. 부사절의 주어가 주절의 주어와 같고 뒤에 be동사가 나오면 '주어+be동사'를 생략할 수 있다.

09 They 대신 Many people in America를 써도 적절하다.

10 Why not 동사원형? = How about ~ing? = Why don't you 동사원형?: '~하는 게 어때?'(제안하는 표현)

11 '필요한 것'은 '요리재료'로 바꿔 쓰는 것이 적절하다. ingredient: (특히 요리 등의) 재료[성분]

12 '달걀과 꿀'을 가리킨다.

13 사역동사 make의 목적격보어로 '원형부정사'를 써야 하므로 tasting을 taste로 고치는 것이 적절하다.

14 not only A but also B = B as well as A: A뿐만 아니라 B도

40 정답 및 해설

01 whereas   02 ②   03 ①

04 You need to breathe through the nose, not through the mouth.

05 ②

06 Pardon? / I beg your pardon? / Pardon me?

07 It is from India.

08 ④   09 ⑤   10 ②   11 ③

12 ⑤   13 ③, ⑤   14 ①, ③   15 ④

16 ②   17 ②   18 ⑤

19 chicken soup

20 a bowl of chicken soup   21 ①   22 served

23 to make it taste better   24 ③

25 The chopped tomato and some water should be mixed in a pan first.

26 ④

---

01 blend(섞다)와 compound(혼합하다, 섞어서 만들다)는 유의어 관계에 있는 단어들이다. 따라서 while과 whereas는 모두 '반면에'라는 뜻을 가진 유의어 관계의 단어들이다.

02 ②에서 사용된 desert는 '사막'이라는 뜻이며, '후식'이라는 뜻을 가진 단어는 dessert이다.

03 주어진 문장에서 warm은 '(날씨, 온도가) 따뜻한'이라는 뜻으로 사용되었다. ①에서 역시 같은 의미로 사용되었다. ②,③,⑤는 '따뜻하다, 따뜻하게 하다', ④는 '(색깔이) 따뜻한'이라는 뜻이다.

04 breathe through ~를 통해서 숨쉬다

05 '어떤 것 안에 혹은 위에, 혹은 하나의 용기에서 다른 용기로 흐르다'라는 뜻의 영영풀이는 pour(붓다, 따르다)를 가리킨다.

06 'Could you say that again?'은 '다시 말해 주세요.'라는 뜻으로 상대방에게 했던 말을 반복해달라고 요청할 때 사용하는 표현이다.

07 위 대화의 마지막 부분에 G가 말했듯이, rasmalai는 인도에서 온 전통 음식이다.

08 'Could you say that again?'은 '다시 말해 주세요.'라는 뜻으로 상대방에게 했던 말을 반복해달라고 요청할 때 사용하는 표현이다.

09 문맥상 빈칸에는 상대방에게 전통 음식 추천을 부탁하는 말이 들어가야 한다. 그러나 ⑤ 'Can I make a recommendation for ~?'는 '제가 추천을 해도 되겠습니까?'라는 뜻으로 상대방에게 추천을 제안하는 표현이다.

10 '나는 한국 음식에 대해 잘 알지 못해.'라는 문장은 대화의 문맥상 한국 음식을 추천해달라는 말 앞인 ②에 오는 것이 가장 적절하다.

11 ③ G가 한국 음식을 먹어본 적이 있는가?(Has G ever tried any Korean food before?)라는 질문에 대한 대답은 위 대화

12 G는 매운 음식을 좋아하고 한국 음식을 먹어 보고 싶다고 말했다. 따라서 G의 심정으로 가장 적절한 것은 ⑤ excited (신난, 흥분한)이다.

13 ③ 'not only A but also B'는 등위접속사이므로 not only 뒤에 명사가 오면, but also 뒤에도 명사에 해당하는 단어가 와야 한다. ⑤ not only가 문두에 와서 주어인 Victor가 아닌 동사 was를 강조하고 있으므로, '도치'가 일어나야 한다. 'Not only was Victor good at ~'이 적절하다.

14 ①, ③ 'Both A and B' 또는 'Either A or B'를 쓰는 것이 적절하다. ①은 or를 and로 고치고, ③은 Either를 Both로 고치는 것이 더 좋은데, 그 반대로 either에 맞춰 고쳐 줄 경우에는 동사들도 모두 is[was]로 바꿔야 하기 때문이다.

15 'Sarah는 그 뉴스를 믿었지만, 반면에 그녀의 딸은 그것을 믿지 않았다.'는 문장이다. '대조'의 역할을 하는 접속사 while이 쓰인 ④가 적절하다.

16 'Harrison은 회사에서 해고를 당했던 반면, 다른 사람들은 직장이 있어서, 생계를 꾸려나갈 수 있었다.'는 문장이다. '대조'의 역할을 하는 접속사 while이 쓰인 ②가 적절하며, ⑤의 during은 전치사이기 때문에, 접속사 자리에 쓸 수 없다.

17 ⓐ와 ②: 관계부사, ①, ④, ⑤: [장소·방향·도착점] 어디에[로] (의문부사), ③: 부사절을 이끄는 접속사

18 이 단순한 음료(양파 우유)는 감기에 좋다. too ~ to: so ~ that ... cannot

19 '닭고기 수프'를 가리킨다.

20 한국 사람들과 핀란드 사람들과는 달리, 미국의 많은 사람들은 아플 때 '닭고기 수프'를 찾는다.

21 ⓐ be made with: ~으로 만들어지다, with 다음에는 재료가 온다. be made from: 화학적 변화가 일어날 때 사용, ⓑ as a dessert: 후식으로

22 후식으로 '제공될 때'라고 해야 하므로 When it is served에서 it is를 생략하고 'served'로 쓰는 것이 적절하다.

23 목적을 나타내는 to부정사를 쓰고, '사역동사 make+목적어+동사원형'의 형식으로 쓰는 것이 적절하다. taste+형용사: ~한 맛이 나다

24 '쌀'은 '인도의 토마토 수프'를 만드는 재료에 속하지 않는다.

25 먼저 잘게 썬 토마토'와 '약간의 물'이 팬에서 섞여야 한다.

26 not A but B: A가 아니라 B, not only/just/simply/merely A but (also) B = not only/just/simply/merely A but B as well = B as well as A = Besides A, B: A뿐만 아니라 B도

01 ①

02 (1) a bottle of   (2) is good for   (3) as well as

03 many places people want to visit in Sydney

04 We recommend visiting the Rocks Markets

05 ③

06 I would recommend cooking something for him.

07 It's easy to make and it's delicious.   08 ④

09 ⑤   10 traditional   11 ①   12 ⑤

13 ③   14 ①   15 ⑤   16 ③

17 Ginger tea is something that people in Korea often drink.

18 ginger tea   19 recipe   20 ②   21 ④

22 called   23 (A) to make   (B) thick   (C) healthy

24 it is usually served cold or at room temperature

01 '열의 결과로 액체에서 기체로 변하다'라는 영영풀이가 가리키는 것은 ① boil(끓다, 끓이다)이다.

02 (1) a bottle of ~ 한 병 (2) be good for ~에 좋다 (3) A as well as B B뿐만 아니라 A도

03 대명사 them은 앞서 언급한 복수 명사를 가리킨다. 이 대화에서는 화자가 말한 시드니에 있는 '당신이 방문하고 싶어 할 많은 장소'(many places you will want to visit)를 가리킨다.

04 recommend는 목적어로 동명사를 취한다. 따라서 recommend to visit이 아니라 recommend visiting이라고 써야 한다.

05 위 글의 중반에 화자는 the Rocks Markets에서 예술 작품, 옷, 책 그리고 많은 다른 것을 살 수 있다고 했으며 그곳에서 지역 음식 역시 먹을 수 있다고 언급했다.

06 'How about ~?'는 상대방에게 추천해 줄 때 쓸 수 있는 표현으로, 'What about ~?', 'I recommend ~.', 'I'd recommend ~.', 'Try ~.' 등으로 대체할 수 있다.

07 easy to make 만들기 쉬운

08 ④ 'B의 아빠가 가장 좋아하는 음식은 무엇인가?'에 대한 대답은 위 대화에서 언급 되지 않았다.

09 (A) tried는 '~ 해 보다, 먹어 보다, 시도해 보다'라는 의미로 사용되었다. ⑤ '자기 전에 아기를 너무 흥분시키지 않도록 해라.'라는 문장에서 try는 '노력하다, 애쓰다'라는 의미로 사용되었다.

10 tradition의 형용사형이 알맞다.

11 'Could you recommend ~?'는 '~를 추천해 주시겠어요?'라는 뜻으로 상대방에게 추천해달라고 요청할 때 사용하는 표현이다.

12 but also 뒤에 형용사 generous가 있으므로, 부사 truly(진심으로, 진정으로)는 적절하지 않다. 나머지는 모두 형용사들이다.

13 not only 뒤에 형용사가 나왔으므로, 형용사 역할이 아닌 것을

찾는다. ③ acts는 동사이다.

14 (A) '수미는 오래 걸었기 때문에, 너무 피곤했다.' (B) '그 쇼를 보고 있던 중에, 나는 무대 뒤에서 무엇인가가 우는 소리를 들을 수 있었다.' (C) '그는 낚시하러 가는 것을 좋아했던 반면에, 그의 아내는 낚시를 몹시 싫어했다.' 등에 적합한 부사절 접속사를 찾는다.

15 접속사 while은 '~하는 동안', '~하는 반면에' 등으로 쓰인다. ①~④ 모두 '~하는 동안'의 의미로 사용되었고, ⑤는 어떤 의미로도 어색하다. If 또는 When으로 고칠 경우, '조금이라도 필요한 것이 있다면, 어느 때든 전화하시오.'라는 의미가 된다.

16 catch/get/have/take a cold = come down with a cold: 감기에 걸리다, catch/get/take/ cold처럼 a를 생략할 수도 있다. ③ have a cough: 기침이 나다

17 'something' 다음에 목적격 관계대명사 'that'이 생략되었다.

18 '생강차'를 가리킨다.

19 recipe: 요리법, 조리법, 재료의 목록과 어떤 것을 요리하는 법을 말해주는 일련의 지시

20 이 글은 '미국의 많은 사람들은 따뜻한 닭고기 수프 한 그릇이 부은 목과 막힌 코에 좋다고 믿으면서 아플 때 닭고기 수프를 원한다'는 내용의 글이므로, 제목으로는 ②번 '미국 사람들은 아플 때 무엇을 원하는가?'가 적절하다.

21 요리 도중에 소금과 후추를 넣는 것이 아니라, 소금과 후추는 '먹기 전'에 넣기도 한다.

22 '고골모골이라는 후식'이라고 해야 하므로, 과거분사 called로 쓰는 것이 적절하다.

23 (A) '그것을 더 맛있게 하기 위해'라고 해야 하므로 to make가 적절하다. (B) '진한' 요구르트라고 해야 하므로 thick이 적절하다. thick: (액체가) 진한, 걸쭉한, huge: (크기·양·정도가) 막대한, 거대한, (C) '건강한' 사람들이라고 해야 하므로 healthy가 적절하다. healthy: 건강한, 건강에 좋은, healthful: 건강에 좋은

24 빈도부사는 be동사, 조동사 뒤, 일반동사 앞에 위치하는 것이 보편적이다. at room temperature: 실온으로

01 G's favorite Korean traditional drink is Maesil-tea.

02 He describes that his favorite drink is cool and sweet.

03 who → that[which]

04 (A) not only[just, simply, merely] (B) but also

05 (1) believe → believes   (2) is → are
   (3) have → has   (4) excited → exciting
   (5) is → are

06 (1) While he talks a lot, he acts little.

(2) While Paula was cooking, her uncle visited her house.

07 (A) clothes   (B) With   (C) other

08 to reduce

09 (A) hot tea   (B) reduce the pain

10 looks → looks like

11 serve

12 They often drink a cup of warm *gogol-mogol*.

01 대화 시작에서 G는 자신이 가장 좋아하는 한국 전통 음료가 매실차라고 밝히고 있다.

02 B에 따르면 그가 좋아하는 한국 전통 음료인 식혜가 시원하고 달콤하다고 언급했다.

03 위 대화에서 B의 말에서 poke가 하와이에서 인기 있는 샐러드라고 말한다. 이때 관계대명사 who가 쓰였는데, 이는 선행사가 사람일 때만 쓰일 수 있다. 따라서 관계대명사 that[which]으로 고쳐야 한다.

04 빈칸이 포함된 문장은 '그것은 맛도 좋고 매우 건강하다'라는 뜻의 문장이다. not only[just, simply, merely] A but also B A뿐만 아니라 B도

05 (1), (5) but also 뒤의 주어에 일치시킨다. (1)은 Julie가 (5)는 the stores가 주어이다. (2) 'both A and B'가 주어일 때는 항상 복수 동사가 온다. (3) 'either A or B'는 동사와 가까운 주어에 수를 일치시킨다. (4) 노래가 사람의 흥미를 유발하는 것이므로 excited가 아니라 현재분사형의 형용사 exciting을 쓰는 것이 적절하다.

06 (1) 3인칭 단수 현재시제임을 유의한다. (2) 과거진행시제와 과거시제에 유의한다.

07 (A) '옷'을 더 입을 것이라고 해야 하므로 clothes가 적절하다. clothes: 옷, 의복, cloths: 옷감들, 직물의 종류를 나타낼 때의 복수 형태, (B) 특별한 맛과 '함께'라고 해야 하므로 With가 적절하다. (C) 'another' 뒤에는 단수 명사를 써야 하므로 other가 적절하다.

08 help+원형부정사 = help+to부정사

09 사람들이 감기에 걸릴 때 그들 중 몇몇은 생강차와 같은 '따뜻한 차'를 마시는 것을 좋아한다. 그것은 특별한 맛을 가지고 있고 몸을 따뜻하게 해주면서 목 '통증을 완화하는 데' 도움을 준다.

10 'looks' 뒤에 '명사인 yogurt'가 나오기 때문에, 'looks'를 'looks like'로 고치는 것이 적절하다. looks+형용사, looks like+명사: ~처럼 보이다

11 people[they]을 주어로 하여 능동태로 고치는 것이 적절하다.

12 러시아와 동유럽에서, 사람들은 목이 아플 때 종종 '따뜻한 고골모골 한 잔'을 마신다.

창의사고력 서술형 문제   p.218

|모범답안|

01 (1) While Hana wears glasses, Duna does not.

(2) Hana likes singing while Duna likes dancing.

(3) While Hana got an A in math, Duna got a C.

02 (A) chop   (B) pour some water

(C) for ten minutes   (D) to cool down

(E) blend it   (F) some black pepper and salt

01 표의 단어들을 적절히 조합하여 어법에 맞게 영작한 답이면 된다.

단원별 모의고사   p.219~223

01 ③   02 ①

03 (1) added   (2) held   (3) mix   04 ⑤

05 They're sweet and made with rice cake powder.

06 Could you recommend something?

07 It's made with lots of vegetables, beef and an egg over rice.

08 ②, ⑤   09 (C) – (B) – (A)   10 ⑤

11 ②   12 ④   13 ①   14 ③

15 ④   16 ④

17 (1) broke the speed limit, but also made an illegal

(2) a guitar, while I was interested in

18 Onion milk   19 ⑤   20 ②

21 They can add salt and pepper before eating.

22 ①   23 ⑤   24 ④   25 ③

01 '표준 척도를 기준으로 한 물체의 온기 측정'은 ③ temperature(온도, 기온)를 가리킨다.

02 '우리가 집을 비운 사이에 도둑이 들었다.'라는 문장에서 들어갈 것으로 가장 적절한 것은 ① while(~하는 동안, 반면에)이다.

03 (1) add 더하다, 첨가하다 (2) hold 열다, 개최하다 (3) mix 섞다

04 'Could you say that again?'은 '다시 말해 주세요.'라는 뜻으로 상대방에게 했던 말을 반복해달라고 요청할 때 사용하는 표현이다. 따라서 ⑤ 'G에게 했던 말을 반복해달라고 요청하기 위해'이다.

05 be made with ~로 만들어지다 / rice cake powder 쌀가루

06 상대방에게 추천해달라고 요청할 때 '~를 추천해 주시겠어요?'라는 뜻을 가진 'Could you recommend ~?'를 사용할 수 있다.

07 be made with ~로 만들어지다 / lots of ~ 많은 ~

08 ② G가 B에게 한국 음식을 먹어 보라고 하는 것은 옳지 않다. ⑤ G는 매운 음식을 좋아한다고 말한다.

09 (C)가 rasmalai를 먹어 본 적이 있는지 물어보자 (B)에서 상

대방이 다시 말해 달라고 요청하며 (A)에서 다시 반복하여 말해 주면서 덧붙여 설명해 주는 순서로 이어지는 것이 가장 자연스럽다.

10 주어진 문장의 대명사 They가 무엇을 가리키는지 아는 것이 중요하다. 이때 복수형 대명사 they가 fantastic하다고 말했으므로, 문맥상 the onion rings를 가리킨다.

11 ② '누가 파티에 초대될 것인가?'라는 질문에 대한 대답은 위 대화에서 언급되어 있지 않다.

12 ④ '제 여동생을 위한 책을 추천해 주시겠어요?'(Could you recommend a good book for my sister?)라는 질문에 B가 '다시 말해 주시겠어요? 이 이야기는 감동적이에요.'(Pardon me? The story is touching.)라는 대답은 문맥상 어색하다.

13 'not only ~ but also' 구문의 영작이다. delicious와 too much가 병렬이 된 ①이 정답이다. ④는 Not only를 문두로 보내 ①을 도치한 문장인데, too much 뒤의 is가 없다면, 옳은 문장이 될 수 있다.

14 not only와 but also 뒤의 동사가 병렬이 되므로, 조동사 can이 동시에 동사를 받는다. ①에서 solves의 s를 빼면 정답이 될 수 있다. ①을 도치시킨 문장이 ③이다. 동사를 받는 Not only가 문두로 나오면, 주어와 동사는 '도치'된다. 원형동사 solve가 바르게 나왔다. ⑤는 but also 뒤에 he를 다시 썼기 때문에, 앞의 can을 받을 수 없으므로 부적절하다.

15 접속사 while은 '~하는 동안', '~하는 반면에' 등으로 쓰인다. ①, ②, ③, ⑤ 모두 '~하는 반면에'의 의미로 사용되었고, ④는 '~하는 동안'이다.

16 ①, ②, ③, ⑤ 모두 '~하는 동안'의 의미로 사용되었고, ④는 '~하는 반면에'이다. 'Walter의 여자친구 Celine은 한국사를 매우 좋아하는 반면에, Walter는 그렇지 않다.'

17 (1) 그 차는 속도 제한을 위반했을 뿐 아니라, 불법 차선 변경도 했다. (2) 그녀는 나에게 기타를 팔려고 했는데, 반면 나는 다른 악기들에 관심이 있었다.

18 '양파 우유'를 가리킨다.

19 '왜 양파 우유가 감기에 좋은지'는 알 수 없다. ① It is very cold. ② They drink a cup of onion milk. ③ I need onion and milk. ④ It is to put chopped onion in milk and boil it over low heat for half an hour.

20 ⓐ: 대조를 나타내는 접속사, '~인 반면에', ③ 그렇지 않으면, ④ ~이 아닌 한, 만약 ~이 아니면, ⑤ ~하는 한

21 막연한 사람을 나타내는 They를 주어로 하여 능동태로 고치는 것이 적절하다.

22 ⓐ와 ①: 부사적 용법, ②, ④, ⑤: 명사적 용법, ③: 형용사적 용법

23 고골모골은 감기에 걸린 사람들에게 좋을 뿐만 아니라 '건강한 사람들의 후식으로도 인기가 있다.'

24 ⓐ 음식들에 '대해' 알아본 것이므로 about이 적절하다. ⓑ pour A into B: A를 B에 붓다

25 (A)와 ③: (음식의 양이) 돌아가다, ③ 이 한 접시면 배고픈 사람 네 명에게 돌아간다[4인분이 된다]. ① (특히 다른 것을 구할 수 없을 때 특정한 용도로) 쓰일 수 있다[적합하다], ② ~에 봉사하다, ~을 섬기다, ④ ~에 근무[복무]하다, ⑤ (상점에서) 손님을 접대하다, serve behind a counter: 점원으로 일하다

A Christmas Miracle

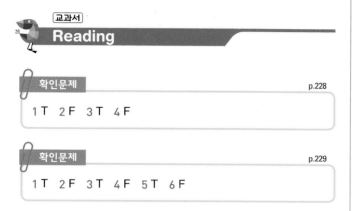

교과서 Reading

확인문제   p.228

1 T   2 F   3 T   4 F

확인문제   p.229

1 T   2 F   3 T   4 F   5 T   6 F

교과서 확인학습 A   p.230~231

01 Miracle	02 the first year
03 were facing, had done	04 cold and wet
05 all the more so	06 was heard coming
07 carol	08 going on
09 might be a trick	10 boldly looked out of
11 One by one	12 What
13 lit with lanterns	
14 one Christmas song after another	
15 by also singing	16 made them forget
17 came out from	
18 whose aim, exchange greetings	
19 in several months	20 It truly was
21 came	22 on both sides
23 in the no man's land	24 such as
25 sang carols	26 exchanged addresses
27 unbelievable, about	28 between the two lines
29 had bike races	30 were at war
31 Here we were	
32 like us, waiting to welcome	

교과서 확인학습 B   p.232~233

1 A Christmas Miracle

2 It was Christmas Eve in 1914, the first year of World War I.

3 English soldiers were facing German soldiers from

---

their trenches as they had done for the last few months.

4 The trenches were cold and wet.

5 The soldiers were tired and missed their home, all the more so because it was Christmas.

6 Suddenly, a familiar song was heard coming from the German trenches.

7 It was a Christmas carol!

8 What's going on?

9 It might be a trick to make them come out of the trenches.

10 A few English soldiers boldly looked out of their trenches.

11 One by one, other soldiers followed their example.

12 What they saw was a sight they never expected.

13 Along the German trenches, Christmas trees were standing lit with lanterns!

14 The German soldiers sang one Christmas song after another.

15 The English soldiers began to answer by also singing Christmas songs.

16 The warm lights and the Christmas carols made them forget they were on the front line.

17 Then a shout came out from the German side: "Happy Christmas! You no shoot, we no shoot!"

18 Soon, soldiers whose aim had been to kill each other just a few hours before began to exchange greetings.

19 For the first time in several months, the soldiers were able to spend a night in peace.

20 It truly was a silent night.

21 Christmas morning came.

22 Soldiers on both sides put down their weapons and came out of their trenches.

23 They met in the no man's land between their trenches and shook hands.

24 They exchanged small gifts such as wine and cake.

25 They sang carols together.

26 Some even exchanged addresses and played football.

27 This unbelievable Christmas Day was written about in letters English soldiers sent home.

28 One soldier wrote, "On Christmas Day, English and German soldiers met between the two lines

and had talks.

29 We also had bike races."

30 Another wrote, "We didn't think that we were at war.

31 Here we were, enemy talking to enemy.

32 They were like us, with mothers, with friends, with wives who were waiting to welcome their men home again."

서술형 실전문제

p.234~235

01 unfamiliar 02 for the first time

03 (1) come out (2) one by one (3) have a talk

04 (1) They had to think of a trick to get past the teacher.

(2) The early morning street was silent.

(3) Lana shares a house with three other students.

05 (1) They fell in love with each other.

(2) You have to follow the example of great scientists.

(3) The marathon runners arrived at the finish line one after another.

06 World War One 또는 the First World War

07 had done 08 Because it was Christmas.

09 forgetting → forget 10 whose

11 (A) singing Christmas songs (B) peacefully

01 begin(시작하다)과 end(끝나다)는 반의어 관계에 있는 단어들이다. 따라서 familiar(익숙한, 친숙한)과 반의어 관계에 있는 단어는 unfamiliar(익숙지 못한)이다.

02 for the first time 처음으로

03 (1) come out 나오다 (2) one by one 차례로 (3) have a talk 이야기하다

04 (1) trick 속임수 (2) silent 고요한 (3) share 공유하다, 나누다

05 (1) each other 서로 (2) follow one's example ~의 사례를 따르다, 모범으로 삼다 (3) one after another 잇따라서

06 제일차 세계 대전은 World War부터 읽으면 'I'을 'One'으로 읽고, 'I'을 먼저 읽으면 'I'을 'the First'로 읽는 것이 적절하다.

07 과거에 일어났던 일보다 더 앞서 일어난 일에 대해 언급하는 것이므로, 과거완료 'had done'으로 쓰는 것이 적절하다.

08 글의 마지막 문장에서 그 이유를 설명하고 있다.

09 '사역동사 make+목적어+목적격 보어' 구문에서 목적격 보어에는 '동사원형'을 쓰는 것이 적절하다.

10 소유격 관계대명사 'whose'가 적절하다.

11 독일 군인들이 크리스마스 캐럴을 연이어 불렀을 때. 영국 군인들도 '크리스마스 캐럴을 부르며' 화답하기 시작했다. 몇 달 만에 처음으로, 군인들은 '평화롭게' 밤을 지낼 수 있었다. in peace = peacefully

단원별 예상문제

p.236~239

01 quiet 02 ③

03 Although it is small, the kitchen is well designed.

04 ② 05 such as 06 ⑤

07 English soldiers 08 ②, ④

09 They were facing the German soldiers.

10 ② 11 ③ 12 ③

13 soldiers whose aim had been to kill each other just a few hours before began to exchange greetings

14 ⑤ 15 changed → exchanged

16 ⑤ 17 ②

18 (A) unbelievable (B) between (C) like 19 ④

20 English soldiers heard a familiar song coming from the German trenches

21 English soldiers

22 looked out of their trenches

01 entire(전체의)와 whole(전체의, 모든)은 유사한 뜻을 가진 단어들이다. 따라서 silent(고요한)와 유사한 뜻을 가진 quiet(조용한)이다.

02 ③ aim은 '목표'라는 뜻이 아니라 '~를 겨냥하다'라는 뜻으로 사용되었다.

03 although 비록 ~이긴 하지만

04 주어진 문장에서 light는 '불을 붙이다'라는 뜻으로 사용되었다. ①, ③ 빛, ④, ⑤ 가벼운

05 such as ~와 같은

06 '보이는 어떤 사물이나 볼 가치가 있는 것'이라는 뜻을 가진 영영풀이가 가리키는 것은 ⑤ sight(광경)이다.

07 '영국 군인들'을 가리킨다.

08 ⓑ와 ②, ④: 계속 용법, ①, ⑤: 경험 용법, ③ 완료 용법

09 1914년의 크리스마스 이브에 영국 군인들이 그들의 참호에서 대치하고 있었던 것은 '독일 군인들'이었다.

10 (B)에서 그들이 무인 지대에서 만났다고 한 다음에 (A)에서 그들이 작은 선물도 교환했다고 해야 하므로 (B) 다음에 (A)가 이어지고 (C)의 'even exchanged addresses'는 (A)의 'exchanged small gifts'에 이어 '심지어 주소를 교환하기도

했다'는 것이므로 (A) 다음에 (C)가 와야 한다. 그러므로 (B)-(A)-(C)의 순서가 적절하다.

11 'what'은 선행사를 포함하고 있는 관계대명사로 'The thing which[that]'로 풀어 쓸 수 있다.

12 주어진 문장의 also singing Christmas songs에 주목한다. ③번 앞 문장에서 '독일 군인들이 크리스마스 캐럴을 연이어 부른 것'에 '영국 군인들이 크리스마스 캐럴을 부르며 화답한 것'이므로 ③번이 적절하다.

13 'whose'는 소유격 관계대명사로, 사람 또는 사물을 선행사로 취하며 생략할 수 없다.

14 '몇 달 동안'이 아니라, '몇 달 만에 처음으로', 군인들은 평화롭게 밤을 지낼 수 있었다

15 몇몇은 심지어 주소를 '교환하기도' 했다고 해야 하므로, changed를 exchanged로 고치는 것이 적절하다. change: 바꾸다, exchange: 교환하다

16 '영국 군인들과 독일 군인들이 얼마나 오래 축구를 했는지'는 대답할 수 없다. ① They met on Christmas morning. ② They put down their weapons and came out of their trenches. ③ They met in the no man's land. ④ They exchanged small gifts such as wine and cake, and some even exchanged addresses.

17 ⓐ 날짜 앞에는 'on'을 쓰는 것이 적절하다. On Christmas Day: 크리스마스에, ⓑ be at war: 전쟁[교전] 중이다

18 (A) 이 '믿을 수 없는' 크리스마스라고 해야 하므로 unbelievable이 적절하다. unbelievable: 믿을 수 없는, (B) '두 경계선 사이에서' 만났으므로 between이 적절하다. among: (셋 이상이 관련된 분배·선택 시) ~ 간에, ~ 중에서, between: (둘) 사이에, (C) 뒤에 'us'가 나오므로 like가 적절하다. alike: 비슷한(뒤에 목적어를 가질 수 없고, 서술적 용법으로만 쓰임), like는 전치사로서 뒤에 목적어를 가진다.

19 '크리스마스 후에 영국 군인들과 독일 군인들이 다시 싸웠을 때 그들이 어떻게 느꼈는지'는 알 수 없다. ① It was written about in letters English soldiers sent home. ② They met between the two lines. ③ They had talks and bike races. ⑤ They thought the German soldiers were like them, with mothers, with friends, with wives.

20 문장의 주어인 a familiar song을 목적어로 바꾸고, 주격보어 coming from the German trenches를 목적격보어로 바꿔서 고치는 것이 적절하다.

21 '영국 군인들'을 가리킨다.

22 '차례차례 다른 군인들도 앞사람을 따랐다'는 것은 '다른 군인들도 용감하게 자신들의 참호 밖을 내다보았다'는 뜻이다. one by one = one after another: 연달아, 차례로

교과서 파헤치기

Lesson 5

단어 TEST Step 1   p.02

01 수단, 방법   02 주의, 집중   03 ~ 아래에
04 의미   05 (긴장을) 늦추다, 휴식을 취하다
06 면밀히, 밀접하게   07 잡지   08 밝은, 긍정적인
09 방울   10 감정   11 발랄한, 쾌활한
12 독립적인, 자립심이 강한   13 기사
14 ~을 관련[연결]시키다   15 성격
16 보호   17 합리적인   18 다름, 차이점
19 의존적인   20 호기심이 있는   21 미루다, 연기하다
22 짜증이 난   23 유용한, 도움이 되는
24 여러 가지의, 다양한   25 편한, 편안한
26 인기 있는   27 세부 사항   28 현실적인
29 상상, 상상력   30 차분한   31 주의 깊은
32 큰 소리로   33 평화로운   34 줄이다
35 매진된, 다 팔린   36 ~을 다루다, ~을 처리하다
37 (사람들과) 잘 어울리다   38 동시에, 함께
39 다시 말하면   40 ~와 연관되다   41 ~와 관련되다
42 ~에 따르면, ~에 따라
43 반면에, 한편으로는

단어 TEST Step 2   p.03

01 article   02 situation   03 difference
04 relax   05 magazine   06 creative
07 emotion   08 drop   09 relate
10 independent   11 cheerful   12 comfortable
13 recipe   14 curious   15 reasonable
16 dependent   17 personality   18 various
19 protection   20 imagination   21 calm
22 reduce   23 popular   24 detail
25 realistic   26 careful   27 peaceful
28 delay   29 express   30 closely
31 annoyed   32 meaning   33 means
34 opinion   35 in other words   36 deal with
37 get along   38 be related to   39 according to
40 have to do with   41 at the same time
42 on the other hand
43 draw attention to oneself

단어 TEST Step 3   p.04

1 reasonable, 합리적인   2 frightened, 겁먹은, 두려워하는
3 recipe, 조리[요리]법   4 delay, 미루다, 연기하다
5 calm, 차분한   6 comfortable, 편안한
7 seat, 자리, 좌석   8 focus, 집중하다   9 reduce, 줄이다
10 hopeful, 희망찬   11 attitude, 태도
12 independent, 독립적인, 자립심이 강한
13 express, 표현하다   14 difference, 다름, 차이점
15 article, 기사   16 personality, 성격

대화문 TEST Step 1   p.05~06

Listen and Speak 1 Listen

1. does, mean / nervous, frightened, doing
2. does, mean / feel sad
3. does, mean / means, look sad
4. does, mean / means, give up

Listen and Speak 1 A

1. How, doing / for / does, mean / means, happy, excited
2. personality test, had to draw / According to, a lot, by, mine / do, mean / mean, open, other

Listen and Speak 2 Listen

1. sold out / Are there, other seats / some tickets
2. spicy, sweet / other sauces / only two
3. would, like to, maybe / any other, too much sugar / too
4. the most popluar / other colors / lots, over here

Listen and Speak 2 A

1. reading / says, change people's feelings / surprising / For example, help us focus / useful colors / helps,   relax
2. more, yourself, kinds of, other tests / calling to take, test / any time before

Real-Life Zone

what kind of, to try / like fun / afraid of, one of, spiders / dark places, without, on, mean / says, full of, That's why, fill, with, scary things / about, anything, afraid of / big imagination / any other tests, take / a lot of

Wrap Up 1~2

blood type / an article, says / your personality / type A / with, calm, listeners, too

대화문 TEST Step 2   p.07~08

Listen and Speak 1 Listen

1. G: What does "be in a cold sweat" mean?

B: It means "to be nervous or frightened before doing something."

2. B: What does "feel blue" mean?

G: It means "to feel sad."

3. G: What does "have a long face" mean?

B: It means "to look sad."

4. B: What does "throw up one's hands" mean?

G: It means "to give up."

Listen and Speak 1 A

1. G: Hi, Jack! How are you doing?

B: I'm on cloud nine! I got a concert ticket for my favorite band.

G: What does "on cloud nine" mean?

B: It means I'm really happy and excited.

2. G: I took a personality test today. I had to draw a house.

B: A house?

G: Yeah. According to the test, you can tell a lot about a person by their drawing. Here's mine.

B: Interesting. So what do these big windows mean?

G: They mean I'm open to other people.

Listen and Speak 2 Listen

1. M: Sorry. The tickets for the blue zone are all sold out.

G: Are there any other seats?

M: Yes, we have some tickets for the red zone.

2. W: What would you like on your hot dog? We have spicy sauce and sweet sauce.

B: Are there any other sauces?

W: Sorry. Those are the only two we have.

3. M: What would you like to drink? A soft drink maybe?

G: Are there any other drinks? Soft drinks have too much sugar in them.

M: We have apple juice too.

4. W: This is the most popluar cap in our store.

B: Are there any other colors?

W: Sure, we have lots more. They're over here. I'll show you.

Listen and Speak 2 A

1. B: Jane, what are you reading?

G: I'm reading an interesting magazine. It says colors can change people's feelings.

B: That's surprising.

G: Yes. For example, the color red can help us focus better.

B: Are there any other useful colors?

G: Yes. The color blue helps people relax.

2. M: EDPI Test Center. Do you want to learn more about yourself? We have many kinds of personality tests. If there are any other tests you want to learn more about, we are here to help you.

B: Hi, I'm calling to take a personality test. Can I do one this afternoon?

M: Sure, you can come any time before 5 o'clock.

Real-Life Zone

Hajun: Look! I found this test on an app that tells what kind of person you are. Do you want to try it?

Emma: Sure. Sounds like fun.

Hajun: Okay, listen. What are you afraid of? Choose one of these: crowds, spiders, or dark places.

Emma: I hate dark places. I cannot sleep without a night light on. What does that mean?

Hajun: It says you are full of imagination. That's why you fill dark places with all kinds of scary things.

Emma: That's very interesting. What about you? Is there anything you are afraid of?

Hajun: I chose dark places too. But I don't think I have a big imagination.

Emma: This is fun. I want to do some more. Are there any other tests we can take?

Hajun: Sure. This app has a lot of them.

Wrap Up 1~2

B: What's your blood type?

G: Type A. Why?

B: I'm reading an article. It says that blood type tells something about your personality.

G: Wow. Then what does type A mean?

B: People with blood type A are calm. They are good listeners, too.

본문 TEST Step 1   p.09~10

01 Everything, do says something

02 wear, even, raise, kind

03 things, draw, much different

04 What, how, related, personality

05 using various, better understand

06 One, those tests, test   07 Study, below

08 person, holding, light rain

09 other hand, heavy, no

10 there, dark, above, person

11 What, differences mean

12 rain, stress, who, under

13 bigger, drops, heavily, falling

14 waiting, happen, hopeful, future

15 Second, protection, stressful situation

16 big, shows, plans, protection

17 drawing, means, deal with

18 details, have, with, attitude

19 example, draws, without, attention

20 right side, ready to

21 hand, may, worried, happened

22 possible meanings, part, drawings

23 go back, at look   24 Try reading, yourself

25 what kind, each one   26 your opinion

---

01 Everything, says something

02 use, wear, even, raise, what kind of person you are

03 draw, much

04 What, how, are related to, personality

05 have been using, to better understand

06 One, those tests   07 Study, below

08 holding, light

09 On the other hand, heavy, no

10 there are, above   11 differences mean

12 stress, who, under

13 The bigger, the more heavily, the bigger

14 waiting, happen, hopeful, future

15 Second, protection, stressful situation

16 big, shows, a lot of plans, protection

17 drawing, means, deal with difficult situations

18 Third, details, have to do, attitude

19 example, who, without, attention, himself, herself

20 who, right, is ready to meet

21 hand, may, worried, happened

22 possible meanings, part, drawings

23 back, look at   24 reading, yourself

25 what kind, drew each one 26 opinion

---

1 당신이 하는 모든 행동은 당신에 대해 말해 줍니다.

2 당신이 사용하는 언어, 당신이 입는 옷, 그리고 당신이 기르는 애완동물까지도 당신이 어떤 종류의 사람인지 보여 줍니다.

---

3 당신이 그리는 그림도 마찬가지입니다.

4 당신이 무엇을 그리는지 그리고 그것을 어떻게 그리는지는 당신의 성격과 관련이 있습니다.

5 의사들은 사람들을 더 잘 이해하기 위해 다양한 그림 그리기 검사를 사용해 오고 있습니다.

6 이런 검사들 중 하나는 빗속의 사람 그리기 검사입니다.

7 아래의 그림들을 연구해 봅시다.

8 A 그림 속의 사람은 가벼운 빗속에서 우산을 들고 있습니다.

9 반면에, B 그림 속의 사람은 거센 빗속에서 우산을 가지고 있지 않습니다.

10 또한, 검은 구름들이 B 그림의 사람 머리 위에 있습니다.

11 이런 차이는 무엇을 의미하는 걸까요?

12 첫 번째, 비는 그림을 그린 사람이 받고 있는 스트레스를 보여줍니다.

13 빗방울의 크기가 크면 클수록, 혹은 비가 더 세게 내리면 내릴수록 스트레스는 더 큽니다.

14 구름은 앞으로 벌어질 문제를 의미하기 때문에, 큰 구름은 그림을 그린 사람이 미래에 대해 그다지 희망적이지 않다는 것을 나타냅니다.

15 두 번째, 우산은 스트레스를 받는 상황에서 그 사람이 가지고 있는 보호 기제를 의미합니다.

16 큰 우산은 그림을 그린 사람이 많은 계획이나 보호 기제를 가지고 있음을 보여 줍니다.

17 만약 그림에 우산이 없다면, 그 그림을 그린 사람은 어려운 상황을 헤쳐 나갈 어떤 방법도 가지고 있지 않습니다.

18 세 번째, 그림 속 사람의 세부적인 것들은 그 그림을 그린 사람이 스트레스를 받을 때의 태도와 관련이 있습니다.

19 예를 들어, 얼굴이 없는 사람을 그린 사람은 사람들의 관심을 끌기를 원하지 않습니다.

20 사람을 종이의 오른쪽에 그린 사람은 미래를 맞이할 준비가 되어 있습니다.

21 반면에, 사람을 왼쪽에 그린 사람은 과거에 일어났던 일에 대해 걱정하고 있을 수도 있습니다.

22 이것들은 그림 각 부분의 가능한 의미 풀이 중 일부입니다.

23 이제, 돌아가서 두 그림을 보세요.

24 그 그림들을 스스로 읽으려고 시도해 보세요.

25 당신은 각 그림을 그린 사람이 어떤 사람인지 알 수 있나요?

26 당신의 의견은 어떤가요?

---

1 Everything you do says something about you.

2 The language you use, the clothes you wear, and even the pets you raise somehow show what kind of person you are.

3 The things you draw are not much different.

4 What you draw and how you draw it are related to your personality.

5 Doctors have been using various drawing tests to better understand people.

6 One of those tests is the Draw–a–Person–in–the–Rain (DAPR) test.

7 Study the pictures below.

8 The person in Drawing A is holding an umbrella in a light rain.

9 On the other hand, the person in Drawing B is in a heavy rain and has no umbrella.

10 Also, there are dark clouds above the person in Drawing B.

11 What can these differences mean?

12 First, the rain shows the stress the person who drew the picture is under.

13 The bigger the drops are or the more heavily the rain is falling, the bigger the stress is.

14 The clouds mean problems waiting to happen, so a big cloud shows the drawer is not very hopeful about the future.

15 Second, the umbrella means the protection the person has in a stressful situation.

16 A big umbrella shows that the drawer has a lot of plans or protection.

17 If there's no umbrella in the drawing, the drawer does not have any means to deal with difficult situations.

18 Third, the details in the drawing of the person have to do with the drawer's attitude under stress.

19 For example, someone who draws a person without a face does not want to draw people's attention to himself or herself.

20 Someone who draws the person on the right side of the paper is ready to meet the future.

21 On the other hand, someone who draws the person on the left side may be worried about things that have happened in the past.

22 These are some of the possible meanings of each part of the drawings.

23 Now, go back and look at the two drawings.

24 Try reading them yourself.

25 Can you understand what kind of person drew each one?

26 What's your opinion?

구석구석지문 TEST Step 1 p.19

Before You Read

1. closely related to what
2. When, draw, shows your feelings
3. In other words, can be expressed
4. Therefore, find out, pay careful attention to

Writing Workshop

1. have been doing, different kinds of
2. had to talk about, own personalities
3. saw myself, shy, friendly
4. What, said, quite different
5. active, curious, get along well with, lots of clubs

Wrap Up 3~4

1. need to go, no train tickets left
2. any other ways
3. take a bus, comfortable
4. do that

구석구석지문 TEST Step 2 p.20

Before You Read

1. A picture is often closely related to what you're feeling in your mind.
2. When you draw a picture, it shows your feelings.
3. In other words, your various feelings can be expressed through pictures.
4. Therefore, you can find out other people's feelings if you pay careful attention to their drawings.

Writing Workshop

1. This year, we have been doing a lot of different kinds of activities at school.
2. Today, we had to talk about our own personalities and then talk about a friend's personality.
3. I saw myself as shy and friendly.
4. What my friend said about me was quite different.
5. She said I am active and curious because I get along well with others and am in lots of clubs.

Wrap Up 3~4

1. G: I need to go to Daegu today, but there are no train tickets left.
2. Are there any other ways to get there?
3. B: You can take a bus. It's fast and comfortable.
4. G: That's a great idea. I'll do that.

15 account, 은행 계좌　**16** scratch, 긁힌 자국

단어 TEST Step 1　p.21

01 광고	02 성급한	03 몇몇의
04 범주, 부류	05 앞으로	06 그러나, 하지만
07 갑자기	08 언급	09 ~을 통해
10 긁힌 자국	11 연락, 접촉	12 추천하다
13 ~처럼 보이다, ~인 것 같다		14 구매자
15 고객	16 결국에	17 배달하다
18 예금	19 은행 계좌	20 아마도
21 매력적인	22 기대	23 보통, 보통 때는
24 식료품, 식료품점	25 묘사	26 욕심 많은
27 깨닫다	28 할인 판매	29 훌륭한, 탁월한
30 빌려주다	31 (무례나 실수 등을) 용서하다	
32 각도	33 실내의	34 중고의
35 ~만큼 좋은	36 ~에 비교해서	37 밀어 내리다
38 하루 종일	39 ~을 건네주다	40 ~의 수/숫자
41 ~을 요청하다	42 다른 각도에서	43 ~에 좋은

단어 TEST Step 2　p.22

01 account	02 scratch	03 maybe
04 savings	05 normally	06 accept
07 posting	08 greedy	09 comment
10 through	11 used	12 seem
13 advertisement	14 recommend	15 ahead
16 description	17 angle	18 suddenly
19 realize	20 buyer	21 grocery
22 category	23 deliver	24 excuse
25 contact	26 hasty	27 customer
28 attractive	29 expectation	30 finally
31 indoors	32 mix	33 several
34 post	35 grow up	36 ask for
37 get a reply	38 as good as ~	39 hand over
40 good for ~	41 a whole day	42 push down
43 compared to ~		

단어 TEST Step 3　p.23

1 used, 중고의　**2** excuse, 용서하다　**3** ugly, 못생긴

4 normally, 보통, 보통 때는　**5** comment, 언급

6 search, 찾다, 검색하다　**7** accept, 받아들이다

8 expectation, 기대　**9** contact, 연락, 접촉

10 lend, 빌려주다　**11** sink, 가라앉다　**12** savings, 예금

13 act, 행동하다　**14** experience, 경험

대화문 TEST Step 1　p.24~26

Listen and Speak 1 Listen

1. mind, lean / at all

2. mind / don't

3. change seats / with

4. shut / ahead

Listen and Speak 1 A-1

Excuse, return / why, to return / dirt, haven't, worn / mind, a look / all, Here

Listen and Speak 1 A-2

What / open, should / fill out, form / use / at all

Listen and Speak 1 B-1

lean / at all

Listen and Speak 1 B-2

Do, mind, seats

Listen and Speak 1 B-3

Do, eat / ahead

Listen and Speak 2 Listen

1. look around / afraid, open

2. pictures during / afraid, can't, disturb other

3. Can, anywhere / afraid

Listen & Speak 2 A-1

Look, Let's check / can't, inside / haven't finished, yet / first, can

Listen & Speak 2 A-2

come / afraid / That's, special, various games / heard, going, then / Let's, together

Listen & Speak 2 B-1

around / open only

Listen & Speak 2 B-2

Can, use / sorry, only, online orders

Listen & Speak 2 B-3

Can / can't, on

Real-Life Zone

to find, mind, take / at all, favorites / looking, over, lend / afraid, Actually / okay / used, online / Used bookstores, thought, idea / together, think / cheap, get

Wrap Up 1-2

mind, a look / Not, called, bought / putting / means, bringing / interesting, where, get / afraid, contact with

Wrap Up 3~4

some, place to buy / been, lots of / never been / about / afraid, What / fine

Listen and Speak 1 Listen

1. M: Do you mind if I lean my seat back?

G: No, not at all.

2. B: Mom do you mind if I use your smartphone?

W: I don't mind.

3. G: Do you mind if I change seats with you?

B: I'm sorry. I'm with my friend.

4. B: Do you mind if I shut the blinds?

G: No, go ahead.

Listen and Speak 1 A-1

B: Excuse me. I want to return these sneakers.

W: Okay. Can I ask why you want to return them?

B: There's dirt on them and I haven't even worn them yet.

W: Do you mind if I have a look?

B: Not at all. Here.

Listen and Speak 1 A-2

M: What can I help you with?

G: I'd like to open a bank account. What should I do?

M: First, you need to fill out this form.

G: Sure. Do you mind if I use your pen?

M: Not at all.

Listen and Speak 1 B-1

A: Do you mind if I lean my seat back?

B: No, not at all.

Listen and Speak 1 B-2

A: Do you mind if I change seats with you?

B: No, not at all.

Listen and Speak 1 B-3

A: Do you mind if I eat this snack here?

B: No, go ahead.

Listen and Speak 2 Listen

1. G: Can I look around the stage?

M: I'm sorry. I'm afraid you can't. It's open only for the actors.

2. B: Can I take pictures during the play?

W: I'm sorry. I'm afraid you can't. It can disturb other people.

3. B: Can I sit anywhere I want?

M: I'm afraid you can't. Your seat number is on your ticket.

Listen & Speak 2 A-1

G: Look! This jacket is really cute. Let's check out this store.

B: Wait, I'm afraid we can't take our drinks inside.

G: But I haven't finished mine yet.

B: Let's finish our drinks first. Then we can go inside.

Listen & Speak 2 A-2

G: Minho, can you come with us to the game expo this Sunday?

B: I'd love to, but I'm afraid I can't. I have an important test next week.

G: That's too bad. They're having a special show of various games.

B: Yeah, I've heard it's really great. What about going with me next Saturday then?

G: Sure. Let's go together next Saturday.

Listen & Speak 2 B-1

A: Can I look around the stage?

B: I'm sorry. I'm afraid you can't. It's open only for the actors.

Listen & Speak 2 B-2

A: Can I use this coupon?

B: I'm sorry. I'm afraid you can't. The coupon is only for online orders.

Listen & Speak 2 B-3

A: Can I seat anywhere I want?

B: I'm sorry. I'm afraid you can't. Your seat number is on your ticket.

Real-Life Zone

Ben: Wow! This comic book is really hard to find. Do you mind if I take a look at it?

Dana: Not at all. It's one of my favorites. I've read it maybe a hundred times.

Ben: I've been looking all over for it. Can you lend it to me?

Dana: I'm afraid I can't. Actually, it's not mine. It's my sister's. Sorry.

Ben: Oh, that's okay. I understand.

Dana: You know, if you really want it, you should check used bookstores online.

Ben: Used bookstores online? I've never thought of that. That's a good idea.

Dana: Let's look together. Oh, here's one! It says it's "like new." What do you think?

Ben: Great! And it's cheap! I'll get it. Thanks!

Wrap Up 1-2

B: The toy on your desk is so cute. Do you mind if I take a look at it?

G: Not at all. It's called a maneki-neko, or a good luck cat. My friend bought it for me when she went to Japan.

B: Why is it putting its hand up?

G: That means it is bringing you money.

B: Really? That's interesting. Could you ask your friend where she got it? I'm going to Japan next week and I'd like to get one.

G: I'm sorry. I'm afraid I can't. I lost contact with her.

Wrap Up 3~4

B: I want to buy some traditional Korean gifts for my friends. Where's a good place to buy them?

G: Have you been to Insa-dong? They have lots of traditional Korean things there.

B: No, I've never been there.

G: How about I take you there this Friday afternoon?

B: Oh, I'm afraid I can't. I have other plans. What about Saturday?

G: That's fine with me.

01 First Online Sale

02 rides, bike, every day

03 taller and stronger, year   04 become too, for, one

05 However, enough, savings account

06 What can, do

07 Suddenly, had an idea   08 almost as good, one

09 Maybe, sell, add, money   10 acted fast

11 posted, with, comment, excellent

12 excited, thinking, planned, buy

13 himself riding, shiny new

14 could, wait, reply, advertisement

15 Every, minutes, checked, hits

16 As, went up, expectations

17 passed, whole, received, texts

18 Nobody seemed, bike

19 postings, pushed, post down

20 heart, to sink

21 wrong with, postings

22 bike, attractive enough

23 searched on, tips, sell

24 realized what, done wrong

25 been, hasty, greedy

26 enough information, possible buyers

27 compared to, price, high

28 wrote, posting, longer description

29 added, from different angles

30 kept indoors, like, scratches

31 got several texts

32 Sadly, asked, lower price   33 to accept, sold, for

34 buyer, handed over, needed

35 could get, new bike   36 felt both happy, sad

37 himself, grown, through, experience

01 Online Sale

02 rides his bike, every day

03 taller and stronger

04 too small for him, bigger, faster

05 enough money, savings account

06 What

07 Suddnely, had an idea   08 almost as good as

09 add the money   10 acted fast

11 posted, with a short comment, Used bike, text

12 thinking about   13 himself riding, shiny

14 could not wait, advertisement

15 Every few minutes

16 As, went up, went up

17 finally, whole day, received no texts

18 Nobody seemed

19 postings, pushed his post down

20 to sink   21 wrong with

22 attractive enough

23 for tips on how to sell

24 what he had done wrong   25 hasty, greedy

26 possible buyers

27 compared to, price, high

28 with a longer description

29 added, from different angles

30 kept indoors, scratches   31 several texts

32 asked for, lower price   33 to accept, finally, for

34 handed over   35 could get

36 both happy and sad

37 go, himself, grown up, through the experience

1 세윤이의 첫 온라인 판매

2 세윤이는 매일 학교에 자전거를 타고 갑니다.

3 세윤이는 자신의 자전거를 좋아하지만, 그는 올해 키가 더 크고 힘도 더 세졌습니다.

4 그의 자전거는 그에게 너무 작아져서, 그는 더 크고 더 빠른 자전거를 사기를 원합니다.

5 하지만, 그는 자신의 예금 계좌에 충분한 돈을 가지고 있지 않습니다.

6 그가 무엇을 할 수 있을까요?

7 갑자기, 세윤이는 아이디어가 떠올랐습니다.

8 "내 오래된 자전거는 거의 새것과 다름없이 좋아.

9 아마 나는 그것을 팔고 새것을 사기 위한 돈에 보탤 수 있을 거야."

10 그는 빠르게 행동했습니다.

11 그는 스마트폰으로 자신의 자전거 사진을 찍었고, 짧은 설명과 함께 온라인 장터에 사진을 게시했습니다. "훌륭한 상태의 중고 자전거. 겨우 십만 원. 문자 주세요."

12 세윤이는 자신이 구입하려고 계획한 자전거에 대해 생각하며 신이 났습니다.

13 그는 자신이 빛나는 새 자전거를 타고 있는 것을 상상할 수 있었습니다.

14 세윤이는 자신의 온라인 광고에 대한 대답이 오는 것을 무척 기다렸습니다.

15 몇 분마다 그는 조회 수를 체크했습니다.

16 숫자가 올라갈수록 그의 기대도 덩달아 올라갔습니다.

17 한 시간이 지나고, 두 시간이 지나고, 마침내 하루가 지났지만 세윤이는 문자를 받지 못했습니다.

18 아무도 그의 자전거를 원하지 않는 것처럼 보였습니다.

19 다른 사람들의 새 게시물이 그의 게시물을 리스트에서 밀어냈습니다.

20 세윤이의 가슴이 내려앉기 시작했습니다.

21 '내 포스팅에 무슨 문제가 있지?

22 내 자전거가 충분히 매력적이지 못한가?'

23 세윤이는 온라인에서 판매하는 방법에 대한 조언을 찾기 위해 인터넷을 검색했습니다.

24 곧 그는 자신의 잘못을 깨달았습니다.

25 세윤이는 너무 성급했고 너무 욕심이 많았습니다.

26 그는 구매 가능성이 있는 사람들에게 충분한 정보를 주지 않았습니다.

27 또한, 다른 자전거들과 비교했을 때 그의 가격은 너무 높았습니다.

28 세윤이는 자신의 자전거에 대한 더 긴 묘사가 있는 새 게시물을 작성했습니다.

29 그는 자신의 자전거를 다른 각도에서 보여 주기 위해서 더 많은 사진들을 첨부했습니다.

30 "24인치 자전거. 훌륭한 상태. 항상 실내에 보관했음. 새것처럼 탐. 스크래치 매우 적음. 12-14세에게 좋음. 8만 원."

31 이번에 그는 여러 통의 문자 메시지를 받았습니다.

32 애석하게도, 그들은 모두 더 낮은 가격을 요청했습니다.

33 처음에는 받아들이기 어려웠지만, 마침내 그는 자신의 자전거를 칠만 원에 팔았습니다.

34 세윤이는 구매자를 만나 자전거를 건네주고, 그가 필요했던 돈을 받았습니다.

35 이제 세윤이는 새 자전거를 살 수 있습니다.

36 그는 기쁘고 슬픈 감정을 동시에 느꼈습니다.

37 세윤이는 자신의 오래된 자전거가 떠나는 것을 봐서 슬펐지만, 이 경험을 통해 자신이 많은 것을 배우고 조금 더 성장한 것이 기뻤습니다.

1 Seyun's First Online Sale.

2 Seyun rides his bike to school every day.

3 He likes his bike, but he is taller and stronger this year.

4 His bike has become too small for him, so he wants to buy a bigger, faster one.

5 However, he does not have enough money in his savings account.

6 What can he do?

7 Suddenly, Seyun had an idea.

8 "My old bike is almost as good as a new one.

9 Maybe I can sell it and add the money to buy a new one."

10 He acted fast.

11 He took a photo of his bike with his smartphone and posted the picture, with a short comment, on an online market: "Used bike in excellent condition. Only 100,000 won. Please text me."

12 He was excited, thinking about the bike he planned to buy.

13 He could see himself riding the shiny new bike.

14 He could not wait to get a reply to his online advertisement.

15 Every few minutes he checked the number of hits.

16 As the number of hits went up, his expectations went up too.

17 One hour passed, then two, and finally a whole day, but he received no texts.

18 Nobody seemed to want his bike.

19 New postings by other people pushed his post down the list.

20 His heart began to sink.

21 "What's wrong with my posting?

22 Is my bike not attractive enough?"

23 He searched on the Internet for tips on how to sell online.

24 Then he realized what he had done wrong.

25 He had been too hasty and too greedy.

26 He had not given enough information to the possible buyers.

27 Also, when compared to other bicycles, his price was too high.

28 He wrote a new posting with a longer description of the bike.

29 He added more photos to show his bike from different angles.

30 "Twenty-four inch bicycle. Excellent condition.

Always kept indoors. Rides just like new. Very few scratches. Good for someone 12–14 years old. 80,000 won."

31 This time he got several texts.

32 Sadly, they all asked for a lower price.

33 It was hard to accept at first, but finally he sold his bike for 70,000 won.

34 He met the buyer, handed over his bike, and got the money he needed.

35 Now he could get a new bike.

36 He felt both happy and sad.

37 He was sad to see his old bike go, but he was happy with himself because he had learned a lot and grown up a bit through the experience.

구석구석지문 TEST Step 1 p.40

After You Read B

1. who posted a bike for sale
2. me
3. check, to see, as you wrote
4. has, few scratches, ugly
5. Let, check, seems good enough
6. Perfect
7. By the way, why you want to sell
8. grown more than, this year, too small for me
9. see

Writing Workshop

1. If, are looking for, would be perfect
2. as cheap as, on sale
3. bought one, it
4. would advise, to buy a bigger size, what you usually buy
5. Even though, the same, as what, normally wear, too small for

Wrap Up 7

1. September 8th
2. Last spring, with my grandfather
3. visited, watered the potatoes often
4. had never planted, before
5. dug some of
6. looked as good as, there were
7. can take some of, to the market, sell
8. will be really exciting

구석구석지문 TEST Step 2 p.41

After You Read B

1. Buyer: Hello? Are you the one who posted a bike for sale?
2. Seyun: Yes, that's me.
3. Buyer: Can I check your bike to see if it's in good condition as you wrote?
4. Seyun: Sure. It has very few scratches but nothing ugly.
5. Buyer: Let me check…. Yeah, it seems good enough.
6. Seyun: Perfect!
7. Buyer: By the way, can I ask why you want to sell this bike?
8. Seyun: I've grown more than 10 cm this year, so it's too small for me now.
9. Buyer: Oh, I see.

Writing Workshop

1. If you are looking for a new swimming suit, this one would be perfect. It is beautiful.
2. Also, it is as cheap as the one that is on sale.
3. I bought one, and I really like it.
4. However, I would advise you to buy a bigger size than what you usually buy.
5. Even though I had ordered the same size as what I normally wear, it was too small for me.

Wrap Up 7

1. September 8th, Monday
2. Last spring, I planted some potatoes with my grandfather in his garden.
3. I visited the garden and watered the potatoes often.
4. I had never planted potatoes before. It was fun.
5. Today, my grandfather and I dug some of the potatoes.
6. They looked as good as the ones you see in the market, and there were so many of them.
7. My grandfather says we can take some of them to the market and sell them!
8. That will be really exciting.

Lesson **7**

단어 TEST Step 1
p.42

01 주의 깊은, 조심스러운, 세심한	02 판유리
03 놀랍게도	04 바삭한	05 아마, 어쩌면
06 삼키다	07 결과	08 돌리다, 비틀다
09 막다	10 환상적인	11 수리하다
12 압력	13 알아채다, 의식하다	
14 수증기, 김	15 끓기; 끓이다	
16 주의 깊게, 조심스럽게	17 죽음
18 비상사태	19 양, 총계	20 지붕
21 균형; 균형을 잡다	22 호흡, 숨	23 특히
24 소파, 긴 의자	25 필수적인	26 최근에
27 ~ 모양의	28 숨기다, 숨다	29 뚜껑
30 안개; 수증기가 서리다	31 회사, 동료
32 ~을 야기하다; 원인	33 생산물, 상품
34 유용한, 도움이 되는	35 점점 커지다
36 A가 ~하는 것을 방지하다	37 끓어 넘치다
38 안개로 흐려지다, 김이 서리다	39 내보내다
40 주위를 둘러보다	41 ~로 구성되다	42 ~의 결과
43 거쳐 지나가다, 통과하다	

단어 TEST Step 2
p.43

01 surprisingly	02 twist	03 hide
04 crispy	05 notice	06 pane
07 hidden	08 breathing	09 swallow
10 couch	11 helpful	12 repair
13 death	14 recently	15 shaped
16 product	17 emergency	18 amount
19 pressure	20 lid	21 carefully
22 boil	23 especially	24 prevent
25 balance	26 fog	27 careful
28 necessary	29 result	30 perhaps
31 cause	32 company	33 roof
34 steam	35 boil over	36 let out
37 the result of ~	38 look out	39 pass through
40 look around	41 keep A from -ing	
42 be made up of	43 in an emergency	

단어 TEST Step 3
p.44

1 recently, 최근에 2 swallow, 삼키다

3 helpful, 유용한, 도움이 되는 4 notice, 알아채다, 의식하다

5 normally, 보통, 보통 때는 6 emergency, 비상사태

7 necessary, 필수적인 8 couch, 소파, 긴 의자

9 repair, 수리하다 10 roof, 지붕 11 breathing, 호흡, 숨

12 especially, 특히, 특별히 13 prevent, 막다

14 amount, 양, 총계 15 product, 생산물, 상품

16 balance, 균형을 잡다

대화문 TEST Step 1
p.45~47

Listen and Speak 1 Listen

1. picture, those / invented
2. why, front / sold, repaired
3. what, looked / looked like
4. wonder, tried / tested

Listen and Speak 1 A-1

invention, cook without electricity / possible, how it works / sunlight / helpful

Listen and Speak 1 A-2

Have, heard, shaped, Most, tall, wondering how people moved, searched, learned, ropes, amazing

Listen and Speak 1 B-1

who / invented

Listen and Speak 1 B-2

looked like / model, like

Listen and Speak 1 B-3

wonder, country, from / from

Listen and Speak 2 Listen

1. What, with / Let, Maybe
2. How, float / pushes, up
3. move / see, with
4. with / pictures

Listen & Speak 2 A-1

Look, going up quickly / pass, increases / mean / Let, step, made, amount / amazing

Listen & Speak 2 A-2

field, Invention / creative inventions / excited, planning / Good, Let, museum / Let's, started

Listen & Speak 2 B-1

What, with / Let, see, play

Listen & Speak 2 B-2

with / see, from

Listen & Speak 2 B-3

What, with / send text messages

Real-Life Zone

these / why, little holes / think, maybe, make, look tastier / possible, must, reasons / look, what / says during, through, thin / make, crispy / why

Wrap Up 1-2

what, going / sounds, that, Saturdays, what they are / advertisement, Here / say / says / both, fantastic / call, what

Wrap Up 3~4

invention competition / sounds / enter, ideas / when, competition is / from / wonder, have / talk, science

대화문 TEST Step 2

p.48~50

Listen and Speak 1 Listen

1. G: Look at this picture. I wonder who those men are.
   B: They're the Wright brothers. They invented the airplane.

2. G: I wonder why they are standing in front of the bicycle shop.
   B: They had a bicycle shop. They sold and repaired bicycles.

3. G: I wonder what the first plane looked like.
   B: Look! There is a model. It looked like a big bird.

4. G: I wonder where they first tried to fly their airplane.
   B: They tested their airplane on a hill in North Carolina.

Listen and Speak 1 A-1

B: Look at this invention. It can help us cook without electricity.
G: Is that possible? I wonder how it works.
B: It uses sunlight to cook food.
G: Wow. That would be really helpful when you go camping.

Listen and Speak 1 A-2

B: Hi, class. Have you ever heard about the Moai? They are tall, human-shaped stones in Chile. Most of the stones are four meters tall, but the tallest one is 20 meters tall. I was wondering how people moved them long ago. So I searched the Internet and learned that they used ropes. Isn't that amazing?

Listen and Speak 1 B-1

A: I wonder who those men are.
B: They're the Wright brothers. They invented the airplane.

Listen and Speak 1 B-2

A: I wonder what the first plane looked like.
B: Look! There is a model. It looked like a big bird.

Listen and Speak 1 B-3

A: I wonder what country they're from.
B: They're from the U.S.

Listen and Speak 2 Listen

1. G: What can we do with these VR glasses?
   B: Let me see.... Maybe we can play soccer.

2. B: How does the ball float in the air?
   G: Let me see.... I think air pushes the ball up.

3. G: How does this train start to move?
   B: Let me see.... I think you can move it with a smartphone app.

4. B: What can we do with this drone?
   G: Well, let me see.... Maybe we can take pictures from the sky.

Listen & Speak 2 A-1

G: Look at the number. It's going up quickly.
B: When people pass by, the number increases.
G: Oh, you're right. What does the number mean?
B: Let me see.... Oh, when people step on the floor, energy is made. It shows the amount of energy that is made.
G: Wow, that's amazing!

Listen & Speak 2 A-2

G: We're going on a field trip tomorrow to the Invention Museum.
B: I've heard that it has a lot of creative inventions.
G: That's why I'm so excited. How about planning the tour before we go?
B: Good idea. Let me see.... I have the school letter and a map of the museum.
G: Perfect. Let's get started.

Listen & Speak 2 B-1

A: What can we do with this VR glasses?
B: Let me see... We can play soccer.

Listen & Speak 2 B-2

A: What can we do with this drone?
B: Let me see... We can take pictures from the sky.

Listen & Speak 2 B-3

A: What can we do with the smart watch?
B: Let me see... We can send text messages.

Real-Life Zone

G: I like these crackers. They're really good.
B: Yeah, me, too. I wonder why crackers have these little holes in them.
G: I don't know. Let me think.... Um ... well ... maybe it's because the holes make the crackers look tastier.
B: That's possible, but there must be some other

reasons.

G: Let's look up crackers on the Internet and see what it says.

B: Okay. Oh, look at this.

G: It says during baking, steam comes out through the holes and that makes the crackers thin.

B: It also says that the holes make the crackers crispy.

G: Wow! So that's why they have holes!

Wrap Up 1-2

B: Hi, Kate. Today's Saturday, so what about going to the Einstein Science Park today?

G: That sounds like a good idea. I heard that they have special programs on Saturdays. I wonder what they are.

B: Let me see…. I saw an advertisement in the newspaper. Here it is.

G: What does it say?

B: It says that today they have two shows: the Smart Design Show and the International Drone Show in Einstein Hall 101.

G: They both sound fantastic.

B: I'll call them and ask what time they start.

Wrap Up 3~4

G: John, look. The school is having an invention competition.

B: Really? That sounds interesting.

G: Yeah. You should enter that. You always have great ideas.

B: Does it say when the competition is?

G: Let me see…. It says it's November 11. That's two weeks from today.

B: I wonder what I have to do to enter the competition.

G: It says here you should talk to Mr. Harrison, the science teacher.

본문 TEST Step 1   p.51~52

01 Hidden Holes

02 Think, hole, seen recently

03 Was, good, or, bad   04 If, hole, sock, bad

05 hole, for, button, good

06 There, holes everywhere   07 so, may, even notice

08 hidden, make, life safe   09 Take, pen

10 Look at, carefully   11 small hole, cap

12 why it is there   13 hole, help save lives

14 especially, put, like, in

15 Sometimes, even swallow

16 stop, breathing, cause death

17 famous, company, putting, hole

18 lets, pass through, lives

19 look around, helpful role

20 with, lid, perhaps, noticed 21 hole, too, safety

22 cooking, pressure, builds up

23 inside, boil over, hole

24 out, keeps, from coming   25 Have, ever been on

26 Wasn't it exciting, below

27 Surprisingly, there was, in

28 are made up of   29 in the middle pane

30 balances, air pressure

31 Without, little, break, emergency

32 prevents, from fogging up

33 more products, hidden holes

34 why it is there

35 result, careful, life safer

본문 TEST Step 2   p.53~54

01 Hidden   02 have seen recently

03 good, bad   04 in your sock

05 for a button   06 There, everywhere

07 so small, notice

08 well hidden, make your life safe

09 Take   10 Look at, carefully

11 a small hole   12 why it is there

13 help save lives   14 put, like, in

15 Sometimes, swallow them

16 stop their breathing, cause death

17 putting a small hole

18 lets, pass through, saved lives

19 look around, play a helpful role

20 with a lid, noticed, lid   21 for safety

22 When cooking, pressure, builds up

23 boil over

24 steam out, keeps, from coming

25 Have, been

26 Wasn't it exciting, look out

27 Surprisingly

28 are made up of   29 in the middle pane

30 balances, air pressure

31 Without, little hole, in an emergency

32 prevents, from fogging up, fantastic view

33 that have, hidden holes   34 why it is there

35 the result, to make your life safer

1 숨겨진 구멍들

2 여러분이 최근에 본 구멍에 대해 생각해 보라.

3 그것은 좋은 구멍이었는가, 아니면 나쁜 구멍이었는가?

4 만약 그것이 여러분의 양말에 있는 구멍이었다면, 그것은 좋지 않은 것이었다.

5 만약 그것이 단추를 위해 셔츠에 있는 구멍이었다면, 그것은 좋은 것이었다.

6 구멍은 어디에나 있다.

7 어떤 것들은 너무 작아서 인지하지 못할 수도 있다.

8 그것들은 잘 숨겨져 있지만, 이 작은 구멍들 중 많은 것들이 매우 중요하고 여러분의 삶을 안전하게 해 준다.

9 펜을 꺼내라.

10 그것을 자세히 관찰해 보라.

11 뚜껑에 작은 구멍이 보이는가?

12 여러분은 왜 거기에 구멍이 있는지 아는가?

13 펜 뚜껑에 있는 구멍이 생명을 구하는 데 도움을 줄 수 있기 때문이다.

14 사람들, 특히 아이들은 종종 펜 뚜껑 같은 작은 것들을 그들의 입에 넣는다.

15 때때로 그들은 심지어 그것들을 삼키기도 한다.

16 이것은 그들의 호흡을 막고 죽음을 초래할 수도 있다.

17 유명한 펜 회사가 자사의 펜 뚜껑에 작은 구멍을 넣기 시작했다.

18 뚜껑에 있는 그 구멍은 공기를 통하게 해 주고 생명들을 구했다.

19 여러분이 주위를 둘러본다면, 여러분의 생활에 도움을 주는 다른 구멍들을 보게 될 것이다.

20 만약 여러분이 뚜껑 있는 냄비에 어떤 것을 요리해 본 적이 있다면, 아마도 여러분은 뚜껑에 작은 구멍이 있다는 것을 알아챘을 수도 있다.

21 이 구멍 역시 안전을 위해 존재한다.

22 뚜껑이 있는 냄비에 무언가를 요리할 때, 냄비 안쪽의 압력이 상승한다.

23 만약 뚜껑에 그 구멍이 없다면, 그 안의 물은 금방 끓어 넘칠 것이다.

24 그 구멍이 수증기를 나가게 해 주고 물이 밖으로 넘치는 것을 막아 준다.

25 비행기를 타 본 적이 있는가?

26 창밖을 내다보고 아래에 있는 세상을 보는 것이 신나지 않았는가?

27 놀랍게도, 여러분의 창문에는 작은 구멍이 하나 있었다.

28 비행기 창문은 세 개의 유리판으로 구성되어 있다.

29 그 중간 유리판에 구멍이 있다.

30 그것은 기압의 균형을 맞춰 준다.

31 이 작은 구멍이 없다면, 비행기 창문은 비상시에 깨질 수 있다.

32 그 구멍은 또한, 멋진 경치를 즐길 수 있도록 창문에 김이 서리는 것을 막아 준다.

33 숨겨진 작은 구멍들이 있는 더 많은 제품들이 있다.

34 앞으로, 여러분이 어떤 물건에서 작은 구멍을 본다면, 왜 그것이 거기에 있는지 자신에게 물어보라.

35 아마도 그것은 여러분의 삶을 더 안전하게 만들려는 사려 깊은 디자인의 결과일 것이다.

1 Hidden Holes

2 Think about a hole that you have seen recently.

3 Was it a good hole or a bad hole?

4 If it was a hole in your sock, it was bad.

5 If it was a hole in your shirt for a button, it was good.

6 There are holes everywhere.

7 Some are so small you may not even notice them.

8 They are well hidden, but many of these small holes are very important and make your life safe.

9 Take a pen.

10 Look at it carefully.

11 Do you see a small hole in the cap?

12 Do you know why it is there?

13 The hole in a pen cap can help save lives.

14 People, especially children, often put small things like pen caps in their mouths.

15 Sometimes they even swallow them.

16 This can stop their breathing and cause death.

17 A famous pen company started putting a small hole in their pen caps.

18 The hole in the cap lets air pass through and has saved lives.

19 If you look around, you will see other holes that play a helpful role in your life.

20 If you have ever cooked anything in a pot with a lid, perhaps you noticed a small hole in the lid.

21 This hole, too, is there for safety.

22 When cooking something in a pot with a lid, the pressure inside the pot builds up.

23 The water inside would quickly boil over if the lid did not have that hole.

24 The hole lets steam out and keeps the water from coming out.

25 Have you ever been on an airplane?

26 Wasn't it exciting to look out the window and see the world below?

27 Surprisingly, there was a small hole in your window.

28 Airplane windows are made up of three panes.

29 There is a hole in the middle pane.

30 It balances the air pressure.

31 Without this little hole, airplane windows might break in an emergency.

32 The hole also prevents the window from fogging up so that you can enjoy that fantastic view.

33 There are many more products that have small hidden holes.

34 In the future, when you see a little hole in something, ask yourself why it is there.

35 Maybe it is the result of a careful design to make your life safer.

구석구석지문 TEST Step 1　　　p.61

After You Read B

1. lets the air pass through, swallow
2. balances the air pressures
3. lets steam out, prevents, from boiling over

Work Together

1. Sweet Dream
2. helps people dream sweet dreams
3. have a sweet dream every night
4. select the type of dream, so that, while you are sleeping

Writing Workshop

1. Refrigerator
2. Can, imagine without
3. so that, keep food cool, fresh
4. invented, form of the refrigerator
5. developed through, has become a necessary part of modern life
6. If, did not have, would not be able to enjoy

구석구석지문 TEST Step 2　　　p.62

After You Read B

1. It lets the air pass through even when people swallow the pen cap.
2. It balances the air pressures.
3. It lets steam out and prevents the water in the pot from boiling over.

Work Together

1. Sweet Dream Helmet
2. This invention helps people dream sweet dreams.
3. If you use the Sweet Dream Helmet, you will have a sweet dream every night.
4. You can even select the type of dream you want to dream so that you can have different experiences while you are sleeping.

Writing Workshop

1. A Refrigerator
2. Can you imagine without a refrigerator?
3. We use it every day so that we can keep food cool and fresh.
4. In 1755, William Cullen invented the first form of the refrigerator.
5. After that, it developed through the years and has become a necessary part of modern life.
6. If we did not have refrigerators in today's world, we would not be able to enjoy ice cream on hot summer days.

Lesson 8

7 boil, 끓이다   8 mixture, 혼합물

9 recommend, 추천하다   10 pour, 붓다, 따르다

11 stay, 그대로 있다   12 stir, 휘젓다

13 temperature, 온도, 기온   14 melt, 녹다

15 local, 지역의, 현지의   16 ginger, 생강

단어 TEST Step 1   p.63

01 끓다, 끓이다   02 감동적인

03 따뜻하게 하다, 따뜻한   04 잘게 썰다

05 반면에, ~하는 동안에   06 제공하다

07 더하다, 첨가하다   08 섞다   09 생강

10 식히다   11 보물   12 맛

13 아픔, 통증   14 고루 잘 섞인, 매끄러운

15 열다, 개최하다   16 목구멍, 목   17 후추, 고추

18 온도, 기온   19 줄이다   20 녹다

21 지역의, 현지의   22 코가 막힌, 답답한   23 두꺼운, 걸쭉한

24 낮은   25 그대로 있다   26 약

27 해산물   28 추천하다   29 휘젓다

30 혼합물   31 아픈, 따가운   32 붓다, 따르다

33 섞다   34 요리법   35 A와 같은

36 ~로 만들어지다   37 알아내다, 발견하다

38 ~ 한 그릇   39 ~에 더하여, 게다가

40 ~와 다르다   41 A에게 B를 둘러보도록 안내하다

42 ~에 좋다   43 A뿐만 아니라 B도

단어 TEST Step 2   p.64

01 pour   02 recipe   03 cool

04 hold   05 add   06 blend

07 recommend   08 chop   09 boil

10 medicine   11 smooth   12 eastern

13 ginger   14 mixture   15 serve

16 stuffy   17 taste   18 while

19 pain   20 melt   21 pepper

22 temperature   23 thick   24 throat

25 stir   26 reduce   27 touching

28 treasure   29 seafood   30 local

31 mix   32 lamb   33 stay

34 sore   35 be different from

36 a plate of   37 as well as   38 find out

39 put on   40 for the first time

41 such as A   42 not only A but also B

43 be made with

단어 TEST Step 3   p.65

1 pain, 아픔, 통증   2 touching, 감동적인

3 chop, 잘게 썰다   4 treasure, 보물

5 thick, 두꺼운, 걸쭉한   6 reduce, 줄이다

대화문 TEST Step 1   p.66~68

Listen and Speak 1 Listen 1

they called / called / Could, again / made with, from

Listen and Speak 1 Listen 2

eating / say, again / like, traditional food

Listen and Speak 1 Listen 3

that, eating, looks like / Sorry, again / tasty, popular

Listen and Speak 1 A-1

favorite, What / traditional drink / say, again / sweet / try

Listen and Speak 1 A-2

tried / could / salad, popular / special / with rice, fish, only, but, healthy

Listen and Speak 1 B

1. Have, tried / Sorry / traditional dessert

2. tried / traditional

3. ever tried / that / in

Listen and Speak 2 Listen

1. recommend, traditional / Try

2. Could, for / touching

3. beginners / about

4. snack / How

Listen & Speak 2 A-1

something special / How, cooking, would / recommend, easy / about, easy, delicious / idea

Listen & Speak 2 B-2

Welcome, many, visit, There, clothing, other, tasty local, recommend visiting, enjoying

Real-Life Zone

for / Here, back, take / much, recommend / recommend / Could / made, over, good, health / try / served, spicy, pepper, okay / problem

Wrap Up 1-2

Are, have / Can, place / recommend, enough / would, recommend / fantastic / thinking, makes, water

---

Listen and Speak 1 Listen 1

B: Hi, Grace. Those are pretty. What are they called?

G: They're called *dango*.

B: I'm sorry. Could you say that again?

G: *Dan-go*. They're sweet and made with rice cake powder. They're from Japan.

Listen and Speak 1 Listen 2

B: Alice, what's that you're eating?

G: It's *rasmalai*.

B: *Ra....* Could you say that again?

G: *Ras-ma-lai*. It's like a cheesecake in a sweet cream. It's a traditional food in India.

Listen and Speak 1 Listen 3

G: What's that you're eating, David? It looks like a chocolate ball.

B: It's *brigadeiro*.

G: Sorry? Could you say that again?

B: *Bri-ga-dei-ro*. It's sweet and tasty. It's popular in Brazil.

Listen and Speak 1 A-1

G: My favorite Korean traditional drink is Maesil-tea. What about you, Jinsu?

B: Well, my favorite traditional drink is Sikhye.

G: Sik.... Can you say that again?

B: Sik-hye. It's sweet and cool.

G: I want to try it.

Listen and Speak 1 A-2

B: Have you ever tried *poke*?

G: Sorry, could you say that again, please?

B: *Po-ke*. It's a salad that is popular in Hawaii.

G: What's so special about it?

B: It's made with rice and fish. It's not only delicious but also very healthy.

Listen and Speak 1 B

1. A: Have you ever tried *rasmalai*?

    B: Sorry, could you say that again?

    A: *Rasmalai*. It's a traditional dessert in India.

2. A: Have you ever tried *brigadeiro*?

    B: Sorry, could you say that again?

    A: *Brigadeiro*. It's a traditional dessert in Brazil.

3. A: Have you ever tried *macaron*?

    B: Sorry, could you say that again?

    A: *Macaron*. It's a traditional dessert in France.

Listen and Speak 2 Listen

1. B: Could you recommend a good traditional dish?

    W: Try Samgyetang. It'll give you energy.

2. G: Could you recommend a good book for my little sister?

    M: I recommend this one. The story is touching.

3. B: Could you recommend a guitar for beginners?

    W: How about this one? Many beginners play it.

4. G: Could you recommend a snack for my dog?

    M: Sure. How about this? Dogs really like it.

Listen & Speak 2 A-1

B: Tomorrow is my dad's birthday. I'd like to do something special for him.

G: How about cooking something for him? He would really like that.

B: That sounds great. Can you recommend something easy to cook?

G: Umm. How about Gimchijeon? It's easy to make and it's delicious.

B: Oh, that's a good idea. He'll love it.

Listen & Speak 2 B-2

M: Welcome to the Sydney Information Center. Sydney has many places you will want to visit. The Rocks Markets is one of them. There you can buy art, clothing, books and many other things. You can also eat fresh, tasty local food. We recommend visiting the Rocks Markets and enjoying the food and the fun there.

Real-Life Zone

M: Good afternoon. A table for two?

B: Yes.

M: This way please. Here is the menu. I'll be back in a few minutes and take your order.

B: Okay. Thank you.

G: I don't know much about Korean food. Could you recommend something?

B: Well, I'd recommend the Bibimbap.

G: I'm sorry. Could you say that again, please?

B: This one. Bi-bim-bap. It's made with lots of vegetables, beef and an egg over rice. It's tasty and it's also good for your health.

G: That sounds great. I'll try it.

B: It's served with a spicy red pepper sauce. Is that okay?

G: No problem. I like spicy food.

Wrap Up 1-2

B: Tomorrow is my birthday.

G: I know. Are you going to have a birthday party, Alex?

B: Yes. Can you recommend a good place to have the party?

G: I'd recommend the Happy Snack House. The

food is really good and it'll be large enough.

B: What dish would you recommend?

G: I'd recommend the onion rings. They're fantastic!

B: Oh, just thinking about them makes my mouth water.

01 Foods, Fight Colds
02 when, catch, cold
03 stay warm, put, clothes
04 Some, drink hot tea
05 something people, often drink
06 taste, warms, reduce, pain
07 What, other countries, cold
08 Let's find out
09 have, special drink, catch
10 cup, onion milk
11 chopped, over low, half
12 simple, said, be good
13 While, drinks, sick, bowl
14 recipe, one, to another
15 can be added, eating
16 sore throat, suffy nose
17 Eastern, get sick, called
18 is made with
19 to make, taste better
20 looks like thick
21 warm, have, sore throat
22 only, but, popular, healthy
23 served, usually, cold, temperature
24 Why not, found, about
25 fun, good for, health
26 How to Make
27 You need, honey
28 Put, in, mix them
29 Pour half, in, pan
30 Add, butter
31 Warm, until, melts
32 Pour, hot, into, with
33 Stir as, pour
34 Drink while, hot

01 Fight Colds
02 catch a cold
03 stay warm, put on
04 to drink hot tea
05 something, often drink
06 helps reduce the pain, throat
07 What do people drink or eat
08 find out
09 have a special drink
10 a cup of onion milk
11 chopped onion, over low heat, half an hour
12 is said to be good
13 While, look for, a bowl of chicken soup
14 from one family to another

15 can be added, eating
16 great for a sore throat and a stuffy nose
17 called
18 is made with
19 add, to make it taste better
20 looks like thick
21 have a sore throat
22 not only, but also, healthy
23 served, served, at room temperature
24 Why not, found out about
25 good for
26 How to Make
27 You need
28 Put, in, mix them
29 Pour
30 Add
31 Warm, until, melts
32 Pour, into, with
33 Stir as, pour
34 while

1 감기와 싸우는 음식들

2 여러분은 감기에 걸리면 어떻게 하는가?

3 당연히, 따뜻함을 유지하고자 할 것이고, 아마도 옷을 더 입을 것이다.

4 몇몇 사람들은 따뜻한 차를 마시는 것을 좋아한다.

5 생강차는 한국인들이 자주 마시는 것이다.

6 특별한 맛과 함께, 그것은 여러분의 몸을 따뜻하게 하고 목 통증을 완화하는 데 도움을 준다.

7 다른 나라에서는 사람들이 감기에 걸렸을 때 무엇을 마시거나 먹을까?

8 함께 알아보자.

9 겨울이 매우 추운 핀란드에서는 사람들이 감기에 걸리면 특별한 음료를 마신다.

10 그것은 양파 우유이다.

11 그들은 우유에 잘게 썬 양파를 넣고 30분 동안 약한 불에서 끓인다.

12 이 단순한 음료는 감기에 좋다고 한다.

13 한국 사람들과 핀란드 사람들이 아플 때 음료를 찾는 반면, 미국의 많은 사람들은 닭고기 수프를 원한다.

14 그것은 보통 닭고기와 야채로 만들어지는데, 요리법은 가정마다 다르다.

15 소금과 후추를 먹기 전에 넣기도 한다.

16 미국인들은 따뜻한 닭고기 수프 한 그릇이 부은 목과 막힌 코에 좋다고 믿는다.

17 러시아와 동유럽에서는 사람들이 아플 때, 고골모골이라는 후식을 먹는다.

18 그것은 달걀과 꿀로 만든다.

19 어떤 사람들은 그것을 더 맛있게 하기 위해 초콜릿, 버터, 레몬주스, 또는 우유를 첨가한다.

20 그것은 진한 요구르트처럼 보인다.

21 사람들은 목이 아플 때 종종 따뜻한 고골모골 한 잔을 마신다.

22 고골모골은 감기에 걸린 사람들에게 좋을 뿐만 아니라 건강한 사람들의 후식으로도 인기가 있다.

23 후식으로 제공될 때에는 보통 차갑게 또는 실온으로 제공된다.

24 여러분이 알아본 음식들 중 하나를 만들어 보는 것은 어떨까?

25 그것은 재미있고 여러분의 건강에 좋을 것이다.

26 고골모골 만드는 방법 (1인분)

27 필요한 것: 달걀 1개, 우유 1/2컵, 꿀 5g, 버터 15g

28 1. 달걀과 꿀을 큰 컵에 넣고 섞는다.

29 2. 우유 반 컵을 팬에 붓는다.

30 버터를 추가한다.

31 버터가 녹을 때까지 데운다.

32 3. 뜨거운 우유와 버터를 달걀과 꿀이 있는 컵에 붓는다.

33 부으면서 젓는다.

34 4. 뜨거울 때 마신다.

본문 TEST Step 4-Step 5　　　p.78~81

1 Foods That Fight Colds

2 What do you do when you catch a cold?

3 Of course, you want to stay warm, so maybe you put on more clothes.

4 Some people like to drink hot tea.

5 Ginger tea is something people in Korea often drink.

6 With its special taste, it warms your body and helps reduce the pain in your throat.

7 What do people drink or eat in other countries when they catch a cold?

8 Let's find out.

9 In Finland, where it is very cold in winter, people have a special drink when they catch a cold.

10 It is a cup of onion milk.

11 They put chopped onion in milk and boil it over low heat for half an hour.

12 This simple drink is said to be good for a cold.

13 While people in Korea and Finland look for drinks when sick, many people in America want a bowl of chicken soup.

14 It is usually made with chicken and vegetables, but the recipe is different from one family to another.

15 Salt and pepper can be added before eating.

16 People in America believe that a bowl of warm chicken soup is great for a sore throt and a suffy nose.

17 In Russia and in Eastern Europe, when people get sick, they eat a dessert called *gogol-mogol*.

---

18 It is made with eggs and honey.

19 Some people add chocolate, butter, lemon juice, or milk to make it taste better.

20 It looks like thick yogurt.

21 People often drink a cup of warm *gogol-mogol* when they have a sore throat.

22 *Gogol-mogol* is not only good for people with a cold but also popular as a dessert for healthy people.

23 When served as a dessert, it is usually served cold or at room temperature.

24 Why not try making one of the foods you have found out about?

25 It will be fun and good for your health.

26 How to make *Gogol-mogol* (Serves one)

27 You need: 1 egg, 1/2 cup of milk, honey (5 g), butter (15 g)

28 1. Put the egg and the honey in a large cup and mix them.

29 2. Pour half a cup of milk in a pan.

30 Add the butter.

31 Warm it until the butter melts.

32 3. Pour the hot milk and butter into the cup with the egg and the honey.

33 Stir as you pour.

34 4. Drink while it is hot.

구석구석지문 TEST Step 1　　　p.82

After You Read B

1. I've made

2. What is

3. that, in Eastern Europe, when, are sick

4. looks delicious, made with

5. made with eggs

6. put on top of it

7. to make, taste better

8. when they're not sick

9. popular dessert. When served, usually served, at room temperature

Writing Workshop

1. While, when they are sick, many people in India

2. how to make

3. You need, black pepper, salt

4. chop, put, chopped, in, pour, over

5. boil the mixture, turn off, leave, to cool down

6. blend, until, is, add, black pepper, salt

7. can enjoy

8. not only healthy but also delicious

구석구석지문 TEST Step 2   p.83

After You Read B

1. Look! I've made *gogol-mogol*.

2. Happy07: What is *gogol-mogol*?

3. Bora: It's a dessert that people in Russia and in Eastern Europe eat when they are sick.

4. Yumyum: It looks delicious. What is it made with?

5. Bora: It's made with eggs and honey.

6. Yumyum: What's that you put on top of it?

7. Bora: I put chocolate on top to make it taste better.

8. Happy07: Do people also eat it when they're not sick?

9. Bora: Sure. It's a popular dessert. When served as a dessert, it's usually served cold or at room temperature.

Writing Workshop

1. While many Koreans eat Samgyetang when they are sick, many people in India eat tomato soup.

2. Here is how to make it.

3. You need: 1 tomato, some water, black pepper, salt

4. First, chop one fresh tomato. Then put the chopped tomato in a pan and pour some water over it.

5. Next, boil the mixture for ten minutes. Then turn off the heat and leave it to cool down.

6. Next, blend it until it is smooth. Finally, add some black pepper and salt.

7. Now you can enjoy the tomato soup.

8. This tomato soup is not only healthy but also delicious.

Lesson **S**

단어 TEST Step 1   p.84

01 목표	02 무기	03 ~를 따라
04 갑자기	05 일어나다	06 마주하다
07 인간, 사람	08 놀라게 하다	09 기적
10 참호	11 전체의	12 광경
13 비록 ~이긴 하지만		14 젖은
15 ~일지도 모른다	16 따라가다	17 사실은
18 믿기 힘든	19 군인, 병사	20 주소
21 최전선, 최전방	22 인사, 안부의 말	23 그리워하다
24 정말로, 진심으로	25 대담하게	26 교환하다
27 외침, 고함	28 ~도, ~ 또한	29 적군, 적
30 속임수	31 익숙한, 친숙한	32 공유하다, 나누다
33 몇의, 수개의	34 유지하다, 계속 있다	
35 ~ 밖을 내다보다	36 더욱 더	
37 서로	38 평화 속에서	39 전쟁 중인
40 사망하다	41 ~와 같은	42 내려놓다
43 잇따라서		

단어 TEST Step 2   p.85

01 several	02 entire	03 trick
04 actually	05 miss	06 along
07 shout	08 aim	09 face
10 light	11 address	12 truly
13 weapon	14 soldier	15 familiar
16 unbelievable	17 miracle	18 boldly
19 sight	20 wet	21 suddenly
22 enemy	23 exchange	24 surprise
25 trench	26 greeting	27 human
28 expect	29 lantern	30 although
31 happen	32 share	33 either
34 follow	35 one after another	
36 at war	37 one by one	38 put down
39 shake hands	40 such as	
41 on the front line		42 pass away
43 look out of		

단어 TEST Step 3   p.86

1 carol, 캐럴   2 shout, 외침, 고함

3 greeting, 인사, 안부의 말   4 share, 공유하다, 나누다

5 sight, 광경   6 trick, 속임수   7 aim, 목표

8 exchange, 교환하다   9 peace, 평화

10 race, 경주, 시합　11 shoot, 쏘다　12 boldly, 대담하게
13 address, 주소　14 weapon, 무기
15 soldier, 군인, 병사　16 surprise, 놀라게 하다

본문 TEST Step 1　　　　　　　　　p.87~88

01 Christmas Miracle　02 It, in, first year
03 facing, had done, few　04 trenches, cold, wet
05 tired, missed, more so
06 Suddenly, familiar, heard coming
07 It, Christmas carol　08 going on
09 might be, trick, out　10 boldly looked out of
11 by, other, followed, example
12 What, sight, never expected
13 Along, standing lit with
14 one, song after another
15 answer by also singing
16 lights, made, forget, front
17 came out from, shoot
18 whose aim, exchange greetings
19 several, able, in peace　20 truly, silent night
21 morning came　22 on both sides, down
23 man's land between, and
24 exchanged, gifts such as
25 sang carols together
26 Some even exchanged addresses
27 unbelievable, written, letters, soldiers
28 wrote, between, lines, talks
29 also had, races　30 Another, think, at war
31 Here, were, talking, enemy
32 like, wives, waiting, welcome

본문 TEST Step 2　　　　　　　　　p.89~90

01 Miracle　02 the first year
03 were facing, had done, few months
04 cold and wet
05 missed, all the more so because
06 Suddenly, was heard coming
07 carol　08 going on
09 might be a trick, trenches
10 boldly looked out of　11 One by one, followed
12 What, sight, expected　13 lit with lanterns
14 one Christmas song after another
15 by also singing
16 made them forget, front line

17 came out from, shoot
18 whose aim, each other, exchange greetings
19 in several months, in peace
20 It truly was　21 came
22 on both sides, came out of
23 in the no man's land, shook hands
24 such as　25 sang carols
26 exchanged addresses
27 unbelievable, about, sent
28 between the two lines
29 had bike races　30 were at war
31 Here we were, enemy
32 like us, waiting to welcome

본문 TEST Step 3　　　　　　　　　p.91~92

1 크리스마스의 기적
2 제일차 세계 대전의 첫해였던 1914년의 크리스마스이브였습니다.
3 영국 군인들은 지난 몇 달 동안 그래왔듯이 그들의 참호에서 독일 군인들과 대치하고 있었어요.
4 참호는 춥고 축축했습니다.
5 군인들은 지쳤고 자신들의 집을 그리워했는데, 크리스마스라는 이유로 더욱 더 그랬습니다.
6 갑자기 익숙한 노래가 독일 군인들의 참호로부터 들려왔습니다.
7 그것은 크리스마스 캐럴이었어요!
8 무슨 일이 벌어지고 있는 걸까요?
9 어쩌면 그들을 참호 밖으로 유인하고자 하는 속임수일지도 모릅니다.
10 몇몇 영국 군인들이 용감하게 자신들의 참호 밖을 내다보았어요.
11 차례차례 다른 군인들도 앞사람을 따랐습니다.
12 영국 군인들이 본 것은 그들이 절대 예상하지 못한 광경이었어요.
13 독일 군인들의 참호를 따라, 크리스마스트리들이 랜턴으로 밝혀진 채 있었습니다!
14 독일 군인들은 크리스마스 캐럴을 연이어 불렀어요.
15 영국 군인들도 크리스마스 캐럴을 부르며 화답하기 시작했습니다.
16 따뜻한 불빛과 크리스마스 캐럴은 그들이 최전선에 있다는 것을 잊게 만들었어요.
17 그리고 독일 군인들 쪽에서 고함이 터져 나왔습니다. "행복한 크리스마스예요! 당신들이 쏘지 않는다면, 우리도 쏘지 않을게요!"
18 곧, 단지 몇 시간 전까지만 해도 서로를 죽이는 것이 목적이었던 군인들은 인사를 나누기 시작했습니다.
19 몇 달 만에 처음으로, 군인들은 평화롭게 밤을 지낼 수 있었어요.

20 그날은 정말로 조용한 밤이었습니다.

21 크리스마스 아침이 밝았습니다.

22 양편의 군인들은 자신들의 무기를 내려놓고 참호 밖으로 나왔어요.

23 그들은 무인 지대에서 만났고 악수를 했습니다.

24 그들은 와인과 케이크 같은 작은 선물도 교환했어요.

25 그들은 캐럴을 함께 불렀습니다.

26 몇몇은 심지어 주소를 교환하기도 했고 함께 축구를 했습니다.

27 이 믿을 수 없는 크리스마스는 영국 군인들이 집으로 보낸 편지에 적혀 있었습니다.

28 한 군인은 "크리스마스에 영국 군인들과 독일 군인들은 두 경계선 사이에서 만났고 대화를 나눴어.

29 우리는 자전거 시합도 했어."라고 적었어요.

30 다른 군인은 "우리는 전쟁 중이라는 생각이 들지 않았어.

31 여기서 우리는 적대 관계인 서로와 대화를 나누고 있는 상황이었어.

32 그들은 우리와 마찬가지로, 그들의 남자들이 집으로 다시 돌아오기를 고대하는 어머니와, 친구들, 부인이 있는 사람들이었어."라고 썼습니다.

본문 TEST Step 4–Step 5   p.93~96

1 A Christmas Miracle

2 It was Christmas Eve in 1914, the first year of World War I.

3 English soldiers were facing German soldiers from their trenches as they had done for the last few months.

4 The trenches were cold and wet.

5 The soldiers were tired and missed their home, all the more so because it was Christmas.

6 Suddenly, a familiar song was heard coming from the German trenches.

7 It was a Christmas carol!

8 What's going on?

9 It might be a trick to make them come out of the trenches.

10 A few English soldiers boldly looked out of their trenches.

11 One by one, other soldiers followed their example.

12 What they saw was a sight they never expected.

13 Along the German trenches, Christmas trees were standing lit with lanterns!

14 The German soldiers sang one Christmas song after another.

15 The English soldiers began to answer by also singing Christmas songs.

16 The warm lights and the Christmas carols made them forget they were on the front line.

17 Then a shout came out from the German side: "Happy Christmas! You no shoot, we no shoot!"

18 Soon, soldiers whose aim had been to kill each other just a few hours before began to exchange greetings.

19 For the first time in several months, the soldiers were able to spend a night in peace.

20 It truly was a silent night.

21 Christmas morning came.

22 Soldiers on both sides put down their weapons and came out of their trenches.

23 They met in the no man's land between their trenches and shook hands.

24 They exchanged small gifts such as wine and cake.

25 They sang carols together.

26 Some even exchanged addresses and played football.

27 This unbelievable Christmas Day was written about in letters English soldiers sent home.

28 One soldier wrote, "On Christmas Day, English and German soldiers met between the two lines and had talks.

29 We also had bike races."

30 Another wrote, "We didn't think that we were at war.

31 Here we were, enemy talking to enemy.

32 They were like us, with mothers, with friends, with wives who were waiting to welcome their men home again."

2학기 전과정

적중 100 plus

영어 기출 문제집

정답 및 해설

시사 | 송미정

적중 100 + 특별부록

Plan B

우리학교
최신기출

시사 · 송미정 교과서를 배우는

학교 시험문제 분석 · 모음 · 해설집

전국단위 학교 시험문제 수집 및 분석
출제 빈도가 높은 문제 위주로 선별
문제 풀이에 필요한 상세한 해설

중3-2
영어

시사 · 송미정

적중 1OO + 특별부록

Plan B

우리학교
최신기출

중3-2
영어

시사 · 송미정

◎ 선택형 문항의 답안은 컴퓨터용 수정 싸인펜을 사용하여 OMR 답안지에 바르게 표기하시오.
◎ 서술형 문제는 답을 답안지에 반드시 검정 볼펜으로 쓰시오.
◎ 총 30문항 100점 만점입니다. 문항별 배점은 각 문항에 표시되어 있습니다.

[전북 ○○중]

01 다음 우리말 뜻에 알맞은 단어는?　(3점)

> 노력하다, 시도하다, 애를 쓰다

① try　② lean　③ fire
④ leave　⑤ raise

[부산 ○○중]

02 다음 중 영영 풀이가 올바른 것은?　(3점)

① category: extremely good
② dig: break up and move earth with a tool or with your hand
③ search: a long and thin mark made with a sharp object
④ comment: communication or touch between people or things
⑤ lend: an area of ground, especially used for a particular purpose such as farming or building

[전북 ○○중]

03 다음 빈칸에 공통으로 들어갈 말로 알맞은 것은?　(3점)

> • What did you _____ in the art class?
> • A man is _____ing people's attention in the train station by playing his guitar.

① pay　② teach　③ draw
④ drop　⑤ mean

[경기 ○○중]

04 다음 중 우리말을 적절하게 영작한 것은?　(3점)

① 그 음식의 대부분은 맛있어요.
　→ Most of the food are delicious.
② 저 꽃들 중 하나가 장미야.
　→ One of those flowers are a rose.
③ 그 돈의 일부는 은행으로 보내진다.
　→ Some of the money are sent to the bank.
④ 그 음악은 오늘 축제와 관련이 있어.
　→ The music has to do with the festival today.
⑤ 나의 동생은 내가 요리하는 것을 좋아해.
　→ My brother likes that I cook.

[부산 ○○중]

05 다음 밑줄 친 what과 쓰임이 <u>다른</u> 것은? (정답 두 개)　(3점)

> This book is <u>what</u> I read when I was young.

① <u>What</u> size do you wear?
② You should choose <u>what</u> you like.
③ <u>What</u> he says is always different.
④ <u>What</u> do you want to achieve in 2022?
⑤ Do your best for <u>what</u> you want to get.

[전북 ○○중]

06 다음 문장의 빈칸에 들어갈 말로 알맞은 것은?　(3점)

> I can't believe _____ you did last night.

① when
② what
③ that
④ where
⑤ which

07 다음 중 어법상 옳은 문장은? (3점)

① Sandra has been lived in Korea for seven years.

② Bill has taking a walk every day since last week.

③ We have been wait in line for thirty minutes.

④ Fred has been living in Seoul since 2010.

⑤ I have be reading this book since last week.

09 다음 〈조건〉에 맞게 영작하시오. (한 칸에 한 단어) (5점)

조건

• 'Andy는 얼마나 오래 스페인어를 배우고 있나요?' 라는 뜻의 문장으로 완성할 것
• long / Spanish / learn / be를 사용하되 필요 시 변형할 것

→ _____ _____ _____ _____

_____ _____ _____?

08 다음 〈보기〉에서 어법상 어색한 문장을 2개 찾아 고치시오. (5점)

ⓐ Do you think that this book is interesting?
ⓑ He always does that we don't understand.
ⓒ This air ticket is what I've been looking for since morning.
ⓓ She is different from what she was.
ⓔ Judy had been practiced tennis since she was seven.

(1) 어색한 것 : _____

고쳐 쓴 것 : _____

(2) 어색한 것 : _____

고쳐 쓴 것 : _____

10 다음 두 문장의 (A)와 (B)에 들어갈 말이 순서대로 짝지어진 것은? (3점)

• When I got to the bakery, my favorite chocolate cake (A)_____.
• My teacher wondered if I (B)_____ _____ London before.

	(A)	(B)
①	has been sold out	had been to
②	had been sold out	had been to
③	had been sold out	has been to
④	have been sold out	had been to
⑤	had been sold out	have been to

11 Eric went to the shopping mall to buy shoes. He found the shoes he liked, but they didn't fit him. In this case, what should Eric ask the clerk? (3점)

① Can I try these shoes on?

② Are there any other sizes?

③ Can you call another clerk?

④ Can I take a photo of these shoes?

⑤ I'm sorry, but I don't have any shoes that I like.

13 위 대화의 주제로 가장 적절한 것은? (3점)

① Colors can affect people's feelings.

② Reading magazines is interesting.

③ All colors can help people relax.

④ There is a color many people like the most.

⑤ Reading many kinds of books is useful.

[12~13] 다음 대화를 읽고 물음에 답하시오.

K: Jane, what are you reading?

(A) That's surprising.
(B) I'm reading an interesting magazine. It says colors can change people's feelings.
(C) Are there any other useful colors?
(D) Yes. For example, the color red can help us focus better.

J: Yes. The color blue helps people relax.

*K: Kevin, J: Jane

14 다음 대화 중 <u>어색한</u> 것은? (3점)

① A: What does "have a long face" mean?

　B: It means "to look sad."

② A: Hi, Jack! How are you doing?

　B: I'm on cloud nine! I got a concert ticket for my favorite band.

③ A: Sorry. The tickets for the blue zone are all sold out.

　B: Are there any other seats?

④ A: Jane, what are you reading?

　B: I'm reading an interesting magazine. It says colors can change people's feelings.

⑤ A: Hi, I'm calling to take a personality test. Can I do one this afternoon?

　B: You can come any time before afternoon.

12 위 대화가 자연스러운 대화가 되도록 (A)~(D)가 바르게 배열된 것은? (3점)

① (B) - (A) - (C) - (D)

② (B) - (C) - (D) - (A)

③ (B) - (D) - (A) - (C)

④ (B) - (A) - (D) - (C)

⑤ (B) - (C) - (A) - (D)

15 다음 대화 이후에 이어질 행동으로 가장 적절한 것은? (4점)

> H: Look! I found this test on an app that tells what kind of person you are. Do you want to try it?
> E: Sure. Sounds like fun.
> H: Okay, listen. What are you afraid of? Choose one of these: crowds, spiders, or dark places.
> E: I hate dark places. I cannot sleep without a night light on. What does that mean?
> H: It says you are full of imagination. That's why you fill dark places with all kinds of scary things.
> E: This is fun. I want to do some more. Are there any other tests we can take?
> H: Sure. This app has a lot of them.
> *H: Hajun, E: Emma

① To take another test
② To look for another app
③ To talk about scary things
④ To talk about the result of the test
⑤ To think why they choose dark places

16 다음 대화의 내용과 일치하는 것은? (3점)

> R: EDPI Test Center. Do you want to learn more about yourself? We run many kinds of on-site personality tests. Also, if there are any other tests you want to learn more about, please visit our office. Business hours are from 9AM to 6PM, Monday to Friday.
> T: Hi, I'm calling to take a personality test. Can I take one this Thursday afternoon?
> M: Sure, for the test, you should visit our center. You can come any time before 5 o'clock. You will get the result after a few days.
> *R: Recorded voice, T: Tom, M: Man

① EDPI only offers one kind of a test.
② People can know themselves through a test.
③ EDPI offers its services on weekends.
④ Tom can have a test at his home.
⑤ Tom can know the result right after the test.

17 다음 글의 '어조'(말하는 투)로 가장 적절한 것은? (3점)

This *Draw-a-Person-in-the-Rain* Test Will Reveal Your True Self. Psychologists believe that it's possible to evaluate different areas of your subconscious, such as fears, dreams, and main personality traits in general. The test will reveal your attitude toward tolerance, pressure and frustration, your defense mechanisms, and level of anxiety. The main objective is to obtain information about your personality through the image of the individual under certain unpleasant circumstances.

① informative

② humorous

③ defensive

④ competitive

⑤ pessimistic

[18~19] 다음 글을 읽고 물음에 답하시오.

Everything you do (A)[says / tells] something about you. The language you use, the clothes you wear, and even the pets you (B)[rise / raise] somehow show what kind of person you are. The things you draw are not much different. What you draw and how you draw it (C)[is / are] related to your personality. Doctors have been using various drawing tests to better understand people.

18 위 글의 괄호 (A), (B), (C) 안에 가장 적절한 것은? (3점)

	(A)	(B)	(C)
①	says	raise	are
②	says	raise	is
③	says	rise	are
④	tells	rise	is
⑤	tells	raise	is

19 위 글에서 어떤 사람인지 알 수 있는 정보로 언급되지 않은 것은? (3점)

① Everything you eat

② The language you use

③ The clothes you put on

④ The pets you keep

⑤ The picture you paint

[20~22] 다음 글을 읽고 물음에 답하시오.

Doctors have been using various drawing tests to better understand people. First, the rain shows the stress ⓐ_____ the person who drew the picture ⓑis under. The bigger the drops are or the more heavily the rain is falling, the bigger the stress is. (A)_____, so a big cloud shows the drawer is not very hopeful about the future. Second, the umbrella means the protection ⓒ_____ the person has in a stressful situation. A big umbrella shows ⓓthat the drawer has a lot of plans or protection. If there's no umbrella in the drawing, the drawer does not have any ⓔmeans ⓕto deal with difficult situations.

21 위 글의 내용과 아래 그림을 해석한 내용이 일치하지 <u>않는</u> 것은? (4점)

ⓐThere are various drawing tests to understand people. ⓑThe person who drew this picture was under a lot of stress because it rained a lot. However, ⓒhe is holding an umbrella, so the drawer has some protection to deal with stress. However, ⓓsince the umbrella is not big, the drawer has a few plans to control the stress. And ⓔhe is anxious about the future because there are no clouds.

① ⓐ　　　　② ⓑ　　　　③ ⓒ

④ ⓓ　　　　⑤ ⓔ

20 다음은 위 글에 대한 설명이다. 옳은 설명은 몇 개인가? (4점)

<u>보기</u>

(A) ⓐ에 생략된 것은 관계대명사 who이다.

(B) ⓑ의 주어는 stress이다.

(C) ⓒ는 목적격 관계대명사이므로 생략할 수 있다.

(D) ⓓ는 목적격 관계대명사이다.

(E) ⓔ는 '의미하다'라는 뜻으로 쓰였다.

(F) ⓕ는 to부정사의 명사적 용법으로 쓰였다.

① 1개　　　　② 2개　　　　③ 3개

④ 4개　　　　⑤ 5개

22 위 글의 (A)에 들어갈 말을 〈조건〉에 맞게 완성하시오. (4점)

<u>조건</u>

• '구름들은 일어날 문제들을 의미한다.'라는 뜻의 문장으로 완성할 것

• wait / cloud / happen을 사용하되 필요시 변형할 것

→ _____

[23~25] 다음 글을 읽고 물음에 답하시오.

The details in the drawing of the person have to do with the drawer's attitude under stress. For example, someone who ⓐdraws a person without a face does not want to ⓑdraw people's attention to himself or herself. Someone who ⓒdraws the person on the right side of the paper is ready to meet the future. On the other hand, someone who ⓓdraws the person on the left side may be worried about things that have happened in the past. He or she isn't hopeful about the future. In the center, if the person that you ⓔdraw occupies a central position, it means you're quite competitive.

These are some of the possible meanings of each part of the drawings. Now, go back and look at the two drawings. Try reading them yourself. Can you understand (A)what kind of person drew each one? What's your opinion?

23 위 글의 밑줄 친 ⓐ~ⓔ 중 의미가 <u>다른</u> 것은? (3점)

① ⓐ   ② ⓑ   ③ ⓒ

④ ⓓ   ⑤ ⓔ

24 위 글의 밑줄 친 (A)와 쓰임이 같은 것은? (3점)

① <u>What</u> I bought for my mom is a rose.

② This is <u>what</u> I can do to make a living.

③ I don't know <u>what</u> the movie's ending is.

④ This book is <u>what</u> I read when I was young.

⑤ <u>What</u> Thomas will buy at the mall is a shirt.

25 다음 밑줄 친 부분 중 위 글의 내용과 일치하지 <u>않은</u> 것은? (4점)

The Orientation of the Drawing

On the right, if the person on your sheet of paper is located on the right, ⓐit indicates your desire to grow professionally in the future and ⓑyour confidence in what will happen in the future. On the left, if the person is located on the left part of the paper, ⓒit shows your positive attitude about the future and also that ⓓsomething from your past prevents you from being happy in the future. In the center, if your person occupies a central position, ⓔit means you're quite competitive.

① ⓐ   ② ⓑ   ③ ⓒ

④ ⓓ   ⑤ ⓔ

[26~29] 다음 글을 읽고 물음에 답하시오.

The person in Drawing A ⓐare holding an umbrella in a light rain. (A) On the other hand, the person in Drawing B is in a heavy rain and ⓑhas no umbrella. (B) Also, there are dark clouds above the person in Drawing B. What can these differences mean?

First, (가)the rain shows the stress the person who drew the picture ⓒare under. (C) The clouds mean problems ⓓwaiting to happen, so a big cloud shows the drawer ⓔis not very hopeless about the future. Second, the umbrella means the protection the person has in a stressful situation. (D) A big umbrella shows that the drawer has a lot of plans or protection. If there's ⓕno umbrella in the drawing, the drawer does not have any ⓖmean to deal with difficult situations. (E)

26 위 글에 주어진 문장이 들어갈 위치로 가장 적절한 곳은? (3점)

> The bigger the drops are or the more heavily the rain is falling, the bigger the stress is.

① (A)　　　② (B)　　　③ (C)

④ (D)　　　⑤ (E)

29 위 글의 내용과 일치하게 말한 사람은? (3점)

① 순희: 폭우를 그린 것을 보니 스트레스가 많은가 보네.

② 영희: 그림 속의 구름은 너무나 행복하다는 것을 의미해.

③ 철수: 큰 구름은 미래에 큰 꿈을 가지고 있다는 것이지.

④ 은수: 그림에서 우산이 의미하는 것은 자신을 드러내고 싶지 않다는 심리를 나타낸 거야.

⑤ 미아: 그림에서 우산이 없다는 것은 힘든 상황을 견뎌낼 의지가 있다는 것을 의미하지.

27 위 글의 ⓐ~ⓖ 중 어법이나 문법상 적절한 것을 <u>모두</u> 고른 것은? (3점)

① ⓐ, ⓒ

② ⓐ, ⓓ, ⓔ

③ ⓑ, ⓓ, ⓕ

④ ⓒ, ⓓ, ⓕ, ⓖ

⑤ ⓑ, ⓒ, ⓓ, ⓔ, ⓖ

30 다음 글에서 당신의 성향을 보여주는 예시가 <u>아닌</u> 것은? (4점)

> Everything you do says something about you. The language you use, the clothes you wear, and even the pets you raise somehow show what kind of person you are. The things you draw are not much different. What you draw and how you draw it are related to your personality.

① 입는 옷

② 사용하는 말

③ 기르는 애완동물

④ 남에게서 받은 그림

⑤ 여러분이 그리는 그림

28 위 글의 밑줄 친 (가)가 의미하는 것은? (3점)

① level of stress

② problems waiting to happen

③ protections the person has in a stressful situation

④ the drawer who is not very hopeful about the future

⑤ the drawer who has a lot of plans or protection

문항수 : 선택형(25문항) 서술형(5문항)   20 . . .

◎ 선택형 문항의 답안은 컴퓨터용 수정 싸인펜을 사용하여 OMR 답안지에 바르게 표기하시오.
◎ 서술형 문제는 답을 답안지에 반드시 검정 볼펜으로 쓰시오.
◎ 총 30문항 100점 만점입니다. 문항별 배점은 각 문항에 표시되어 있습니다.

01 다음 어구 중 그 의미가 <u>잘못</u> 연결된 것은?   [경기 ○○중]   (3점)

① feel blue - to feel happy

② hang in there - do not give up

③ out of hand - not able to deal with

④ see eye to eye - to agree with each other

⑤ be over the moon - to feel very happy

02 다음 영영 풀이에 해당하는 단어가 <u>아닌</u> 것은?   [부산 ○○중]   (4점)

- to have a connection between two or more things
- a settled way of thinking or feeling about something
- lower in position, rank, or degree than something else
- the combination of characteristic or qualities that form a person's distinctive character

① below

② relate

③ attitude

④ personality

⑤ frighten

03 다음 설명에 알맞은 말을 고른 것은?   [전북 ○○중]   (3점)

What kind of personality does someone have if he/she can do things on their own very well?

① kind

② lazy

③ funny

④ dependent

⑤ independent

04 다음 글의 빈칸에 알맞은 것은?   [경기 ○○중]   (3점)

A _____ is often closely related to what you're feeling in your mind. When you draw one, it shows your feelings. In other words, your various feelings can be expressed through it. Therefore you can find out other people's feelings if you pay careful attention to their drawings.

① sign

② picture

③ gesture

④ photograph

⑤ facial expression

05 다음 문장의 오류를 적절하게 수정한 것은? (3점)

> 비가 3시간째 내리는 중이다.
> → It has raining on three hour.

① It is raining to three hour.
② It is rained for three hours.
③ It had been rained for three hour.
④ It has been raining for three hours.
⑤ It has been rained for three hours.

08 다음 문장의 빈칸에 들어갈 말로 알맞은 것은? (3점)

> The students _____ on the project since yesterday.

① work
② worked
③ are worked
④ are working
⑤ have been working

06 다음 괄호 안에서 알맞은 말을 고르고, 우리말로 해석하시오. (4점)

> The witness remembered (that / what) the thief was wearing.

(1) 단어: _____
(2) 해석: _____

09 다음 단어들을 바르게 배열하여 문장을 완성하시오. (4점)

> for / waiting / been / you / me / have / ?
> → How long _____?

→ _____

07 다음 중 밑줄 친 부분의 쓰임이 나머지와 다른 것은? (3점)

① I can't hear <u>what</u> you said.
② I know <u>what</u> you did yesterday.
③ <u>What</u> she wants to be is a farmer.
④ <u>What</u> I want for dinner is Chinese food.
⑤ Please tell me <u>what</u> color you like the most.

10 다음 〈조건〉에 맞게 영작하시오. (4점)

> 조건
> • 'Sara를 무섭게 한 것은 그가 흘린 피였다.' 라는 뜻의 문장으로 완성할 것
> • scare / which / thing / spill을 사용하되 필요 시 변형할 것

→ _____.

11 다음 밑줄 친 부분의 쓰임이 <u>다른</u> 것은? (3점)

① My brother likes <u>what</u> I cook.

② <u>What</u> I bought for my wife is a ring.

③ This package is <u>what</u> I ordered yesterday.

④ <u>What</u> do you do when you have free time?

⑤ This is <u>what</u> I want to eat for breakfast.

12 주어진 대화 다음에 이어질 대화의 순서로 가장 적절한 것은? (3점)

L: I took a personality test today. I had to draw a house.

J: A house?

(A) They mean I'm open to other people.

(B) Interesting. So what do these big windows mean?

(C) According to the test, you can tell a lot about a person by their drawings. Here's mine.

*L: Laura, J: Jack

① (A) - (B) - (C)

② (A) - (C) - (B)

③ (B) - (A) - (C)

④ (C) - (A) - (B)

⑤ (C) - (B) - (A)

[13~14] 다음 대화를 읽고 물음에 답하시오.

Hajun: Look! I found this test on an app that tells what kind of person you are. Do you want to try it?

Emma: Sure. Sounds like fun.

Hajun: Okay, listen. What are you afraid of? Choose one of these crowds, spiders, or dark places.

Emma: I hate dark places. I cannot sleep without a night light on. What does that mean?

Hajun: It says you are full of imagination. That's why you fill dark places with all kinds of scary things.

Emma: That's very interesting. What about you? Is there anything you are afraid of?

Hajun: I chose dark places too. But I don't think I have a big imagination.

Emma: This is fun. I want to do some more. (A)우리가 할 수 있는 다른 검사들이 있니?

Hajun: Sure. This app has a lot of them.

13 위 대화의 내용과 일치하는 것은? (3점)

① Hajun은 책을 소개하는 중이다.

② Hajun은 심리학에 많은 관심이 있다.

③ Emma는 거미에 대한 두려움이 있다.

④ Hajun과 Emma 모두 상상력이 풍부하다.

⑤ Hajun과 Emma 모두 어두운 곳을 무서워한다.

14 위 대화의 우리말 (A)를 바르게 영작한 것은? (3점)

① Can we take are there any other tests?

② Can we any other tests there are take?

③ Are there we can take tests any other?

④ Are there any other tests we can take?

⑤ We can take are there any other tests?

15 다음 대화의 빈칸에 들어갈 말로 알맞은 것은? (3점)

> A: I'm reading an article about blood type. It says that blood type tells something about your personality.
> B: Wow. Then _____?
> A: People with blood type A are calm. They are good listeners too.

① what's your blood type

② what does type A mean

③ have you read the article

④ what are good listeners for

⑤ how would you describe your personality

17 다음 대화의 빈칸에 알맞은 말은? (3점)

> J: Bob, you look so sad. What's wrong?
> B: I have been solving this math problem since last night. But I haven't found the answer. So I threw up my hands.
> J: That's too bad. Anyway, I don't understand what you said. _____
> _____
> B: I gave up solving this problem.
> J: Oh, let's ask the math teacher about the problem.
> B: I think I should do that. Can you come with me?
> J: Of course.

① Do you want to throw my hands?

② I think you should study math harder.

③ What does "threw up my hands" mean?

④ Should I know how to solve this problem?

⑤ I can explain the meaning of "throw up my hands".

16 다음 글에서 옳지 않은 것은? (4점)

> I ⓐhave read an article yesterday. It said that many scientists ⓑresearched how color and personality were related. People who like green are polite and diligent. People who like blue are cautious and patient. People who like red are passionate and active. When I ⓒasked Tommy ⓓwhat color he liked, he said he liked blue. I thought it was correct that the color ⓔwas related to personality.

① ⓐ   ② ⓑ   ③ ⓒ

④ ⓓ   ⑤ ⓔ

ⓐ_____. The language you use, the clothes you wear, and even the pets you (가)raise somehow show what kind of person you are. The things you draw are not much different. What you draw and how you draw it are related to your personality.

[부산 ○○중]

18 What are the TWO things mentioned in the article above that show a person's personality? (3점)

① 당신이 먹는 음식
② 당신이 그리는 그림
③ 당신이 사용하는 언어
④ 당신이 여행하는 나라
⑤ 당신이 좋아하는 계절

[부산 ○○중]

19 위 글의 밑줄 친 (가)raise와 같은 뜻으로 쓰인 문장은? (3점)

① You don't have to raise your voice.
② How can we raise standards in schools?
③ Raise your leg and hold for a count of ten.
④ Can anybody think of a way to raise money?
⑤ I can't raise a dog because I have fur allergies.

[부산 ○○중]

20 위 글의 ⓐ에 들어갈 말을 〈조건〉에 맞게 완성하시오. (4점)

조건
• '당신이 하는 모든 것은 당신에 대한 어떤 것을 말한다'라는 뜻의 문장으로 완성할 것
• say / something / about을 사용하되 필요시 변형할 것

→ _____

[21~24] 다음 글을 읽고 물음에 답하시오.

First, the rain shows the stress the person who drew the picture is under. (A) The bigger the drops are or the more heavily the rain is falling, the ⓐ[bigger / smaller] the stress is. (B) The clouds mean problems waiting to happen, so a big cloud shows the drawer is not very ⓑ[anxious / hopeful] about the future. (C) A big umbrella shows that the drawer has a lot of plans or protection. (D) If there's no umbrella in the drawing, the drawer does not have any (가)means to deal with difficult situations. (E)

[전북 ○○중]

21 위 글의 (A)~(E) 중 주어진 문장이 들어가기에 가장 적절한 곳은? (4점)

Second, the umbrella means the protection the person has in a stressful situation.

① (A)　　② (B)　　③ (C)
④ (D)　　⑤ (E)

[충남 ○○중]

22 위 글의 밑줄 친 (가)means의 의미는? (3점)

① 수단
② 마음
③ 태도
④ 지혜
⑤ 용기

23 위 글의 내용과 일치하지 <u>않는</u> 것은? (3점)

① 구름은 앞으로 다가올 문제를 의미한다.

② 빗방울이 클수록 스트레스가 더 크다는 그것을 의미한다.

③ 비는 그림을 그린 사람이 받고 있는 스트레스를 보여 준다.

④ 우산이 없다는 것은 더 이상의 고민이 없음을 의미한다.

⑤ 큰 우산을 그린 사람은 보호 기제를 가지고 있다는 것을 의미한다.

24 위 글의 괄호 ⓐ, ⓑ 안에서 문맥상 적절한 말을 골라 쓰시오. (4점)

ⓐ_____ ⓑ_____

[25~27] 다음 글을 읽고 물음에 답하시오.

Third, ⓐthe details in the drawing of the person have to do with the drawer's attitude under stress. For example, ⓑsomeone who draws a person without a face do not want to draw people's attention to himself or herself. ⓒSomeone who draws the person on the right side of the paper are ready to meet the future. On the other hand, ⓓsomeone who draws the person on the left side may be worried about things that have happened in the past.

These (가)_____ some of the possible meanings of each (나)_____ of the drawings. Now, go back and look (다)_____ the two drawings. ⓔTry to reading them yourself. Can you understand what kind of person drew each one? What's your opinion?

25 위 글의 밑줄 친 ⓐ~ⓔ 중 어법상 맞는 문장의 개수는? (3점)

① 1개   ② 2개   ③ 3개

④ 4개   ⑤ 5개

26 위 글의 빈칸 (가)~(다)에 들어갈 말이 알맞게 배열된 것은? (4점)

	(가)	(나)	(다)
①	is	part	at
②	is	parts	in
③	are	part	to
④	are	part	at
⑤	are	parts	to

27 위 글의 내용과 일치하는 것은? (3점)

① 그림 속 사람의 세부사항은 그림을 그린 사람의 자존심과 관련이 있다.

② 얼굴을 안 그린 사람은 사람들로부터 관심 끌기를 원한다.

③ 사람을 종이의 왼쪽에 그린 사람은 과거의 일을 걱정하고 있다.

④ 그림을 해석할 때 그림의 일부로는 어떤 의미도 알 수 없다.

⑤ 그림을 해석하는 것은 전문가들만 해야 한다.

The person in Drawing A is holding an umbrella in a light rain. On the other hand, the person in Drawing B is in a heavy rain and has no umbrella. Also, there are big and dark clouds above the person in Drawing B. What can these differences mean?

(A) First, the rain shows the stress the person who drew the picture is under. (B) The bigger the drops are or the more heavily the rain is falling, the bigger stress is. (C) The clouds mean problems waiting to happen, so a big cloud shows the drawer is not very hopeful about the future. (D) Second, the umbrella means the protection the person has in a stressful situation. (E) If there's no umbrella in the drawing, the drawer does not have any means to deal with difficult situations.

29 위 글에서 그림 B를 그린 사람의 심정으로 가장 적절한 것은?

(3점)

① frustrated

② delighted

③ comforted

④ indifferent

⑤ embarrassed

30 위 글의 내용을 바탕으로 추론할 수 있는 것은? (4점)

① The painter of Drawing A seems to be under huge amount of stress.

② The size of a raindrop or the amount of rain determines the stress level.

③ The clouds in drawing B show that the drawer couldn't overcome the problems in the past.

④ The umbrella in the drawing can be read both positively and negatively.

⑤ The painter of Drawing B can find out some solutions to make situations better.

28 위 글의 (A)~(E) 중 주어진 문장이 들어가기에 가장 적절한 곳은?

(3점)

A big umbrella shows that the drawer has a lot of plans or protection.

① (A)   ② (B)   ③ (C)

④ (D)   ⑤ (E)

◎ 선택형 문항의 답안은 컴퓨터용 수정 싸인펜을 사용하여 OMR 답안지에 바르게 표기하시오.
◎ 서술형 문제는 답을 답안지에 반드시 검정 볼펜으로 쓰시오.
◎ 총 30문항 100점 만점입니다. 문항별 배점은 각 문항에 표시되어 있습니다.

[경기 ○○중]

01 다음 빈칸 (A)에 공통으로 들어갈 말로 적절한 것은? (3점)

> • To (A)_____ for information, most people use the Internet.
> • You can (A)_____ the website for a cheap hotel.

① add
② sell
③ accept
④ search
⑤ receive

[전북 ○○중]

02 다음 중 영영 풀이가 <u>어색한</u> 것은? (3점)

① various: of many different kinds
② suddenly: quickly and unexpectedly
③ search: to advise and suggest something
④ attractive: beautiful and pleasant to look at
⑤ angle: a position from which something is viewed

[전북 ○○중]

03 다음 문장에서 철자가 뒤섞인 단어를 찾아서 바르게 쓰시오. (4점)

> There was only 10,000 won in my bank occnatu.

→ _____

[전북 ○○중]

04 다음 빈칸 (A), (B)에 들어갈 말이 바르게 짝지어진 것은? (3점)

> • My dad asked me to hand (A)_____ the salt.
> • It's very important to know how to ask (B)_____ help in a polite way.

	(A)	(B)
①	over	in
②	for	in
③	over	for
④	for	with
⑤	over	with

[전북 ○○중]

05 다음 주어진 단어와 'as+형용사/부사의 원급+as' 구문을 이용해 문장을 완성하시오. (4점)

> Fred is _____ a lion. (brave)

→ _____

[충남 ○○중]

06 다음 밑줄 친 부분의 쓰임이 <u>잘못된</u> 것은? (3점)

① An apple is <u>as</u> expensive as an orange.
② My bag is as <u>light</u> as a feather.
③ Tim earns as <u>many</u> as I do.
④ Dogs are not <u>so</u> fast as cheetahs.
⑤ Linda doesn't move as slowly <u>as</u> a turtle.

07 다음 글의 빈칸 ⓐ~ⓒ에 들어갈 단어와 문장을 〈조건〉에 맞게 작성하시오. (6점)

> 조건
> • start / enter / leave / wake up을 사용하되 필요시 변형할 것
> • 시제에 유의하여 작성할 것

> Last Monday, I watched TV until late at night. So, next day I ⓐ_____ very late. So I had to run to the train station. When I got there, the train already ⓑ_____ the station. But, fortunately ⓒ나는 수업이 시작하기 전에 교실에 들어갔다.

ⓐ_____

ⓑ_____

ⓒ_____

08 다음 글의 빈칸 (A)에 들어갈 말로 알맞은 것은? (3점)

> Last spring, I planted some potatoes with my grandfather in his garden. I visited the garden and watered the potatoes often. I (A)_____ potatoes before. It was fun.

① have never plant
② had planted never
③ had never planted
④ have never planted
⑤ have planted never

09 다음 대화의 밑줄 친 ⓐ~ⓔ 중 흐름상 어색한 것은? (4점)

> A: ⓐThe toy on your desk is so cute. Do you mind if I take a look at it?
> B: ⓑYes, I do. It's called maneki-neko, or a good luck cat. ⓒMy friend bought it for me when she went to Japan.
> A: ⓓWhy is it putting its hands up?
> B: ⓔThat means it is bringing you money.

① ⓐ
② ⓑ
③ ⓒ
④ ⓓ
⑤ ⓔ

10 What are they going to do right after the conversation? (3점)

> D: Look! This jacket is really cute. Let's check out this store.
> M: Wait, I'm afraid we can't take our drinks inside.
> D: But I haven't finished mine yet.
> M: Let's finish our drinks first. Then we can go inside.
>
> *M: Mike, D: Diana

① To wear clothes
② To buy some drinks
③ To finish their drinks
④ To wait for other friends
⑤ To buy tickets to enter the store

[11~12] 다음 대화를 읽고 물음에 답하시오.

Nana: Minho, can you come with us to the game expo this Sunday?
Minho: ⓐ<u>나도 그러고 싶지만 유감스럽게도 갈 수 없어.</u> (love, but, I'd, to, afraid, I, I'm, can't). I have an important test next week.
Nana: That's too bad. They're having a special show of various games.
Minho: Yeah, I've heard it's really great. What about going with me next Saturday then?
Nana: Sure. Let's go together next Saturday.

[부산 ○○중]

11 위 대화의 ⓐ를 주어진 단어를 배열하여 영어로 쓸 때, 다음 ★에 들어갈 단어는? (4점)

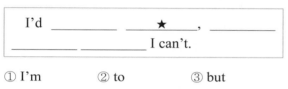

I'd _____ ____★____, _____ _____ _____ I can't.

① I'm   ② to   ③ but
④ love   ⑤ afraid

[부산 ○○중]

12 다음 중 위 대화의 내용과 일치하는 것은? (3점)

① Minho는 다음 주에 중요한 시험이 있다.
② Minho는 Nana와 함께 전시회를 가고 싶지 않다.
③ Nana는 이번 주 토요일에 게임 전시회를 가려고 한다.
④ Minho와 Nana는 이번 주 일요일에 게임 전시회에 갈 것을 약속했다.
⑤ Nana는 Minho에게 다음 주 토요일에 게임 전시회에 함께 가자고 제안한다.

[13~15] 다음 대화를 읽고 물음에 답하시오.

Boy: Wow! This comic book is really hard to find. Do you mind if I take a look at it?
Girl: (A)_____ It's one of my favorites. I've read it maybe a hundred times.
Boy: I've been looking all over for it. Can you lend it to me?
Girl: I'm afraid I can't. Actually, it's not mine. It's my sister's. Sorry.
Boy: Oh, that's okay. I understand.
Girl: You know, if you really want it, you should check used bookstores online.
Boy: Used bookstores online? I've never thought of that. That's a good idea.
Girl: Let's look together. Oh, here's one! It says it's "like new." What do you think?
Boy: Great! And it's cheap! I'll get it. Thanks!

[경기 ○○중]

13 위 대화의 빈칸 (A)에 들어갈 말로 알맞지 <u>않은</u> 것은? (3점)

① Why not?
② Not at all.
③ No, go ahead.
④ Of course not.
⑤ Yes. I'm sorry.

14 What did the boy ask the girl? (3점)

① He asked the girl to have lunch with him.

② He asked the girl to go to the movies with him.

③ He asked the girl if he could borrow the comic book.

④ He asked the girl if she could buy the comic book.

⑤ He asked the girl to go to the used bookstore with him.

16 주어진 대화 다음에 이어질 대화의 순서로 적절한 것은? (3점)

Jack: I want to buy some traditional Korean gifts for my friends. Where's a good place to buy them?

(A) Oh, I'm sorry. I have other plans. What about Saturday?

(B) No, I've never been there.

(C) Have you been to Insa-dong? They have lots of traditional Korean things there.

(D) How about visiting there with me this Friday afternoon?

Nara: That's fine with me.

① (A)-(B)-(C)-(D)

② (B)-(C)-(D)-(A)

③ (C)-(B)-(D)-(A)

④ (C)-(D)-(B)-(A)

⑤ (D)-(B)-(C)-(A)

15 위 대화의 내용과 일치하는 것은? (3점)

① The comic book is easy to find.

② The comic book is one of the girl's favorites.

③ The girl does not care about lending the book to the boy.

④ The girl tells the boy to buy a new book.

⑤ The boy has thought of buying the comic book in used bookstores online before.

This time Seyun got ⓐunderline:several text. Sadly, they all asked for a lower price. It was hard to accept at first, but finally he sold his bike for 70,000 won. He met the (A)buyer, ⓑhand over his bike, and got the money he needed. Now he could get a new bike. He felt ⓒeither happy and sad. He was sad to see his old bike ⓓto go, but he was happy with himself because he had learned a lot and ⓔgrown up a bit through the experience.

17 위 글의 ⓐ~ⓔ 중 어법상 옳은 것은? (3점)

① ⓐ   ② ⓑ   ③ ⓒ

④ ⓓ   ⑤ ⓔ

18 위 글의 내용과 일치하는 것은? (3점)

① He could not get any texts.

② He sold his bike at a lower price.

③ He was sad with his new bike.

④ The buyer handed over his bike.

⑤ He could not buy a new bike after he sold his old bike.

19 위 글 (A)buyer의 입장에 맞도록 아래 〈조건〉에 맞게 (B)에 들어갈 문장을 완성하시오. (4점)

> **조건**
> • '부탁을 하나만 들어 줄 수 있나요?'라는 뜻의 문장으로 쓸 것
> • favor를 사용할 것

> Buyer: Wow! Your bike looks really nice. How much is it?
> Seyun: It almost a new bike. I want 80,000 won.
> Buyer: I think that's a bit expensive. (B)_____?
> Seyun: What is it?
> Buyer: I really want this bike. Could you sell this bike at 70,000 won? I am just 10 years old.
> Seyun: Oh, I understand. OK.
> Buyer: Great! Thanks.

→ _____

[20~22] 다음 글을 읽고 물음에 답하시오.

"What's wrong with my posting? Is my bike not attractive enough? Seyun searched on the Internet for tips on how to sell online. (A) Then he realized what he had done wrong. (B) He had not given enough information to the possible buyers. (C) He wrote a new posting with a longer description of the bike. (D) He added more photos to show his bike from different angles. (E) "Twenty-four inch bicycle. Excellent condition. Always kept indoors. Rides just like new. Very few scratches. Good for someone 12-14 years old. 80,000 won."

20 위 글의 흐름에 따라, (A)~(E) 중 다음 문장이 들어갈 위치로 가장 알맞은 것은? (3점)

> Also, when compared to other bicycles, this price was too high.

① (A)   ② (B)   ③ (C)
④ (D)   ⑤ (E)

22 다음은 세윤이가 자전거 판매를 위한 게시글을 아래와 같이 수정한 것이다. 수정한 내용으로 옳지 <u>않은</u> 것은? (4점)

Before	After
· Used bike in excellent condition · Only 100,000 won · Please text me.	· Twenty-four inch bicycle · Excellent condition · Always kept indoors when not used. · Rides just like new · Very few scratches · Good for someone 12-14 years old · 80,000 won

① Seyun wrote a longer explanation.
② It seemed that Seyun rode the bike very carefully.
③ Seyun didn't put his bike outside when he didn't ride it.
④ Seyun added more photos of his bike from different angles.
⑤ Seyun gave ten percent off the price that he had suggested.

21 위 글의 내용과 일치하지 <u>않는</u> 것은? (3점)

① Seyun의 자전거 가격은 다른 것들에 비해 높았다.
② Seyun은 그가 충분한 정보를 주지 않았음을 깨달았다.
③ Seyun의 자전거는 12-14년을 탔지만, 여전히 좋은 상태이다.
④ Seyun의 게시물에 따르면 그의 자전거는 항상 실내에 보관되었다.
⑤ Seyun의 새로운 게시물에는 자전거에 대한 보다 긴 설명과 많은 그림이 있었다.

He acted fast. He took a photo of ⓐhis bike with his smartphone and posted the picture, with a short comment, on an online market: "ⓑUsed bike in excellent condition. Only 100,000 won. Please text me." He was excited (A)_____ about ⓒ the bike he planned to buy. He could see himself riding the shiny new bike. He could not wait to get a reply to his online advertisement of ⓓthe bike. Every few minutes he checked the number of hits. As the number of hits went up, his expectations went up too. One hour (B)_____, then two, and finally a whole day, but he received no texts. (C)_____ seemed to want ⓔhis bike. New postings by other people pushed his post down the list. His heart began to sink.

24 위 글의 ⓐ~ⓔ 중 지칭하는 것이 <u>다른</u> 것은?　(3점)

① ⓐ　　　② ⓑ　　　③ ⓒ

④ ⓓ　　　⑤ ⓔ

25 위 글의 내용과 일치하는 것은?　(3점)

① He posted the advertisement with a lot of photos.

② He took a photo of his bike with his new camera.

③ He wanted to sell his bike for 80,000 won.

④ He got many replies to his online advertisement.

⑤ His post was pushed down by other new postings.

23 위 글의 (A)~(C)에 들어갈 형태를 바르게 짝지은 것은?　(3점)

	(A)	(B)	(C)
①	thinks	passing	Nobody
②	thought	pass	No
③	thought	passed	Anybody
④	thinking	passed	Nobody
⑤	thinking	passing	Anybody

Seyun rides his bike to school every day. He likes his bike, but he is taller and stronger this year. His bike has become too small for him, so he wants to buy a bigger, faster one. (A)_____, he does not have enough money in his savings account. What can he do? Suddenly, Seyun had an idea. "My old bike is almost as (B)_____ as a new one. Maybe I can sell it and add the money to buy a new one."

26 위 글의 빈칸 (A)에 들어갈 말로 알맞은 것은? (3점)

① Finally

② However

③ Therefore

④ In addition

⑤ In other words

29 아래의 글은 위 글에서 Seyun이가 더 크고, 빠른 자전거를 사려는 이유를 쓴 글이다. <u>어색한</u> 부분을 바르게 수정하시오. (4점)

Seyun is as weaker and smaller as he was last year.

조건
• 위 글의 내용과 일치하도록 수정할 것
• 필요한 단어를 추가할 수 있음
• as ... as를 사용할 것
• 밑줄 친 Seyun과 he was last year은 고치지 말 것

→ _____

27 위 글의 빈칸 (B)에 들어갈 말로 알맞은 것은? (3점)

① bad

② worse

③ good

④ better

⑤ worst

30 위 글의 내용과 일치하지 <u>않는</u> 것은? (3점)

① 세윤이는 매일 자전거를 타고 학교에 간다.

② 세윤이의 자전거는 세윤이에게 너무 작아졌다.

③ 세윤이는 자전거를 살 충분한 돈이 없다.

④ 세윤이의 자전거는 너무 오래 타서 상태가 아주 좋지 않다.

⑤ 세윤이는 자전거를 팔아서 새 자전거를 살 때 보태기로 했다.

28 위 글을 읽고 답할 수 <u>없는</u> 것은? (3점)

① Does he like his old bike?

② Why does he want to sell his old bike?

③ How is his old bike's condition?

④ What idea does he come up with?

⑤ How much does he need to buy a new bike?

◎ 선택형 문항의 답안은 컴퓨터용 수정 싸인펜을 사용하여 OMR 답안지에 바르게 표기하시오.

◎ 서술형 문제는 답을 답안지에 반드시 검정 볼펜으로 쓰시오.

◎ 총 30문항 100점 만점입니다. 문항별 배점은 각 문항에 표시되어 있습니다.

[경기 ○○중]

01 다음 영영 풀이에 해당하는 단어로 알맞은 것은? (3점)

an arrangement with a bank or other institutions to keep money there and take some out when the user needs it

① account
② comment
③ description
④ expectation
⑤ experience

[전북 ○○중]

02 다음 우리말과 일치하도록 빈칸에 알맞은 글자를 쓰시오. (3점)

게시하다, 공고하다
p ____ ____ ____

→ _____

[전북 ○○중]

03 다음 우리말과 일치하도록 주어진 말을 알맞게 배열하시오. (4점)

내가 기차역에 도착했을 때, 기차는 이미 떠났다.
→ When I arrived at the train station, _____.
(left / the train / already / had)

→ _____

[대전 ○○중]

04 다음 표의 내용과 같은 것은? (4점)

	Sweetness (★)	Price (원)	Weight (g)
Lemon	★★	1,000	100
Apple	★★★	2,000	150
Orange	★★★	2,000	100

① An apple is as cheap as a lemon.
② An apple is as heavy as a lemon.
③ A lemon is not as heavy as an orange.
④ An orange is as expensive as an apple.
⑤ An orange is not as sweet as an apple.

[충남 ○○중]

05 다음 A, B의 대화가 가장 자연스러운 것은? (3점)

① A : What does "feel blue" mean?
   B : It means "I'm really happy."
② A : Could you recommend a good dish?
   B : Try *Samgyetang*. It'll give you energy.
③ A : Do you mind if I lean my seat back?
   B : Yes, not at all.
④ A : What does "be in a cold sweat" mean?
   B : I'm not cold.
⑤ A : I wonder who those men are.
   B : Look! There is a model.

06 다음 대화의 빈칸에 들어갈 말로 알맞은 것은? (3점)

> A: Excuse me. I want to return these sneakers.
> B: Okay. Can I ask why you want to return them?
> A: There's dirt on them and I haven't even worn them yet.
> B: Do you mind if I have a look?
> A: _____. Here.

① Yes.

② Of course.

③ Not at all.

④ Yes, I do.

⑤ Yes, I mind.

08 다음 대화의 흐름에 맞게 (A)~(C)를 배열한 것으로 가장 적절한 것은? (4점)

> G: Minho, can you come with us to the game expo this Sunday?
>
> (A) Yeah, I've heard it's really great. What about going with me next Saturday then?
> (B) I'd love to, but it's not a good time. I have an important test next week.
> (C) That's too bad. They're having a special show of various games.
>
> G: Sure. Let's go together next Saturday.

① (A) - (B) - (C)

② (A) - (C) - (B)

③ (B) - (A) - (C)

④ (B) - (C) - (A)

⑤ (C) - (B) - (A)

07 Why is the girl visiting the bank? (3점)

> M: What can I help you with?
> G: I'd like to open a bank account. What should I do?
> M: First, you need to fill out this form.
> G: Sure. Do you mind if I use your pen?
> M: Not at all.
> *M: Man, G: Girl

① 현금 인출

② 계좌 이체

③ 카드 신청하기

④ 은행 계좌 개설

⑤ 통장에 저축하기

B: Wow! This comic book is really hard to find. Do you mind if I take a look at it?

D: (A)_____. It's one of my favorites. I've read it maybe a hundred times.

B: I've been looking all over for it. Can you lend it to me?

D: (B)_____. Actually, it's not mine. It's my sister's. Sorry.

B: Oh, that's okay. I understand.

D: You know, if you really want it, you should check used bookstores online.

B: Used bookstores online? I've never thought of that. That's a good idea.

D: Let's look together. Oh, here's one! It says it's "like new." What do you think?

B: Great! And it's cheap! I'll get it. Thanks!

*B: Ben, D: Dana

09 위 대화의 흐름상 빈칸 (A)에 들어갈 표현으로 적절하지 <u>않은</u> 것은? (3점)

① Not at all.

② No, go ahead.

③ No, I don't mind.

④ Of course not.

⑤ I'm sorry, but I can't.

10 위 대화의 빈칸 (B)에 들어갈 말로 가장 적절한 것은? (3점)

① Go ahead.

② I'm afraid I can't.

③ Do what you want.

④ I agree very strongly.

⑤ I'm so sure about that.

11 위 대화의 내용을 적절하게 설명한 학생으로 알맞게 짝지어진 것은? (4점)

- 민호: Ben asked Dana to have lunch with him.
- 채아: Ben asked Dana if he could borrow a comic book.
- 수민: Dana suggested Ben should search online stores.
- 정은: Dana suggested Ben should walk to a bookstore.
- 지훈: The condition of the comic book in the used bookstore is very old and dirty.
- 은정: The condition of the comic book in the online bookstore is a few pages missing.

① 민호, 채아

② 채아, 수민

③ 수민, 정은

④ 정은, 지훈

⑤ 지훈, 은정

12 What did Ben ask Dana? (3점)

① To have lunch with him

② To search online stores

③ To borrow a comic book

④ To go to the movies with him

⑤ To help him find a book at a bookstore

[13~14] 다음 글을 읽고 물음에 답하시오.

Seyun rides his bike to school every day. He likes his bike, but he is taller and stronger this year. His bike has become too small for him, so he wants to buy a bigger, faster one. However, _____. What can he do? Suddenly, Seyun had an idea. "My old bike is almost as good as a new one. Maybe I can sell it and add the money to buy a new one."

[전북 ○○중]

13 위 글의 빈칸에 들어갈 말로 가장 적절한 것은?　(4점)

① he wants to borrow his brother's bike

② he already saved enough money for a new bike

③ his mother doesn't want him to buy a new bike

④ he can't find any new models that he wants to buy

⑤ he does not have enough money in his savings account

[대전 ○○중]

14 위 글을 읽고 아래 질문에 대한 답으로 옳은 것은?　(3점)

Q: What is Seyun's problem?

① His bike is big and fast.

② He likes his bike too much.

③ He doesn't have any friends at school.

④ His bike is almost as good as a new one.

⑤ He doesn't have enough money to buy a new bike.

[15~20] 다음 글을 읽고 물음에 답하시오.

Seyun rides his bike to school every day. He likes his bike, but he is taller and stronger this year. His bike has become too small for him, so he wants to buy a bigger, faster one. (가)_____, he does not have enough money in his savings account. What can he do? Suddenly, Seyun had an idea. "My old bike is almost as good as a new one. Maybe I can sell it and add the money to buy a new one."

He acted ⓐfast. He took a photo (A)_____ his bike (B)_____ his smartphone and posted the picture, with a short (나)comment, on an online market: "Used bike (C)_____ excellent condition. Only 100,000 won. Please text me." He was excited, ⓑthinking about the bike he planned to buy. He could see himself ⓒriding the shiny new bike. He could not wait to get a reply to his online advertisement. ⓓEvery few minutes he checked the number of hits. (D)_____ ⓔa number of hits went up, his expectations went up too. One hour passed, then two, and finally a whole day, but he received no texts. (다)_____. New postings (E)_____ other people pushed his post down the list. His heart began to sink. He thought he needed to identify the reason and find a proper solution.

[경기 ○○중]

15 위 글의 밑줄 친 ⓐ~ⓔ 중 문맥상 옳지 <u>않은</u> 것은?　(4점)

① ⓐ　　　② ⓑ　　　③ ⓒ

④ ⓓ　　　⑤ ⓔ

16 위 글의 빈칸 (가)에 가장 적절한 것은? (3점)

① Despite
② However
③ Because of
④ By the way
⑤ For instance

19 위 글의 빈칸 (A)~(E)에 들어갈 말이 알맞지 <u>않은</u> 것은? (4점)

① (A) - of
② (B) - with
③ (C) - in
④ (D) - As
⑤ (E) - from

17 위 글의 흐름상 밑줄 친 (나)와 바꿔 쓸 수 있는 것은? (3점)

① sample
② instance
③ explanation
④ condition
⑤ reason

18 위 글의 빈칸 (다)에 들어갈 말로 가장 적절한 것은? (3점)

① Everything looked so bright.
② His bike does not seem to be attracting buyers.
③ He decided to sell it at the flea market face to face.
④ He had to choose one buyer to contact for the sale.
⑤ Seyun and a buyer needed to agree on a price for the bike.

20 위 글의 Seyun에 관한 내용과 일치하는 것은? (3점)

① No one visited his posting.
② He got many texts from people.
③ He doesn't like his bike anymore.
④ He has enough money on his bank account.
⑤ He thought that the condition of his bike was good.

This time he got several texts. (가)_____, they all ⓐasked for a lower price. It was hard to accept ⓑat first, but finally he ⓒsold his bike for 70,000 won. He met the buyer, ⓓhanded over his bike, and got the money he needed. Now he could get a new bike. He felt both happy and sad. He was sad to see his old bike go, but he was happy with himself because he had learned a lot and ⓔ grown up a bit through the experience.

[전북 ○○중]

21 위 글의 빈칸 (가)에 들어갈 말로 알맞은 것은? (3점)

① Sadly　　　　② Happily

③ Lonely　　　　④ Lovely

⑤ Friendly

[충남 ○○중]

22 위 글의 밑줄 친 ⓐ~ⓔ 중 의미가 어색한 것은? (3점)

① ⓐ: ~을 요청했다

② ⓑ: 처음에는

③ ⓒ: 그의 자전거를 ~에 팔았다

④ ⓓ: 건네주었다

⑤ ⓔ: 재배했다

[전북 ○○중]

23 위 글을 읽고 대답할 수 없는 질문은? (4점)

① Did Seyun accept a lower price?

② How much was Seyun's bike sold for?

③ Did Seyun get any messages this time?

④ How much did Seyun pay for his new bike?

⑤ How did Seyun feel after he handed over his old bike?

"What's wrong with my posting? Does my bike not look good enough?" Seyun searched (A)_____ the Internet for tips (B)_____ how to sell online. Then (가)he realized what he had done wrong. He had been too hasty and too greedy. He had not given enough information to the possible buyers. Also, when ⓐcompared to other bicycles, his price was too high. He wrote a new posting with a longer description of the bike. He added more photos to show his bike from different angles. "Twenty-four inch bicycle. Excellent condition. Always kept indoors. Rides just like new. Very few scratches. Good for someone ⓑthat is 12-14 years old. 80,000 won."

This time he got several texts. Sadly, they all asked for a lower price. It was hard to ⓒaccepting at first, but finally he sold his bike for 70,000 won. He met the buyer, handed over his bike, and got the money he needed. Now he could get a new bike. He felt both happy and sad. He was sad to see his old bike ⓓgo, but he was happy with himself because he had learned a lot and ⓔgrown up a bit through his experience selling online.

[대전 ○○중]

24 위 글의 밑줄 친 ⓐ~ⓔ 중, 어법상 옳지 않은 것은? (4점)

① ⓐ　　　　② ⓑ　　　　③ ⓒ

④ ⓓ　　　　⑤ ⓔ

25 위 글의 (A), (B)에 공통으로 들어갈 말로 알맞은 것은? (3점)

① on

② in

③ of

④ for

⑤ with

28 위 글을 읽고 대답할 수 없는 질문은? (3점)

① What did Seyun add to his posting?

② What did people ask Seyun for in texts?

③ How much did Seyun finally sell his bike for?

④ When Seyun first bought his bike, how much was it?

⑤ What did Seyun do to find tips on how to sell his bike?

26 위 글의 밑줄 친 (가)와 바꿔 쓸 수 있는 것은? (3점)

① he realized who he had done wrong.

② he realized which he had done wrong.

③ he realized in which he had done wrong.

④ he realized the thing that he had done wrong.

⑤ he realized the thing what he had done wrong.

29 위 글의 제목으로 가장 적절한 것은? (4점)

① How to Get a Refund

② Tips to Be a Sensible Consumer

③ Learning to Become a Wise Online Seller

④ The Reason for Increasing Online Shopping

⑤ Traditional Markets are My Favorite Place

30 위 글의 내용과 일치하지 <u>않는</u> 것은? (3점)

① 세윤이는 자신의 게시물의 문제점을 찾기 위해 인터넷을 검색했다.

② 다른 자전거들과 비교했을 때 세윤이의 자전거의 첫 제시 가격은 합리적이었다.

③ 세윤이는 자신의 자전거에 대한 더 긴 설명과 사진을 담아 새 게시물을 작성했다.

④ 수정된 게시물을 보고 몇몇 구매자로부터 연락이 왔으나 가격을 낮춰 달라고 요청했다.

⑤ 온라인 판매를 통해 세윤이는 조금 더 성장한 것이 기뻤다.

27 위 글에서 언급된 자전거에 대한 내용과 일치하는 것은? (3점)

① 바퀴는 22인치이다.

② 상태가 훌륭하다.

③ 항상 실외에 보관했다.

④ 스크래치가 상당히 많은 편이다.

⑤ 키가 큰 아이에게 적당하다.

3학년 영어 2학기 기말고사(7과) 1회

문항수 : 선택형(30문항) 서술형(0문항) | 20 . . .

◎ 선택형 문항의 답안은 컴퓨터용 수정 싸인펜을 사용하여 OMR 답안지에 바르게 표기하시오.

◎ 서술형 문제는 답을 답안지에 반드시 검정 볼펜으로 쓰시오.

◎ 총 30문항 100점 만점입니다. 문항별 배점은 각 문항에 표시되어 있습니다.

[서울 양천구 ○○중]

01 다음 빈칸에 공통으로 들어갈 단어로 가장 적절한 것은? (3점)

> • The _____ is concentrating on developing new products.
> • I enjoyed her _____ very much.

① condition
② balance
③ choice
④ company
⑤ interest

[충남 ○○중]

02 다음 중 어법상 어색한 문장은? (3점)

① Turn around for me see your face.
② Turn around for me to see your face.
③ Turn around in order for me to see your face.
④ Turn around so that I can see your face.
⑤ Turn around in order that I can see your face.

[충남 ○○중]

03 다음 두 문장의 (A)와 (B)에 들어갈 말이 순서대로 짝지어진 것은? (3점)

> • What would you do if you (A)_____ in my shoes?
> • If I didn't have any classes today, I (B)_____ go to an amusement park.

	(A)	(B)
①	are	will
②	were	will
③	were	would
④	are	would
⑤	was	would

[대전 ○○중]

04 다음 문장을 가정법과거를 사용하여 옳게 바꾼 것은? (4점)

> As I have homework, I cannot play outside.

① I can play outside if I don't have homework.
② If I didn't have homework, I played outside.
③ I could play outside if I didn't have homework.
④ If I didn't have homework, I could have played outside.
⑤ If I don't have homework, I could have been playing outside.

[6~10] 다음 대화를 읽고 물음에 답하시오.

05 다음 그림을 보고 유추한 대화문의 내용으로 바르지 <u>않은</u> 것은? (4점)

[대전 ○○중]

All about Wright Brothers!

① A: Look at this picture. They're the Wright brothers. I wonder what they did.

B: They invented the airplane.

② A: I wonder who inspired them to make the plane.

B: I heard they sold their bicycles to prepare money for making the airplane.

③ A: I wonder why they are standing in front of the bicycle shop.

B: They had a bicycle shop. They sold and repaired bicycles.

④ A: I wonder what the first plane looked like.

B: Look! There's a model over there.

⑤ A: I wonder where they tested flying their airplane.

B: There is a picture of their plane being tested on a hill.

G: I like these crackers. They're really good.

B: Yeah, me, too. I wonder why crackers have these little holes in them.

G: I don't know. Let me (A)<u>see</u>.... Um... well... maybe it's because (B)<u>그 구멍들이 크래커를 더욱 맛있게 보이도록 해준다</u>.

B: That's possible, but there must be some other reasons.

G: Let's look up crackers on the Internet and see what it says.

B: Okay. Oh, look at this.

G: It says during baking, steam comes out through the holes and that makes the crackers thin.

B: It also says that the holes make the crackers crispy.

G: Wow! So that's why they have holes!

*B: Boy, G: Girl

[대전 ○○중]

06 위 대화의 밑줄 친 (A)와 바꿔 쓸 수 있는 것은? (3점)

① know ② think
③ have ④ make
⑤ move

[서울 양천구 ○○중]

07 위 대화의 밑줄 친 (B)를 영어로 표현했을 때 가장 적절한 것은? (4점)

① the holes look tastier crackers

② the holes make to look tastier crackers

③ the holes make the crackers look tastier

④ the holes make the crackers looking tastier

⑤ the holes make the crackers to look tastier

Lesson 7 Small Ideas, Big Differences **33**

08 What do the holes do? (4점)

① To make people eat more

② To let water drain out

③ To look the crackers tastier

④ To prevent water from overflowing

⑤ To make the crackers thin and crispy

09 위 대화의 내용과 일치하지 <u>않는</u> 것은? (3점)

① 소년과 소녀 둘 다 이 크래커를 좋아한다.

② 소년은 크래커에 작은 구멍들이 왜 있는지 궁금해한다.

③ 처음에 소녀는 크래커를 더 맛있어 보이게 하기 위해 작은 구멍을 만드는 줄 알았다.

④ 크래커의 구멍은 구워지는 동안 증기를 들어오게 한다.

⑤ 그들은 크래커에 구멍이 있는 이유를 알게 되었다.

10 위 대화를 읽고 답할 수 <u>없는</u> 질문은? (3점)

① Does the girl like the crackers?

② Do the crackers have holes in them?

③ How long does it take to bake the crackers?

④ Did the girl know why crackers have these little holes in them?

⑤ Where did they find some information about the holes in crackers?

[11~12] 다음 글을 읽고 물음에 답하시오.

A Butter Stick

What does it look like? Maybe a glue stick? Well, (A)(what, is, it, not, is, that) at all. It is butter in a stick. We call it a butter stick. The butter stick was invented (B)<u>빵에 버터를 바를 수 있도록</u> without using a knife. What a great invention!

11 위 글의 흐름에 맞게 (A)를 배열할 때, 다섯 번째로 오는 단어는? (3점)

① it

② is

③ not

④ that

⑤ what

12 위 글의 (B)를 영어로 옮긴 것 중 옳지 <u>않은</u> 것은? (3점)

① to put butter on your bread

② in order to put butter on your bread

③ so that you can put butter on your bread

④ so as that you can put butter on your bread

⑤ in order that you can put butter on your bread

If you look around, you will see other holes that play a helpful role in your life. If you have ever cooked anything in a pot with a lid, perhaps you noticed a small hole in the lid. This hole, too, is there for safety. When cooking something in a pot with a lid, the pressure inside the pot builds up. The water inside (가)quickly boil over if the lid did not have that hole. The hole lets steam out and keeps the water from (A)_____ out.

13 위 글의 빈칸 (A)에 들어갈 알맞은 것은?   (3점)
[충남 ○○중]

① comes

② coming

③ come

④ came

⑤ be coming

14 위 글의 밑줄 친 (가)의 가정법과거 형태로 가장 적절한 것은?
[대전 ○○중]
(4점)

① quickly boils

② quickly boiled

③ is quickly boiling

④ would quickly boil

⑤ would have quickly boiled

15 위 글의 제목으로 가장 적절한 것은?   (3점)
[대전 ○○중]

① Tips to Make Good Holes

② The Importance of Kitchen Safety

③ The Role of the Small Hole in a Pot Lid

④ How to Use a Pressure Cooker Safely

⑤ Influences of the Small Hole in the Window

16 위 글을 읽고, 다음 질문에 가장 알맞은 대답을 고르면? (3점)
[충남 ○○중]

Q: What happens when you cook something in a pot with a lid?

① You notice a small hole in the lid.

② This hole, too, is there for safety.

③ The pressure inside the pot builds up.

④ The water inside doesn't boil over quickly.

⑤ A small hole in the lid doesn't let steam out.

[17~19] 다음 글을 읽고 물음에 답하시오.

Have you ever been on an airplane? Wasn't it exciting ⓐto look out the window and see the world below? Surprisingly, there was a small hole in your window. Airplane windows ⓑare made up of three panes. There is a hole in the middle pane. It balances the air pressure. Without this little hole, airplane windows ⓒmight break in an emergency. The hole also prevents the window from fogging up ⓓso that you can enjoy that fantastic view.

There are many more products ⓔwhat have small hidden holes. In the future, when you see a little hole in something, ask yourself why it is there. Maybe it is the result of a careful design (A)to make your life safer.

18 위 글의 밑줄 친 (A)와 어법상 쓰임이 같은 것은? (3점)

① My job is to teach English.

② It is not easy to know oneself.

③ To play the piano is my new hobby.

④ If it starts to rain, the river might overflow.

⑤ The easiest way to make strong bones is to go outside.

19 위 글의 내용과 일치하는 것은? (3점)

① 비행기 창문은 네 개의 판으로 구성되어 있다.

② 중간 유리판의 구멍은 기압의 균형을 맞춰 준다.

③ 작은 구멍이 있으면, 비행기 창문은 비상시에 깨질 수 있다.

④ 구멍은 창문에 김이 서리는 것을 유발한다.

⑤ 숨겨진 작은 구멍들이 있는 제품은 많지 않다.

17 위 글의 밑줄 친 ⓐ~ⓔ 중, 어법상 옳지 않은 것은? (4점)

① ⓐ   ② ⓑ   ③ ⓒ

④ ⓓ   ⑤ ⓔ

Think about a hole that you have seen recently. Was it a good hole or a bad hole? If it was a hole in your sock, it was bad. If it was a hole in your shirt for a button, it was good. There are holes everywhere. (a)_____. They are well hidden, but many of these small holes are very important and make your life safe.

(A) Take a (가)pen. Look at it carefully. Do you see a small hole in the (나)cap? (B) Do you know why it is there? The hole in a pen cap can help save lives. (C) People, especially children, often put small things like pen caps in their mouths. Sometimes they even swallow them. (D) A famous pen (다)company started putting a small hole in their pen caps. (E) The hole in the cap lets air pass through and has saved lives.

20 위 글의 (A)~(E) 중 주어진 문장이 들어가기에 가장 적절한 곳은? (4점)

> If so, this can stop their breathing and cause death.

① (A) ② (B) ③ (C)
④ (D) ⑤ (E)

21 위 글의 밑줄 친 (가)~(다)와 다른 의미로 쓰인 것은? (3점)

① ⓐ You need to borrow a pen to write.
② ⓐ She asked for some paper and a pen.
③ ⓑ He twisted the cap several times but it didn't open.
④ ⓒ Steve joined the company in 2019.
⑤ ⓒ I enjoyed her company very much.

22 위 글의 제목으로 가장 적절한 것은? (3점)

① Check How Deep the Hole Is
② Dangerous Experiences You Have Had
③ Exercising Is the Best Way to Keep Healthy
④ A Goal You Have Set for Product Development
⑤ Changes in Our Lives that Small Ideas Have Brought about

23 위 글의 빈칸 (a)에 들어갈 말로 가장 적절한 것은? (4점)

① They are getting faster and better.
② That's how science is used in making steam.
③ They can also be used for pouring engine oil.
④ The small hole helps liquid inside flow out smoothly.
⑤ Some are so small that you may not even notice them.

24 위 글을 읽고 답할 수 없는 질문은? (3점)

① Are the holes that we see around us all good holes?
② What is an example of a bad hole?
③ What do children often put in their mouths?
④ What design of pen caps do people like?
⑤ Why is there a hole in a pen cap?

[25~27] 다음 글을 읽고 물음에 답하시오.

If you look around, you will see other holes that play a helpful role in your life. If you have ever cooked anything in a pot with a lid, perhaps you noticed a small hole in the lid. This hole, too, is there for safety. When cooking something in a pot with a lid, the pressure inside the pot builds up. The water inside would quickly boil over if the lid (A)[does not / did not] have that hole. The hole lets steam out and keeps the water from coming out.

Have you ever been on an airplane? Wasn't it exciting to look out the window and see the world below? Surprisingly, there was a small hole in your window. Airplane windows (B)[are composed of / made up of] three panes. There is a hole in the middle pane. It balances the air pressure. ⓐ이 작은 구멍이 없다면, 비행기 창문은 비상시에 깨질 수 있다. The hole also (C)[prevents / promotes] the window from fogging up so that you can enjoy that fantastic view.

26 위 글의 밑줄 친 ⓐ를 영어로 표현했을 때 가장 적절한 것은?
(3점)

① If it were not for this little hole, airplane windows might not break in an emergency.

② If it were not for this little hole, airplane windows might break in an emergency.

③ With this little hole, airplane windows might break in an emergency.

④ With this little hole, airplane windows might be strong enough in an emergency.

⑤ Without this big hole, airplane windows might break in an emergency.

27 위 글을 읽고 답할 수 없는 질문은?
(3점)

① What is the tiny hole in a pot lid for?

② What will happen if we boil water in a pot without a lid hole?

③ How does the hole in the lid help us cook faster?

④ Where is a small hole in the three panes of airplane windows?

⑤ What does the hole in the middle pane do?

25 위 글의 괄호 (A), (B), (C) 안에서 문맥에 맞는 낱말로 적절한 것은?
(4점)

	(A)	(B)	(C)
①	does not	are composed of	prevents
②	does not	are composed of	promotes
③	did not	are composed of	prevents
④	did not	made up of	prevents
⑤	did not	made up of	promotes

Have you ever been on an airplane? ⓐWasn't it excited to look out the window and see the world below? Surprisingly, there was a small hole in your window.

(A) Without this little hole, airplane windows might break in an emergency.
(B) Airplane windows are made up of three panes.
(C) It balances the air pressure.
(D) There is a hole in the middle pane.

ⓑThe hole also prevents the window from fogging up so that you can enjoy that fantastic view.
ⓒThere are many more products that has small hidden holes. In the future, when you see a little hole in something, ⓓask yourself why is it there. Maybe ⓔit is the result of a careful design to make your life safer.

[대전 ○○중]

29 위 글의 흐름에 맞게 (A)~(D)를 순서대로 배열한 것은? (4점)

① (B)-(A)-(C)-(D)
② (B)-(D)-(C)-(A)
③ (C)-(D)-(A)-(B)
④ (D)-(A)-(C)-(B)
⑤ (D)-(C)-(A)-(B)

[대전 ○○중]

30 위 글을 읽고 답할 수 있는 것만을 〈보기〉에서 있는 대로 고른 것은? (3점)

> **보기**
> ⓐ What is an example of a bad hole?
> ⓑ What does the hole in the middle pane do?
> ⓒ How many windows does an airplane have?
> ⓓ What might happen if there were no holes in the airplane windows?
> ⓔ What does the writer want you to do when you see a small hole in something?

① ⓐ, ⓒ
② ⓑ, ⓔ
③ ⓓ, ⓔ
④ ⓑ, ⓒ, ⓓ
⑤ ⓑ, ⓓ, ⓔ

[대전 ○○중]

28 위 글의 밑줄 친 ⓐ~ⓔ 중 어법상 옳은 것만을 있는 대로 고른 것은? (3점)

① ⓐ, ⓑ
② ⓐ, ⓓ
③ ⓑ, ⓔ
④ ⓐ, ⓑ, ⓔ
⑤ ⓒ, ⓓ, ⓔ

◎ 선택형 문항의 답안은 컴퓨터용 수정 싸인펜을 사용하여 OMR 답안지에 바르게 표기하시오.
◎ 서술형 문제는 답을 답안지에 반드시 검정 볼펜으로 쓰시오.
◎ 총 28문항 100점 만점입니다. 문항별 배점은 각 문항에 표시되어 있습니다.

[충남 ○○중]

01 다음 밑줄 친 단어의 의미가 <u>다른</u> 것은? (3점)

① Hajin likes soccer <u>while</u> Daniel likes baseball.

② Hajin likes Gimchi fried rice <u>while</u> Daniel likes potato soup.

③ Hajin likes comedy movies <u>while</u> Daniel likes action movies.

④ <u>While</u> I was sleeping, I had a nightmare.

⑤ <u>While</u> I work at a company, Jay works at home.

[서울 양천구 ○○중]

02 다음 중 A와 B의 대화가 <u>어색한</u> 것은? (4점)

① A: Do you mind if I change seats with you?
   B: Yes, go ahead. I'm with my friend.

② A: Can I look around the stage?
   B: I'm afraid you can't. It's open only for the actors.

③ A: I wonder what the first plane looked like.
   B: Look! There is a model. It looked like a big bird.

④ A: Could you recommend a good traditional dish?
   B: Try *Samgyetang*.

⑤ A: What can we do with this ball?
   B: Let me see. We can play soccer.

[3~6] 다음 대화를 읽고 물음에 답하시오.

M: Good afternoon. (가)A table for two?
B: Yes.
M: This way, please. Here is the menu. I'll be back in a few minutes and take your order.
B: Okay. Thank you.
G: I don't know much about Korean food. Could you recommend something?
B: (나)I'd recommend Bibimbap.
G: (A)_____
B: Bi-bim-bap. It's made with lots of vegetables, beef and an egg over rice. It's tasty and it's also good for your health.
G: That sounds great. I'll try it.
B: It's served with a spicy red pepper sauce. Is that okay?
G: No problem. I like spicy food.

*M: Waiter, G: Sophie, B: Hajun

[서울 양천구 ○○중]

03 위 대화의 흐름상 밑줄 친 (가)의 의미로 가장 적절한 것은? (4점)

① Do you need two tables?

② Do you need a table for two people?

③ Do you need a table to use for two hours?

④ Did you make a reservation for a table at 2 pm?

⑤ Did you make a reservation for the table number 2?

04 위 대화의 밑줄 친 (나)와 바꿔 쓸 수 <u>없는</u> 것은? (3점)

① Try Bibimbap.

② How about Bibimbap?

③ What about Bibimbap?

④ What's so special about Bibimbap?

⑤ Bibimbap will be good for you.

[7~8] 다음 대화를 읽고 물음에 답하시오.

> A: Have you ever tried poke?
>
> (A) Poke. It's a salad that is popular in Hawaii.
> (B) Sorry. ⓐCould you say that again?
> (C) What's so special about it?
> (D) It's made with rice and fish. It's not only delicious but also very healthy.

07 주어진 대화 다음에 이어질 대화의 순서를 바르게 배열한 것은? (4점)

① (B)-(A)-(C)-(D)

② (B)-(D)-(A)-(C)

③ (C)-(A)-(D)-(B)

④ (C)-(B)-(A)-(D)

⑤ (D)-(A)-(B)-(C)

05 위 대화의 빈칸 (A)에 들어갈 표현으로 적절하지 <u>않은</u> 것은? (3점)

① Pardon?

② Excuse me?

③ I beg your pardon?

④ Could you give it to me?

⑤ Could you say that again?

06 위 대화의 내용과 일치하는 것은? (4점)

① Sophie does not enjoy spicy food.

② The Bibimbap has an egg under rice.

③ Sophie knows a lot about Korean dishes.

④ Sophie has been to Korean restaurants many times.

⑤ Hajun recommends the food that is not only tasty but also good for the health.

08 위 대화의 ⓐ와 바꿔 쓸 수 <u>없는</u> 것은? (4점)

① Excuse me?

② I beg your pardon?

③ Can you repeat that, please?

④ Could you say it one more time?

⑤ Can you tell me more about that?

09 다음 대화의 주제로 가장 적절한 것은? (4점)

> B: Tomorrow is my birthday.
> G: I know. Are you going to have a birthday party, Alex?
> B: Yes. Can you recommend a good place to have the party?
> G: I'd recommend the Happy Snack House. The food is really good and it'll be large enough.
> B: What dish would you recommend?
> G: I'd recommend the onion rings. They're fantastic!
> B: Oh, just thinking about them makes my mouth water.

① A place to hold a party

② A place to go shopping

③ A place to take a walk

④ A place to do a project

⑤ A place to read books

[10~12] 다음 대화를 읽고 물음에 답하시오.

> W: Good afternoon. Did you make a call?
> B: No. We would like a table for two.
> W: This way, please. Here is the menu. I'll be back in a few minutes and __(A)__ your order.
> B: Okay. Thank you.
> G: I don't know much about Korean food. Could you recommend something?
> B: Well, what about Bibimbap?
> G: I'm sorry. Could you say that again, please?
> B: Bi-bim-bap. It's made with lots of vegetables, beef and an egg over rice. It's tasty and it's also good for your health.
> G: That sounds great. I'll try it.
> B: It's served with a spicy red pepper sauce. Is that okay?
> G: (B)No problem. I like spicy food.
>
> *W: Waiter, B: Boy, G: Girl

10 위 대화의 빈칸 (A)에 알맞은 것은? (3점)

① let

② allow

③ make

④ take

⑤ leave

11 위 대화의 (B)가 의미하는 바로 가장 적절한 것은? (4점)

① She can eat what her friend suggests.

② She has a good relationship with him.

③ She has enough money to pay the bill.

④ She doesn't have any problems these days.

⑤ She doesn't know what kind of food the Bibimbap is.

13 다음 글을 볼 수 있는 곳으로 가장 적절한 것은? (3점)

> Have you seen the two sisters at our school who look so much alike? They are Hana and Duna. While Hana has short hair, Duna has long hair. Also, while Hana wears glasses, Duna does not. They both are not only very kind but also smart.

① Diary

② Scientific journal

③ School newspaper

④ Fashion magazine

⑤ Advertisement paper

14 다음 글의 흐름과 관련 <u>없는</u> 문장은? (4점)

> *Customer Reviews* ★★★★★
> This one would be perfect if you are looking for a new swimming suit. ⓐIt is beautiful and unique at the same time. ⓑAlso, it is as cheap as the one that is on sale. ⓒThe color is the same as the one I saw on the website, so I like it. ⓓHowever, I would advise you to buy a bigger size than what you usually buy. ⓔIn terms of buying a swimming suit, you need to buy a smaller size because it can be stretched after you wear it several times. Even though I had ordered the same size as what I usually wear, it was too small for me.

① ⓐ   ② ⓑ   ③ ⓒ

④ ⓓ   ⑤ ⓔ

12 위 대화의 내용과 일치하는 것은? (4점)

① Two customers come to the restaurant.

② They made a reservation for the table.

③ The girl recommends the Bibimbap to the boy.

④ The Bibimbap doesn't have vegetables.

⑤ The girl doesn't like vegetables.

15 다음 글의 내용과 일치하는 것은? (4점)

September 8th, Monday

Last spring, I planted some potatoes with my grandfather in his garden. I visited the garden and watered the potatoes often. I had never planted potatoes before. It was fun.

Today, my grandfather and I dug some of the potatoes. They looked as good as the ones you see in the market, and there were so many of them. My grandfather says we can take some of them to the market and sell them! That will be really exciting.

I = Mike

① Mike는 올봄에 자신의 정원에 감자를 심었다.
② Mike는 이전에도 감자를 심은 적이 있었다.
③ Mike는 할아버지를 포함한 가족 모두와 감자를 캤다.
④ 수확한 감자는 시장에서 파는 것만큼 상태가 좋았다.
⑤ 감자를 시장에 팔고 남는 것을 이웃 사람에게 나누어 주었다.

[16~17] 다음 글을 읽고 물음에 답하시오.

My foreign friend, Paul, is coming to Gyeongju this weekend, so we're planning to show him around. First, we're going to take him to Bulguksa Temple. We want to show some of the national treasures of Korea. Then we'll eat Kongguksu for lunch. I think he'll like it. After eating it, we'll have Gyeongju Bread for dessert. In the evening, we'll visit Donggung Palace and Wolji Pond and enjoy how beautiful it looks at night.

16 위 글을 쓴 목적으로 가장 적절한 것은? (3점)

① to guide my friend
② to study Korean history
③ to visit my friend's house
④ to have some Korean food
⑤ to enjoy the beauty of the temple

17 위 글을 읽고 답할 수 있는 것은? (3점)

① Where is Paul from?
② When will Paul visit Gyeongju?
③ What food does Paul like?
④ How's the taste of Gyeongju Bread?
⑤ How many people will visit Gyeongju?

18 다음 글을 읽고, 'Moai'에 관해 답할 수 <u>없는</u> 질문은? (4점)

Hi, class. Have you ever heard about the Moai? They are tall, human-shaped stones in Chile. Most of the stones are four meters tall, but the tallest one is 20 meters tall. I was wondering how people moved them long ago. So I searched the Internet and learned that they used ropes. Also, I found that people built them to honor their leaders or other important people who had passed away. Isn't that amazing?

① What do they look like?

② Where are they located now?

③ What is their average height?

④ How could the people carve them?

⑤ Why did the people make the stones?

19 다음 글을 읽고 알 수 있는 내용으로 적절하지 <u>않은</u> 것은? (4점)

Gobol-mogol is not only good for people with a cold but also popular as a dessert for healthy people. When served as a dessert, it is usually served cold or at room temperature.

Why not try making Gogol-mogol? It will be fun and good for your health.

How to Make Gogol-mogol
(Serves one)

You need: 1 egg, 1/2 cup of milk, honey (5g), butter (15g)

1. Put the egg and the honey in a large cup and mix them.

2. Pour half a cup of milk in a pan. Add the butter. Warm it until the butter melts.

3. Pour the hot milk and butter into the cup with the egg and the honey. Stir as you pour.

4. Drink while it is hot or at room temperature.

① Gogol-mogol is popular as a dessert for healthy people as well as good for people with a cold.

② You can enjoy Gogol-mogol even at room temperature as a dessert.

③ Making Gogol-mogol is not only fun but also good for health.

④ When you make Gogol-mogol that serves two, you need half a cup of milk.

⑤ An egg and honey should be mixed in the cup first.

[20~21] 다음 글을 읽고 물음에 답하시오.

Foods That (A)_____ Colds

What do you do when you catch a cold? Of course, you want to stay warm, so maybe you put on more clothes. Some people like to drink hot tea. Ginger tea is something people in Korea often drink. ⓐWith its special taste, it warms your body and helps worsen the pain in your throat. What do people drink or eat in other countries when they catch a cold? Let's find out.

In Finland, where it is very cold in winter, people have a special drink when they catch a cold. It is a cup of onion milk. ⓑThey put chopped onion in milk and boil it over low heat for half an hour. This simple drink is said to be good for a cold.

While people in Korea and Finland look for drinks when sick, many people in America want a bowl of chicken soup. ⓒIt is usually made with chicken and vegetables, but the receipt is different from one family to another. Salt and pepper can be added before eating. ⓓPeople in America believe that a bowl of warm chicken soup is great for a sore throat and a stuffy nose.

In Russia and in Eastern Europe, when people get sick, they eat a dessert called gogol-mogol. It is made with eggs and honey. ⓔSome people add chocolate, butter, lemon juice, or milk to make it taste better. It looks like thick yogurt. People often drink a cup of warm gogol-mogol when they have a sore throat.

20 위 글의 밑줄 친 ⓐ~ⓔ 중 문맥상 어색한 것으로 짝지어진 것은? (4점)

① ⓐ, ⓑ
② ⓐ, ⓒ
③ ⓑ, ⓓ
④ ⓒ, ⓓ
⑤ ⓓ, ⓔ

21 위 글의 빈칸 (A)에 가장 적절한 말은? (3점)

① Fight
② Invite
③ Catch
④ Enable
⑤ Warm

[22~24] 다음 글을 읽고 물음에 답하시오.

(A) What do you do when you catch a cold? Of course, you want to stay warm, so maybe you put on more clothes. Some people like to drink hot tea. Ginger tea is something people in Korea often drink. With its special taste, it warms your body and helps ⓐreduce the pain in your throat. What do people drink or eat in other countries when they catch a cold? Let's find out.

(B) In Finland, ⓑwhere it is very cold in winter, people have a special drink when they catch a cold. It is ⓒa cup of onion milk. They put ⓓchop onion in milk and boil it over low heat for half an hour. This simple drink ⓔis said to be good for a cold.

22 위 글의 밑줄 친 ⓐ~ⓔ 중, 어법상 옳지 <u>않은</u> 것은? (3점)

① ⓐ   ② ⓑ   ③ ⓒ

④ ⓓ   ⑤ ⓔ

23 위 글 (A) 다음에 이어질 내용으로 알맞은 것은? (4점)

① What kind of food do Koreans like?

② How can people wear clothes well?

③ What is the benefit of drinking ginger tea?

④ Why do Korean people like to drink ginger tea?

⑤ What food do people eat in other countries when they have a cold?

24 위 글 (A), (B)의 공통된 주제로 가장 적절한 것은? (3점)

① People like to drink hot tea.

② Koreans like to drink ginger tea.

③ There are some foods that fight colds.

④ There are many kinds of tea in the world.

⑤ What kind of food do people like the most?

[25~26] 다음 글을 읽고 물음에 답하시오.

While people in Korea and Finland look for drinks when sick, many people in America want a bowl of chicken soup. ⓐ<u>It is usually made with chicken and vegetables, but the recipe is different from one family to another.</u> Salt and pepper can be added before eating. ⓑ<u>Why not try making one of the foods you have found out?</u> ⓒ<u>People in America believe that a bowl of warm chicken soup is great for a sore throat and a stuffy nose.</u>

In Russia and in Eastern Europe, when people get sick, they eat a dessert called gogol-mogol. It is made with eggs and honey. ⓓ<u>Some people add chocolate, butter, lemon juice, or milk to make it taste better.</u> It looks like thick yogurt. People often drink a cup of warm gogol-mogol when they have a sore throat. Gogol-mogol is not only good for people with a cold but also popular as a dessert for healthy people. ⓔ<u>When served as a dessert, it is usually served cold or at room temperature.</u>

25 위 글의 밑줄 친 ⓐ~ⓔ 중, 전체 흐름과 관계 <u>없는</u> 문장은? (4점)

① ⓐ   ② ⓑ   ③ ⓒ

④ ⓓ   ⑤ ⓔ

26 위 글의 내용과 일치하는 것은? (3점)

① People in Finland and America eat the same food when they are sick.

② Americans use the same recipe to make chicken soup.

③ Americans believe that chicken soup is also good as a dessert.

④ Some people add some foods when they make Gogol-mogol.

⑤ Gogol-mogol is always served cold.

27 위 글의 흐름으로 보아, 주어진 문장이 들어가기에 가장 적절한 곳은? (4점)

While people in Korea and Finland look for drinks when sick, many people in America want a bowl of chicken soup.

① (A) ② (B) ③ (C)
④ (D) ⑤ (E)

[27~28] 다음 글을 읽고 물음에 답하시오.

(A) In Finland, where it is very cold in winter, people have a special drink when they catch a cold. (B) It is a cup of onion milk. (C) They put chopped onion in milk and boil it over low heat for half an hour. (D) This simple drink is said to be good for a cold. (E) It is usually made with chicken and vegetables, but the recipe is different from one family to another. Salt and pepper can be added before eating. People in America believe that a bowl of warm chicken soup is great for a sore throat and a stuffy nose.

28 위 글에서 미국인들의 닭고기 수프에 대한 생각으로 가장 알맞은 것은? (3점)

① 인후통과 코막힘에 좋다.

② 복통을 완화하고, 인후통에 좋다.

③ 기침 감기를 예방하는 데 좋다.

④ 열을 내리는 데 도움이 된다.

⑤ 몸을 따뜻하게 하는 데 도움이 된다.

정답 및 해설

Lesson 5 (중간)

01 ①	**02** ②	**03** ③	**04** ④	**05** ①, ④	**06** ②	**07** ④

08 ⓑ that → what ⓔ practiced → practicing

09 How long has Andy been learning Spanish?

10 ② **11** ② **12** ④ **13** ① **14** ⑤ **15** ① **16** ② **17** ①

18 ① **19** ① **20** ① **21** ⑤

22 The clouds mean problems waiting to happen

23 ② **24** ③ **25** ③ **26** ③ **27** ③ **28** ① **29** ① **30** ④

01 lean: 기울다; 기대다   fire: 불; 사격하다
leave: 떠나다; 남기다   raise: 올리다; 모으다

02 category: 범주, 범위   dig: 파다
search: 찾다   comment: 언급하다; 언급
lend: 빌려주다

03 빈칸에 공통으로 들어가기에 가장 적절한 것은 ③ draw(그리다; 끌다)이다.

04 ① are → is / ② are → is / ③ are → is / ⑤ that → what으로 고쳐야 어법상 적절한 문장이 된다.

05 주어진 문장의 what은 선행사를 포함한 관계대명사로 사용되었다. ①, ④ what은 의문사로 사용되었다.

06 빈칸에는 what 또는 the thing that[which]이 들어가는 것이 적절하다.

07 ① has been lived → has lived / ② has taking → has taken / ③ have been wait → have been waiting / ⑤ have be reading → have been reading으로 고쳐야 어법상 적절한 문장이 된다.

08 ⓑ that we don't understand는 목적어이므로 that이 아니라 선행사를 포함하는 관계대명사 what이 이끄는 관계대명사절이 되는 것이 적절하다.
ⓔ Judy가 7살 때부터 계속 테니스 연습을 해왔다는 내용이므로 현재완료진행 시제를 이용해 'Judy had been practicing tennis since she was seven.'이라고 쓰는 것이 어법상 적절하다.

09 과거의 어느 시점부터 현재까지 이어져 오고 있는 일을 표현할 때 현재완료 진행형 시제(has/have been ~ing)를 이용해 나타낼 수 있다. 따라서 주어진 문장을 의문문으로 영작하면, 'How long has Andy been learning Spanish?'라고 할 수 있다.

10 과거의 특정 시점보다 앞서 일어난 일을 나타낼 경우에 과거완료 시제인 'had (not)+p.p'를 쓸 수 있다. 따라서 (A)에는 과거완료 시제의 수동태 동사인 had been sold out이, (B)에는 과거완료

시제인 had been to가 적절하다.

11 Eric이 신발을 사기 위해 쇼핑몰에 갔다. 마음에 드는 신발을 찾았지만 크기가 맞지 않았다고 한다. 따라서 Eric이 점원에게 할 말로 가장 적절한 것은 ② Are there any other sizes?(다른 사이즈가 있나요?)이다.

12 Kevin이 무엇을 읽냐고 물어보았고, Jane이 흥미로운 잡지를 읽고 있다고 대답하면서 색깔이 사람의 감정을 바꿀 수 있다는 내용이라고 말한다(B). Kevin이 놀랍다고 대답하자(A), Jane은 빨간색이 집중력을 높이게 도와준다고 말한다(D). 이에 Kevin이 다른 유용한 색깔이 있냐고(C) 물어보는 순서로 이어지는 것이 흐름상 가장 자연스럽다.

13 위 대화에서는 Jane이 잡지에서 읽은 색깔이 사람의 감정을 바꿀 수 있다는 내용에 대해서 이야기하고 있다.

14 "성격 테스트를 하려고 전화했습니다. 오늘 오후에 테스트할 수 있나요?"라는 A의 질문에 "오후 전에는 언제든 오셔도 됩니다."라는 B의 대답은 대화 흐름상 적절하지 않다.

15 위 대화의 후반부에 Emma가 다른 테스트도 해보고 싶다고 말하자 하준이가 어플리케이션에 많다고 대답하고 있다. 따라서 대화 후에 이어질 행동으로 가장 적절한 것은 ① To take another test(다른 테스트를 해보는 것)이다.

16 위 글에 따르면, 녹음된 음성은 테스트를 통해서 자신에 대해서 더 잘 알 수 있다고('Do you want to learn more about yourself? We run many kinds of on-site personality tests.') 말하고 있다.

17 위 글에서는 '빗속에 있는 사람 그리기' 테스트를 통해서 자신의 성격에 대해 더 잘 알 수 있다고 말하고 있다. 따라서 위 글의 어조로 가장 적절한 것은 ① informative(유용한 정보를 제공하는)이다.

18 (A) '당신이 하는 모든 일이 당신에 대해서 말해준다'는 의미의 문장이다. 따라서 동사로 says가 적절하다.
(B) raise(기르다)가 적절하다.
(C) 주어가 What you draw and how you draw it이므로 동사 are가 적절하다.

19 위 글에서는 ① Everything you eat(당신이 먹는 모든 것)에 대해서는 언급된 바 없다.

20 (A) ⓐ에 생략된 것은 관계대명사 that이다.
(B) ⓑ의 주어는 the person이다.
(D) ⓓ는 두 문장을 연결하는 접속사이다.
(E) ⓔ는 '수단', '방법'이라는 의미의 명사로 사용되었다.
(F) ⓕ는 to부정사의 형용사적 용법으로 사용되었다.

21 본문에 따르면, 구름은 일어날 문제들을 의미한다고 언급되어 있다. 따라서 구름이 없다는 것은 미래에 대한 걱정이 없거나 적다고 볼 수 있다.

22 관계대명사 that 또는 which를 이용해 The clouds mean problems that[which] are waiting to happen으로 쓸 수 있다. 이때 주격 관계대명사+be동사는 생략 가능하다.

23 ⓑdraw는 '(주의를) 끌다'라는 뜻의 동사로 사용되었다. 나머지는 모두 '그리다'라는 뜻의 동사로 사용되었다.

24 (A)what은 간접의문문에서 의문사로 쓰였다. ①, ②, ④, ⑤는 모두 선행사를 포함한 관계대명사 what이다.

25 본문에 따르면, 종이 왼쪽에 사람을 그림 사람은 과거의 일에 대해 걱정하고 있을지도 모른다고 언급했다. 따라서 ⓒ it shows your positive attitude about the future는 문맥상 적절하지 않다.

26 '빗방울이 더 크거나 비가 심하게 내릴수록, 스트레스는 더 크다'라는 문장이 들어가기에 가장 적절한 곳은 비는 그림을 그린 사람이 받는 스트레스를 의미한다고 말하고 있는 곳인 (C)이다.

27 ⓐ are → is / ⓒ are → is / ⓔ is not very hopeless → is not very hopeful / ⓖ mean to deal → means to deal로 고쳐야 어법상 적절한 문장이 된다.

28 위 글에 따르면, 비는 그림을 그린 사람이 받는 스트레스를 의미한다고('the rain shows the stress the person who drew the picture is under.') 언급되어 있다

29 비는 그림을 그린 사람이 받는 스트레스를 의미하며, 빗방울이 더 크거나 비가 심하게 내릴수록, 스트레스는 더 크다('the rain shows the stress the person who drew the picture is under. The bigger the drops are or the more heavily the rain is falling, the bigger the stress is.')라고 언급되어 있다.

30 위 글에서는 당신의 성향에 대해서 보여주는 것으로 ④ '남에게서 받은 그림'에 대해서는 언급된 바 없다.

Lesson 5 (중간)

> **01** ① **02** ⑤ **03** ⑤ **04** ② **05** ④
>
> **06** (1) what (2) 그 목격자는 도둑이 입고 있었던 것을 기억했다.
>
> **07** ⑤ **08** ⑤ **09** have you been waiting for me
>
> **10** The thing which scared Sara was the blood he spilled.
>
> **11** ④ **12** ⑤ **13** ⑤ **14** ④ **15** ② **16** ① **17** ③
>
> **18** ②, ③ **19** ⑤
>
> **20** Everything you do says something about you.
>
> **21** ③ **22** ① **23** ④ **24** ⓐ bigger ⓑ hopeful **25** ②
>
> **26** ④ **27** ③ **28** ⑤ **29** ① **30** ②

01 ① feel blue는 '우울함을 느끼다'라는 뜻으로 쓰이는 표현이다.

02 위에서부터 순서대로, ② relate(관련시키다), ③ attitude(태도), ① below(~ 아래의), ④ personality(성격, 개성)를 가리키는 영영 풀이이다.

03 어떤 사람이 자신의 일을 스스로 잘한다면 ⑤ 'independent'(독립적인)이라는 성향을 가진 것이라고 말하는 것이 적절하다.

04 위 글에서는 어떤 그림을 그리면 그것이 당신의 감정을 보여준다고 말하고 있다. 따라서 빈칸에 들어갈 말로 가장 적절한 것은 ② picture(그림)이다.

05 과거의 어느 시점부터 현재까지 이어져 오고 있는 일을 표현할 때 현재완료 진행형 시제(has/have been ~ing)를 이용해 나타낼 수 있다. 이때 전치사 for와 함께 쓰면 '~ 동안'이라는 뜻을 나타낸다.

06 관계대명사 what은 선행사를 포함하는 관계대명사로 명사절을 이끌며, '~하는 것'으로 해석된다. what이 이끄는 절은 문장 내에서 주어, 목적어, 또는 보어 역할을 한다.

07 ⑤ what은 의문형용사로 쓰였다. 나머지 what은 모두 선행사를 포함하는 관계대명사로 사용되었다.

08 과거의 어느 시점부터 현재까지 이어져 오고 있는 일을 표현할 때 현재완료 진행형 시제(has/have been ~ing)를 이용해 나타낼 수 있다. 이때 전치사 since와 함께 쓰면 '~ 이후로'라는 뜻을 나타낸다.

09 과거의 어느 시점부터 현재까지 이어져 오고 있는 일을 표현할 때 현재완료 진행형 시제(has/have been ~ing)를 이용해 나타낼 수 있다. 따라서 주어진 문장을 바르게 배열하면, 'How long have you been waiting for me?'라고 할 수 있다.

10 관계대명사 what은 선행사를 포함하는 관계대명사로 두 문장을 연결하는 역할을 하며, 명사절을 이끌어 '~하는 것'으로 해석된다. 이때 what은 the thing(s) which 또는 the thing(s) that으로 바꿔 쓸 수 있다.

11 ④What은 의문사로 쓰여서 의문문을 이끈다. 나머지 what은 모두 선행사를 포함하는 관계대명사로 쓰였다.

12 Laura가 성격 테스트로 집을 그렸다고 말하자, Jack은 집이냐고 되물었다. Laura는 테스트에 따르면, 그림을 통해서 한 사람에 대해서 많은 걸 알 수 있다고 말한다(C). Jack이 흥미롭다고 대답하면서, 큰 창문들은 무슨 의미냐고 묻는다(B). 이에 Laura가 자기가 다른 사람들에게 개방적이라는 의미라고(A) 대답하는 순서로 이어지는 것이 흐름상 가장 자연스럽다.

13 위 글에 따르면, Hajun("I chose dark places too.")과 Emma("I hate dark places.") 모두 어두운 곳을 무서워한다고 언급되어 있다.

14 "Are there any other+복수명사 ~?"는 "다른 ~는 없나요?"라는 의미의 문장이다.

15 B의 말에 대한 A의 대답이 "A형은 침착하고 말을 잘 들어주는 사람이래."였다. 따라서 빈칸에 들어갈 B의 말로 가장 적절한 것은 ② what does type A mean(혈액형 A형은 무슨 의미니?)이다.

16 ⓐ have read → read로 고쳐야 어법상 적절한 문장이 된다.

17 J의 말에 대한 B의 대답이 "나는 이 문제 풀기를 포기했다는 거

야."였다. 따라서 빈칸에 들어갈 J의 말로 가장 적절한 것은 ③ What does "threw up my hands" mean?(손을 들다라는 말이 무슨 의미니?)이다.

18 위 글에서 사람의 성격을 보여주는 것으로 언급된 것은 사용하는 언어, 입는 옷, 기르는 동물, 그리는 그림을 언급했다.

19 (가)raise는 '키우다, 기르다'라는 뜻의 동사로 사용되었다.
① (소리를) 높이다, ② (수준을) 올리다, ③ (다리를) 올리다, ④ (돈을) 모으다

20 주어 Everything you do는 단수 취급한다.

21 '둘째, 우산은 스트레스의 상황에서 사람이 가진 보호를 의미한다'라는 문장이 들어가기에 가장 적절한 곳은 큰 우산은 보호할 수 있는 능력이 크다고 말하고 있는 곳 앞인 (C)이다.

22 (가)means는 '수단', '방법'을 의미한다.

23 위 글에 따르면, 우산은 스트레스 상황에서 사람이 가진 보호를 의미한다. 따라서 우산이 없다는 것은 어려운 상황을 다룰 수 있는 방법이 없다는 것을 의미한다고('If there's no umbrella in the drawing, the drawer does not have any means to deal with difficult situations.') 언급되어 있다.

24 (A) 빗방울이 크거나 폭우가 내리는 것은 스트레스가 심하다는 의미라고 언급되어 있다. 따라서 bigger가 적절하다.
(B) 큰 구름은 문제가 발생할 수 있다는 걱정을 나타내므로 미래에 대해 희망적이지 않다는 것을 의미한다. 따라서 hopeful이 적절하다.

25 ⓑ do not → does not / ⓒ are → is / ⓔ to reading → reading으로 고쳐야 어법상 적절한 문장이 된다.

26 (가) 주어가 These이므로 동사 are가 적절하다.
(나) each 다음에는 단수 명사를 쓴다. 따라서 part가 적절하다.
(다) look at: ~을 보다

27 첫 문단에 따르면, 종이 왼쪽에 사람을 그린 사람은 과거의 일을 걱정하고 있을지도 모른다고('someone who draws the person on the left side may be worried about what have happened in the past.') 언급되어 있다.

28 '큰 우산은 그림을 그린 사람이 계획이나 보호물을 많이 갖고 있다는 것을 보여준다.'라는 문장이 들어가기에 가장 적절한 곳은 우산이 스트레스 상황에서 사람이 갖는 보호를 의미한다고 말하고 있는 곳인 (E)이다.

29 위 글에 따르면, 그림 B에는 폭우가 내리고 있으며 큰 먹구름이 있고 우산이 없다고 한다. 폭우는 스트레스의 수준, 우산은 보호를 의미한다고 언급되어 있다. 따라서 그림 B를 그린 사람의 심정으로 가장 적절한 것은 ① frustrated(좌절한)이다.

30 위 글에 따르면, 빗방울의 크기나 비의 양이 스트레스 수준을 의미한다고('First, the rain shows the stress the person who drew the picture is under.') 언급되어 있다.

Lesson 6 (중간)

> 01 ④ 02 ③ 03 occnatu → account 04 ③
> 05 as brave as 06 ③
> 07 ⓐ woke up ⓑ had left
> ⓒ I (had) entered the classroom before class started
> 08 ③ 09 ② 10 ③ 11 ③ 12 ① 13 ⑤ 14 ③ 15 ②
> 16 ③ 17 ⑤ 18 ② 19 Can you do me a favor? 20 ③
> 21 ③ 22 ⑤ 23 ④ 24 ③ 25 ⑤ 26 ② 27 ③ 28 ⑤
> 29 Seyun is not as weak and small as he was last year.
> 30 ④

01 빈칸 (A)에 공통으로 들어갈 말로 가장 적절한 것은 ④ search(~를 찾다, 검색하다)이다.

02 ③ search: ~를 찾다, 검색하다

03 account: 계좌

04 (A) hand over: ~를 건네주다
(B) ask for help: 도움을 요청하다

05 '~만큼 …한'이라는 동등 비교 표현은 'as (형용사/부사) as ~'의 형태로 쓸 수 있다.

06 ③ many → much로 고쳐야 어법상 적절한 문장이 된다.

07 과거의 특정 시점을 기준으로 그보다 더 이전에 시작된 일이 그 시점까지 영향을 미치는 경우 혹은 과거의 특정 시점보다 앞서 일어난 일을 나타낼 경우에 과거완료 시제인 'had (not)+p.p'를 쓸 수 있다.

08 지난 봄 이전에는 한 번도 감자를 심어본 적 없었지만 지난 봄에 감자를 심어봤다는 내용이다. 따라서 과거완료 시제인 ③ had never planted가 들어가는 것이 적절하다.

09 "Do you mind ~?"는 "제가 ~해도 될까요?"라는 뜻으로 상대방의 허락을 구하는 표현이다. 동사 mind는 '~를 꺼리다'라는 뜻을 갖고 있기 때문에 이에 대한 대답은 허락할 때는 "No, I don't."를, 거절할 때는 "Yes, I do."를 쓴다.

10 위 대화에 따르면, 옷가게에 들어가려고 하지만 음료 반입이 금지여서 먼저 음료를 다 마시자고("Let's finish our drinks first. Then we can go inside.") 말하고 있다.

11 "I'd love to, but I'm afraid I can't."는 "그리고 싶지만, 유감스럽게도 안 될 것 같아."라는 의미의 문장으로 상대방의 제안을 거절하는 표현이다.

12 위 대화에 따르면, 게임 엑스포에 같이 가자는 나나의 제안에 민호는 "I have an important test next week."라고 대답했다.

13 "Do you mind ~?"는 "제가 ~해도 될까요?"라는 뜻으로 상대방의 허락을 구하는 표현이다. 동사 mind는 '~를 꺼리다'라는 뜻을 갖고 있기 때문에 이에 대한 대답은 허락할 때는 "No, I don't."를, 거절할 때는 "Yes, I do."를 쓴다.

14 위 대화에 따르면, 남학생은 여학생에게 만화책을 빌려줄 수 있냐고("Can you lend it to me?") 물어보고 있다.

15 위 대화에 따르면, 여학생은 만화책에 대해서 "It's one of my favorites."라고 언급했다.

16 Jack이 친구들을 위해 한국 전통 선물을 사고 싶다고 말하면서 그 것들을 구매할 곳을 추천해 달라고 말한다. Nara는 인사동을 들어 봤냐고 물어보면서 그곳에 한국 전통 물건이 많다고 말한다(C). Jack이 그곳에 가 본 적이 없다고 대답하자(B), Nara는 이번주 금요일 오후에 자신과 그곳에 방문하는 건 어떠냐고 묻는다(D). 이에 Jack이 다른 약속이 있어서 안 되지만 토요일은 어떠냐고 묻고(A) Nara가 좋다고 말하는 순서로 이어지는 것이 흐름상 가장 자연스럽다.

17 ⓐ several text → several texts / ⓑ hand over → handed over / ⓒ either happy and sad → both happy and sad / ⓓ to go → go로 고쳐야 어법상 적절한 문장이 된다.

18 위 글에 따르면, 구매자가 낮은 가격을 제시했고 그는 처음에 받아 들이기 힘들었지만 낮은 가격에 자전거를 팔았다고('Sadly, they all asked for a lower price. It was hard to accept at first, but finally he sold his bike for 70,000 won.) 언급되어 있다.

19 위 대화에서 구매자는 낮은 가격을 제시하고 있다. 따라서 빈칸에 들어갈 말로 가장 적절한 것은 Can you do me a favor?(부탁을 들어주시겠어요?)이다.

20 '또한, 다른 자전거에 비해서 이 가격은 너무 높았다.'라는 문장이 들어가기에 가장 적절한 곳은 세윤이가 자전거 게시글에 설명을 충분히 하지 않았다는 내용 뒤인 (C)이다.

21 위 글에 따르면, Seyun의 자전거는 12-14년을 탄 것이 아니라 12~14세 사이의 아이가 타기에 좋다고 설명글을 쓴 것이다.

22 위 글에 따르면, 세윤이는 10만원이었던 자전거 가격을 8만원으로 내렸다. 따라서 10퍼센트가 아니라 20퍼센트 할인되었다.

23 (A) 분사구문으로 현재분사인 thinking이 적절하다.
(B) 한 시간이 지났다라는 의미이므로 동사 passed가 적절하다.
(C) 그가 올린 자전거 중고 판매글에 아무런 답장도 없었고 아무도 그의 자전거를 원하지 않는 것처럼 보였다는 내용이므로 Nobody 가 적절하다.

24 ⓒthe bike는 세윤이가 새로 사려고 하는 자전거를 가리킨다. 나머지는 모두 세윤이가 사용하던 중고 자전거를 가리킨다.

25 위 글에 따르면, 세윤이가 올린 게시글은 다른 사람들이 올린 게시글 때문에 밀려 내려갔다고('New postings by other people pushed his post down the list.') 언급되어 있다.

26 위 글에 따르면, 그가 새 자전거를 사고 싶지만 충분한 돈이 없다는 내용이다. 따라서 빈칸에는 ② However(그러나)가 적절하다.

27 세윤이는 자신이 타던 자전거가 새 것만큼 좋다고 생각했다. 따라

서 빈칸 (B)에는 형용사 good이 들어가는 것이 적절하다.

28 위 글에서는 ⑤ How much does he need to buy a new bike?(그가 새 자전거를 사기 위해서는 얼마가 필요한가?)에 대해서는 언급된 바 없다.

29 '~만큼 …한'이라는 동등 비교 표현은 'as+형용사/부사+as ~'의 형태로 쓸 수 있다. 이때 형용사와 부사는 모두 원급으로 쓰는 것이 어법상 적절하다.

30 세윤이는 그가 쓰던 자전거가 새것만큼 상태가 좋아서 그것을 팔아서 새 자전거를 살 때 보태기로 했다고("My old bike is almost as good as a new one. Maybe I can sell it and add the money to buy a new one.") 언급되어 있다.

Lesson 6 (중간) 2회

01 ①	**02** post	**03** the train had already left	**04** ④
05 ②	**06** ③	**07** ④	**08** ④	**09** ⑤	**10** ②	**11** ②	**12** ③
13 ⑤	**14** ⑤	**15** ⑤	**16** ②	**17** ③	**18** ②	**19** ⑤	**20** ⑤
21 ①	**22** ⑤	**23** ④	**24** ③	**25** ①	**26** ④	**27** ②	**28** ④
29 ③	**30** ②		

01 '돈을 보관하고 필요할 때 인출하기 위한 은행 또는 다른 기관과의 합의'라는 영영 풀이가 가리키는 것은 ① account(계좌)이다.

02 post: 게시하다, 공고하다

03 과거의 특정 시점을 기준으로 그보다 더 이전에 시작된 일이 그 시점까지 영향을 미치는 경우 혹은 과거의 특정 시점보다 앞서 일어난 일을 나타낼 경우에 과거완료 시제인 'had+p.p'를 쓸 수 있다.

04 위 표에 따르면, 오렌지는 사과와 가격이 동일하다.

05 "좋은 음식을 추천해줄 수 있니?"라는 A의 질문에 "삼계탕을 먹어봐. 기운이 보충될 거야."라는 B의 대답이 대화 흐름상 가장 자연스럽다.

06 "Do you mind ~?"는 "제가 ~해도 될까요?"라는 뜻으로 상대방의 허락을 구하는 표현이다. 동사 mind는 '~를 꺼리다'라는 뜻을 갖고 있기 때문에 이에 대한 대답은 허락할 때는 "No, I don't."를, 거절할 때는, "Yes, I do."를 쓴다.

07 위 대화에 따르면, 여학생은 은행 계좌를 열고 싶다고("I'd like to open a bank account.") 말하고 있다.

08 여학생이 민호에게 이번주 일요일에 함께 게임 엑스포에 가자고 제안하고 있다. 민호는 가고 싶지만 다음주에 중요한 시험이 있다고 대답한다(B). 여학생이 아쉽다고 말하면서, 특별 게임쇼도 한다고 말한다(C). 이에 민호가 자신도 들었다고 말하면서, 다음주 토요일에 같이 가는건 어떠냐고 묻자(A) 여학생이 좋다고 대답하는 순서로 이어지는 것이 흐름상 가장 자연스럽다.

09 "Do you mind ~?"는 "제가 ~해도 될까요?"라는 뜻으로 상대

방의 허락을 구하는 표현이다. 동사 mind는 '~를 꺼리다'라는 뜻을 갖고 있기 때문에 이에 대한 대답은 허락할 때는 "No, I don't.", 거절할 때는, "Yes, I do."를 쓴다.

10 "I'm afraid I can't."는 "미안하지만, 안 될 것 같아."라는 의미의 문장으로 상대방의 제안을 거절하는 표현이다.

11 위 대화에 따르면, Ben은 Dana에게 만화책을 빌려줄 수 있는지 물어보았다("Can you lend it to me?"). 이에 Dana는 그 만화책이 자신의 것이 아니므로 빌려줄 수 없다고 말하면서 인터넷에 중고 제품을 찾아보라고("if you really want it, you should check used bookstores online") 제안했다.

12 위 대화에 따르면, Ben은 Dana에게 만화책을 빌려달라고 요청하고 있다.

13 문맥상 그가 새 자전거를 사고 싶지만 충분한 돈이 없다는 내용이 들어가는 것이 적절하다. 따라서 빈칸에는 ⑤ 'he does not have enough money in his savings account'가 적절하다.

14 위 글에 따르면, 세윤이는 키가 커지고 힘이 세져서 원래 갖고 있던 자전거가 그에게 너무 작아졌다고 한다. 그래서 더 크고 빠른 자전거를 사고 싶지만 충분한 돈이 없다고 한다.

15 ⓔ a number of → the number of로 고쳐야 어법상 적절한 문장이 된다.

16 세윤이가 새 자전거를 사고 싶지만 자전거를 살 수 있는 충분한 돈이 없다는 내용이다. 따라서 빈칸에는 ② However(그러나)가 적절하다.

17 (나)comment는 '언급'이라는 뜻이다. 따라서 ③ explanation(설명)으로 바꿔 쓸 수 있다.

18 위 글에 따르면, 세윤이는 새 자전거를 사기 위해 쓰던 자전거를 중고 판매하기 위해 게시글을 올렸고 새 자전거를 살 수 있다는 기대에 부풀었다고 한다. 그러나 시간이 지나도 그의 자전거를 산다는 답장이 없었다고 한다. 따라서 빈칸 (다)에 들어갈 말로 가장 적절한 것은 ② His bike does not seem to be attracting buyers.(그의 자전거는 구매자를 유혹하지 못하는 것처럼 보인다.)이다.

19 (E)에는 by(~에 의한)가 들어가는 것이 적절하다.

20 위 글에 따르면, 세윤이는 중고 판매로 올린 자전거 게시글에 '아주 좋은 상태'라고 써놓았다고 언급되어 있다.

21 세윤이가 자전거를 중고 판매하려고 게시글을 올려놓았지만 사람들이 모두 가격을 깎아달라고 요청했다고 이야기하고 있다. 따라서 빈칸에는 ① Sadly(슬프게도, 아쉽게도)가 적절하다.

22 ⓔ (had) grown up은 문맥상 경험을 통해 조금 더 '성장했다'는 의미로 사용되고 있다.

23 위 글에서는 ④ How much did Seyun pay for his new bike?(세윤이는 새 자전거를 얼마를 지불하고 샀는가?)에 대해서는 언급된 바 없다.

24 ⓒ accepting → accept로 고쳐야 어법상 적절한 문장이 된다.

25 빈칸 (A), (B)에 공통으로 들어갈 말로 알맞은 것은 ① on(~에; ~에 대해서)이다.

26 관계대명사 what은 선행사를 포함하는 관계대명사로 두 문장을 연결하는 역할을 하며, 명사절을 이끌어 '~하는 것'으로 해석된다. 이때 what은 the thing(s) which 또는 the thing(s) that으로 바꿔 쓸 수 있다.

27 위 글에 따르면, 세윤이는 중고 판매하려고 하는 자전거의 설명글에 "Twenty-four inch bicycle. Excellent condition. Always kept indoors. Rides just like new. Very few scratches. Good for someone that is 12-14 years old. 80,000 won."이라고 적었다고 언급되어 있다.

28 위 글에서는 ④ When Seyun first bought his bike, how much was it?(세윤이가 처음 자전거를 샀을 때, 그것은 얼마였는가?)에 대해서는 언급된 바 없다.

29 위 글에서는 세윤이가 쓰던 자전거를 중고로 판매하는 과정을 보여주면서 온라인에서 현명하게 물건을 판매하는 방법에 대해서 설명하고 있다. 따라서 위 글의 제목으로 가장 적절한 것은 ③ Learning to Become a Wise Online Seller(현명한 온라인 판매자가 되는 법)이다.

30 첫 문단에 따르면, 다른 자전거들과 비교했을 때 세윤이의 자전거의 첫 제시 가격은 합리적이지 않았다고('when compared to other bicycles, his price was too high.') 언급되어 있다.

Lesson 7 (기말) 1회

01 ④	**02** ①	**03** ③	**04** ③	**05** ②	**06** ②	**07** ③	**08** ⑤
09 ④	**10** ③	**11** ①	**12** ④	**13** ②	**14** ④	**15** ②	**16** ③
17 ⑤	**18** ⑤	**19** ④	**20** ④	**21** ⑤	**22** ②	**23** ⑤	**24** ④
25 ③	**26** ②	**27** ③	**28** ③	**29** ②	**30** ⑤		

01 빈칸에 공통으로 들어갈 단어로 가장 적절한 것은 ④ company(회사; 함께 있음)이다.

02 ①은 Turn around for me to see your face.라고 바꾸면 어법상 적절한 문장이 된다.

03 (A) 가정법과거가 쓰인 If 절에서 be동사가 쓰일 때에는 인칭에 관계없이 were를 쓴다.
(B) 가정법과거 문장은 'If+주어+were/동사의 과거형 ~, 주어+조동사의 과거형(would/should/could/might)+동사원형 ….'의 형식으로 쓴다.

04 가정법과거 문장은 'If+주어+were/동사의 과거형 ~, 주어+조동사의 과거형(would/should/could/might)+동사원형 ….'의 형식으로 현재 사실과 반대되는 가정을 나타낼 때 쓸 수 있다.

05 "난 누가 그들이 비행기를 만들도록 영감을 주었는지 궁금해."라는 A의 질문에 대해 "난 그들이 비행기 제작을 위한 돈을 벌기 위해 자전거를 팔았다고 들었어."라는 B의 대답은 흐름상 자연스럽지 않다.

06 "Let me see."는 "어디 보자.", "글쎄."라는 의미의 문장이다. "Let me think."로 바꿔 쓸 수 있다.

07 행동의 주체가 자발적으로 어떤 행동을 하는 것이 아니라 '주어가 목적격보어에게 ~하게 하다'라는 뜻으로 쓰이는 동사를 사역동사라고 한다. 사역동사에는 make(~하게 하다), let(~하도록 허락하다), have(~하게 하다) 등이 있다. 이때 「사역동사+목적어+목적격보어(동사원형)」의 순서로 쓴다.

08 위 대화에 따르면, 크래커에 있는 구멍들이 크래커를 얇고 바삭하게 만들어 준다고 언급되어 있다.

09 위 대화에 따르면, 크래커의 구멍은 구워지는 동안 증기를 내보낼 수 있도록 만든다("It says during baking, steam comes out through the holes and that makes the crackers thin.").

10 위 글에서는 ③ How long does it take to bake the crackers?(크래커를 굽는데는 시간이 얼마나 걸리는가?)에 대해서는 언급된 바 없다.

11 주어진 단어를 배열하면, that is not what it is(그것은 전혀 딱풀이 아니다)가 된다.

12 '~하기 위해서, ~하도록'이라는 의미를 나타내는 표현으로 「(so as) to+동사원형」, 「in order to+동사원형」, 「so that+주어+can/may ~」, 「in order that+주어+can/may ~」 등을 쓸 수 있다.

13 전치사 from이 쓰였으므로 빈칸 (A)에는 동명사형인 coming이 들어가는 것이 적절하다.

14 가정법과거 문장은 'If+주어+were/동사의 과거형 ~, 주어+조동사의 과거형(would/should/could/might)+동사원형 ….'의 형식으로 현재 사실과 반대되는 가정을 나타낼 때 쓸 수 있다.

15 위 글에서는 구멍이 유용한 역할을 하는 사례 중 하나로 냄비에 있는 구멍이 요리할 때 증기를 빼줘 물이 흘러넘치는 것을 방지한다고 이야기하고 있다. 따라서 위 글의 제목으로 가장 적절한 것은 ③ The Role of the Small Hole in a Pot Lid(냄비 뚜껑에 있는 작은 구멍의 역할)이다.

16 위 글에 따르면, 뚜껑이 있는 냄비에 무언가를 요리할 때, 냄비 내부의 압력이 올라간다고('When cooking something in a pot with a lid, the pressure inside the pot builds up.') 언급되어 있다.

17 ⓔ what have small hidden holes → that have small hidden holes로 고쳐야 어법상 적절한 문장이 된다.

18 (A)to make는 to부정사의 형용사적 용법으로 사용되어 명사를 수식한다. 따라서 이와 쓰임이 같은 것은 ⑤ The easiest way to make strong bones is to go outside.(뼈를 튼튼하게 만드는 가장 빠른 방법은 야외로 나가는 것이다.)이다.

19 위 글에 따르면, 중간 유리판의 구멍은 기압의 균형을 맞춘다고('There is a hole in the middle pane. It balances the air pressure.') 언급되어 있다.

20 '그렇다면, 이것은 호흡을 막아서 죽음으로 이어질 수 있다.'라는 문장이 들어가기에 가장 적절한 곳은 어린이가 작은 물건들을 입에 넣기도 하며 심하면 삼킬 수도 있다고 말하고 있는 곳인 (D)이다.

21 ⑤ company는 '함께 있음'이라는 뜻으로 사용되었다.
(가)pen: 펜, (나) cap: (펜 등의) 뚜껑, (다) company: 회사

22 위 글에서는 물건들에 있는 작은 구멍이 중요한 역할을 하고 더 나아가서는 생명을 살리기도 한다고 이야기하면서 펜의 뚜껑에 있는 작은 구멍을 예시로 들고 있다. 따라서 위 글의 제목으로 가장 적절한 것은 ⑤ Changes in Our Lives That Small Ideas Have Brought About(작은 아이디어가 우리의 삶에 가져온 변화들)이다.

23 첫 문단에서, 이것들은 매우 잘 숨겨져 있지만 매우 중요하고 사람의 생명을 살리기도 한다고 이야기하고 있다. 따라서 빈칸에 들어갈 말로 가장 적절한 것은 ⑤ Some are so small that you may not even notice them.(몇몇 구멍들은 너무 작아서 심지어는 알아챌 수도 없다.)이다.

24 위 글에서는 ④ What design of pen caps do people like?(어떤 펜 뚜껑 디자인을 사람들이 좋아하는가?)에 대해서는 언급된 바 없다.

25 (A) 가정법과거 문장은 'If+주어+were/동사의 과거형 ~, 주어+조동사의 과거형(would/should/could/might)+동사원형 ….'의 형식으로 쓴다.
(B) be composed of ~: ~로 구성되어 있다 (= be made up of)
(C) prevent A from ~ing: A가 ~하는 것을 방지하다

26 현재 사실과 반대되는 가정을 나타낼 때, 'If+주어+were/동사의 과거형 ~, 주어+조동사의 과거형(would/should/could/might)+동사원형 ….'의 형식의 가정법 과거 형식을 쓰며, '만약 ~라면, …할 텐데.'로 해석한다.

27 위 글에서는 ③ How does the hole in the lid help us cook faster?(뚜껑에 있는 구멍이 더 빨리 요리할 수 있도록 어떻게 도와주는가?)에 대해서는 언급된 바 없다.

28 ⓐ excited → exciting / ⓒ that has → that have / ⓓ why is it → why it is로 고쳐야 어법상 적절한 문장이 된다.

29 첫 문단에서 비행기의 창문에는 작은 구멍이 있다고 말하고 있다. 비행기 창문은 총 3장의 유리로 구성 되어 있는데(B), 중간 유리판에 구멍이 있다(D). 그 구멍은 기압의 균형을 맞추어 주는데(C), 이 작은 구멍이 없다면 비상상황에서 비행기의 창문이 부서질지도

모른다고(A) 말하는 순서로 이어지는 것이 흐름상 가장 자연스럽다.

30 위 글에서 ⓐ What is an example of a bad hole?(나쁜 구멍의 예시는 무엇인가?)와 ⓒ How many windows does an airplane have?(비행기는 총 몇 개의 창문을 갖고 있는가?)에 대해서는 언급된 바 없다.

Lesson 8 (기말)

01 ④	**02** ①	**03** ②	**04** ④	**05** ④	**06** ⑤	**07** ①	**08** ⑤
09 ①	**10** ④	**11** ①	**12** ①	**13** ③	**14** ⑤	**15** ④	**16** ①
17 ②	**18** ④	**19** ②	**20** ②	**21** ①	**22** ④	**23** ⑤	**24** ③
25 ②	**26** ④	**27** ⑤	**28** ①				

01 ④ while은 '~하는 동안에'라는 뜻으로 사용되었다. 나머지는 모두 '~인 반면에'라는 뜻으로 사용되었다.

02 "제가 당신과 좌석을 바꿔도 될까요?"라는 A의 질문에 "안 돼요. 좋아요. 친구와 같이 앉을 거예요."라는 B의 대답은 대화 흐름상 적절하지 않다.

03 웨이터가 말한 "A table for two?"는 "두 명이 앉을 테이블을 원하십니까?"라는 의미의 문장이다.

04 위 대화에 따르면, Sophie는 하준이에게 한국 음식을 추천해 달라고 했고, 하준이는 비빔밥이 어떠냐고 추천하고 있다. ④ What's so special about Bibimbap?(비빔밥이 특별한 점이 무엇이니?)는 적절하지 않다.

05 Sophie의 질문에 대해 Hajun이는 비빔밥을 다시 말해주었다. 따라서 빈칸에는 다시 말해달라고 요청하는 표현이 적절하다. ④ Could you give it to me?는 "그것을 나에게 줄 수 있니?"라는 의미의 문장이다.

06 위 대화에 따르면, 하준이는 Sophie에게 비빔밥을 추천하면서 그것이 맛도 있고 건강에도 좋다고("It's tasty and it's also good for your health.") 말하고 있다.

07 A가 포케를 먹어본 적이 있냐고 물어보자, B는 무슨 말인지 몰라서 다시 한번 말해달라고 말한다(B). A는 포케가 하와이에서 유명한 샐러드라고 대답하고(A), B는 무엇이 특별한 점인지 묻는다(C). 이에 A가 쌀이랑 생선으로 만들어진 것이며 맛도 있고 건강에도 좋다고(D) 말하는 순서로 이어지는 것이 흐름상 가장 자연스럽다.

08 "Could you say that again?"은 "다시 말씀해주시겠어요?"라는 의미의 문장이다. ⑤ Can you tell me more about that?은 "그것에 대해 자세히 설명해주시겠어요?"라는 의미의 문장이다.

09 위 대화에서는 B가 G에게 생일 파티를 할 장소를 추천해 달라고 요청했고, G는 B에게 파티에 적합한 장소를 추천해 주고 있다.

10 take one's order: 주문을 받다

11 위 대화에 따르면, 남학생은 비빔밥에 매운 고추장 소스가 들어간다고 말하면서 괜찮냐고 물어보았다. 여학생이 "문제 없다."고 말하면서 매운 음식을 좋아한다고 대답하고 있다. 따라서 밑줄 친 (B)가 의미하는 바로 가장 적절한 것은 ① She can eat what her friend suggests.(그녀는 친구가 추천한 음식을 먹을 수 있다.)이다.

12 위 대화는 여학생과 남학생이 식당에 한국 음식을 먹으러 와서 나누고 있는 대화이다.

13 위 글에서는 글쓴이가 자신의 학교에서 하나와 두나라는 쌍둥이를 본 적이 있는지에 대해서 묻고 그들의 외모와 성격에 대해서 설명하고 있다. 따라서 위 글을 볼 수 있는 곳으로 가장 적절한 곳은 ③ School newspaper(학교 신문)이다.

14 위 글에서는 수영복을 구매하고 쓴 후기이다. ⓔIn terms of buying a swimming suit, you need to buy a smaller size because it can be stretched after you wear it several times.(수영복 구매에 관해서는, 수영복을 여러번 입으면 늘어날 수 있기 때문에 작은 사이즈를 사야 한다.)는 문맥상 적절하지 않다.

15 위 글에 따르면, ④ 수확한 감자는 시장에서 파는 것만큼 상태가 좋았다고('They looked as good as the ones you see in the market') 언급되어 있다.

16 위 글에서는 외국인 친구 Paul이 주말에 경주에 방문할 것이며 경주를 안내를 해줄 것이라고 말하고 있다.

17 위 글에 따르면, Paul은 이번 주말에 경주에 방문할 것이라고 ('My foreign friend, Paul, is coming to Gyeongju this weekend') 언급되어 있다.

18 위 글에서는 ④ How could the people carve them?(그들은 어떻게 모아이를 조각할 수 있었는가?)에 대해서는 언급된 바 없다.

19 위 글에 언급된 Gogol-mogol 요리법은 한 사람 기준으로 우유를 반 컵 넣는다고 언급되어 있다. 따라서 두 사람 기준으로 만들면 한 컵의 우유가 필요하다.

20 ⓐ worsen → reduce / ⓒ receipt → recipe로 고쳐야 문맥상 적절한 문장이 된다.

21 위 글에서는 감기를 물리칠 수 있게 도와주는 세계의 여러 음식에 대해서 소개하고 있다. 따라서 빈칸 (A)에 가장 적절한 말은 ① Fight이다.

22 ⓓ chop → chopped로 고쳐야 어법상 적절한 문장이 된다.

23 (A)문단에서는 다른 나라들에서는 감기를 물리치기 위해 무엇을 먹고 마시는지에 대해서 알아보자고 말하고 있다. 따라서 (A) 다음에 이어질 내용으로 알맞은 것은 ⑤ What food do people eat in other countries when they have a cold?이다.

24 (A), (B) 문단에서는 모두 감기를 물리치기 위해 세계 사람들이 먹는 음식에 대해서 이야기하고 있다.

25 첫 문단에서는 핀란드나 한국과 달리 미국 사람들은 감기에 걸렸을 때 닭고기 수프를 먹는다고 소개하고 있다. 따라서 ⓑWhy not try making one of the foods you have found out?(당신이 알게 된 음식 중 하나를 만들어 보는 건 어떤가요?)는 문맥상 적절하지 않다.

26 두 번째 문단에 따르면, 몇몇 사람들은 Gogol-mogol을 만들 때 몇 가지 음식을 추가한다고('Some people add chocolate, butter, lemon juice, or milk to make it taste better.') 언급하고 있다.

27 '한국과 핀란드 사람들은 아플 때 마실 것을 찾는 반면에, 미국의 많은 사람들은 닭고기 수프를 원한다.'라는 문장이 들어가기에 가장 적절한 곳은 닭고기 수프를 만드는 법에 대해서 말하고 있는 곳 앞인 (E)이다.

28 위 글에 따르면, 미국 사람들은 닭고기 수프가 인후염과 코막힘에 좋다고 믿는다고('People in America believe that a bowl of warm chicken soup is great for a sore throat and a stuffy nose.') 언급되어 있다.

적중 100 + 특별부록

Plan B

우리학교
최신기출

시사·송미정 교과서를 배우는

학교 시험문제 분석·모음·해설집

전국단위 학교 시험문제 수집 및 분석
출제 빈도가 높은 문제 위주로 선별
문제 풀이에 필요한 상세한 해설

중3-2
영어

시사·송미정

값 6,000원